The Lives and Stories
of Early Asian Americans

The Lives and Stories
of Early Asian Americans

An Anthology of Asian American Literature
from 1887 to 1923

Edited with an Introduction by
Charles A. McAllister Jr.

WHITLOCK PUBLISHING
Alfred, New York

The Lives and Stories of Early Asian Americans
First Whitlock Publishing edition 2019

Whitlock Publishing
Alfred, New York
http://www.whitlockpublishing.com

Editorial matter © Charles A. McAllister Jr.

ISBN: 978-1-943115-33-4

For my parents,
Charles A. McAllister Sr. and Sharon Neypes McAllister,
and my sister, Chaslynn McAllister

TABLE OF CONTENTS

Eurasian Authors

Onoto Watanna

JAPANESE AMERICAN AUTHORS

JENICHIRO OYABE

A Japanese Robinson Crusoe

YONE NOGUCHI

Selected Poems of Yone Noguchi, Selected by Himself

JUN FUJITA

Tanka: Poems in Exile

PREFACE

IN PREPARATION FOR WRITING THIS ANTHOLOGY, I decided to perform a quick experiment by looking for the authors in a local bookstore. I was staying at my grandparents' home for another Christmas break, and I drove to a Books-A-Million in Bridgeport, West Virginia to check their shelves. Growing up with Filipino and American heritages, I was much more familiar with my American side. As for my Filipino identity, my exposure has been limited, just as it is with the lack of Asian American representation in mainstream media. I felt ready to learn more about the Oriental side of my identity, but I kept my expectations low.

I walked into the store and started my search for Asian American authors. Every bookshelf was neatly cluttered with books of various heights and sizes and a semblance of alphabetical order. The first authors on my list started with "E" for the Eaton sisters. I scanned each row of books and remarked multiple copies of *Middlemarch* by George Elliot lined up next to each other. Winnifred and Edith Maud Eaton were absent front the bookshelf, but this was not too disconcerting for me—perhaps they were published under their pseudonyms Onoto Watanna and Sui Sin Far. *Mrs. Spring Fragrance* has been reclaimed in American literature anthologies, so I felt certain that Far's short story collection would be here. I walked to the "F" section, and I saw a row of William Faulkner's books. The spines of *As I Lay Dying* mocked me. Then, I continued my search to look for Onoto Watanna, only to see two thick copies of David Foster Wallace's *Infinite Jest* instead.

I did not stop looking. I crossed several names off my list: I saw Oscar Wilde but not Yung Wing, Harper Lee but not Yan Phou Lee, Aldous Huxley but not Sadakichi Hartmann. The latter perplexed me the most. Hartmann's social circle with Walt Whitman, Ezra Pound, and Stéphane Mallarmé should have merited at least one book of his poetry in circulation. Being one of the first authors who introduced the haiku and tanka into American literature, his lack of inclusion was significant.

I knew it would be challenging to find the works of late-nineteenth and early-twentieth century Asian American authors, so I tried looking for works by contemporary authors instead. Alas, there were no copies of any novels by Ha Jin nor Maxine Hong Kingston. Within the shelf, I eyed copies of *Dubliners* and *Ulysses* by James Joyce. In the "K" section, Stephen King's novels occupied multiple shelves. Of the present authors, Amy Tan was represented by a single, lonely copy of *The Joy Luck Club*, and Ruth Ozeki was represented by two copies of *A Tale for the Time Being*. Diversity began to look more hopeful when I saw a quarter of a bookshelf filled with Celeste Ng's novels *Little Fires* and *Everywhere and I Never Told You*. At the front of the bookstore, the *Crazy Rich Asians* fever was still happening with copies of Kevin Kwak's novel placed on the best-seller table.

Near the end of my visit at the Books-A-Million, I walked past a carousel of Penguin Classics Editions and recognized all the works from having taken surveys of English and American literature. Each of these authors, who were all peculiarly men, influenced literature with bold ideas and innovation. I turned the carousel, and it squeaked as I read the names of these great authors: Herman Melville, Mark Twain, Henry David Thoreau, Ken Kesey, Nathanial Hawthorne, Joseph Conrad, and Robert Louis Stevenson. The United States was built on immigration, so why is there such a disparity when it comes to inclusion? The United States is supposed to be a country that takes pride in its immigrant history, but the general public and mainstream media continue to focus all of their attention on Anglo-Americans.

I stood there for a few more minutes, thinking about the lack of the earliest Asian American literature. In the seventies, Frank Chin, Jeffrey Paul Chan, Lawson Fusao Inada, and Shawn Wong had anthologized the *Aiiieeeee! An Anthology of Asian-American Writers*, but it failed to cover authors reaching further back into the late-nineteenth century. I thought about my education in high school and the lack of coverage about Asian Americans in both history and literature. We learned all about the foundation of our nation with the Puritans and the Civil War. The Reconstruction era never focused on the Chinese immigrants, and the World War II section never focused on the Japanese internment camps. Even the Civil Rights section, which was a tremendous feat for all racial minorities, never focused on Asian American issues. Whenever it came to Asian American inclusion, it was almost always abbreviated into a single paragraph in a history book. Perhaps the Cold War is to blame for creating the Model Minority stereotype to erase and devalue actual Asian American issues.

Still standing and thinking, I scratched my cheek and appreciated that I was given the opportunity to learn more about my own pan-ethic group. I could already feel the weight and burden of having to learn and research this topic on my own, and it became clear to me that this would be a life-long battle to advance Asian American inclusion in the western canon of literature. But then, a woman's voice disrupted my thoughts; I did not know how long she was standing there. She smiled at me and asked if I needed help finding anything. I told her that I had found what I needed and thanked her.

INTRODUCTION

With the rise of Asian American voices in American literature, it is important to look back at their origins. These voices reveal their experiences primarily through their memoirs and autobiographies. In *When I Was A Boy in China*, Yan Phou Lee describes his first experience in the land of the free with a train robbery. Lee Chew, on the other hand, describes his struggles to adapt to a capitalist society to earn a wage as a laundryman in San Francisco.

While traces of Asian Americans can be found sporadically through early records of America's colonialization, large waves of Asian American immigrants arrived in the United States with the discovery of gold in the mid-nineteenth century. The Gold Rush, lasting from 1848 to 1855, brought over 20,000 Chinese immigrants who tried their luck in finding gold. By 1870, the population rose to over 63,000 (Lee 59). As a result of this rapid immigration, white Americans began to fear for the integrity of the country's genetic makeup, and Chinese immigrants were isolated into Chinatowns to prevent their integration. While this allowed Chinese immigrants to maintain solidarity within their own ethnic group, it also hindered their ability to develop English speaking skills.[1]

Chinese American Authors

English language Asian American literature began with the education of Chinese immigrants in higher education. The first of all Asian immigrants to obtain a bachelor's degree was Yung Wing. Graduating from Yale College in 1855, Wing devoted the rest of his life to improving relations between America and China. After returning to China, he organized the Chinese Educational Program under the supervision of the Qing Dynasty.

The Chinese Educational Program sent 120 Chinamen to the United States in 1873, a year after the program's creation. Among these Chinamen was Yan Phou Lee, who published the first English autobiography by an Asian American

---

1 As a result, the earliest examples of Asian American literature are written in Chinese, an issue explored by Xiao-huang Yin in Chinese American Literature since the 1850s.

in 1887. A result of limited communication between English speakers and Chinese speakers allowed his autobiography *When I Was a Boy in China* to provide answers for the common American about the Chinamen who had rapidly immigrated to the United States. Likewise, Wing would publish his autobiography *My Life in China and America* later in his life in 1909. While Wing's experiences predate those of Lee's, Lee would not have been able to study in the United States without Wing's involvement.

In 1904, Henry Pearson Gratton published a collection of letters from an anonymous Chinese American in *As a Chinaman Saw Us: Passages from His Letters to a Friend at Home*. Throughout these letters, the narrator offers a humorous portrayal of an Oriental immigrant's perspective of American life. "I am going to ask you to behold the American as he is, as I honestly found him—great, small, good, bad, self-glorious, egotistical, intellectual, supercilious, ignorant, superstitious, vain, and bombastic." The selected chapters in this anthology focus on different parts of American life, from the disposition of an American man versus an American woman to critiques on American mannerisms and religions.

Similarly, Tingfang Wu's *America Through the Spectacles of an Oriental Diplomat* offers a more serious examination of American life. Wu's stay in the United States was intended to improve China's international relations and help modernize the Qing Dynasty, but the hypocrisies of America did not hide from him (Pomerantz-Zhang 104). Throughout his memoir, Wu compares American life and culture to his native Chinese and mentions the mindset of some Americans when talking about immigration: "The cry of 'America for the Americans' . . . is most illogical, for those people were not the original owners of the soil." *America Through the Spectacles of an Oriental Diplomat* allows its readers to see how the ideals of an everyday American have both remained stagnant and evolved liberally to acceptance.

The Chinese Exclusion Act was passed in 1882. A reaction against the quick growth of Chinese immigration within the past forty years, this federal law halted Chinese immigration. However, an exception to the Chinese Exclusion Act exempted male Chinese immigrants who were immigrating to the United States for primarily scholastic purposes. For this reason, the Chinese American authors in this anthology are predominantly educated men who had the chance to attend schools and universities (Lee 67). Nevertheless, the American government normalized Sinophobia, further alienating Chinese Americans from integrating into American society. Wing, who had already been naturalized in 1852, had his citizenship removed as a result of this law. Race-related massacres also occurred during this time, including the 1885 Rock Springs massacre that killed 28 coal miners (Lee 93). This period of Yellow Peril was heightened by white man's perceived threat of Chinese immigrants coming into the United States to steal their jobs. One example of this perceived fear can be seen with the "[d]emagogues . . . [who] capitalized on the deep sense of economic insecurity among the working classes" (Lee 91). Despite Chinese American immigrants taking jobs with low-paying wages, many Americans still resented the fact that they are taking jobs, causing "insecurity" in the economy.

Other forms of racism were created to instill fear and concern for the protection of women and children due to their "unassimilability" and "immorality." Caricatures of Chinese American men build off of this stereotype by portraying their facial features into exaggerated rat-like proportions to show uncleanliness (Lee 91). In continuation to this line of thought, Chinese Americans were accused of being sexually deviant and volatile men who would rape white women if given the opportunity; the sexual danger associated with Chinese Americans was produced due to their work in mines and railroads throughout the mid-nineteenth century (Lee 91).

However, this stereotype of sexual deviancy among Chinese Americans shifts away during the early-twentieth century when Chinese American men take more domestic jobs. In Lee Chew's "The Biography of a Chinaman," he explains the reasoning behind Chinese American discrimination: "The reason why so many Chinese go into the laundry business in this country is because it requires little capital and is one of the few opportunities that are open." With the resentment of Chinese Americans still being alive and strong, Chinese American men had few options to choose from for income. With an increase of Chinese American men working in domestic spheres, they were easy targets for being harassed and targeted for effeminacy due to doing "woman's work." Before the Chinese Exclusion Act was passed, the Page Act of 1875 barred Chinese American women from immigrating to the United States (Lee 67). By the late-nineteenth century, a disproportionate ratio between Chinese American men and women existed, thus creating a high percentage of unmarried Chinese American men. Coupled with the societal disapproval of interracial relationships, the stereotype of Chinese American men was born (Wang 60-61).

Moving forward, other federal laws continued to discourage Chinese Americans from journeying in the United States. Some discriminating laws that have yet to be mentioned include the Scott Act of 1888 which prevented Chinese immigrants who left the United States from ever reentering the country, the Expatriate Act of 1907 which relinquished American identity from any woman who married a foreign man of Asian descent, and the Immigration Act of 1917 which regulated literacy exams during the immigration process to deter uneducated immigrants.

The Chinese American authors in the first section of this anthology all strive for a common goal: to convince their readers they are human. Yung Wing and Yan Phou Lee begin their autobiographies by declaring basic information regarding their place and year of birth. From thereon, Wing and Lee detail their Chinese culture, frequently comparing it back to an American perspective to help American readers understand their culture. Similarly, the anonymous letters from *As a Chinaman Saw Us* and Tingfang Wu's *America Through the Spectacles of an Oriental Diplomat* allow American readers to see the frank perceptions of Chinese immigrants. Using these authors as the foundation of Asian American literature allows us to see that the beginnings are focused on autobiographical texts which allow white American readers to better understand Chinese immigrants' perspectives.

Eurasian Authors

Eurasian individuals are defined by having mixed heritages, usually of Asian and European descent. The three authors represented in this section are Sadakichi Hartmann, Sui Sin Far, and Onoto Watanna. In the late-nineteenth century, it was especially rare for mixed race individuals to be born, so the lives of these Eurasian authors are steered by race and identity.

The first of these three authors is Carl Sadakichi Hartmann, born in Dejima, Japan to a German father and Japanese mother in 1867. Due to his mother dying two months after his birth, Hartmann was raised in Germany to receive a western education (Peters 14). He developed an inclination to the arts and later in 1882 arrived to Philadelphia, Pennsylvania to stay with his granduncle. (Peters 39-41). Given the circumstances of his limited exposure to his Japanese mother, he was more attuned to his western identity and claimed that his ability to assimilate into American culture was advantageous when compared to other minorities (Peters 47).

At the start of Hartmann's writing career, one of his first projects was a short play titled *Christ: A Dramatic Poem in Three Acts*, published in 1893. The reception of the play was galvanizing due to its graphic portrayal of sexual indulgence and religion. It showed once in Boston before Hartmann was briefly arrested and ordered to destroy every copy of the play by the New England Watch and Ward Society (Peters 160). A year later, he published *Conversations with Walt Whitman* journaling his mentorship with the aging author from 1884 to 1891. His friendship with Whitman influenced his poetic style, but when he befriended Stéphane Mallarmé while serving as a foreign correspondent for the McClure's Syndicate, his poetic style gained another influence from the Symbolist movement (Xu *Historical Dictionary*).

Hartmann's childhood in Europe allowed him to have an expansive worldview of literature, being able to draw influences from French, German, and Japanese literature. Exploring the Japanese side of his identity, he borrowed the forms of the haiku, tanka, and dodoitsu in his collection of poetry *Japanese Rhythms*.[1] His contemporaries Ezra Pound and Gertrude Stein praised his literary career, as well, proving him to be a lost voice in the American canon ("Sadakichi Hartmann"). At the end of his life, the mass incarceration of Japanese Americans during World War II occurred after President Franklin D. Roosevelt ordered Executive Order 9066. Hartmann was one of the few Japanese Americans to avoid internment due to old age. He died in 1944 in Florida.

The next author, Sui Sin Far, was born as Edith Maud Eaton in 1865 in Macclesfield, England to an English father and a Chinese mother. Being another biracial figure, she was raised with western values. During her childhood, she lived in England and the United States before settling in Montreal (Madsen 75). After turning eighteen years old, she was hired as a staff writer for the *Montreal Star* where she began writing about local Chinese communities, and Eaton's interest in learning about her mother's heritage increased. Thus, she began to focus on shedding light on the Chinese immigrant experience (Madsen 76). During a short time during which she worked as a journalist in Jamaica in 1896, she created her penname "Sui Sin Far." The translation of her name is a type of narcissus flower in Cantonese, marking the full embrace of her Chinese American identity (Madsen 77).

Following her return to North America, the rest of Eaton's life was spent working in American coastal cities where she would interview Chinese communities in effort to have the general public sympathize with Chinese American immigrants (Madsen 78-79). Despite her determination to aid her fellow Chinese Americans, she sometimes faced rejection from the Chinatown communities due to her inability to properly speak her mother's tongue, a challenge she reflected in "Leaves from the Mental Portfolio of an Eurasian": "I am unacquainted with my mother tongue. How, then, can I expect these people to accept me as their own countrywoman? The Americanized Chinamen actually laugh in my face when I tell them that I am of their race." Excluding the significant number of articles she published for newspaper businesses during her

---

1 Not included in this anthology.

lifetime, Eaton published only one collection of short stories in her lifetime titled *Mrs. Spring Fragrance*. Eaton died in Montreal in 1914.

The last Eurasian author in this section is Onoto Watanna, sister of Edith Maud Eaton. Born in Montreal as Winnifred Eaton in 1875, her success as a writer was greater than her sister's. She was inspired by her elder sister, but she did not feel the same connection to their mother's Chinese heritage. Rather, Winnifred Eaton took a Japanese pseudonym, Onoto Watanna, finding that a false Japanese pseudonym would allow her to hide from the Chinese prejudice (Madsen 86). She published at least ten romance novels, which often focused on the relationships between Japanese women and white men (Xu *Historical Dictionary*). Depending heavily on the conventions of romance novels, they were written with a readership of white women in mind. Included here is a brief selection from her first novel, *Miss Numè of Japan*, published in 1899. Her portrayal of Japanese characters is problematic at times, often conforming to American stereotypes of people of Asian descent. An passage from the third chapter highlights a moment when Cleo comments on Takashima's eyes: "You are really very fine looking . . . —for a Japanese."

The other two works in this section of the anthology—*Marion: The Story of an Artist's Model* and *Me: A Book of Remembrance*—are autobiographies, originally published anonymously. Despite these memoirs containing Winnifred Eaton's most honest accounts of her life, she chooses to portray herself as ethnically ambiguous. In *Me: A Book of Remembrance*, she describes herself as "not beautiful to look at [with] black and shining eyes, and black and shining hair. . . . I was a little thing, and, like my mother, foreign-looking." She identified with her Canadian identity more than anything else, and her self-inflicted racial erasure was evidently problematic when she wrote these memoirs. Winnifred Eaton later explored Hollywood, writing screenplays for Universal and Metro-Goldwyn-Mayer. Unfortunately, most of her screenplays did not credit her due to her Asian descent (Madsen 91-92). Winnifred Eaton died in Butte, Montana in 1954.

Japanese American Authors

The addition of new poetry forms from Japanese literature was perhaps the most prominent contribution to American and British literature from Japanese American poets.

Yone Noguchi, born in Japan in 1875, encouraged English-speaking authors to experiment with the form of haikus. In his article "A Proposal to American Poets," he describes them as tiny stars for Americans to experiment with.

The compressed format of haiku poetry forces writers to consider every syllable carefully, as they can only use seventeen. In his own anthology of his poetry, *Selected Poems by Yone Noguchi, Selected by Himself,* he highlights his favorite poems from his literary career.

Like Hartmann, Noguchi also had connections with literary figures—Joaquin Miller and Charles Warren Stoddard. Noguchi arrived in San Francisco in 1893 to pursue a more intellectual life. Although his arrival was met with tribulations speaking English and encountering racism, he eventually found a job working as a dishwasher and was able to attend classes at Stanford in exchange for custodial work (Sueyoshi 19-21). Through Japanese acquaintances, he learned about Miller who was also warmhearted towards Japanese immigrants. Needing a residence, he was able to live with Miller for four years, and it is through their cohabitation that Noguchi met Stoddard (Sueyoshi 24-25, 32). In 1887, Noguchi and Stoddard began having a sexual affair, which in turn allowed Noguchi to learn more about American literature. Although Stoddard was partially attracted to Noguchi for his foreign and Oriental ethnicity, Noguchi appreciated his intimacy, nevertheless (Sueyoshi 34, 41).

Another form of Japanese literature that Noguchi helped popularize into the western sphere was Noh Theater. Though it did not make the same impact as the haikus, it was another endeavor within his literary career (Xu *Historical Dictionary*). When Noguchi returned to Japan in 1904, he never returned to the United States. He became a professor of what is now Keio University for forty years, writing propaganda-fueled poetry when World War II began. His reasoning was to "advance the cause of Japan's imperialism" (Xu *Historical Dictionary*).

Also a contributor to Japanese American literature was Jun Fujita who influenced American literature with his tanka poems. His book of poetry, *Tanka: Poems in Exile,* was notably the first American tanka collection. Very minimalist with its compact format, each tanka is stylized and centered on separate pages with white space engulfing the poems. Fujita was born in Hiroshima in 1888 and settled in Chicago, working for various newspapers as a photojournalist. He died in 1963 (Xu *Historical Dictionary*).

Unlike the two poets in this section, Jenichiro Oyabe wrote the autobiography *A Japanese Robinson Crusoe.* This text fulfills a similar purpose to the Chinese American autobiographies, showing his determination to be Christianized and attend a school in the United States. Oyabe wants to present to his readers an origin story stating why and where he came from: "how I happened to leave Japan, what strange experiences I had during my roving, and how I was converted?" His interest in Christianity and lifelong voyage serves to be a lesson of both warning and inspiration.

Conclusion

Asian American literature exists, and acknowledging its existence in a special-ized anthology is a step in constructing awareness. The first steps are small but important in this journey to augment the visibility of diversity and inclusion. As of 2019, anthologies from large publishers have already begun to reevaluate their voices to be mindful of *all* American immigrant groups.

To illustrate the current state of Asian American diversity in the *Norton Anthology of American Literature*, its ninth edition currently contains five voices: Sui Sin Far, Maxine Hong Kingston, Amy Tan, Li-Young Lee, and Michiko Kakutani. Interestingly, all five are East Asian authors. With the exception of Kakutani, they are all Chinese American writers, yet Kakutani's inclusion in the anthology is merely an essay that follows *Huckleberry Finn*. Without the essay, only four Chinese American authors represent all of Asian American literature for many students in college literature classes. The numbers diminish more in the shorter edition—Tan is excluded from the anthology, leaving all of Asian American literature to be represented by three authors.

While the selections made in this anthology contain authors of Chinese and Japanese descent, this choice was not intentional. The context of Asian immigration created a situation where it was primarily Chinese and Japanese immigrants coming from Asia. After 1923, we see more diversity within Asian American authors, but before then, it is almost exclusively Chinese and Japa-nese Americans. The journey to have our voices be told will be rocky, so for now here are the voices of the earliest Asian American authors. Perhaps in the future, these voices will gain more recognition and be heard outside of an anthology specializing in such a topic.

The decision for this anthology's time frame being from 1887 to 1923 was an arbitrary choice due to copyright. Texts from 1924 to 1945 are listed in the "Suggested Reading."

BIBLIOGRAPHY

Lee, Erika. *The Making of Asian America*. Simon and Schuster, 2015. Print.

Peters, James S. *Sadakichi Hartmann: Alien Son*. Sunstone Press, 2017. Print.

Pomerantz-Zhang, Linda. *Wu Tingfang (1842-1922): Reform and Modernization in Modern Chinese History*. Hong Kong University Press, 1992. ProQuest Ebook Central.

"Sadakichi Hartmann." *Contemporary Authors Online*, Gale, 2003. *Literature Resource Center*.

Sueyoshi, Amy H. *Queer Compulsions: Race, Nation, and Sexuality in the Affairs of Yone Noguchi*. University of Hawaii Press, 2012. ProQuest Ebook Central.

Wang, Joan S. "Race, Gender, and Laundry Work: The Roles of Chinese Laundrymen and American Women in the United States, 1850-1950." *Journal of American Ethnic History*, vol. 24, no. 1, 2004, pp. 58–99. *JSTOR*, www.jstor.org/stable/27501531.

Xu, Wenying. *Historical Dictionary of Asian American Literature and Theater*. Lanham: Scarecrow Press, 2012. eBook Collection (EBSCOhost).

ACKNOWLEDGEMENTS

First and foremost, I would like to thank my dear friends Jessica Cheng, David Gong, and Amanda Godsil for being the catalysts of my political awakening into the foray of race politics. Through Dr. Allen Grove's publishing practicum, I am thankful for the opportunity of creating an anthology of Asian American literature. To Dr. Grove, Haley Ruffner, and my peers, their advice helped influence the creation of this anthology.

Without Alfred University's English Division, I would not have the same understanding of the canon of American and British literature. I am indebted to my professors for sharing their expansive knowledge of literature and concisely laying its foundation: Dr. Robert Reginio, Dr. Melissa Ryan, Dr. Allen Grove, Dr. Susan Mayberry, Prof. Susan Morehouse, and Dr. Juliana Gray.

My gratitude extends to Dr. Brian Saltsman and Associate Dean Patricia Debertolis for their sensible discussions of diversity and inclusion during the making of this anthology. A special thanks is also due to librarian Ellen Bahr for her invaluable help in finding the texts "The Biography of a Chinaman" by Lee Chew, *Christ: A Dramatic Poem in Three Acts* by Sadakichi Hartmann, and *Tanka: Poems in Exile* by Jun Fujita. The first-edition copies of these works had proven to be well-hidden compared to the other works in this anthology.

Lastly, I would like to thank the Asian American pioneers in this anthology and the voices that remain unknown. These texts lay the foundation of Asian American literature, and through their writings I am able to learn about the history and treatment of Asian Americans. Racism in American society has improved greatly since the nineteenth century, but it is still an ongoing battle today. I am optimistic for the future of diversity and inclusion, now having the knowledge of their accomplishments.

NOTE ON THE TEXT

In editing the texts for this anthology, I retained most archaic spellings. Except when appearing in poetry, I did change some words such as "any one," "some one," "every one," and "any more" to conform to modern spelling.

CHINESE AMERICAN AUTHORS

My Life in China and America

Yung Wing

CHAPTER I
BOYHOOD

I WAS BORN ON THE 17TH OF November, 1828, in the village of Nam Ping (South Screen) which is about four miles southwest of the Portuguese Colony of Macao, and is situated on Pedro Island lying west of Macao, from which it is separated by a channel of half a mile wide.

I was one of a family of four children. A brother was the eldest, a sister came next, I was the third, and another brother was the fourth and the youngest of the group. I am the only survivor of them all.

As early as 1834, an English lady, Mrs. Gutzlaff, wife of the Rev. Charles Gutzlaff, a missionary to China, came to Macao and, under the auspices of the Ladies' Association in London for the promotion of female education in India and the East, immediately took up the work of her mission by starting a girls' school for Chinese girls, which was soon followed by the opening of a school for boys also.

Mrs. Gutzlaff's comprador or factotum happened to come from the village I did and was, in fact, my father's friend and neighbor. It was through him that my parents heard about Mrs. Gutzlaff's school and it was doubtless through his influence and means that my father got me admitted into the school. It has always been a mystery to me why my parents should take it into their heads to put me into a foreign school, instead of a regular orthodox Confucian school, where my brother much older than myself was placed. Most assuredly such a step would have been more in play with Chinese public sentiment, taste, and the wants of the country at large, than to allow me to attend an English school; moreover, a Chinese cult is the only avenue in China that leads to political preferment, influence, power and wealth. I can only account for the departure thus taken on the theory that as foreign intercourse with China was just beginning to grow, my parents, anticipating that it might soon assume the proportions of a tidal wave, thought it worth while to take time by the forelock and put one of their sons to learning English that he might become one of

3

the advanced interpreters and have a more advantageous position from which
to make his way into the business and diplomatic world. This I take to be the
chief aim that influenced my parents to put me into Mrs. Gutzlaff's Mission
School. As to what other results or sequences it has eventually brought about
in my subsequent life, they were entirely left to Him who has control of all our
devising and planning, as they are governed by a complete system of divine laws
of antecedents and consequents, or of cause and effect.

In 1835, when I was barely seven years of age, my father took me to Macao.
Upon reaching the school, I was brought before Mrs. Gutzlaff. She was the first
English lady I had ever seen. On my untutored and unsophisticated mind she
made a deep impression. If my memory serves me right, she was somewhat tall
and well-built. She had prominent features which were strong and assertive; her
eyes were of clear blue lustre, somewhat deep set. She had thin lips, supported
by a square chin,—both indicative of firmness and authority. She had flaxen
hair and eyebrows somewhat heavy. Her features taken collectively indicated
great determination and will power.

As she came forward to welcome me in her long and full flowing white
dress (the interview took place in the summer), surmounted by two large globe
sleeves which were fashionable at the time and which lent her an exaggerated
appearance, I remember most vividly I was no less puzzled than stunned. I ac-
tually trembled all over with fear at her imposing proportions—having never in
my life seen such a peculiar and odd fashion. I clung to my father in fear. Her
kindly expression and sympathetic smiles found little appreciative response at
the outset, as I stood half dazed at her personality and my new environment.
For really, a new world had dawned on me. After a time, when my homesick-
ness was over and the novelty of my surroundings began gradually to wear away,
she completely won me over through her kindness and sympathy. I began to
look upon her more like a mother. She seemed to take a special interest in me; I
suppose, because I was young and helpless, and away from my parents, besides
being the youngest pupil in the school. She kept me among her girl pupils and
did not allow me to mingle with what few boys there were at the time.

There is one escapade that I can never forget! It happened during the first
year in the school, and was an attempt on my part to run away. I was shut up
in the third story of the house, which had a wide open terrace on the top,—the
only place where the girls and myself played and found recreation. We were
not allowed to go out of doors to play in the streets. The boy pupils had their
quarters on the ground floor and had full liberty to go out for exercise. I used
to envy them their freedom and smuggled down stairs to mingle with them in
their sports after school hours. I felt ill at ease to be shut up with the girls all

alone way up in the third story. I wanted to see something of the outside world. I occasionally stole down stairs and ventured out to the wharves around which were clustered a number of small ferry boats which had a peculiar fascination to my young fancy. To gain my freedom, I planned to run away. The girls were all much older than I was, and a few sympathized with me in my wild scheme; doubtless, from the same restlessness of being too closely cooped up. I told them of my plan. Six of the older ones fell in with me in the idea. I was to slip out of the house alone, go down to the wharf and engage a covered boat to take us all in.

The next morning after our morning meal, and while Mrs. Gutzlaff was off taking her breakfast, we stole out unbeknown to anyone and crowded into the boat and started off in hot haste for the opposite shore of Pedro Island. I was to take the whole party to my home and from there the girls were to disperse to their respective villages. We were half way across the channel when, to my great consternation, I saw a boat chasing us, making fast time and gaining on us all the while. No promise of additional pay was of any avail, because our two oars against their four made it impossible for us to win out; so our boatmen gave up the race at the waving of handkerchiefs in the other boat and the whole party was captured. Then came the punishment. We were marched through the whole school and placed in a row, standing on a long narrow school table placed at one end of the school room facing all the pupils in front of us. I was placed in the center of the row, with a tall foolscap mounted on my head, having three girls on the right and three on the left. I had pinned on my breast a large square placard bearing the inscription, "Head of the Runaways;" there we stood for a whole hour till school was dismissed. I never felt so humiliated in my life as I did when I was undergoing that ordeal. I felt completely crestfallen. Some of the mischievous fellows would extract a little fun out of this display by taking furtive glances and making wry faces at us. Mrs. Gutzlaff, in order to aggravate our punishment, had ordered ginger snaps and oranges to be distributed among the other pupils right before us.

Mrs. Gutzlaff's school, started in September, 1835, was originally for girls only. Pending the organization and opening of the so-called "Morrison Education Society School," in the interval between 1835 and 1839, a department for boys was temporarily incorporated into her school, and part of the subscription fund belonging to the M. E. S. School was devoted to the maintenance of this one.

This accounts for my entrance into Mrs. Gutzlaff's School, as one of only two boys first admitted. Her school being thus enlarged and modified temporarily, Mrs. Gutzlaff's two nieces—the Misses Parkes, sisters to Mr. Harry Parkes who was afterwards knighted, by reason of the conspicuous part he played in the second Opium War, in 1864, of which he was in fact the originator—came out to China as assistants in the school. I was fortunately placed under their instruction for a short time.

Afterwards the boys' school under Mrs. Gutzlaff and her two nieces, the Misses Parkes, was broken up; that event parted our ways in life in divergent directions. Mrs. Gutzlaff went over to the United States with three blind girls,—Laura, Lucy and Jessie. The Misses Parkes were married to missionaries, one to Dr. William Lockhart, a medical missionary; the other to a Rev. Mr. MacClatchy, also a missionary. They labored long in China, under the auspices of the London Missionary Society. The three blind girls whom Mrs. Gutzlaff took with her were taught by me to read on raised letters till they could read from the Bible and Pilgrim's Progress.

On my return to my home village I resumed my Chinese studies.

In the fall of 1840, while the Opium War was still going on, my father died, leaving four children on my mother's hands without means of support.

Fortunately, three of us were old enough to lend a helping hand. My brother was engaged in fishing, my sister helped in housework, and I took to hawking candy through my own village and the neighboring one. I took hold of the business in good earnest, rising at three o'clock every morning, and I did not come home until six o'clock in the evening. My daily earnings netted twenty-five cents, which I turned over to my mother, and with the help given by my brother, who was the main stay of the family, we managed to keep the wolf away from our door. I was engaged in hawking candy for about five months, and when winter was over, when no candy was made, I changed my occupation and went into the rice fields to glean rice after the reapers. My sister usually accompanied me in such excursions. But unlike Ruth of old, I had no Boaz to help me out when I was short in my gleaning. But my knowledge of English came to my rescue. My sister told the head reaper that I could speak, read and write English. This awakened the curiosity of the reaper. He beckoned me to him and asked me whether I wouldn't talk some "Red Hair Men" talk to him. He said he never heard of such talk in his life. I felt bashful and diffident at first, but my sister encouraged me and said "the reaper may give you a large bundle of rice sheaf to take home." This was said as a kind of prompter. The reaper was shrewd enough to take it up, and told me that if I would talk, he would give me a bundle heavier than I could carry. So I began and repeated the alphabet to him. All the reapers as well as the gleaners stood in vacant silence, with mouths wide open, grinning with evident delight. A few minutes after my maiden speech was delivered in the paddy field with water and mud almost knee deep, I was rewarded with several sheaves, and I had to hurry away in order to get two other boys to carry what my sister and I could not lug. Thus I came home loaded with joy and sheaves of golden rice to my mother, little dreaming that my smattering knowledge of English would serve me such a turn so early in my career. I was then about twelve years old. Even Ruth with her six measures of corn did not fare any better than I did.

Soon after the gleaning days, all too few, were over, a neighbor of mine who was a printer in the printing office of a Roman Catholic priest happened to be home from Macao on a vacation. He spoke to my mother about the priest wanting to hire a boy in his office who knew enough English to read the numerals correctly, so as to be able to fold and prepare the papers for the binders. My mother said I could do the work. So I was introduced to the priest and a bargain was struck. I returned home to report myself, and a few days later I was in Macao and entered upon my duty as a folder on a salary of $4.50 a month. My board and lodging came to $1.50—the balance of $3.00 was punctually sent to my mother every month. I did not get rich quickly in this employment, for I had been there but four months when a call for me to quit work came from a quarter I least expected. It had more the sound of heaven in it. It came from a Dr. Benjamin Hobson, a medical missionary in Macao whose hospital was not more than a mile from the printer's office. He sent word that he wanted to see me; that he had been hunting for me for months. I knew Dr. Hobson well, for I saw him a number of times at Mrs. Gutzlaff's. So I called on him. At the outset, I thought he was going to take me in to make a doctor of me, but no, he said he had a promise to fulfill. Mrs. Gutzlaff's last message to him, before she embarked for America with the three blind girls, was to be sure to find out where I was and to put me into the Morrison Education Society School as soon as it was opened for pupils.

"This is what I wanted to see you for," said Dr. Hobson. "Before you leave your employment and after you get the consent of your mother to let you go to the Morrison School, I would like to have you come to the hospital and stay with me for a short time so that I may become better acquainted with you, before I take you to the Morrison School, which is already opened for pupils, and introduce you to the teacher."

At the end of the interview, I went home to see my mother who, after some reluctance, gave her consent. I returned to Macao, bade farewell to the priest who, though reticent and reserved, not having said a word to me during all the four months I was in his employ, yet did not find fault with me in my work. I went over to the hospital. Dr. Hobson immediately set me to work with the mortar and pestle, preparing materials for ointments and pills. I used to carry a tray and accompany him in his rounds to visit the patients, in the benevolent work of alleviating their pains and sufferings. I was with him about a couple of months in the hospital work, at the end of which time he took me one day and introduced me to the Rev. Samuel Robins Brown, the teacher of the Morrison Education Society School.

CHAPTER II
SCHOOL DAYS

THE MORRISON SCHOOL WAS OPENED ON the 1st of November, 1839, under the charge of the Rev. S. R. Brown who, with his wife, Mrs. Brown, landed at Macao on the 19th of February, 1839. Brown, who was afterwards made a D.D., was a graduate of Yale of the class of 1832. From his antecedents, he was eminently fitted to pioneer the first English school in China. I entered the school in 1841. I found that five other boys had entered ahead of me by one year. They were all studying primary arithmetic, geography, and reading. I had the start of them only in reading and pronouncing English well. We studied English in the forenoon, and Chinese in the afternoon. The names of the five boys were: 1. Wong Shing; 2. Li Kan; 3. Chow Wan; 4. Tong Chik; 5. Wong Foon. I made the sixth one and was the youngest of all. We formed the first class of the school, and became Brown's oldest pupils throughout, from first to last, till he left China in December, 1846, on account of poor health. Half of our original number accompanied him to this country, on his return.

The Morrison Education Society School came about in this way: Not long after the death of Dr. Robert Morrison, which occurred on the 1st of August, 1834, a circular was issued among the foreign residents on the 26th of January, 1835, calling for the formation of an Association to be named the "Morrison Education Society." Its object was to "improve and promote English education in China by schools and other means." It was called "Morrison" to commemorate the labors and works of that distinguished man who was sent out by the London Missionary Society as the first missionary to China in 1807. He crossed the Atlantic from London to New York where he embarked for China in the sailing vessel "Trident" on the 31st of January, 1807. He tried to land in Macao, but the jealousy of the Jesuits thwarted his purpose. He was obliged to go up to Canton. Finally, on account of the unsettled relations between the Chinese government and the foreign merchants there, he repaired to Malacca, and made that place the basis of his labors. He was the author of the first Anglo-Chinese dictionary, of three quarto volumes. He translated the Bible into Chinese; Leang Afah was his first Chinese convert and trained by him to preach. Leang afterwards became a powerful preacher. The importance and bearing of his dictionary and the translation of the Bible into Chinese, on subsequent missionary work in China, were fundamental and paramount. The preaching of his convert, Leang Afah, likewise contributed in no small degree towards opening up a new era in the religious life of China. His memory, therefore, is worthy of being kept alive by the establishment of a school named after him. Indeed, a university ought to have been permanently founded for that purpose instead of a school, whose existence was solely dependent upon the precarious and ephemeral subscriptions of transient foreign merchants in China.

At the close of the Opium War in 1840, and after the Island of Hong Kong had been ceded to the British government, the Morrison school was removed to Hong Kong in 1842. The site chosen for it was on the top of a hill about six hundred feet above the level of the sea. The hill is situated on the eastern end of Victoria Colony and was called "Morrison Hill" after the name of the school. It commands a fine view of the harbor, as that stretches from east to west. The harbor alone made Hong Kong the most coveted concession in Southern China. It is spacious and deep enough to hold the Navy of Great Britain, and it is that distinguishing feature and its strategic location that have made it what it is. On the 12th of March, 1845, Mr. Wm. Allen Macy arrived in Hong Kong as an assistant teacher in the school. His arrival was timely, because the school, since its removal from Macao to Hong Kong, had been much enlarged. Three more classes of new pupils had been formed and the total number of pupils all told was more than forty. This was more than one man could manage. The assistant teacher was much needed. Brown continued his work in the school till the fall of 1846. Macy had a whole year in which to be broken into the work.

Between Brown and Macy there was a marked difference in temperament and character. Brown, on the one hand, showed evidences of a self-made man. He was cool in temperament, versatile in the adaptation of means to ends, gentlemanly and agreeable, and somewhat optimistic. He found no difficulty in endearing himself to his pupils, because he sympathized with them in their efforts to master their studies, and entered heart and soul into his work. He had an innate faculty of making things clear to the pupils and conveying to them his understanding of a subject without circumlocution, and with great directness and facility. This was owing in a great measure to his experience as a pedagogue, before coming out to China, and even before he entered college. He knew how to manage boys, because he knew boys' nature well, whether Chinese, Japanese or American. He impressed his pupils as being a fine teacher and one eminently fitted from inborn tact and temperament to be a successful school master, as he proved himself to be in his subsequent career in Auburn, N. Y., and in Japan.

Macy, the assistant teacher, was likewise a Yale man. He had never taught school before in his life, and had no occasion to do so. He possessed no previous experience to guide him in his new work of pedagogy in China. He was evidently well brought up and was a man of sensitive nature, and of fine moral sensibilities,—a soul full of earnestness and lofty ideals.

After the Morrison School was broken up in 1850, he returned to this country with his mother and took up theology in the Yale Theological Seminary. In 1854, he went back to China as a missionary under the American Board. I had graduated from Yale College then and was returning to China with him. We were the only passengers in that long, wearisome and most trying passage of 154 days from Sandy Hook to Hong Kong.

Brown left China in the winter of 1846. Four months before he left, he one day sprang a surprise upon the whole school. He told of his contemplated return to America on account of his health and the health of his family. Before closing his remarks by telling us of his deep interest in the school, he said he would like to take a few of his old pupils home with him to finish their education in the United States, and that those who wished to accompany him would signify it by rising. This announcement, together with his decision to return to America, cast a deep gloom over the whole school. A dead silence came over all of us. And then for several days afterwards the burden of our conversation was about Brown's leaving the school for good. The only cheerful ones among us were those who had decided to accompany him home. These were Wong Shing, Wong Foon and myself. When he requested those who wished to accompany him to the States to signify it by rising, I was the first one on my feet. Wong Foon was the second, followed by Wong Shing. But before regarding our cases as permanently settled, we were told to go home and ask the consent of our respective parents. My mother gave her consent with great reluctance, but after my earnest persuasion she yielded, though not without tears and sorrow. I consoled her with the fact that she had two more sons besides myself, and a daughter to look after her comfort. Besides, she was going to have a daughter-in-law to take care of her, as my elder brother was engaged to be married.

It may not be out of place to say that if it had depended on our own resources, we never could have come to America to finish our education, for we were all poor. Doubtless Brown must have had the project well discussed among the trustees of the school months before he broached the subject to his pupils.

It was also through his influence that due provision was made for the support of our parents for at least two years, during our absence in America. Our patrons who bore all our expenses did not intend that we should stay in this country longer than two years. They treated us nobly. They did a great work for us. Among those who bore a conspicuous part in defraying our expenses while in America, besides providing for the support of our aged parents, I can recall the names of Andrew Shortrede, proprietor and editor of the "Hong Kong China Mail" (he was a Scotchman, an old bachelor, and a noble and handsome specimen of humanity), A. A. Ritchie, an American merchant, and A. A. Campbell, another Scotchman. There were others unknown to me. The Olyphant Sons, David, Talbot and Robert, three brothers, leading merchants of New York, gave us a free passage from Hong Kong to New York in their sailing vessel, the "Huntress," which brought a cargo of tea at the same time. Though late in the day for me to mention the names of these benefactors who from pure motives of Christian philanthropy aided me in my education, yet it may be a source of satisfaction to their descendants, if there are any living in different parts of the world, to know that their sires took a prominent part in the education of the three Chinese youths,—Wong Shing, Wong Foon and myself.

CHAPTER III
JOURNEY TO AMERICA AND FIRST EXPERIENCES THERE

BEING THUS GENEROUSLY PROVIDED FOR, WE embarked at Whompoa on the 4th of January, 1847, in the good ship "Huntress" under Captain Gillespie. As stated above, she belonged to the Olyphant Brothers and was loaded with a full cargo of tea. We had the northeast trade wind in our favor, which blew strong and steady all the way from Whompoa to St. Helena. There was no accident of any kind, excepting a gale as we doubled the Cape of Good Hope. The tops of the masts and ends of the yards were tipped with balls of electricity. The strong wind was howling and whistling behind us like a host of invisible Furies. The night was pitch dark and the electric balls dancing on the tips of the yards and tops of the masts, back and forth and from side to side like so many infernal lanterns in the black night, presented a spectacle never to be forgotten by me. I realized no danger, although the ship pitched and groaned, but enjoyed the wild and weird scene hugely. After the Cape was doubled, our vessel ploughed through the comparatively smooth waters of the Atlantic until we reached the Island of St. Helena where we were obliged to stop for fresh water and provisions. Most sailing vessels that were bound from the East for the Atlantic board were accustomed to make St. Helena their stopping place. St. Helena, as viewed from the shipboard, presented an outward appearance of a barren volcanic rock, as though freshly emerged from the baptism of fire and brimstone. Not a blade of grass could be seen on its burnt and charred surface. We landed at Jamestown, which is a small village in the valley of the Island. In this valley there was rich and beautiful vegetation. We found among the sparse inhabitants a few Chinese who were brought there by the East India Company's ships. They were middle-aged people, and had their families there. While there, we went over to Longwood where was Napoleon's empty tomb. A large weeping willow hung and swept over it. We cut a few twigs, and kept them alive till we reached this country and they were brought to Auburn, N. Y., by Mr. Brown, who planted them near his residence when he was teaching in the Auburn Academy for several years before his departure for Japan. These willows proved to be fine, handsome trees when I visited Auburn in 1854.

From St. Helena we took a northwesterly course and struck the Gulf Stream, which, with the wind still fair and favorable, carried us to New York in a short time. We landed in New York on the 12th of April, 1847, after a passage of ninety-eight days of unprecedented fair weather. The New York of 1847 was altogether a different city from the New York of 1909. It was a city of only 250,000 or 300,000 inhabitants; now it is a metropolis rivaling London in population, wealth and commerce. The whole of Manhattan Island is turned into a city of skyscrapers, churches and palatial residences.

Little did I realize when in 1845 I wrote, while in the Morrison School, a composition on "An Imaginary Voyage to New York and up the Hudson," that I was to see New York in reality. This incident leads me to the reflection that sometimes our imagination foreshadows what lies uppermost in our minds and brings possibilities within the sphere of realities. The Chinese Education Scheme is another example of the realities that came out of my day dreams a year before I graduated. So was my marrying an American wife. Still there are other day dreams yet to be realized; whether or no they will ever come to pass the future will determine.

Our stay in New York was brief. The first friends we had the good fortune to make in the new world, were Prof. David E. Bartlett and his wife. He was a professor in the New York Asylum for the Deaf and Dumb, and was afterwards connected with a like institution in Hartford. The Professor died in 1879. His wife, Mrs. Fanny P. Bartlett, survived him for nearly thirty years and passed away in the spring of 1907. She was a woman highly respected and beloved for her high Christian character and unceasing activities for good in the community in which she lived. Her influence was even extended to China by the few students who happened to enjoy her care and instruction. I count her as one of my most valued friends in America.

From New York we proceeded by boat to New Haven where we had an opportunity to see Yale College and were introduced to President Day. I had not then the remotest idea of becoming a graduate of one of the finest colleges of the country, as I did a few years afterwards. We went by rail from New Haven to Warehouse Point and from there to East Windsor, the home of Mrs. Elizabeth Brown, wife of Dr. Brown. Her parents were then living. Her father, the Rev. Shubael Bartlett, was the pastor of the East Windsor Congregational Church. I well remember the first Sabbath we attended his church. We three Chinese boys sat in the pastor's pew which was on the left of the pulpit, having a side view of the minister, but in full view of the whole congregation. We were the cynosure of the whole church. I doubt whether much attention was paid to the sermon that day.

The Rev. Shubael Bartlett was a genuine type of the old New England Puritan. He was exact and precise in all his manners and ways. He spoke in a deliberate and solemn tone, but full of sincerity and earnestness. He conducted himself as though he was treading on thin ice, cautiously and circumspectly. One would suppose from his appearance that he was austere and exacting, but he was gentle and thoughtful. He would have his family Bible and hymn book placed one on top of the other, squared and in straight lines, on the same spot on the table every morning for morning prayers. He always sat in the same spot for morning prayers. In other words, you always knew where to find him. His habits and daily life were as regular as clock work. I never heard him crack a joke or burst out in open laughter.

Mrs. Bartlett, Mrs. Brown's mother, was of a different makeup. She was always cheerful. A smile lighted up her features nearly all the time and for everyone she had a kind and cheerful word, while the sweet tone of her voice always carried with it cheerfulness and good will. Her genial temperament and her hospitality made the parsonage a favorite resort to all the friends and relatives of the family, who were quite numerous. It was always a puzzle to me how the old lady managed to make ends meet when her husband's salary was not over $400 a year. To be sure, the farm annually realized something, but Daniel, the youngest son, who was the staff of the old couple, had to work hard to keep up the prestige of the parsonage. It was in this parsonage that I found a temporary home while at school in Monson, and also in Yale.

CHAPTER IV
AT MONSON ACADEMY

W E WERE IN EAST WINDSOR FOR about a week; then we went up to Monson, Mass., to enter the Academy there. Monson Academy was, at one time, quite a noted preparatory school in New England, before high schools sprang into existence. Young men from all parts of the country were found here, undergoing preparation for colleges. It was its fortune, at different periods of its history, to have had men of character and experience for its principals. The Rev. Charles Hammond was one of them. He was in every sense a self-made man. He was a graduate of Yale; he was enthusiastically fond of the classics, and a great admirer of English literature. He was a man of liberal views and broad sympathies. He was well-known in New England as an educator and a champion of temperance and New England virtues. His high character gave the Academy a wide reputation and the school was never in a more prosperous condition than when he was principal. He took a special interest in us, the three Chinese students—Wong Shing, Wong Foon and myself—not so much from the novelty of having Chinese in the school as from his interest in China, and the possible good that might come out of our education.

In our first year in the Academy, we were placed in the English department. Greenleaf's Arithmetic, English Grammar, Physiology, and Upham's Mental Philosophy were our studies. In the last two studies we recited to the new preceptress, Miss Rebekah Brown, a graduate of Mt. Holyoke, the valedictorian of her class. She afterwards became the wife of Doctor A. S. McClean, of Springfield, Mass. She was a fine teacher and a woman of exceptional Christian virtues. She had an even and sweet temper, and was full of good will and good works. She and her husband, the good Doctor, took a genuine interest in me; they gave me a home during some of my college vacations, and helped me in various ways in my struggle through Yale. I kept up my correspondence with them after my return to China, and upon my coming back to this country, I was always cordially invited to their home in Springfield. It was on account of such a genuine friendship that I made Springfield my headquarters in 1872, when I brought the first installment of Government students to this country.

Brown placed us under the care of his mother, Mrs. Phoebe H. Brown. We boarded with her, but had a separate room assigned us in a dwelling right across the road, opposite to her cottage. Her widowed daughter with her three boys had taken up all the spare rooms in the cottage, which accounts for the want of accommodation for us.

In those primitive days, board and lodging in the country were very reasonable. Indigent students had a fair chance to work their way for an education. I remember we paid for board and lodging, including fuel, light and washing, only $1.25 a week for each, but we had to take care of our own rooms and, in the winter, saw and split our own wood, which we found to be capital exercise.

Our lodging was about half a mile from the academy. We had to walk three times a day to school and back, in the dead of winter when the snow was three feet deep; that gave us plenty of exercise, keen appetites and kept us in fine condition.

I look back upon my acquaintance with Mrs. Phoebe H. Brown with a mingled feeling of respect and admiration. She certainly was a remarkable New England woman—a woman of surpassing strength of moral and religious character. Those who have had the rare privilege of reading her stirring biography, will, I am sure, bear me out in this statement. She went through the crucible of unprecedented adversities and trials of life and came out one of the rare shining lights that beautify the New England sky. She is the authoress of the well-known hymn, "I love to steal awhile away from every cumbering care," etc., which breathes the calm spirit of contentment and resignation wherever sung.

The Rev. Charles Hammond, the principal of the academy when we joined it, was a graduate of Yale, as I stated before, and a man of a fine cultivated taste. He was an enthusiastic admirer of Shakespeare, who was his favorite poet; among orators, he was partial to Daniel Webster. He had the faculty of inspiring his pupils with the love of the beautiful, both in ancient and modern literature. In our daily recitations, he laid a greater stress on pointing out the beauties of a sentence and its construction, than he did on grammatical rules, moods and tenses. He was a fine writer. His addresses and sermons were pointed and full of life. Like Dr. Arnold of Rugby, he aimed to build character in his pupils and not to convert them into walking encyclopedias, or intelligent parrots. It was through him that I was introduced to Addison, Goldsmith, Dickens, Sir Walter Scott, the Edinburgh Reviews, Macaulay and Shakespeare, which formed the bulk of my reading while in Monson.

During my first year in the Monson Academy, I had no idea of taking a collegiate course. It was well understood that I was to return to China at the end of 1849, and the appropriation was made to suit such a plan. In the fall of 1848, after Wong Shing—the eldest of the three of us—had returned to China on account of his poor health, Wong Foon and myself, who were left behind to continue our studies for another year, frequently met to talk over future plans for the end of the prescribed time. We both decided finally to stay in this country to continue our studies, but the question arose, who was going to back us financially after 1849? This was the Gordian Knot. We concluded to consult Mr. Hammond and Mr. Brown on the subject. They both decided to have the matter referred to our patrons in Hong Kong. Reply came that if we wished to prosecute our studies after 1849, they would be willing to continue their support through a professional course, if we were willing to go over to Scotland to go through the University of Edinburgh. This was a generous and noble-hearted proposal.

Wong Foon, on his part, after much deliberation, decided to accept the offer and go over to Scotland at the end of 1849, while, on my part, I preferred to remain in this country to continue my studies here with the view of going to Yale. Wong Foon's decision had relieved him of all financial anxieties, while the problem of how I was to pay my education bills after 1849, still remained to be solved. But I did not allow the perplexities of the future to disturb my peace of mind. I threw all my anxieties to the wind, trusting to a wise Providence to care for my future, as it had done for my past.

Wong Foon and I, having taken our decisive steps, dropped our English studies at the close of the school year of 1849, and in the fall of the same year we began the A B C's of our classical course. In the summer of 1850, we graduated from the academy. Wong Foon, by previous arrangements, went over to Scotland and entered the University of Edinburgh. I remained in this country and finally entered Yale. It was fully a decade since we had met for the first time in the Morrison School in Macao, in 1840, to become school-mates as well as class-mates. Now that link was broken.

Wong was in the University seven years. After completing his professional studies as a doctor, he returned to China in 1857. He was a fine scholar. He graduated the third man in his medical class. He also distinguished himself in his profession. His ability and skill secured for him an enviable reputation as one of the ablest surgeons east of the Cape of Good Hope at that time. He had a fine practice in Canton, where the foreign residents retained him as their physician in preference to European doctors. He was very successful and made quite a fortune before his death, which took place in 1879. Both the native and foreign communities felt his loss. He was highly respected and honored by Chinese and foreigners for his Christian character and the purity of his life.

CHAPTER V
MY COLLEGE DAYS

BEFORE ENTERING YALE, I HAD NOT solved the problem of how I was to be carried through the collegiate course without financial backing of a definite and well-assured character. It was an easy matter to talk about getting an education by working for it, and there is a kind of romance in it that captivates the imagination, but it is altogether a different thing to face it in a business and practical way. So it proved to me, after I had put my foot into it. I had no one except Brown, who had already done so much for me in bringing me to this country, and Hammond, who fitted me for college. To them I appealed for advice and counsel. I was advised to avail myself of the contingent fund provided for indigent students. It was in the hands of the trustees of the academy and so well guarded that it could not be appropriated without the recipient's signing a written pledge that he would study for the ministry and afterwards become a missionary. Such being the case, I made up my mind that it would be utterly useless for me to apply for the fund. However, a day was appointed for me to meet the trustees in the parsonage, to talk over the subject. They said they would be too glad to have me avail myself of the fund, provided I was willing to sign a pledge that after graduation I should go back to China as a missionary. I gave the trustees to understand that I would never give such a pledge for the following reasons: First, it would handicap and circumscribe my usefulness. I wanted the utmost freedom of action to avail myself of every opportunity to do the greatest good in China. If necessary, I might be obliged to create new conditions, if I found old ones were not favorable to any plan I might have for promoting her highest welfare.

In the second place, the calling of a missionary is not the only sphere in life where one can do the most good in China or elsewhere. In such a vast empire, there can be hardly any limit put upon one's ambition to do good, if one is possessed of the Christ-spirit; on the other hand, if one has not such a spirit, no pledge in the world could melt his ice-bound soul.

In the third place, a pledge of that character would prevent me from taking advantage of any circumstance or event that might arise in the life of a nation like China, to do her a great service.

"For these reasons," I said, "I must decline to give the pledge and at the same time decline to accept your kind offer to help me. I thank you, gentlemen, very much, for your good wishes."

Both Brown and Hammond afterwards agreed that I took the right view on the subject and sustained me in my position. To be sure, I was poor, but I would not allow my poverty to gain the upper hand and compel me to barter away my inward convictions of duty for a temporary mess of pottage.

During the summer of 1850, it seems that Brown who had been making a visit in the South to see his sister, while there had occasion to call on some of the members of "The Ladies' Association" in Savannah, Ga., to whom he mentioned my case. He returned home in the nick of time, just after I had the interview with the board of trustees of the academy. I told him of the outcome, when, as stated above, he approved of my position, and told me what he had done. He said that the members of the association agreed to help me in college. On the strength of that I gathered fresh courage, and went down to New Haven to pass my examination for entrance. How I got in, I do not know, as I had had only fifteen months of Latin and twelve months of Greek, and ten months of mathematics. My preparation had been interrupted because the academy had been broken up by the Palmer & New London R.R. that was being built close by. As compared with the college preparations of nine-tenths of my class-mates, I was far behind. However, I passed without condition. But I was convinced I was not sufficiently prepared, as my recitations in the class-room clearly proved. Between the struggle of how to make ends meet financially and how to keep up with the class in my studies, I had a pretty tough time of it. I used to sweat over my studies till twelve o'clock every night the whole Freshman year. I took little or no exercise and my health and strength began to fail and I was obliged to ask for a leave of absence of a week. I went to East Windsor to get rested and came back refreshed.

In the Sophomore year, from my utter aversion to mathematics, especially to differential and integral calculus, which I abhorred and detested, and which did me little or no good in the way of mental discipline, I used to fizzle and flunk so often that I really thought I was going to be dropped from the class, or dismissed from college. But for some unexplained reasons I was saved from such a catastrophe, and I squeezed through the second year in college with so low a mark that I was afraid to ask my division tutor, who happened to be Tutor Blodget, who had me in Greek, about it. The only redeeming feature that saved me as a student in the class of 1854, was the fortunate circumstance that I happened to be a successful competitor on two occasions in English composition in my division. I was awarded the first prize in the second term, and the first prize in the third term of the year. These prizes gave me quite an éclat in the college as well as in the outside world, but I was not at all elated over them on account of my poor scholarship which I felt keenly through the whole college course.

Before the close of my second year, I succeeded in securing the stewardship of a boarding club consisting of sophomores and juniors. There were altogether twenty members. I did all the marketing and served at the table. In this way, I earned my board through the latter half of my college course. In money matters, I was supplied with remittances from "The Ladies' Association" in Savannah, and also contributions from the Olyphant Brothers of New York. In addition to these sources of supply, I was paid for being an assistant librarian to the "Brothers in Unity," which was one of the two college debating societies that owned a library, and of which I was a member.

In my senior year I was again elected librarian to the same Society and got $30.00. These combined sums were large enough to meet all my cash bills, since my wants had to be finely trimmed to suit the cloth. If most of the country parsons of that period could get along with a salary of $200 or $300 a year (supplemented, of course, with an annual donation party, which sometimes carried away more than it donated), having as a general thing a large family to look after, I certainly ought to have been able to get through college with gifts of nearly a like amount, supplemented with donations of shirts and stockings from ladies who took an interest in my education.

The class of 1854, to which I had the honor and the good fortune to belong, graduated ninety-eight all told. Being the first Chinaman who had ever been known to go through a first-class American college, I naturally attracted considerable attention; and from the fact that I was librarian for one of the college debating societies (Linonia was the other) for two years, I was known by members of the three classes above, and members of the three classes below me. This fact had contributed toward familiarizing me with the college world at large, and my nationality, of course, added piquancy to my popularity.

As an undergraduate, I had already acquired a factitious reputation within the walls of Yale. But that was ephemeral and soon passed out of existence after graduation.

All through my college course, especially in the closing year, the lamentable condition of China was before my mind constantly and weighed on my spirits. In my despondency, I often wished I had never been educated, as education had unmistakably enlarged my mental and moral horizon, and revealed to me responsibilities which the sealed eye of ignorance can never see, and sufferings and wrongs of humanity to which an uncultivated and callous nature can never be made sensitive. The more one knows, the more he suffers and is consequently less happy; the less one knows, the less he suffers, and hence is more happy. But this is a low view of life, a cowardly feeling and unworthy of a being bearing the impress of divinity. I had started out to get an education. By dint of hard work and self-denial I had finally secured the coveted prize and although it might not be so complete and symmetrical a thing as could be desired, yet I had come right up to the conventional standard and idea of a liberal education. I could, therefore, call myself an educated man and, as such, it behooved me to ask, "What am I going to do with my education?" Before the close of my last year in college I had already sketched out what I should do. I was determined that the rising generation of China should enjoy the same educational advantages that I had enjoyed; that through western education China might be regenerated, become enlightened and powerful. To accomplish that object became the guiding star of my ambition. Towards such a goal, I directed all my mental resources and energy. Through thick and thin, and the vicissitudes of a checkered life from 1854 to 1872, I labored and waited for its consummation.

CHAPTER VI
RETURN TO CHINA

IN ENTERING UPON MY LIFE'S WORK WHICH TO me was so full of meaning and earnestness, the first episode was a voyage back to the old country, which I had not seen for nearly ten years, but which had never escaped my mind's eye nor my heart's yearning for her welfare. I wanted very much to stay a few years longer in order to take a scientific course. I had taken up surveying in the Sheffield Scientific School just as that department was starting into existence under Professor Norton. Had I had the means to prosecute a practical profession, that might have helped to shorten and facilitate the way to the goal I had in view; but as I was poor and my friends thought that a longer stay in this country might keep me here for good, and China would lose me altogether, I was for this and other reasons induced to return. The scientific course was accordingly abandoned. The persons who were most interested in my return to China were Pelatiah Perit of Messrs. Goodhue & Co., merchants in the China trade, and the Olyphant Brothers, who had taken such a lively interest eight years before in helping me to come over in their ship, the "Huntress." These gentlemen had no other motive in desiring me to return to China than that of hoping to see me useful in Christianizing the Chinese, which was in harmony with their well-known broad and benevolent characters.

On the 13th of November, 1854, the Rev. William Allen Macy, who went out to Hong Kong to take the place of the Rev. Dr. Brown, as teacher in the Morrison Education Society School in 1845, went back to China as a missionary under the American Board, and we were fellow-passengers on board the sailing clipper ship "Eureka," under Captain Whipple, of Messrs. Chamber, Heisser & Co., of New York.

Winter is the worst season of the year to go on an eastern voyage in a sailing vessel, via the Cape of Good Hope. The northeast trade winds prevail then and one is sure to have head winds all the way. The "Eureka," in which Macy and myself were the only passengers, took that route to Hong Kong. We embarked on board of her as she rode in midstream of the East River. The day was bleak and bitingly cold. No handkerchiefs were fluttering in the air, waving a good voyage; no sound from the shore cheered us as the anchor was weighed, and as the tug towed us out as far as Sandy Hook. There we were left to our own resources. The sails were not furled to their full extent, but were reefed for tacking, as the wind was nearly dead ahead and quite strong. We found the "Eureka" to be empty of cargo, and empty even of ballast of any kind; for that reason she acted like a sailor who had just had his nip before he went out to sea. She tossed up and down and twisted from right to left, just as though she had a little too much to keep her balance. It was in such a fashion that she reeled her way from Sandy Hook to Hong Kong—a distance of nearly 13,000 nautical miles, which took her 154 days to accomplish. It was decidedly the most uninteresting and wearisome voyage I ever took in my life. The skipper was a Philadelphian. He had the unfortunate habit of stuttering badly, which tended to irritate a temper naturally quick and fiery. He was certainly a ludicrous object to look at. It was particularly in the morning that he might be seen pacing the quarter deck, scanning the sky. This, by the spectator, was deemed necessary for the skipper to work himself up to the right pitch, preliminary to his pantomimic performances in his battle with the head wind. All at once, he halted, stared at the quarter of the sky from whence the malicious head wind came. With a face all bloated and reddened by intense excitement, his eyes almost standing out of their sockets, and all ablaze with uncontrollable rage, with arms uplifted, he would clutch his hair as if plucking it out by the roots, gnash his teeth, and simultaneously he would jump up and down, stamping on the deck, and swear at the Almighty for sending him head winds. The air for the moment was split with his revolting imprecations and blasphemous oaths that were ejaculated through the laborious process of stammering and stuttering, which made him a most pitiable object to behold. In the early part of the voyage it was a painful sight to see him working himself up to that pitch of contortion and paroxysm of rage which made him appear more like an insane than a sane man, but as these exhibitions were of daily occurrence for the greater part of the voyage, we came to regard him as no longer deserving of sympathy and pity, but rather with contempt. After his passion had spent its force, and he subsided into his calmer and normal mood, he would drop limply into a cane chair, where he would sit for hours all by himself. For the sake of diversion, he would rub his hands together, and soliloquize quietly to himself, an occasional smile breaking over his face, which made him look like an innocent idiot. Before the voyage was half through, the skipper had made such a fool of himself through his silly and insane conduct about the wind, that he became the laughing stock of the whole crew, who, of course, did not dare to show any outward signs of insubordination. The sailing of the vessel was entirely in the hands of the first mate, who was literally a sea-tyrant. The crew was composed of Swedes and Norwegians. If it had been made up of Americans, the inhuman treatment by the officers might have driven them to desperate extremities, because the men were over-worked night and day in incessant tacking. The only time that they found a resting spell was when the ship was becalmed in the tropics when not a breath of wind was to be had for several days at a time. Referring to my diary kept in that memorable voyage,—it took us nearly two weeks to beat up the Macassar straits. This event tried our patience sorely. After it was passed, the skipper made the remark within the hearing of the Rev. Macy that the reason he had bad luck was because he had a Jonah on board. My friend Macy took the remark in a good-natured way and gave me a significant smile. We were just then discussing the feat of going through the Macassar straits and I remarked in a tone just loud enough to be heard by the old skipper that if I had charge of the vessel, I could take her through in less than ten days. This was meant as a direct reflection on the poor seamanship of the old fellow (for he really was a miserable sailor), as well as to serve as a retaliation for what he said a few minutes before, that there was a Jonah on board.

In the dead of winter, the passage to the East should have been taken around Cape Horn instead of the Cape of Good Hope, in which case we would no doubt have had strong and fair wind all the way from New York to Hong Kong, which would not only have shortened the voyage but also saved the captain a world of swearing and an incalculable amount of wear and tear on his nervous system. But as a passenger only, I had no idea of the financial motive back of the move to send the ship off perfectly empty and unballasted, right in the teeth of the northeast monsoon. I would have been glad to go around Cape Horn, as that would have added a new route to my journeying around the world, and furnished me with new incidents as well.

As we approached Hong Kong, a Chinese pilot boarded us. The captain wanted me to ask him whether there were any dangerous rocks and shoals nearby. I could not for the life of me recall my Chinese in order to interpret for him; the pilot himself understood English, and he was the first Chinese teacher to give me the terms in Chinese for dangerous rocks and shoals. So the skipper and Macy, and a few other persons who were present at the time, had the laugh on me, who, being a Chinese, yet was not able to speak the language.

My first thought upon landing was to walk up to the office of the "China Mail," to pay my respects to Andrew Shortrede, the proprietor and editor of the paper, and the friend who supported me for over a year, while I was in Monson Academy. After seeing him and accepting his hospitality by way of an invitation to take up my quarters in his house, I lost no time in hastening over to Macao to see my aged and beloved mother, who, I knew, yearned to see her long-absent boy. Our meeting was arranged a day beforehand. I was in citizen's dress and could not conveniently change the same for my Chinese costume. I had also allowed a pair of mustaches to grow, which, according to Chinese custom, was not becoming for an unmarried young man to do. We met with tears of joy, gratitude and thanksgiving. Our hearts were too full even to speak at first. We gave way to our emotions. As soon as we were fairly composed, she began to stroke me all over, as expressive of her maternal endearment which had been held in patient suspense for at least ten years. As we sat close to each other, I gave her a brief recital of my life in America, for I knew she would be deeply interested in the account. I told her that I had just finished a long and wearisome voyage of five months' duration, but had met with no danger of any kind; that during my eight years of sojourn in the United States, I was very kindly treated by the good people everywhere; that I had had good health and never been seriously sick, and that my chief object during the eight years was to study and prepare myself for my life work in China. I explained to her that I had to go through a preparatory school before entering college; that the college I entered was Yale—one of the leading colleges of the United States, and that the course was four years, which accounted for my long stay and delayed my return to China. I told her that at the end of four years I had graduated with the degree of A.B.,—analogous to the Chinese title of Siu Tsai, which is interpreted "Elegant Talent;" that it was inscribed on a parchment of sheep skin and that to graduate from Yale College was considered a great honor, even to a native American, and much more so to a Chinese. She asked me naïvely how much money it conferred. I said it did not confer any money at once, but it enabled one to make money quicker and easier than one can who has not been educated; that it gave one greater influence and power among men and if he built on his college education, he would be more likely to become the leader of men, especially if he had a well-established character. I told her my college education was worth more to me than money, and that I was confident of making plenty of money.

"Knowledge," I said, "is power, and power is greater than riches. I am the first Chinese to graduate from Yale College, and that being the case, you have the honor of being the first and only mother out of the countless millions of mothers in China at this time, who can claim the honor of having a son who is the first Chinese graduate of a first-class American college. Such an honor is a rare thing to possess." I also assured her that as long as I lived all her comforts and wants would be scrupulously and sedulously looked after, and that nothing would be neglected to make her contented and happy. This interview seemed to give her great comfort and satisfaction. She seemed very happy over it. After it was ended, she looked at me with a significant smile and said, "I see you have already raised your mustaches. You know you have a brother who is much older than you are; he hasn't grown his mustaches yet. You must have yours off." I promptly obeyed her mandate, and as I entered the room with a clean face, she smiled with intense satisfaction, evidently thinking that with all my foreign education, I had not lost my early training of being obedient to my mother. And if she could only have read my heart, she would have found how every throb palpitated with the most tender love for her. During the remaining years of her life, I had the rare privilege of seeing her often and ministered to her every comfort that it was in my power to bestow. She passed away in 1858, at the age of sixty-four, twenty-four years after the death of my father. I was in Shanghai at the time of her death. I returned to my native village in time to attend her funeral.

In the summer of 1855, I took up my residence in Canton, with the Rev. Mr. Vrooman, a missionary under the American Board. His headquarters were in Ham Ha Lan, in the vicinity of the government execution ground, which is in the southwestern outskirts of the city, close to the bank of the Pearl River. While there, I began my Chinese studies and commenced to regain the dialect of Canton, which I had forgotten during my stay in the United States. In less than six months, the language came back to me readily, although I was still a little rusty in it. I was also making slow progress in recovering the written language, in which I was not well-grounded before leaving China, in 1846. I had studied it only four years, which was considered a short time in which to master the written language. There is a greater difference between the written and the spoken language of China than there is between the written and spoken English language. The Chinese written language is stilted and full of conventional forms. It is understood throughout the whole empire, but differently pronounced in different provinces and localities. The spoken language is cut up into endless dialects and in certain provinces like Fuhkien, Anhui and Kiangsu, the people are as foreigners to each other in the matter of dialects. Such are the peculiar characteristics of the ideographic and spoken languages of China.

During the six months of my residence in Canton, while trying to recover both the written and spoken languages, Kwang Tung province was thrown into a somewhat disorganized condition. The people of Canton attempted to raise a provincial insurrection or rebellion entirely distinct from the Taiping rebellion which was being carried on in the interior of China with marked success. To suppress and nip it in the bud, drastic measures were resorted to by Viceroy Yeh Ming Hsin, who, in the summer of 1855, decapitated seventy-five thousand people, most of whom, I was told, were innocent. My residence was within half a mile of the execution ground, as stated above, and one day, out of curiosity, I ventured to walk over to the place. But, oh! what a sight. The ground was perfectly drenched with human blood. On both sides of the driveway were to be seen headless human trunks, piled up in heaps, waiting to be taken away for burial. But no provision had been made to facilitate their removal.

The execution was carried on on a larger scale than had been expected, and no provision had been made to find a place large enough to bury all the bodies. There they were, left exposed to a burning sun. The temperature stood from morning to night in midsummer steadily at 90° Fahrenheit, and sometimes higher. The atmosphere within a radius of two thousand yards of the execution ground was heavily charged with the poisonous and pestilential vapor that was reeking from the ground already over-saturated with blood and from the heaps of corpses which had been left behind for at least two days, and which showed signs of rapid decomposition. It was a wonder to me that no virulent epidemic had sprung up from such an infectious spot to decimate the compact population of the city of Canton. It was a fortunate circumstance that at last a deep and extensive ravine, located in the far-off outskirts of the western part of the city, was found, which was at once converted into a sepulchral receptacle into which this vast human hecatomb was dumped. It was said that no earth was needed to be thrown over these corpses to cover them up; the work was accomplished by countless swarms of worms of a reddish hue and of an appearance that was perfectly hideous and revolting.

I was told that during the months of June, July and August, of 1855, seventy-five thousand people had been decapitated; that more than half of that number were declared to be innocent of the charge of rebellion, but that the accusation was made as a pretext to exact money from them. This wholesale slaughter, unparalleled in the annals of modern civilization, eclipsing even the enormities and blood-thirstiness of Caligula and Nero, or even the French Revolution, was perpetrated by Yeh Ming Hsin, who was appointed viceroy of Kwang Tung and Kwangsi in 1854.

Yeh Ming Hsin was a native of Han-Yang. Han-Yang is a part of the port of Hankau, and was destroyed with it when the Taiping rebels took possession of it. It was said that Yeh Ming Hsin had immense estates in Han-Yang, which were completely destroyed by fire. This circumstance embittered him towards the Taiping rebels and as the Taiping leaders hailed from Kwang Tung and Kwangsi, he naturally transferred his hatred to the people of those two provinces. It was in the lofty position of a viceroy that he found his opportunity to wreak his private and personal vengeance upon the Canton people. This accounts for his indiscriminate slaughter of them, and for the fact that he did not deign to give them even the semblance of a trial, but hurried them from life to death like packs of cattle to the shambles.

But this human monster did not dream that his day of reckoning was fast approaching. Several years after this appalling sacrifice of human life, in 1855, he got into trouble with the British government. He was captured by the British forces and banished to some obscure and remote corner in India where he led a most ignominious life, hated by the whole Chinese nation, and despised by the world at large.

On my return to headquarters, after my visit to the execution ground, I felt faint-hearted and depressed in spirit. I had no appetite for food, and when night came, I was too nervous for sleep. The scene I had looked upon during the day had stirred me up. I thought then that the Taiping rebels had ample grounds to justify their attempt to overthrow the Manchu régime. My sympathies were thoroughly enlisted in their favor and I thought seriously of making preparations to join the Taiping rebels, but upon a calmer reflection, I fell back on the original plan of doing my best to recover the Chinese language as fast as I possibly could and of following the logical course of things, in order to accomplish the object I had at heart.

CHAPTER VII
EFFORT TO FIND A POSITION

HAVING AT LAST SUCCEEDED IN MASTERING THE SPOKEN language sufficiently to speak it quite fluently, I at once set to work to find a position in which I could not only support myself and mother, but also form a plan for working out my ideas of reform in China.

Doctor Peter Parker, who had been a medical missionary under the American Board for many years in Canton, was at that time made United States Commissioner as a temporary expedient, to take the place of an accredited minister plenipotentiary—a diplomatic appointment not yet come into existence, because the question of a foreign minister resident in Peking was still under negotiation, and had not been fully settled as a permanent diplomatic arrangement between the Peking government and the Treaty Powers. Dr. Parker was given the appointment of commissioner on account of his long residence in China and his ability to speak the Chinese language, but not on account of any special training as a diplomat, nor for legal knowledge. It was through Mr. M. N. Hitchcock, an American merchant of the firm of Messrs. King & Co., and a mutual friend of Dr. Parker and myself, that I became the Doctor's private secretary. I knew Dr. Parker while I was at Mrs. Gutzlaff's School, and he doubtless knew I had recently graduated from Yale, which was his Alma Mater also. His headquarters were in Canton, but he spent his summers in Macao. I was with him only three months. My salary was $15 a month (not large enough to spoil me at any rate). He had very little for me to do, but I thought that by being identified with him, I might possibly come in contact with Chinese officials. However, this was far from being the case. Seeing that I could neither learn anything from him, nor enlarge my acquaintance with the Chinese officials, I gave up my position as his secretary and went over to Hong Kong to try to study law. Through my old friend, Andrew Shortrede, who generously extended to me the hospitality of his house, I succeeded in securing the position of the interpretership in the Hong Kong Supreme Court. The situation paid me $75 a month. Having this to fall back upon, I felt encouraged to go ahead in my effort to study law. Accordingly, I was advised to apprentice myself to an attorney or solicitor-at-law. In the English court of practice, it seems that there are two distinct classes of lawyers—attorneys or solicitors, and barristers. The first prepares in writing all evidences, facts, and proofs of a case, hands them to the barrister or counsel, who argues the case in court according to law.

I apprenticed myself to an attorney, who was recommended to me by my old patron and friend, Shortrede. I was not aware that by going into the British Colony in Hong Kong to become an attorney, I was stepping on the toes of the British legal fraternity, nor that by apprenticing myself to an attorney instead of to the new attorney-general of the Colony, who, without my knowledge, wanted me himself, I had committed another mistake, which eventually necessitated my leaving Hong Kong altogether.

First of all, all the attorneys banded themselves together against me, because, as they openly stated in all the local papers except the "China Mail," if I were allowed to practice my profession, they might as well pack up and go back to England, for as I had a complete knowledge of both English and Chinese I would eventually monopolize all the Chinese legal business. So they made it too hot for me to continue in my studies.

In the next place, I was not aware that the attorney-general wanted me to apprentice myself to him, for he did all he could in his capacity as attorney-general of the Colony to use his influence to open the way for me to become an attorney, by draughting a special colonial ordinance to admit Chinese to practice in the Hong Kong Colony as soon as I could pass my examinations. This ordinance was sent to the British government to be sanctioned by Parliament before it became valid and a colonial law. It was sanctioned and thus became a colonial ordinance.

In the meanwhile, Anstey, the attorney-general, found out that I had already apprenticed myself to Parson, the attorney. From that time forth I had no peace. I was between two fires—the batteries operated by the attorneys opened on me with redoubled energy, and the new battery, operated by the attorney-general, opened its fire. He found fault with my interpreting, which he had never done previously. Mr. Parson saw how things stood. He himself was also under a hot fire from both sides. So in order to save himself, he told me plainly and candidly that he had to give me up and made the article of apprenticeship between us null and void. I, on my part, had to give up my position as interpreter in the Supreme Court. Parson, himself, not long after I had abandoned my apprenticeship and my position as interpreter, for reasons satisfactory to himself, gave up his business in Hong Kong and returned to England. So master and pupil left their posts at pretty nearly the same time.

A retrospective view of my short experience in Hong Kong convinced me that it was after all the best thing that I did not succeed in becoming a lawyer in Hong Kong, as the theatre of action there would have been too restricted and circumscribed. I could not have come in touch with the leading minds of China, had I been bound up in that rocky and barren Colony. Doubtless I might have made a fortune if I had succeeded in my legal profession, but as circumstances forced me to leave the Colony, my mind was directed northward to Shanghai, and in August, 1856, I left Hong Kong in the tea clipper, "Florence," under Captain Dumaresque, of Boston. He was altogether a different type of man from the captain of the "Eureka" which brought me out in 1855. He was kind, intelligent and gentlemanly. When he found out who I was, he offered me a free passage from Hong Kong to Shanghai. He was, in fact, the sole owner of the vessel, which was named after his daughter, Florence. The passage was a short one—lasting only seven days—but before it was over, we became great friends.

Not long after my arrival in Shanghai, I found a situation in the Imperial Customs Translating Department, at a salary of Tls. 75 a month, equivalent to $100 Mexican. For want of a Chinese silver currency the Mexican dollar was adopted. This was one point better than the interpretership in the Hong Kong Supreme Court. The duties were not arduous and trying. In fact, they were too simple and easy to suit my taste and ambition. I had plenty of time to read. Before three months of trial in my new situation, I found that things were not as they should be, and if I wished to keep a clean and clear record and an untarnished character, I could not remain long in the service. Between the interpreters who had been in the service many years and the Chinese shippers there existed a regular system of graft. After learning this, and not wishing to be implicated with the others in the division of the spoils in any way or shape, I made up my mind to resign. So one day I called upon the Chief Commissioner of Customs, ostensibly to find out what my future prospects were in connection with the Customs Service—whether or not there were any prospects of my being promoted to the position of a commissioner. I was told that no such prospects were held out to me or to any other Chinese interpreter. I, therefore, at once decided to throw up my position. So I sent in my resignation, which was at first not accepted. A few days after my first interview, Lay, the chief commissioner, strenuously tried to persuade me to change my mind, and offered as an inducement to raise my salary to Tls. 200 a month, evidently thinking that I was only bluffing in order to get higher wages. It did not occur to him that there was at least one Chinaman who valued a clean reputation and an honest character more than money; that being an educated man, I saw no reason why I should not be given the same chances to rise in the service of the Chinese government as an Englishman, nor why my individuality should not be recognized and respected in every walk of life. He little thought that I had aspirations even higher than his, and that I did not care to associate myself with a pack of Custom-house interpreters and inspectors, who were known to take bribes; that a man who expects others to respect him, must first respect himself. Such were my promptings. I did not state the real cause of my quitting the service, but at the end of four months' trial I left the service in order to try my fortune in new fields more congenial.

My friends at the time looked upon me as a crank in throwing up a position yielding me Tls. 200 a month for something uncertain and untried. This in their estimation was the height of folly. They little realized what I was driving at. I had a clean record and I meant to keep it clean. I was perfectly aware that in less than a year since my return to China, I had made three shifts. I myself began to think I was too mercurial to accomplish anything substantial, or that I was too dreamy to be practical or too proud to succeed in life. But in a strenuous life one needs to be a dreamer in order to accomplish possibilities. We are not called into being simply to drudge for an animal existence. I had had to work hard for my education, and I felt that I ought to make the most of what little I had, not so much to benefit myself individually as to make it a blessing common to my race. By these shifts and changes I was only trying to find my true bearing, and how I could make myself a blessing to China.

CHAPTER VIII
EXPERIENCES IN BUSINESS

THE NEXT TURN I TOOK, AFTER LEAVING THE Imperial Customs, was clerk in an English house—tea and silk merchants. During the few months that I was with them, I gained quite an insight into mercantile business, and the methods of conducting it, which proved to be profitable knowledge and experience to me later on. Six months after I had entered upon my new sphere as a make-shift, the firm dissolved partnership, which once more threw me out of a position, and I was again cast upon the sea of uncertainty. But during my connection with the firm, two little incidents occurred which I must not fail to relate.

One Thursday evening, as I was returning home from a prayer meeting held in the Union Chapel in Shanghai, I saw ahead of me on Szechuen Road in front of the Episcopal church, a string of men; each had a Chinese lantern swinging in the air over his head, and they were singing and shouting as they zigzagged along the road, evidently having a jolly, good time, while Chinese on both sides of the road were seen dodging and scampering about in great fright in all directions, and acting as though they were chased by the Old Nick himself. I was at a distance of about one hundred yards from the scene. I took in the situation at once. My servant, who held a lantern ahead of me, to light the way, was so frightened that he began to come back towards me. I told him not to be afraid, but walk right straight ahead. Pretty soon we confronted three or four of the fellows, half tipsy. One of them snatched the lantern from my servant and another, staggering about, tried to give me a kick. I walked along coolly and unconcerned till I reached the last batch of two or three fellows. I found these quite sober and in their senses and they were lingering behind evidently to enjoy the fun and watch the crowd in their hilarious antics. I stopped and parleyed with them, and told them who I was. I asked them for the names of the fellows who snatched my boy's lantern and of the fellow who tried to kick me. They declined at first, but finally with the promise that I would not give them any trouble, they gave me the name of one of the fellows, his position on the vessel, and the name of the vessel he belonged to. It turned out that the man was the first mate of the ship "Eureka," the very vessel that brought me out to China, in 1855, and which happened to be consigned to the firm I was working for. The next morning, I wrote a note to the captain, asking him to hand the note to his first officer. The captain, on receiving the note, was quite excited, and handed it to the first mate, who immediately came ashore and apologized. I made it very pleasant for him and told him that Americans in China were held in high esteem by the people, and every American landing in China should be jealous of the high estimation in which they were held and not do anything to compromise it. My motive in writing the note was merely to get him on shore and give him this advice. He was evidently pleased with my friendly attitude and extended his hand for a shake to thank me for the advice. He invited me to go on board with him to take a glass of wine and be good friends. I thanked him for his offer, but declined it, and we parted in an amicable way.

My second incident, which happened a couple of months after the first, did not have such a peaceful ending.

After the partnership of the firm, in whose employ I was, dissolved, an auction sale of the furniture of the firm took place. In the room where the auction was proceeding, I happened to be standing in a mixed crowd of Chinese and foreigners. A stalwart six-footer of a Scotchman happened to be standing behind me. He was not altogether a stranger to me, for I had met him in the streets several times. He began to tie a bunch of cotton balls to my queue, simply for a lark. But I caught him at it and in a pleasant way held it up and asked him to untie it. He folded up his arms and drew himself straight up with a look of the utmost disdain and scorn. I at once took in the situation, and as my countenance sobered, I reiterated my demand to have the appendage taken off. All of a sudden, he thrust his fist against my mouth, without drawing any blood, however. Although he stood head and shoulders above me in height, yet I was not at all abashed or intimidated by his burly and contemptuous appearance. My dander was up and oblivious to all thoughts of our comparative size and strength, I struck him back in the identical place where he punched me, but my blow was a stinger and it went with lightning rapidity to the spot, without giving him time to think. It drew blood in great profusion from lip and nose. He caught me by the wrist with both his hands. As he held my right wrist in his powerful grasp, for he was an athlete and a sportsman, I was just on the point of raising my right foot for a kick, which was aimed at a vital point, when the head partner of the firm, who happened to be near, suddenly stepped in between and separated us. I then stood off to one side, facing my antagonist, who was moving off into the crowd. As I moved away, I was asked by a voice from the crowd:

"Do you want to fight?"

I said, "No, I was only defending myself. Your friend insulted me and added injury to insult. I took him for a gentleman, but he has proved himself a blackguard."

With this stinging remark, which was heard all over the room, I retired from the scene into an adjoining room, leaving the crowd to comment on the incident. The British Consul, who happened to be present on the occasion, made a casual remark on the merits of the case and said, as I was told afterwards by a friend, that "The young man was a little too fiery; if he had not taken the law into his own hands, he could have brought suit for assault and battery in the consular court, but since he has already retaliated and his last remark before the crowd has inflicted a deeper cut to his antagonist than the blow itself, he has lost the advantage of a suit."

The Scotchman, after the incident, did not appear in public for a whole week. I was told he had shut himself up in his room to give his wound time to heal, but the reason he did not care to show himself was more on account of being whipped by a little Chinaman in a public manner; for the affair, unpleasant and unfortunate as it was, created quite a sensation in the settlement. It was the chief topic of conversation for a short time among foreigners, while among the Chinese I was looked upon with great respect, for since the foreign settlement on the extra-territorial basis was established close to the city of Shanghai, no Chinese within its jurisdiction had ever been known to have the courage and pluck to defend his rights, point blank, when they had been violated or trampled upon by a foreigner. Their meek and mild disposition had allowed personal insults and affronts to pass unresented and unchallenged, which naturally had the tendency to encourage arrogance and insolence on the part of ignorant foreigners. The time will soon come, however, when the people of China will be so educated and enlightened as to know what their rights are, public and private, and to have the moral courage to assert and defend them whenever they are invaded. The triumph of Japan over Russia in the recent war has opened the eyes of the Chinese world. It will never tolerate injustice in any way or shape, much less will it put up with foreign aggression and aggrandizement any longer. They see now in what plight their national ignorance, conceit and conservatism, in which they had been fossilized, had placed them. They were on the verge of being partitioned by the European Powers and were saved from that catastrophe only by the timely intervention of the United States government. What the future will bring forth, since the Emperor Kwangsu and Dowager Empress Chi Hsi have both passed away, no one can predict.

The breaking up of the firm by which I was employed, once more, as stated before, and for the fourth time, threw me out of a regular business. But I was not at all disconcerted or discouraged, for I had no idea of following a mercantile life as a permanent calling. Within the past two years, my knowledge of the Chinese language had decidedly improved. I was not in hot haste to seek for a new position. I immediately took to translating as a means of bridging over the breaks of a desultory life. This independent avocation, though not a lucrative one, nevertheless led the way to a wider acquaintance with the educated and mercantile classes of the Chinese; to widen my acquaintance was my chief concern. My translating business brought me in contact with the comprador of one of the leading houses in Shanghai. The senior partner of this house died in 1857. He was well-known and thought much of by both the Chinese and the foreign mercantile body. To attest their high regard for his memory, the prominent Chinese merchants drew up an elaborate and eulogistic epitaph on the occasion of his death. The surviving members of the firm selected two translators to translate the epitaph. One was the interpreter in the British Consulate General, a brother to the author of "The Chinese and their Rebellions," and the other was (through the influence of the comprador) myself. To my great surprise, my translation was given the preference and accepted by the manager of the firm. The Chinese committee were quite elated that one of their countrymen knew enough English to bring out the inner sense of their epitaph. It was adopted and engraved on the monument. My name began to be known among the Chinese, not as a fighter this time, but as a Chinese student educated in America.

Soon after this performance, another event unexpectedly came up in which I was again called upon to act; that was the inundation of the Yellow River, which had converted the northern part of Kiangsu province into a sea, and made homeless and destitute thousands of people of that locality. A large body of refugees had wandered to and flocked near Shanghai. A Chinese deputation, consisting of the leading merchants and gentry, who knew or had heard of me, called and asked me to draw up a circular appealing to the foreign community for aid and contributions to relieve the widespread suffering among the refugees. Several copies were immediately put into circulation and in less than a week, no less than $20,000 were subscribed and paid. The Chinese Committee were greatly elated over their success and their joy was unbounded. To give a finishing touch to this stroke of business, I wrote in the name of the committee a letter of acknowledgment and thanks to the foreign community for the prompt and generous contribution it had made. This was published in the Shanghai local papers—"The Shanghai Mail" and "Friend of China"—so that inside of three months after I had started my translating business, I had become widely known among the Chinese as the Chinese student educated in America. I was indebted to Tsang Kee Foo, the comprador, for being in this line of business, and for the fact that I was becoming known in Shanghai. He was a well-educated Chinese—a man highly respected and trusted for his probity and intelligence. His long connection with the firm and his literary taste had gathered around him some of the finest Chinese scholars from all parts of China, while his business transactions brought him in touch with the leading Chinese capitalists and business men in Shanghai and elsewhere. It was through him that both the epitaph and the circular mentioned above were written; and it was Tsang Kee Foo who introduced me to the celebrated Chinese mathematician, Li Jen Shu, who years afterwards brought me to the notice of Viceroy Tsang Kwoh Fan—the distinguished general and statesman, who, as will be seen hereafter, took up and promoted the Chinese Education Scheme. In the great web of human affairs, it is almost impossible to know who among our friends and acquaintances may prove to be the right clue to unravel the skein of our destiny. Tsang Kee Foo introduced me to Li Jen Shu, the latter introduced me to Tsang Kwoh Fan, who finally through the Chinese Education Scheme grafted Western education to the Oriental culture, a union destined to weld together the different races of the world into one brotherhood.

My friend Tsang Kee Foo afterwards introduced me to the head or manager of Messrs. Dent & Co., who kindly offered me a position in his firm as comprador in Nagasaki, Japan, soon after that country was opened to foreign trade. I declined the situation, frankly and plainly stating my reason, which was that the compradorship, though lucrative, is associated with all that is menial, and that as a graduate of Yale, one of the leading colleges in America, I could not think of bringing discredit to my Alma Mater, for which I entertained the most profound respect and reverence, and was jealous of her proud fame. What would the college and my class-mates think of me, if they should hear that I was a comprador—the head servant of servants in an English establishment? I said there were cases when a man from stress of circumstances may be compelled to play the part of a menial for a shift, but I was not yet reduced to that strait, though I was poor financially. I told him I would prefer to travel for the firm as its agent in the interior and correspond directly with the head of the firm. In that case, I would not sacrifice my manhood for the sake of making money in a position which is commonly held to be servile. I would much prefer to pack tea and buy silk as an agent--either on a salary or on commission. Such was my ground for declining. I, however, thanked him for the offer. This interview took place in the presence of my friend, Tsang Kee Foo, who without knowing the details of the conversation, knew enough of the English language to follow the general tenor of the talk. I then retired and left the manager and my friend to talk over the result. Tsang afterwards told me that Webb said, "Yung Wing is poor but proud. Poverty and pride usually go together, hand in hand." A few days afterwards Tsang informed me that Webb had decided to send me to the tea districts to see and learn the business of packing tea.

CHAPTER XVI
PROPOSAL OF MY EDUCATIONAL SCHEME

HAVING SCORED IN A SMALL WAY THIS EDUCATIONAL victory, by inducing the Viceroy to establish a mechanical training school as a corollary to the arsenal, I felt quite worked up and encouraged concerning my educational scheme which had been lying dormant in my mind for the past fifteen years, awaiting an opportunity to be brought forward.

Besides Viceroy Tsang Kwoh Fan, whom I counted upon to back me in furthering the scheme, Ting Yih Chang, an old friend of mine, had become an important factor to be reckoned with in Chinese politics. He was a man of progressive tendencies and was alive to all practical measures of reform. He had been appointed governor of Kiangsu province, and after his accession to his new office, I had many interviews with him regarding my educational scheme, in which he was intensely interested. He told me that he was in correspondence with Wen Seang, the prime minister of China, who was a Manchu, and that if I were to put my scheme in writing, he would forward it to Peking, and ask Wen Seang to use his influence to memorialize the government for its adoption. Such an unexpected piece of information came like a clap of thunder and fairly lifted me off my feet. I immediately left Suchau for Shanghai. With the help of my Nanking friend, who had helped me in the work of translating "Parsons on Contracts," I drew up four proposals to be presented to Governor Ting, to be forwarded by him to Minister Wen Seang, at Peking. They were as follows:

FIRST PROPOSAL

The first proposal contemplated the organization of a Steamship Company on a joint stock basis. No foreigner was to be allowed to be a stockholder in the company. It was to be a purely Chinese company, managed and worked by Chinese exclusively.

To insure its stability and success, an annual government subsidy was to be made in the shape of a certain percentage of the tribute rice carried to Peking from Shanghai and Chinkiang, and elsewhere, where tribute rice is paid over to the government in lieu of taxes in money. This tribute rice heretofore had been taken to Peking by flat-bottom boats, via the Grand Canal. Thousands of these boats were built expressly for this rice transportation, which supported a large population all along the whole route of the Grand Canal.

On account of the great evils arising from this mode of transportation, such as the great length of time it took to take the rice to Peking, the great percentage of loss from theft, and from fermentation, which made the rice unfit for food, part of the tribute rice was carried by sea in Ningpo junks as far as Tiensin, and from thence transhipped again in flat-bottom boats to Peking. But even the Ningpo junk system was attended with great loss of time and much damage, almost as great as by flat-bottom scows. My proposition was to use steam to do the work, supplanting both the flat-bottomed scows and the Ningpo junk system, so that the millions who were dependent on rice for subsistence might find it possible to get good and sound rice. This is one of the great benefits and blessings which the China Merchant Steamship Co. has conferred upon China.

SECOND PROPOSAL

The second proposition was for the government to send picked Chinese youths abroad to be thoroughly educated for the public service. The scheme contemplated the education of one hundred and twenty students as an experiment. These one hundred and twenty students were to be divided into four installments of thirty students each, one installment to be sent out each year. They were to have fifteen years to finish their education. Their average age was to be from twelve to fourteen years. If the first and second installments proved to be a success, the scheme was to be continued indefinitely. Chinese teachers were to be provided to keep up their knowledge of Chinese while in the United States. Over the whole enterprise two commissioners were to be appointed, and the government was to appropriate a certain percentage of the Shanghai customs to maintain the mission.

THIRD PROPOSAL

The third proposition was to induce the government to open the mineral resources of the country and thus in an indirect way lead to the necessity of introducing railroads to transport the mineral products from the interior to the ports.

I did not expect this proposition to be adopted and carried out, because China at that time had no mining engineers who could be depended upon to develop the mines, nor were the people free from the Fung Shui superstition.[1]

FOURTH PROPOSAL

The encroachment of foreign powers upon the independent sovereignty of China has always been watched by me with the most intense interest. No one who is at all acquainted with Roman Catholicism can fail to be impressed with the unwarranted pretensions and assumptions of the Romish church in China. She claims civil jurisdiction over her proselytes, and takes civil and criminal cases out of Chinese courts. In order to put a stop to such insidious and crafty workings to gain temporal power in China, I put forth this proposition: to prohibit missionaries of any religious sect or denomination from exercising any kind of jurisdiction over their converts, in either civil or criminal cases. These four propositions were carefully drawn up, and were presented to Governor Ting for transmission to Peking.

Of the four proposals, the first, third and fourth were put in to chaperone the second, in which my whole heart was enlisted, and which above all others was the one I wanted to be taken up; but not to give it too prominent a place, at the suggestion of my Chinese teacher, it was assigned a second place in the order of the arrangement. Governor Ting recognized this, and accordingly wrote to Prime Minister Wen Seang and forwarded the proposals to Peking. Two months later, a letter from Ting, at Suchau, his headquarters, gave me to understand that news from Peking had reached him that Wen Seang's mother had died, and he was obliged, according to Chinese laws and customs, to retire from office and go into mourning for a period of twenty-seven months, equivalent to three years, and to abstain altogether from public affairs of all kinds. This news threw a cold blanket over my educational scheme for the time being. No sooner had one misfortune happened than another took its place, worst than the first--Wen Seang

---

1 The doctrine held by the Chinese in relation to the spirits or genii that rule over winds and waters, especially running streams and subterranean waters. This doctrine is universal and inveterate among the Chinese, and in a great measure prompts their hostility to railroads and telegraphs, since they believe that such structures anger the spirits of the air and waters and consequently cause floods and typhoons.—*Standard Dictionary.*

himself, three months afterwards, was overtaken by death during his retirement. This announcement appeared in the Peking "Gazette," which I saw, besides being officially informed of it by Governor Ting. No one who had a pet scheme to promote or a hobby to ride could feel more blue than I did, when the cup of joy held so near to his lips was dashed from him. I was not entirely disheartened by such circumstances, but had an abiding faith that my educational scheme would in the end come out all right. There was an interval of at least three years of suspense and waiting between 1868 and 1870. I kept pegging at Governor Ting, urging him to keep the subject constantly before Viceroy Tsang's mind. But like the fate of all measures of reform, it had to abide its time and opportunity. The time and the opportunity for my educational scheme to materialize finally came. Contrary to all human expectations, the opportunity appeared in the guise of the Tientsin Massacre. No more did Samson, when he slew the Timnath lion, expect to extract honey from its carcass than did I expect to extract from the slaughter of the French nuns and Sisters of Charity the educational scheme that was destined to make a new China of the old, and to work out an Oriental civilization on an Occidental basis.

The Tientsin Massacre took place early in 1870. It arose from the gross ignorance and superstition of the Tientsin populace regarding the work of the nuns and Sisters of Charity, part of whose religious duty it was to rescue foundlings and castaway orphans, who were gathered into hospitals, cared for and educated for the services of the Roman Catholic church. This beneficent work was misunderstood and misconstrued by the ignorant masses, who really believed in the rumors and stories that the infants and children thus gathered in were taken into the hospitals and churches to have their eyes gouged out for medical and religious purposes. Such diabolical reports soon spread like wild-fire till popular excitement was worked up to its highest pitch of frenzy, and the infuriated mob, regardless of death and fearless of law, plunged headlong into the Tientsin Massacre. In that massacre a Protestant church was burned and destroyed, as was also a Roman Catholic church and hospital; several nuns or Sisters of Charity were killed.

At the time of this occurrence, Chung Hou was viceroy of the Metropolitan province. He had been ambassador to Russia previously, but in this unfortunate affair, according to Chinese law, he was held responsible, was degraded from office and banished. The whole imbroglio was finally settled and patched up by the payment of an indemnity to the relatives and friends of the victims of the massacre and the rebuilding of the Roman Catholic and Protestant churches, another Catholic hospital, besides a suitable official apology made by the government for the incident. Had the French government not been handicapped by the impending German War which threatened her at the time, France would certainly have made the Tientsin Massacre a *casus belli*, and another slice of the Chinese Empire would have been annexed to the French possessions in Asia. As it was, Tonquin, a tributary state of China, was afterwards unscrupulously wrenched from her.

In the settlement of the massacre, the Imperial commissioners appointed were: Viceroy Tsang Kwoh Fan, Mow Chung Hsi, Liu * * * and Ting Yih Chang, Governor of Kiang Su. Li Hung Chang was still in the field finishing up the Nien-fi rebellion, otherwise he, too, would have been appointed to take part in the proceedings of the settlement. I was telegraphed for by my friend, Ting Yih Chang, to be present to act as interpreter on the occasion, but the telegram did not reach me in time for me to accompany him to Tientsin; but I reached Tientsin in time to witness the last proceedings. The High Commissioners, after the settlement with the French, for some reason or other, did not disband, but remained in Tientsin for several days. They evidently had other matters of State connected with Chung Hou's degradation and banishment to consider.

CHAPTER XVII
THE CHINESE EDUCATIONAL MISSION

TAKING ADVANTAGE OF THEIR PRESENCE, I SEIZED THE opportunity to press my educational scheme upon the attention of Ting Yih Chang and urged him to present the subject to the Board of Commissioners of which Tsang Kwoh Fan was president. I knew Ting sympathized with me in the scheme, and I knew, too, that Tsang Kwoh Fan had been well informed of it three years before through Governor Ting. Governor Ting took up the matter in dead earnest and held many private interviews with Tsang Kwoh Fan as well as with the other members of the Commission. One evening, returning to his headquarters very late, he came to my room and awakened me and told me that Viceroy Tsang and the other Commissioners had unanimously decided to sign their names conjointly in a memorial to the government to adopt my four propositions. This piece of news was too much to allow me to sleep anymore that night; while lying on my bed, as wakeful as an owl, I felt as though I were treading on clouds and walking in air. Two days after this stirring piece of news, the memorial was jointly signed with Viceroy Tsang Kwoh Fan's name heading the list, and was on its way to Peking by pony express. Meanwhile, before the Board of Commissioners disbanded and Viceroy Tsang took his departure for Nanking, it was decided that Chin Lan Pin, a member of the Hanlin College, who had served twenty years as a clerk in the Board of Punishment, should be recommended by Ting to co-operate with me in charge of the Chinese Educational Commission. The ground upon which Chin Lan Pin was recommended as a co-commissioner was that he was a Han Lin and a regularly educated Chinese, and the enterprise would not be so likely to meet with the opposition it might have if I were to attempt to carry it out alone, because the scheme in principle and significance was against the Chinese theory of national education, and it would not have taken much to create a reaction to defeat the plan on account of the intense conservatism of the government. The wisdom and the shrewd policy of such a move appealed to me at once, and I accepted the suggestion with pleasure and alacrity. So Chin Lan Pin was written to and came to Tientsin. The next day, after a farewell dinner had been accorded to the Board of Commissioners before it broke up, Governor Ting introduced me to Chin Lan Pin, whom I had never met before and who was to be my associate in the educational scheme. He evidently was pleased to quit Peking, where he had been cooped up in the Board of Punishment for twenty years as a clerk. He had never filled a government position in any other capacity in his life, nor did he show any practical experience in the world of business and hard facts. In his habits he was very retiring, but very scholarly. In disposition he was kindly and pleasant, but very timid and afraid of responsibilities of even a feather's weight.

In the winter of 1870, Tsang Kwoh Fan, after having settled the Tientsin imbroglio, returned to Nanking, his headquarters as the viceroy of the two Kiangs. There he received the imperial rescript sanctioning his joint memorial on the four proposals submitted through Ting Yih Chang for adoption by the government. He notified me on the subject. It was a glorious piece of news, and the Chinese educational project thus became a veritable historical fact, marking a new era in the annals of China. Tsang invited me to repair to Nanking, and during that visit the most important points connected with the mission were settled, viz.: the establishment of a preparatory school; the number of students to be selected to be sent abroad; where the money was to come from to support the students while there; the number of years they were to be allowed to remain there for their education.

The educational commission was to consist of two commissioners, Chin Lan Pin and myself. Chin Lan Pin's duty was to see that the students should keep up their knowledge of Chinese while in America; my duty was to look after their foreign education and to find suitable homes for them. Chin Lan Pin and myself were to look after their expenses conjointly. Two Chinese teachers were provided to keep up their studies in Chinese, and an interpreter was provided for the Commission. Yeh Shu Tung and Yung Yune Foo were the Chinese teachers and Tsang Lai Sun was the interpreter. Such was the composition of the Chinese Educational Commission.

As to the character and selection of the students: the whole number to be sent abroad for education was one hundred and twenty; they were to be divided into four installments of thirty members each, one installment to be sent each year for four successive years at about the same time. The candidates to be selected were not to be younger than twelve or older than fifteen years of age. They were to show respectable parentage or responsible and respectable guardians. They were required to pass a medical examination, and an examination in their Chinese studies according to regulation--reading and writing in Chinese--also to pass an English examination if a candidate had been in an English school. All successful candidates were required to repair every day to the preparatory school, where teachers were provided to continue with their Chinese studies, and to begin the study of English or to continue with their English studies, for at least one year before they were to embark for the United States.

Parents and guardians were required to sign a paper which stated that without recourse, they were perfectly willing to let their sons or protégés go abroad to be educated for a period of fifteen years, from the time they began their studies in the United States until they had finished, and that during the fifteen years, the government was not to be responsible for death or for any accident that might happen to any student.

The government guaranteed to pay all their expenses while they were being educated. It was to provide every installment with a Chinese teacher to accompany it to the United States, and to give each installment of students a suitable outfit. Such were the requirements and the organization of the student corps.

Immediately upon my return to Shanghai from Nanking after my long interview with the Viceroy, my first step was to have a preparatory school established in Shanghai for the accommodation of at least thirty students, which was the full complement for the first installment. Liu Kai Sing, who was with the Viceroy for a number of years as his first secretary in the Department on Memorials, was appointed superintendent of the preparatory school in Shanghai. In him, I found an able coadjutor as well as a staunch friend who took a deep interest in the educational scheme. He it was who prepared all the four installments of students to come to this country.

Thus the China end of the scheme was set afloat in the summer of 1871. To make up the full complement of the first installment of students, I had to take a trip down to Hong Kong to visit the English government schools to select from them a few bright candidates who had had some instruction both in English and Chinese studies. As the people in the northern part of China did not know that such an educational scheme had been projected by the government, there being no Chinese newspapers published at that time to spread the news among the people, we had, at first, few applications for entrance into the preparatory school. All the applications came from the Canton people, especially from the district of Heang Shan. This accounts for the fact that nine-tenths of the one hundred and twenty government students were from the south.

In the winter of 1871, a few months after the preparatory school had begun operations, China suffered an irreparable loss by the death of Viceroy Tsang Kwoh Fan, who died in Nanking at the ripe age of seventy-one years. Had his life been spared even a year longer, he would have seen the first installment of thirty students started for the United States,—the first fruit of his own planting. But founders of all great and good works are not permitted by the nature and order of things to live beyond their ordained limitations to witness the successful developments of their own labor in this world; but the consequences of human action and human character, when once their die is cast, will reach to eternity. Sufficient for Tsang Kwoh Fan that he had completed his share in the educational line well. He did a great and glorious work for China and posterity, and those who were privileged to reap the benefit of his labor will find ample reason to bless him as China's great benefactor. Tsang, as a statesman, a patriot, and as a man, towered above his contemporaries even as Mount Everest rises above the surrounding heights of the Himalaya range, forever resting in undisturbed calmness and crowned with the purity of everlasting snow. Before he breathed his last, I was told that it was his wish that his successor and protégé, Li Hung Chang, be requested to take up his mantle and carry on the work of the Chinese Educational Commission.

Li Hung Chang was of an altogether different make-up from his distinguished predecessor and patron. He was of an excitable and nervous temperament, capricious and impulsive, susceptible to flattery and praise, or, as the Chinese laconically put it, he was fond of wearing tall hats. His outward manners were brusque, but he was inwardly kind-hearted. As a statesman he was far inferior to Tsang; as a patriot and politician, his character could not stand a moment before the searchlight of cold and impartial history. It was under such a man that the Chinese Educational Commission was launched forth.

In the latter part of the summer of 1872 the first installment of Chinese students, thirty in number, were ready to start on the passage across the Pacific to the United States. In order that they might have homes to go to on their arrival, it devolved upon me to precede them by one month, leaving Chin Lan Pin, the two Chinese teachers and their interpreter to come on a mail later. After reaching New York by the Baltimore and Ohio, via Washington, I went as far as New Haven on my way to Springfield, Mass., where I intended to meet the students and other members of the commission on their way to the East by the Boston and Albany Railroad. At New Haven, the first person I called upon to announce my mission was Prof. James Hadley. He was indeed glad to see me, and was delighted to know that I had come back with such a mission in my hands. After making my wants known to him, he immediately recommended me to call upon Mr. B. G. Northrop, which I did. Mr. Northrop was then Commissioner of Education for Connecticut. I told him my business and asked his advice. He strongly recommended me to distribute and locate the students in New England families, either by twos or fours to each family, where they could be cared for and at the same time instructed, till they were able to join classes in graded schools. This advice I followed at once. I went on to Springfield, Mass., which city I considered was the most central point from which to distribute the students in New England; for this reason I chose Springfield for my headquarters. This enabled me to be very near my friends, Dr. A. S. McClean and his worthy wife, both of whom had been my steadfast friends since 1854.

But through the advice of Dr. B. G. Northrop and other friends, I made my permanent headquarters in the city of Hartford, Conn., and for nearly two years our headquarters were located on Sumner Street. I did not abandon Springfield, but made it the center of distribution and location of the students as long as they continued to come over, which was for three successive years, ending in 1875.

In 1874, Li Hung Chang, at the recommendation of the commission, authorized me to put up a handsome, substantial building on Collins Street as the permanent headquarters of the Chinese Educational Commission in the United States. In January, 1875, we moved into our new headquarters, which was a large, double three-story house spacious enough to accommodate the Commissioners, teachers and seventy-five students at one time. It was provided with a school-room where Chinese was exclusively taught; a dining room, a double kitchen, dormitories and bath rooms. The motive which led me to build permanent headquarters of our own was to have the educational mission as deeply rooted in the United States as possible, so as not to give the Chinese government any chance of retrograding in this movement. Such was my proposal, but that was not God's disposal as subsequent events plainly proved.

CHAPTER XIX
END OF THE EDUCATIONAL MISSION

IN THE FALL OF 1875 THE LAST INSTALLMENT of students arrived. They came in charge of a new commissioner, Ou Ngoh Liang, two new Chinese teachers and a new interpreter, Kwang Kee Cheu. These new men were appointed by Viceroy Li Hung Chang. I knew them in China, especially the new commissioner and the interpreter.

These changes were made at the request of Chin Lan Pin, who expected soon to return to China on a leave of absence. He was going to take with him the old Chinese teacher, Yeh Shu Tung, who had rendered him great and signal service in his trip to Cuba on the coolie question the year before. Tsang Lai Sun, the old interpreter, was also requested to resign and returned to China. These changes I had anticipated some time before and they did not surprise me.

Three months after Chin Lan Pin's arrival in Peking, word came from China that he and I were appointed joint Chinese ministers to Washington, and that Yeh Shu Tung, the old Chinese teacher, was appointed secretary to the Chinese Legation. This was great news to me to be sure, but I did not feel ecstatic over it; on the contrary, the more I reflected on it, the more I felt depressed. But my friends who congratulated me on the honor and promotion did not take in the whole situation as it loomed up before my mind in all its bearings. As far as I was concerned, I had every reason to feel grateful and honored, but how about my life work—the Chinese educational mission that I had in hand—and which needed in its present stage great watchfulness and care? If, as I reflected, I were to be removed to Washington, who was there left behind to look after the welfare of the students with the same interest that I had manifested? It would be like separating the father from his children. This would not do, so I sat down and wrote to the Viceroy a letter, the tenor of which ran somewhat as follows: I thanked him for the appointment which I considered to be a great honor for any man to receive from the government; and said that while I appreciated fully its significance, the obligations and responsibilities inseparably connected with the position filled me with anxious solicitude that my abilities and qualifications might not be equal to their satisfactory fulfillment. In view of such a state of mind, I much preferred, if I were

44

allowed to have my preference in the matter, to remain in my present position as a commissioner of the Chinese mission in Hartford and to continue in it till the Chinese students should have finished their education and were ready to return to China to serve the State in their various capacities. In that event I should have discharged a duty to "Tsang the Upright," and at the same time fulfilled a great duty to China. As Chin Lan Pin had been appointed minister at the same time, he would doubtless be able alone to meet the expectations of the government in his diplomatic capacity.

The letter was written and engrossed by Yung Yune Foo, one of the old Chinese teachers who came over with the first installment of students at the same time Yeh Shu Tung came. In less than four months an answer was received which partially acceded to my request by making me an assistant or associate minister, at the same time allowing me to retain my position as Commissioner of Education, and in that capacity, to exercise a general supervision over the education of the students.

Ou Ngoh Liang, the new commissioner, was a much younger man than Chin. He was a fair Chinese scholar, but not a member of the Hanlin College. He was doubtless recommended by Chin Lan Pin. He brought his family with him, which consisted of his second wife and two children. He was a man of a quiet disposition and showed no inclination to meddle with settled conditions or to create trouble, but took rather a philosophical view of things; he had the good sense to let well enough alone. He was connected with the mission but a short time and resigned in 1876.

In 1876 Chin Lan Pin came as minister plenipotentiary and brought with him among his numerous retinue Woo Tsze Tung, a man whom I knew in Shanghai even in the '50's. He was a member of the Hanlin College, but for some reason or other, he was never assigned to any government department, nor was he ever known to hold any kind of government office. He showed a decided taste for chemistry, but never seemed to have made any progress in it, and was regarded by all his friends as a crank.

After Ou's resignation, Chin Lan Pin before proceeding to Washington to take up his official position as Chinese minister, strongly recommended Woo Tsze Tung to succeed Ou as commissioner, to which Viceroy Li Hung Chang acceded without thinking of the consequences to follow. From this time forth the educational mission found an enemy who was determined to undermine the work of Tsang Kwoh Fan and Ting Yih Cheong, to both of whom Woo Tsze Tung was more or less hostile. Woo was a member of the reactionary party, which looked upon the Chinese Educational Commission as a move subversive of the principles and theories of Chinese culture. This was told me by one of

Chin's suite who held the appointment of *chargé d'affaires* for Peru. The making of Woo Tsze Tung a commissioner plainly revealed the fact that Chin Lan Pin himself was at heart an uncompromising Confucian and practically represented the reactionary party with all its rigid and uncompromising conservatism that gnashes its teeth against all and every attempt put forth to reform the government or to improve the general condition of things in China. This accounts for the fact that in the early stages of the mission, I had many and bitter altercations with him on many things which had to be settled for good, once and for all. Such as the school and personal expenses of the students; their vacation expenses; their change of costume; their attendance at family worship; their attendance at Sunday School and church services; their outdoor exercises and athletic games. These and other questions of a social nature came up for settlement. I had to stand as a kind of buffer between Chin and the students, and defended them in all their reasonable claims. It was in this manner that I must have incurred Chin's displeasure if not his utter dislike. He had never been out of China in his life until he came to this country. The only standard by which he measured things and men (especially students) was purely Chinese. The gradual but marked transformation of the students in their behavior and conduct as they grew in knowledge and stature under New England influence, culture and environment produced a contrast to their behavior and conduct when they first set foot in New England that might well be strange and repugnant to the ideas and senses of a man like Chin Lan Pin, who all his life had been accustomed to see the springs of life, energy and independence, candor, ingenuity and open-heartedness all covered up and concealed, and in a great measure smothered and never allowed their full play. Now in New England the heavy weight of repression and suppression was lifted from the minds of these young students; they exulted in their freedom and leaped for joy. No wonder they took to athletic sports with alacrity and delight!

Doubtless Chin Lan Pin when he left Hartford for good to go to Washington carried away with him a very poor idea of the work to which he was singled out and called upon to perform. He must have felt that his own immaculate Chinese training had been contaminated by coming in contact with Occidental schooling, which he looked upon with evident repugnance. At the same time the very work which he seemed to look upon with disgust had certainly served him the best turn in his life. It served to lift him out of his obscurity as a head clerk in the office of the Board of Punishment for twenty years to become a commissioner of the Chinese Educational Commission, and from that post to be a minister plenipotentiary in Washington. It was the stepping stone by which he climbed to political prominence. He should not have kicked away the ladder under him after he had reached his dizzy elevation. He did all he could to break up the educational scheme by recommending Woo Tsze Tung to be the Commissioner of Education, than whom he could not have had a more pliant and subservient tool for his purpose, as may be seen hereinafter.

Woo Tsze Tung was installed commissioner in the fall of 1876. No sooner was he in office than he began to find fault with everything that had been done. Instead of laying those complaints before me, he clandestinely started a stream of misrepresentation to Peking about the students; how they had been mismanaged; how they had been indulged and petted by Commissioner Yung; how they had been allowed to enjoy more privileges than was good for them; how they imitated American students in athletics; that they played more than they studied; that they formed themselves into secret societies, both religious and political; that they ignored their teachers and would not listen to the advice of the new commissioner; that if they were allowed to continue to have their own way, they would soon lose their love of their own country, and on their return to China, they would be good for nothing or worse than nothing; that most of them went to church, attended Sunday Schools and had become Christians; that the sooner this educational enterprise was broken up and all the students recalled, the better it would be for China, etc., etc.

Such malicious misrepresentations and other falsehoods which we knew nothing of, were kept up in a continuous stream from year to year by Woo Tsze Tung to his friends in Peking and to Viceroy Li Hung Chang. The Viceroy called my attention to Woo's accusations. I wrote back in reply that they were malicious fabrications of a man who was known to have been a crank all his life; that it was a grand mistake to put such a man in a responsible position who had done nothing for himself or for others in his life; that he was only attempting to destroy the work of Tsang Kwoh Fan who, by projecting and fathering the educational mission, had the highest interest of China at heart; whereas Woo should have been relegated to a cell in an insane asylum or to an institution for imbeciles. I said further that Chin Lan Pin, who had recommended Woo to His Excellency as commissioner of Chinese Education, was a timid man by nature and trembled at the sight of the smallest responsibilities. He and I had not agreed in our line of policy in our diplomatic correspondence with the State Department nor had we agreed as commissioners in regard to the treatment of the Chinese students. To illustrate his extreme dislike of responsibilities: He was requested by the Governor to go to Cuba to find out the condition of the coolies in that island in 1873. He waited three months before he started on his journey. He sent Yeh Shu Tung and one of the teachers of the Mission accompanied by a young American lawyer and an interpreter to Cuba, which party did the burden of the work and thus paved the way for Chin Lan Pin and made the work easy for him. All he had to do was to take a trip down to Cuba and return, fulfilling his mission in a perfunctory way. The heat of the day and the burden of the labor were all borne by Yeh Shu Tung, but Chin Lan Pin gathered in the laurel and was made a minister plenipotentiary, while Yeh was given the appointment of a secretary of the legation. I mention these things not from any invidious motive towards Chin, but simply to show that often in the official and political world one man gets more praise and glory than he really deserves, while another is not rewarded according to his intrinsic worth. His Excellency was well aware that I had no axe to grind in making the foregoing statement. I further added that I much preferred not to accept the appointment of a minister to Washington, but rather to remain as commissioner of education, for the sole purpose of carrying it through to its final success. And, one time in the heat of our altercation over a letter addressed to the State Department, I told Chin Lan Pin in plain language that I did not care a rap either for the appointment of an assistant minister, or for that matter, of a full minister, and that I was ready and would gladly resign at any moment, leaving him free and independent to do as he pleased.

This letter in answer to the Viceroy's note calling my attention to Woo's accusations gave the Viceroy an insight into Woo's antecedents, as well as into the impalpable character of Chin Lan Pin. Li was, of course, in the dark as to what the Viceroy had written to Chin Lan Pin, but things both in the legation and the Mission apparently moved on smoothly for a while, till some of the students were advanced enough in their studies for me to make application to the State Department for admittance to the Military Academy at West Point and the Naval Academy in Annapolis. The answer to my application was: "There is no room provided for Chinese students." It was curt and disdainful. It breathed the spirit of Kearnyism and Sandlotism with which the whole Pacific atmosphere was impregnated, and which had hypnotized all the departments of the government, especially Congress, in which Blaine figured most conspicuously as the champion against the Chinese on the floor of the Senate. He had the presidential bee buzzing in his bonnet at the time, and did his best to cater for the electoral votes of the Pacific coast. The race prejudice against the Chinese was so rampant and rank that not only my application for the students to gain entrance to Annapolis and West Point was treated with cold indifference and scornful hauteur, but the Burlingame Treaty of 1868 was, without the least provocation, and contrary to all diplomatic precedents and common decency, trampled under foot unceremoniously and wantonly, and set aside as though no such treaty had ever existed, in order to make way for those acts of congressional discrimination against Chinese immigration which were pressed for immediate enactment.

When I wrote to the Viceroy that I had met with a rebuff in my attempt to have some of the students admitted to West Point and Annapolis, his reply at once convinced me that the fate of the Mission was sealed. He too fell back on the Burlingame Treaty of 1868 to convince me that the United States government had violated the treaty by shutting out our students from West Point and Annapolis.

Having given a sketch of the progress of the Chinese Educational Mission from 1870 to 1877-8, my letter applying for their admittance into the Military and Naval Academies might be regarded as my last official act as a commissioner. My duties from 1878 onwards were chiefly confined to legation work.

When the news that my application for the students to enter the Military and Naval Academies of the government had proved a failure, and the displeasure and disappointment of the Viceroy at the rebuff were known, Commissioner Woo once more renewed his efforts to break up the Mission. This time he had the secret co-operation of Chin Lan Pin. Misrepresentations and falsehoods manufactured out of the whole cloth went forth to Peking in renewed budgets in every mail, till a censor from the ranks of the reactionary party came forward and took advantage of the strong anti-Chinese prejudices in America to memorialize the government to break up the Mission and have all the students recalled.

The government before acceding to the memorial put the question to Viceroy Li Hung Chang first, who, instead of standing up for the students, yielded to the opposition of the reactionary party and gave his assent to have the students recalled. Chin Lan Pin, who from his personal experience was supposed to know what ought to be done, was the next man asked to give his opinion. He decided that the students had been in the United States long enough, and that it was time for them to return to China. Woo Tsze Tung, the Commissioner, when asked for his opinion, came out point blank and said that they should be recalled without delay and should be strictly watched after their return. I was ruled out of the consultation altogether as being one utterly incompetent to give an impartial and reliable opinion on the subject. Thus the fate of the educational mission was sealed, and all students, about one hundred in all, returned to China in 1881.

The breaking up of the Chinese Educational Commission and the recall of the young students in 1881, was not brought about without a strenuous effort on the part of some thoughtful men who had watched steadfastly over the

development of human progress in the East and the West, who came forward
in their quiet and modest ways to enter a protest against the revocation of the
Mission. Chief among them were my lifelong friend, the Rev. J. H. Twichell,
and Rev. John W. Lane, through whose persistent efforts Presidents Porter and
Seelye, Samuel Clemens, T. F. Frelinghuysen, John Russell Young and others
were enlisted and brought forward to stay the work of retrogression of the part
of the Chinese. The protest was couched in the most dignified, frank and manly
language of President Porter of Yale and read as follows:

To The Tsung Li Yamun
or
Office for Foreign Affairs.

"The undersigned, who have been instructors, guardians and friends of
the students who were sent to this country under the care of the Chinese Edu-
cational Commission, beg leave to represent:

"That they exceedingly regret that these young men have been withdrawn
from the country, and that the Educational Commission has been dissolved.

"So far as we have had opportunity to observe, and can learn from the
representations of others, the young men have generally made a faithful use
of their opportunities, and have made good progress in the studies assigned to
them, and in the knowledge of the language, ideas, arts and institutions of the
people of this country.

"With scarcely a single exception, their morals have been good; their man-
ners have been singularly polite and decorous, and their behavior has been such
as to make friends for themselves and their country in the families, the schools,
the cities and villages in which they have resided.

"In these ways they have proved themselves eminently worthy of the con-
fidence which has been reposed in them to represent their families and the
great Chinese Empire in a land of strangers. Though children and youths, they
have seemed always to understand that the honor of their race and their nation
was committed to their keeping. As the result of their good conduct, many of
the prejudices of ignorant and wicked men towards the Chinese have been re-
moved, and more favorable sentiments have taken their place.

"We deeply regret that the young men have been taken away just at the
time when they were about to reap the most important advantages from their
previous studies, and to gather in the rich harvest which their painful and labo-
rious industry had been preparing for them to reap. The studies which most of
them have pursued hitherto have been disciplinary and preparatory. The studies

of which they have been deprived by their removal, would have been the bright flower and the ripened fruit of the roots and stems which have been slowly reared under patient watering and tillage. We have given to them the same knowledge and culture that we give to our own children and citizens.

"As instructors and guardians of these young men, we should have welcomed to our schools and colleges the Commissioners of Education or their representatives and have explained to them our system and methods of instruction. In some cases, they have been invited to visit us, but have failed to respond to their invitations in person or by their deputies.

"We would remind your honorable body that these students were originally received to our homes and our colleges by request of the Chinese government through the Secretary of State with the express desire that they might learn our language, our manners, our sciences and our arts. To remove them permanently and suddenly without formal notice or inquiry on the ground that as yet they had learned nothing useful to China when their education in Western institutions, arts and sciences is as yet incomplete, seems to us as unworthy of the great Empire for which we wish eminent prosperity and peace, as it is discourteous to the nation that extended to these young men its friendly hospitality.

"We cannot accept as true the representation that they have derived evil and not good from our institutions, our principles and our manners. If they have neglected or forgotten their native language, we never assumed the duty of instructing them in it, and cannot be held responsible for this neglect. The Chinese government thought it wise that some of its own youth should be trained after our methods. We have not finished the work which we were expected to perform. May we not reasonably be displeased that the results of our work should be judged unfavorably before it could possibly be finished?

"In view of these considerations, and especially in view of the injury and loss which have fallen upon the young men whom we have learned to respect and love, and the reproach which has implicitly been brought upon ourselves and the great nation to which we belong,—we would respectfully urge that the reasons for this sudden decision should be reconsidered, and the representations which have been made concerning the intellectual and moral character of our education should be properly substantiated. We would suggest that to this end, a committee may be appointed of eminent Chinese citizens whose duty it shall be to examine into the truth of the statements unfavorable to the young men or their teachers, which have led to the unexpected abandonment of the Educational Commission and to the withdrawal of the young men from the United States before their education could be finished."

CHAPTER XX
JOURNEY TO PEKING AND DEATH OF MY WIFE

THE TREATMENT WHICH THE STUDENTS RECEIVED AT THE hands of Chinese officials in the first years after their return to China as compared with the treatment they received in America while at school could not fail to make an impression upon their innermost convictions of the superiority of Occidental civilization over that of China—an impression which will always appeal to them as cogent and valid ground for radical reforms in China, however altered their conditions may be in their subsequent careers. Quite a number of the survivors of the one hundred students, I am happy to say, have risen to high official ranks and positions of great trust and responsibility. The eyes of the government have been opened to see the grand mistake it made in breaking up the Mission and having the students recalled. Within only a few years it had the candor and magnanimity to confess that it wished it had more of just such men as had been turned out by the Chinese Educational Mission in Hartford, Conn. This confession, though coming too late, may be taken as a sure sign that China is really awakening and is making the best use of what few partially educated men are available. And these few Occidentally educated men have, in their turn, encouraged and stimulated both the government and the people. Since the memorable events of the China and Japan war, and the war between Japan and Russia, several hundreds of Chinese students have come over to the United States to be educated. Thus the Chinese educational scheme which Tsang Kwoh Fan initiated in 1870 at Tientsin and established in Hartford, Conn., in 1872, though rolled back for a period of twenty-five years, has been practically revived.

Soon after the students' recall and return to China in 1881, I also took my departure and arrived in Tientsin in the fall of that year on my way to Peking to report myself to the government after my term of office as assistant minister had expired. This was the customary step for all diplomatic officers of the government to take at the close of their terms. Chin Lan Pin preceded me by nearly a year, having returned in 1880.

While paying my visit to Li Hung Chang in Tientsin, before going up to Peking, he brought up the subject of the recall of the students. To my great astonishment he asked me why I had allowed the students to return to China.

Not knowing exactly the significance of the inquiry, I said that Chin Lan Pin, who was minister, had received an imperial decree to break up the Mission; that His Excellency was in favor of the decree, so was Chin Lan Pin and so was Woo Tsze Tung. If I had stood out alone against carrying out the imperial mandate, would not I have been regarded as a rebel, guilty of treason, and lose my head for it? But he said that at heart he was in favor of their being kept in the States to continue their studies, and that I ought to have detained them. In reply I asked how I could have been supposed to read his heart at a distance of 45,000 lis, especially when it was well known that His Excellency had said that they might just as well be recalled. If His Excellency had written to me beforehand not to break up the Mission under any circumstances, I would then have known what to do; as it was, I could not have done otherwise than to see the decree carried out. "Well," said he, in a somewhat angry and excited tone, "I know the author of this great mischief." Woo Tsze Tung happened to be in Tientsin at the time. He had just been to Peking and sent me word begging me to call and see him. Out of courtesy, I did call. He told me he had not been well received in Peking, and that Viceroy Li was bitter towards him when he had called and had refused to see him a second time. He looked careworn and cast down. He was never heard of after our last interview.

On my arrival in Peking, one of my first duties was to make my round of official calls on the leading dignitaries of the government—the Princes Kung and Ching and the presidents of the six boards. It took me nearly a month to finish these official calls. Peking may be said to be a city of great distances, and the high officials live quite far apart from each other. The only conveyances that were used to go about from place to place were the mule carts. These were heavy, clumsy vehicles with an axle-tree running right across under the body of a box, which was the carriage, and without springs to break the jolting, with two heavy wheels, one at each end of the axle. They were slow coaches, and with the Peking roads all cut up and seldom repaired, you can imagine what traveling in those days meant. The dust and smell of the roads were something fearful. The dust was nothing but pulverized manure almost as black as ink. It was ground so fine by the millions of mule carts that this black stuff would fill one's eyes and ears and penetrate deep into the pores of one's skin, making it impossible to cleanse oneself with one washing. The neck, head and hands had to have suitable coverings to keep off the dust. The water is brackish, making it difficult to take off the dirt, thereby adding to the discomforts of living in Peking.

I was in Peking about three months. While there, I found time to prepare a plan for the effectual suppression of the Indian opium trade in China and the extinction of the poppy cultivation in China and India. This plan was submitted to the Chinese government to be carried out, but I was told by Whang Wen Shiu, the president of the Tsung Li Yamun (Foreign Affairs), that for want of suitable men, the plan could not be entertained, and it was shelved for nearly a quarter of a century until recently when the subject became an international question.

I left Peking in 1882. After four months' residence in Shanghai, I returned to the United States on account of the health of my family.

I reached home in the spring of 1883, and found my wife in a very low condition. She had lost the use of her voice and greeted me in a hoarse low whisper. I was thankful that I found her still living though much emaciated. In less than a month after my return, she began to pick up and felt more like herself. Doubtless, her declining health and suffering were brought on partly on account of my absence and her inexpressible anxiety over the safety of my life. A missionary fresh from China happened to call on her a few days before my departure for China and told her that my going back to China was a hazardous step, as they would probably cut my head off on account of the Chinese Educational Mission. This piece of gratuitous information tended more to aggravate a mind already weighed down by poor health, and to have this gloomy foreboding added to her anxiety was more than she could bear. I was absent in China from my family this time nearly a year and a half, and I made up my mind that I would never leave it again under any conditions whatever. My return in 1883 seemed to act on my wife's health and spirit like magic, as she gradually recovered strength enough to go up to Norfolk for the summer. The air up in Norfolk was comparatively pure and more wholesome than in the Connecticut valley, and proved highly salubrious to her condition. At the close of the summer, she came back a different person from what she was when she went away, and I was much encouraged by her improved health. I followed up these changes of climate and air with the view of restoring her to her normal condition, taking her down to Atlanta, Georgia, one winter and to the Adirondacks another year. It seemed that these changes brought only temporary relief without any permanent recovery. In the winter of 1885, she began to show signs of a loss of appetite and expressed a desire for a change. Somerville, New Jersey, was recommended to her as a sanitarium. That was the last resort she went to for her health, for there she caught a cold which resulted in her death. She lingered there for nearly two months till she was brought home, and died of Bright's disease on the 28th of June, 1886. She was buried in Cedar Hill Cemetery in the home lot I secured for that purpose. Her death made a great void in my after-life, which was irreparable, but she did not leave me hopelessly deserted and alone; she left me two sons who are constant reminders of her beautiful life and character. They have proved to be my greatest comfort and solace in my declining years. They are most faithful, thoughtful and affectionate sons, and I am proud of their manly and earnest Christian characters. My gratitude to God for blessing me with two such sons will forever rise to heaven, an endless incense.

The two blows that fell upon me one after the other within the short span of five years from 1880 to 1886 were enough to crush my spirit. The one had scattered my life work to the four winds; the other had deprived me of a happy home which had lasted only ten years. The only gleam of light that broke through the dark clouds which hung over my head came from my two motherless sons whose tender years appealed to the very depths of my soul for care and sympathy. They were respectively seven and nine years old when deprived of their mother. I was both father and mother to them from 1886 till 1895. My whole soul was wrapped up in their education and well-being. My mother-in-law, Mrs. Mary B. Kellogg, assisted me in my work and stood by me in my most trying hours, keeping house for me for nearly two years.

WHEN I WAS A BOY IN CHINA

YAN PHOU LEE

CHAPTER I.
INFANCY.

O N A CERTAIN DAY IN THE YEAR 1861, I was born. I cannot give you the exact date, because the Chinese year is different from the English year, and our months being lunar, that is, reckoned by the revolution of the moon around the earth, are consequently shorter than yours. We reckon time from the accessions of Emperors, and also by cycles of sixty years each. The year of my birth, 1861, was the first year of the Emperor Tung-che. We have twelve months ordinarily; and we say, instead of "January, February," etc., "Regular Moon, Second Moon, Third Moon," etc. Each third year is a leap year, and has an extra month so as to make each of the lunar years equal to a solar year. Accordingly, taking the English calendar as a standard, our New Year's Day varies. Therefore, although I am sure that I was born on the twenty-first day of the Second Moon, in Chinese, I don't know my exact birthday in English; and consequently, living in America as I have for many years, I have been cheated of my birthday celebration.

Being born a boy, there was a deal of rejoicing in the family, and among numerous relatives. If I had happened to be a girl, it would have been very different; the reason for which I will tell in a chapter on "Girls of my Acquaintance." My aged grandfather smiled with satisfaction when the news reached him in Fungshun, three hundred miles away to the East, where he was holding office as Literary Sub-Chancellor. Congratulations poured in in the shape of presents of rich cloths, jewelry and pigs' feet. These gifts came a month after my birth, which day is always celebrated as a christening-day is in England. On that day, which we call the "Completion of the Moon," my name was given to me. I started with the surname "Lee" which my family and clan possess in common; and to that "Yan Phou," which signifies "Wealth by Imperial Favor," was added—Lee Yan Phou. But I now arrange my name in accordance with American custom.

The names given on those occasions are not like your "Jack," "Harry," or "Dick," but are usually words chosen "from the dictionary" for their lucky import, or because they are supposed to possess the power of warding off evil influences in the child's horoscope. You should know that in China a baby's fortune is told almost as soon as he is born, the events of his life being foretold with surprising particularity.

In order to ward off malignant influences from the future of their child, rich people often spend great sums of money. To some deities, especially to the God of Longevity, vows are made, and promises of presents annually, if the god will protect baby and bring him through certain crises in his life; and thus, willing or unwilling, the idol is supposed bound to be the child's tutelary guardian.

Also blind fortune-tellers are paid to intercede for the infant with their particular idol. If you were living in China, you would notice the strings of amulets which youngsters wear. They are sometimes made of gold and silver; but often these necklaces are composed of mere scraps of paper with talismanic characters penned by priests; they are supposed to be efficacious in scaring away evil spirits. The priests, fortune-tellers, lessees of temples, clairvoyants, and astrologers drive a flourishing trade in these mysterious wares. For these charms, and the friendliness of the idols being a matter of life or death, of future happiness or misery to the beloved child, of course the poor are just as eager to spend money in this way as the rich, and through baby's life they continue to pay annual installments of money for these things.

On my christening-day friends came to see me and to congratulate my family, and a feast was made in my honor. When the guests departed they carried each a slice of roast pork as a return-gift. Roast pig is the national festal dish in China, as you will learn. No occasion is complete without it, whether it be a religious festival, the worship of ancestors, a wedding, or a birthday celebration. One feature of my christening feast was that my mother was permitted to have all she wanted of pigs' feet and ginger pickled together. It is believed that baby's food will be more abundant if the mother eat plentifully of this delicacy.

From what I have since observed I suppose that as it was the winter season I was wrapped in "swaddling clothes;" and I think the layers of garments would have caused the death of any ordinary American baby. First came much underwear of cotton cloth; then a jacket; then another jacket; then a gown padded with cotton; then still another quilted coat of bright calico; and over all a bib. I wore a cap too, but no shoes until I was able to walk. My hair was shaved off except a small tuft, which was the beginning, the embryo, you may say, of the queue of the future.

Speaking of the winter season: The climate in the city of my nativity is like that of Canton which lies seventy-five miles to the north. Although no snow falls, and although ice is an unknown quality there, yet the weather is sufficiently chilly to make a fire desirable. But Chinese houses, strangely enough I now think, are built for summer, and to counteract heat rather than to keep off cold; and no such furniture as a heating stove is known, neither furnaces, nor steam-heaters. So for warmth we resort to thick clothing, and all sleeves are cut long with that end in view. A funny consequence is that old and young look twice as big in winter as in summer.

As a baby I had my playthings bells, rattles and other knick-knacks. But there is no such blessed thing as a cradle among the Chinese in which baby may be soothed and rocked to sleep, neither the healthful, separate "crib." I had to sleep with my mother; and I have not a doubt that I used to cry a deal because I felt too warm, for the bedclothes which were plentiful and heavily padded would sometimes cover me all up and make it difficult for me to breathe. I would be suffocated, smothered, and of course I would cry; and my mother would do everything except give me air and liberty; numberless were the medicines administered, for Chinese doctors pretend they can cure the crying of children at night. American mothers have no idea what impositions Chinese mothers suffer from physicians and sellers of charms, on account of their superstitious fears concerning the health and welfare of their children.

In the daytime I used to sit in a bamboo chair which had a board in front that slid back and forth and served both as a table to hold my playthings and a lock to keep me in my seat, for it came up to my waist, so it was not possible for me to leap out. In this stiff fixture I used to sit hours at a time and watch my mother spin flax.

Our Oriental tastes are too simple to contrive such luxuries as baby-carriages. We have instead our "carrying tie." This consists of a piece of thick cloth, about two feet square, lined inside, and embroidered outside with beautiful figures, and having four bands sewed on, one at each corner. To put me into this cloth carriage, the one who was to carry me, my mother or a servant, would lean over; I was then laid on her back, the "carriage" thrown over me, and the upper bands tied around the bosom of the carrier, the lower ones around her waist. My legs, of course, dangled outside; but it was nevertheless a very comfortable seat for me, though I doubt if it were so pleasant for the one who lugged me about. The primary object of this contrivance was to get me to sleep, and many a fine nap I must have had in my "carriage." If I persisted in keeping awake, my carrier would sing to me a lullaby which, being ordinary conversation put to music more or less tuneful, is hardly worth a translation.

My earliest recollections are of a sitting-room on the ground floor of my grandsire's house, the right wing of which was assigned to my father at the time of his marriage. It was very long and narrow, with bare brick walls in which no windows opened upon the street; all the light and ventilation came through a long narrow opening in the roof. Rain came through too, as well as light and air, and had to be drained off.

The furniture of this room was simple; a bamboo sofa, a square table, a few stiff-backed chairs, three long and narrow benches and a couple of stools. This ascetic simplicity in furnishings, may be noticed everywhere in China; nowhere or even the rich inclined to indulge in luxury to any extent.

I remember very well the comfortless Chinese bed. Boards took the place of springs, and benches supported these boards. In ours, surmounting all as a heavy canopy frame, which, when new, was evidently gilded and carved. By this frame was suspended mosquito nettings, an absolutely necessary arrangement. The ground was our floor, overlaid with bricks a foot square as carpet. No chimney was to be seen anywhere, no heating apparatus, hardly any ornaments. In summer these rooms were cool and comfortable; but the winter's wind and cold rendered them cheerless.

There is only one event of my infant life worth of record, the death of my adopted father. He was my father's brother and had accompanied my grandfather to the city of his literary administration. He was but a youth of twenty-one, unmarried and studying for the public examinations. On his deathbed, he designated me as his adopted son and heir. My grandfather ratified the choice, so that without my consent I was transferred from my father's hands into my uncle's.

This mode of adoption is common. Usually the adopted son belongs to the same family or clan, but not always; in any case he has the rights, privileges and duties of a born son. Among the rights may be mentioned the inheriting of property, and among the duties the annual offerings at the family altar and the grave, and the daily burning of remembrance incense.

CHAPTER X.
HOW I WENT TO SHANGHAI.

ABOUT FORTY YEARS AGO, THERE CAME TO THIS country under the auspices of the Rev. Dr. Brown, an American missionary in China, a Chinese youth—who was destined to exert a potent influence on the future of the Chinese Empire. Many have heard of him or read about him; his name is Yung Wing. Inspired by a lofty ambition, he worked his way through preparatory school and college, graduating from Yale in 1854 with high honors.

He went back to China soon after his graduation and engaged in business in Shanghai. But the business with the incidental pleasure of money-making, did not entirely absorb his attention. China was at that time having troublesome diplomatic negotiations with foreign powers, and was being taken advantage of right and left for want of men in office who understood the customs, the laws and the civilization of Western countries.

Dr. Wing, indignant at the wrongs with China had suffered and was suffering at the hands of so-called "Christian" and "enlightened" nations, sought for a remedy, and conceived the brilliant project of educating a number of Chinese boys in America for future service at the government expense.

He made his plan known to prominent Chinese officials. At first he met with no sympathy, no encouragement. Still, he persevered; and after twelve years of patient waiting and active labor, he succeeded in convincing two of the most powerful ministers at the court of Pekin of the feasibility of his scheme. In consequence, an edict was issued by the emperor to enforce its execution.

A school was established in Shanghai to receive candidates, and announcement made that the government had appropriated a large sum of money to educate one hundred and twenty boys in America, who were to be sent in four detachments, in four successive years, beginning with 1872; and that a candidate, on his election after a term of probation at the school, should have the cadet's button and rank conferred on him; and that after fifteen years of residence in America, during which period the government promised to defray all expenses and exercise parental care over the youths, they were to return for entrance into its service.

Such an offer was unheard of. People doubtless were dazzled by its splendor, as many as came in view of it. But as no newspapers existed there, excepting at

Pekin and some of the treaty ports, the news did not spread far. Only faint and vague rumors reached the inland towns. Hence, comparatively few candidates presented themselves and these hailed, for the most part, from the maritime provinces. In fact, parents were not overeager to send their sons away so far, for so long a time, and to a land unknown to them, the inhabitants of which they heard and believed were barbarians.

A cousin of mine, however, who was in business then at Shanghai, thought differently; and was not deterred by any such considerations. He came home with glowing accounts of the new movement; and so painted the golden prospects of the successful candidate that he persuaded my mother to let me go. I was then twelve years old; my father had died three years before and my mother had assumed the sole charge of her three sons. But she was not going to force me to go, whether willing or unwilling; and so left the matter to me to decide.

I was more or less adventurous in disposition. A chance to see the world was just what I wanted. I said yes without hesitation. My mother, if she had any misgivings, wisely kept them to herself; and, like a brave woman who has resolved to deny herself for the good of her child, she set to work to prepare me for the journey to Shanghai.

For a whole month, I reveled at the sight of new clothes that were made for me. Friends and relatives made presents of food for the voyage, sweetmeats predominating. At last, after bidding farewell to all my uncles, aunts and cousins, with others of my kith and kin, I paid my last respects to my mother in the conventional way. I did not embrace her and kiss her. O no! that would have been un-Chinese and undignified. What I actually did was to bow my head four times to the ground upon my knees. She tried to appear cheerful, but I could see that her eyes were moistened with tears. I did not think much of it then, but I remembered it in after-time. Ah! a mother's love is strong wherever it is found. She gave me some pocket-money and bade me be a good boy and write often.

With those words ringing in my ears and the memory of that sad face fresh in my mind, I walked briskly by the side of my cousin down to the wharf at which the junk was moored, which vessel, of a style well-known by picture to American boys and girls, was to carry us to Hongkong, whence we expected to take steamer for Shanghai. We sailed down the narrow river with a stiff breeze in our favor, after offerings had been made to the river-god, and the gong had announced to the world that "we were off."

The river was so serpentine with its numerous bends that the men often had to take a run on the banks to pull the boat along. The sun was just tinging the western cloud-castles with crimson and gold and as we went further and fur-

ther from the town a panorama of great beauty passed before our eyes. Moun-
tains and stream, and fields wavy with golden grain, and towering pagodas, all
gemmed by the setting sun, composed this kaleidoscopic scene. But I had no
heart to enjoy it. I was homesick for the first time in my life. A sense of solitude,
of desolation—a feeling of loss possessed me—and I retired into a small cabin
to weep unseen. Before long, a tossing of the boat announced the awful pres-
ence of the sea, and soon after I realized what seasickness meant.

We arrived at Hongkong the next morning. It was a wonderful place to
me. I never wearied with gazing at the vessels, which were of all sorts and all
nationalities. The foreigners too were strange sights. How I stared at them and
wondered how they could move with their "straitjackets and tight pantaloons!"

I had an adventure which I can never forget. My cousin left me behind
with friends while he went to the theatre. I inwardly rebelled at this treatment,
and, against the advice of the people at the store where we stayed, set out in
that strange place to find the theatre, taking the money which my mother
had given me to buy a ticket. I walked quite a distance, stopping frequently
to gaze at the show windows and at the foreigners, till I came upon one at
last. Although I had seen theatrical performances before, I had never been in
a permanent theatre, so I was determined to enjoy my new experience. But
alas! no enjoyment came to me. I felt uneasy the whole time and looked all
over the auditory to see if my cousin was there. But he was nowhere to be
seen. Scared and trembling for the consequences, I left the building before the
grand climax when one hero was to distinguish himself by killing another and
went my way back to the store. My cousin returned before long and, being
informed of my escapade gave me a sound whipping. In two days we went
on board a steamer and arrived at Shanghai after a four days' journey from
Hongkong, without any incident or accident.

CHAPTER XI.
HOW I PREPARED FOR AMERICA.

ON OUR ARRIVAL TO SHANGHAI, MY COUSIN took me to see our aunt
whose husband was a compradôr in an American tea warehouse. A
compradôr is usually found in every foreign *hong* or firm. He acts as
interpreter and also as agent for the company. He has a corps of accountants
called *shroffs*, assistants and workmen under him.

My uncle was rich and lived in a fine house built after European models. It
was there that I first came in immediate contact with Western civilization. But

it was a long time before I got used to those red-headed and tight-jacketed foreigners. "How can they walk or run?" I asked myself curiously contemplating their close and confining garments. The dress of foreign ladies was still another mystery to me. They shocked my sense of propriety also, by walking arm-in-arm with the men. "How peculiar their voices are! how screechy! how sharp!" Such were some of the thoughts I had about these peculiar people.

A few days after, I was taken to the Tung Mim Kuen, or Government School, where I was destined to spend a whole year, preparatory to my American education. It was established by the government and was in charge of a commissioner, a deputy-commissioner, two teachers of Chinese, and two teachers of English. The building was quite spacious, consisting of two stories. The large schoolroom, library, dining-rooms and kitchen occupied the first floor. The offices, reception room and dormitories were overhead. The square tables of the teachers of Chinese were placed at each end of the schoolroom; between them were oblong tables and stools of the pupils.

I was brought into the presence of the commissioners and teachers; and having performed my *kow-tow* to each, a seat was assigned me among my mates, who scanned me with a good deal of curiosity. It was afternoon, and then Chinese lessons were being recited. So while they looked at me through the corners of their eyes, they were also attending to their lessons with as much vim and voice as they could command. Soon recitations were over, not without one or two pupils being sent back to their seats to study their tasks over again, a few blows being administered to stimulate the intellect and quicken memory.

At half-past four o'clock, school was out and the boys, to the number of forty, went forth to play. They ran around, chased each other and wasted their cash on fruits and confections. I soon made acquaintance with some of them, but I did not experience any of the hazing and bullying to which new pupils in American and English schools are subject. I found that there were two parties among the boys. I joined one of them and had many friendly encounters with the rival party. As in America, we had a great deal of generous emulation, and consequently much boasting of the prizes and honors won by the rival societies. Our chief amusements were sight-seeing, shuttle-cock-kicking and penny-guessing.

Supper came at six when we had rice, meats and vegetables. Our faces invariably were washed after supper in warm water. This is customary. Then the lamps were lighted; and when the teachers came down, full forty pairs of lungs were at work with lessons of next day. At eight o'clock, one of the teachers read and explained a long extract from Chinese history, which, let me assure you, is replete with interest. At nine o'clock we were sent to our beds. Nothing ever happened of special interest. I remember that we used to talk till pretty late, and that some of the nights that I spent there were not of the pleasantest kind because I was haunted by the fear of spirits.

After breakfast the following morning we assembled in the same school-room to study our English lessons. The teacher of this branch was a Chinese gentleman who learned his English at Hongkong. The first thing to be done with me was to teach me the alphabet. When the teacher grew tired he set some advanced pupils to teach me. The letters sounded rather funny, I must say. It took me two days to learn them. The letter R was the hardest one to pronounce, but I soon learned to give it, with a peculiar roll of the tongue even. We were taught to read and write English and managed by means of primers and phrase-books to pick up a limited knowledge of the language. A year thus passed in study and pastime. Sundays were given to us to spend as holidays.

It was in the month of May when we were examined in our English studies and the best thirty were selected to go to America, their proficiency in Chinese, their general deportment and their record also being taken into account.

There was great rejoicing among our friends and kindred. For the cadet's gilt button and rank were conferred on us, which, like the first literary degree, was a step towards fortune, rank and influence. Large posters were posted up at the front doors of our homes, informing the world in gold characters of the great honor which had come to the family.

We paid visits of ceremony to the *Tautai*, chief officer of the department, and to the American consul-general, dressed in our official robes and carried in fine carriages. By the first part of June, we were ready for the ocean journey. We bade our farewell with due solemnity, for thought that on our return after fifteen years of study abroad half of them might be dead, made us rather serious. But the sadness of parting was soon over and homesickness and dreariness took its place, as the steamer steamed out of the river and our native country grew indistinct in the twilight.

CHAPTER XII.
FIRST EXPERIENCES IN AMERICA.

AFTER A STORMY VOYAGE OF ONE WEEK, with the usual accompaniment of seasickness, we landed at Yokohama, in the Country of the Rising Sun. For Japan means "sun-origin." The Japanese claim to be descendants of the sun, instead of being an off-shoot of the Chinese race.

During the four days on shore we young Chinese saw many strange things; the most remarkable being the steam-engine. We were told that those iron rails running parallel for a long distance were the "fire-car road." I was wondering how a car could run on them, and driven by fire, too, as I understood it, when a locomotive whizzed by screeching and ringing its bell. That was the first iron-horse we had ever seen, and it made a profound impression on us. We made a number of other remarkable and agreeable discoveries. We were delighted to learn that the Japanese studied the same books as we and worshiped our Confucius, and that we could converse with them in writing, pretty much as deaf and dumb people do. We learned that the way they lived and dressed was like that in vogue in the time of Confucius. Their mode of dressing the hair and their custom of sitting on mats laid on the floor is identical with ancient Chinese usage.

When our brief stay came to an end, we went aboard the steamer *City of Peking*, which reached San Francisco in nineteen days. Our journey across the Pacific was made in the halcyon weather. The ocean was as gentle as a lamb for the most part, although at times it acted in such a way as to suggest a raging lion.

San Francisco in 1873 was the paradise of the self-exiled Chinese. We boys who came to study under the auspices of the Chinese government and under the protection of the American eagle, were objects of some attention from the press. Many of its representatives came to interview us.

The city impressed my young imagination with its lofty buildings—their solidity and elegance. The depot with its trains running in and out was a great attraction. But the "modern conveniences" of gas and running water and electric bells and elevators were what excited wonder and stimulated investigation.

Nothing occurred on our Eastward journey to mar the enjoyment of our first ride on the steam-cars—excepting a train robbery, a consequent smash-up of the engine, and the murder of the engineer. We were quietly looking out of the windows and gazing at the seemingly interminable prairies when the train suddenly bounded backward, then rushed forward a few feet, and, then meeting some resistance, started back again. Then all was confusion and terror. Pistol-shots could be made out above the cries of frightened passengers. Women shrieked and babies cried. Our party, teachers and pupils, jumped from our seats in dismay and looked out through the windows for more light on the subject. What we saw was enough to make our hair stand on end. Two ruffianly men held a revolver in each hand and seemed to be taking aim at us from the short distance of forty feet or thereabouts. Our teachers told us to crouch down for our lives. We obeyed with trembling and fear. Doubtless many prayers were most fervently offered to the gods of China at the time. Our teachers certainly prayed as they had never done before. One of them was overhead calling upon all the gods of the Chinese Pantheon to come and save him. In half an hour the agony and suspense were over. A brakeman rushed through with a lamp in his hand. He told us that the train had been robbed of its gold bricks, by five men, three of whom, dressed like Indians, rifled the baggage car while the others held the passengers at bay; that the engine was hopelessly wrecked, the engineer killed; that the robbers had escaped on horseback with their booty; and that men had been sent to the nearest telegraph station to "wire" for another engine and a supply of workmen. One phase of American civilization was thus indelibly fixed upon our minds.

We reached Springfield, Mass., in due time, where we were distributed among some of the best families in New England. As liberal provision having been made for our care by the Chinese government, there was no difficulty in finding nice people to undertake our "bringing-up," although I now know that a philanthropic split must have inspired all who assumed the responsibility of our training and education. We were assigned two by two; and it was my good fortune to be put into the hands of a most motherly lady in Springfield. She came after us in a hack. As I was pointed out to her, she put her arms around and kissed me. This made the rest of the boys laugh, and perhaps I got rather red in the face; however, I would say nothing to show my embarrassment. But that was the first kiss I ever had had since my infancy.

Our first appearance in an American household must have been a funny occurrence to its members. We were dressed in our full Chinese costume, consisting of cue, satin shoes, skull-cap, silk gown, loose jacket and white linen blouse. We were both thirteen years of age, but smaller than American boys at eleven.

Sunday came. After lunch, the lady and her son came up to our room to tell us to get ready to go to Sabbath-school with them. We knew very little English at the time. The simplest Anglo-Saxon words were still but slightly known to us. We caught the word "school" only. We supposed that at last our ordeal in an American school was at hand. We each took a cloth-wrapper and began to tie up a pile of books with it, *à la Chinoise*, when our guardians, returning, made us understand by signs and otherwise that no books were needed.

Well, we four set out, passed Court Square, and walked up the steps of the First Church.

"It is a church," said my companion in Chinese.

We were confirmed in our suspicions on peeping in and seeing the people rise to sing. "Church! church!" we muttered, and rushed from the edifice with all the speed we could command. We did not stop till we got into our room, while our American friends, surprised at this move on our part and failing to overtake us, went back to the church.

We learned English by object-lessons. At table we were always told the names of certain dishes, and then assured that if we could not remember the name we were not to partake of that article of food. Taught by this method, our progress was rapid and surprising.

THE AMERICAN MISSIONARY
VOL. XLI. SEPTEMBER, 1887. NO.9

Graduating Address of Yan Phou Lee, at Yale College.

The Other Side of the Chinese Question.

THE TORRENTS OF HATRED AND ABUSE WHICH have periodically swept over the Chinese industrial class in America had their sources in the early California days. They grew gradually in strength, and, uniting in one mighty stream, at last broke the barriers with which justice, humanity and the Constitution of the Republic had until then restrained their fury.

The catastrophe was too terrible, and has made too deep an impression to be easily forgotten. Even if Americans are disposed to forget, the Chinese will not fail to keep the sad record of faith unkept, of persecution permitted by an enlightened people, of rights violated without redress in a land where all are equal before the law.

Sad it is that in a Christian community only a feeble voice here and there has been raised against this public wrong; while the enemies of the Chinese laborer may be counted by the million. Yet these men, having everything their own way, are still dissatisfied and cannot rest secure until all the Chinese laborers have been driven out or killed off with the connivance of a perverted public opinion. Is it not high time for good men to ____[1] themselves and say to the enemy of industry and order, "Halt! thus far shalt though go, and no farther"? For be assured that after the Chinese have all departed, those men who are determined to get high wages for doing nothing will turn against other peaceful sons of toil; and who would venture to say that there will be absolute safety for the native American? Mob-rule knows no respect for persons; the Chinese were attached first simply because they were the weakest. I do not deny that the anti-Chinese agitation has some show reason. But its strength rests on three erroneous assumptions, by proving the groundlessness of which the whole superstructure of fallacy and falsehood can be made to totter.

1 This word is unreadable in the original document. It could be a four letter word that ends with "E."

First, it is assumed that the work to be done and the fund for labor's remuneration are fixed quantities, and that if the Chinese are employed so much will be taken from other laborers. It is sufficient to reply that no economist holds that view.

Secondly, it is assumed that the Pekin authorities are anxious to get rid of its redundant population. Nothing can be more absurd. They have been always, and are still, averse to the emigration of their subjects; so much so that they yielded only to the inducements and concessions offered by this Government, which are embodies in the Burlingame Treaty. Another proof is the readiness with which they consented to the limitation of Chinese immigration when the Angell Treaty was negotiated.

Thirdly, it is assumed that China's four hundred millions are only waiting for an opening to "inundate" this country. This is soberly asserted and has the effect of the Gorgon-head; for who is not stunned at the bare mention of this appalling and impending disaster? It would be terrible if it were possible—if it could be true.

But there is no cause for apprehension. The immigration of my compatriots has been exclusively from Canton and the region around it within a radius of a hundred miles. The population of this district is estimated at 5,000,000. Not a single immigrant has hailed from any other part of the Empire. The Mongolization of America, therefore, is an event as far off as the Millennium. For after twenty-five years of unrestricted immigration, your patriotic agitators could muster up only 200,000 Chinese laborers in all the States and Territories. Now place this figure side by side with the 3,000,000 of immigrant princes from the "English Poland," which has never had more than 8,000,000 inhabitants at any one time, and you will be struck with the contrast.

What reason can we give why so few comparatively come from China? The Chinese are by nature and from habit gregarious, but not migratory. hey dislike to cut adrift from the ties of kindred, the associations of home, the traditions of fatherland. The belief that their welfare in the future life depends on the proper burial of their remains in home-soil, followed by sorrowing children and tearful widow, curbs their desire to go abroad, even with the hope of bettering their condition. But as only the poorest are tempted to lead a life of adventure, and as the good Emperor does not pay their passage money, the number that can leave their native land is very small. Thus you will find that Chinese immigrants are usually poor on landing, for they bring no votes in their pockets which can immediately be turned into money, and so they must rely upon their countrymen who have preceded them for assistance. This is afforded by the Six Companies, who accordingly have a lien on their prospective wages. From this practice of advancing money arises the terrible accusation that Chinese labor is contract labor—is slave labor. We know with what reluctance they first made their way to this country. Oftentimes they had to be drugged and kidnapped. It was thought necessary, for labor in those days was in great demand; the Western country was wild; its resources wanted development. Laborers were welcome irrespective of race or nationality.

But the times soon changed; California had grown rich and flourishing; the Pacific Railroad had been built; wages had fallen; the Chinese became superfluous, and the corals which constructed the reef must go or die. From being an economic question, the expulsion of the Chinese laborers was made a political question. Disinterested demagogues easily won mob-favor by advocating the cause of the sand-lot, and the Chinese workmen were sacrificed to the Moloch of political ambition. The matter was carried to the National Council, and you would suppose that Congress at least would be just and dispassionate, but it, too, was borne along the waves of prejudice.

In every such conflict might is right; the weakest goes to the wall. Two parties were bidding for the Pacific vote—that of great moral principles as well as that of no principles. The Chinese came in like cloth between the blades of the scissors, like Mr. Pickwick between the infuriated rival editors of Eatanswill. When 80,000 offices were at stake, and the hoodlums of California had to be petted, it was not hard to make the Chinese out to be undesirable immigrants and to hoodwink the public with charges against them which are false, or which may be preferred against all immigrants.

Sand-lotters were scandalized by the alleged immoral practices of the Asiatics; were in trembling and fear lest their Christianity should suffer by contact with Chinese paganism. I believe the cesspool once complained of the influx of muddy water. Californians prohibited the Chinese from becoming citizens and then accused them of failure to become naturalized. People in general were staggered at the imminent danger of the Mongolization of American and at the same time found fault with the Chinese for not making the United States their home. "Consistency, thou art a jewel."

Those who make America a catspaw to secure home-rule chestnuts proved most conclusively the non-assimilability of the Chinese race—said they came simply to make money which eventually found its way to the old country. I admit both points: I admit that they do not come to America for the good of their fatherland and mother church, and that they do come here to make money. So do Americans in China. They are wicked enough to send money home to support wife and children, but they give an equivalent in work. Gold and silver are things you can most conveniently spare; but if you must keep them at home, why then make a law forbidding their export.

I also admit that the Chinese laborer does not assimilate with your enlightened Hibernian citizens. Thank God for that! If he did, he would not be compelled to do menial work through fear of starvation. If he did he might have become a saloon statesman by this time, or even a much-envied "boodler." If he did, he might be even now luxuriating in Sing Sing at the public expense.

But why pursue this theme further? The bill was passed which excluded both skilled as well as unskilled Chinese laborers, though the Court of Pekin diplomatically understood that the restriction was to affect common workmen alone. Natives of China are forbidden to become citizens of this Republic, which takes to its bosom the off-scouring, the garbage, and the dynamite of Europe. Never had there been seen such pandering to the worst passion of an insignificant faction!

Were it not for the tragic events which trod on the heels of the Chinese Immigration Bill, one might be inclined to laugh at the absurdities in the bill itself. If the law is faithfully executed (and to be worth anything it must be), all Americans born in China are disfranchised, and all Chinese natives of British colonies, like Hong Kong and India, have free access to this country. But who could laugh in the midst of indignant tears? By passing a discriminating law against an already persecuted class, the Central Government yielded to the demands of the mob, and to that extent countenanced its violence and lawlessness. The Anti-Chinese Act is a cause of all the outrages and massacres that have been since committed in Rock Springs and Denver, in Portland, San Francisco and other parts, which, if they had been perpetrated in China against Americans, would have resounded from Bedloe's Island (whereon stands the Statue of Liberty) to the Golden Gate. But the criminals in these cases were not punished, and even the pitiful indemnity was voted down until Congress could not withhold it from very shame.

I have stated facts which are well known. It is not necessary to exaggerate. I now ask you Christian people of America whether you have not failed in your duties as lovers of justice and fatherland, in not enforcing your opinions in public and in private, as well as in church as in State. I ask those who gallantly sided with the strong against the weak, whether they do not think they have done enough for glory and personal ambition? If there is an avenging Deity, (and we believe there is), ought you not to beware of the retribution which is sure to overtake a nation that permits the cold-blooded murder of innocent strangers within its gates to go unpunished?

THE BIOGRAPHY OF A CHINAMAN

LEE CHEW

[Mr. Lee Chew is a representative Chinese business man who expresses with much force views that are generally held by his countrymen throughout America. The Interview that follows is strictly as he gave it, except as to detail of arrangement and mere verbiage. Mr. Lee was assisted by the well-known Chinese Interpreter, Mr. Joseph M. Singleton, of 24 Pell Street.—EDITOR.]

THE VILLAGE WHERE I WAS BORN IS situated in the province of Canton, on one of the banks of the Si-Kiang River. It is called a village, altho it is really as big as a city, for there are about 5.000 men in it over eighteen years of age—women and children and even youths are not counted in our villages.

All in the village belonged to the tribe of Lee. They did not intermarry with one another, but the men went to other villages for their wives and brought them home to their fathers' houses, and men from other villages—Wus and Wings and Sings and Fongs, etc.—chose wives from among our girls.

When I was a baby I was kept in our house all the time with my mother, but when 1 was a boy of seven I had to sleep at nights with other boys of the village— about thirty of them in one house. The girls are separated the same way—thirty or forty of them sleeping together in one house away from their parents—and the widows have houses where they work and sleep, tho they go to their fathers' houses to eat.

My father's house is built of fine blue brick, better than the brick in the houses here in the United States. It is only one story high, roofed with red tiles and surrounded by a stone wall which also encloses the yard. There are four rooms in the house, one large living room which serves for a parlor and three private rooms, one occupied by my grandfather, who is very old and very honorable; another by my father and mother, and the third by my oldest brother and his wife and two little children. There are no windows, but the door is left open all day.

All the men of the village have farms, but they don't live on them as the farmers do here; they live in the village, but go out during the day time and work their farms, coming home before dark. My father has a farm of about ten acres, on which he grows a great abundance of things—sweet potatoes, rice, beans, peas, yams, sugar cane, pineapples, bananas, lychee nuts and palms. The palm leaves are useful and can be sold. Men make fans of the lower part of each leaf near the stem, and water proof coats and hats, and awnings for boats, of the parts that are left when the fans are cut out.

So many different things can be grown on one small farm, because we bring plenty of water in a canal from the mountains thirty miles away, and every farmer takes as much as he wants for his fields by means of drains. He can give each crop the right amount of water.

Our people all working together make these things, the mandarin has nothing to do with it, and we pay no taxes, except a small one on the land. We have our own Government, consisting of the elders of our tribe—the honorable men. When a man gets to be sixty years of age he begins to have honor and to become a leader, and then the older he grows the more he is honored. We had some men who were nearly one hundred years, but very few of them.

In spite of the fact that any man may correct them for a fault, Chinese boys have good times and plenty of play. We played games like tag, and other games like shinny and a sort of football called yin.

We had dogs to play with—plenty of dogs and good dogs—that understand Chinese as well as American dogs understand American language. We hunted with them, and we also went fishing and had as good a time as American boys, perhaps better, as we were almost always together in our house, which was a sort of boys' club house, so we had many playmates. Whatever we did we did all together, and our rivals were the boys of other club houses, with whom we sometimes competed in the games. But all our play outdoors was in the daylight, because there were many graveyards about and after dark, so it was said, black ghosts with naming mouths and eyes and long claws and teeth would come from these and tear to pieces and devour anyone whom they might meet.

It was not all play for us boys, however. We had to go to school, where we learned to read and write and to recite the precepts of Kong-foo-tsze and the other Sages, and stories about the great Emperors of China, who ruled with the wisdom of gods and gave to the whole world the light of high civilization and the culture of our literature, which is the admiration of all nations.

I went to my parents' house for meals, approaching my grandfather with awe, my father and mother with veneration and my elder brother with respect. I never spoke unless spoken to, but I listened and heard much concerning the red haired, green eyed foreign devils with the hairy faces, who had lately come out of the sea and clustered on our shores. They were wild and fierce and wicked, and paid no regard to the moral precepts of Kong-foo-tsze and the Sages; neither did they worship their ancestors, but pretended to be wiser than their fathers and grandfathers. They loved to beat people and to rob and murder. In the streets of Hong Kong many of them could be seen reeling drunk. Their speech was a savage roar, like the voice of the tiger or the buffalo, and they wanted to take the land away from the Chinese. Their men and women lived together like animals, without any marriage or faithfulness, and even were shameless enough to walk the streets arm in arm in daylight. So the old men said.

All this was very shocking and disgusting, as our women seldom were on the street, except in the evenings, when they went with the water jars to the three wells that supplied all the people. Then if they met a man they stood still, with their faces turned to the wall, while he looked the other way when he passed them. A man who spoke to a woman on the street in a Chinese village would be beaten, perhaps killed.

My grandfather told how the English foreign devils had made wicked war on the Emperor, and by means of their enchantments and spells had defeated his armies and forced him to admit their opium, so that the Chinese might smoke and become weakened and the foreign devils might rob them of their land. My grandfather said that it was well known that the Chinese were always the greatest and wisest among men. They had invented and discovered everything that was good. Therefore the things which the foreign devils had and the Chinese had not must be evil. Some of these things were very wonderful, enabling the red haired savages to talk with one another, tho they might be thousands of miles apart. They had suns that made darkness like day, their ships carried earthquakes and volcanoes to fight for them, and thousands of demons that lived in iron and steel houses spun their cotton and silk, pushed their boats, pulled their cars, printed their newspapers and did other work for them. They were constantly showing disrespect for their ancestors by getting new things to take the place of the old.

I heard about the American foreign devils, that they were false, having made a treaty by which it was agreed that they could freely come to China, and the Chinese as freely go to their country. After this treaty was made China opened its doors to them and then they broke the treaty that they had asked for by shutting the Chinese out of their country.

When I was ten years of age I worked on my father's farm, digging, hoeing, manuring, gathering and carrying the crop. We had no horses, as nobody under the rank of an official is allowed to have a horse in China, and horses do not work on farms there, which is the reason why the roads there are so bad. The people cannot use roads as they are used here, and so they do not make them.

I worked on my father's farm till I was about sixteen years of age, when a man of our tribe came back from America and took ground as large as four city blocks and made a paradise of it. He put a large stone wall around and led some streams through and built a palace and summer house and about twenty other structures, with beautiful bridges over the streams and walks and roads. Trees and flowers, singing birds, water fowl and curious animals were within the walls.

The man had gone away from our village a poor boy. Now he returned with unlimited wealth, which he had obtained in the country of the American wizards. After many amazing adventures he had become a merchant in a city called Mott Street, so it was said.

When his palace and grounds were completed he gave a dinner to all the people who assembled to be his guests. One hundred pigs roasted whole were served on the tables, with chickens, ducks, geese and such an abundance of dainties that our villagers even now lick their fingers when they think of it. He had the best actors from Hong Kong performing, and every musician for miles around was playing and singing. At night the blaze of the lanterns could be seen for many miles.

Having made his wealth among the barbarians this man had faithfully returned to pour it out among his tribesmen, and he is living in our village now very happy, and a pillar of strength to the poor.

The wealth of this man filled my mind with the idea that I, too, would like to go to the country of the wizards and gain some of their wealth, and after a long time my father consented, and gave me his blessing, and my mother took leave of me with tears, while my grandfather laid his hand upon my head and told me to remember and live up to the admonitions of the Sages, to avoid gambling, bad women and men of evil minds, and so to govern my conduct that when I died my ancestors might rejoice to welcome me as a guest on high.

My father gave me $100, and I went to Hong Kong with five other boys from our place and we got steerage passage on a steamer, paying $50 each. Everything was new to me. All my life I had been used to sleeping on a board bed with a wooden pillow, and I found the steamer's bunk very uncomfortable, because it was so soft. The food was different from that which I had been used to, and I did not like it at all. I was afraid of the stews, for the thought of what they might be made of by the wicked wizards of the ship made me ill. Of the great power of these people I saw many signs. The engines that moved the ship were wonderful monsters, strong enough to lift mountains. When I got to San

Francisco, which was before the passage of the Exclusion act, I was half starved, because I was afraid to eat the provisions of the barbarians, but a few days' living in the Chinese quarter made me happy again. A man got me work as a house servant in an American family, and my start was the same as that of almost all the Chinese in this country.

The Chinese laundryman does not learn his trade in China; there are no laundries in China. The women there do the washing in tubs and have no wash-boards or flat irons. All the Chinese laundry men here were taught in the first place by American women just as I was taught.

When I went to work for that American family I could not speak a word of English, and I did not know anything about housework. The family consisted of husband, wife and two children. They were very good to me and paid me $3.50 a week, of which I could save $3.

I did not know how to do anything, and I did not understand what the lady said to me, but she showed me how to cook, wash, iron, sweep, dust, make beds, wash dishes, clean windows, paint and brass, polish the knives and forks, etc., by doing the things herself and then overseeing my efforts to imitate her. She would take my hands and show them how to do things. She and her husband and children laughed at me a great deal, but it was all good natured. I was not confined to the house in the way servants are confined here, but when my work was done in the morning I was allowed to go out till lunch time. People in California are more generous than they are here.

In six months I had learned how to do the work of our house quite well, and I was getting $5 a week and board, and putting away about $4.25 a week. I had also learned some English, and by going to a Sunday school I learned more English and something about Jesus, who was a great Sage, and whose precepts are like those of Kong-foo-tsze.

It was twenty years ago when I came to this country, and I worked for two years as a servant, getting at the last $35 a month. I sent money home to comfort my parents, but tho I dressed well and lived well and had pleasure, going quite often to the Chinese theater and to dinner parties in Chinatown, I saved $50 in the first six months, $90 in the second, $120 in the third and $150 in the fourth. So I had $410 at the end of two years, and I was now ready to start in business.

When I first opened a laundry it was in company with a partner, who had been in the business for some years. We went to a town about 500 miles inland, where a railroad was building. We got a board shanty and worked for the men employed by the railroads. Our rent cost us $10 a month and food nearly $5 a week each, for all food was dear and we wanted the best of everything—we lived principally on rice, chickens, ducks and pork, and did our own cooking. The Chinese take naturally to cooking. It cost us about $50 for our furniture and apparatus, and we made close upon $60 a week, which we divided between us. We had to put up with many insults and some frauds, as men would come in and claim parcels that did not belong to them, saying they had lost their tickets, and would fight if they did not get what they asked for. Sometimes we were taken before Magistrates and fined for losing shirts that we had never seen. On the other hand, we were making money, and even after sending home $3 a week I was able to save about $15. When the railroad construction gang moved on we went with them. The men were rough and prejudiced against us, but not more so than in the big Eastern cities. It is only lately in New York that the Chinese have been able to discontinue putting wire screens in front of their windows, and at the present time the street boys are still breaking the windows of Chinese laundries all over the city, while the police seem to think it a joke.

We were three years with the railroad, and then went to the mines, where we made plenty of money in gold dust, but had a hard time, for many of the miners were wild men who carried revolvers and after drinking would come into our place to shoot and steal shirts, for which we had to pay. One of these men hit his head hard against a flat iron and all the miners came and broke up our laundry, chasing us out of town. They were going to hang us. We lost all our property and $365 in money, which members of the mob must have found.

Luckily most of our money was in the hands of Chinese bankers in San Francisco. I drew $500 and went East to Chicago, where I had a laundry for three years, during which I increased my capital to $2,500. After that I was four years in Detroit. I went home to China in 1897, but returned in 1898, and began a laundry business in Buffalo. But Chinese laundry business now is not as good as it was ten years ago. American cheap labor in the steam laundries has hurt it. So I determined to become a general merchant, and with this idea I came to New York and opened a shop in the Chinese quarter, keeping silks, teas, porcelain, clothes, shoes, hats and Chinese provisions, which include shark's fins and nuts, lily bulbs and lily flowers, lychee nuts and other Chinese dainties, but do not include rats, because it would be too expensive to import them. The rat which is eaten by the Chinese is a field animal which lives on rice, grain and sugar cane. Its flesh is delicious. Many Americans who have tasted shark's fin and bird's nest soup and tiger lily flowers and bulbs are firm friends of Chinese cookery. If they could enjoy one of our fine rats they would go to China to live, so as to get some more.

American people eat ground hogs, which are very like these Chinese rats, and they also eat many sorts of food that our people would not touch. Those that have dined with us know that we understand how to live well.

The ordinary laundry shop is generally divided into three rooms. In front is the room where the customers are received, behind that a bedroom and in the back the work shop, which is also the dining room and kitchen. The stove and cooking utensils are the same as those of the Americans.

Work in a laundry begins early on Monday morning—about seven o'clock. There are generally two men, one of whom washes while the other does the ironing. The man who irons does not start in till Tuesday, as the clothes are not ready for him to begin till that time. So he has Sundays and Mondays as holidays. The man who does the washing finishes up on Friday night, and so he has Saturday and Sunday. Each works only five days a week, but those are long days—from seven o'clock in the morning till midnight.

During his holidays the Chinaman gets a good deal of fun out of life. There's a good deal of gambling and some opium smoking, but not so much as Americans imagine. Only a few of New York's Chinamen smoke opium. The habit is very general among rich men and officials in China, but not so much among poor men. I don't think it does as much harm as the liquor that the Americans drink. There's nothing so bad as a drunken man. Opium doesn't make people crazy.

Gambling is mostly fan tan, but there is a good deal of poker, which the Chinese have learned from Americans and can play very well. They also gamble with dominoes and dice.

The fights among the Chinese and the operations of the hatchet men are all due to gambling. Newspapers often say that they are feuds between the six companies, but that is a mistake. The six companies are purely benevolent societies, which look after the Chinaman when he first lands here. They represent the six southern provinces of China, where most of our people are from, and they are like the German, Swedish, English, Irish and Italian societies which assist emigrants. When the Chinese keep clear of gambling and opium they are not blackmailed, and they have no trouble with hatchet men or any others.

About 500 of New York's Chinese are Christians, the others are Buddhists, Taoists, etc., all mixed up. These haven't any Sunday of their own, but keep New Year's Day and the first and fifteenth days of each month, when they go to the temple in Mott Street.

In all New York there are only thirty-four Chinese women, and it is impossible to get a Chinese woman out here unless one goes to China and marries her there, and then he must collect affidavits to prove that she really is his wife. That is in case of a merchant. A laundryman can't bring his wife here under any circumstances, and even the women of the Chinese Ambassador's family had trouble getting in lately.

Is it any wonder, therefore, or any proof of the demoralization of our people if some of the white women in Chinatown are not of good character? What other set of men so isolated and so surrounded by alien and prejudiced people are more moral? Men, wherever they may be, need the society of women, and among the white women of Chinatown are many excellent and faithful wives and mothers.

Recently there has been organized among us the Oriental Club, composed of our most intelligent and influential men. We hope for a great improvement in social conditions by its means, as it will discuss matters that concern us, bring us in closer touch with Americans and speak for us in something like an official manner.

Some fault is found with us for sticking to our old customs here, especially in the matter of clothes, but the reason is that we find American clothes much inferior, so far as comfort and warmth go. The Chinaman's coat for the winter is very durable, very light and very warm. It is easy and not in the way. If he wants to work he slips out of it in a moment and can put it on again as quickly. Our shoes and hats also are better, we think, for our purposes, than the American clothes. Most of us have tried the American clothes, and they make us feel as if we were in the stocks. I have found out, during my residence in this country, that much of the Chinese prejudice against Americans is unfounded, and I no longer put faith in the wild tales that were told about them in our village, tho some of the Chinese, who have been here twenty years and who are learned men, still believe that there is no marriage in this country, that the land is infested with demons and that all the people are given over to general wickedness.

I know better. Americans are not all bad, nor are they wicked wizards. Still, they have their faults, and their treatment of us is outrageous.

The reason why so many Chinese go into the laundry business in this country is because it requires little capital and is one of the few opportunities that are open. Men of other nationalities who are jealous of the Chinese, because he is a more faithful worker than one of their people, have raised such a great outcry about Chinese cheap labor that they have shut him out of working on farms or in factories or building railroads or making streets or digging sewers. He cannot practice any trade, and his opportunities to do business are limited to his own countrymen. So he opens a laundry when he quits domestic service.

The treatment of the Chinese in this country is all wrong and mean. It is persisted in merely because China is not a fighting nation. The Americans would not dare to treat Germans, English, Italians or even Japanese as they treat the Chinese, because if they did there would be a war.

There is no reason for the prejudice against the Chinese. The cheap labor cry was always a falsehood. Their labor was never cheap, and is not cheap now. It has always commanded the highest market price. But the trouble is that the Chinese are such excellent and faithful workers that bosses will have no others when they can get them. If you look at men working on the street you will find an overseer for every four or five of them. That watching is not necessary for Chinese. They work as well when left to themselves as they do when someone is looking at them.

It was the jealousy of laboring men of other nationalities—especially the Irish— that raised all the outcry against the Chinese. No one would hire an Irishman, German, Englishman or Italian when he could get a Chinese, because our countrymen are so much more honest, industrious, steady, sober and painstaking. Chinese were persecuted, not for their vices, but for their virtues. There never was any honesty in the pretended fear of leprosy or in the cheap labor scare, and the persecution continues still, because Americans make a mere practice of loving justice. They are all for money making, and they want to be on the strongest side always. They treat you as a friend while you are prosperous, but if you have a misfortune they don't know you. There is nothing substantial in their friendship.

Wu Tingfang talked very plainly to Americans about their ill treatment of our countrymen, but we don't see any good results. We hoped for good from Roosevelt, we thought him a brave and good man, but yet he has continued the exclusion of our countrymen, tho all other nations are allowed to pour in here —Irish, Italians, Jews, Poles, Greeks, Hungarians, etc. It would not have been so if Mr. McKinley had lived.

Irish fill the almshouses and prisons and orphan asylums, Italians are among the most dangerous of men, Jews are unclean and ignorant. Yet they are all let in, while Chinese, who are sober, or duly law abiding, clean, educated and industrious, are shut out. There are few Chinamen in jails and none in the poor houses. There are no Chinese tramps or drunkards. Many Chinese here have become sincere Christians, in spite of the persecution which they have to endure from their heathen countrymen. More than half the Chinese in this country would become citizens if allowed to do so, and would be patriotic Americans. But how can they make this country their home as matters now are! They are not allowed to bring wives here from China, and if they marry American women there is a great outcry.

All Congressmen acknowledge the injustice of the treatment of my people, yet they continue it. They have no backbone.

Under the circumstances, how can I call this my home, and how can anyone blame me if I take my money and go back to my village in China?

NEW YORK.

As a Chinaman Saw Us
Passages from His Letters to a Friend at Home

Anonymous

PREFACE

Since the publication in 1832 of that classic of cynicism, *The Domestic Manners of the Americans*, by Mrs. Trollope, perhaps nothing has appeared that is more caustic or amusing in its treatment of America and the Americans than the following passages from the letters of a cultivated and educated Chinaman. The selections have been made from a series of letters covering a decade spent in America, and were addressed to a friend in China who had seen few foreigners. The writer was graduated from a well-known college, after he had attended an English school, and later took special studies at a German university. Americans have been informed of the impressions they make on the French, English, and other people, but doubtless this is the first unreserved and weighty expression of opinion on a multiplicity of American topics by a Chinaman of cultivation and grasp of mind.

It will be difficult for the average American to conceive it possible that a cultivated Chinaman, of all persons, should have been honestly amused at our civilization; that he should have considered what Mrs. Trollope called "our great experiment" in republics a failure, and our institutions, fashions, literary methods, customs and manners, sports and pastimes as legitimate fields for wit and unrepressed jollity. Yet in the unbosoming of this cultivated "heathen" we see our fads and foibles held up as strange gods, and must confess some of them to be grotesque when seen in this yellow light.

It is doubtless true that the masses of Americans do not take the Chinaman seriously, and an interesting feature of this correspondence is the attitude of the Chinaman on this very point and his clever satire on our assumption of perfection and superiority over a nation, the habits of which have been fixed and settled for many centuries. The writer's experiences in society, his acquaintance with American women of fashion and their husbands, all ingeniously set forth, have the hall-mark of actual novelty, while his loyalty to the traditions of his country and his egotism, even after the Americanizing process had exercised its influence over him for years, add to the interest of the recital.

In revising the correspondence and rearranging it under general heads, the editor has preserved the salient features of it, with but little essential change and practically in its original shape. If the reader misses the peculiar idioms, or the pigeon-English that is usually placed in the mouth of the Chinaman of the novel or story, he or she should remember that the writer of the letters, while a "heathen Chinee," was an educated gentleman in the American sense of the term. This fact should always be kept in mind because, as the author remarks, to many Americans whom he met, it was "incomprehensible that a Chinaman can be educated, refined, and cultivated according to their own standards."

With pardonable pride he tells how, on one occasion, when a woman in New York told him she knew her ancestral line as far back as 1200 A. D., he replied that he himself had "a tree without a break for thirty-two hundred years." He was sure she did not believe him, but he found her "indeed!" delightful. The author's name has been withheld for personal reasons that will be sufficiently obvious to those who read the letters. The period during which he wrote them is embraced in the ten years from 1892 to 1902.

HENRY PEARSON GRATTON.
SAN FRANCISCO, CALIFORNIA,
MAY 10TH, 1904.

CHAPTER I
THE AMERICAN—WHO HE IS

MANY OF THE GREAT POWERS BELIEVE themselves to be passing through an evolutionary period leading to civic and national perfection. America, or the United States, has already reached this state; it is complete and finished. I have this from the Americans themselves, so there can be no question about it; hence it requires no little temerity to discuss, let alone criticize, them.

Yet I am going to ask you to behold the American as he is, as I honestly found him—great, small, good, bad, self-glorious, egotistical, intellectual, supercilious, ignorant, superstitious, vain, and bombastic. In truth, so very remarkable, so contradictory, so incongruous have I found the American that I hesitate. Shall I give you a satire; shall I devote myself to eulogy; shall I tear what they call the "whitewash" aside and expose them to the winds of excoriation; or shall I devote myself to an introspective, analytical *divertissement*? But I do not wish to educate you on the Americans, but to entertain, to make you laugh by the recital of comical truths; so without system I am going to tell you of these Americans as I found them, day by day, month by month, officially, socially; in their homes, in politics, trade, sorrow, despair, and in their pleasures.

You will remember when the Evil Spirit is asked by the modest Spirit of Good to indicate his possessions he tucks the earth under one arm, drops the sun into one pocket, the moon into another, and the stars into the folds of his garment. In a word, to use the saying of my friends, he "claims everything in sight;" and this is certainly a characteristic of the American: he is all-perspective, he claims to have all the virtues, and in his ancestry embraces the entire world. At a dinner at the —— in Washington during the egg stage of my experience I sat next to a charming lady; and having been told that it was a custom of the French to compliment women, I remarked that her cheeks bloomed like our poppy of the Orient. She laughed, and responded, "Yes, I get that from my English grandfather." "But your eyes are like black pearls," I continued, seeing that I was on what a general on my right called the "right trail." "I got them from my Italian grandmother," she replied. "And your hair?" I pressed. "Must be Irish," was the answer, "for my paternal grandmother was Irish and her husband Scotch." It is true that this charmingly beautiful and composite goddess (at least she would have been one had she not been naked like a geisha at a men's dinner) was the product of a dozen nations, and a typical American.

The original Americans appear to have been English, despite the fact that the Spaniards discovered the country, though a high official, a Yankee whom I met at a reception, told me that this was untrue. His ancestor had discovered North America, and I believe he had written a book to prove it. (*En passant*, all Americans write books; those who have not, fully intend to write one). I listened complacently, then said, "My dear ——, if I am not mistaken the Chinese discovered America." I recalled the fact to his mind that the northwestern Eskimos and the Indians were essentially Asiatic in type; and it is true that he had never heard of the ethnologic map at his National Museum, which shows the location of Chinese junks blown to American shores within a period of three hundred years. I explained that junks had been blown over to America for the last *three thousand* years, and that in my country there were many records of voyages to the Western land, ages before 1492.

You see I soon began to be Americanized and to claim things. China discovered America and gave her the compass as well as gunpowder. The first Americans were in the nature of emigrants; men and women who did not succeed well in their own country and so sought new fields, just as people are doing to-day. They came over in a ship called the "Mayflower," and were remarkably prolific, as I have met thousands who hail from this stock. At one time England sent her criminals to Virginia—one of the United States—and many of the refuse of the home country were sent to other parts of America in the early days. Younger sons of good families were also sent over for various reasons. Women of all classes were sent by the ship-load, and sold for wives. I reminded a lady of this, who was lamenting the fact that in China some women are sold for wives. She was absolutely ignorant of this well-known fact in American history, and forgot the selling of black women. Among the men were many representatives of old and noble families; but the bulk, I judge from their colonial histories, were people of low degree. Very soon other countries began to ship people to America. Italy, Germany, Russia, Norway, Sweden, and other lands were drawn upon for constantly increasing numbers as years went by. All tumbled into the American hopper. Imagine a coffee-grinder into which have been thrown Greek, Roman, Jew, Gentile, and all the rest, and then let what they call Uncle Sam—a heroic, paternal, and comical figure, representing the government—turn the handle and grind out the American who is neither Jew, Gentile, Greek, Roman, Russe, or Swede, but a new product, *sui generis*, and mostly Methodist.

This process has never ceased for an hour. America has been from 1492 to the present time, in the language of the American "press," the "dumping-ground" of the nations of the world, the real open door; yet this grinding assimilation has gone on. It is, perhaps, due to the climate, perhaps the water, or the air; but the product of these people born on the soil is described by no other word than American. It may be Irish-American, very offensive; Dutch-American, very strenuous, like the Vice-President;[1] Jewish-American, very commercial; Italian-American, very dirty and reeking with garlic; but it is American, totally unlike its progenitor, a something into which is blown a tremendous energy, that is very wearisome, a bombast which is the sum of that of all nations, and a conceit like that possessed by —— alone. You see it is incurable, also offensive—at least to the Oriental mind. Yet I grant you the American is great; I have it from him and from her; it must be so.

You have the spectacle here of the nations of the world pouring a stream, that is not pactolean, and not perfumed with the gums of Araby, flowing in and peopling the country. In time they had grievances more fancied than real, yet grievances. They rose against the home government, threw off the English yoke, and became a republic with a division into States, which I will write of when I tell you of the American politician. This was the first trust—what they

---

1 This passage was written just before the assassination of President McKinley.

call a merger—but it occurred in politics. They have killed off a fair percentage of the actual owners of the soil, the Indians, swindling them out of the balance, and driving them back to a sort of ever-changing dead-line. Without delay they assumed the form of a dominant nation, and announced themselves the greatest nation on the earth.

Immigration was resumed, and all nations again sent their refuse population to America. I have facts showing that for years English poorhouses and hospitals were emptied of their inmates and shipped to America. It was a distinct policy of the anti-home-rule party in Ireland to encourage the poor Irish to go to America; and now when there are more Irish in America than in Ireland the fate of Ireland is assured. Yet the American air takes the fight out of the Irishman, the rose from his cheek, and makes a natural-born politician out of him. America still continued to receive immigrants, and not satisfied with the natural flow of the human current, began to import African slaves to a country founded for the benefit of those who desired an asylum where they could enjoy religious and political freedom. The Africans were sold in the cotton belt, their existence virtually creating two distinct political parties. America long remained a dumping-ground for nearly all the nations of the world having an excess of population. Great navigation companies were built up, to a large extent, on this trade. They sent agents to every foreign country, issued pamphlets in every European language, and uncounted thousands were brought over—the scum of the earth in many instances. There was no restriction to immigration until the Chinese were barred out. After accepting the outlaws of every European state, the poor of all lands, they shut the door on our "coolie" countrymen.

In this way, briefly, America has grown to her present population of 80,000,000. The remarkable growth and assimilation is still going on—a menace to the world, but in a constantly decreasing ratio, which has become so marked that the leading Americans, the class which corresponds to our scholars, are aghast at the singular conditions which exist. Non-assimilation shows itself in labor riots, in the murder of two Presidents—Garfield and Lincoln—in socialistic outbreaks in every quarter, and in signal outbreaks in various sections, at lynchings, and other unlawful performances. I am attempting to give you an idea of the constituents of America to-day; but so interesting is the subject, so prolific in its warnings and possibilities, that I find myself wandering.

To glance at conditions at the present time, about 600,000 aliens are coming to America yearly. What is the result? I was invited to meet a distinguished German visiting in New York last month, and at the dinner a young lady who sat by my side said to me, "I wish I could puzzle him." "Why?" I asked, in amazement. "Oh," was her reply, "he looks so cram full of knowledge; I would like to take him down." "Ah," I said. "Ask him which is the third largest German city in the world. It is New York; he will never guess it." She did so, and I assure you he was "puzzled," and would scarcely believe it until a well-known man assured him it was true. There are more Germans in Chicago than in Leipsic, Cologne, Dresden, Munich, or a dozen small towns joined in one. Half of the Chicago Germans speak their own tongue. This city is the third Swedish city of the world in population. It is the fourth Polish city and the second Bohemian city. I was informed by a professor in the University of Chicago that, in that strange city, the number of people who speak the language of the Bohemians equaled the combined inhabitants of Richmond, Atlanta, Portland, and Nashville—all large cities. "What do you think of it?" I asked. "We are up against it," was the reply. I can not explain this retort so that you would understand it, but it had great significance. The professor, a distinguished philologist, was worried, and he looked it. A lady who was a club woman—and by this I do not mean that she was armed with a club, but merely a member of clubs or societies for educational advancement and social aggrandizement—said it was merely his digestion.

I learned from my friend, the dyspeptic professor, that over forty dialects are spoken in Chicago. About one-half only of the total population speak or understand English. There are 500,000 Germans, 125,000 Poles, 100,000 Swedes, 90,000 Bohemians, 50,000 Yiddish, 25,000 Dutch, 25,000 Italians, 15,000 French, 10,000 Irish, 10,000 Servians, 10,000 Lutherans, 7,000 Russians, and 5,000 Hungarians in Chicago. You will be surprised to learn that numbers do not count. The 500,000 Germans are not the dominating power, nor are the 100,000 Swedes. The 10,000 Irish are said absolutely to control the political situation. You will ask if I believe that this monster foreign element can be reduced to a homogeneous unit. I reply, yes. Fifty years from to-day they will all be Americans, and a majority will, doubtless, show you their family tree, tracing their ancestry back to the Mayflower.

CHAPTER II
THE AMERICAN MAN

HASH—AND I DO NOT MEAN BY this word a corruption of hasheesh—is a term indicating in America a food formed of more than one article chopped and cooked together. I was told by a very witty and charming lady that hash was a synonym for *E pluribus unum* (one from many), the motto of the Government, but I did not find it on the American arms. This was an American "dinner joke," of which more anon; nevertheless, hash represents the American people of to-day. The millions of all nations, which have swarmed here since 1492, may be represented by this delectable dish, which, after all, has a certain homogeneity. Englishmen are at once recognized here, and so are Chinamen. You would never mistake one of our people for a Japanese; an Italian you would know across the way; but an American not always in America. He may be a Swede, a German, or a Canadian; he is not an American until he opens his mouth. Then there is no mistake as to what he is. He has a nasal tone that is purely American.

All the old cities, as Boston, New York, Richmond, and Philadelphia, have certain nasal peculiarities or variants. The Bostonian affects the English. The New Englander, especially in the north, has a comical twang, which you can produce by holding the nose tightly and attempting to speak. When he says *down* it sounds like *daoun*. It is impossible for him not to overvowel his words, and nothing is more amusing than to hear the true Yankee countryman talk. The Philadelphian is quite as marked in tone and enunciation. A well-educated Philadelphian will say where is *me* wife for *my*. I have also been asked by a Philadelphian, "Where are you going at?" It would be impossible to mistake the intonation of a Philadelphian, even though you met him in the wilds of Manchuria in the depths of night.

Among the most charming and delightfully cultured people I met in America were Philadelphians of old families. The New Yorker is more cosmopolitan, while the Southern men, to a certain extent, have caught the inflection of the negro, who is the nurse in the South for all white children. The Americans are taught that the principal and chief end of man is to make a fortune and get married; but to accomplish this it is necessary first to "sow wild oats," become familiar with the vices of drink, smoking, and other forms of dissipation, a sort of test of endurance possibly, such as is found among many native races; yet one scarcely expects to find it among the latest and highest exponents of perfection in the human race.

The American pretends to be democratic; scoffs at England and other European lands, but at heart he is an aristocrat. His tastes are only limited by his means, and not always then. Any American, especially a politician, will tell you that there is but one class—the people, and that all are born equal. In point of fact, there are as many classes as there are grades of pronounced individuality, and all are very unequal, as everyone knows. They are included in a general way in three classes: the upper class (the refined and cultivated); the middle class (represented by the retail shop-keepers); and last, the rest. The cream of society will be found in all the cities to be among the professional men, clergymen, presidents of colleges, long-rich wholesale merchants, judges, authors, etc.

The distinctions in society are so singular that it is almost impossible for a foreigner to understand them. There are persons who make it a life study to prepare books and papers on the subject, and whose opinions are readily accepted; yet such a person might not be accepted in the best society. What constitutes American society and its divisions is a mystery. In a general sense a retail merchant, a man who sold shoes or clothes, a tailor, would under no circumstances find a place in the first social circles; yet if these same tradesmen should change to wholesalers and give up selling one article at a time, they would become eligible to the best society. They do not always get in, however. At a dinner my neighbor, an attractive matron, was much dismayed by my asking if she knew a certain Mr. ——, a well-known grocer. "I believe our supplies (groceries) come from him," was her chilly reply. "But," I ventured, "he is now a wholesaler." "Indeed!" said madam; "I had not heard of it." The point, very inconceivable to you, perhaps, was that the grocer, whether wholesale or retail, was not readily accepted; yet the man in the wholesale business in drugs, books, wine, stores, fruit, or almost anything else, had the *entrée*, if he was a gentleman. The druggist, the hardware man, the furniture dealer, the grocer, the retailer would constitute a class by themselves, though of course there are other subtle divisions completely beyond my comprehension.

At some of the homes of the first people I would meet a president of a university, an author of note, an Episcopal bishop, a general of the regular army (preferably a graduate of the West Point Academy), several retired merchants of the highest standing, bankers, lawyers, a judge or two of the Supreme Bench, an admiral of good family and connections. I have good reason to think that a Methodist bishop would not be present at such a meeting unless he was a remarkable man. There were always a dozen men of well-known lineage; men who knew their family history as far back as their great-grandparents, and whose ancestors were associated with the history of the country and its development. The men were all in business or the professions. They went to their offices at nine or ten o'clock and remained until twelve; lunched at their clubs or at a restaurant, returned at one, and many remained until six before going to their homes. The work is intense. A dominating factor or characteristic in the American man is his pursuit of the dollar. That he secures it is manifest from the miles of beautiful residences, the show of costly equipages and plate, the unlimited range of "stores" or shops one sees in large cities. The millionaire is a very ordinary individual in America; it is only the billionaire who now really attracts attention. The wealth and splendors of the homes, the magnificent *tout ensemble* of these establishments, suggests the possibility of degeneracy, an appearance of demoralization; but I am assured that this is not apparent in very wealthy families.

It is not to be understood that wealth always gives social position in America. By reading the American papers you might believe that this is all that is necessary. Some wealth is of course requisite to enable a family to hold its own, to give the social retort courteous, to live according to the mode of others; yet mere wealth will not buy the *entrée* to the very best society, even in villages. Culture, refinement, education, and, most important, *savoir faire*, constitute the "open sesame." I know a billionaire, at least this is his reputation, who has no standing merely because he is vulgar—that is, ill-bred. I have met another man, a great financier, who would give a million to have the *entrée* to the very best houses. Instances could be cited without end.

Such men and women generally have their standing in Europe; in a word, go abroad for the position they can not secure at home. A family now allied to one of the proudest families in Europe had absolutely no position in America previous to the alliance, and doubtless would not now be taken up by some. You will understand that I am speaking now of the most exclusive American society, formed of families who have age, historical associations, breeding, education, great-grandparents, and always have had "manners." There are other social sets which pass as representative society, into which all the ill-mannered *nouveau riche* can climb by the golden stairs; but this is not real society. The richest man in America, Rockefeller, quoted at over a billion, is a religious worker, and his indulgences consist in gifts to universities. Another billionaire, Mr. Carnegie, gives his millions to found libraries. Mr. Morgan, the millionaire banker, attends church conventions as an antipodal diversion. There is no conspicuous millionaire before the American public who has earned a reputation for extreme profligacy.

There is a leisure class, the sons of wealthy men, who devote their time to hunting and other sports; but in the recent war this class surged to the front as private soldiers and fought the country's battles. I admire the American gentleman of the select society class I have described. He is modest, intelligent, learned in the best sense, magnanimous, a type of chivalry, bold, vigorous, charming as a host, and the soul of honor. It is a regret that this is not the dominating and best-known class in America, but it is not; and the alien, the stranger coming without letters of introduction, would fall into other hands. A man might live a lifetime in Philadelphia or Boston and never meet these people, unless he had been introduced by someone who was of the same class in some other city. Such strange social customs make strange bedfellows. Thus, if you came to America to-day and had letters to the Vice-President, you would, without doubt, if properly accredited, see the very best society. If, on the other hand, you had letters to the President at his home in the State of Ohio you would doubtless meet an entirely different class, eminently respectable, yet not the same. It would be impossible to ignore the inference from this. The Vice-President is in society (the best); the President is not. Where else could this hold? Nowhere but in America.

The Americans affect to scorn caste and sect, yet no nation has more of them. Sets or classes, even among men, are found in all towns where there is any display of wealth. The best society of a small town consists of its bank presidents, its clergymen, its physicians, its authors, its lawyers. No matter how educated the grocer may be, he will not be received, nor the retail shoe dealer, though the shoe manufacturer, the dealer in many shoes, may be the virtual leader, at least among the men. Each town will have its clubs, the members ranging according to their class; and while it seems a paradox, it is true that this classification is mainly based upon the refinement, culture, and family of the man. A well-known man once engaged me in conversation with a view to finding out some facts regarding our social customs, and I learned from him that a dentist in America would scarcely be received in the best society. He argued, that to a man of refinement and culture, such a profession, which included the cleaning of teeth, would be impossible; consequently, you would not be likely to find a really cultivated man who was a dentist. On the same grounds an undertaker would not be admitted to the first society.

With us a gentleman is born; with Americans it is possible to create one, though rarely. An American gentleman is described as a product of two generations of college men who have always had association with gentlemen and the advantages of family standing. Political elevation can not affect a man's status as a gentleman. I heard a lady of unquestioned position say that she admired President McKinley, but regretted that he was not a gentleman. She meant that he was not an aristocrat, and did not possess the *savoir faire*, or the family associations, that completely round out the American or English gentleman. I asked this lady to indicate the gentlemen Presidents of the country. There were very few that I recall. There were Washington, Harrison, Adams, and Arthur. Doubtless there were others, which have escaped me. Lincoln, the strongest American type, she did not consider in the gentlemen class, and General Grant, the nation's especial pride, did not fulfill her ideas of what a gentleman should be.

You will perceive, then, that what some American people consider a gentleman and what its most exclusive society accepts for one, comprise two entirely different personages. I found this emphasized especially in the old society of Washington, which takes its traditions from Washington's time or even the pre-Revolutionary period. For such society a self-made man was impossible. Such are the remarkable, indeed astounding, ramifications of the social system of a people who cry to heaven of their democracy. "Americans are all equal—this is one of the gems in our diadem." This epigram I heard drop from the lips of a senator who was the recognized aristocrat of the chamber; yet a man of peculiar social reserve, who would have nothing to do with the other "equals." In a word, all the talk of equality is an absurd figure of speech. America is at heart as much an aristocracy as England, and the social divisions are much the same under the surface.

You will understand that social rules and customs are all laid down and exacted by women and from women. From them I obtained all my information. No American gentleman would talk (to me at least) on the subject. Ask one of them if there is an American aristocracy, and he will pass over the question in an engaging manner, and tell you that his government is based on the principle of perfect equality—one of the most transparent farces to be found in this interesting country. I have outlined to you what I conceived to be the best society in each city, and in the various sections of the country. In morality and probity I believe them to stand very high; lapses there may be, but the general tone is good. The women are charming and refined; the men chivalrous, brave, well-poised, and highly educated. Unfortunately, the Americans who compose this "set" are numerically weak. They are not represented to the extent of being a dominating body, and oddly enough, the common people, the shopkeepers, the people in the retail trades, do not understand them as leaders from the fact that they are so completely aloof that they never meet them. A sort of inner "holy of holies" is the real aristocracy of America. What goes for society among the people, the mob, and the press is the set (and a set means a faction, a clique) known as the Four Hundred, so named because it was supposed to represent the "blue blood" of New York ten years ago in its perfection. This Four Hundred has its prototype in all cities, and in some cities is known as the "fast set." In New York it is made up often of the descendants of old families, the heads of whom in many instances were retail traders within one hundred and fifty years ago; but the modern wealthy representatives endeavor to forget this or skip over it. It is, however, constantly kept alive by what is termed the "yellow press," which delights in picturing the ancestor of one family as a pedler and an itinerant trader, and the head of another family as a vegetable vender, and so on, literally venting its spleen upon them.

In my studies in American sociology I asked many questions, and obtained the most piquant replies from women. One lady, a leader in New York in what I have termed the exclusive set, informed me with a laugh that the ancestor of a well-known family of to-day, one which cuts a commanding figure in society, was an ordinary laborer in the employ of her grandfather. "Yet you receive them?" I suggested. The reply was a shrug of charming shoulders, which, translated, meant that great wealth had here enabled them to "bore" into the exclusive circle. I found that even among these people, the *crème de la crème* in the eyes of the people, there were inner circles, and these were not on intimate terms with the others. Here I met a member of the Washington and Lee family, a descendant of Bishop Provoost, the first Episcopal bishop of New York, and friend of Washington and Hamilton. This latter family is notable for an ancestry running back to the massacre of St. Bartholomew and even beyond. I astonished its charming descendant, who very delicately informed me that she knew her ancestry as far back as 1200 A. D., when I told her that I had my "family tree," as they call it, without a break for thirty-two hundred years. I am confident she did not believe me, but her "Indeed!" was delightful. In fact, I assure you I have lost my heart to these American women. I met representatives of the Adams, Dana, Madison, Lee, and other families identified with American history in a most honorable way.

The continuity of the Four Hundred idea as a logical system was broken by the quality of some of its members. Compared to the society I have previously mentioned it was as chaff. There was a total lack of intellectuality. Degeneracy marked some of their acts; divorce blackened their records, and shameless affairs marked them. In this "set," and particularly its imitators throughout the United States, the divorce rate is appalling. Men leave their wives and obtain a divorce for no other reason than that a woman falls in love with another woman's husband. On a yacht we will say there is some scandal. A divorce ensues, and afterward the parties are remarried. Or we will say a wife succumbs to the blandishments of another man. The conjugal arrangements are rearranged, so that, as a very merry New York club man told me, "It is difficult to tell where you are at." In a word, the morale of the men of this set is low, their standard high, but not always lived up to. I believe that I am not doing the American of the middle class wrong and the ultra-fashionable class an injustice in saying that it is as a class immoral.

Americans make great parade of their churches. Spires rise like the pikes of an army in every town, yet the morality of the men is low. There are in this land 600,000 prostitutes—ruined women. But this is not due entirely to the Four Hundred, whose irregularities appear to be confined to inroads upon their own set. Nearly all these men are club men; two-thirds are in business as brokers, bankers, or professional men; and there is a large percentage of men of leisure and vast wealth. They affect English methods, and are, as a rule, not highly intelligent, but *blasé*, often effeminate, an interesting spectacle to the student, showing that the downfall of the American Republic would come sooner than that of Rome if the "fast set" were a dominating force, which it is not.

In the great middle class of the American men I find much to admire; half educated, despite their boasted school system, they put up, to quote one of them, "a splendid bluff" of respectability and morality, yet their statistics give the lie to it. Their divorces are phenomenal, and they are obtained on the slightest cause. If a man or woman becomes weary of the other they are divorced on the ground of incompatibility of temper.

A lady, a descendant of one of the oldest families, desired to marry her friend's husband. He charged his wife with various vague acts, one of which, according to the press, was that she did not wear "corsets"—a sort of steel frame which the American women wear to compress the waist. This was not accepted by the learned judge, and the wife then left her husband and went away on a six or eight months' visit. This enabled the husband to put in a claim of desertion, and the decree of divorce was granted. A quicker method is to pretend to throw the breakfast dishes at your wife, who makes a charge of "extreme incompatibility," and a divorce is at once obtained. Certain Territories bank on their divorce laws, and the mismated have but to go there and live a few months to obtain a separation on almost any claim. Many of the most distinguished statesmen have been charged with certain moral lapses in the heat of political fights, which, in almost every instance, are ignored by the victims, their silence being significant to some, illogical to others; yet the fact remains that the press goes to the greatest extremes. No family secret is considered sacred to the American politician in the heat of a campaign; to win, he would sacrifice the husband, father, mother, and children of his enemy. So remarkable is the rage for divorce that many of the great religious denominations have taken up arms against it. Catholics forbid it. Episcopalians resent it by ostracism if the cause is trivial, and a "separation" is denounced in the pulpit.

CHAPTER III
AMERICAN CUSTOMS

THE AMERICAN IS AN INTERESTING, THOUGH NOT always pleasant, study. His perfect equipoise, his independence, his assumption that he is the best product of the best soil in the world, comes first as a shock; but when you find this but one of the many national characteristics it merely amuses you. One of the extraordinary features of the American is his attitude toward the Chinese, who are taken on sufferance. The lower classes absolutely can conceive of no difference between me and the "coolie." As an example, a boy on the street accosts me with "Hi, John, you washee, washee?" Even a representative in Congress insisted on calling me "John." On protesting to another man, he laughed, and said, "Oh, the man don't know any better." "But," I replied, "if he does not know any better how is it he is a lawmaker in your lower house?" "I give it up," was his answer, and he ordered what they term a "high-ball." After we had tried several, he laughed and asked, "Shall we consider the matter a closed incident?" Many diplomatic, social, and political questions are often settled with a "high-ball."

It is inconceivable to the average American that there can be an educated Chinese gentleman, a man of real refinement. They know us by the Cantonese laundrymen, the class which ranks with their lowest classes. At dinners and receptions I was asked the most atrocious questions by men and women. One charming young girl, who I was informed was the relative of a Cabinet officer, asked me if I would not sometime put up my "pig-tail," as she wished to photograph me. Another asked if it was really true that we privately considered all Americans as "white devils." All had an inordinate curiosity to know my "point of view;" what I thought of them, how their customs differed from my own. Of course, replies were manifestly impossible. At a dinner a young man, who, I learned, was a sort of professional diner-out, remarked to a lady: "None of the American girls will have me for a husband; do you not think that if I should go to China some pretty Chinese girl would have me?" This was said before all the company. Everyone was silent, waiting for the response. Looking up, she replied, with charming *naïveté*, "No, I do not think so," which produced much laughter. Now you would have thought the young man would have been slightly discomfited, but not at all; he laughed heartily, and plumed himself upon the fact that he had succeeded in bringing out a reply.

American men have a variety of costumes for as many occasions. They have one for the morning, which is called a sack-coat, that is, tailless, and is of mixed colors. With this they wear a low hat, an abomination called the derby. After twelve o'clock the frock-coat is used, having long tails reaching to the knees. Senators often wear this costume in the morning—why I could not learn, though I imagine they think it is more dignified than the sack. With the afternoon suit goes a high silk hat, called a "plug" by the lower classes, who never wear them. After dark two suits of black are worn: one a sack, being informal, the other with tails, very formal. They also have a suit for the bath—a robe—and a sleeping-costume, like a huge bag, with sleeves and neck-hole. This is the night-shirt, and formerly a "nightcap" was used by some. There is also a hat to go with the evening costume—a high hat, which crushes in. You may sit on it without injury to yourself or hat. I know this by a harrowing experience.

Many of the customs of the Americans are strange. Their social life consists of dinners, receptions, balls, card-parties, teas, and smokers. At all but the last women are present. At the dinner everyone is in evening dress; the men wear black swallowtail coats, following the English in every way, low white vest, white starched shirt, white collar and necktie, and black trousers. If the dinner does not include women the coat-tails are eliminated, and the vest and necktie are black. Exactly why this is I do not understand, nor do the Americans. The dinner is begun with the national drink, the "cocktail;" then follow oysters on the half-shell, which you eat with an object resembling the trident carried in the ceremony of Ah Dieu at the Triennial. Each course of the dinner is accompanied by a different wine, an agreeable but exhilarating custom. The knife and fork are used, the latter to go into the mouth, the former not, and here you see a singular ethnologic feature. Class distinctions may at times be recognized by the knife or fork. Thus I was informed that you could at once recognize a person of the gentleman class by his use of the knife and fork. "This is infallible," said my young lady companion. If he is a commoner, he eats with his knife; if a gentleman, with his fork. This was a very nice distinction, and I looked carefully for a knife eater, but never saw one.

There is a vast amount of ceremony and etiquette about a dinner and various rules for eating, to break which is a social offense. I heard that a certain Madam —— gave lessons in "good form" after the American fashion, so that one could learn what was expected, and at my first dinner I regretted that I had not availed myself of the services of the lady, as at each plate there were nearly a dozen solid silver articles to be used in the different courses, but I endeavored to escape by watching my companion and following her example. But here the impossibility of an American girl resisting a joke caused my downfall. She at once saw my dilemma, and would take up the wrong implement, and when I followed suit she dropped it and took another, laughing in her eyes in a way in which the American girl is a prodigious adept; but completely deceived by her nearly every time, knowing that she was amusing herself at my expense, I said nothing. The Americans have a peculiar term for the mental attitude I had during this trial. I "sawed wood." The saying was particularly applicable to my situation. My young companion was most engaging, and presently began to talk of the superiority of America, her inventions, etc., mentioning the telephone, printing, and others. "Yes, wonderful," I replied; "but the Chinese had the telephone ages ago. They invented printing, gunpowder, the mariner's compass, and it would be difficult," I said, "for you to mention an object which China has not had for ages." She was amazed that I, a Chinaman, should "claim everything in sight."

There is a peculiar etiquette relating to every course in a dinner. The soup is eaten with a bowl-like spoon, and it is the grossest breach to place this in your mouth, or approach it, endwise. You approach the side and suck the soup from it. To make a noise would attract attention. The etiquette of the fish is to eat it with a fork; to use the knife even to cut the fish would be unpardonable, or to touch it to take out the bones; the fork alone must be used. The punch course is often an embarrassment to the previous wines, and is followed by what the French call the *entrée*. In fact, while the Americans boast that everything American is the best, French customs are followed at banquets invariably, this being one of the strange inconsistencies of the Americans. Their clothes are copied from the English, though they will claim in the same breath that their tailors are the best in the world. For wines they claim to be unsurpassed, producing the finest; yet the wines on their tables are French or bear French labels. Game is served—a grouse or perhaps a hare, and then a vast roast, possibly venison, or beef, and there are vegetables, followed by a salad of some kind. Then comes the dessert—an iced cream, cakes, nuts, raisins, cheese, and coffee with brandy, and then cigars and vermuth or some cordial. After such a dinner of three hours a Southern gentleman clapped me on the back and said, "Great dinner, that; but let's go and get a drink of something solid," and I saw him take what he termed "two fingers" of Kentucky Bourbon whisky—a very stiff drink. I often wondered how the guests could stand so much.

The dinner has no attendant amusement, no dancing, no professional entertainers, and rarely lasts over two hours. Some houses have stringed bands concealed behind barriers of flowers playing soft music, but in the main the dinner is a jollification, a symposium of stories, where the guests take a turn at telling tales. Story-tellers can not be hired, and the guest at the proper moment says (after having prepared himself beforehand), "That reminds me of a story," and he relates what he has learned with great *éclat* and applause, as every American will applaud a good story, even if he has heard it time and again. At one dinner which I attended in New York story-telling had been going on for some time when a well-known man came in late. He was received with applause, and when called on for a speech told exactly the same story, by a strange coincidence, that had been told by the last speaker. Not a guest interfered; he was allowed to proceed, and at the end the point was greeted with a roar of laughter. This appeared to me to be an excellent quality in the American character. I was informed that these stories, forming so important a feature of American dinners, are the product mainly of drummers and certain prominent men; but why men that drum are more skillful in story inventing I failed to learn. President Lincoln and a lawyer named Daniel Webster originated a large percentage of the current stories. It is difficult to understand exactly what the Americans mean.

The American story is incomprehensible to the average foreigner, but it is good form to laugh. I will relate several as illustrative of American wit, and I might add that many of these have been published in books for the benefit of the diner-out. A Cabinet minister told of a prisoner who was called to the bar and asked his name. The man had some impediment in his speech, one of the hundred complaints of the tongue, and began to hiss, uttering a strange stuttering sound like escaping steam. The judge listened a few moments, then turning to the guard said, "Officer, what is this man charged with?" "Soda-water, I think, your honor," was the reply. This was unintelligible to me until my companion explained it. You must understand that soda-water is a drink that is charged with gas and makes a hissing, spluttering noise when opened. Hence when the judge asked what the prisoner was charged with the policeman, an Irishman, retorted with a joke, the story-teller disregarding the fact that it was an impertinence.

A distinguished New York judge told the following: Two tenement harridans look out of their windows simultaneously. "Good-morning, Mrs. Moriarity," says one. "Good-morning, Mrs. Gilfillan," says the other, adding, "not that I care a d——, but just to make conversation." This was considered wit of the sharpest kind, and was received with applause. In their stories the Americans spare neither age, sex, nor relatives. The following was related by a general of the army. He said he took a friend home to spend the night with him, the guest occupying the best room. When he came down in the morning he turned to the hostess and said, "Mrs. ——, that was excellent tooth-powder you placed at my disposal; can you give me the name of the maker?" The hostess fairly screamed. "What," she exclaimed, "the powder in the urn?" "Yes," replied the officer, startled; "was it poison?" "Worse, worse," said she; "you swallowed Aunt Jane!" Conceive of this wretched taste. The guest had actually cleaned his teeth with the cremated dust of the general's aunt; yet he told the story before a dinner assemblage, and it was received with shouts of laughter.

I did not hear the intellectual conversation at dinner I had expected. Art, science, literature, were rarely touched upon, although I invariably met artists, litterateurs, and scientific men at these dinners. They all talked small talk or "told stories." I was informed that if I wished to hear the weighty questions of the day discussed I must go to the women's clubs, or to Madam ——'s Current

Topics Society. The latter is an extraordinary affair, where society women who have no time to read the news of the day listen to short lectures on the news of the preceding week, discussed pro and con, giving these women in a nutshell material for intelligent conversation when they meet senators and other men at the various receptions before which they wish to make an agreeable impression.

The American has many clubs, but is not entirely at home in them. He uses them as places in which to play poker or whist, to dine his men friends, and in a great measure because it is the "proper thing." At many a room is set apart for the national game of poker—a fascinating game to the player who wins. Poker was never mentioned in my presence that some did not make a joke on a supposed Chinaman named Ah Sin; but the obscurity of the joke and my lack of knowledge regarding American literature caused the point to elude me at first, which was true of many jokes. The Americans are preeminently practical jokers, and the ends to which they go is beyond belief. I heard of jokes which, if perpetrated in China, would have resulted in the loss of someone's head. To illustrate this, in the Spanish-American War the camps at Tampa were besieged with newspaper reporters, and one from a large journal was constantly trying to secure secret news by entertaining certain officers with wine and cigars; so they determined to get rid of his importunities, and what is known as a "job" in America was "put up" on him. He was told that Colonel —— had a detailed map of the forthcoming battle, and if he could get the officer intoxicated he doubtless could secure the map. This looked very easy to the correspondent, so the story goes, and he dropped into the colonel's tent one night with a basket of wine, and began to celebrate its arrival from some friends. Soon the colonel pretended to become communicative, and the map was brought out and finally loaned to the correspondent under the promise that it would not be used. This was sufficient. The correspondent hied him to his tent, wrote an article and sent the map to his paper in one of the large cities, where it was duly published. It proved to be what dressmakers call a "Butterick pattern," a maze of lines for cutting out dresses for women. The lines looked like roads, and the practical jokers had merely added towns and forts and bridges here and there.

The Americans are excellent parents, though small families are general. The domestic life is charming. The family is denied nothing needed, the only limit being the purse of the head of the family, so called, the real head in many cases being the wife, who does not fail to assert herself if the proper occasion opens. Well-to-do families have every luxury, and no nation is apparently so well off, so completely supplied with the necessities of life as the American. One is impressed by their business sagacity, their cleverness in finance, their complete grasp of all questions, yet no people are easier gulled or more readily victimized. An instance will suffice. In making my investigations regarding methods of managing railroads, I not only obtained information from the road officials, but questioned the employees whenever it happened that I was traveling. One day, observing that it was the custom to "tip" the porters (give money), I asked the conductor what the men were paid. "Little or nothing," was the reply; "they get from seventy-five to one hundred dollars a month out of the *passengers* on a long run." "But the passengers paid the road for the service?" "Yes, and they pay the salary of the porter also," said the man. With that in view the men are poorly paid, and the railroad knows that the people will make up their salaries, as they do. If you refused you would have no service.

This rule holds everywhere, in hotels and restaurants. Servants receive little pay where the patronage is rich, with the understanding that they will make it up out of the customers. Thus if you go to a hotel you fee the bell-boy for bringing you a glass of water. If you order one of the seductive cocktails you fee the man who brings it; you fee the chambermaid who attends to your room. Infinite are the resources of these servants who do not receive a fee. You fee the elevator or lift boy, or he will take the opportunity to jerk you up as though shot out of a gun. You fee the porter for taking up your trunk, and give a special fee for unstrapping it. You fee the head waiter, and when you fee the table waiter he whispers in your ear that a slight fee will be acceptable to the cook, who will see that the *Count* or the *Judge* will be cared for as becomes his station. When you leave, the sidewalk porter expects a fee; if he does not receive it the door of the carriage may possibly be slammed on the tail of your coat. Then you pay the cabman two dollars to carry you to the station, and fee him. Arriving at the station, he hands you over to a red-hatted porter, who carries your baggage for a fee. He puts you in charge of the railroad porter, who is feed at the rate of about fifty cents per diem.

The American submits to this robbery without a murmur; yet he is sagacious, prudent. I can only explain his gullibility on the ground of his innate snobbery; he thinks it is the "thing to do," and does it, and for this reason it is carried to the most merciless lengths. To illustrate. In the season of 1902, when I was at Newport, Mr. ———, a conspicuous member of the New York smart set, known as the "Four Hundred," lost his hat in some way and rode to his home without one. The ubiquitous reporter saw him, and photographed him, bareheaded, and his paper, the New York ———, gave a column the following day to a description of the new fad of going without a hat. Thus the fashion started, and the amazing spectacle was seen the summer following of men and women of fashion riding and walking for miles without hats. This is beyond belief, yet it attracted no attention from the common people, who perhaps got the cast-off hats. Despite this, the Americans are hard-fisted, shrewd, and as a nation a match for any in the field of cunning.

I can explain it in no way than by assuming that it is due to over-anxiety to do the correct thing. Their own actors satirize them, one especially taking them off in a jingle which read, "It's English, quite English, you know." It is said of the men of the "Four Hundred" that they turn up their trousers when it rains in London, special reports of the weather being sent to the clubs for the purpose; but I cannot vouch for this. I have seen the trousers turned up in all weathers, and found no one who could explain why he did so. What can you make of so contradictory a people?

CHAPTER IV
THE AMERICAN WOMAN

THE MOST REMARKABLE FEATURE OF AMERICA is the women. Divest your mind of any woman you know in order to prepare yourself to receive my impressions. To begin with, the American woman ranks with her husband; indeed, she is his superior in that all men render her homage and deference. It is accounted a point of chivalry to stand as the defender of the weaker sex. The American girl is educated with the boys in the public school, grows up with them, and studies their studies, that she may be their intellectual equal, and there is a strong party, led by masculine women, who contend for complete political rights for women. In some States they vote, and in nearly all may be elected to boards of various kinds and to minor offices. The Government departments are filled with women clerks, and all, from the lowest to the highest, are equal; hence, it is a difficult matter to find a native-born American who will become a servant. They all aspire to be ladies, and even aliens become salesladies, cook ladies, laundry ladies. They are on their dignity, and able to protect it from any point of attack.

The lower classes are particularly uninteresting, for they have no individuality, and ape the class above them, the result being a cheap, ludicrous imitation of a lady—an absurd abstraction. The women of the lower classes who are unmarried work in shops, factories, and restaurants, often in situations the reverse of sanitary; yet prefer this to good situations in families as servants, service being beneath their dignity and tending to disturb the balance of equality. I doubt if a native-born woman would permit herself to be called a servant; indeed, all the servants are Irish, Swedes, Norwegians, French, German, or negroes; the American girls fill the factories and the sweat-shops of the great cities. When I refer these girls to the lower classes it is merely to classify them, as morally and intellectually they are sometimes the equal of the higher classes. The middle-class women or girls are an attractive type, well educated and often beautiful. You obtain an idea of them in the great shops and bazaars of the great cities, where they fill every conceivable position and receive from five to six dollars per week.

But it is with the higher classes that you will be most interested, and when I say that the American girl, the product of the first families, is at once beautiful, refined, cultured, charming physically and mentally, I have but faintly expressed it; yet the most pronounced characteristic is their "daring," or temerity. There is no word exactly to cover it. I frequently met women at dinners. With few exceptions, it appears impossible for the American girl to take one of our race, an Oriental, seriously. She can not conceive that he may be a man of intelligence and education, and I can not better describe her than to sketch in its detail a dinner to which I was invited by the —— at Washington. The invitation was engraved on a small card and read "The —— and Mrs. —— request the honor of the presence of the —— at dinner on Wednesday at eight o'clock, etc." I immediately sent my valet with an acceptance and a basket of orchids to the hostess, this being the mode among the men who are *au fait*.

A week later I went to the dinner, and was taken up to the dressing-room for men, where I found a dozen or more, all in the conventional evening dress I have described—now with tails, it being a ladies' affair. In a corner was a table, and by it stood a negro, also in a dress suit, identical with that of the others. I was cordially greeted by a guest, who said, "Let me introduce you to our American minister to Ijiji and Zanzibar," and he presented me to the tall negro, who was turning out some bottled "cocktail." I shook hands with him, and he laughed, showing a set of teeth like an elephant's tusks, and asked me "what I would have." He was a servant dealing out "appetizers," and this was an American joke. The perpetrator of this joke was a minor official in the State Department, yet the entire party apparently considered it a good joke. Fortunately, I could disguise my real feeling, and I merely relate the incident to give you an idea of the sense of the proprieties as entertained by certain Americans. All that winter the story of the American minister to Zanzibar was told at my expense without doubt.

Having been "fortified," and some of the men took two or three "cocktails" before they became "tuned up," we went down to the drawing-room, where I paid my respects to the host and hostess, who stood at the end of a beautiful room. As I approached the lady greeted me with a charming smile, extending her gloved hand almost on a direct line with her face, grasping it firmly, not shaking it, saying, "Very kind of you, ——. Delighted, I am sure. General"—

turning to her husband—"you know the ——, of course," and the general shook my hand as he would a pump-handle, and whispered, "Our minister to Zanzibar treated you all right, eh?" and with a wink indescribable, closing the right eye for a second, passed me on. The story had got down-stairs before me. Americans of the official class have, as a rule, an absolute lack of *savoir faire* and social refinement; lack them so utterly as to become comical.

I now joined other groups of officers and officials, there being about thirty guests, half of whom were ladies. The latter were all in what is termed full dress. Why "full" I do not know. Here you see one of the most extraordinary features of American life—the dress of women. The Americans make claim to being among the most modest, the most religious, the most proper people in the world, yet the appearance of the ladies at many public functions is beyond belief. All the women in this house were beautiful and covered with jewels. They wore gowns in the French court fashion, with trains a yard or two in length, but the upper part cut so low that a large portion of the neck and shoulders was exposed. I was embarrassed beyond expression; such an exhibition in China could only be made by a certain class. These matrons were of the highest respectability. This remarkable custom of a strange people, who deluge China with missionaries from every sect under the sun and at home commit the grossest solecisms, is universal, and not thought of as improper. There was not much opportunity for introspective analysis, yet I could not but believe that such a custom must have its moral effect upon a nation in the long run.

It was a mystery to me how the upper part of some of the gowns was supported. In some instances there was no strap over the shoulders, the upper third of these alabaster torsos and arms being absolutely naked, save for a band of pearls, diamonds, or other gems, of a size rarely seen in the Orient; but I learned later that the bone or steel corset, which molds the form, constituted the support of the gown. I gradually became habituated to the custom, and did not notice it. My friend ——, an artist of repute, explained that it all depends on the point of view. "Our people are essentially artistic," he said. "There is nothing more beautiful than the divine female contour; the American women realize this, and sacrifice themselves at the altar of art." Yet the Americans are such jokers that exactly what my friend had in mind it was difficult to arrive at.

After being presented to these marvelously arrayed ladies we passed into the dining-room, where I found myself with one of the most charming of divinities, a woman famous for her wit and literary success. I have described the typical dinner, so I need not repeat my words. My companion held the same extraordinary attitude toward me that all American women do; amused, half laughing, refusing absolutely to take me seriously, and probing me with so many absurd questions that I was forced to ask some very pointed ones, which only succeeded in making her laugh. The conversation proceeded something as follows: "I am charmed that I have fallen to your Highness." "Equally charmed," I replied; "but my rank does not admit the adjective you do me the honor to apply." "No?" was the answer. "Well, I'll wager you anything that when the butler pours your wine in the first course he will call you Count, and in the next Prince. You see, they become exhilarated as the dinner progresses. But tell me, how many wives have you in China, you look *very* wicked?" Imagine this! But I rallied, and replied that I had none—a statement received with incredulity. Her next question was, "Have you ever been a highbinder?" Ministers of grace! and this from a people who profess to know more than any nation on earth! I explained that a highbinder ranked with a professional murderer in this country, whereupon she again laughed, and, turning to General ——, in a loud voice said, "General, I have been calling the —— a highbinder," at which the company laughed at my expense. In China, as you know, a guest or a host would have killed himself rather than commit so gross a solecism; but this is America.

The second course was oysters served in the shell, and my companion, assuming that I had never seen an oyster [ignorant that our fathers ate oysters thousands of years before America was heard of and when the Anglo-Saxon was living in a cave], in a confidential and engaging whisper remarked, "This, your 'Highness,' is the only animal we eat alive." "Why alive?" I asked, looking as innocent as possible; "why not kill them?" "Oh, the Society for the Prevention of Cruelty to Animals will not permit it," was her reply. "You see, if they are swallowed alive they are immediately suffocated, but if you cut them up they suffer horribly while the soup is being served. How large a one do you think you can swallow?" Fancy the daring of a young girl to joke with a man twice her age in this way! I did not undeceive her, and allowed her to enlighten me on various subjects of contemporaneous interest. "It's so strange that the Chinese never study mathematics," she next remarked. "Why, all our public schools demand higher mathematics, and in the fourth grade you could not find a child but could square the circle."

In this manner this volatile young savage entertained me all through the dinner, utterly superficial herself, yet possessed of a singular sharpness and wit, mostly at my expense; yet she was so charming I forgave her. There is no denying that you become enraged, insulted, chagrined by these women, who, however, by a look, dispel your annoyance. I do not understand it. I found that while an author of a novel she was grossly ignorant of the literature of her own country, yet she possessed that consummate American froth by which she could convince the average person that she was brilliant to the point of scintillation. I fancy that any keen, well-educated woman must have seen that I was laughing at her, yet so inborn was her belief that a Chinaman must be an imbecile that she was ever joking at my expense. The last story she told me illustrates the peculiar fancy for joking these women possess. I had been describing a storm at Manchester-by-the-Sea and the splendor of the ocean. "Did you see the tea-leaves?" she asked, solemnly. "No," I replied. "That is strange," she said. "I fear you are not very observing. After every storm the tea-leaves still wash up all along Massachusetts Bay," alluding to the fact that loads of tea on ships were tossed over by the Americans during the quarrel with England before the Revolution.

The daring of the American woman impressed me. This same lady asked me not to remain with the men to smoke but go on the veranda with her, where *tête-à-tête* she produced a gold cigarette-case and offered me a cigarette. This I found not uncommon. American women of the fast sets drink at the clubs; an insidious drink—the "high-ball"—is a common one, yet I never saw a woman under the influence of wine or liquor. The amount of both consumed in America, is amazing. The consumption per head in the United States for beer alone is ten and a half gallons for each of the eighty millions. My friend, a prohibitionist, a member of a political party whose object is to ruin the wine industry of the world, put it stronger, and, backed by facts, said that if the wine, beer, whisky, gin, and alcoholic drinks of all kinds and the tea and coffee drank yearly by the Americans could be collected it would make a lake two miles square and ten feet deep. The alcoholic drinks alone if collected would fill a canal one hundred miles long, one hundred feet wide, and ten feet deep. May their saints propitiate this insatiate thirst!

It would amuse you to hear the American women of literary tendency boast of their schools, yet when educational facilities are considered the average American is ignorant. They are educated in lines. Thus a girl graduate will speak French with a good accent, or she will converse in Milwaukee German. She can prove her statement in conic sections or algebra, but when it comes to actual knowledge she is deficient. This is due to the ignorance of the teachers in the public schools and their lack of inborn culture. No better test of the futility of the American public-school education can be seen than the average girl product of the public school of the lower class in a city like Chicago or New York. Americans affect to despise Chinese methods because the Chinese girl or boy is not crammed with a thousand thoughts of no relative value. China has existed thousands of years; her people are happy; happiness and content are the chief virtues, and if China is ever overthrown it will be not because, as the Americans put it, she is behind the times, but because the fever of unrest and the craze for riches has become a contagion which will react upon her. The development of China is normal, that of America hysterical. Our growth has been along the line of peace; that of other nations has been entirely opposed to their own religious teaching, showing it to be farcical and pure sophistry.

If I should tell you how many American women asked me why Chinese women bandage their feet you would be amazed; yet everyone of these submitted to and practised a deformity that has seriously affected the growth and development of the race. I am no iconoclast, but listen to the story of the American woman who, with one hand, deforms her waist in the most barbarous fashion, while waving the other in horror at her Chinese sister with the bound feet. American women change their fashions twice a year or more. Fashions are in the hands of the middle classes, and the highest lady in the land is completely at their mercy; to disobey the mandates of fashion is to become ridiculous. The fashion is set in Paris and various cities by men and women who have skilled artists to draw patterns and paint pictures showing the new mode. These are published in certain papers and issued by millions, republished in America, and no woman here would have the temerity to ignore them. The laws of the Medes and Persians are not more inexorable.

It is not a suggestion but an order, a fiat, a command, so we see this free nation really truckling to or dominated by a class of tradesmen. The object of the change of style is to create a sale for new goods, give work for laborers, and enable the producer to reach the pocketbook of the rich man; but the "fashions" have become so fixed, so thoroughly a national feature, that they affect rich and poor, and we have the spectacle of every woman studying these guides and conforming to them with a servility beyond belief. I once said to a lady, "The Chinese lady dresses richer than the American, but her styles have been very much the same for thousands of years," but I believe she doubted it. It would be futile, indeed impossible, for me to explain the extravagances of American fashion. Their own press and stage use it as a standard butt. At the present time tablets or plates of fashion insist upon an outline which shows the form completely, the antipodes of a Chinese woman; and this is intensified by some of the women who, when in the street, grasp the skirt and in an ingenious way wrap it about so that the outline of the American divinity is sufficiently well defined to startle one. Such a trick in China could but originate with the demimonde, yet it is taken up by certain of the Americans who are constantly seeking for variety. There can be no question but that the middle-class fashion designer revenges himself upon the *beau monde*. They will not receive him socially, so he forces them to wear his clothes.

Some years ago women were made to wear "hoops," pictures of which I have seen in old publications. Imagine, if you can, a bird-cage three feet high and four feet across, formed of bone of the whale or some metal. This was worn beneath the dress, expanding it on either side so that it was difficult to approach a lady. A later order was given to wear a camel-like "hump" at the base of the vertebral column, which was called the "bustle"—a contrivance calculated to unnerve the wearer, not to speak of the looker-on; yet the American woman adopted it, distorted her body, and aped the gait of the kangaroo, the form being called the "Grecian bend." This lasted six months or more; first adopted by the aristocracy, then by the common people, and by the time the latter had it well in hand the *bon ton* had cast it aside and were trying something else.

A close study of this mad dressing shows that there is always a "hump." At one time it went all around; later appeared only behind, like an excrescence on a bilbol-tree. At the present time the designer has drawn his picture showing it as a pendent bag from the "shirtwaist," like the pouch of the bird pelican. A few years ago the designer, in a delirium, placed the humps on the tops of the sleeves, then snatched them away and tipped them upside down. Finally he appeared to go utterly mad with the desire to humiliate the woman, and created a fashion that entailed dragging the skirt on the ground from one to two feet.

Did the American woman resent the insult; did she refuse to adopt a custom not only disgusting but really filthy, one that a Chinese lady would have died rather than have accepted? By no means; she seized upon it with the ardor of a child with a new toy, and for a year the side-paths of the great cities of the country were swept by women's skirts, clouds of dust following them. The press took up the question, but without effect; the fashion dragged its nauseating and frightful course from rich and poor, and I was told by an official that it was impossible to stop it or to force a glimmer of reason into the minds of these women. Then they gave it up, and passed a law making it a statutory offense, with heavy fines, for anyone to "expectorate" on the sidewalk or anywhere else where the saliva could be swept up by the trains of the women of nearly all classes who followed the fashion. The American woman, as I have said, looks askance at the footgear of the Chinese—high, warm, dry, sanitary, yet revels in creations which cramp the feet and distort the anatomy. The shoes are made of leather, inflexible, pointed; and to enable them to deceive the men into the belief that they have high insteps (a sign of good blood here) the women wear stilt-like heels, which throw the foot forward and elevate the heel from two to three inches above the ground.

But all this is but a bagatelle to the fashions in deformity which we find among nearly all American women. There are throughout the country numbers of large manufactories which make "corsets"—a peculiar waist and lung compressor, used by nearly every woman in America. These men are as dogmatic as the designers of the fashion-plates. They also issue plates or guides showing new changes, and the women, like sheep, adopt them. The American woman believes that a narrow waist enhances her beauty, and the corset-maker works upon the national weakness and builds creations that put to shame and ridicule the bound feet of the aristocratic Chinese woman. The corset is a lace and ribbon-decorated armor, made either of steel ribs or whale-bone, which fits the waist and clings to the hips. It is laced up, and the degree of tightness depends upon the will or nerve of the wearer. It compresses the heart and lungs, and wearing it is a most barbarous custom—a telling argument against the assumption of high intelligence on the part of the Americans, who, in this respect, rank with the flat-headed Indians of the northwest American coast, whose heads I have seen in their medical offices side by side with a diagram showing the abnormal conditions caused by the corset.

A year ago the fiat went forth that the American woman must have wide hips. Presto! there appeared especially devised machinery, advertised in all the journals, accomplishing the condition for those whom nature had not well endowed. Now the dressmaker has decided that they must be narrow-hipped, and half a million dollars in false hips, rubber pads, and other properties are cast aside. No extravaganza is too absurd for these people who are abject slaves to the whimsicalities of the designer, who is a wag in his way, as has been well shown in a story told to me. The designers for a famous man dressmaker in Paris had a habit of taking sketches of the latest creations to their club meetings. One evening a clever caricaturist took a caricature of a fashion showing a woman with enormous and outlandish sleeves. It created a laugh. "As impossible as it is," said the artist, "I will wager a dinner that if I present it seriously to a certain fashion paper they will take it up." This is said to be the history of the "big-sleeve" fashion that really amazed the Americans themselves.

The customs of women here are so at variance with those of China that they are not readily understood. Our ways are those culled from a civilization of thousands of years; theirs from one just beginning; yet they have the temerity to speak of China as effete and behind the times. In writing, the women affect the English round hand and write across from left to right, and then beginning at the left of the page again. They are fond of perfumes, especially the lower classes, and display a barbaric taste for jewels. It is not uncommon to see the wife of a wealthy man wear half a million pounds sterling in diamonds or rubies at the opera. I was told that one lady wore a $5,000 diamond in her garter. The utterly strange and contradictory customs of these women are best observed at the beach and bath. In China if a woman is modest she is so at all times; but this is not true with some Americans, who appear to have the desire to attract attention, especially that of men, by an appeal to the beautiful in nature and art; at least this is the impression the unprejudiced looker-on gains by a sojourn in the great cities and fashionable resorts. If you happen to be riding horseback, or walking in the street with a lady, and any accident occurs to her costume whereby her neck, her leg, or her ankle is exposed, she will be mortified beyond expression; yet the night previous you might have sat in the box with her at the opera, when her décolleté gown had made her the mark for hundreds of lorgnettes. Again, this lady the next morning might bathe with me at the beach and lie on the sand basking in the sun like a siren in a costume that would arrest the attention of a St. Anthony.

Let me describe such a costume: A pair of skin-tight black stockings, then a pair of tights of black silk and a flimsy black skirt that comes just to the knee; a black silk waist, armless, and as low in the neck as the moral law permits, beneath which, to preserve her contour, is a water-proof corset. Limbs, to expose which an inch on the street were a crime, are blazoned to the world at Newport, Cape May, Atlantic City, and other resorts, and often photographed and shown in the papers. To explain this manifest contradiction would be beyond the powers of an Oriental, had he the prescience of the immortal Confucius and the divination of a Mahomet and Hilliel combined.

CHAPTER VIII
PECULIARITIES AND MANNERISMS

ONE FINDS IT DIFFICULT TO LEARN THE language fluently because of a peculiar second language called "slang," which is in use even among the fashionable classes. I despair of conveying any clear idea of it, as we have no exact equivalent. As near as I can judge, it is first composed by professional actors on the stage. Some funny remark being constantly repeated, as a part of a taking song, becomes slang, conveying a certain meaning, and is at once adopted by the people, especially by a class who pose as leaders in all towns, but who are not exactly the best, but charming imitations of the best, we may say. To illustrate this "jargon," I took a drive with a young lady at Manchester—a seaside resort. Her father was a man of good family, an official, and she was an attendant at a fashionable school. The following occurred in the conversation. Her slang is italicized:

Heathen Chinee: "It is very dull this week, Miss ———."

Young lady, sententiously: "*Bum.*"

Heathen Chinee: "I hope it will be less bum soon."

Young lady: "*It's all off with me all right*, if it don't change soon, *and don't you forget it!*"

Heathen Chinee: "I wish I could do something."

Young lady: "Well, you'll have to *get a move on you*, as I go back to school to-morrow; then there'll be *something doing*."

Heathen Chinee: "Have you seen —— lately?"

Young lady: "Yes, and isn't he *a peach*? Ah, he's a *peacharina*, and *don't you forget it!*"

Young lady (passing a friend): "*Ah, there*! why *so toppy*? *Nay, nay, Pauline*," this in reply to remarks from a friend; then turning to me, "Isn't she a *jim dandy*? *Say*, have you any girls in China that can *top* her?"

These are only a few of the slang expressions which occur to me. They are countless and endless. Such a girl in meeting a friend, instead of saying good-morning, says, "*Ah, there*," which is the slang for this salutation. If she wished to express a difference of opinion with you she would say, "*Oh, come off*." This girl would probably outgrow this if she moved in the very best circle, but the shop-girl of a common type lives in a whirl of slang; it becomes second nature, while the young men of all classes seem to use nothing else, and we often see the jargon of the lowest class used by some of the best people. There has been compiled a dictionary of slang; books are written on it, and an adept, say a "rough" or "hoodlum," it is said can carry on a conversation with nothing else. Thus, "Hi, cully, what's on?" to which comes in answer, "Hunki dori." All this means that a man has said, "How do you do, how are you, and what are you doing?" and thus learned in reply that everything is all right. A number of gentlemen were posing for a lady before a camera. "Have you finished?" asked one. "Yes, *it's all off*," was the reply, "and *a peach*, I think." It is unnecessary to say that among really refined people this slang is never heard, and would be considered a gross solecism, which gives me an opportunity to repeat that the really cultivated Americans, and they are many, are among the most delightful and charming of people.

They have strange habits, these Americans. The men chew tobacco, especially in the South, and in Virginia I have seen men spitting five or six feet, evidently taking pride in their skill in striking a "cuspidore." In every hotel, office, or public place are cuspidores—which become targets for these chewers. This is a national habit, extraordinary in so enlightened a people. So ridiculous has it made the Americans, so much has been written about it by such visitors as Charles Dickens, that the State governments have determined to take up the "spitting" question, and now there is a fine of from $10 to $100 for anyone spitting in a car or on a hotel floor. Nearly all the "up-to-date" towns have passed anti-spitting laws. Up to this time, or even during my college days in America, this habit made walking on the sidewalk a most disagreeable function, and the interior of cars was a horror. Is not this remarkable in a people who claim so much? In the South certain white men and women chew snuff—a gross habit.

In the North they also have a strange custom, called chewing gum. This gum is the exudation from certain trees, and is manufactured into plates and sold in an attractive form, merely to chew like tobacco, and young and old may be seen chewing with great velocity. The children forget themselves and chew with great force, their jaws working like those of a cow chewing her cud, only more rapidly; and to see a party of three or four chewing frantically is one of the "sights" in America, which astonishes the Heathen Chinee and convinces him that, in the slang of the country, "*there are others*" who are peculiar. There are many manufactories of this stuff, which is harmless, though such constant chewing can but affect the size of the muscles of the jaw if the theory of evolution is to be believed; at least there will be no atrophy of these parts.

In New England, the northeastern portion of the country, this habit appeared to be more prevalent, and I asked several scientific persons if they had made any attempt to trace the history of the habit or to find anything to attribute it to. One learned man told me that he had made a special study of the habit, and believed that it was merely the modern expression in human beings of the cud chewing of ruminating mammals, as cows, goats, etc. In a word, the gum-chewing Americans are trying to chew their cud as did their ancestors. Any habit like this is seized upon by manufacturers for their personal profit, and every expedient is employed to induce people to chew. The gum is mixed with perfumes, and sold as a breath purifier; others mix it with pepsin, to aid the digestion; some with something else, which is sold on ships and excursion-boats as a cure or preventive for seasickness, all of which finds a large sale among the credulous Americans, who by a clever leader can be made to take up any fad or habit.

The Americans have a peculiar habit of "treating;" that is, one of a party will "treat" or buy a certain article and distribute it gratuitously to one or ten people. A young lady may treat her friends to gum, ice-cream, soda-water, or to a theater party. A matron may treat her friends to "high-balls" or cocktails at the club. The man confines his "treats" to drinks and cigars. Thus five or six Americans may meet in a club or barroom for the sale of liquors. One says, "Come up and have something;" or "What will you have, gentlemen; this is on me;" or in some places the treater says, "Let's liquor," and all step up, the drinks are dispensed, and the treater pays. You might suppose that he was deserving of some encomium, but not at all; he expects that the others will take their turn in treating, or at least this is the assumption; and if the party is engaged in social conversation each in turn will "treat," the others taking what they wish to drink or smoke. There is a code of etiquette regarding the treat. Thus, unless you are invited, it would be bad form among gentlemen to order wine when invited to drink unless the "treater" asks you to have wine; he means a drink of whisky, brandy, or a mixed drink, or you may take soda or a cigar, or you may refuse. It is a gross solecism to accept a cigar and put it in your pocket; you should not take it unless you smoke it on the spot.

Drinking to excess is frowned upon by all classes, and a drunkard is avoided and despised; but the amount an American will drink in a day is astonishing. A really delightful man told me that he did not drink much, and this was his daily experience: before breakfast a champagne cocktail; two or three drinks during the forenoon; a pint of white or red wine at lunch; two or three cocktails in the afternoon; a cocktail at dinner, with two glasses of wine; and in the evening at the club several drinks before bedtime! This man was never drunk, and never *appeared* to be under the influence of liquor, yet he was in reality never actually sober; and he is a type of a large number in the great cities who constitute what is termed the "man about town."

The Americans are not a wine-drinking people. Whisky, and of a very excellent quality, is the national drink, while vast quantities of beer are consumed, though they make the finest red and white wines. All the grog-shops are licensed by the Government and State—that is, made to pay a tax; but in the country there is a political party, the Prohibitionists, who would drive out all wine and liquor. These, working with the conservative people, often succeed in preventing saloons from opening in certain towns; but in large cities there are from one to two saloons to the block in the districts where they are allowed.

Taking everything into consideration, I think the Americans a temperate people. They organize in a thousand directions to fight drinking and other vices, and millions of dollars are expended yearly in this direction. A peculiar quality about the American humor is that they joke about the most serious things. In fact, drink and drinking afford thousands of stories, the point of which is often very obscure to an alien. Here is one, told to illustrate the cleverness of a drinker. He walked into a bar and ordered a "tin-roof cocktail." The barkeeper was nonplussed, and asked what a tin-roof cocktail was. "Why, it's on the house." I leave you to figure it out, but the barkeeper paid the bill. The ingenuity of the Americans is shown in their mixed drinks. They have cocktails, highballs, ponies, straights, fizzes, and many other drinks. Books are written on the subject. I have seen a book devoted entirely to cocktails. Certain papers offer prizes for the invention of new drinks. I have told you that, all in all, America is a temperate country, especially when its composite character is considered; yet if the nation has a curse, a great moral drawback, it is the habit of drinking at the public bar.

CHAPTER IX
LIFE IN WASHINGTON

One of the best-known American authors has immortalized the Chinaman in some of his verses. It was some time before I understood the smile which went around when someone in my presence suggested a game of poker. I need not repeat the poem, but the essence of it is that the "Heathen Chinee is peculiar." Doubtless Mr. Harte is right, but the Chinaman and his ways are not more peculiar to the American than American customs and contradictions are to the Chinaman. If there is any race on the earth that is peculiar, it is the "Heathen Yankee," the good-hearted, ingenuous product of all the nations of the earth—black, red, white, brown, all but "yellow." Imagine yourself going out to what they call a "stag" dinner, and having an officer of the ranking of lieutenant shout, "Hi, John, pass the wine!"

Washington can not be said to be a typical American city. It is the center of *official* life, and abounds in statesmen of all grades. I have attended one of the President's receptions, to which the diplomats went in a body; then followed the army and navy, General Miles, a good-looking, soldier-like man, leading the former, and Admiral Dewey the latter, a fine body of men, all in full uniform, unpretentious, and quiet compared to similar men in other nations. I passed in line, and found the President, standing with several persons, the center of a group. The announcement and presentation were made by an officer in full uniform, and beyond this there was no formality, indeed, an abundance of republican simplicity; only the uniforms saved it from the commonplace.

The President is a man of medium size, thick-set, and inclined to be fleshy, with an interesting, smooth face, eye clear and glance alert. He grasped me quickly by the hand, but shook it gingerly, giving the impression that he was endeavoring to anticipate me, called me by name, and made a pleasant allusion to —— of ——. He has a high forehead and what you would term an intelligent face, but not one you would pick out as that of a great man; and from a study of his work I should say that he is of a class of advanced politicians, clever in political intrigue, quick to grasp the best situation for himself or party; a man of high moral character, but not a great statesman, only a man with high ideals and sentiments and the faculty of impressing the masses that he is great.

The really intelligent class regard him as a useful man, and safe. It is a curious fact that the chief appreciation of President McKinley, I was informed, came from the masses, who say, "He is so kind to his wife" (a great invalid); or "He is a model husband." Why there should be anything remarkable in a man's being kind, attentive, and loyal to an invalid spouse I could not see. Her influence with him is said to be remarkable. One day she asked the President to promote a certain officer, the son of one of the greatest of American generals, to a very high rank. He did so, despite the fact that, as an officer said, the army roared with laughter and rage.

The influence of women is an important factor in Washington life. I was presented to an officer who obtained his commission in the following manner: Two very attractive ladies in Washington were discussing their relative influence with the powers that be, when one remarked, "To show you what I can do, name a man and I will obtain a commission in the army for him." The other lady named a private soldier, whose stupidity was a matter of record, and a few days later he became an officer; but the story leaked out.

President McKinley is a popular President with the masses, but the aristocrats regard him with indifference. It is a singular fact, but the Vice-President, Mr. Roosevelt, attracts more attention than the President. He is a type that is appreciated in America, what they term in the West a "hustler;" active, wide-awake, intense, "strenuous," all these terms are applied to him. Said an officer in the field service to me, "Roosevelt is playing on a ninety-nine-year run of luck; he always lands on his feet at the right time and place." "What they call a man of destiny," I suggested. "Yes," he replied; "he is the Yankee Oliver Cromwell. He can't help 'getting there,' and he has a sturdy, evident honesty of purpose that carries him through. A team of six horses won't keep him out of the White House." This is the general opinion regarding the Vice-President, that while he is not a remarkable statesman, he already overshadows the President in the eyes of the public. I think the secret is that he is young and a hero, and what the Americans call an all-around man; not brilliant in any particular line, but a man of energy, like our ——.

He looks it. A smooth face, square, determined jaw, with a look about the eye suggestive that he would ride you down if you stood in the way. I judge him to be a man of honor, high purpose, as my friend said, of the Cromwell type, inclined to preach, and who also has what the Americans call the "get-there" quality. In conversation Vice-President Roosevelt is hearty and open, a poor diplomat, but a talker who comes to the point. He says what he thinks, and asks no favor. He acts as though he wished to clap you on the shoulder and be familiar. It will be difficult for you to understand that such a man is second in

rank in this great nation. There are no imposing surroundings, no glamor of at-
tendance, only Roosevelt, strong as a water-ox in a rice-field, smiling, all on the
surface, ready to fight for his friend or his country. Author, cowboy, stockman,
soldier, essayist, historian, sportsman, clever with the boxing-gloves or saber,
hurdle-jumper, crack revolver and rifle shot, naturalist and aristocrat, such is
the all-around Vice-President of the United States—a man who will make a
strong impression upon the history of the century if he is not shot by Socialists.

I have it from those who know, that President McKinley would be killed
in less than a week if the guards about the White House were removed. He
never makes a move without guards or detectives, and the secret-service men
surround him as carefully as possible. It would be an easy matter to kill him.
Like all officials, he is accessible to almost anyone with an apparently legitimate
object. Two Presidents have been murdered; all are threatened continually by
half-insane people called "cranks," and by the professional Socialists, mainly
foreigners. Both the President and Vice-President are well-dressed men. Presi-
dent McKinley, when I was granted an audience, wore a long-tailed black "frock
coat" and vest, light trousers, and patent leather or varnished shoes, and standing
collar. The Vice-President was similarly dressed, but with a "turn-down" collar.
The two men are said to make a "strong team," and it is a foregone conclusion
that the Vice-President will succeed President McKinley. This is already talked
of by the society people at Newport. "It is a long time," said a lady at Newport,
"since we have had a President who represented an old and distinguished family.
The McKinleys were from the ordinary ranks of life, but eminently respectable,
while Roosevelt is an old and honored name in New York, identified with the
history of the State; in a word, typical of the American aristocracy, bearing arms
by right of heritage."

I have frequently met Admiral Dewey, already so well known in China. He
is a small man, with bright eyes, who already shows the effects of years. Nothing
could illustrate the volatile, uncertain character of the American than the down-
fall of the admiral as a popular idol. Here a "peculiarity" of the American is seen.
Carried away by political and public adulation, the old sailor's new wife, the sister
of a prominent politician, became seized with a desire to make him President.
Then the hero lovers raised a large sum and purchased a house for the admiral;
but the politicians ignored him as a candidate, which was a humiliation, and the
donors of the house demanded their money returned when the admiral placed
the gift in the name of his wife; and so for a while the entire people turned against
the gallant sailor, who was criticized, jeered at, and ridiculed. All he had accom-
plished in one of the most remarkable victories in the history of modern warfare
was forgotten in a moment, to the lasting disgrace of his critics.

One of the interesting places in Washington is the Capitol, perhaps the most splendid building in any land. Here we see the men whom the Americans select to make laws for them. The looker-on is impressed with the singular fact that most of the senators are very wealthy men; and it is said that they seek the position for the honor and power it confers. I was told that so many are millionaires that it gave rise to the suspicion that they bought their way in, and this has been boldly claimed as to many of them. This may be the treasonable suggestion of some enemy; but that money plays a part in some elections there is little doubt. I believe this is so in England, where elections have often been carried by money.

The American Senate is a dignified body, and I doubt if it have a peer in the world. The men are elected by the State legislatures, not by the people at large, a method which makes it easy for an unprincipled millionaire or his political manager to buy votes sufficient to seat his patron. The fact that senators are mainly rich does not imply unfitness, but quite the contrary. Only a genius can become a multi-millionaire in America, and hence the senators are in the main bright men. When observing these men and enabled to look into their records, I was impressed by the fact that, despite the advantages of education, this wonderful country has produced few really great men, and there is not at this time a great man on the horizon.

America has no Gladstone, no Salisbury, no Bright. Lincoln, Blaine and Sumner are names which impress me as approximating greatness; they made an impression on American history that will be enduring. Then there are Frye, Reed, Garfield, McKinley, Cleveland, who were little great men, and following them a distinguished company, as Hanna, Conkling, Hay, Hayes, and others, who were superior men of affairs. A distinctly great national figure has not appeared in America since Daniel Webster, Henry Clay, and Rufus Choate—all men too great to become President. It appears to be the fate of the republic not to place its greatest men in the White House, and by this I mean great statesmen. General Grant was a great man, a heroic figure, but not a statesman. Lincoln is considered a great man. He is called the "Liberator;" but I can conceive that none but a very crude mind, inspired by a false sentiment, could have made a horde of slaves, the most ignorant people on the globe, the political equals of the American people. A great man in such a crisis would have resisted popular clamor and have refused them suffrage until they had been prepared to receive it by at least some education. Americans are prone to call their great politicians statesmen. Blaine, Reed, Conkling, Harrison were types of statesmen; Hanna, Quay, and others are politicians.

The Lower House was a disappointment to me. There are too many ordinary men there. They do not look great, and at the present time there is not a really great man in the Lower House. There are too many cheap lawyers and third-rate politicians there. Good business men are required, but such men can not afford to take the position. I heard a great captain of industry, who had been before Congress with a committee, say that he never saw "so many asses together in all his life;" but this was an extreme view. The House may not compare intellectually with the House of Commons, but it contains many bright men. A fool could hardly get in, though the labor unions have placed some vicious representatives there. The lack of manners distressed a lady acquaintance of mine, who, in a burst of indignation at seeing a congressman sitting with his feet on his desk, said that there was not a man in Congress who had any social position in Washington or at home, which, let us trust, is not true.

As I came from the White House some days ago I met a delegation of native Indians going in, a sad sight. In Indian affairs occurs a page of national history which the Americans are not proud of. In less than four hundred years they have almost literally been wiped from the face of the earth; the whites have waged a war of extermination, and the pitiful remnant now left is fast disappearing. In no land has the survival of the fittest found a more remarkable illustration. But the Indians are having their revenge. The Americans long ago brought over Africans as slaves; then, as the result of a war of words and war of fact, suddenly released them all, and, at one fell move, in obedience to the hysterical cries of their people, gave these ignorant semisavages and slaves the same political rights as themselves.

Imagine the condition of things! The most ignorant and debased of races suddenly receives rights and privileges and is made the equal of American citizens. So strange a move was never seen or heard of elsewhere, and the result has been relations more than strained and always increasing between the whites and the blacks in the South. As voters the negroes secure many positions in the South above their old masters. I have seen a negro[1] sitting in the Vice-President's chair in the United States Senate; while white Southern senators were pacing the outer corridors in rage and disgust. There are generally one or more black men in Congress, and they are given a few offices as a sop. With one hand the Americans place millions of them on a plane with themselves as free and independent citizens, and with the other refuse them the privileges of such citizenship. They may enter the army as privates, but any attempt to make them officers is a failure—white officers will not associate with them. It is impossible for a negro to graduate from the Naval Academy, though he has the right to

1 Probably Senator Bruce.

do so. I was told that white sailors would shoot him if placed over them. Several negroes have been appointed as students, but none as yet have been able to pass the examination. Here we see the strange and contradictory nature of the Americans. The white master of the South had the black woman nurse his children. Thousands of mulattoes in the country show that the whites took advantage of the women in other ways, marriage between blacks and whites being prohibited. When it comes to according the blacks recognition as social equals, the people North and South resent even the thought. The negro woman may provide the sustenance of life for the white baby, but I venture to say that any Southern man, or Northern one for that matter, would rather see his daughter die than be married to a negro. So strong is this feeling that I believe in the extreme South if a negro persisted in his addresses to a white woman he would be shot, and no jury or judge could be found to convict the white man.

In the North the negro has certain rights. He can ride in the street-cars, go to the theater, enter restaurants, but I doubt if large hotels would entertain him. In the South every train has its separate cars for negroes; every station its waiting-room for them; even on the street-cars they are divided off by a wire rail or screen, and sit beneath a sign, which advertises this free, independent, but black American voter as being not fit to sit by the side of his political brother. This causes a bitter feeling, and the time is coming when the blacks will revolt. Already criminal attacks upon white women are not uncommon, and a virtual reign of terror exists in some portions of the South, where it is said that white women are never left unprotected; and the negro, if he attacks a white woman, is almost invariably burned alive, with the horrible ghastly features that attend an Indian scalping. The crowd carry off bits of skin, hair, finger-nails, and rope as trophies. In fact, these "burnings" are the most extraordinary features in this "enlightened" country. The papers denounce them and compare the people to ghouls; yet these same people accuse the Chinese of being cruel, barbarous, insensible to cruelty, and "pagans." It is true we have pirates and criminals, but the horrible features of the lynchings in America during the last ten years I believe have no counterpart in the history of China in the last five hundred.

In Washington the servants are blacks; irresponsible, childlike, aping the vanities of the white people. They are "niggers;" the mulattoes, the illegitimate offspring of whites, form another and totally distinct class of colored society, and are the aristocracy. Rarely will a mulatto girl marry a black man, and *vice versa*. They have their clubs and their functions, their professional men, including lawyers and doctors, as have the white people. They present a strange and singular feature. Despised by their fathers, half-sisters, and brothers, denied any social recognition, hating their black ancestry, they are socially "between the devil and the deep sea." The negro question constitutes the gravest one now before the American people. He is increasing rapidly, but in the years since the civil war no pure-blooded negro has given evidence of brilliant attainments. Frederick Douglas, Senator Bruce, and Booker T. Washington rank with many white Americans in authorship, diplomacy, and scholarship; but Douglas and Bruce were mulattoes, and Booker Washington's father was an unknown white man. These men are held in high esteem, but the social line has been drawn against them, though Douglas married a white woman.

Balls are a feature of life in Washington. The women appear in full dress, which means that the arms and neck are exposed, and the men wear evening dress. The dances are mostly "round." The man takes a lady to the ball, and when he dances seizes her in an embrace which would be considered highly improper under ordinary circumstances, but the etiquette of the dance makes it permissible. He places his right arm around her waist, takes her left hand in his, holds her close to him, and both begin to move around to the special music designed for this peculiar motion, which may be a "waltz," or a "two-step," or a "gallop," or a "schottische," all being different and having different music or time, or there may be various kinds of music for each. At times the music is varied, being a gliding, scooping, swooping slide, indescribable. When the dancers feel the approach of giddiness they reverse the whirl or move backward.

Many Washington men have become famous as dancers, and quite outshadow war heroes. All the officers of the army and navy are taught these dances at the Military and Naval Academies, it being a national policy to be agreeable to ladies; at least this must be so, as the men never dance together. To see several hundred people whirling about, as I have seen them at the inaugural of the President, is one of the most remarkable scenes to be observed in America. The man in Washington who can not dance is a "wallflower"—that is, he never leaves the wall. There is a professional champion who has danced eight out of twenty-four hours without stopping. A yearly convention of dancing-school professors is held. These men, with much dignity, meet in various cities and discuss various dances, how to grasp the partner, and other important questions. Some time ago the question was whether the "gent" should hold a handkerchief in the hand he pressed upon the back of the lady, a professor having testified before the convention that he had seen the imprint of a man's hand on the white dress of a lady. The acumen displayed at these conventions is profound and impressive. Here you observe a singular fact. The good dancer may be an officer of high social standing, but the dancing-teacher, even though he be famous as such, is *persona non grata*, so far as society is concerned. A professional dancer, fighter, wrestler, cook, musician, and a hundred more are not acceptable in society except in the strict line of their profession; but a professional civil or naval engineer, an organist, an artist, a decorator (household), and an architect are received by the elect in Washington.

I have alluded to the craze for joking among young ladies in society. At a dinner a reigning beauty, and daughter of ——, who sat next to me, talked with me on dancing. She told me all about it, and, pointing to a tall, distinguished-looking man near by, said that he had received his degree of D. D. (Doctor of Dancing) from Harvard University, and was extremely proud of it; and, furthermore, it would please him to have me mention it. I did not enlighten the young lady, and allowed her to continue, that I might enjoy her animation and superb "nerve" (this is the American slang word for her attitude). The gentleman was her uncle, a doctor of divinity, who was constitutionally opposed to dancing; and I learned later that he had a cork leg. Such are some of the pitfalls in Washington set for the pagan Oriental by charming Americans.

Dancing parties, in fact, all functions, are seized upon by young men and women who anticipate marriage as especially favorable occasions for "courtship." The parents apparently have absolutely nothing to do with the affair, this being a free country. The girl "falls in love" with someone, and the courtship begins. In the lower classes the girl is said to be "keeping company" with so and so, or he is "her steady company." In higher circles the admirer is "devoted to the lady." This lasts for a year, perhaps longer, the man monopolizing the young lady's time, calling so many times a week, as the case may be, the familiarity between the two increasing until they finally exchange kisses—a popular greeting in America. About now they become affianced or "engaged," and the man is supposed to ask the consent of the parents. In France the latter is supposed to give a *dot*; in America it is not thought of. In time the wedding occurs, amid much ceremony, the bride's parents bearing all the expense; the groom is relieving them of a future expense, and is naturally not burdened. The married young people then go upon a "honeymoon," the month succeeding the wedding, and this is long or brief, according to the wealth of the parties. When they return they usually live by themselves, the bride resenting any advice or espionage from her husband's mother, who is the mother-in-law, a relation as much joked about in America as revered in China.

Sometimes the "engaged" couple do not marry. The man perhaps in his long courtship discovers traits that weary him, and he breaks off the match. If he is wealthy the average American girl may sue him for damages, for laceration of the affections. One woman in the State of New York sued for the value of over two thousand kisses her "steady company" had taken during a number of years' courtship, and was awarded three thousand dollars. The journal from which I took this made an estimate that the kisses had cost the man one dollar and a half each! Sometimes the girl breaks the engagement, and if presents have been given she returns them, the man rarely suing; but I have seen record of a case where the girl refused to return the presents, and the man sued for them; but no jury could be found to decide in his favor. A distinguished physician has written a book on falling in love. It is recognized as a contagious disease; men and women often die of it, and commit the most extraordinary acts when under its influence. I have observed it, and, all things considered, it has no advantages over the Chinese method of attaining the marriage state. The wisdom of some older person is certainly better than what the American would call the "snap judgment" of two young people carried away by passion. One might find the chief cause of divorce in America to lie in this strange custom.

I was invited by a famous wag last week to meet a man who could claim that he was the father of fifty-three children and several hundred grandchildren. I fully expected to see the *Gaikwar of Baroda*, or some such celebrity, but found a tall, ministerial, typical American, with long beard, whom —— introduced to me as a Mormon bishop, who, he said, had a virtual *congé d'élire* in the Church, at the same time referring to me as a Chinese Mormon with "fifty wives." I endeavored to protest, but —— explained to the bishop that I was merely modest. The Mormons are a sect who believe in polygamy. Each man has as many wives as he can support, and the population increases rapidly where they settle. The ludicrous feature of Mormonism is that the Government has failed to stop it, though it has legislated against it; but it is well known that the Mormon allows nothing to interfere with his "revelations," which are on "tap" in Utah.

I was much amused at the bishop's remarks. He said that if the American politicians who were endeavoring to kill them off would marry their actual concubines, and *all* Americans would do the same, the United States would have a Mormon majority the next day. The bishop had the frailties and moral lapses of prominent people in all lands at his fingers' ends, and his claim was that the whole civilized world was practising polygamy, but doing it illegally, and the Mormons were the only ones who had the honor to legitimatize it. The joke was on ——, who was literally bottled up by the flow of facts from the bishop, who referred to me to substantiate him, which I pretended to do, in order totally to crush ——, who had tried to make me a party to his joke. The bishop, who invited me to call upon him in Utah, said that he hoped some time to be a United States senator, though he supposed the women of the East could create public sentiment sufficient to defeat him.

I once stopped over in Utah and visited the great Mormon Temple, and I must say that the Mormon women are far below the average in intelligence, that is, if personal appearances count. I understand they are recruited from the lowest and most ignorant classes in Europe, where there are thousands of women who would rather have a fifth of a husband than work in the field. In the language of American slang, I imagine the Americans are "up against it," as the country avowedly offers an asylum for all seeking religious liberty, and the Mormons claim polygamy as a divine revelation and a part of their doctrine.

The bishop, I believe, was not a bishop, but a proselyting elder, or something of the kind. The man who introduced me to him was a type peculiar to America, a so-called "good fellow." People called him by his first name, and he returned the favor. The second time I met him he called me Count, and upon my replying that I was not a count he said, "Well, you look it, anyway," and he has always called me Count. He knows everyone, and everyone knows him—a good-hearted man, a spendthrift, yet a power in politics; a *remarkable* poker player, a friend worth knowing, the kind of man you like to meet, and there are many such in this country.

CHAPTER X
THE AMERICAN IN LITERATURE

I HAVE BEEN A GUEST AT THE ANNUAL DINNER of the ——, one of the leading literary associations in America, and later at a "reception" at the house of ——, where I met some of the most charming men and delightful women, possessed of manners that marked the person of culture and the *savoir faire* that I have seen so little of among other "sets" of well-known public people. But what think you of an author of note who knew absolutely nothing of the literature of our country? There were Italians, French, and Swedes at the dinner, who were called upon to respond to toasts on the literature of their country; but was I called upon? No, indeed. I doubt if in all that *entourage* there was more than one or two who were familiar with the splendid literature of China and its antiquity.

But to come to the "shock." My immediate companion was a lady with just a *soupçon* of the masculine, who, I was told, was a distinguished novelist, which means that her book had sold to the limit of 30,000 copies. After a toast and speech in which the literature of Norway and Sweden had been extolled, this charming lady turned to me and said, "It is too bad, ——, that you have no literature in China; you miss so much that is enjoyed by other nations." This was too much, and I broke one of the American rules of chivalry—I became disputatious with a lady and slightly cynical; and when I wish to be cynical I always quote Mr. Harte, which usually "brings down the house." To hear a Chinese heathen quote the "Heathen Chinee" is supposed to be very funny.

I said, "My dear madam, I am surprised that you do not know that China has the finest and oldest literature known in the history of the world. I assure you, my ancestors were writing books when the Anglo-Saxon was living in caves."[1] She was astonished and somewhat dismayed, but was not cast down— the clever American woman never is. I told her of our classics, of our wonderful Book of Changes, written by my ancestor Wan Wang in 1150 B. C. I told her of his philosophy. I compared his idea of the creation to that in the Bible. I explained the loss of many rare Chinese books by the piratical order of destruction by Emperor Che Hwang-ti, calling attention to the fact that the burning of the famous library of Alexandria was a parallel. I asked her if it were possible that she had never heard of the *Odes of Confucius*, or his *Book of History*, which was supposed to have been destroyed, but which was found in the walls of his home one hundred and forty years before Christ, and so saved to become a part of the literature of China.

Finally she said, "I have studied literature, but that of China was not included." "Your history," I continued, "begins in 1492; our written history begins in the twenty-third century before Christ, and the years down to 720 B. C. are particularly well covered, while our legends run back for thousands of years." But my companion had never heard of the *Shoo-King*. It was so with the *Chun Tsew*[2] of Confucius and the *Four Books—Ta-he-o*[3], *Chung-yung*[4], *Lun-yu*[5], *Măng-tsze*[6]. She had never heard of them. I told her of the invention of paper by the Marquis Tsae several centuries before Christ, and she laughingly replied that she supposed that I would claim next that the Chinese had libraries like those Mr. Carnegie is founding. I was delighted to assure her that her assumption was correct, and drew a little picture of a well-known Chinese library, founded two thousand years ago, the Han Library, with its 3,123 classics, its 2,706 works on philosophy, its 2,528 books on mathematics, its 790 works on war, its 868 books on medicine, 1,318 on poetry, not to speak of thousands of essays.

---

1 As a frontispiece to this volume, the cover design used on one of these old Chinese books is shown.

2 Spring and Autumn Annals.

3 Great Learning.

4 Confucian Analects.

5 Doctrine of the Mean.

6 Works of Mencius.

I could not but wonder as I talked, where were the Americans and their literature when our fathers were reading these books two thousand years ago! Even the English people were wild savages, living in caves and huts, when our people were printing books and encyclopedias of knowledge. I dwelt upon our poetry, the National Airs, Greater Eulogies, dating back several thousand years. I told her of the splendors of our great versifier, *Le-Tai-Pih*; and I might have said that many American poets, like Walt Whitman, had doubtless read the translations to their advantage. I had the pleasure at least of commanding this lady's attention, and I believe she was the first American who deigned to take a Chinaman seriously. The facts of our literature are available, but only scholars make a study of it, and so far as I could learn not a word of Chinese literature is ever taught in American schools, though in the great universities there are facilities, and the best educated people are familiar with our history.

The American authors, especially novelists, who constitute the majority of authors, are by no means all well educated. Many appear to have a faculty of "story-telling," which enables them to produce something that will sell; but that all American authors, and this will surprise you, are included among the great scholars, is far from true. Some, yes many, are deplorably ignorant in the sense of broad learning, and I believe this is a universal, national fault. If one thing Chinese more than another is ridiculed in America it is our drama. I met a famous "play-writer" at the —— dinner, who thought it a huge joke. I heard that his income was $30,000 per annum from plays alone; yet he had never heard of our "Hundred Plays of the Yuen Dynasty," which rests in one of his own city libraries not a mile distant, and he laughed good-naturedly when I remarked that the modern stage obtained its initiative in China.

A listener did me the honor to question my statement that Voltaire's "*L'Orphelin de la Chine*" was taken from the *Orphan of Chaou* of this collection, which I thought everyone knew. All the authors whom I met seemed surprised to learn that I was familiar with their literature and could not compare it synthetically with that of other nations, and even more so when I said that all well-educated Chinamen endeavored to familiarize themselves with the literature of other countries.

I continually gain the impression that the Americans "size us up," as they say, and "lump" us with the "coolie." We are "heathen Chinee," and it is incomprehensible that we should know anything. I am talking now of the half-educated people as I have met them. Here and there I meet men and women of the highest culture and knowledge, and this class has no peer in the world. If I were to live in America I should wish to consort with her real scholars, culled from the best society of New York, Boston, Philadelphia, Washington, Baltimore, and other cities. In a word, the aristocracy of America is her educated class, the education that comes from association year after year with other cultivated people. I understand there is more of it in Boston and Philadelphia than anywhere; but you find it in all towns and cities. This I grant is the real American, who, in time—several thousand years perhaps—as in our own case, will demonstrate the wonderful possibilities of the human race in the West.

I would like to tell you something about the books of the literary men and women I have met, but you will be more interested in the things I have seen and the mannerisms of the people. I was told by a distinguished writer that America had failed to produce any really great authors—I mean to compare with other nations—and I agreed with him, although appreciating what she has done. There is no one to compare with the great minds of England—Scott, Dickens, Thackeray. There is no American poet to compare with Tennyson, Milton, and a dozen others in England, France, Italy, and Germany; indeed, America is far behind in this respect, yet in the making of books there is nothing to compare with it. Every American, apparently, aspires to become an author, and I really think it would be difficult to find a citizen of the republic who had not been a contributor to some publication at some time, or had not written a book. The output of books is extraordinary, and covers every field; but the class is not in all cases such as one might expect. The people are omnivorous readers, and "stories," "novels," are ground out by the ton; but I doubt if a book has been produced since the time of Hawthorne that will really live as a great classic.

The American authors are mainly collected in New York, where the great publishing houses are located, and are a fine representative class of men and women, of whom I have met a number, such as Howells, the author and editor, and Mark Twain, the latter the most brilliant litterateur in the United States. This will be discovered when he dies and is safe beyond receiving all possible benefits from such recognition. Many men in America make reputations as humorists, and find it impossible to divest their more serious writings from this "taint," if so it may be called. They are not taken seriously when they seriously desire it; a fact I fully appreciate, as I am taken as a joke, my "pigtail," my "shoes," my "clothes," my way of speaking, all being objects of joking.

The literary men have several clubs in New York, where they can be found, and many have marked peculiarities, which are interesting to a foreigner. Several artists affect a peculiar style of dress to advertise their wares. One, it is said, lived in a tree at Washington. It is not so much with the authors as with the methods of making books that I think you will be interested. I met a rising young author at a dinner in Washington who confided to me that the "book business" was really ruined in America by reason of the mad craze of nearly all

Americans to become writers. He said that he as an editor had been offered money to publish a novel by a society woman who desired to pose as an authoress. This author said that there were in America a dozen or more of the finest and most honorable publishing houses in the world, but there were many more in the various cities which virtually preyed upon this "literary disease" of the people. No country in the world, said my acquaintance, produces so many books every year as America; so many, in fact, that the shops groan with them and the forests of America threaten to give out, and the supply virtually clogs and ruins the market. So crazy are the people to be authors and see themselves in print that they will go to any length to accomplish authorship.

He cited a case of a carpenter, a man of no education, who was seized with the desire to write a book, which he did. It was sent to all the leading publishers, and promptly returned; then he began the rounds of the second-class houses, of which there are legion. One of the latter wrote him that they published on the "cooperative" plan, and would pay *half* the expenses of publishing if he would pay the other half. Of course *his* share paid for the entire edition and gave the clever "cooperative" publisher a profit, whether the edition sold or not. And my informant said that at least twenty firms were publishing books for such authors, and encouraging people to produce manuscripts that were so much "dead wood" in the real literary field. He later sent me the prospectus of several such houses which would take any manuscript, if the author would pay for the publishing, revise it and send it forth. I was assured that thousands of books are produced yearly by these houses, who are really "printers," who advertise in various ways and encourage would-be authors, the idea being to get their money, a species of literary "graft," according to my literary informant, who assured me I must not confuse such parasites with the large publishers of America, who will not produce a book unless their skilled readers consider it a credit to them and to the country, a high standard which I believe is maintained.

Perhaps the most interesting phase of literature in America is found in the weekly and monthly magazines, of which there is no end. Every sport has its "organ," every great trade, every society, every religion; even the missionaries sent to China have their organs, in which is reported their success in saving *us* and divorcing us from our ancient beliefs. The great literary magazines number perhaps a dozen, with a few in the front rank, such as the Century, Harper's, Scribner's, The Atlantic, Cosmopolitan, McClure's, Dial, North American Review, Popular Science Monthly, Bookman, Critic, and Nation. Such magazines I conceive to be the universities of the people, the great educators in art, literature, science, etc. Nothing escapes them. They are timely, beautiful, exact, thorough, scientific, the reflex of the best and most artistic minds in America; and many are so cheap as to be within the reach of the poor. It is interesting to know that most of these magazines are sources of wealth, the money coming from the advertisements, published as a feature in the front and back. These notices are in bulk often more than the literary portion, and the rate charged, I was told, from $100 to $1,000 per page for a single printing.

The skill with which appeals are made to the weaknesses of readers is well shown in some of the minor publications not exactly within the same class as the literary magazines. One that is devoted to women is a most clever appeal to the idiosyncrasies of the sex: There are articles on cooking, dinners, luncheons, how to set tables, table manners, etiquette (one would think they had read Confucius), how to dress for these functions; and, in fact, every occupation in life possible to a woman is dealt with by an extraordinary editor who is a man. Whenever I was joked with about our men acting on the stage as women, I re-torted by quoting Mr. ———, the male editor of the female ———, who is either a consummate actor or a remarkably composite creature, to so thoroughly antic-ipate his audience. The mother, the widow, the orphan, the young maiden, the "old maid," are all taken into the confidence of this editor, who in his editorials has what are termed "heart to heart" talks.

I send you a copy of this paper, which is very clever and very successful, and a good illustration of the American magazine that, while claiming to be literature, is a mechanical production, "machine made" in every sense. One can imagine the introspective editor entering all the foibles and weaknesses of women in a book and in cold blood forming a department to appeal to each. I was informed that the editors of such publications were "not in business for their health," but for money; and their energies are all expended on projects to hold present readers and obtain others. The more readers the more they can charge the "advertiser" in the back or side pages, who here illustrate their deadly corsets, their new dye for the hair, their beauty doctors, freckle eradicators, powders for the toilet, bustles, and the thousand and one things which shrewd dealers are anxious to have women take up.

The children also have their journals or "magazines." One in New York deals with fairies and genii, on the ground that it is good for the imagination. Another, published in Boston, denounces the fairy-story idea, and gives the children stories by great generals, princes of the blood, captains of industry, admirals, etc.; briefly, the name of the writer, not the literary quality of the tale, is the important feature. There are papers for babes, boys, girls, the sick and the well.

The most conspicuous literary names before the people are Howells, Twain, and Harte, though one hears of scores of novelists, who, I believe, will be forgotten in a decade or so. As I have said previously, I am always joked with about the "Heathen Chinee." I have really learned to play "poker," but I seldom if ever sit down to a game that someone does not joke with me about "Ah Sin." Such is the American idea of the proprieties and their sense of humor; yet I finally have come to be so good an American that I can laugh also, for I am confident the jokers mean it all in the best of feeling.

There are in America a class of litterateurs who are rarely heard of by the masses, but to my mind they are among the greatest and most advanced Americans. They are the astronomers, geologists, zoologists, ornithologists, and others, authors of papers and articles in the Government Reports of priceless value. These writers appear to me, an outsider, to be the real safety-valves, the real backbone of the literary productions of the day. With them science is but a synonym of truth; they fling all superstition and ignorance to the winds, and should be better known. Such names as Edison, Cope, Marsh, Hall, Young, Field, Baird, Agassiz, and fifty more might be mentioned, all authors whose books will give them undying fame, men who have devoted a lifetime to research and the accumulation of knowledge; yet the author of the last novel, "My Mule from New Jersey," will, for the day, have more vogue among the people than any of these. But such is fame, at least in America, where erudition is not appreciated as it is in "pagan" China.

CHAPTER XI
THE POLITICAL BOSS

AT AN ASSEMBLY-ROOM IN NEW YORK I MET a famous American political "boss." Many governors in China do not have the same power and influence. I had letters to him from Senators —— and ——. I expected to meet a man of the highest culture, but what was my surprise to see a huge, overgrown, uneducated Irishman, gross in every particular, who used the local "slang" so fiercely that I had difficulty in understanding him. He had been a police officer, and I understand was a "grafter," but that may have been a report of his enemies, as he commanded attention at the time of the election.

This man had a fund of humor, which was displayed in his clapping me on the back and calling me "John," introducing me to a dozen or so of as hard-looking men in the garb of gentlemen as I have ever seen. I heard them described later as "ward beetles," and they looked it, whatever it meant. The "Boss" appeared much interested in me; said he had heard I was no "slouch," and knew I must have a "pull" or I would not be where I am. He wished to

know how we run elections on "the Ho-Hang-Ho." When I told him that a
candidate for a governmental office never obtained it until he passed one of
three very difficult literary examinations in our nine classics, and that there
were thousands competing for the office, he was "paralyzed"—that is, he said he
was, and volunteered the information that "he would not be 'in it' in China." I
thought so myself, but did not say so.

I told him that the politicians in China were the greatest scholars; that the
policy of the Government was to make all offices competitive, as we thus se-
cured the brightest, smartest, and most gifted men for officials. "Smart h——!"
retorted the "Boss." "Why, we've got smart men. Look at our school-teachers.
Them guys[1] is crammed with guff[2], and passing examinations all the time; but
there ain't one in a thousand that's got sense enough to run a tamale[3] conven-
tion. The State governor would get left here if all the boys that wanted office had
to pass an examination. We've got something like it here," he said, "that blank
Civil Service, that keeps many a natural-born genius out of office; but it don't
'cut ice with me.' I'm the whole thing in the ward."

Despite his rough exterior, —— was a good-hearted fellow, as they say,
no rougher than his constituents, and I was with him several days during a
local election with a view to studying American politics. Much of the time was
spent in the saloons of the district where the "Boss" held out, and where I was
introduced as a "white Chinee," or as a "white Chink," and "my friend." I wish I
had kept a list of the drinks the "Boss" took and the cigars he smoked *per diem*.
Perhaps it is as well I did not; you would not believe me. I was always "John"
to this crowd, that was made up of laboring people in the main, of whom Irish
and Germans predominated. The "Boss" was what they called a "bulldozer." If
a man differed with him he tried to talk or drink him down; if it was an enemy
and he became too disputatious, he would knock him out with his fist. In this
way he had acquired a reputation as a "slugger," that counted for much in such
an assemblage, and he confided to me one evening that it was the easiest way to
"stop talk," and that if he "laid down," the opposition would walk off with all
his "people." He was "Boss" because he was the boss slugger, the best executive,
the best drinker and smoker, the best "persuader," and the best public speaker in
his ward. So you see he had a variety of talents. In China I can imagine such a
man being beheaded as a pirate in a few weeks; this would be as good an excuse
as any; yet men like this have grown and developed into respectable persons in
New York and other cities.

---

1 Slang for citizens.

2 Slang for information, facts.

3 Mexican hash in corn-husk.

"For ways that are dark and tricks that are vain, the Heathen Chinee is peculiar," but I doubt if he is more so than the political system of the United States, where every man is supposed to be free, but where a few men in each town own everything and everybody politically. The American thinks he is free, but he has in reality no more freedom than the Englishman; in fact, I am inclined to think that the latter is the freest of them all, and I doubt if too much freedom is good for man. Politics in America is a profession, a trade, a science, a perfect system by which one or two men run or control millions. Politics means the attainment of political power and influence, which mean office. Some men are in politics for the love of power, some for spoils ("graft" they call it in slang), and some for the high offices. In America there are two large parties, the Republican and the Democratic. Then there are the Labor, Prohibition (non-drinking), and various other parties, which, in the language of politics, "cut no ice." The real issues of a party are often lost sight of. The Republicans may be said to favor a high tariff; the Democrats a low tariff or free trade; and when there is not sufficient to amuse the people in these, then other reasons for being a Democrat or a Republican are raised, and a platform is issued. Lately the Democrats have espoused "free silver," and the Republicans have "buried" them. The Democrats are now trying to invent some new "platform;" but the Republicans appear to have included about all the desirable things in their platform, and hence they win.

In a small town one or two men are known as "bosses." They control the situation at the primaries; they manage to get elected and keep before the people. Generally they are natural leaders, and fill some office. When the senator comes to town they "escort" him about and advise him as to the votes he may expect. Sometimes the ward man is the postmaster, sometimes a national congressman, again a State senator; but he is always in evidence, and before the people, a good speaker and talker and the "boss." Every town has its Republican and Democratic "boss," always striving to increase the vote, always striving for something. The larger the city, the larger the "boss," until we come to a city like New York, where we find, or did find, Boss Tweed, who absolutely controlled the political situation for years.

This means that he was in politics, and manipulated all the offices in order to steal for himself and his friends; this is of public record. He was overthrown or exposed by the citizens, but was followed by others, who manipulated the affairs of the city for money. Offices were sold; anyone who had a position either bought it or paid a percentage for it. Gambling-dens and other "resorts" paid large sums to "sub-bosses," who become rich, and if the full history of some of the "bosses" of New York, Philadelphia, Chicago, or any great American city could be exposed, it would show a state of affairs that would display the American politician in a dark light. Repeatedly the machinations of the politicians have been exposed, yet they doubtless go on in some form. And this is true to some extent of the Government. The honor of no President has been impugned; they are men of integrity, but the enormous appointing power which they have is a mere form; they do not and could not appoint many men. The little "boss" in some town desires a position. He has been a spy for the congressman or senator for years, and now aspires to office. He obtains the influence of the senator and the congressman, and is supported by a petition of his friends, and the President names him for the office, taking the senator for his sponsor. If the man becomes a grafter or thief, the President is attacked by the opposition.

In a large city like New York each ward will have its "boss," who will report to a supreme "boss," and by this system, often pernicious, the latter acquires absolute control of the situation. He names the candidates for office, or most of them, and is all powerful. I have met a number of "bosses," and all, it happened, were Irish; indeed, the Irish dominate American politics. One, a leader of Tammany in New York, was a most preposterous person, well dressed, but not a gentleman from any standpoint; ignorant so far as education goes, yet supremely sharp in politics. Such a man could not have led a fire brigade in China, yet he was the leader of thousands, and controlled Democratic New York for years. He never held office, I was told, yet grew very rich.

The Republican "boss" was a tall, thin, United States senator. I was also introduced to him—a Mephistophelian sort of an individual—to me utterly without any attraction; but I was informed that he carried the vote of the Republican party in his pocket. How? that is the mystery. If you desired office you went to him; without his influence one was impotent. Thousands of office-holders felt his power, hated him, perhaps, but did not dare to say it.

The "boss" controls the situation, gives and "takes," and the other citizens get the satisfaction of thinking they are a free people. In reality, they are political slaves, and the "boss," "sub-boss," and the long line of smaller "bosses" are their masters. Very much the same situation is seen in national politics. The party is controlled by a "boss," and at the present this personage is a millionaire, named Hanna, said to be an honest, upright man, with a genius for political diplomacy, a puller of wires, a maker of Presidents, having virtually placed President McKinley where he is. This man I met. Many of the politicians called him "Uncle Mark." He has a familiar way with reporters. He is a man of good size, with a face of a rather common type, with very large and protruding ears, but two bright, gleaming eyes, that tell of genius, force, intelligence, power, and executive talents of an exalted order. I recall but one other such pair of eyes, and those were in the head of Senator James G. Blaine, whom I saw during my first visit to America. Hanna is famous for his *bonhomie*, and is a fine story-teller. Indeed, unless a man can tell stories he had better remain out of politics, or rather he will never get into politics.

As an outsider I should say that the power of the "boss" was due to the fact that the best classes will have none of him, as a rule (I refer to the ordinary "boss"), and as a consequence he and his henchmen control the situation. I think I am not overstating the truth when I say that every city in the United States has been looted by the politicians of various parties. It is of public record that Philadelphia, Chicago, St. Louis, and New York citizens have repeatedly risen and shown that the city was being robbed in the most bare-handed manner. Bribery and corruption have been found to exist to-day in the entire system, and if the credit of the republic stands on its political *morale* this vast union of States is a colossal failure, as it is being pillaged by politicians. Every "boss" has what are termed "heelers," one function of whom is to buy votes and do other work in the interest of "reform." A friend told me that he spent election day in the office of a candidate for Congress in a certain Western town, and the candidate had his safe heaped full of silver dollars. All day long men were coming and going, each taking the dollars to buy votes. By night the supply was exhausted, and the man defeated. I expressed satisfaction at this, but my friend laughed; the other fellow who won paid more for votes, he said. I was told that all the great senatorial battles were merely a question of dollars; the man with the largest "sack" won.

On the other hand, there are senators who not only never paid for a vote but never expressed a wish to be elected. The foreign vote—Italians and others—are swayed by cash considerations; the negroes are bought and sold politically. The "bosses" handle the money, and the senators consider it as "expenses," and doubtless do not know that some of it has been used to influence legislators. The Americans have a remarkable network of laws to prevent fraudulent voting. Each candidate in some States is required to swear to an expense account, yet the wary politician, with his "ways that are dark," evades the law. The entire system, the control of the political fortunes of 80,000,000 Americans, is in the hands of a small army of political "bosses," some of whom, had they figured as grafters in "effete" China, would have been beheaded without mercy.

CHAPTER XII
EDUCATION IN AMERICA

A FUNDAMENTAL IDEA WITH THE AMERICAN IS TO educate children. This is carried to the extent of making it an offense not to send those above a certain age to school, while State or town officers, called "truant police," are on the alert to arrest all such children who are not in school. The following was told me by a Government official in Washington, who had obtained it from a well-known literary man who witnessed the incident. The literary man was invited to visit a Boston school of the lower grade, where he found the teacher, an attractive woman, engaged in teaching a class of "youngsters," the progeny of the working class. After the visitor had listened to the recitations for some time, he remarked to the teacher, "How do you account for the neatness and cleanliness of these children?" "Oh, I insist upon it," was the reply. "The Board of Education does not anticipate all the desiderata, but I make them come clean and make it a part of the course;" then rising and tapping on the table, she said, "Prepare for the sixth exercise." All the children stood up. "One," said the teacher, whereupon each pupil took out a clean cloth handkerchief. "Two," counted the teacher, and with one concerted blast every pupil blew his or her nose in clarion notes. "Three," came again after a few seconds, and the handkerchiefs were replaced. At "four" the student body sank back to their seats without even smiling, or without having "cracked a smile." You could search the world over and not find a prototype. It goes without saying that the teacher was a wit and wag, but the lesson of handkerchiefs and their use was inculcated.

Education is a part of the scheme to make all Americans equal. A more splendid *system* it is impossible to conceive. Every possible facility is afforded the poorest family to educate their children. Public schools loom up everywhere, and are increased as rapidly as the children, so there is no excuse for ignorance. The schools are graded, and there is no expense or fee. The parents pay a tax, a small sum, those who have no children being taxed as well as those who have many. There are schools to train boys to any trade; normal free schools to make teachers; night schools for working boys; commercial schools to educate clerks; ship schools to train sailors and engineers. Then come the great universities, in part free, with all the splendid paraphernalia, some being State institutions and others memorials of dead millionaires. Then there are the great technical schools, as well as universities (where one can study Chinese, if desired). There are schools of art, law, medicine, nature, forestry, sculpture; schools to teach one how to write, how to dress, how to eat, and how to keep well; schools to teach one how to write advertisements, to cultivate the memory, to grow strong; schools for shooting, boxing, fencing; schools for nurses and cooks; summer schools; winter schools.

And yet the American is not profoundly educated. He has too much within his reach. I have been distinctly surprised at crude specimens I have met who were graduates of great universities. The well-educated Englishman, German, and American are different things. The American is far behind in the best sense, which I am inclined to think is due to the teachers. Anyone can get through a normal school and become a teacher who can pass the examination, and I have seen some singular instances. If all the teachers were obliged to pass examinations in culture, refinement, and the art of *conveying* knowledge, there would be a falling of pedagogic heads. The free and over education of the poor places them at once above their parents. They are free, and the daughter of a ditch laborer, whose wife is a floor scrubber, upon being educated is ashamed of her parents, learns to play the piano, apes the rich, and is at least unhappy.

The result is, there remains no peasant class. The effect of education on the country boy is to make him despise the farm and go to the city, to become a clerk and ape the fashions of the wealthy at six or eight dollars a week. He has been educated up to the standard of his "boss" and to be his equal. The over-education of the poor is a heartless thing. The women vie with the men, and as a result women graduates, taking positions at half the price that men demand, crowd them out of the fields of skilled labor, whereas the man, not crowded out, should, normally, marry the girl. In power, strength, and progress the American nation stands first in the world, and all this may be due to splendid educational facilities. But this is not everything. There result strife, unhappiness, envy, and a craze for riches. I do not think the Americans as a race are as happy as the Chinese. Religious denominations try to have their own schools, so that children shall not be captured by other denominations. Thus the Roman Catholics have parochial schools, under priests and sisters, and colleges of various grades. They oppose the use of the Bible in the public school, and in some States their influence has helped to suppress its use. The Quakers, with a following of only eighty thousand, have colleges and schools. The Methodists have universities, as have the Presbyterians, Episcopalians, and others. All denominations have institutions of learning. These schools are in the hands of clergymen, and are often endowed or supported by wealthy members of the denomination.

A remarkable feature of American life is the college of correspondence. A man or firm advertises to teach by correspondence at so much a month. Many branches are taught, and if the student is in earnest a certain amount of information can thus be accumulated. Among the people I have met I have observed a lack of what I term full, broad education, producing a well-rounded mind, which is rare except among the class that stands first in America—the refined, cultured, educated man of an old family, who is the product of many generations. The curriculum of the high school in America would in China seem sufficient to equip a student for any position in diplomatic life; but I have found that a majority of graduates become clerks in a grocery or in other shops, car conductors, or commercial travelers, where Latin, Greek, and other higher studies are absolutely useless. The brightest educational sign I see in America is the attention given to manual training. In schools boys are taught some trade or are allowed to experiment in the trades in order to find out their natural bent, so that the boy can be educated with his future in view. As a result of education, women appear in nearly every field except that of manual labor on farms, which is performed in America only by alien women.

The richest men in America to-day, the multi-millionaires, are not the product of the universities, but mainly of the public schools. Carnegie, Rockefeller, Schwab, men of the great steel combine, the oil magnates, the great railway magnates, the great mine owners, were all men of limited education at the beginning. Among great merchants, however, the university man is found, and among the Harvard and Yale graduates, for example, may be found some of America's most distinguished men. But Lincoln, the martyred President, had the most limited education, and among public men the majority have been the product of the public school, which suggests that great men are natural geniuses, who will attain prominence despite the lack of education. The best-educated men in America to my mind are the graduates of West Point and Annapolis, the military and naval academies. These two institutions are extremely rigorous, and are open to the most humble citizens. They so transform men in four years that people would hardly recognize them. The result is a highly educated, refined, cultivated, practical man, with a high sense of honor and patriotism. If America would have a school of this kind in every State there would be no limit to her power in two decades.

Despite education, the great mass of the people are superficial; they have a smattering of this and that. An employer of several thousand men told the Superintendent of Education of the District of Columbia that he had selected the brightest boy graduate of a high school for a position which required only a knowledge of simple arithmetic. The graduate proved to be totally unfit for the position and was discharged. Later he became the driver of a team of horses. America abounds in thousands of educational institutions, yet there is not one so well endowed that it can say to the world we wish no more money. It is singular that some multi-millionaire does not grasp this opportunity to donate one hundred millions to a great national school or university, to be placed at Washington, where the buildings would all be lessons in architecture of marble after the plans of a world's fair. Instead they leave a few thousands here and a few there. Carnegie, the leading millionaire, gives libraries to cities all over the States, each of which bears the name of the giver. The object is too obvious, and is cheap in conception. In San Francisco some years ago a citizen tried the same experiment. He proposed to give the city a large number of fountains. When they were finished *each* one was seen to be surmounted by his own statue. A few were put up, how many I do not recall, but one night some citizens waited on a statue, fastened a rope to its neck, and hauled it down. So peculiar are the Americans that I believe if Mr. Carnegie should place his name on ten thousand libraries, with the object of attaining undying fame, the people, by a concerted effort, would forget all about him in a few decades. Such an attempt does not appeal to any side of the American character. I have known the best Americans, but Mr. Carnegie has not known the best of his own countrymen or he would not attempt to perpetuate his memory in this way.

CHAPTER XV
THE DARK SIDE OF REPUBLICANISM

THE QUESTIONS I KNOW YOU WILL WISH answered are, Whether this stupendous aggregation of States is a success? Does it possess advantages beyond those of the Chinese Empire? Does it fulfill the expectations of its own people? Frankly, I do not consider myself competent to answer. I have studied America and the Americans for many years during my visits to this country and Europe, and while I have seen many accounts of the country, written after several months of observation, I believe that no just estimate of the republican form of government can be formed after such experience. My private impression, however, is that the republic falls far short of what the men in Washington's time expected, and it is also my private opinion that it has not so many advantages as a government like that of England.

It is too splendid an organization to be lightly denounced. The idea of the equality of men is noble, and I would not wish to be arraigned among its critics. There is too much good to offset the bad. I have been attempting to amuse you by analyzing the Americans, pointing out their frailties as well as their good qualities. I tell you what I see as I run, always, I hope, remembering what is good in this spontaneous and open-hearted people. The characteristic claim of the people is that the Government offers freedom to its citizens; yet every man is quite as free in China if he behaves himself, and he can rise if he possesses brains.

Any native-born citizen in the United States may become the head of the nation has he the courage of his convictions, the many accomplishments which equip the great leader, and should the hour and the man meet opportunity. This is the one prize which distinguishes America from England. The latter in other respects offers exactly as much freedom with half the wear and tear; in fact, to me the freedom of America is one of her disadvantages. Everyone knows, and the American best of all, that all men are *not equal*, never were and never can be. Yet this false doctrine is their standard, and they swear by it, though some will explain that what is meant is political freedom. Freedom accounts for the gross impertinence of the ignorant and lower classes, the laughable assumptions of servants, and the illogical pretenses of the *nouveau riche*, which make America impossible to some people. Cultivated Americans are as thoroughly aristocratic as the nobility of England. There are the same classes here as there. A grocer becomes rich and retires or dies; his children refuse to associate with the families of other grocers; in a word, the Americans have the aristocratic feeling, but they have no peasant class; the latter would be, in their own estimation, as good as anyone. One class, the lower and poorer, is arraigned against the upper and richer, and the gap is growing daily.

But this would not prove that the republic is a failure. What then? It is, in the opinion of many of its clergymen, a great moral failure. No nation in history has lasted many centuries after having developed the "symptoms" now shown in the United States. I quote their own press, "the States are morally rotten," and you have but to turn to these organs and the magazines of the past decade, which make a feature of holding up the shortcomings of cities and millionaires, to read the details of the tragedy. Thieves—grafters—have seized upon the vitals of the country. St. Louis, Philadelphia, New York, Chicago, great representative cities—what is their history? The story of dishonesty among officials, of bribery, stealing, and every possible crime that a man can devise to wring money from the people. This is no secret. It has all been exposed by the friends of morality. City governments are overthrown, the rascals are turned out, but in a few months the new officers are caught devising some new "grafting" operation.

I have it from a prominent official that there is not an honest State or city administration in America. What can a nation say when for years it has known that a large and influential lobby has been maintained to influence statesmen, a lobby comprising a corps of "persuaders" in the pay of business men? How do they influence them? The great fights waged to defeat certain measures are well known, and it is known that money was used. Certain congressmen have been notoriously receptive. I have seen the following story in print in many forms. I took the trouble to ask a well-known man if it was possible that it could be founded on fact; his reply was, "Certainly it is a fact." A briber entered the private room of a congressman. "Mr. ——, to come right to the point, I want the —— bill to pass, and I will give you five hundred dollars for the vote and your interest." The congressman rose to his feet, purple with rage. "You dare to offer me this insulting bribe? You infernal scoundrel, I will throw you out." "Well, suppose we make it one thousand," said the imperturbable visitor. "Well," replied the congressman, cooling down, "that is a little better put. We will talk it over."

The American Government had been attempting, since 1859, to build a canal across the Isthmus. I believe surveys were made earlier than that, but bribery and corruption and "graft" enabled the friends of transcontinental railroads to stop the canals. It would be a disadvantage to the railroads to have a canal across the Isthmus. So in some mysterious way the canal, which the people wished, has not been built, and will not be until the people rise and demand it. Corruption has stood on the Isthmus with a flaming sword and struck down every attempt to build the canal. The morality of the people is low. Divorce is rampant, the daily journals are filled with accounts of divorces, and daily lists of crimes are printed that would seem impossible to a nation that can raise millions to send to China to convert the "heathen." If they would only divert these Chinese missionaries from China to their own heathen and grafters, but they will not. The peculiar freedom of the country, which is nothing less than the most atrocious license, tends to drag it down.

The papers have absolutely no check on their freedom. Men and women are attacked by them, ruined, held up to scorn and ridicule, and the victim has no recourse but to shoot the editor and thus embroil himself. That it is a crime to ridicule a man and make him the butt of a nation or the world seems never to occur to these men. Certain statesmen have been so lampooned by the "hired" libelers that they have been ruined. The press hires a class of men, called cartoonists, usually ill-bred fellows of no standing, yet clever, in their business, whose duty it is to hold up public men to ridicule in every possible way and make them infamous before the people. This is called the freedom of the press, and its attitude, or the sensational part of it, in presenting crime in an alluring manner, is having its effect upon the youth of the country. Young girls and boys become familiar with every feature of bestial crime through the "yellow journals," so called, and that the republic will reap sorely from this sowing I venture to prophesy.

I asked one of the great insurance men why it was that great financial institutions took so strong an interest in politics. He laughed, and said, "If I am not mistaken, not long since your country repudiated its Government bonds, and they are not negotiable to any great extent among your people." Hearing this I assumed the American attitude and "sawed wood." "We take an interest in politics," he continued, "to offset the professional blackmailer and thief. Now in the case of your repudiation I understand all about it. The Chinese Government was in straits, and suddenly some seemingly patriotic citizen started a petition, stating to the Government that the subscribers offered their Government securities to the Government as a gift. By no means all the bondholders signed, but enough, I understand, to have justified your Government in repudiating the bonds—'at the request of the people'—thus destroying the national credit at home and abroad. Now in America that would be called 'graft.' The act would be done by a few grafters in the hope of reward, or by some unscrupulous statesmen to save the Government from bankruptcy during their term of office. I conceive this to be what was done in China. If we do not keep eternal watch we shall be bled every day. It is done in this way: a grafter becomes an assemblyman, and with others lays a plan of graft. It is to get up a bill, so offensive to our corporation that it would mean ruin if passed. The grafter has no idea that it will pass, but it is made much of, and of course reaches our ears, and the question is how to stop it. We are finally told that we had better see Mr. ——, in our own city. He is accordingly looked up and found to be a cheap and ignorant politician, who, if there are no witnesses, tells our agent plainly that it can be stopped for ten thousand dollars. Perhaps we beat him down to eight thousand, but we pay it. Hundreds of firms have been blackmailed in this way. Now we keep an agent in the State Capitol to attend to our interests, and we take an interest in politics to head off the election of professional grafters."

One of the most serious things in this phase of national immorality is showing itself in what are termed "lynchings;" that is, a negro commits a crime against a white woman, and instead of permitting the law to run its course, the people rise, seized with a savage craze for revenge, batter in the jails, take the criminal, and burn him at the stake. This burning is sometimes attended by thousands, who display the most remarkable *abandon* and savagery. Some African chiefs have sacrificed more people at one time, but no savage has ever displayed greater bestiality, gloated over his victim with more real satisfaction, than these free Americans in numerous instances when shouting and yelling about the burning body of some unfortunate whose crime has aroused their ferocity to the point of madness.

Not one but many clergymen have denounced this. They compare it to the most brutal acts of savagery, and we have the picture of a country posing as civilized, with the temerity to point out the sins of others, giving themselves over to orgies that would disgrace the lowest of races. I have it from the lips of a clergyman that during the past twelve years over twenty-five hundred men have been lynched in the United States. In a single year two hundred and forty men were killed by mobs in this way, many being burned at the stake. If any excuse is offered, it is said that most of these were negroes, and the crime was rape, and the victims white women; but of the number mentioned only forty-six were charged with this crime and but two-thirds were black. Many confessed as the torch was applied, many died protesting their innocence, and in no case was the offense legally proved. This lynching seems to be a mania with the people. It began with the attack of negroes on white women. The repetition of similar cases so enraged the whites that they have become mad upon the subject. The feeling is well illustrated by the remark of a Southerner to me. "If a woman of my family was attacked by a negro I must be his executioner. I could not wait for the law." This man told me that no lynching would ever have taken place had it not been for the uncertainty of the law. Men who were known to be guilty of the grossest of crimes had been virtually protected by the law, and their cases dragged along at great expense to the State, this occurring so many times that the patience of the people became exhausted. This man forgot that the law was instigated for the purpose of justice.

The negro is an issue in America and a cause of much crime, a vengeance on the people who held them as slaves. The negro has increased so rapidly that in forty years he has doubled in number, there now being over nine millions in the country. At the present rate there will be twenty-five millions in 1930—a black menace to the white American.

The negro is a factor in the national unrest. They outnumber the whites in some localities, and hence vote themselves many offices, while the few whites pay eighty or eighty-five per cent of the taxes and the negroes supply from eighty to ninety per cent of the criminals. While this is going on in the South and the whites are rising and preparing to disfranchise the blacks in many States, the people of Boston and Cambridge are discussing the propriety of the whites and blacks marrying to settle the question of social equality. Such proposals I have read. Reprinted in the South, they added fuel to the flame.

Another element of distress in America is the attitude of labor, the policy of the Government of letting in the lowest of the low from every nation except the Chinese, against whom the only charge has been that they are too industrious and thus a menace to the whites. The swarms of people from the low and criminal classes of Europe have enabled the anarchists to obtain such a foothold that in this free country the President of the United States is almost as closely guarded as the Emperor of Russia. The White House is surrounded and guarded by detectives of various kinds. The secret-service department is equal in its equipment to that of many European nations, and millions are spent in watching criminals and putting down their strikes and riots. The doctrine of freedom to all appeals so well to the ignorant laborer that he has decided to control the entire situation, and to this end labor is divided into "unions," and in many sections business has been ruined.

The demands of these ignorant men are so preposterous that they can scarcely be credited. The merchant no longer owns his business or directs it. The laborer tells him what to pay, how to pay it, when and how long the hours shall be—in fact, undertakes to usurp entire control. If the owner protests, the laborers all stop work, strike, appoint guards, who attack, kill, or intimidate anyone who attempts to take their place. In this way it is said that one billion dollars have been lost in the last few years. Contracts have been broken, men ruined, localities and cities placed in the greatest jeopardy, and hundreds of lives lost. Every branch of trade has its "union," and in so many cases have the laborers been successful that a national panic comes almost in sight. Never was there a more farcical illustration of freedom. Irrational, ignorant Irishmen, who had not the mental capacity to earn more than a dollar a day, dictated to merchant princes and millionaire contractors. In New York it was proved that the leaders of the strikers sold out to employers, and accepted bribes to call off strikes.

The question before the American people is, Has an American citizen the right to conduct his own business to suit himself and employ whom he wishes? Has the laborer the right to work for whom and what rate he pleases? The imported socialists, anarchists, and their converts among Americans say no, and it will require but little to precipitate a bloody war, when labor, led by red-handed murderers, will enact in New York and all over the United States the horrors of the French Commune.

The republic for a great and enlightened country has too many criminals. I am told by a prohibition clergyman that the curse of drink and license has its fangs in the heart of the land. He tells me that the Americans pay yearly $1,172,000,000 for their alcoholic drink; for bread, $600,000,000; for tobacco, $625,000,000; for education, $197,000,000; for ministers' salaries, $14,000,000. It has been found that the downfall of eighty-one per cent of criminals is traceable to drink. He said: "Our republic is a failure morally, as we have 2,550,000 drunkards and people addicted to drink. We have 600,000 prostitutes, and many more doubtless that are not known, and in nine cases out of ten their downfall can be traced to drink."

I listen to this side of the story, and then I see wonderful philanthropy, institutions for the prevention of crime, good men at work according to their light, millions employed to educate the young, thousands of churches and societies to aid man in making man better. When I listen to these men, and see tens of thousands of Christian men and women living pure lives, building up vast cities, great monuments for the future, I feel that I can not judge the Americans. They perhaps expect too much from their freedom and their republican ideas. I shall never be a republican. I believe that we all have all the freedom we deserve. It is well to remember that man is an animal. After all his polish and refinement, he has animal tastes and desires, and if he makes laws that are in direct opposition to the indulgence which his animal nature suggests, he certainly must have some method of enforcing the laws. Like all animals, some men are easily influenced and others not, and the human animal has not made progress so far but that he needs watching in order to make him conform to what he has decided or elected to call right.

You will expect me to compare the American to the Chinaman, but it is impossible. Some things which we look upon as right, the American considers grievous sins. The point of view is entirely at variance, but I have boundless faith in the brilliant and good men and women I have met in America. I say this despite my other impressions, which also hold.

The great political scheme of the people is poorly devised and crude. It is so arranged that in some States governors are elected every year or two and other officers every year, representatives of the people in Congress every two years, senators every six, Presidents every four years. Thus the country is constantly in a whirl, and as soon as the rancor of one national election is over begins the scheming for another. The people have really little to do with the selection of a President. A small band of rich and influential schemers generally have the entire plan or "slate" laid out. A plan, natural in appearance, is *arranged* for the public, and at the right time the slated program is sprung. Senators should be elected by the people, congressmen should be elected for a longer period, and Presidents should have twice the terms they do. But it is easy to suggest, and I confess that my suggestions are those of many American people themselves which I hear reformers cry abroad.

The vital trouble with America to-day is that she can not assimilate the 600,000 debased, ignorant, poverty-stricken foreigners who are coming in every year. They keep out the one peaceful nation. They exclude the Chinese and take to the national heart the Jew, the Socialist, the Italian, the Roumanian and others who constitute a nation of unrest. What America needs is the "rest cure" that you hear so much about here. She should close her seaports to these aliens for ten years, allow the people here to assimilate; but they can not do it. The foreign transportation lines under foreign flags are in the business to load up America with the dregs of Europe. I know of one family of Jews, four brothers, who wished to come to America, but found that they would have to show that they were not paupers. They mustered about one thousand dollars. One came over, and sent back the money by draft. The second brought it back as his fortune, then immediately sent it back for another brother to bring over, and so on until they all arrived, each proving that he was not a pauper. Yet these same brothers, each with several children, became an expense to the Government before they were earners. The children were sent to industrial homes, and later entered the sweat-shops. In America there is not a Chinaman to-day in a work-house, or a pauper[1] at the expense of the Government; yet the Chinese are not wanted here.

CHAPTER XVI
SPORTS AND PASTIMES

I HAD NOT BEEN IN WASHINGTON A MONTH before I received invitations to a "country club golf" tournament, to a "rowing club," to a "pink tea," to a "polo game," to a private "boxing" bout between two light-weight professionals, given in Senator ——'s stable, to a private "cock-fight" by the brother of ——'s wife, to a gun club "shoot," not to speak of invitations to several "poker games." From this you may infer that Americans are fond of sport. The official sport—that is, the game I heard of most among Government officials, senators, and others—was "poker," and the sums played for at times I am assured are beyond belief. There are rules and etiquette for poker, and one of the most distinguished of American diplomatists of a past generation, General Schenck, emulated the Marquis of Queensberry in boxing by writing a book on the national game, that has all the charm claimed for it. It is seductive, and doubtless has had its influence on the people who employ the "bluff" in diplomacy, war, business, or poker, with equal tact and cleverness.

Middle-class Americans are fond of sport in every way, but the aristocrats lack sporting spontaneity; they like it, or pretend to like it, because it is the fashion, and they take up one sport after another as it becomes the fad. That this

---

1 This is doubtful.—Editor

is true can be shown by comparing the Englishman and the American of the fashionable class. The Englishman is fond of sport because it is in his blood; he does not like golf to-day and swimming to-morrow, but he likes them all, and always has done so. He would never give up cricket, golf, or any of his games because they go out of fashion; he does not allow them to go out of fashion; but with the American it is different.

Hence I assume that the average American of the better class is not imbued with the sporting spirit. He wears it like an ill-fitting coat. I find a singular feature among the Americans in connection with their sports. Thus if something is known and recognized as sport, people take to it with avidity, but if the same thing is called labor or exercise, it is considered hard work, shirked and avoided. This is very cleverly illustrated by Mark Twain in one of his books, where a boy makes his companions believe that white-washing a fence is sport, and so relieves himself from an arduous duty by pretending to share the great privilege with them.

No one would think of walking steadily for six days, yet once this became sport; dozens of men undertook it, and long walks became a fad. If a man committed a crime and should be sentenced to play the modern American game of football every day for thirty days as a punishment, there are some who might prefer a death sentence and so avoid a lingering end; but under the title of "sport" all young men play it, and a number are maimed and killed yearly.

Sport is in the blood of the common people. Children begin with tops, marbles, and kites, yet never appreciate our skill with either. I amazed a boy on the outskirts of Washington one day by asking him why he did not *irritate* his kite and make it go through various evolutions. He had never heard of doing that, and when I took the string and began to jerk it, and finally made the kite plunge downward or swing in circles, and always restored it by suddenly slacking off the cord, he was astonished and delighted. The national game is baseball, a very clever game. It is nothing to see thousands at a game, each person having paid twenty-five or fifty cents for the privilege. In summer this game, played by experts, becomes a most profitable business. Rarely is anyone hurt but the judge or umpire, who is at times hissed by the audience and mobbed, and at others beaten by either side for unfair decisions; but this is rare.

Football is dangerous, but is even more popular than the other. You might imagine by the name that the ball is kicked. On the contrary the real action of the game consists in running down, tripping up, smashing into, and falling on whomever has the ball. As a consequence, men wear a soft armor. There are fashions in sports which demonstrate the ephemeral quality of the American love for sport. A while ago "wheeling" was popular, and everybody wheeled.

Books were printed on the etiquette of the sport; roads were built for it and improved; but suddenly the working class took it up and fashion dropped it. Then came golf, imported from Scotland. With this fad millions of dollars were expended in country clubs and greens all over the United States, as acres of land were necessary. People seized upon this with a fierceness that warmed the hearts of dealers in balls and clubs. The men who edited wheel magazines now changed them to "golf monthlies." This sport began to wane as the novelty wore off, until golf is now played by comparatively few experts and lovers.

Society introduced the automobile, and we have the same thing— more magazines, the spending of millions, the building of the *garage*, and the appearance of the *chaufeur* or driver. Then came the etiquette of the auto—a German navy cap, rubber coat, and Chinese goggles. This peculiar uniform is of course only to be worn when racing, but you see the American going out for a slow ride solemnly attired in rubber coat and goggles. The moment the auto comes within reach of the poor man it will be given up; but it is now the fad and a most expensive one, the best machines costing ten thousand dollars or more, and I have seen races where the speed exceeded a mile a minute.

All sports have their ethics and rules and their correct costuming. Baseball men are in uniform, generally white, with various-colored stockings. The golfer wears a red coat and has a servant or valet, who carries his bag of clubs, de-signed for every possible expediency. To hear a group of golfers discuss the merits of these tools is one of the extraordinary experiences one has in America. I have been made fairly "giddy," as the Englishmen say, by this anemic conver-sation at country clubs. The "high-ball" was the saving clause—a remarkable invention this. Have I explained it? You take a very tall glass, made for the purpose, and into it pour the contents of a small cut-glass bottle or decanter of whisky, which must be Scotch, tasting of smoke. On this you pour seltzer or soda-water, filling up the glass, and if you take enough you are "high" and feel like a rolling ball. It is the thing to take a "high-ball" after every nine holes in golf. Then after the game you bathe, and sit and drink as many as your skin will hold. I got this from a professional golf-teacher in charge of the —— links, and hence it is official.

The avidity with which the Americans seize upon a sport and the sudden-ness with which they drop it, illustrating what I have said about the lack of a na-tional sporting taste, is well shown by the coming of a game called "ping pong," a parlor tennis, with our battledores for rackets. What great mind invented this game, or where it came from, no one seems to know, but as a wag remarked, "When in doubt lay it to China." Some suppose it is Chinese, the name suggest-ing it. So extraordinary was the early demand for it that it appeared as though everybody in America was determined to own and play ping pong. The dealers could not produce it fast enough. Factories were established all over the country, and the tools were ground out by the ten thousands. Books were written on the ethics of the game; experts came to the front; ping pong weeklies and monthlies were founded, to dumfound the masses, and the very air vibrated with the "ping" and the "pong."

The old and young, rich and poor, feeble and herculean, all played it. Doctors advised it, children cried for it, and a fashionable journal devised the correct ping-pong costume for players. Great matches were played between the experts of various sections, and this sport, a game really for small children, after the fashion of battledore and shuttlecock, ran its course among young and old. Pictures of adult ping-pong champions were blazoned in the public print; even churchmen took it up. Public gardens had special ping-pong tables to relieve the stress. At last the people seized upon ping pong, and it became common. Then it was dropped like a dead fish. If some cyclonic disturbance had swept all the ping-pong balls into space, the disappearance could not have been more complete. Ping pong was put out of fashion. All this to the alien suggests something, a want of balance, a "youngness" perhaps.

At the present time the old game of croquet is being revived under another name, and tennis is the vogue among many. Among the fashionable and wealthy men polo is the vogue, but among a few everything goes by fads for a few years. Everyone will rush to see or play some game; but this interest soon dies out, and something new starts up. Such games as baseball and football, tennis and polo are, in a sense, in a class by themselves, but among the pastimes of the people a wide vogue belongs to fishing, and shooting wild fowl and large game. The former is universal, and the Americans are the most skilled anglers with artificial lures in the world, due to the abundance of game-fish, trout, and others, and the perfect Government care exercised to perfect the supply.

As an illustration, each State considers hunting and fishing a valuable asset to attract those who will come and spend money. I was told by a Government official that the State of Maine reckoned its game at five million dollars per annum, which means that the sport is so good that sportsmen spend that amount there every year; but I fancy the amount is overestimated. The Government has perfect fish hatcheries, constantly supplying young fish to streams, while the business in anglers' supplies is immense. There are thousands of duck-shooting clubs in the United States. Men, or a body of men, rent or buy marshes, and keep the poor man out. Rich men acquire hundreds of acres, and make preserves. Possibly the sport of hunting wild fowl is the most characteristic of American sports. This also has its etiquette, its costumes, its club-houses, and its poker and high-balls. I know of one such club in which almost all the members are millionaires. A humorous paper stated that they used "gold shot."

As a nation the Americans are fond of athletics, which are taught in the schools. There are splendid gymnasiums, and boys and girls are trained in athletic exercises. Athletics are all in vogue. It is fashionable to be a good "fencer." All the young dance. I believe the Americans stand high as a nation in all-around athletics; at least they are far ahead of China in this respect.

I have reserved for mention last the most popular fashion of the people in sport, which is prize-fighting. Here again you see a strange contradiction. The people are preeminently religious, and prize-fighting and football are the sports of brutes; yet the two are most popular. No public event attracts more attention in America than a gladiatorial fight to the finish between the champion and some aspirant. For months the papers are filled with it, and on the day of the event the streets are thronged with people crowding about the billboards to receive the news. No national event, save the killing of a President, attracted more universal attention than the beating of Sullivan by Corbett and the beating of Corbett by Fitzsimmons, and "Fitz" in turn by Jeffries. I might add that I joined with the Americans in this, as the modern prize-fighter is a fine animal. If all boys were taught to believe that their fists are their natural weapons, there would be fewer murders and sudden deaths in America. I have seen several of these prize-fights and many private bouts, all with gloves. They are governed by rules. Such a combat is by no means as dangerous as football, where the obvious intention seems to be to break ribs and crush the opponent.

Rowing is much indulged in, and yachting is a great national maritime sport, in which the Americans lead and challenge the world. In no sport is the wealth of the nation so well shown. Every seaside town has its yacht or boat club, and in this the interest is perpetual. Even in winter the yacht is rigged into an "ice-boat." I have often wondered that fashionable people do not take up the romantic sport of falconry, as they have the birds and every facility. I suggested this to a lady, who replied, "Ah, that is too barbaric for us." "More barbaric than cock-fighting?" I asked, knowing that her brother owned the finest game-cocks in the District of Columbia. Among the Americans there is a distinct love for fair play, and such sports as "bull-baiting," "bull-fights," "dog-fights," and "cock-fights" have never attained any degree of popularity. There are spasmodic instances of such indulgences, but in no sense can they be included, as in England and Spain, among the national sports, which leads me to the conclusion that, aside from the many peculiarities, as taking up and dropping sports, America, all in all, is the greatest sporting nation of the world. It leads in fist-fighting, rifle-shooting, in skillful angling, in yachting, in rowing, in running, in six-day walking, in auto-racing, in trotting and running horses, and in trap-shooting, and if its champions in all fields could be lined up it would make a surprising showing. I am free to confess and quite agree with a vivacious young woman who at the country club told me that it was very nice of me to uphold my country, but that we were "not in it" with American sports.

The Presidents are often sportsmen. President Cleveland and President Harrison both have been famous, the former as a fisherman, the latter as well as the former as a duck-shooter. President McKinley has no taste for sport, but the Vice-President is a promoter of sport of each and every kind. He is at home in polo or hurdle racing, with the rifle or revolver. This calls to mind the national weapon—the revolver. Nine-tenths of all the shooting is done with this weapon, that is carried in a special pocket on the hips, and I venture to say that a pair of "trousers" was never made without the pistol pocket. Even the clergymen have one. I asked an Episcopal clergyman why he had a pistol pocket. He replied that he carried his prayer-book there. The Southern people use a long curved knife, called a bowie, after its inventor. Many people have been cut by this weapon. The negro, for some strange reason, carries a razor, and in a fight "whips out" this awful weapon and slashes his enemy. I have asked many negroes to explain this habit or selection. One replied that it was "none of my d—— business." Nearly all the others said they did not know why they carried it.

CHAPTER XVII
THE CHINAMAN IN AMERICA

THE AVERAGE IRISHMAN WHOM ONE MEETS IN AMERICA, and he is legion, is a very different person from the polished gentleman I have met in Belfast, Dublin, and other cities in Ireland; but I never heard that the American Irishman, the product of an ignorant peasantry crowded out of Ireland, had been accepted as a type of the race. Peculiar discrimination is made in America against the Chinese. Our lower classes, "coolies" from the Cantonese districts, have flocked to America. Americans "lump" all Chinese under this head, and can not conceive that in China there are cultivated men, just as there are cultivated men in Ireland, the antipodes of the grotesque Irish types seen in America.

I believe there are seventy-five or eighty thousand Chinamen in America. They do not assimilate with the Americans. Many are common laborers, laundrymen, and small merchants. In New York, Chicago, San Francisco, and other cities there are large settlements of them. In San Francisco many have acquired wealth. The Chinese quarter is to all intents and purposes a

Chinese city. None of these people, or very few, are Americanized in the sense of taking an active part in the government; Americans do not permit it. I was told that the Chinese were among the best citizens, the percentage of criminals being very small. They are honest, frugal, and industrious—too industrious, in fact, and for this very reason the ban has been placed upon them. Red-handed members of the Italian Mafia—a society of murderers— the most ignorant class in Ireland, Wales, and England, the scum of Russia, and the human dregs of Europe generally are welcome, but the clean, hard-working Chinaman is excluded.

Millions are spent yearly in keeping him out after he had been invited to come. He built many American railroads; he opened the door between the Atlantic and the Pacific; he worked in the mines; he did work that no one else would or could do, and when it was completed the American laborer, the product of this scum of all nations, demanded that the Chinaman be "thrown out" and kept out. America listened to the blatant demagogues, the "sand-lot orators," and excluded the Chinese. To-day it is almost impossible for a Chinese gentleman to send his son to America to travel or study. He will not be distinguished from laundryman "John," and is thrown back in the teeth of his countrymen; meanwhile China continues to be raided by American missionaries. The insult is rarely resented. In the treaty ratified by the United States Senate in 1868 we read:

"The United States of America and the Empire of China cordially recognize the inherent right of man to change his home and allegiance, and also the mutual advantage of the free immigration and emigration of their citizens and subjects respectively from the one country to the other for purposes of curiosity, of trade or as permanent residents."

Again we read, in the treaty ratified under the Hayes administration, that the Government of the United States, "if its labor interests are threatened by the incoming Chinese, may regulate or limit such coming, but may not *absolutely prohibit* it." The United States Government has disregarded its solemn treaty obligations. Not only this, our people, previous to the Exclusion Act, were killed, stoned, and attacked time and again by "hoodlums." The life of a Chinaman was not safe. The labor class in America, the lowest and almost always a foreign class, wished to get rid of the Chinaman so that they could raise the price of labor and secure all the work. China had reason to go to war with America for her treatment of her people and for failure to observe a treaty. The Scott Exclusion Act was a gratuitous insult. I hope our people will continue to retaliate by refusing to buy anything from the Americans or sell anything to them. Let us deal with our friends.

Then came the Geary Bill, which was an outrage, our people being thrown into jail for a year and then sent back. I might quote some of the charges made against our people. Mr. Geary, I understand, is an Irish ex-congressman from the State of California, who, while in Congress, was the mouthpiece of the worst anti-Chinese faction ever organized in America. He was ultimately defeated, much to the delight of New England and many other people in the East. Mr. Geary's chief complaint against the Chinese was that they work too cheaply, are too industrious, and do not eat as much as an American. He obtained his information from Consul Bedloe, of Amoy. He says the average earnings of the Chinese adult employed as mechanic or laborer (in China) is five dollars per month, and states that this is ten per cent above the average wages prevailing throughout China.

The wages paid, according to his report, per month, to blacksmiths are $7.25; carpenters, $8.50; cabinet-makers, $9; glass-blowers, $9; plasterers, $6.25; plumbers, $6.25; machinists, $6; while other classes of skilled labor are paid from $7.25 to $9 per month, and common laborers receive $4 per month. In European houses the average wages paid to servants are from $5 to $6 a month, without board. Clothing costs per year from 75 cents to $1.50. Out of these incomes large families are maintained. He says: "The daily fare of an Amoy working man and its cost are about as follows: 1½ pounds of rice, 3 cents; 1 ounce of meat, 1 ounce of fish, 2 ounces of shell-fish, 1 cent; 1 pound of cabbage or other vegetable, 1 cent; fuel, salt, and oil, 1 cent; total, 6 cents.

"Here," said Mr. Geary, "is a condition deserving of attention by all friends of this country, and by all who believe in the protection of the working classes. Is it fair to subject our laborer to a competitor who can measure his wants by an expenditure of six cents a day, and who can live on an income not exceeding five dollars a month? What will become of the boasted civilization of our country if our toilers are compelled to compete with this class of labor, with more competitors available than twice the entire population of France, Germany, Austria, Belgium, Denmark, Switzerland, Italy, Netherlands, Portugal, and Spain?

"The Chinese laborer brings neither wife nor children, and his wants are limited to the immediate necessities of the individual, while the American is compelled to earn income sufficient to maintain the wife and babies. There can be but one end to this. If this immigration is permitted to continue, American labor must surely be reduced to the level of the Chinese competitor—the American's wants measured by his wants, the American's comforts be made no greater than the comforts of the Chinaman, and the American laborer, not having been educated to maintain himself according to this standard, must either meet his Chinese competitor on his own level, or else take up his pack and leave his native land. The entire trade of China, if we had it all, is not worth such a sacrifice."

Mr. Geary forgets that when Chinamen go to America they adapt themselves to prevailing conditions. Chinese cooks in the States to-day receive from $30 to $50 per month and board; Chinese laborers from $20 to $30, and some of them $2 per day. In China, where there is an enormous population, prices are lower, people are not wasteful, and the necessities of life do not cost so much. The Chinaman goes to America to obtain the benefit of *high* wages, not to *reduce* wages. I have never seen such poverty and wretchedness in China as I have seen in London, or such vice and poverty as can be seen in any large American city. Mr. Geary scorns the treaties between his country and China, and laughs at our commercial relations. He says, "There is nothing in the Chinese trade, or rather the loss of it, to alarm any American. We would be better off without any part or portion of it."

In answer to this I would suggest that China take him at his word, and I assure you that if every Chinaman could be recalled, if in six months or less we could take the eighty or one hundred thousand Chinamen out of the country, the region where they now live would be demoralized. The Chinese control the vegetable-garden business on the Pacific Coast; they virtually control the laundry business; and that the Americans want them, and want cheaper labor than they are getting from the Irish and Italians, is shown by the fact that they continue to patronize our people, and that in various lines Chinamen have the monopoly. Even when the "hoodlums" of San Francisco were fighting the Chinese, the American women did not withdraw their patronage, and while the men were off speaking on the sand-lots against employing our people their wives were buying vegetables from them.

Why? Because their hypocritical husbands and brothers refused to pay higher prices. America is suffering not for want of the cheapest labor, but for a laborer like the Chinese, and until they have him industries will languish. With American labor and American "union" prices it is impossible for the American farmer or rancher to make money. The vineyardist, the orange, lemon, olive, and other fruit raisers can not compete with Europe. Labor is kept up to such a high rate that the country is obliged to put on a high tariff to keep out foreign competition, and in so doing they "cut off the nose to spite the face." The common people are taxed by the rich. The salvation of industrial America is a cheap, but not degraded, labor. America desires house-servants at from $10 to $12 per month; this is all a mere servant is worth. She wants good cooks at $12 or $15 per month. She wants fruit-pickers at $10 to $12 per month and board. She wants vineyard men, hop-pickers, cherry, peach, apricot and berry pickers, and people to work in canneries at these prices. She wants gardeners, drivers, railroad laborers at lower rates, and, to quote an American, "wants them 'bad.'"

When in San Francisco I made a thorough investigation of the "house-servant" question, and learned that our people as cooks in private houses were receiving from $30 to $50 per month and board. A friend tells me there is continued protest against this. Housekeepers on the Pacific coast are complaining of the lack of "Chinese boys," and want more to come over so that prices shall go down. The American wants the Chinaman, but the American *foreign laborer*, the Irishman, the Italian, the Mexican, and others who dominate American politics, do not want him and will not have him. As a result of this bending to the alien vote the Americans find themselves in a most serious and laughable position in their relations to domestic labor.

I am not overstating the fact when I say that the "servant-girl" question is going to be a political issue in the future. The man may howl against the Chinese, but his wife will demand that "John" be admitted to relieve a situation that is becoming unbearable. As the Americans are all equal, there are no servants among them. The poor are as good as the "boss," and won't be called servants. You read in the papers, "A lady desires a position as cook in a small family, no children; wages, $35." "A young lady wishes a position to take care of children; salary, $30." "A saleslady wants position." "A lady (good scrubber) will go out by the day; $2." When you meet these "ladies," in nine cases out of ten they are Irish from the peasant class—untidy, insolent, often dissipated in the sense of drink. When they apply for a position they put the employer through a course of questions. Some want references from the last girl, I am told. Some want one thing, some another, and all must have time for pleasure. Few have the air of servants or inferiors, but are often offensive in appearance and manners. I have never been called "John" by the girls who came to the door where I called to pay a visit, but I could see that they all wished so to address me. In England, where classes are acknowledged and a servant is hired as a servant, and is one, an entirely different state of affairs holds. They are respectful, having been educated to be servants, know that they are servants, and as a result are cared for and treated as old retainers and pensioners of the family.

The whole story of exclusion is a blot upon the American national honor, and the most mystifying part of it is that intelligent people, the best people, are not a party to it. The railroads want the Chinese laborer. The great ranches of the West need him; people want cooks at $15 and $20 a month instead of $30 or $50. In a word, America is suffering for what she must have some time—cheap labor; yet the low elements force the issue. Congressmen are dominated by labor organizations on the Pacific slope, and there are hundreds of Dennis

Kearneys to-day where there was one a few years ago. To make the case more ex-asperating, the Americans, in their dire necessity, have imported swarms of low Mexicans to take the place of the Chinese on the railroads, against whom there seems to be no Irish hand raised. The Irish and Mexicans are of a piece. I know from inquiry everywhere that the country at large would welcome thousands of servants and field-workers in vineyards and orchards which can not be made to pay if worked by expensive labor.

The Americans try to keep us out, but they also try to convert those who get in. They have what they call Chinese missions, to which Chinamen go. To be converted? No. To learn the language? Yes. I am told by an American friend that here and in China over fifty thousand Chinese have embraced Christianity. On the Atlantic coast I am assured that eight hundred Chinamen are Chris-tians, and on the Pacific slope two thousand have embraced the faith of the Christians. There is a Christian Chinese evangelist working among our people in the West, Lum Foon, and I have met the pastor of a Pacific coast church who told me that nearly a third of his congregation were Chinamen, and he esteemed them highly. But the most conclusive evidence that the Americans are succeeding in their proselyting is that in one year a single denomination received as a donation from Chinamen $6,000. The Americans have a saying, "Money talks," which is much like one of our own.

On the other hand, a clergyman told me that it was discouraging work to some, so few Chinamen were "converted" compared to the great mass of them. The Chinese of California have sent $1,000 to Canton to build a Christian church, and the Chinese members of the Presbyterian Church of California sent $3,000 in one year for the same purpose. I am told that the Chinese Meth-odists of one church in California give yearly from $1,000 to $1,800 for the various purposes of the church. The Christians have captured some brilliant men, such as Sia Sek Ong, who is a Methodist; Chan Hon Fan, who ought to be in our army from what I hear; Rev. Tong Keet Hing, the Baptist, a noted Biblical scholar; Rev. Wong, of the Presbyterians; Rev. Ng Poon Chiv, famous as a Greek and Hebrew reader; Gee Gam and Rev. Le Tong Hay, Methodists; and there are many more, suggestive that our people are interested in Christianity, against the *moral* teachings of which no one could seriously object.

I dined some time ago with a merchants' club, and was much pleased at the eulogy I heard on the Chinese. A merchant said, "My firm deals largely with the Chinese and Japanese. When I make a trade with the Japanese I tie them up with a written contract, but I have always found that the word of a Chinese mer-chant was sufficient." This I found to be the universal feeling, and yet Americans exclude us at the bidding of "hoodlums," a term applied to the lowest class of young men on the Pacific coast. In the East he is a "tough" or "rough" or "rowdy." "Tough nut" and "hard nut" are also applied to such people, the Americans having numbers of terms like these, which may be called "nicknames," or false names. Thus a man who is noted for his dress is a "swell," a "dude," or a "sport."

The United States Government does not allow the Chinese to vote, yet tens of thousands of poor Americans, "white trash" in the South, ignorant negroes, low Irish and Italians who can not speak the tongue, are welcome and courted by both parties. It is difficult for me to overlook this insult on the part of America. There is a large settlement of Chinese in New York, but they are as isolated as if they were in China. In San Francisco there is the largest settlement, and many fine merchants live there, and also in Los Angeles.

In the latter city —— told me that the best of feeling existed between the Chinese and Americans; and at the American Festival of the Rose the Chinese joined in the procession. The dragon was brought out, and all the Chinese merchants appeared; but these gentlemen are never consulted by the Americans, never allowed to vote or take any interest in the growth of the city, and —— informed me that none of them had ever been asked to join a board of trade. It is the same everywhere; the only advances the Americans make is to try and "convert" us to their various religious denominations. While the Chinese are not allowed to vote or to have any part in the affairs of government, they are taxed. "Taxation without representation" was the cause of the war of the American Revolution, but that is another matter.

Yet our people have ways of influencing the whites with the "dollar," for which some officials will do anything, and, I regret to say, all Chinamen are not above bribing Americans. I have heard that the Chinese of San Francisco for years were blackmailed by Americans, and obliged to raise money to fight bills in the Legislature. In 1892 the Six Companies raised $200,000 to defeat the "Geary Bill." The Chinese merchants have some influence. Out of the 110,000 Chinamen in America hardly ten per cent obeyed the iniquitous law and registered. The Chinese societies contracted to defend all who refused to register.

Our people have a strong and influential membership in the Sam Yup, Hop Wo, Yan Wo, Kong Chow, Ning Yeong, and Yeong Wo companies. These societies practically control everything in America relating to the Chinese, and they retain American lawyers to fight their battles. I have met many of the officers of these companies, and China has produced no more brilliant minds than some, and, *sub rosa*, they have been pitted against the Americans on more than one occasion and have outwitted them. Among these men are Yee Ha Chung, Chang Wah Kwan, Chun Ti Chu, Chu Shee Sum, Lee Cheang Chun, and others. Many of these men have been presidents of the Six Companies in San

Francisco, and rank in intelligence with the most brilliant American statesmen. I regret to see them in America.

Chun Ti Chu especially, at one time president of the Sam Yuz, should be in China. I met this brilliant man some years ago in San Francisco. After dinner he took me to a place and showed me a placard which was a reward of $300 for his head. He had obtained the enmity of criminal Chinamen on the Pacific coast, but when I last heard of him he was still alive. There are many criminals here who do not dare to return to China, who left their country for their country's good. These are the cause of much trouble here, and bring discredit upon the better class of our people. Our people in America are loyal to the Government. It was interesting to see at one time a proclamation from the Emperor brought over by Chew Shu Sum and posted in the streets of an American city: "By order of his Imperial Majesty, the Emperor of China." The President, the mayor of San Francisco, was not thought of; China was revered, and is to-day holding her government over the Chinese in every American city where they have a stronghold. So much for the loyalty of our people.

CHAPTER XVIII
THE RELIGIONS OF THE AMERICANS

THOMAS J. GEARY, THE FORMER CONGRESSMAN, is an avowed enemy of the Chinese and the author of the famous Geary bill, but I condone all he has said against us for one profound utterance made in a published address or article, in which he said: "As to the missionaries (in China), it wouldn't be a national loss if they were required to return home. If the American missionary would only look about him in the large cities of the Union he would find enough of misery, enough of suffering, enough people falling away from the Christian churches, enough of darkness, enough of vice in all its conditions and all its grades, to furnish him work for years to come." This is a sentiment Americans may well think of; but there are "none so blind as those who will not see." There will always be women and men willing to spend their time in picturesque China at the expense of foreign missions. China has never attempted to convert the Americans to her religion, believing she has all she can do to keep her people within bounds at home.

In my search for information in America I have had some singular experiences. I have made an examination of the many religions of the Americans, and they have been remarkably prolific in this respect. While we are satisfied with Taoism, Buddhism, but mostly with Confucianism, I have observed the following sects in America: Baptists of two kinds, Congregationalists, Methodists, Quakers of three kinds, Catholics, Unitarians, Universalists, Presbyterians, Swedenborgians, Spiritualists, Christian Scientists (healers), Episcopalians (high and low), Jews, Seventh-Day Adventists, and many more. Nearly all are Christians, as we are nearly all Confucians. Unitarians, Universalists, Jews, and several others believe in the moral teachings of Christ, but hold that he was not of divine origin. America was first settled to supply room for religious liberty, which perhaps explains the remarkable number of religions. They are constantly increasing. Nearly all of these denominations hold that their own belief is the right one. Much proselyting is going on among them, with which one would take no exception if there was no denouncing of one another. Our religion, founded in the faith of Confucius, seems satisfying to us. Some of us believe that at least we are not savages.

Some American friends once invited me to go to a negro church in Washington. Upon arriving we were given a seat well down in front. The pastor was a "visiting evangelist," and in a short time had these excitable and ignorant people in a frenzy, several being carried out of the church in a semicataleptic condition. Suddenly the minister began to pray for the strangers, and especially "for the heathen in our midst," for the unsaved from pagan lands, that they might be saved; and I could not but wonder at the conceit and ignorance that would ask a believer in the splendid philosophy of Confucius to throw it aside for this African religion. This idea that a Chinaman is a "pagan" and idolator is found everywhere in America, and every attempt is made to "save" him.

I very much fear that many of our countrymen go to the American missions and Sunday-schools merely to learn the language and enjoy the social life of those who are interested in this special work. I was told by a well-to-do Chinaman that he knew Chinamen who were both Catholic and Protestant, and who attended all the Chinese missions without reference to sect. They were Methodist when at the Methodist mission, Catholic when at mass, and when they returned to their home slipped back into Confucianism. Let us hope this is not universal, though I venture the belief that the witty Americans would see the humor of it.

I was told by a prominent patron of the Woman's Christian Union that she felt very sorry I did not have the consolation of religion, coming as I did from a heathen land. Some "heathens" might have been insulted, but I had come to know the Americans and was aware that she really felt a kindly interest in me. I replied that we could find some consolation in the sayings of our religious teachers, as the great guide of our life is, "What you do not like when done to yourself do not do to others."

"Why," said the lady, "that is Christian doctrine, our 'Golden Rule.'"

"Pardon me," I answered, "this is the golden rule of Confucius, written four hundred years or so before Christ was born."

"I think you must be mistaken," she continued; "this is a fundamental pillar of the Christian belief."

"True," I retorted; "but none the less Christians obtained it from Confucius."

She did not believe me, and we referred the question to Bishop ———, who sat near us. Much to her confusion he agreed with me, and then quoted the well-known lines of one of our religious writers who lived twelve hundred years before Christ: "The great God has conferred on the people a moral sense, compliance with which would show their nature inevitably right," and remarked that it was a splendid sentiment.

"Then you believe in a God," said the lady, turning to me.

"I trust so," was my answer.

Now this lady, who believed me to be a "pagan" and unsaved, was a product of the American school system, yet she had never read a line of Confucius, having been "brought up" to consider him an infidel writer.

I have seen many of the great Western nations and observed their religions. My conclusion is that none make so general and united an attempt to be what they consider "good and moral" as the Americans; but the Americans scatter their efforts like shot fired from a gun, and the result is a multiplicity of religious beliefs beyond belief. I do not forget that America was settled to afford an asylum for religious belief, where men could work out their salvation in peace. If Americans would grant us the same privilege and not send missionaries to fight over us, all would be well. No one can dispute the fact that the Americans are in earnest; the greater number believe they are right, and that they possess true zeal all China knows.

The impression the convert in China obtains is that the United States is a sort of paradise, where Christians live in peace and happiness, loving one another, doing good to those who ill-treat them, turning the cheek to those who strike them, etc.; but the Chinaman soon finds after landing in America that this is often "conspicuous by its absence." These ideas are preached, and doubtless thousands follow them or attempt to do so, but that they are common practises of the people is not true. There is great need of Christian missions in America as well as in China. I told a clergyman that our people believed the Christian religion was very good for the Americans, and we had no fault to find with it, nor had we the temerity to insinuate that our own was superior.

A Roman Catholic young lady whom I met spoke to me about burning our prayers, our joss-houses, and our dragon, which she had seen carried about the streets of San Francisco. "Pure symbolism," I answered, and then told her of the Christian dragon in the Divine Key of the Revelation of Jesus Christ as Given to John, by a Christian writer, William Eugene Brown. This dragon had nine heads, while ours has only one. I believe I had the best of the argument so far as heads went. This young woman, a graduate of a large college, wore an amulet, which she believes protects her from accident. She possessed a bottle of water from a miraculous spring in Canada, which she said would cure any disease, and she told me that one of the Catholic churches there, Ste. Anne de Beaupré, had a small piece of the wrist-bone of the mother of the Virgin, which would heal and had healed thousands. She had a picture of the church, showing piles of crutches thrown aside by cured and grateful patients. Can China produce such credulity? I think not.

All nations may be wrong in their religious beliefs, but certainly "pagan China" is outdone in religious extravaganza by America or any European state. Our joss-houses and our feasts are nothing to the splendors of American churches. An American girl laughed at the bearded figures in a San Francisco joss-house, but looked solemn when I referred to the saints in a Catholic cathedral in the same city. If I were "fancy free" I should like to lecture in America on the inconsistencies of the Caucasian. They really challenge our own. Instead of having one splendid church and devoting themselves to the real ethics of Christianity, these Christians have divided irrevocably, and so lost strength and force. They are in a sense turned against themselves, and their religious colleges are graduating men to perpetuate the differences. No more splendid religion than that expounded by Christ could be imagined if they would join hands and, like the Confucians, devote their attention not to rites and theological differences but to the daily conduct of men.

The Americans have a saying, "Take care of the pennies and the dollars will care for themselves." We believe that in taking care of the morals of the individual the nation will take care of itself. I took the liberty of commending this Confucian doctrine to a Methodist brother, but he had never been allowed to read the books of Confucius. They are classed with those of Mohammed, Voltaire, and others. So what can one do with such people, who have the conceit of the ages and the ignorance of all time? Their great scholars see their idiosyncrasies, and I can not begin to describe them. One sect believes that no one can be saved unless immersed in water; others believe in sprinkling. Others, as the Quakers, denounce all this as mummery. One sect, the Shakers, will have no marriages. Another believes in having as many wives as they can support—the Mormons. The Jews and Quakers oblige members to marry in the society; in the latter instance the society is dying out, and the former from constant intermarriage has resulted in conspicuous and marked facial peculiarities. These different sects, instead of loving, despise one another. Episcopalians look down upon the Methodists, and the latter denounce the former because the priests sometimes smoke and drink. The Unitarians are not regarded well by the others, yet nearly all the other bodies contain Unitarians, who for business and other reasons do not acknowledge the fact. A certain clergyman would not admit a Catholic priest to his platform. All combine against the poor Jew.

So strong is the feeling against this people among the best of American citizens that they are almost completely ostracised, at least socially. In all the years spent in America I do not recall meeting a Jew at dinner in Washington, New York, or Newport. They are disliked, and as a rule associate entirely with themselves, having their own churches, clubs, etc. Yet they in large degree control the finances of America. They have almost complete control of the textile-fabric business, clothing, and many other trades. Why the American Christians dislike the American Jews is difficult to understand, but the invariable reply to this question is that their manners are so offensive that Christians will not associate with them. I doubt if in any of the first circles of any city you would meet a Jew. In the fashionable circles of New York I heard that it would be "easier for a camel to pass through the eye of a needle" than for a Jew to enter these circles. Many hotels will not receive them. In fact, the ban is on the Jew as completely in America as in Russia. I was strongly tempted to ask if this was the brotherly love I heard so much about, but refrained. I heard the following story at a dinner: A Chinese laundryman received a call from a Jew, who brought with him his soiled clothing. The Chinaman, glancing at the Jew, refused to take the package. "But why?" asked the Jew; "here's the money in advance." "No washee," said the Christian Chinaman; "you killed Melican man's Joss," meaning that the Jews crucified the Christ.

The more you delve into the religions of the Americans the more anomalies you find. I asked a New York lady at Newport if she had ever met Miss ———, a prominent Chinese missionary. She had never heard of her, and considered most missionaries very ordinary persons. This same lady, when someone spoke about laxity of morals, replied, "It is not morals but manners that we need;" and I can assure you that this high-church lady, a model of propriety, judged her men acquaintances by that standard. If their manners were correct, she apparently did not care what moral lapses they committed when out of her presence. Briefly, I looked in vain for the religion in everyday life preached by the missionary. Doubtless many possess it, but the meek and humble follower of the head of the Christian Church, the American who turned his cheek for another blow, the one who loved his enemies, or the one who was anxious to do unto others as he would have them do unto him, all these, whom I expected to see everywhere, were not found, at least in any numbers.

In visiting a certain village I dined with several clergymen. One told me he was the Catholic priest, and invited me to visit his chapel. Not long after I met another clergyman. I do not recall his denomination, but his work he told me was undoing that of the Catholic priest. The latter converted the people to Catholicism, while the former tried to reclaim them from Catholicism. I heard much about our joss-houses, but they fade into insignificance when compared with the splendid religious palaces of the Americans, and particularly those of the Catholics and Episcopalians. Their religious customs are beyond belief. As an illustration, their religion teaches them that the dead, if they have led a good life, go at once to heaven, though the Catholics believe in a purgatory, a half-way house, out of which the dead can be bought by the payment of money.

Now the simple Chinaman would naturally believe that the relatives would be pleased at the death of a friend who was *immediately* transported to paradise and freed from the worries of life, but not at all; at the death of a relative the friends are plunged into such grief that they have been known to hire professional mourners, and instead of putting on clothes indicative of joy and thanksgiving array themselves in somber black, the token of woe, and wear it for years. Everything is black, and the more fashionable the family the deeper the black. The deepest crape is worn by the women. Writing-paper is inscribed with a deep band, also visiting cards. Women use jet as jewelry, and white pearls are replaced by black ones. Even servants are garbed in mourning for the departed, who, they believe, have gone to the most beautiful paradise possible to conceive. Contemplating all these inconsistencies one is amazed, and the amazement is ever increasing as one delves deeper into the ways of the inconsistent American.

The credulity of the American is nowhere more singularly shown than in his susceptibility to religion. At a dinner given by the —— of —— in Washington, conversation turned on religion, and Senator ——, a very clever man, told me in a burst of confidence, "Our people are easily led; it merely requires a leader, a bright, audacious man, with plenty of 'cheek,' to create a following." There are hundreds of examples of this statement. No matter how idiotic the religion or philosophy may be, a following can be established among Americans. A man of the name of Dowie, "ignorant, impertinent, but with a superabundance of cheek" (I quote an American journal), announced himself as the prophet Elijah, and obtained a following of thousands, built a large city, and lives upon the credulity of the public.

Three different "healers" have appeared within a decade in America, each by inference claiming to be the Christ and imitating his wanderings and healing methods. All, even the last, grossest, and most impudent impostor, who advertised himself in the daily press, the picture showing him posing after one of the well-known pictures of Christ, had many followers. I hoped to hear that this fellow had been "tarred and feathered," a happy American remedy for gross things. This fellow, as the Americans say, "went beyond the limit." I asked the senator how he accounted for Americans, well educated as they are, taking up these strange impostors. "Well," he replied, puffing on a big cigar, "between you and me and the lamp-post it's on account of the kind of schooling they get. I didn't get much myself—I'm an old-timer; but I accumulated a lot of 'horse sense,' that has served me so well that I never have my leg pulled, and I notice that all these 'suckers' are graduates from something; but don't take this as gospel, as I'm always getting up minority reports."

The religion of the Americans, as diffuse as it is, is one of the most remarkable factors you meet in the country. Despite its peculiar phases you can not fail to appreciate a people who make such stupendous attempts to crush out evil and raise the morals of the masses. We may differ from them. We may resent their assumption that we are pagans and heathens, but this colossal series of movements, under the banner of the Cross, is one of the marvels of the world. Surely it is disinterested. It comes from the heart. I wish the Americans knew more of Confucius and his code of morals; they would then see that we are not so "pagan" as they suppose.

THE END

America
Through the Spectacles
of an Oriental Diplomat

Tingfang Wu

Introduction

While this book is by no means famous, it is a remarkable chance to look at America of 1914 through the eyes of an outsider. Wu Tingfang shows evidence of having thought through many issues of relevance to the United States, and while some of his thoughts are rather odd—such as his suggestion that the title of President be replaced by the title of Emperor; and others are unfortunately wrong—such as his hopes for peace, written on the eve of the First World War; they are all well-considered and sometimes show remarkable insight into American culture.

Even so, it should be remarked that he makes some errors, including some misunderstandings of American and Western ideas and an idealization of Chinese culture, and humanity in general, in some points—while I do not wish to refute his claims about China, I would simply point out that many of the things he praises have been seen differently by many outside observers, just as Wu Tingfang sometimes looks critically at things in America which he does not fully understand (and, unfortunately, he is sometimes all too correct)—in all these cases (on both sides) some leeway must be given to account for mutual misunderstandings. Still, his observations allow us to see ourselves as others see us—and regardless of accuracy those observations are useful, if only because they will allow us to better communicate.

The range of topics covered is also of particular interest. Wu Tingfang wrote this book at an interesting juncture in history—airplanes and motion pictures had recently been invented, (and his expectations for both these inventions have proven correct), and while he did not know it, a tremendous cultural shift was about to take place in the West due to the First World War and other factors. I will leave it to the reader to see which ideas have caught on and which have not. The topics include:

Immigration; the Arms Race and changes in technology; one-time six year terms for the office of President; religion and/or ethics in the classroom; women's equality; fashion; violence in the theatre (violence on television); vegetarianism; and, cruelty to animals.

I will also note that a few passages seem satiric in nature, though I am not certain that it isn't merely a clash of cultures.

ALAN R. LIGHT. BIRMINGHAM, ALABAMA. MAY, 1996.

Late Chinese Minister to the United States of America, Spain, Peru, Mexico and Cuba; recently Minister of Foreign Affairs and Minister of Justice for the Provincial Government of the Republic of China, etc.

Preface

Of all nations in the world, America is the most interesting to the Chinese. A handful of people left England to explore this country: gradually their number increased, and, in course of time, emigrants from other lands swelled the population. They were governed by officials from the home of the first settlers, but when it appeared to them that they were being treated unjustly, they rebelled and declared war against their rulers, the strongest nation on the face of the earth. After seven years of strenuous, perilous, and bloody warfare, during which thousands of lives were sacrificed on both sides, the younger race shook off the yoke of the older, and England was compelled to recognize the independence of the American States. Since then, in the comparatively short space of one hundred and thirty years, those revolutionists and their descendants, have not only made the commonwealth the richest in the world, but have founded a nation whose word now carries weight with all the other great powers.

The territory at first occupied was not larger than one or two provinces of China, but by purchase, and in other ways, the commonwealth has gradually grown till now it extends from the Atlantic to the Pacific Ocean, from the north where ice is perpetual to the south where the sun is as hot as in equatorial Singapore. This young republic has already produced many men and women who are distinguished in the fields of literature, science, art and invention. There hosts of men, who in their youth were as poor as church mice, have, by dint of perseverance and business capacity, become multi-millionaires. There you may see the richest man in the world living a simple and abstemious life, without pomp and ostentation, daily walking in the streets unattended even by a servant. Many of them have so much money that they do not know what to do with it. Many foreign counts, dukes, and even princes have been captured by their wealthy and handsome daughters, some of whom have borne sons who have become high officers of state in foreign lands. There you find rich people who devote their time and wealth to charitable works, sometimes endowing libraries not only in their own land, but all over the world; there you will find lynching tolerated, or impossible of prevention; there one man may kill another, and by the wonderful process of law escape the extreme penalty of death; there you meet the people who are most favorably disposed toward the maintenance of peace, and who hold conferences and conventions with that object in view almost every year; there an American multi-millionaire devotes a great proportion of his time to the propaganda of peace, and at his own expense has built in a foreign country a palatial building to be used as a tribunal of peace[1]. Yet these people have waged war on behalf of other nationalities who they thought were being unjustly treated and when victorious they have not held on to the fruits of their victory without paying a reasonable price[2]. There the inhabitants are, as a rule, extremely patriotic, and in a recent foreign war many gave up their businesses and professions and volunteered for service in the army; one of her richest sons enlisted and equipped a whole regiment at his own expense, and took command of it. In that country all the citizens are heirs apparent to the throne, called the White House. A man may become the chief ruler for a few years, but after leaving the White House he reverts to private citizenship; if he is a lawyer he may practise and appear before a judge, whom he appointed while he was president. There a woman may become a lawyer and plead a case before a court of justice on behalf of a male client; there freedom of speech and criticism are allowed to the extreme limit, and people are liable to be annoyed by slanders and libels without much chance of obtaining satisfaction; there you will see women wearing "Merry Widow" hats who are not widows but spinsters, or married women whose husbands are very much alive, and the hats

---

1 This magnificent building at The Hague, which is aptly called the Palace of Peace, was formally opened on the 28th of August, 1913, in the presence of Queen Wilhelmina, Mr. Carnegie (the founder) and a large assembly of foreign representatives.
2 I refer to the Spanish-American War. Have captured the Philippine Islands, the United States paid $20,000,000, gold, for it to the Spanish Government.

in many cases are as large as three feet in diameter[1]; there you may travel by rail most comfortably on palace cars, and at night you may sleep on Pullman cars, to find in the morning that a young lady has been sleeping in the berth above your bed. The people are most ingenious in that they can float a company and water the stock without using a drop of fluid; there are bears and bulls in the Stock Exchange, but you do not see these animals fight, although they roar and yell loudly enough. It is certainly a most extraordinary country. The people are wonderful and are most interesting and instructive to the Chinese.

Such a race should certainly be very interesting to study. During my two missions to America where I resided nearly eight years, repeated requests were made that I should write my observations and impressions of America. I did not feel justified in doing so for several reasons: first, I could not find time for such a task amidst my official duties; secondly, although I had been travelling through many sections of the country, and had come in contact officially and socially with many classes of people, still there might be some features of the country and some traits of the people which had escaped my attention; and thirdly, though I had seen much in America to arouse my admiration, I felt that here and there, there was room for improvement, and to be compelled to criticize people who had been generous, courteous, and kind was something I did not wish to do. In answer to my scruples I was told that I was not expected to write about America in a partial or unfair manner, but to state impressions of the land just as I had found it. A lady friend, for whose opinion I have the highest respect, said in effect, "We want you to write about our country and to speak of our people in an impartial and candid way; we do not want you to bestow praise where it is undeserved; and when you find anything deserving of criticism or condemnation you should not hesitate to mention it, for we like our faults to be pointed out that we may reform." I admit the soundness of my friend's argument. It shows the broad-mindedness and magnanimity of the American people. In writing the following pages I have uniformly followed the principles laid down by my American lady friend. I have not scrupled to frankly and freely express my views, but I hope not in any carping spirit; and I trust American readers will forgive me if they find some opinions they cannot endorse. I assure them they were not formed hastily or unkindly. Indeed, I should not be a sincere friend were I to picture their country as a perfect paradise, or were I to gloss over what seem to me to be their defects.

---

1 This was several years ago. Fashions change every year. The present type is equally ludicrous.

Chapter 1. The Importance of Names

"What's in a name? That which we call a rose
By any other name would smell as sweet."

NOTWITHSTANDING THESE LINES, I MAINTAIN that the selection of names is important. They should always be carefully chosen. They are apt to influence friendships or to excite prejudices according to their significance. We Chinese are very particular in this matter. When a son is born the father or the grandfather chooses a name for the infant boy which, according to his horoscope, is likely to insure him success, or a name is selected which indicates the wish of the family for the new-born child. Hence such names as "happiness," "prosperity," "longevity," "success," and others, with like propitious import, are common in China. With regard to girls their names are generally selected from flowers, fruits, or trees. Particular care is taken not to use a name which has a bad meaning. In Washington I once met a man in an elevator whose name was "Coffin." Was I to be blamed for wondering if the elevator would be my coffin? On another occasion I met a man whose name was "Death," and as soon as I heard his name I felt inclined to run away, for I did not wish to die. I am not superstitious. I have frequently taken dinner with thirteen persons at the table, and I do not hesitate to start on a journey on a Friday. I often do things which would not be done by superstitious persons in China. But to meet a man calling himself "Coffin" or "Death" was too much for me, and with all my disbelief in superstition I could not help showing some repugnance to those who bore such names.

Equally important, if not more so, is the selection of a name for a state or a nation. When the several states of America became independent they called themselves the "United States of America"—a very happy idea. The Union was originally composed of thirteen states, covering about 300,000 square miles; it is now composed of forty-eight states and three territories, which in area amount to 3,571,492 square miles, practically as large in extent as China, the oldest nation in the world. It should be noted that the name is most comprehensive: it might comprise the entire continent of North and South America. It is safe to say that the founders of the nation did not choose such a name without consideration, and doubtless the designation "United States of America" conceals a deep motive. I once asked a gentleman who said he was an American whether he had come from South or North America, or whether he was a Mexican, a Peruvian or a native of any of the countries in Central America? He replied with emphasis that he was an American citizen of the United States. I said it might be the United States of Mexico, or Argentina, or other United States, but he answered that when he called himself a citizen it could not mean any other than that of the United States of America. I have asked many other Americans similar questions and they all have given me replies in the same way. We Chinese call our nation "The Middle Kingdom;" it was supposed to be in the center of the earth. I give credit to the founders of the United States for a better knowledge of geography than that possessed by my countrymen of ancient times and do not assume that the newly formed nation was supposed to comprise the whole continent of North and South America, yet the name chosen is so comprehensive as to lead one naturally to suspect that it was intended to include the entire continent. However, from my observation of their national conduct, I believe their purpose was just and humane; it was to set a noble example to the sister nations in the Western Hemisphere, and to knit more closely all the nations on that continent through the bonds of mutual justice, goodwill and friendship. The American nation is, indeed, itself a pleasing and unique example of the principle of democracy. Its government is ideal, with a liberal constitution, which in effect declares that all men are created equal, and that the government is "of the people, for the people, and by the people." Anyone with ordinary intelligence and with open eyes, who should visit any city, town or village in America, could not but be impressed with the orderly and unostentatious way in which it is governed by the local authorities, or help being struck by the plain and democratic character of the people. Even in the elementary schools, democracy is taught and practised. I remember visiting a public school for children in Philadelphia, which I shall never forget. There were about three or four hundred children, boys and girls, between seven and fourteen years of age. They elected one of their students as mayor, another as judge, another as police commissioner, and in fact they elected for the control of their school community almost all the officials who usually govern a city. There were a few Chinese children among the students, and one of them was pointed out to me as the police superintendent. This not only eloquently spoke of his popularity, but showed goodwill and harmony among the several hundred children, and the entire absence of race feeling. The principals and teachers told me that they had no difficulty whatever with the students. If one of them did anything wrong, which was not often, he would be taken by the student policeman before the judge, who would try the case, and decide it on its merits, and punish or discharge his fellow student as justice demanded. I was assured by the school authorities that this system of self-government worked admirably; it not only relieved the teachers of the burden of constantly looking after the several hundred pupils, but each of them felt a moral responsibility to behave well, for the sake of preserving the peace and good name of the school. Thus early imbued with the idea of self-government, and entrusted with the responsibilities of its administration, these children when grown up, take a deep interest in federal and municipal affairs, and, when elected for office, invariably perform their duties efficiently and with credit to themselves.

It cannot be disputed that the United States with its democratic system of government has exercised a great influence over the states and nations in Central and South America. The following data showing the different nations of America, with the dates at which they turned their respective governments from Monarchies into Republics, all subsequent to the independence of the United States, are very significant.

Mexico became a Republic in 1823, Honduras in 1839, Salvador in 1839, Nicaragua in 1821, Costa Rica in 1821, Panama in 1903, Colombia in 1819, Venezuela in 1830, Ecuador in 1810, Brazil in 1889, Peru in 1821, Bolivia in 1825, Paraguay in 1811, Chile in 1810, Argentina in 1824, and Uruguay in 1828.

These Republics have been closely modelled upon the republican form of government of the United States; thus, nearly all the nations or states on the continent of America have become Republics. Canada still belongs to Great Britain. The fair and generous policy pursued by the Imperial Government of Great Britain accounts for the Canadians' satisfaction with their political position, and for the fact that they do not wish a change. It must be noted, however, that a section of the American people would like to see Canada incorporated with the United States. I remember that at a public meeting held in Washington, at which Sir Wilfrid Laurier, then Premier of Canada, was present, an eminent judge of the Federal Supreme Court jocularly expressed a wish that Canada should be annexed to the United States. Later, Mr. Champ Clark, a leader of the Democratic party in the House of Representatives, addressed the House urging the annexation of Canada. Even if these statements are not taken seriously they at least show the feelings of some people, and he would be a bold man who would prophesy the political status of Canada in the future. There is, however, no present indication of any change being desired by the Canadians, and it may be safely presumed that the existing conditions will continue for many years to come. This is not to be wondered at, for Canada though nominally a British colony practically enjoys almost all the privileges of an independent state. She possesses a constitution similar to that of the United Kingdom, with a parliament of two houses, called the "Senate," and the "House of Commons." The Sovereign of Great Britain appoints only the Governor General who acts in his name, but the Dominion is governed by a responsible Ministry, and all domestic affairs are managed by local officials, without interference from the Home Government. Canadians enjoy as many rights as the inhabitants of England, with the additional advantage that they do not have to bear the burden of maintaining an army and navy. Some years ago, if I remember rightly, in consequence of some agitation or discussion for independence, the late Lord Derby, then Secretary of State for the Colonies, stated that if the Canadians really wished for independence, the Home Government would not oppose, but that they should consider if they would gain anything by the change, seeing that they already had self-government, enjoyed all the benefits of a free people, and that the only right the Home Government reserved was the appointment of the Governor-General, although it assumed the responsibility of protecting every inch of their territory from encroachment. Since this sensible advice from the Colonial Secretary, I have heard nothing more of the agitation for independence.

From a commercial point of view, and for the welfare of the people, there is not much to choose to-day between a Limited Monarchy and a Republic. Let us, for instance, compare England with the United States. The people of England are as free and independent as the people of the United States, and though subjects, they enjoy as much freedom as Americans. There are, however, some advantages in favor of a Republic. Americans until recently paid their President a salary of only $50,000 a year; it is now $75,000 with an additional allowance of $25,000 for travelling expenses. This is small indeed compared with the Civil List of the King or Emperor of any great nation. There are more chances in a Republic for ambitious men to distinguish themselves; for instance, a citizen can become a president, and practically assume the functions of a king or an emperor. In fact the President of the United States appoints his own cabinet officials, ambassadors, ministers, etc. It is generally stated that every new president has the privilege of making more than ten thousand appointments. With regard to the administration and executive functions he has in practice more power than is usually exercised by a king or an emperor of a Constitutional Monarchy. On the other hand, in some matters, the executive of a Republic cannot do what a king or an emperor can do; for example, a president cannot declare war against a foreign nation without first obtaining the consent of Congress. In a monarchical government the king or the cabinet officials assume enormous responsibilities. Lord Beaconsfield (then Mr. D'Israeli), while he was Prime Minister of England, purchased in 1875 from the Khedive of Egypt 176,602 Suez Canal shares for the sum of 3,976,582 Pounds on his own responsibility, and without consulting the Imperial Parliament. When Parliament or Congress has to be consulted about everything, great national opportunities to do some profitable business must undoubtedly be sometimes lost. No such bold national investment as that made by Lord Beaconsfield could have been undertaken by any American president on his own responsibility. Mr. Cleveland, when president of the United States, said that "the public affairs of the United States are transacted in a glass house."

Washington, in his farewell address, advised his compatriots that on account of the detached and distant situation of their country they should, in extending their commercial relations with foreign nations, have as little political connection with them as possible; and he asked this pertinent and pregnant question, "Why, by interweaving our destiny with that of any part of Europe, entangle our peace and prosperity in the toils of European ambition, rivalship, interest, humor, or caprice?" In 1823, twenty-seven years after Washington's celebrated address, President Monroe in his annual message to Congress warned the European Powers not to plant any new colonies on any portion of the American hemisphere, as any attempt on their part to extend their system in that part of the world would be considered as dangerous to the peace and safety of the United States. This "Monroe Doctrine," as it has since been called, practically protects every state and country on the American continent from attack or interference by any foreign power, and it cannot be denied that it has been and is now the chief factor in preserving the integrity of all the countries on that continent. Thus the United States is assuming the role of guardian over the other American nations. In the city of Washington there is an International Bureau of the American Republics, in which all the Republics of Central and South America are represented. It is housed in a magnificent palace made possible by the beneficence of Mr. Andrew Carnegie, the American multi-millionaire and philanthropist, and the contributions of the different governments. It cost 750,000 gold dollars, and Mr. John Barrett, the capable and popular director of the Bureau, has well called it "a temple of friendship and commerce and a meeting place for the American Republics." The Bureau is supported by the joint contributions of the twenty-one American Republics, and its affairs are controlled by a governing board composed of their diplomatic representatives in Washington, with the American Secretary of State as chairman ex officio. This institution no doubt strengthens the position of the United States and is calculated to draw the American Republics into closer friendship.

Chapter 4. America and China

AMERICA HAS PERFORMED GREAT SERVICE FOR the Orient and especially for China. If, however, the people of the latter country were asked to express their candid opinion on the matter, the verdict would not be altogether pleasant, but would be given with mixed feelings of gratitude and regret. Since the formal opening of China to foreign trade and commerce, people of all nationalities have come here, some to trade, some for pleasure, some to preach Christianity, and others for other purposes. Considering that the Chinese have a civilization of their own, and that their modes of thoughts, ideas, and habits are, in many respects, different from those of the western people, it is not surprising that frictions and disputes have occasionally occurred and that even foreign wars have been waged between China and the Occident, but it is gratifying to observe that no force has ever been resorted to against China by the United States of America. Now and then troublesome questions have arisen, but they have always been settled amicably. Indeed the just and friendly attitude taken by the American officials in China had so won the esteem and confidence of the Chinese Government that in 1867, on the termination of Mr. Anson Burlingame's term as American Minister to Peking, he was appointed by the Manchu Government as Chief of a special mission to America and Europe. In that capacity he performed valuable services for China, although his work was unfortunately cut short by his untimely death. The liberal and generous treatment accorded to the Chinese students in America is another source of satisfaction. They have been admitted freely to all educational institutions, and welcomed into American families. In whatever school or college they enter they are taught in the same way as the American boys and girls, and enjoy equal opportunities of learning all that the American students learn[1]. That America has no desire for territorial acquisition in China is well known. During the Boxer movement the American Government took the lead in initiating the policy of maintaining the open door, and preserving the integrity of China, a policy to which the other great powers readily consented. It was well known at the time, and it is no breach

---

1 I need hardly say that our students are also well treated in England, France, Germany, Japan, and other countries in Europe, but I am dealing in this chapter with America.

of confidence to mention the fact here, that Mr. John Hay, American Secretary of State, with the permission of President McKinley, was quite willing that America's indemnity demanded from China as her share of the compensation for losses sustained during the Boxer upheaval, should be reduced by one-half, provided the other powers would consent to similar reductions. Unfortunately, Mr. Hay's proposal could not be carried out for want of unanimity. However, to show the good faith, and the humane and just policy of America, she has since voluntarily refunded to China a considerable portion of her indemnity, being the surplus due to her after payment of the actual expenses incurred. This is the second occasion on which she has done this, although in the previous case the refund was smaller. These are some of the instances for which the people of China have good reasons to be grateful to America and her people.

There is, however, another side to the picture; the Chinese students in America, who may be roughly calculated by the thousands, and whose number is annually increasing, have been taught democratic principles of government. These could not but be detrimental to the welfare of the late Manchu Government. They have read the history of how the American people gained their independence, and naturally they have been imbued with the idea of inaugurating a similar policy in China. Chinese merchants, traders, and others who have been residing in America, seeing the free and independent manner in which the American people carry on their government, learned, of course, a similar lesson. These people have been an important factor in the recent overthrow of the Manchu dynasty. Added to this, the fact that America has afforded a safe refuge for political offenders was another cause of dissatisfaction to the Manchus. Thus it will be seen that the Manchu Government, from their point of view, have had many reasons for entertaining unfavorable sentiments toward America.

This view I need hardly say is not shared by the large majority of Chinese. Persons who have committed political offenses in their own country find protection not only in America but in all countries in Europe, Japan, and other civilized lands. It is an irony of fate that since the establishment of the Chinese Republic, Manchu and other officials under the old regime, now find secure asylums in Hongkong, Japan, and Tsingtao, while hundreds of ex-Manchu officials have fled to the foreign settlements of Shanghai, Tientsin, and other treaty ports, so reluctantly granted by the late Manchu Government. Thus the edge of their complaint against America's policy in harboring political refugees has been turned against themselves, and the liberality against which they protested has become their protection.

The more substantial cause for dissatisfaction with the United States is, I grieve to say, her Chinese exclusion policy. As long as her discriminating laws against the Chinese remain in force a blot must remain on her otherwise good name, and her relations with China, though cordial, cannot be perfect. It is beyond the scope of this chapter to deal with this subject exhaustively, but in order to enable my readers to understand the exact situation it is necessary to supply a short historical summary. In 1868, on account of the pressing need of good laborers for the construction of railways and other public works in America, the Governments of China and the United States, concluded a treaty which provided that "Chinese subjects visiting or residing in the United States shall enjoy the same privileges, immunities, and exemptions in respect to travel or residence as may be enjoyed by the citizens or subjects of the most favored nation." It was a treaty negotiated by that great American statesman, Secretary Seward, and announced by the President of the United States to Congress as a "liberal and auspicious treaty." It was welcomed by the United States as a great advance in their international relations. It had also the double significance of having been negotiated by a Chinese special embassy, of which a distinguished American diplomat, Mr. Anson Burlingame, who was familiar with the wishes and interests of the American people, was the head.

But within a few years the labor unions on the Pacific coast began to object to the competition of Chinese laborers. Soon afterward the Chinese Government, to its intense surprise, was informed that the President of the United States had delegated a commission to come to Peking to solicit an abrogation of the treaty clause to which reference has been made. The Chinese Government was naturally unwilling to abrogate a treaty which had been urged on her by the United States with so much zeal, and which had so lately been entered upon on both sides with such high hopes. Long and tedious negotiations ensued, and finally a short treaty was concluded, the first and second Articles of which are as follows:

Article I

"Whenever in the opinion of the Government of the United States, the coming of Chinese laborers to the United States, or their residence therein, affects or threatens to affect the interests of that country, or to endanger the good order of the said country or of any locality within the territory thereof, the Government of China agrees that the Government of the United States may regulate, limit, or suspend such coming or residence, but may not absolutely prohibit it. The limitation or suspension shall be reasonable and shall apply only to Chinese who may go to the United States as laborers, other classes not being included in the limitations. Legislation taken in regard to Chinese laborers will be of such a character only as is necessary to enforce the regulation, limitation, or suspension of immigration, and immigrants shall not be subject to personal maltreatment or abuse."

Article II

"Chinese subjects, whether proceeding to the United States as teachers, students, merchants, or from curiosity, together with their body and household servants, and Chinese laborers who are now in the United States shall be allowed to go and come of their own free will and accord, and shall be accorded all the rights, privileges, immunities, and exceptions which are accorded to the citizens and subjects of the most favored nations."

It would seem reasonable to expect that in yielding so fully to the wishes of the United States in this second negotiation the Chinese Government would not be called upon to make any further concessions in the interests or at the demand of the labor unions on the Pacific coast, but in this China was disappointed. Within a period of less than ten years an urgent application was made by the American Secretary of State for a new treaty amended so as to enable the Congress of the United States to still further restrict the privileges of Chinese laborers who had come to the United States. And when the Chinese Government hesitated to consent to the withdrawal of rights which the United States granted to the subjects of other Governments, Congress passed the Scott Act of 1888 prohibiting any Chinese person from entering the United States except Chinese officials, teachers, students, merchants or travellers for pleasure or curiosity and forbidding also Chinese laborers in the United States, after having left, from returning thereto. This, in the words of Hon. J. W. Foster, ex-Secretary of State and a distinguished international lawyer, "was a deliberate violation of the Treaty of 1880 and was so declared by the Supreme Court of the United States." In order to save the Executive of the United States from embarrassment, the Chinese Government, contrary to its own sense of justice, and of international comity, for a third time yielded to the wishes of the United States, and concluded the amended treaty of 1894 which gave Congress additional power of legislation respecting Chinese laborers. By Article I of this treaty it was agreed that for a term of ten years the coming of Chinese laborers to the United States should be absolutely prohibited. Article III distinctly provided that "the provisions of this convention shall not affect the right at present enjoyed of Chinese subjects, being officials, teachers, students, merchants, or travellers for curiosity or pleasure, but not laborers, of coming to the United States and residing therein." Thus it is clear that the prohibition affects only laborers, and not the other classes of Chinese. For a few years after the signing of this convention this was the view adopted and acted upon by the immigration officials, but afterward they changed their attitude, and the foregoing Article has since been interpreted to mean that only the above-mentioned five classes can be admitted into the United States, and that all the other classes of Chinese, however respectable and honorable, must be refused admission. Will my readers believe that a Chinese banker, physician, lawyer, broker, commercial agent, scholar or professor could all be barred out of the United States of America under the provisions of this convention? In the face of the plain language of the text it seems too absurd and unreasonable to be contemplated, and yet it is a fact.

This convention was proclaimed in December, 1894. According to its provisions, it was to remain in force only for a period of ten years, but that if six months before the end of that period neither Power should give notice of denunciation it should be extended for a similar period. Such notice was, however, given by China to the United States and accordingly the convention expired in December, 1904, and is now no longer in force. No serious attempt has since been made by the United States Government to negotiate a new treaty regarding Chinese laborers, so the customs and immigration officials continue to prohibit Chinese laborers from coming to America by virtue of the law passed by Congress. It will be seen that by the treaty of 1868, known as the "Burlingame Treaty," the United States Government formally agreed that Chinese subjects, visiting or residing in the United States, should enjoy the same privileges and immunities as were enjoyed by the citizens or subjects of the most favored nation; that being so, and as the convention of 1894 has expired, according to the legal opinion of Mr. John W. Foster, and other eminent lawyers, the continuation of the exclusion of Chinese laborers and the restrictions placed upon Chinese merchants and others seeking admission to the United States are not only without international authority but in violation of treaty stipulations.

The enforcement of the exclusion laws against Chinese in the Hawaiian and Philippine Islands is still more inexcusable. The complaint in America against the immigration of Chinese laborers was that such immigration was detrimental to white labor, but in those Islands there has been no such complaint; on the contrary the enforcement of the law against the Chinese in Hawaii has been, and is, contrary to the unanimous wish of the local Government and the people. Free intercourse and immigration between those Islands and China have been maintained for centuries. What is most objectionable and unfair is that the Chinese should be singled out for discrimination, while all other Asiatics such as Japanese, Siamese, and Malays are allowed to enter America and her colonies without restraint. It is my belief that the gross injustice that has been inflicted upon the Chinese people by the harsh working of the exclusion law is not known to the large majority of the American people, for I am sure they would not allow the continuation of such hardships to be suffered by those who are their sincere friends. China does not wish special treatment, she only asks that her people shall be treated in the same way as the citizens or subjects of other countries. Will the great American nation still refuse to consent to this?

To solve the problem of immigration in a manner that would be satisfactory to all parties is not an easy task, as so many conflicting interests are involved. But it is not impossible. If persons interested in this question be really desirous of seeing it settled and are willing to listen to reasonable proposals, I believe that a way may be found for its solution. There is good reason for my optimistic opinion. Even the Labor Unions, unless I am mistaken, would welcome an amicable settlement of this complicated question. In 1902, while at Washington, I was agreeably surprised to receive a deputation of the leaders of the Central Labor Union of Binghamton, New York, inviting me to pay a visit there and to deliver an address. As I did not wish to disappoint them I accepted their invitation. During my short stay there, I was very cordially and warmly received, and most kindly treated not only by the local authorities and inhabitants, but by the members of the Labor Union and the working men also. I found that the Union leaders and the working men were most reasonable, their platform being, as far as I could learn, to have no cheap labor competition but not necessarily discrimination against any race. If the United States Government would appoint a commission composed of members representing the Labor Unions, manufacturers and merchants, to treat with a similar commission nominated by the Chinese Government, the whole question in all its bearings could be discussed, and I feel certain that after free and candid exchange of views, the joint Commissioners would be able to arrive at a scheme which would put at rest once for all the conflicting claims, and settle the matter satisfactorily to both China and the United States.

When this disagreeable difference has been removed, the friendly relations between the two Republics, cordial even while one was yet an Empire, will leave nothing to be desired and cannot but help to largely affect the trade between the two countries and to contribute to the peace of the Far East.

Chapter 7. American Freedom and Equality

WHEN AN ORIENTAL, WHO, THROUGHOUT HIS LIFE, has lived in his own country where the will of his Sovereign is supreme, and the personal liberty of the subject unknown, first sets foot on the soil of the United States, he breathes an atmosphere unlike anything he has ever known, and experiences curious sensations which are absolutely new. For the first time in his life he feels that he can do whatever he pleases without restraint, and that he can talk freely to people without fear. When he takes up a newspaper and reads statements about different persons in high positions which are not at all creditable to them, and learns that no serious consequences happen to the writers, he is lost in wonderment. After a little time he begins to understand that this is the "land of the free and the home of the brave," and that in America everybody is on an equality. The President, the highest official in the United States, is neither more nor less than a citizen; and should he, which is very unlikely, commit an offense, or do anything in contravention of the law, he would be tried in a Court of Justice in the same manner as the lowest and the poorest citizen. Naturally the new visitor thinks this the happiest people on earth, and wishes that his own country could be governed as happily. Until that lucky day arrives he feels that he would rather stay in free America than return to his native land.

One of the first lessons which is learned by the American child in school, and which is deeply impressed on its mind by its teacher, is that according to the Constitution all persons are born equal, and that no distinction is made between sections, classes, or sects.

No slaves, or persons under bonds, have been allowed in the United States since the abolition of slavery by President Lincoln. The moment a slave, or anyone in bonds, steps on the shores of the United States he is free, and no one, not even his former master, can deprive him of his liberty. America also affords an asylum for oppressed people and for political offenders; people who have been persecuted in their own land, on account of their religion, or for political offenses, find a safe refuge in this country. Every year large numbers of Jews, and other foreigners, emigrate to America for the sake of enjoying religious freedom. Perfect religious liberty is guaranteed to everyone in the United States.

There is equal religious liberty in England, but the King is compelled to belong to a particular section of the Christian Church, whereas in the United States no restriction is placed on the religious belief of the President; thus one President was a Baptist, another a Unitarian, and a third a Congregationalist; and, if elected, a Jew, a Mohammedan, or a Confucianist could become the President. Several Jews have held high Federal offices; they have even been Cabinet Ministers. Article VI of the Constitution of the United States says: "No religious test shall ever be required as a qualification to any office or public trust under the United States."

So ingrained in the minds of the American people is this principle of liberty and freedom of action that I do not believe they would resign it for any consideration whatsoever. Once an English Duke was asked whether he would accept the throne of China on the sole condition that he must reside in the Palace of Peking, and act as the Chinese Emperors have always been accustomed to act. He replied that such an exalted position of power and responsibility would be very great and tempting, but that he would on no account accept such an honor on such terms, as it would practically make him a prisoner. Though a subject under a monarchial form of government, he would not forfeit his right of freedom of action; and much less would a democratic American give up his birthright for any price. I knew an eminent and learned Judge of the Supreme Court in Washington, who used to say that he would never bend his knees to any human being, and that to the Almighty God alone would he ever do homage. He no doubt acted up to his principles, but I much doubt if all Americans observe so lofty an ideal. A young lover in proposing to his sweetheart would not mind kneeling down to support his prayer. I have seen penitent husbands bending their knees to ask the forgiveness of their offended wives. This, however, can be explained by the fact that the act of kneeling is not, in such cases, a sign of inferiority, but the act of one equal asking a favor from another; still it is the bending of the knee which was so solemnly abjured by the learned Judge.

The dislike of distinction of classes which arises from the principle of equality is apparent wherever you go in the States. The railroad cars are not marked first, second, or third, as they are in Europe. It is true that there are Pullman cars, and palace cars, with superior and superb accommodation, and for which the occupant has to pay an extra fare; but the outside of the car simply bears the name "Pullman" without indicating its class, and anyone who is willing to pay the fare may share its luxuries. I should mention that in some of the Southern states negroes are compelled to ride on separate cars. On one occasion, arriving at the railroad station in one of those states, I noticed there were two waiting-rooms, one labelled "For the White," and the other "For the Colored."

The railway porter took my portmanteau to the room for the white, but my conscience soon whispered I had come to the wrong place, as neither of the two rooms was intended for people of my complexion. The street-cars are more democratic; there is no division of classes; all people, high or low, sit in the same car without distinction of race, color or sex. It is a common thing to see a workman, dressed in shabby clothes full of dirt, sitting next to a millionaire or a fashionable lady gorgeously clothed. Cabinet officers and their wives do not think it beneath their dignity to sit beside a laborer, or a coolie, as he is called in China.

Foreign Ministers and Ambassadors coming to Washington soon learn to follow these local customs. In a European country they ride in coronated carriages, with two liverymen; but in Washington they usually go about on foot, or travel by the street-cars. I frequently saw the late Lord Pauncefote, the celebrated British Ambassador to Washington, ride to the State Department in the street-car. My adoption of this democratic way of travelling during the time I was in America was the cause of a complaint being made against me at Peking. The complainants were certain Chinese high officials who had had occasion to visit the States; one of them had had a foreign education, and ought to have known better than to have joined in the accusation that my unpretentious manner of living was not becoming the dignity of a representative of China. They forgot that when in Rome you must do as the Romans do, and that to ride in a sumptuous carriage, with uniformed footmen, is in America not only an unnecessary expense, but a habit which, among such a democratic people as the Americans, would detract from, rather than add to, one's dignity. An envoy residing in a foreign country should be in touch with the people among whom he is sojourning. If he put on unnecessary airs, there will be a coldness and lack of cordiality between him and the community; his sphere of usefulness will be curtailed, and his knowledge of the people and their country limited. Of course, in a European Capital, where every diplomat drives in a carriage, I should follow the example of my colleagues. But even in England, I frequently met high statesmen, such, for example, as Lord Salisbury, walking in the streets. This unrestrained liberty and equality is remarkably conspicuous in the United States; for instance, at the White House official receptions or balls in Washington, I have seen ladies in ordinary dress, while on one occasion a woman appeared in the dress of a man. This was Doctor Mary Walker.

In a democratic country, such as the United States, one would naturally suppose that the people enjoyed a greater degree of freedom than is possible in monarchial countries. But, so far from this being so, in some respects, they appear to be in a worse position. On my return journey from South America, some years ago, our steamer had to stay for four hours outside of New York harbor. We had first to wait for the doctor to come on board to make his inspection of all the passengers, then the Customs officials appeared and examined the luggage and boxes of all the passengers, and then, last but not the least, we had to wait for the immigration officers. All this necessarily took time, and it was not until all these inspections were completed that the steamer was allowed to enter the harbor, and to tie up alongside the dock. And this occurred in the land of freedom and liberty! I spoke to some of my American fellow passengers about the inconvenience and delay, and though they all murmured they quietly submitted. Customs and sanitary inspection should be so conducted as to cause as little delay as possible. I have visited many countries in Europe, in South America, and in Asia, but I have never known of a ship having to stay outside the harbor of the port of her destination for so long a time.

Take another case; some months since, I wished, in compliance with the request of a lady in America, to send her a chow-dog. A mutual friend was willing to take it to her, but, upon making inquiries at the American Consulate as to the Customs regulations, he was informed that it would be impossible for him to undertake the commission, as the Customs officers at San Francisco, besides imposing a heavy duty on the dog, would keep the ship in quarantine because the dog was on board. I could scarcely believe this, but inquiries confirmed the truth of my friend's statement. Customs and immigration laws and sanitary regulations must, of course, be observed, but they should be enforced in such a way as not to work hardship on the people. Officers entrusted with the performance of such duties, while faithfully and conscientiously performing their work, should yet exercise their power with discretion and tact. They are the servants of the people, and ought to look after their interests and convenience as well as after the interests of the State. I would be the last one to encourage smuggling, but would the national interests really suffer if the Custom House officers were to be a little more ready to accept a traveller's word, and if they were less ready to suspect everyone of making false declarations when entering the country? Smuggling must be repressed, but at the same time is it not true that the more imports enter the country the better it is for the State and for the people?

There are no peers in the United States, as the Government has no power to create them; and although America is nominally a free country, yet if a foreign government should confer a decoration on an American citizen for services rendered, he cannot accept it without the consent of Congress, just as under a monarchy a subject must obtain his sovereign's permission to wear a foreign decoration. It is true that there are some such titled persons in America, but they are not treated with any greater respect or distinction than other citizens; yet you frequently find people in America who not only would not disdain, but are actually anxious, to receive decorations from foreign governments. Once, at least, an American high official, just before leaving the country to which he had been accredited, accepted, without permission, a decoration, knowing, that if he had asked for the consent of Congress, he would not have been allowed to receive it.

It is human nature to love change and variety, and for every person to be designated "Mister" is too tame and flat for the go-ahead Americans. Hence many of the people whom you meet daily have some prefix to their names, such as General, Colonel, Major, President, Judge, etc. You will not be far wrong to call a man "Judge" when he is a lawyer; or "General" or "Colonel" if he has served in the army; or "Admiral" or "Captain" if he has been in the navy. Though neither the Federal nor the State Government has power to confer titles, the magnates do so. They see that dukes and other peers are created in Europe, and that the partners in the big, wealthy firms over there, are called "merchant princes," and so to outdo them, they arrogate to themselves a still higher title. Hence there are railroad kings, copper kings, tobacco kings, etc. It is, however, manifestly improper and incongruous that the people should possess a higher title than their President, who is the head of the nation. To make it even, I would suggest that the title "President" be changed to "Emperor," for the following reasons: First, it would not only do away with the impropriety of the chief magistrate of the nation assuming a name below that of some of his people, but it would place him on a level with the highest ruler of any nation on the face of the earth. I have often heard the remark that the President of the United States is no more than a common citizen, elected for four years, and that on the expiration of his term he reverts to his former humble status of a private citizen; that he has nothing in common with the dignified majesty of an Emperor; but were the highest official of the United States to be in future officially known as Emperor, all these depreciatory remarks would fall to the ground. There is no reason whatever why he should not be so styled, as, by virtue of his high office, he possesses almost as much power as the most aristocratic ruler of any nation. Secondly, it would clearly demonstrate the sovereign power of the people; a people who could make and unmake an Emperor, would certainly be highly respected. Thirdly, the United States sends ambassadors to Germany, Austria, Russia, etc. According to international law, ambassadors have what is called the representative character, that is, they represent their sovereign by whom they are delegated, and are entitled to the same honors to which their constituent would be entitled were he personally present. In a Republic where the head of the State is only a citizen and the sovereign is the people, it is only by a stretch of imagination that its ambassador can be said to represent the person of his sovereign. Now it would be much more in consonance with the dignified character of an American ambassador to be the representative of an Emperor than of a simple President. The name of Emperor may be distasteful to some, but may not a new meaning be given to it? A word usually has several definitions. Now, if Congress were to pass a law authorizing the chief magistrate of the United States of America to be styled Emperor, such designation to mean nothing more than the word "President," the title would soon be understood in that sense. There is no reason in history or philology why the word "Emperor" should never mean anything other than a hereditary ruler. I make this suggestion seriously, and hope it will be adopted.

Marriage laws in the United States, as I understand them, are more elastic than those in Europe. In England, until a few years ago, a man could not contract a legal marriage with his deceased wife's sister, although he could marry the betrothed wife of his deceased brother. It is curious to compare the Chinese view of these two cases. Marriage with a deceased wife's sister is, in China, not only lawful, but quite common, while to marry a dead brother's betrothed is strictly prohibited. Doubtless in the United States both are recognized as legal. I was not, however, prepared to hear, and when I did hear it, I could not at first believe that a man is permitted to marry his deceased son's wife. Let me quote from the "China Press" which has special facilities for obtaining news from America. "Boston, March 24. The engagement of Mrs. Katherine M. B., widow of Charles A. B., and daughter of George C. F., chairman of the ...., Board of ...., to her father-in-law, Frank A. B., of ...., became known to-day. Charles A. B. was killed at the .... Road crossing in .... on March 29, 1910, by a locomotive which struck a carriage in which he was driving to the First Congregational Church, to serve as best man at the wedding of Miss H. R. F., another daughter of S. F., to L. G. B. of .... His wife, who was in the carriage with him and was to have been matron at the wedding, was severely injured. Her mother-in-law, Mrs. Frank A. B., died some months later[1]." I suppose the marriage has since been consummated. If a father is permitted to marry his deceased son's wife, in fairness a son should be allowed to marry his deceased father's wife. I presume that there is a law in the United States or in some of the states against marriages within the prohibited degrees of consanguinity and affinity, but I confess that the more I study the subject the more I am confused as to what is or what is not within the prohibited degrees.

---

1 The names of the parties and places were given in full in the "China Press."

In China the law on this subject is extremely rigid, and consequently its infraction is exceedingly rare; I have, as a matter of fact, never heard of the marriage laws in China being broken. In "Liao Chai," a famous collection of Chinese tales, it is recorded that a young widow married her son and moved to another part of the country, so that their identity and relationship should be concealed. They seemed to have lived very happily together. After many years, when they had had children and grandchildren, their true relationship was accidentally discovered. A complaint was laid before the local authorities. After a long deliberation and careful review of the case, and to eradicate such "unnatural offspring," as they were termed, it was decided that the two offenders, and all their children and grandchildren should be burned to death, which sentence was duly carried out. I doubt if the story is authentic. It was probably fabricated by the author that it might serve as a warning. The sentence, if true, was too severe; the offspring who were innocent contributories to the crime deserved pity rather than punishment; the judgment passed on the real offenders was also unduly harsh. My object in citing this unsavory tale is to show the different views held in regard to incestuous marriage in China with its serious consequences.

It is commonly supposed that all men are born equal, and that the United States is the land of perfect equality. Now let us see if this is really so. There are men born into high stations of life, or into wealthy families, with "silver spoons" in their mouths; while there are others ushered into this world by parents who are paupers and who cannot support them. Then there are people born with wit and wisdom, while others are perfect fools. Again there are some who are brought to this life with strong and healthy constitutions, while others are weak and sickly. Thus it is plain that men are not born equal, either physically, intellectually, or socially. I do not know how my American friends account for this undoubted fact, but the Chinese doctrine of previous lives, of which the present are but the continuation, seems to afford a satisfactory explanation.

However, this doctrine of equality and independence has done immense good. It has, as a rule, caused men to think independently, and not to servilely follow the thoughts and ideas of others, who may be quite wrong. It has encouraged invention, and new discoveries in science and art. It has enabled men to develop industries and to expand trade. New York and Chicago, for example, could not have become such huge and prosperous cities within comparatively short periods, but for their free and wise institutions. In countries where personal liberty is unknown, and the rights of person and property are curtailed, people do not exert themselves to improve their environments, but are content to remain quiet and inactive.

By the constitution of the State of California it is declared that "all men are free and independent." It must be conceded that the American people enjoy a greater amount of freedom and independence than other people. But are they perfectly free, and are they really independent? Are they not swayed in politics by their "bosses," and do not many of them act and vote as their bosses dictate? In society are they not bound by conventionalities and, dare they infringe the strict rules laid down by the society leaders? In the matter of dress also are they not slaves, abjectly following new-fangled fashions imported from Paris? In domestic circles are not many husbands hen-pecked by their wives, because they, and not the men, rule the roost? Are not many women practically governed by their husbands, whose word is their law? The eager hunger for "the almighty dollar" leads most Americans to sacrifice their time, health, and liberty in the acquisition of wealth, and, alas, when they have acquired it, they find that their health is broken, and that they themselves are almost ready for the grave. Ought a free and independent people to live after this fashion?

In every well organized community it is essential that people should obey all laws and regulations which are enacted for the greatest good of the greatest number. In domestic circles they should willingly subordinate their own wishes to the wishes of others, for the sake of peace, concord and happiness. Happy that people whose laws and conditions are such that they can enjoy the greatest amount of freedom in regard to person and property, compatible with the general peace and good order of the community, and if I should be asked my opinion, notwithstanding all that I have above said concerning the United States, I should have to acknowledge that I believe that America is one of the few nations which have fairly well approximated the high ideal of a well-governed country.

Chapter 8. American Manners

MUCH HAS BEEN WRITTEN AND MORE SAID ABOUT American manners, or rather the American lack of manners. Americans have frequently been criticized for their bad breeding, and many sarcastic references to American deportment have been made in my presence. I have even been told, I do not know how true it is, that European diplomats dislike being stationed in America, because of their aversion to the American way of doing things.

Much too has been written and said about Chinese manners, not only by foreigners but also by Chinese. One of the classics, which our youth have to know by heart, is practically devoted entirely to manners. There has also been much adverse criticism of our manners or our excess of manners, though I have never heard that any diplomats have, on this account, objected to being sent to China. We Chinese are therefore in the same boat as the Americans. In regard to manners neither of us find much favor with foreigners, though for diametrically opposite reasons: the Americans are accused of observing too few formalities, and we of being too formal.

The Americans are direct and straight-forward. They will tell you to your face that they like you, and occasionally they also have very little hesitation in telling you that they do not like you. They say frankly just what they think. It is immaterial to them that their remarks are personal, complimentary or otherwise. I have had members of my own family complimented on their good looks as if they were children. In this respect Americans differ greatly from the English. The English adhere with meticulous care to the rule of avoiding everything personal. They are very much afraid of rudeness on the one hand, and of insincerity or flattery on the other. Even in the matter of such a harmless affair as a compliment to a foreigner on his knowledge of English, they will precede it with a request for pardon, and speak in a half-apologetic manner, as if complimenting were something personal. The English and the Americans are closely related, they have much in common, but they also differ widely, and in nothing is the difference more conspicuous than in their conduct. I have noticed curiously enough that English Colonials, especially in such particulars as speech and manners, follow their quondam sister colony, rather than the mother country. And this, not only in Canada, where the phenomenon might be explained by climatic, geographic, and historic reasons, but also in such antipodean places as Australia and South Africa, which are so far away as to apparently have very little in common either with America or with each other. Nevertheless, whatever the reason, the transplanted Englishman, whether in the arctics or the tropics, whether in the Northern or the Southern Hemisphere, seems to develop a type quite different from the original stock, yet always resembling his fellow emigrants.

The directness of Americans is seen not only in what they say but in the way they say it. They come directly to the point, without much preface or introduction, much less is there any circumlocution or "beating about the bush." When they come to see you they say their say and then take their departure, moreover they say it in the most terse, concise and unambiguous manner. In this respect what a contrast they are to us! We always approach each other with preliminary greetings. Then we talk of the weather, of politics or friends, of anything, in fact, which is as far as possible from the object of the visit. Only after this introduction do we broach the subject uppermost in our minds, and throughout the conversation polite courtesies are exchanged whenever the opportunity arises. These elaborate preludes and interludes may, to the strenuous ever-in-a-hurry American, seem useless and superfluous, but they serve a good purpose. Like the common courtesies and civilities of life they pave the way for the speakers, especially if they are strangers; they improve their tempers, and place them generally on terms of mutual understanding. It is said that some years ago a Foreign Consul in China, having a serious complaint to make on behalf of his national, called on the Taotai, the highest local authority in the port. He found the Chinese official so genial and polite that after half an hour's conversation, he advised the complainant to settle the matter amicably without troubling the Chinese officials about the matter. A good deal may be said in behalf of both systems. The American practice has at least the merit of saving time, an all important object with the American people. When we recall that this remarkable nation will spend millions of dollars to build a tunnel under a river, or to shorten a curve in a railroad, merely that they may save two or three minutes, we are not surprised at the abruptness of their speech. I, as a matter of fact, when thinking of their time-saving and abrupt manner of address, have been somewhat puzzled to account for that peculiar drawl of theirs. Very slowly and deliberately they enunciate each word and syllable with long-drawn emphasis, punctuating their sentences with pauses, some short and some long. It is almost an effort to follow a story of any length—the beginning often becomes cold before the end is reached. It seems to me that if Americans would speed up their speech after the fashion of their English cousins, who speak two or three times as quickly, they would save many minutes every day, and would find the habit not only more efficacious, but much more economical than many of their time-saving machines and tunnels. I offer this suggestion to the great American nation for what it is worth, and I know they will receive it in the spirit in which it is made, for they have the saving sense of humor.

Some people are ridiculously sensitive. Some years ago, at a certain place, a big dinner was given in honor of a notable who was passing through the district. A Chinese, prominent in local affairs, who had received an invitation, discovered that though he would sit among the honored guests he would be placed below one or two whom he thought he ought to be above, and who, he therefore considered, would be usurping his rightful position. In disgust he refused to attend the dinner, which, excepting for what he imagined was a breach of manners, he would have been very pleased to have attended. Americans are much more sensible. They are not a bit sensitive, especially in small matters. Either they are broad-minded enough to rise above unworthy trifles, or else their good Americanism prevents their squabbling over questions of precedence, at the dinner table or elsewhere.

Americans act up to their Declaration of Independence, especially the principle it enunciates concerning the equality of man. They lay so much importance on this that they do not confine its application to legal rights, but extend it even to social intercourse. In fact, I think this doctrine is the basis of the so-called American manners. All men are deemed socially equal, whether as friend and friend, as President and citizen, as employer and employee, as master and servant, or as parent and child. Their relationship may be such that one is entitled to demand, and the other to render, certain acts of obedience, and a certain amount of respect, but outside that they are on the same level. This is doubtless a rebellion against all the social ideas and prejudices of the old world, but it is perhaps only what might be looked for in a new country, full of robust and ambitious manhood, disdainful of all traditions which in the least savor of monarchy or hierarchy, and eager to blaze as new a path for itself in the social as it has succeeded in accomplishing in the political world. Combined with this is the American characteristic of saving time. Time is precious to all of us, but to Americans it is particularly so. We all wish to save time, but the Americans care much more about it than the rest of us. Then there are different notions about this question of saving time, different notions of what wastes time and what does not, and much which the old world regards as politeness and good manners Americans consider as sheer waste of time. Time is, they think, far too precious to be occupied with ceremonies which appear empty and meaningless. It can, they say, be much more profitably filled with other and more useful occupations. In any discussion of American manners it would be unfair to leave out of consideration their indifference to ceremony and their highly developed sense of the value of time, but in saying this I do not forget that many Americans are devout ritualists, and that these find both comfort and pleasure in ceremony, which suggests that after all there is something to be said for the Chinese who have raised correct deportment almost to the rank of a religion.

The youth of America have not unnaturally caught the spirit of their elders, so that even children consider themselves as almost on a par with their parents, as almost on the same plane of equality; but the parents, on the other hand, also treat them as if they were equals, and allow them the utmost freedom. While a Chinese child renders unquestioning obedience to his parents' orders, such obedience as a soldier yields to his superior officer, the American child must have the whys and the wherefores duly explained to him, and the reason for his obedience made clear. It is not his parent that he obeys, but expediency and the dictates of reason. Here we see the clear-headed, sound, common-sense business man in the making. The early training of the boy has laid the foundation for the future man. The child too has no compunction in correcting a parent even before strangers, and what is stranger still the parent accepts the correction in good part, and sometimes even with thanks. A parent is often interrupted in the course of a narrative, or discussion, by a small piping voice, setting right, or what it believes to be right, some date, place, or fact, and the parent, after a word of encouragement or thanks, proceeds. How different is our rule that a child is not to speak until spoken to! In Chinese official life under the old regime it was not etiquette for one official to contradict another, especially when they were unequal in rank. When a high official expressed views which his subordinates did not endorse, they could not candidly give their opinion, but had to remain silent. I remember that some years ago some of my colleagues and I had an audience with a very high official, and when I expressed my dissent from some of the views of that high functionary, he rebuked me severely. Afterward he called me to him privately, and spoke to me somewhat as follows: "What you said just now was quite correct. I was wrong, and I will adopt your views, but you must not contradict me in the presence of other people. Do not do it again." There is of course much to be said for and against each system, and perhaps a blend of the two would give good results. Anyhow, we can trace in American customs that spirit of equality which pervades the whole of American society, and observe the germs of self-reliance and independence so characteristic of Americans, whether men, women, or children.

Even the domestic servant does not lose this precious American heritage of equality. I have nothing to say against that worthy individual, the American servant (if one can be found); on the contrary, none is more faithful or more efficient. But in some respects he is unique among the servants of the world. He does not see that there is any inequality between him and his master. His master, or should I say, his employer, pays him certain wages to do certain work, and he does it, but outside the bounds of this contract, they are still man and man, citizen and citizen. It is all beautifully, delightfully legal. The washerwoman is the "wash-lady," and is just as much a lady as her mistress. The word "servant" is not applied to domestics, "help" is used instead, very much in the same way that Canada and Australia are no longer English "colonies," but "self-governing dominions."

We of the old world are accustomed to regard domestic service as a profession in which the members work for advancement, without much thought of ever changing their position. A few clever persons may ultimately adopt another profession, and, according to our antiquated conservative ways of thinking, rise higher in the social scale, but, for the large majority, the dignity of a butler, or a housekeeper is the height of ambition, the crowning point in their career. Not so the American servant. Strictly speaking there are no servants in

America. The man, or the woman as the case may be, who happens for the moment to be your servant, is only servant for the time being. He has no intention of making domestic service his profession, of being a servant for the whole of his life. To have to be subject to the will of others, even to the small extent to which American servants are subordinate, is offensive to an American's pride of citizenship, it is contrary to his conception of American equality. He is a servant only for the time, and until he finds something better to do. He accepts a menial position only as a stepping stone to some more independent employment. Is it to be wondered at that American servants have different manners from their brethren in other countries? When foreigners find that American servants are not like servants in their own country, they should not resent their behavior: it does not denote disrespect, it is only the outcrop of their natural independence and aspirations.

All titles of nobility are by the Constitution expressly forbidden. Even titles of honor or courtesy are but rarely used. "Honorable" is used to designate members of Congress; and for a few Americans, such as the President and the Ambassadors, the title "Excellency" is permitted. Yet, whether it is because the persons entitled to be so addressed do not think that even these mild titles are consistent with American democracy, or because the American public feels awkward in employing such stilted terms of address, they are not often used. I remember that on one occasion a much respected Chief Executive, on my proposing, in accordance with diplomatic usage and precedent, to address him as "Your Excellency," begged me to substitute instead "Mr. President." The plain democratic "Mr." suits the democratic American taste much better than any other title, and is applied equally to the President of the Republic and to his coachman. Indeed the plain name John Smith, without even "Mr.," not only gives no offense, where some higher title might be employed, but fits just as well, and is in fact often used. Even prominent and distinguished men do not resent nicknames; for example, the celebrated person whose name is so intimately connected with that delight of American children and grown-ups—the "Teddy Bear." This characteristic, like so many other American characteristics, is due not only to the love of equality and independence, but also to the dislike of any waste of time.

In countries where there are elaborate rules of etiquette concerning titles and forms of address, none but a Master of Ceremonies can hope to be thoroughly familiar with them, or to be able to address the distinguished people without withholding from them their due share of high-sounding titles and epithets; and, be it whispered, these same distinguished people, however broad-minded and magnanimous they may be in other respects, are sometimes extremely sensitive in this respect. And even after one has mastered all the rules and forms, and can appreciate and distinguish the various nice shades which exist between "His Serene Highness," "His Highness," "His Royal Highness," and "His Imperial Highness," or between "Rt. Rev." and "Most Rev.," one has yet to learn what titles a particular person has, and with what particular form of address he should be approached, an impossible task even for a Master of Ceremonies, unless he always has in his pocket a Burke's Peerage to tell him who's who. What a waste of time, what an inconvenience, and what an unnecessary amount of irritation and annoyance all this causes. How much better to be able to address any person you meet simply as Mr. So-and-So, without unwittingly treading on somebody's sensitive corns! Americans have shown their common sense in doing away with titles altogether, an example which the sister Republic of China is following. An illustrious name loses nothing for having to stand by itself without prefixes and suffixes, handles and tails. Mr. Gladstone was no less himself for not prefixing his name with Earl, and the other titles to which it would have entitled him, as he could have done had he not declined the so-called honor. Indeed, like the "Great Commoner," he, if that were possible, endeared himself the more to his countrymen because of his refusal. A name, which is great without resorting to the borrowed light of titles and honors, is greater than any possible suffix or affix which could be appended to it.

In conclusion, American manners are but an instance or result of the two predominant American characteristics to which I have already referred, and which reappear in so many other things American. A love of independence and of equality, early inculcated, and a keen abhorrence of waste of time, engendered by the conditions and circumstances of a new country, serve to explain practically all the manners and mannerisms of Americans. Even the familiar spectacle of men walking with their hands deep in their trousers' pockets, or sitting with their legs crossed needs no other explanation, and to suggest that, because Americans have some habits which are peculiarly their own, they are either inferior or unmanly, would be to do them a grave injustice.

Few people are more warm-hearted, genial, and sociable than the Americans. I do not dwell on this, because it is quite unnecessary. The fact is perfectly familiar to all who have the slightest knowledge of them. Their kindness and warmth to strangers are particularly pleasant, and are much appreciated by their visitors. In some other countries, the people, though not unsociable, surround themselves with so much reserve that strangers are at first chilled and repulsed, although there are no pleasanter or more hospitable persons anywhere to be found when once you have broken the ice, and learned to know them; but it is the stranger who must make the first advances, for they themselves will make no effort to become acquainted, and their manner is such as to discourage any efforts on the part of the visitor. You may travel with them for hours in the same car, sit opposite to them, and all the while they will shelter themselves behind a newspaper, the broad sheets of which effectively prohibit any attempts at closer acquaintance. The following instance, culled from a personal experience, is an illustration. I was a law student at Lincoln's Inn, London, where there is a splendid law library for the use of the students and members of the Inn. I used to go there almost every day to pursue my legal studies, and generally sat in the same quiet corner. The seat on the opposite side of the table was usually occupied by another law student. For months we sat opposite each other without exchanging a word. I thought I was too formal and reserved, so I endeavored to improve matters by occasionally looking up at him as if about to address him, but every time I did so he looked down as though he did not wish to see me. Finally I gave up the attempt. This is the general habit with English gentlemen. They will not speak to a stranger without a proper introduction; but in the case I have mentioned surely the rule would have been more honored by a breach than by the observance. Seeing that we were fellow students, it might have been presumed that we were gentlemen and on an equal footing. How different are the manners of the American! You can hardly take a walk, or go for any distance in a train, without being addressed by a stranger, and not infrequently making a friend. In some countries the fact that you are a foreigner only thickens the ice, in America it thaws it. This delightful trait in the American character is also traceable to the same cause as that which has helped us to explain the other peculiarities which have been mentioned. To good Americans, not only are the citizens of America born equal, but the citizens of the world are also born equal.

Chapter 11. American versus Chinese Civilization

THIS IS A BIG SUBJECT. ITS EXHAUSTIVE TREATMENT would require a large volume. In a little chapter such as this I have no intention of doing more than to cast a glance at its cuff buttons and some of the frills on its shirt. Those who want a thesis must look elsewhere.

Now what is Civilization? According to Webster it is "the act of civilizing or the state of being civilized; national culture; refinement." "Civilization began with the domestication of animals," says Alfred Russell Wallace, but whether for the animal that was domesticated or for the man domesticating it is not clear. In a way the remark probably applies to both, for the commencement of culture, or the beginning of civilization, was our reclamation from a savage state. Burke says: "Our manners, our civilization, and all the good things connected with manners and civilization have in this European world of ours depended for ages upon two principles—the spirit of a gentleman, and the spirit of religion." We often hear people, especially Westerners, calling themselves "highly civilized," and to some extent they have good grounds for their claim, but do they really manifest the qualifications mentioned by Burke? Are they indeed so "highly civilized" as to be in all respects worthy paragons to the so-called semi-civilized nations? Have not some of their policies been such as can be characterized only as crooked and selfish actions which less civilized peoples would not have thought of? I believe that every disinterested reader will be able to supply confirmatory illustrations for himself, but I will enforce the point by giving a few Chinese ideals of a truly civilized man:

"He guards his body as if holding jade;" *i.e.*, he will not contaminate himself with mental or moral filth.

"He does not gratify his appetite, nor in his dwelling place does he seek ease;" *i.e.*, he uses the physical without being submerged by it.

"Without weapons he will not attack a tiger, nor will he dare to cross a river without a boat;" in other words he will never ruin himself and his family by purely speculative practices.

He will "send charcoal in a snowstorm, but he will not add flowers to embroidery," meaning that he renders timely assistance when necessary, but does not curry favor by presents to those who do not need them.

Our most honored heroes are said to have made their virtue "brilliant" and one of them engraved on his bath-tub the axiom—"If you can renovate yourself one day, do so from day to day. Let there be daily renovation." Our ideal for the ruler is that the regulation of the state must commence with his regulation of himself.

It is too often forgotten that civilization, like religion, originally came from the East. Long before Europe and America were civilized, yea while they were still in a state of barbarism, there were nations in the East, including China, superior to them in manners, in education, and in government; possessed of a literature equal to any, and of arts and sciences totally unknown in the West. Self-preservation and self-interest make all men restless, and so Eastern peoples gradually moved to the West taking their knowledge with them; Western people who came into close contact with them learned their civilization. This fusion of East and West was the beginning of Western civilization.

A Chinese proverb compares a pupil who excels his teacher to the color green, which originates with blue but is superior to it. This may aptly be applied to Westerners, for they originally learned literature, science, and other arts from the East; but they have proven apt pupils and have excelled their old masters. I wish I could find an apothegm concerning a former master who went back to school and surpassed his clever pupil. The non-existence of such a maxim probably indicates that no such case has as yet occurred, but that by no means proves that it never will.

Coming now to particulars I would say that one of the distinguishing features in the American people which I much admire is their earnestness and perseverance. When they decide to take up anything, whether it be an invention or the investigation of a difficult problem, they display indomitable perseverance and patience. Mr. Edison, for example, sleeps, it is said, in his factory and is inaccessible for days when he has a problem to solve, frequently even forgetting food and sleep. I can only compare him to our sage Confucius, who, hearing a charming piece of music which he wanted to study, became so engrossed in it that for many days he forgot to eat, while for three months he did not know the taste of meat.

The dauntless courage of the aviators, not only in America, but in Europe also, is a wonderful thing. "The toll of the air," in the shape of fatal accidents from aviation, mounts into the hundreds, and yet men are undeterred in the pursuit of their investigations. With such intrepidity, perseverance, and genius, it is merely a question of time, and I hope it will not be long, when the art of flying, either by aeroplanes or airships, will be perfectly safe. When that time arrives I mean to make an air trip to America, and I anticipate pleasures from the novel experience such as I do not get from travelling by land or sea.

The remarkable genius for organization observable anywhere in America arouses the visitor's enthusiastic admiration. One visits a mercantile office where a number of men are working at different desks in a large room, and marvels at the quiet and systematic manner in which they perform their tasks; or one goes to a big bank and is amazed at the large number of customers ever going in and coming out. It is difficult to calculate the enormous amount of business transacted every hour, yet all is done with perfect organization and a proper division of labor, so that any information required is furnished by the manager or by a clerk, at a moment's notice. I have often been in these places, and the calm, quiet, earnest way in which the employees performed their tasks was beyond praise. It showed that the heads who organized and were directing the institutions had a firm grasp of multiplex details.

We Chinese have a reputation for being good business men. When in business on our own account, or in partnership with a few friends, we succeed marvelously well; but we have yet much to learn regarding large concerns such as corporations or joint stock companies. This is not to be wondered at, for joint stock companies and corporations as conducted in the West were unknown in China before the advent of foreign merchants in our midst. Since then a few joint stock companies have been started in Hongkong, Shanghai, and other ports; these have been carried on by Chinese exclusively, but the managers have not as yet mastered the systematic Western methods of conducting such concerns. Even unpractised and inexpert eyes can see great room for improvement in the management of these businesses. Here, I must admit, the Japanese are ahead of us. Take, for instance, the Yokohama Specie Bank: it has a paid-up capital of Yen 30,000,000 and has branches and agencies not only in all the important towns in Japan, but also in different ports in China, London, New York, San Francisco, Honolulu, Bombay, Calcutta and other places. It is conducted in the latest and most approved scientific fashion; its reports and accounts, published half-yearly, reveal the exact state of the concern's financial position and incidentally show that it makes enormous profits. True, several Chinese banks of a private or official nature have been established, and some of them have been doing a fair business, but candor compels me to say that they are not conducted as scientifically as is the Yokohama Specie Bank, or most American banks. Corporations and joint stock companies are still in their infancy in China; but Chinese merchants and bankers, profiting by the mistakes of the past, will doubtless gradually improve their systems, so that in the future there will be less and less cause to find fault with them.

One system which has been in vogue within the last ten or twenty years in America, and which has lately figured much in the limelight, is that of "Trusts." Here, again, it is only the ingenuity of Americans which could have brought the system to such gigantic proportions as to make it possible for it to wield an immense influence over trade, not only in America but in other countries also. The main object of the Trust seems to be to combine several companies under one direction, so as to economize expenses, regulate production and the price of commodities by destroying competition. Its advocates declare their policy to be productive of good to the world, inasmuch as it secures regular supplies of commodities of the best kind at fair and reasonable prices. On the other hand, its opponents contend that Trusts are injurious to the real interests of the public, as small companies cannot compete with them, and without healthy competition the consumer always suffers. Where experts differ it were perhaps wiser for me not to express an opinion lest I should show no more wisdom than the boy who argued that lobsters were black and not red because he had often seen them swimming about on the seashore, but was confuted by his friend who said he knew they were red and not black for he had seen them on his father's dinner table.

The fact, however, which remains indisputable, is the immense power of wealth. No one boycotts money. It is something no one seems to get enough of. I have never heard that multi-millionaires like Carnegie or Rockefeller ever expressed regrets at not being poor, even though they seem more eager to give money away than to make it. Most people in America are desirous for money, and rush every day to their business with no other thought than to accumulate it quickly. Their love of money leaves them scarcely time to eat, to drink, or to sleep; waking or sleeping they think of nothing else. Wealth is their goal and when they reach it they will probably be still unsatisfied. The Chinese are, of course, not averse to wealth. They can enjoy the jingling coin as much as anyone, but money is not their only thought. They carry on their business calmly and quietly, and they are very patient. I trust they will always retain these habits and never feel any temptation to imitate the Americans in their mad chase after money.

There is, however, one American characteristic my countrymen might learn with profit, and that is the recognition of the fact that punctuality is the soul of business. Americans know this; it is one cause of their success. Make an appointment with an American and you will find him in his office at the appointed time. Everything to be done by him during the course of the day has its fixed hour, and hence he is able to accomplish a greater amount of work in a given time than many others. Chinese, unfortunately, have no adequate conceptions of the value of time. This is due, perhaps, to our mode of reckoning. In the West a day is divided into twenty-four hours, and each hour into sixty minutes, but in China it has been for centuries the custom to divide day and night into twelve (shih) "periods" of two hours each, so that an appointment is not made for a particular minute, as in America, but for one or other of these two-hour periods. This has created ingrained habits of unpunctuality which clocks and watches and contact with foreigners are slow to remove. The time-keeping railway is, however, working a revolution, especially in places where there is only one train a day, and a man who misses that has to wait for the morrow before he can resume his journey.

Some years ago a luncheon—"tiffin" we call it in China—was given in my honor at a Peking restaurant by a couple of friends; the hour was fixed at noon sharp. I arrived on the stroke of twelve, but found that not only were none of the guests there, but that even the hosts themselves were absent. As I had several engagements I did not wait, but I ordered a few dishes and ate what I required. None of the hosts had made their appearance by the time I had finished, so I left with a request to the waiter that he would convey my thanks.

Knowing the unpunctuality of our people, the conveners of a public meeting will often tell the Chinese that it will begin an hour or two before the set time, whereas foreigners are notified of the exact hour. Not being aware of this device I once attended a conference at the appointed time, only to find that I had to wait for over an hour. I protested that in future I should be treated as a foreigner in this regard.

As civilized people have always found it necessary to wear clothes I ought not to omit a reference to them here, but in view of what has already been said in the previous chapter I shall at this juncture content myself with quoting Mrs. M. S. G. Nichols, an English lady who has written on this subject. She characterizes the clothing of men as unbeautiful, but she principally devotes her attention to the dress of women. I quote the following from her book:[1] "The relation of a woman's dress to her health is seldom considered, still less is it contemplated as to its effect upon the health of her children; yet everyone must see that all that concerns the mothers of our race is important. The clothing of woman should be regarded in every aspect if we wish to see its effect upon her health, and consequently upon the health of her offspring. The usual way is to consider the beauty or fashion of dress first, its comfort and healthfulness afterward, if at all. We must reverse this method. First, use, then beauty, flowing from, or in harmony with, use. That is the true law of life" (p. 14). On page 23 she continues: "A great deal more clothing is worn by women in some of fashion's phases than is needed for warmth, and mostly in the form of heavy skirts dragging down upon the hips. The heavy trailing skirts also are burdens upon the spine. Such evils of women's clothes, especially in view of maternity, can hardly be over-estimated. The pains and perils that attend birth are heightened, if not caused, by improper clothing. The nerves of the spine and the maternal system of nerves become diseased together." And on page 32 she writes: "When I first went to an evening party in a fashionable town, I was shocked at seeing ladies with low dresses, and I cannot even now like to see a man, justly called a rake, looking at the half-exposed bosom of a lady. There is no doubt that too much clothing is an evil, as well as too little; but clothing that swelters or leaves us with a cold are both lesser evils than the exposure of esoteric charms to stir the already heated blood of the 'roue'. What we have to do, as far as fashion and the public opinion it forms will allow, is to suit our clothing to our climate, and to be truly modest and healthful in our attire." Mrs. Nichols, speaking from her own experience, has naturally devoted her book largely to a condemnation of woman's dress, but man's dress as worn in the West is just as bad. The dreadful high collar and tight clothes which are donned all the year round, irrespective

---

1 "The Clothes Question Considered in its Relation to Beauty, Comfort and Health," by Mrs. M. S. G. Nichols. Published in London, 32 Fopstone Road, Earl's Court, S.W.

of the weather, must be very uncomfortable. Men wear nearly the same kind of clothing at all seasons of the year. That might be tolerated in the frigid or temperate zones, but should not the style be changed in the tropical heat of summer common to the Eastern countries? I did not notice that men made much difference in their dress in summer; I have seen them, when the thermometer was ranging between 80 and 90, wearing a singlet shirt, waistcoat and coat. The coat may not have been as thick as that worn in winter, still it was made of serge, wool or some similarly unsuitable stuff. However hot the weather might be it was seldom that anyone was to be seen on the street without a coat. No wonder we frequently hear of deaths from sunstroke or heat, a fatality almost unknown among the Chinese.[1]

Chinese dress changes with the seasons, varying from the thickest fur to the lightest gauze. In winter we wear fur or garments lined with cotton wadding; in spring we don a lighter fur or some other thinner garment; in summer we use silk, gauze or grass cloth, according to the weather. Our fashions are set by the weather; not by the arbitrary decrees of dressmakers and tailors from Peking or elsewhere. The number of deaths in America and in Europe every year, resulting from following the fashion must, I fear, be considerable, although of course no doctor would dare in his death certificate to assign unsuitable clothing as the cause of the decease of a patient.

Even in the matter of dressing, and in this twentieth century, "might is right." In the opinion of an impartial observer the dress of man is queer, and that of woman, uncouth; but as all nations in Europe and America are wearing the same kind of dress, mighty Conventionality is extending its influence, so that even some natives of the East have discarded their national dress in favor of the uglier Western attire. If the newly adopted dress were, if no better than, at least equal to, the old one in beauty and comfort, it might be sanctioned for the sake of uniformity, as suggested in the previous chapter; but when it is otherwise why should we imitate? Why should the world assume a depressing monotony of costume? Why should we allow nature's diversities to disappear? Formerly a Chinese student when returning from Europe or America at once resumed his national dress, for if he dared to continue to favor the Western garb he was looked upon as a "half-foreign devil." Since the establishment of the Chinese Republic in 1911, this sentiment has entirely changed, and the inelegant foreign dress is no longer considered fantastic; on the contrary it has become a fashion, not only in cities where foreigners are numerous, but even in interior towns and villages where they are seldom seen.

---

1 There have been a few cases of Chinese workmen who through carelessness have exposed themselves by working in the sun; but such cases are rare.

Chinese ladies, like their Japanese sisters, have not yet, to their credit be it said, become obsessed by this new fashion, which shows that they have more common sense than some men. I have, however, seen a few young and foolish girls imitating the foreign dress of Western women. Indeed this craze for Western fashion has even caught hold of our legislators in Peking, who, having fallen under the spell of clothes, in solemn conclave decided that the frock coat, with the tall-top hat, should in future be the official uniform; and the swallow-tail coat with a white shirt front the evening dress in China. I need hardly say that this action of the Peking Parliament aroused universal surprise and indignation. How could the scholars and gentry of the interior, where foreign tailors are unknown, be expected to dress in frock coats at formal ceremonies, or to attend public entertainments in swallow-tails? Public meetings were held to discuss the subject, and the new style of dress was condemned as unsuitable. At the same time it was thought by many that the present dresses of men and women leave much room for improvement. It should be mentioned that as soon as it was known that the dress uniform was under discussion in Parliament, the silk, hat and other trades guilds, imitating the habits of the wide-world which always everywhere considers self first, fearing that the contemplated change in dress might injuriously affect their respective interests, sent delegates to Peking to "lobby" the members to "go slow" and not to introduce too radical changes. The result was that in addition to the two forms of dress above mentioned, two more patterns were authorized, one for man's ordinary wear and the other for women, both following Chinese styles, but all to be made of home-manufactured material. This was to soothe the ruffled feelings of the manufacturers and traders, for in purchasing a foreign suit some of the materials at least, if not all, must be of foreign origin or foreign make.

During a recent visit to Peking I protested against this novel fashion, and submitted a memorandum to President Yuan with a request that it should be transmitted to Parliament. My suggestion is that the frock-coat and evening-dress regulation should be optional, and that the Chinese dress uniform as sketched by me in my memorandum should be adopted as an alternative. I am in hopes that my suggestion will be favorably considered. The point I have taken is that Chinese diplomats and others who go abroad should, in order to avoid curiosity, and for the sake of uniformity, adopt Western dress, and that those who are at home, if they prefer the ugly change, should be at liberty to adopt it, but that it should not be compulsory on others who object to suffering from cold in winter, or to being liable to sunstroke in summer. I have taken this middle course in order to satisfy both sides; for it would be difficult to induce Parliament to abolish or alter what has been so recently fixed by them.

The Chinese dress, as is well known all over the world, is superior to that worn by civilized people in the West, and the recent change favored by the Chinese is deplored by most foreigners in China. The following paragraph, written by a foreign merchant and published in one of the Shanghai papers, expresses the opinion of almost all intelligent foreigners on this subject:

"Some time back the world was jubilant over the news that among the great reforms adopted in China was the discarding of the Chinese tunic, that great typical national costume. 'They are indeed getting civilized,' said the gossip; and one and all admired the energy displayed by the resolute Young China in coming into line with the CIVILIZED world, adopting even our uncomfortable, anti-hygienic and anti-esthetic costume.

"Foreign 'fashioned' tailor shops, hat stores, shoemakers, etc., sprang up all over the country. When I passed through Canton in September last, I could not help noticing also that those typical streets lined with boat-shaped, high-soled shoes, had been replaced by foreign-style boot and shoemakers.

"Undoubtedly the reform was gaining ground and the Chinese would have to be in the future depicted dressed up as a Caucasian.

"In my simplicity I sincerely confess I could not but deplore the passing away of the century-old tunic, so esthetic, so comfortable, so rich, so typical of the race. In my heart I was sorry for the change, as to my conception it was not in the dress where the Chinese had to seek reform...."

I agree with this writer that it is not in the domain of dress that we Chinese should learn from the Western peoples. There are many things in China which could be very well improved but certainly not dress.

Chapter 12. American versus Chinese Civilization (Continued)

THE QUESTION HAS OFTEN BEEN ASKED "Which are the civilized nations?" And the answer has been, "All Europe and America." To the query, "What about the nations in the East?" the answer has been made that with the exception of Japan, who has now become a great civilized power, the other nations are more or less civilized. When the matter is further pressed and it is asked, "What about China?" the general reply is, "She is semi-civilized," or in other words, not so civilized as the nations in the West.

Before pronouncing such an opinion justifiable, let us consider the plain facts. I take it that civilization inculcates culture, refinement, humane conduct, fair dealing and just treatment. Amiel says, "Civilization is first and foremost a moral thing." There is no doubt that the human race, especially in the West, has improved wonderfully within the last century. Many inventions and discoveries have been made, and men are now able to enjoy comforts which could not have been obtained before.

From a material point of view we have certainly progressed, but do the "civilized" people in the West live longer than the so-called semi-civilized races? Have they succeeded in prolonging their lives? Are they happier than others? I should like to hear their answers. Is it not a fact that Americans are more liable to catch cold than Asiatics; with the least change of air, and with the slightest appearance of an epidemic are they not more easily infected than Asiatics? If so, why? With their genius for invention why have they not discovered means to safeguard themselves so that they can live longer on this earth? Again, can Americans say that they are happier than the Chinese? From personal observation I have formed the opinion that the Chinese are more contented than Americans, and on the whole happier; and certainly one meets more old people in China than in America. Since the United States of America is rich, well governed, and provided with more material comforts than China, Americans, one would think, should be happier than we are, but are they? Are there not many in their midst who are friendless and penurious? In China no man is without friends, or if he is, it is his own fault. "Virtue is never friendless," said Confucius, and, as society is constituted in China, this is literally true. If this is not so in America I fear there is something wrong with that boasted civilization, and that their material triumphs over the physical forces of nature have been paid dearly for by a loss of insight into her profound spiritualities. Perhaps some will understand when I quote Lao Tsze's address to Confucius on "Simplicity." "The chaff from winnowing will blind a man. Mosquitoes will bite a man and keep him awake all night, and so it is with all the talk of yours about charity and duty to one's neighbor, it drives one crazy. Sir, strive to keep the world in its original simplicity—why so much fuss? The wind blows as it listeth, so let virtue establish itself. The swan is white without a daily bath, and the raven is black without dyeing itself. When the pond is dry and the fishes are gasping for breath it is of no use to moisten them with a little water or a little sprinkling. Compared to their original and simple condition in the pond and the rivers it is nothing."

Henry Ward Beecher says, "Wealth may not produce civilization, but civilization produces money," and in my opinion while wealth may be used to promote happiness and health it as often injures both. Happiness is the product of liberality, intelligence and service to others, and the reflex of happiness is health. My contention is that the people who possess these good qualities in the greatest degree are the most civilized. Now civilization, as mentioned in the previous chapter, was born in the East and travelled westward. The law of nature is spiral, and inasmuch as Eastern civilization taught the people of the West, so Western civilization, which is based upon principles native to the East, will return to its original source. No nation can now remain shut up within itself without intercourse with other nations; the East and the West can no longer exist separate and apart. The new facilities for transportation and travel by land and water bring all nations, European, American, Asiatic and African, next door to each other, and when the art of aviation is more advanced and people travel in the air as safely as they now cross oceans, the relationships of nations will become still closer.

What effect will this have on mankind? The first effect will be, I should say, greater stability. As interests become common, destructive combats will vanish. All alike will be interested in peace. It is a gratifying sign that within recent years the people of America have taken a prominent part in peace movements, and have inaugurated peace congresses, the members of which represent different sections of the country. Annual gatherings of this order must do much to prevent war and to perpetuate peace, by turning people's thoughts in the right direction. Take, for instance, the Lake Mohonk Conference on International Arbitration, which was started by a private gentleman, Mr. A. K. Smiley, who was wont every year to invite prominent officials and others to his beautiful summer place at Lake Mohonk for a conference. He has passed away, to the regret of his many friends, but the good movement still continues, and the nineteenth annual conference was held under the auspices of his brother, Mr. Daniel Smiley. Among those present, there were not only eminent Americans, such as Dr. C. W. Eliot, President Emeritus of Harvard University, Ex-American Ambassador C. Tower, Dr. J. Taylor, President of Vassar College, and Dr. Lyman Abbott, but distinguished foreigners such as J. A. Baker, M.P., of England, Herr Heinrich York Steiner, of Vienna, and many others. Among the large number of people who support this kind of movement, and the number is increasing every day, the name of Mr. Andrew Carnegie stands out very prominently. This benevolent gentleman is a most vigorous advocate of International Peace, and has spent most of his time and money for that purpose. He has given ten million dollars (gold) for the purpose of establishing the Carnegie Peace Fund; the first paragraph in his long letter to the trustees is worthy of reproduction, as it expresses his strong convictions:

"I have transferred to you," he says, "as Trustees of the Carnegie Peace Fund, ten million dollars of five per cent. mortgage bonds, the revenue of which is to be administered by you to hasten the abolition of international war, the foulest blot upon our civilization. Although we no longer eat our fellowmen nor torture our prisoners, nor sack cities, killing their inhabitants, we still kill each other in war like barbarians. Only wild beasts are excusable for doing that in this the Twentieth Century of the Christian era, for the crime of war is inherent, since it decides not in favor of the right, but always of the strong. The nation is criminal which refuses arbitration and drives its adversary to a tribunal which knows nothing of righteous judgment."

I am glad to say that I am familiar with many American magazines and journals which are regularly published to advocate peace, and I have no doubt that in every country similar movements are stirring, for the nations are beginning to realize the disastrous effects of war. If I am not mistaken, however, Americans are the most active in this matter. The Permanent Court of Arbitration at The Hague, whose members belong to nearly every nation, is a significant index of the spirit of the times. Yet what an irony of fate that while people are so active in perpetuating peace they cannot preserve it. Look at the recent wars in Europe, first between Italy and Turkey, and afterward in the Balkans, to say nothing of disturbances in China and other parts of the world. It is just like warning a child not to take poison and then allowing him to swallow it and die. Sensible men should consider this question calmly and seriously. We all agree as to the wickedness of war and yet we war with one another; we do not like war yet we cannot help war. There is surely some hidden defect in the way we have been brought up.

Is not the slogan of nationality, to a great extent, the root of the evil? Every schoolboy and schoolgirl is taught the duty of devotion, or strong attachment, to his or her own country, and every statesman or public man preaches the doctrine of loyalty to one's native land; while the man who dares to render service to another country, the interests of which are opposed to the interests of his own land, is denounced a traitor. In such cases the individual is never allowed an opinion as to the right or wrong of the dispute. He is expected to support his own country and to cry at all times, "Our country, right or wrong." A politician's best chance to secure votes is to gloss over the faults of his own party or nation, to dilate on the wickedness of his neighbors and to exhort his compatriots to be loyal to their national flag. Can it be wondered at that men who are imbued with such doctrines become selfish and narrow-minded and are easily involved in quarrels with other nations?

Patriotism is, of course, the national life. Twenty-four centuries ago, speaking in the Greek Colony of Naxos, Pythagoras described this emotion in the following eloquent passage: "Listen, my children, to what the State should be to the good citizen. It is more than father or mother, it is more than husband or wife, it is more than child or friend. The State is the father and mother of all, is the wife of the husband and the husband of the wife. The family is good, and good is the joy of the man in wife and in son. But greater is the State, which is the protector of all, without which the home would be ravaged and destroyed. Dear to the good man is the honor of the woman who bore him, dear the honor of the wife whose children cling to his knees; but dearer should be the honor of the State that keeps safe the wife and the child. It is the State from which comes all that makes your life prosperous, and gives you beauty and safety. Within the State are built up the arts, which make the difference between the barbarian and the man. If the brave man dies gladly for the hearthstone, far more gladly should he die for the State."

But only when the State seeks the good of the governed, for said Pythagoras on another occasion: "Organized society exists for the happiness and welfare of its members; and where it fails to secure these it stands ipso facto condemned."

But to-day should the State be at war with another, and any citizen or section of citizens believe their own country wrong and the opposing nation wronged, they dare not say so, or if they do they run great risk of being punished for treason. Men and women though no longer bought and sold in the market place are subjected to subtler forms of serfdom. In most European countries they are obliged to fight whether they will or not, and irrespective of their private convictions about the dispute; even though, as is the case in some European countries, they may be citizens from compulsion rather than choice, they are not free to abstain from active participation in the quarrel. Chinese rebellions are said to "live on loot," i.e., on the forcible confiscation of private property, but is that worse than winning battles on the forcible deprivation of personal liberty? This is nationalism gone mad! It fosters the desire for territory grabbing and illustrates a fundamental difference between the Orient and the Occident. With us government is based on the consent of the governed in a way that the Westerner can hardly understand, for his passion to expand is chronic. Small nations which are over-populated want territory for their surplus population; great nations desire territory to extend their trade, and when there are several great powers to divide the spoil they distribute it among themselves and call it "spheres of influence," and all in honor of the god Commerce. In China the fundamentals of our social system are brotherhood and the dignity of labor.

What, I ask, is the advantage of adding to national territory? Let us examine the question calmly. If a town or a province is seized the conqueror has to keep a large army to maintain peace and order, and unless the people are well disposed to the new authority there will be constant trouble and friction. All this, I may say, in passing, is opposed to our Confucian code which bases everything on reason and abhors violence. We would rather argue with a mob and find out, if possible, its point of view, than fire on it. We have yet to be convinced that good results flow from the use of the sword and the cannon. Western nations know no other compulsion.

If, however, the acquisition of new territory arises from a desire to develop the country and to introduce the most modern and improved systems of government, without ulterior intentions, then it is beyond praise, but I fear that such disinterested actions are rare. The nearest approach to such high principle is the purchase of the Philippine Islands by the United States. I call it "purchase" because the United States Government paid a good price for the Islands after having seized the territory. The intentions of the Government were well known at the time. Since her acquisition of those Islands, America has been doing her best to develop their resources and expand their trade. Administrative and judicial reforms have been introduced, liberal education has been given to the natives, who are being trained for self-government. It has been repeatedly and authoritatively declared by the United States that as soon as they are competent to govern themselves without danger of disturbances, and are able to establish a stable government, America will grant independence to those islands. I believe that when the proper time comes she will fulfill her word, and thus set a noble example to the world.

The British in Hongkong afford an illustration of a different order, proving the truth of my contention that, excepting as a sphere for the exercise of altruism, the acquisition of new territories is an illusive gain. When Hongkong was ceded to Great Britain at the conclusion of a war in which China was defeated, it was a bare island containing only a few fishermen's huts. In order to make it a trading port and encourage people to live there, the British Government spent large sums of money year after year for its improvement and development, and through the wise administration of the local Government every facility was afforded for free trade. It is now a prosperous British colony with a population of nearly half a million. But what have been the advantages to Great Britain? Financially she has been a great loser, for the Island which she received at the close of her war with China was for many years a great drain on her national treasury. Now Hongkong is a self-supporting colony, but what benefits do the British enjoy there that do not belong to everyone else? The colony is open to all foreigners, and every right which a British merchant has is equally shared with everyone else. According to the census of 1911, out of a population of 456,739 only 12,075 were non-Chinese, of whom a small portion were British; the rest were Chinese. Thus the prosperity of that colony depends upon the Chinese who, it is needless to say, are in possession of all the privileges that are enjoyed by British residents. It should be noticed that the number of foreign firms and stores (*i.e.*, non-British) have been and are increasing, while big British hongs are less numerous than before. Financially, the British people have certainly not been gainers by the acquisition of that colony. Of course I shall be told that it adds to the prestige of Great Britain, but this is an empty, bumptious boast dearly paid for by the British tax-payer.

From an economic and moral point of view, however, I must admit that a great deal of good has been done by the British Government in Hongkong. It has provided the Chinese with an actual working model of a Western system of government which, notwithstanding many difficulties, has succeeded in transforming a barren island into a prosperous town, which is now the largest shipping port in China. The impartial administration of law and the humane treatment of criminals cannot but excite admiration and gain the confidence of the natives. If the British Government, in acquiring the desert island, had for its purpose the instruction of the natives in a modern system of government, she is to be sincerely congratulated, but it is feared that her motives were less altruistic.

These remarks apply equally, if not with greater force, to the other colonies or possessions in China under the control of European Powers, as well as to the other colonies of the British Empire, such as Australia, New Zealand, Canada, and others which are called "self-governing dominions." The Imperial Government feels very tender toward these colonists, and practically they are allowed to manage their affairs as they like. Since they are so generously treated and enjoy the protection of so great a power, there is no fear that these self-governing dominions will ever become independent of their mother country; but if they ever should do so, it is most improbable that she would declare war against them, as the British people have grown wiser since their experience with the American colonists. British statesmen have been awakened to the necessity of winning the good-will of their colonists, and within recent years have adopted the policy of inviting the Colonial premiers to London to discuss questions affecting Imperial and Colonial interests. Imperial federation seems to be growing popular with the British and it is probable that in the future England, Scotland, Wales, and Ireland will each have its own parliament, with an Imperial Parliament, sitting at Westminster, containing representatives from all parts of the British Empire, but America is the only nation which has added to her responsibilities with the avowed purpose of making semi-civilized tribes independent, self-governing colonies, and America is almost the only great power that has never occupied or held territory in China.

Let me ask again what is the object of nations seeking new possessions? Is it for the purpose of trade? If so, the object can be obtained without acquiring territory. In these days of enlightenment anyone can go to any country and trade without restriction, and in the British colonies the alien is in the same position as the native. He is not hampered by "permits" or other "red-tape" methods. Is it for the purpose of emigration? In Europe, America and all the British colonies, so far as I know, white people, unless they are paupers or undesirables, can emigrate to any country and after a short period become naturalized.

Some statesmen would say that it is necessary for a great power to have naval bases or coaling stations in several parts of the world. This presupposes preparations for war; but if international peace were maintained, such possessions would be useless and the money spent on them wasted. In any case it is unproductive expenditure. It is the fashion for politicians (and I am sorry to find them supported by eminent statesmen) to preach the doctrine of armaments; they allege that in order to preserve peace it is necessary to be prepared for war, that a nation with a large army or navy commands respect, and that her word carries weight. This argument cuts both ways, for a nation occupying such a commanding position may be unreasonable and a terror to weaker nations. If this high-toned doctrine continues where will it end? We shall soon see every nation arming to the teeth for the sake of her national honor and safety, and draining her treasury for the purpose of building dreadnaughts and providing armaments. When such a state of things exists can international peace be perpetuated? Will not occasion be found to test those war implements and to utilize the naval and military men? When you purchase a knife don't you expect to use it? Mr. Lloyd George, the English Chancellor of the Exchequer, in a speech in which he lamented the ever-increasing but unnecessary expenditure on armaments, said in Parliament: "I feel confident that it will end in a great disaster—I won't say to this country, though it is just possible that it may end in a disaster here." A man with a revolver sometimes invites attack, lest what was at first intended only for a defense should become a menace.

When discussing the craze of the Western nations for adding to their territories I said that white people can emigrate to any foreign country that they please, but it is not so with the yellow race. It has been asserted with authority that some countries are reserved exclusively for the white races, and with this object in view laws have been enacted prohibiting the natives of Asia from becoming naturalized citizens, besides imposing very strict and almost prohibitory regulations regarding their admission. Those who support such a policy hold that they, the white people, are superior to the yellow people in intellect, in education, in taste, and in habits, and that the yellow people are unworthy to associate with them. Yet in China we have manners, we have arts, we have morals, and we have managed a fairly large society for thousands of years without the bitter class hatreds, class divisions, and class struggles that have marred the fair progress of the West. We have not enslaved our lives to wealth. We like luxury but we like other things better. We love life more than chasing imitations of life.

Our differences of color, like our differences of speech, are accidental, they are due to climatic and other influences. We came originally from one stock. We all started evenly, Heaven has no favorites. Man alone has made differences between man and man, and the yellow man is no whit inferior to the white people in intelligence. During the Russo-Japan War was it not the yellow race that displayed the superior intelligence? I am sometimes almost tempted to say that Asia will have to civilize the West over again. I am not bitter or sarcastic, but I do contend that there are yet many things that the white races have to learn from their colored brethren. In India, in China, and in Japan there are institutions which have a stability unknown outside Asia. Religion has apparently little influence on Western civilization; it is the corner-stone of society in all Asiatic civilizations. The result is that the colored races place morality in the place assigned by their more practical white confreres to economic propositions. We think, as we contemplate the West, that white people do not understand comfort because they have no leisure to enjoy contentment; THEY measure life by accumulation, WE by morality. Family ties are stronger with the so-called colored races than they are among the more irresponsible white races; consequently the social sense is keener among the former and much individual suffering is avoided. We have our vices, but these are not peculiar to US; and, at least, we have the merit of being easily governed. Wherever there are Chinese colonies the general verdict is: "The Chinese make good citizens."

This is what the late Sir Robert Hart, to whom China owes her Customs organization, said about us:

"They (the Chinese) are well-behaved, law-abiding, intelligent, economical, and industrious; they can learn anything and do anything; they are punctiliously polite, they worship talent, and they believe in right so firmly that they scorn to think it requires to be supported or enforced by might; they delight in literature, and everywhere they have their literary clubs and coteries for learning and discussing each other's essays and verses; they possess and practise an admirable system of ethics, and they are generous, charitable, and fond of good work; they never forget a favor, they make rich return for any kindness, and though they know money will buy service, a man must be more than wealthy to win esteem and respect; they are practical, teachable, and wonderfully gifted with common sense; they are excellent artisans, reliable workmen, and of a good faith that everyone acknowledges and admires in their commercial dealings; in no country that is or was, has the commandment 'Honor thy father and thy mother', been so religiously obeyed, or so fully and without exception given effect to, and it is in fact the keynote of their family, social, official and national life, and because it is so their days are long in the land God has given them."

The cry of "America for the Americans" or "Australia for the Australians" is most illogical, for those people were not the original owners of the soil; with far greater reason we in the far East might shout, "China for the Chinese," "Japan for the Japanese." I will quote Mr. T. S. Sutton, English Secretary of the Chinese-American League of Justice, on this point. "The most asinine whine in the world," he says, "is that of 'America for the Americans' or 'China for the Chinese', etc. It is the hissing slogan of greed, fear, envy, selfishness, ignorance and prejudice. No man, no human being who calls himself a man, no Christian, no sane or reasonable person, should or could ever be guilty of uttering that despicable wail. God made the world for all men, and if God has any prefer-ence, if God is any respecter of persons, He must surely favor the Chinese, for He has made more of them than of any other people on the globe. 'America for the aboriginal Indians' was once the cry. Then when the English came over it changed to 'America for the English', later 'America for the Puritans', and around New Orleans they cried 'America for the French'. In Pennsylvania the slogan was 'America for the Dutch', etc., but the truth remains that God has set aside America as 'the melting pot' of the world, the land to which all people may come, and from which there has arisen, and will continue to rise, a great mixed race, a cosmopolitan nation that may, if it is not misled by prejudice and ignorance, yet lead the world." Although Mr. Sutton's phraseology is somewhat strong, his arguments are sound and unanswerable.

I now pass to some less controversial aspects of my theme, and note a praiseworthy custom that is practically unknown in the Far East. I refer to the habit of international marriages which are not only common in cosmopolitan America but are of daily occurrence in Europe also, among ordinary people as well as the royal families of Europe, so that nearly all the European courts are related one to the other. This is a good omen for a permanent world-peace. There have been some marriages of Asiatics with Europeans and Americans, and they should be encouraged. Everything that brings the East and West to-gether and helps each to understand the other better, is good. The offspring from such mixed unions inherit the good points of both sides. The head master of the Queen's College in Hongkong, where there are hundreds of boys of dif-ferent nationalities studying together, once told me that formerly at the yearly examination the prizes were nearly all won by the Chinese students, but that in later years when Eurasian boys were admitted, they beat the Chinese and all the others, and generally came out the best. Not only in school but in business also they have turned out well. It is well known that the richest man in Hongkong is a Eurasian. It is said that the father of Aguinaldo, the well-known Philippine leader, was a Chinese. There is no doubt that mixed marriages of the white with the yellow races will be productive of good to both sides. But do Chinese really make good husbands? my lady friends ask. I will cite the case of an American lady. Some years ago a Chinese called on me at my Legation in Washington accompanied by an American lady and a girl. The lady was introduced to me as his wife and the girl as his daughter; I naturally supposed that the lady was the girl's mother, but she told me that the girl was the daughter of her late intimate friend, and that after her death, knowing that the child's father had been a good and affectionate husband to her friend, she had gladly become his second wife, and adopted his daughter.

Those who believe in reincarnation (and I hope most of my readers do, as it is a clue to many mysteries) understand that when people are reincarnated they are not always born in the same country or continent as that in which they lived in their previous life. I have an impression that in one of my former existences I was born and brought up in the United States. In saying this I do not express the slightest regrets at having now been born in Asia. I only wish to give a hint to those white people who advocate an exclusive policy that in their next life they may be born in Asia or Africa, and that the injury they are now inflicting on the yellow people they may themselves have to suffer in another life.

While admitting that we Chinese have our faults and that in some matters we have much to learn, especially from the Americans, we at least possess one moral quality, magnanimity, while the primal virtues of industry, economy, obedience, and love of peace, combined with a "moderation in all things," are also common among us. Our people have frequently been slighted or ill-treated but we entertain no revengeful spirit, and are willing to forget. We believe that in the end right will conquer might. Innumerable as have been the disputes between Chinese and foreigners it can at least be said, without going into details, that we have not, in the first instance, been the aggressors. Let me supply a local illustration showing how our faults are always exaggerated. Western people are fond of horse-racing. In Shanghai they have secured from the Chinese a large piece of ground where they hold race meetings twice a year, but no Chinese are allowed on the grand-stand during the race days. They are provided with a separate entrance, and a separate enclosure, as though they were the victims of some infectious disease. I have been told that a few years ago a Chinese gentleman took some Chinese ladies into the grand-stand and that they misbehaved; hence this discriminatory treatment of Chinese. It is proper that steps should be taken to preserve order and decency in public places, but is it fair to interdict the people of a nation on account of the misconduct of two or three? Suppose it had been Germans who had misbehaved themselves (which is not likely), would the race club have dared to exclude Germans from sharing with other nations the pleasures of the races?

In contrast with this, let us see what the Chinese have done. Having learned the game of horse-racing from the foreigners in China, and not being allowed to participate, they have formed their own race club, and, with intention, have called it the "International Recreation Club." This Club has purchased a large tract of land at Kiangwan, about five miles from Shanghai, and has turned it into a race-course, considerably larger than that in Shanghai. When a race meeting is held there, IT IS OPEN TO FOREIGNERS AS WELL AS CHINESE, in fact complimentary tickets have even been sent to the members of the foreign race club inviting their attendance. Half of the members of the race committee are foreigners; while foreigners and Chinese act jointly as stewards and judges; the ponies that run are owned by foreigners as well as by Chinese, and Chinese jockeys compete with foreign jockeys in all the events. A most pleasing feature of these races is the very manifest cordial good feeling which prevails throughout the races there. The Chinese have been dubbed "semi-civilized and heathenish," but the "International Recreation Club" and the Kiangwan race-course display an absence of any desire to retaliate and sentiments of international friendship such as it would, perhaps, be difficult to parallel. Should such people be denied admission into Australia, Canada, or the United States? Would not the exclusionists in those countries profit by association with them?

The immigration laws in force in Australia are, I am informed, even more strict and more severe than those in the United States. They amount to almost total prohibition; for they are directed not only against Chinese laborers but are so operated that the Chinese merchant and student are also practically refused admission. In the course of a lecture delivered in England by Mrs. Annie Besant in 1912 on "The citizenship of colored races in the British Empire," while condemning the race prejudices of her own people, she brought out a fact which will be interesting to my readers, especially to the Australians. She says, "In Australia a very curious change is taking place. Color has very much deepened in that clime, and the Australian has become very yellow; so that it becomes a problem whether, after a time, the people would be allowed to live in their own country. The white people are far more colored than are some Indians." In the face of this plain fact is it not time, for their own sake, that the Australians should drop their cry against yellow people and induce their Parliament to abolish, or at least to modify, their immigration laws with regard to the yellow race? Australians are anxious to extend their trade, and they have sent commercial commissioners to Japan and other Eastern countries with the view to developing and expanding commerce. Mr. J. B. Suttor, Special Commissioner of New South Wales, has published the following advertisement:

"NEW SOUTH WALES. The Land of Reward for Capital Commerce and Industry. Specially subsidized steamers now giving direct service between Sydney, THE PREMIER COMMERCIAL CENTER OF AUSTRALIA, AND SHANGHAI. Thus offering special facilities for Commerce and Tourists. NEW SOUTH WALES PRODUCTS ARE STANDARDS OF EXCELLENCE."

Commerce and friendship go together, but how Australians can expect to develop trade in a country whose people are not allowed to come to visit her shores even for the purposes of trade, passes my comprehension. Perhaps, having heard so much of the forgiving and magnanimous spirit of the Chinese, Australians expect the Chinese to greet them with smiles and to trade with them, while being kicked in return.

I believe in the doctrine of the universal brotherhood of men. It is contrary to the law (God) of creation that some people should shut out other people from portions of the earth solely from motives of selfishness and jealousy; the injury caused by such selfish acts will sooner or later react on the doers. "Every man is his own ancestor. We are preparing for the days that come, and we are what we are to-day on account of what has gone before." The dog-in-the-manger policy develops doggish instincts in those who practise it; and, after all, civilization without kindness and justice is not worth having. In conclusion, I will let the English poet, William Wordsworth, state "Nature's case."

Listen to these noble lines from the ninth canto of his "Excursion."

> "Alas! what differs more than man from man,
> And whence that difference? Whence but from himself?
> For see the universal Race endowed
> With the same upright form. The sun is fixed
> And the infinite magnificence of heaven
> Fixed, within reach of every human eye;
> The sleepless ocean murmurs for all years;
> The vernal field infuses fresh delight
> Into all hearts. Throughout the world of sense,
> Even as an object is sublime or fair,
> That object is laid open to the view
> Without reserve or veil; and as a power
> Is salutary, or an influence sweet,
> Are each and all enabled to perceive

That power, that influence, by impartial law,
Gifts nobler are vouchsafed alike to all;
Reason, and, with that reason, smiles and tears;
Imagination, freedom in the will;
Conscience to guide and check; and death to be
Foretasted, immortality conceived
By all—a blissful immortality,
To them whose holiness on earth shall make
The Spirit capable of heaven, assured.

...........................The smoke ascends
To Heaven as lightly from the cottage hearth
As from the haughtiest palace. He whose soul
Ponders this true equality, may walk
The fields of earth with gratitude and hope;
Yet, in that meditation, will he find
Motive to sadder grief, as we have found;
Lamenting ancient virtues overthrown,
And for the injustice grieving, that hath made
So wide a difference between man and man."

Chapter 17. Sports

PERHAPS IN NOTHING DO THE CHINESE DIFFER from their Western friends in the matter of amusements more than in regard to sports. The Chinese would never think of assembling in thousands just to see a game played. We are not modernized enough to care to spend half a day watching others play. When we are tired of work we like to do our own playing. Our national game is the shuttlecock, which we toss from one to another over our shoulders, hitting the shuttlecock with the flat soles of the shoes we are wearing. Sometimes we hit with one part of the foot, sometimes with another, according to the rules of the game. This, like kite-flying, is a great amusement among men and boys.

We have nothing corresponding to tennis and other Western ball games, nor, indeed, any game in which the opposite sexes join. Archery was a health-giving exercise of which modern ideas of war robbed us. The same baneful influence has caused the old-fashioned healthful gymnastic exercises with heavy weights to be discarded. I have seen young men on board ocean-going steamers throwing heavy bags of sand to one another as a pastime. This, though excellent practice, hardly equals our ancient athletic feats with the bow or the heavy weight. Western sports have been introduced into some mission and other schools in China, but I much doubt if they will ever be really popular among my people. They are too violent, and, from the oriental standpoint, lacking in dignity. Yet, when Chinese residing abroad do take up Western athletic sports they prove themselves the equals of all competitors, as witness their success in the Manila Olympiad, and the name the baseball players from the Hawaiian Islands Chinese University made for themselves when they visited America. Nevertheless, were the average Chinese told that many people buy the daily paper in the West simply to see the result of some game, and that a sporting journalism flourishes there, *i.e.*, papers devoted entirely to sport, they would regard the statement as itself a pleasant sport. Personally, I think we might learn much from the West in regard to sports. They certainly increase the physical and mental faculties, and for this reason, if for no other, deserve to be warmly supported. China suffers because her youths have never been trained to team-work. We should be a more united people if as boys and young men we learned to take part in games which took the form of a contest, in which, while each contestant does his best for his own side, the winning or losing of the game is not considered so important as the pleasure of the exercise. I think a great deal of the manliness which I have admired in the West must be attributed to the natural love of healthy sport for sport's sake. Games honestly and fairly played inculcate the virtues of honor, candidness, and chivalry, of which America has produced many worthy specimens. When one side is defeated the winner does not exult over his defeated opponents but attributes his victory to an accident; I have seen the defeated crew in a boat race applauding their winning opponents. It is a noble example for the defeated contestants to give credit to and to applaud the winner, an example which I hope will be followed by my countrymen.

As an ardent believer in the natural, healthy and compassionate life I was interested to find in the Encyclopaedia Britannica how frequently vegetarians have been winners in athletic sports.[1] They won the Berlin to Dresden walking match, a distance of 125 miles, the Carwardine Cup (100 miles) and Dibble Shield (6 hours) cycling races (1901-02), the amateur championship of England in tennis (four successive years up to 1902) and racquets (1902), the cycling championship of India (three years), half-mile running championship of Scotland (1896), world's amateur cycle records for all times from four hours to thirteen hours (1902), 100 miles championship Yorkshire Road Club (1899, 1901), tennis gold medal (five times). I have not access to later statistics on this subject but I know that it is the reverse of truth to say, as Professor Gautier, of

---

1 E. B., 9th ed., vol. 33, p. 649.

the Sarbonne, a Catholic foundation in Paris, recently said, that vegetarians "suffer from lack of energy and weakened will power." The above facts disprove it, and as against Prof. Gautier, I quote Dr. J. H. Kellogg, the eminent physician and Superintendent of Battle Creek Sanitarium in Michigan, U.S.A., who has been a strict vegetarian for many years and who, though over sixty years of age, is as strong and vigorous as a man of forty; he told me that he worked sixteen hours daily without the least fatigue. Mrs. Annie Besant, President of the Theosophical Society, is another example. I am credibly informed that she has been a vegetarian for at least thirty-five years and that it is doubtful if any flesh-eater who is sixty-five can equal her in energy. Whatever else vegetarians may lack they are not lacking in powers of endurance.

It is needless for me to say that hunting, or, as it is called, "sport," is entirely opposed to my idea of the fitness of things. I do not see why it should not be as interesting to shoot at "clay pigeons" as to kill living birds; and why moving targets are not as suitable a recreation as running animals. "The pleasures of the chase" are no doubt fascinating, but when one remembers that these so-called pleasures are memories we have brought with us from the time when we were savages and hunted for the sake of food, no one can be proud of still possessing such tastes. To say that hunters to-day only kill to eat would be denied indignantly by every true sportsman. That the quarry is sometimes eaten afterward is but an incident in the game; the splendid outdoor exercise which the hunt provides can easily be found in other ways without inflicting the fear, distress, and pain which the hunted animals endure. It is a sad commentary on the stage at which humanity still is that even royalty, to whom we look for virtuous examples, seldom misses an opportunity to hunt. When a man has a strong hobby he is unable to see its evil side even though in other respects he may be humane and kind-hearted. Thus the sorry spectacle is presented of highly civilized and humane people displaying their courage by hunting and attacking wild animals, not only in their own native country but in foreign lands as well. Such personages are, I regret to have to add, not unknown in the United States.

The fact that hunting has been followed from time immemorial, that the ancient Egyptians, Assyrians, and Babylonians indulged in this pastime, does not make it any more suitable an occupation for us to-day. The good qualities of temper and patience which hunting demands are equally well developed by athletic sports. I understand that a good hunting establishment will cost as much as $10,000 (2000 Pounds) a year. Surely those who can afford so much on luxuries could find a more refined amusement in yachting and similar recreations. To sail a yacht successfully in half a gale of wind, is, I should imagine, more venturesome, more exciting, and a pastime requiring a manifestation of more of the qualities of daring, than shooting a frightened animal from the safe retreat of the saddle of a trusty horse; and not even the hunt of the wild beast can equal in true sportsmanship a contest with the wind and the waves, for it is only occasionally that a beast shows fight because he is wounded, and even then man is well protected by his gun; but whether yachting or swimming the sportsman's attitude of watchfulness is uninterrupted. I fancy it is convention and custom, rather than conviction of the superiority of the sport, that has given hunting its pre-eminence. It is on record that four thousand years ago the ancient emperors of China started periodically on hunting expeditions. They thus sought relief from the monotony of life in those days; in the days of the Stuarts, in England, royalty found pleasure in shows which were childish and even immoral. Of course in barbarous countries all savages used to hunt for food. For them hunting was an economic necessity, and it is no slander to say that the modern hunt is a relic of barbarism. It is, indeed, a matter of surprise to me that this cruel practice has not ceased, but still exists in this twentieth century. It goes without saying that hunting means killing the defenseless, in-flicting misery and death on the helpless; even if it be admitted that there is some justification for killing a ferocious and dangerous animal, why should we take pleasure in hunting and killing the fox, the deer, the hare, the otter, and similar creatures? People who hunt boast of their bravery and fearlessness, and to show their intrepidity and excellent shooting they go to the wilderness and other countries to carry on their "sport." I admire their fearless courage but I am compelled to express my opinion that such actions are not consistent with those of a good-hearted humane gentleman.

Still less excuse is there for the practice of shooting. What right have we to wantonly kill these harmless and defenseless birds flying in the air? I once watched pigeon shooting at a famous watering place, the poor birds were al-lowed to fly from the trap-holes simply that they might be ruthlessly killed or maimed. That was wanton cruelty; to reprobate too strongly such revolting barbarity is almost impossible. I am glad to say that such cruel practices did not come under my observation during my residence in the States, and I hope that they are not American vices but are prohibited by law. No country, with the least claim to civilization, should allow such things, and our descendants will be astonished that people calling themselves civilized should have indulged in such wholesale and gratuitous atrocities. When people allow animals to be murdered—for it is nothing but murder—for the sake of sport, they ought not to be surprised that men are murdered by criminals for reasons which seem to them good and sufficient. An animal has as much right to its life as man has to his. Both may be called upon to sacrifice life for the sake of some greater good to a greater number, but by what manner of reasoning can killing for killing's sake be justified? Does the superior cunning and intellect of man warrant his taking life for fun? Then, should a race superior to humanity ever appear on the earth, man would have no just cause of complaint if he were killed off for its amusement. There formerly existed in India a "well-organized confederacy of professional assassins" called Thugs, who worshipped the goddess Kali with human lives. They murdered according to "rigidly prescribed forms" and for religious reasons. The English, when they came into power in India, naturally took vigorous measures to stamp out Thuggeeism; but from a higher point of view than our own little selves, is there after all so much difference between the ordinary sportsman and the fanatic Thuggee? If there be, the balance is rather in favor of the latter, for the Thug at least had the sanction of religion, while the hunter has nothing to excuse his cruelty beyond the lust of killing. I do not understand why the humane societies, such as "The Society for the Prevention of Cruelty to Animals," are so supine in regard to these practices. The Chinese are frequently accused of being cruel to animals, but I think that those who are living in glass houses should not throw stones.

In this connection I would remark that birds are shot not only for pleasure and for their flesh, but in some cases for their plumage, and women who wear hats adorned with birds' feathers, do, though indirectly, encourage the slaughter of the innocent. Once a Chinese was arrested by the police in Hongkong for cruelty to a rat. It appeared that the rat had committed great havoc in his household, stealing and damaging various articles of food; when at last it was caught the man nailed its feet to a board, as a warning to other rats. For this he was brought before the English Magistrate, who imposed a penalty of ten dollars. He was astonished, and pleaded that the rat deserved death, on account of the serious havoc committed in his house. The Magistrate told him that he ought to have instantly killed the rat, and not to have tortured it. The amazed offender paid his fine, but murmured that he did not see the justice of the British Court in not allowing him to punish the rat as he chose, while foreigners in China were allowed the privilege of shooting innocent birds without molestation. I must confess, people are not always consistent.

The Peace Societies should take up this matter, for hunting is an imitation of war and an apprenticeship to it. It certainly can find no justification in any of the great world religions, and not even the British, or the Germans, who idolize soldiers, would immortalize a man simply because he was a hunter. From whatever point the subject be viewed it seems undeniable that hunting is only a survival of savagery.

EURASIAN AUTHORS

CHRIST
A DRAMATIC POEM
IN THREE ACTS

SADAKICHI HARTMANN

THIS WORK
IS DEDICATED TO THOSE
WHO HAVE
MISJUDGED, HUMILIATED, OR INJURED
ME
DURING MY PAST LIFE.

INTRODUCTION.

I have written this book because the "great Pan" is not dead yet. Sensuality rules the world as heretofore, and optimists like myself must seize every opportunity to awaken mankind from its Bacchanalian revery.

I am fully aware that mankind cannot be reformed by the medium of printed sheets of papers therefore this book is written merely: to cultivate a consideration for the severe contagious malady of humanity, with the hope of arousing an interest in individual liberty in regard to religion and morality.

In this drama I allow myself a freedom of expression, which will be understood only by the few who are able to rise with me to the height from which I regard man and the universe. Full of contradictions as life itself, it can scarcely be thoroughly appreciated before it has been performed on the stage, with appropriate dramatic music and scenic effects.

Whatever nation gives an ideal representation of my drama "Christ" can claim of having a National Dramatic Art.

THE AUTHOR.

PERSONS REPRESENTED.

JESHUA.

MOTHER MARIA, *his mother.*

MAGDALEN, *his sister.*

    Brothers and sisters to Jeshua.

AN OLD HERMIT.

TUBAL CAIN, *a money-dealer.*

HANNAH, *a pilgrimess.*

EVA, *a young widow.*

AHOLIBAH,

TABEA, } *Young girls of the village.*

HAGAR,

ELLOSAR, *a poet.*

OTHNIEL,

REUBEN, } *Young men of the village.*

SEMAJA,

    Men, women, children, temple-guard, etc.

CARUS MAXIMUS, *a Roman centurion.*

    Roman soldiers.

ZENOBIA, *a foreign queen.*

PRINCE PARSONDES.

CAMILLUS, *a Greek, her steward.*

ATMA, *a dancing-woman.*

    Cortege of Zenobia and Parsondes, stewards, male and female attendants, body-guard, amazons, musicians, palanquin-bearers, etc.

SYNOPSIS.

Act I. *Before Maria's Cottage, First Day, Evening.*

Act II. *1.—Interior of Maria's Cottage, Second Day, Dawn.*

    2.—Among the Sandhills, Second Day, Noon.

    3.—Before Maria's Cottage, Second Day, Afternoon.

Act III. *Zenobia's Camp in the Desert, Third Day, Night.*

Place: A Village in Palestine.

Time: August, 20 A. D.

CHRIST.

ACT I.

SCENE—*To the left Mother Maria's cottage. A road leads across the stage.
In the background a well. View on the sandhills.*

TUBAL CAIN (*enters with Mother Maria.*) Nobody is impatient with his creditors, Mother Maria. As I have said before, my demands you must meet. Old Tubal Cain may be pot-bellied and bandy-legged, but he is not such a fool as to wait until the next festive year, he, he.

MOTHER MARIA (*leaning on a staff.*) You only open your mouth to speak evil.

TUBAL CAIN. The poor can easily be generous. The rich have to be brutal now and then. Yet we two will remain friends, won't we, Mother Maria?

MOTHER MARIA. The desire of gain has no true friends.

TUBAL CAIN. Yet its power is omnipotent.—How is Jeshua? It seems to me that he brings nothing but bitterness upon her who bore him.

MOTHER MARIA. True, he never lends a helping hand in all our distress, and yet he is my favorite son. Sorrow is often the comfort of old age.

TUBAL CAIN. He does not labor, aye? Labor warms the body; he who does not work deserves his poverty.

MOTHER MARIA. He was born for something better. I, his own mother, have never understood the motive of his life. He is different to other human beings.

TUBAL CAIN. No matter whether a goat be white or black, it should give the same amount of milk. That is an old saying. Things learnt in childhood are not forgotten.

MOTHER MARIA. Then remember your mother; she never spoke an unkind word to anyone.

TUBAL CAIN. I remember my mother well, he, he. When a child, I laughingly grasped with my little fingers for the glittering coins, which she was clinking in her hand to please me. Gold rules this world. An ass who denies it.

MOTHER MARIA. Cursed be the man who first brought gold among his fellow men. It dries up every source of kindness and affection.

TUBAL CAIN. Mammon is a lust of possession, and so is love. Like all human efforts it contains as much good as evil. Without these gerahs we would have no temple in Jerusalem, no caravans bringing to us the luxuries of the East and West—no progress could take place. And those who willingly

220

denounce wealth in words would be the very ones to misuse it, if they could, he, he.

MOTHER MARIA. But to what purpose do you toil and struggle? Your gold creates no beneficial influence. Avarice is no enjoyment Tubal Cain. If you would but consent to make my dwelling yours, you would value my frugality. Mother Maria. Be silent— not another word!

TUBAL CAIN. I or another man, what is the difference as long as one is wholesome!

MOTHER MARIA. To insult a woman is an easy task. Tubal Cain.

TUBAL CAIN. Gossip says so, not I. I like you; that's all. I like stout women. Yes, I do. He, he.

MOTHER MARIA. I have loved but once.

TUBAL CAIN. But he was not your husband?

MOTHER MARIA. To the carpenter I was married against my will. It was adultery. I have loved but once. The sun shone hot upon me, but the golden light did not linger upon my head. Like a day of pleasure, it quickly passed. (*As to herself.*) One evening, standing out there in the desert, I mourned and longed for him who had left me for a hermit's life. I felt as if I were alone—alone in this wide, barren world. All springs of nature were at rest; neither bird nor insect seemed to live. All bright colors were lost in the darkness pervading the silent, desolate plain. Time itself stood still, as if hesitating to lift the veil from the immensity of that lonely, immeasurable stretch of sand, where hitherto, only the spirits of perished nations swayed in deep lament. It was a silence which my presence seemed to desecrate. An inexpressible fear came over me—a dream of heavenly love stormed o'er my trembling frame. I saw my lover's pale, wan face in clouds of raining light, and my maternal fruitfulness embraced the seed of Jeshua. (*She stands at the garden gate, in Titanic gloom after her short summer life, like the personification of the Jewish race—a picture, stem and sombre, like the Arabian desert.*)

TUBAL CAIN. Nature cannot be overcome. We all admire purity. It is our body that causes disturbances. We all err through bur temperament. Yes, yes. Mother Maria, love is a burden.

MOTHER MARIA. It is a cruelty to women wherever unlawful maternity is proclaimed a crime. As long as a woman's body glows with the warmth of youth, men will be desirous to test her amativeness. To him it becomes the memory of a radiant hour of joy; while the woman is obliged to suckle a being of whom she owns nothing but the burden and the shame.

TUBAL CAIN. You speak of free copulation, I of marriage.

MOTHER MARIA. Wedlock is but free copulation sanctioned by the law, nothing more. Leave me for tonight, good Tubal Cain. (*Turns to exit.*)

TUBAL CAIN (*shrugs his shoulders; aside.*) How I would like to pet her haunches! (*Exits slowly.*)

JESHUA (*enters, robed in dull red.*) Mother, what are your dealings with this man?

MOTHER MARIA. Those which necessity demand. (*Looks at Jeshua with a yearning expression.*)

JESHUA. Mother?

MOTHER MARIA. My son, why do you act so strangely? People speak of you in a slandering way. They say that you intend renouncing the Mosaic laws. Remember, you are a Jew, even if your father was a stranger to this land. Do not take vengeance upon me and my great sin by casting aside the religion of my forefathers.

JESHUA. Mother, have I ever said a word of reproach to you?

MOTHER MARIA. No, Jeshua.

JESHUA. Why then. Mother, must our roads always cross each other?

MOTHER MARIA. I would do anything, my son, to please you. (*Aside.*) Can I do nothing to draw him to me? (*Exits.*)

JESHUA. Shall I ever be understood? The world is so wide, and I am alone! The world is so wide!—oh, years without fulfillment! how I suffer, wasting *my* energies of youth! In hours of adversity I also grow faithless like the rest. (*Occupies himself in the garden.*)

ELLOSAR (*enters in conversation with* OTHNIEL, REUBEN, *and* SEMAJA.) Day for day, my whole being concentrates itself in a long, lascivious, lambent breath of longing! How can these amorous sighs be satisfied? Youth is troublesome enough without sterility.

OTHNIEL. Virgins, for various reasons, are as inconvenient as lewds. Childless widows and cunning jades seem most commendable.

REUBEN. The guide through all sexual temptations should be health, and health alone.

SEMAJA. Oh, let nature have its way; we can in nowise improve upon it. (*Points to* EVA.) A wind-stirred garment reveals to men all there is and can ever be.

ELLOSAR. True enough. I feel as if dewdrops should impearl her lanuginous chalice of hope. Oh, garden of defloration, what loveless denudations have swept through thy mystic realms!

JESHUA. Innocence in manly strength should consecrate each sexual kiss with salutary gentleness.

OTHNIEL (*to* SEMAJA.) In such company, it were best to be a hermaphrodite.

ELLOSAR. Virtue can only be based on knowledge and conviction. The innocent and ignorant can neither be chaste nor sensual.

JESHUA. Self-denial in love's desire, however fierce or faint it may be!

ELLOSAR. Dear friend, you speak of self-denial and know not what it is. The pregnant lines in which a woman is created would also weave a magic web around your soul while resting in a virgin's arm.

JESHUA (*smiles.*)

OTHNIEL. Oh, abstinent Essenian! For you must know that Jeshua is more modest than a sister of Ammon behind her curtain,

ELLOSAR. And you, wanton Saducee, cannot let a woman pass without insulting and undressing her in your imagination.

OTHNIEL. Can you?

REUBEN (*musingly.*) Jeshua and Othniel are two entirely different representatives of life, and yet alike. Neither will fathom fatherhood. Semaja (*to Jeshua.*) And do you never feel as if you should purify yourself in the ardent glow a deep delight?

JESHUA (*remains silent.*)

REUBEN. You see how natures differ. Othniel, you never knew restraint without dictation. Look at the Arabs, how they breed their horses. They do not allow the stallion to touch the mare after conception, while husbands molest their wives a few hours before delivery.

OTHNIEL. Should they mount their neighbor's mare, perhaps?

ELLOSAR. If men and women would practice purity in married life, what a glorious religion would rise from the present chaos! Science and philosophy, music and poetry, all arts, all noble, unselfish actions would be the children of one mother: Health.

OTHNIEL. When will that be?

ELLOSAR. The future will proudly assert that the seminal fluid of a perfect father is the very essence of life, and that upon the wombs of perfect mothers the happiness of the world depends. Sexual intercourse could be a religion! The wife, trembling with the hopes of maternity, embraces with all her trust and feminine grandeur her husband, who presses all his strength, his manliness, and ideal thought into her sacred body. Such a connection between body and body, soul and soul, is worthy of god—the creation of life, the eternity of nature, divinity itself!

OTHNIEL. If you were god, how different the world would be. (*Murmurs.*) For my part, Aholibah's suit my loins well enough.

SEMAJA. Such idle imaginings remain a blank to me.

REUBEN. It is a pastime. But who comes there?

SEMAJA. The old centurion, who has half persuaded me to join the Roman army.

CARUS MAXIMUS (*enters with soldiers and a crowd of villagers.*) Flock around the Roman eagle, boys! Show courage! Take the chance I offer you. Ovations and trophies shall be yours. Do not hesitate; enter a life of liberty! Nothing more glorious than a life of war!

JESHUA. Will mankind never lead a peaceful life?

CARUS MAXIMUS. Never, youth. War is a necessity; peace unnatural. What would become of man if he could not endure the sight of blood and death? What would become of valor, vigor, vassalage? They soon would have to sound retreat, and power would fall to the vafrous. I spent many years at Augustus' imperial court, unrolled many a parchment scroll, witnessed the devotions of many creeds, gazed at the triumphs of beauty in Rome and in foreign lands, but nothing met my eye that could rival this keen-edged sword. Rather a scabrous gladiator than a decrepit sage! To me, he is a god who knows no fear! Who will enlist?

SEMAJA. Put down my name! I have nothing to lose and much to gain.

YOUNG MEN. Also mine!—And mine!—Would I had no filial piety to perform!—Alas, that I am still so young!

CARUS MAXIMUS. Brave, my boys! You will never repent it. Blow the bugle! strike the drum! We march tomorrow. Now go, and enjoy the last evening at home; and let sweethearts and sisters decorate my future heroes with garlands of flowers. (*Exits with soldiers and young men, who shout and embrace each other!*)
Young girls and women come with jars and vessels to the well, TABEA *and* HAGAR *among them.*

HERMIT (*crosses the stage.*) I once dreamed like you, my boys. I also loved the burning sun; now, I prefer a clear and mellow evening. The feeling of approaching darkness and melancholy solitude of night, puts my mind at rest. All your strength, imagination, ardent zeal of youth, will arrive at the same goal. And as annihilation knows of no restraint, the nations which you conquer, as well as the Roman empire which you serve, will perish. At last all humanity will decay. Sun and stars will extinguish; like this day, the earth will sink into oblivion.

TABEA. She will soon be here. I long to see her.

AHOLIBAH (*enters with* EVA; *a mysterious, sensual smile plays continually about* AHOLIBAH's *lips, she is dressed in green and black!*) Are you speaking of the foreign queen? I am craving to know, how many of her suitors the enchantress has killed.

TABEA. Her camp equipments passed by this morning. At least thirty camels, accompanied by hundreds of slaves.

HAGAR. Why are some people so poor and others so rich?

AHOLIBAH. There is no greater harlot living; they say, she changes her lovers as we change our robes.

TABEA. That takes away all my pleasure of seeing her.

AHOLIBAH. You need not stay. The loom and spindle are waiting for you at home. (*Aside.*) Oh, if I could but lead her wild, unrestrained life! Oh, that there are thousands of men longing for us, and that we dare not satisfy them and ourselves. The thought drives me mad. Why is this forbidden and that not allowed? If it is wrong, why am I so created that at certain moments I feel like throwing myself into the arms of the lowest man?

EVA. Hush!

MOTHER MARIA (*sings inside the cottage.*) Unhappy children, having lost a parent still mother-naked, children growing up in ignorance and want, children bred without a kind word or kiss.

Toil along, toil along!

Unhappy lovers, young widows and widowers, parents sitting at the empty cradle, beggars, all diseased and deformed beings, poets and artists without success.

Toil along, toil along!

Unhappy mortals, struggling with poverty, sickness and sorrow, repentant sinners, all human beings who have a crime on their conscience,

Toil along, toil along, oh, toil along!

ELLOSAR. Look at the last greeting of the setting sun! What color-dreams weave over the distant hills! The evening star steals softly into the trembling air. (*The temple-guard is heard singing.*) Heaven on earth! That my art could hold this picture for eternity! But before we have comprehended it, it fades in its magic flight.

OTHNIEL. Ellosar, write a song on these colors, so hot and so wild!

REUBEN. The golden dust can be seen, but not grasped!

ELLOSAR. Always denying?

REUBEN. Always searching for truth.

ELLOSAR. And never admiring when it reveals itself.

TABEA. How wide the meshes of the spider's web are. A sure sign of bad weather.

AHOLIBAH. I dissolve in pain. (*The languid voluptuousness of Southern climes takes possession of her body.*)

EVA (*in profound silence watches the sunset.* JESHUA *comes into the garden and saws wood.*)

TABEA. Look at Jeshua.

AHOLIBAH. He pretends to be above curiosity.

EVA. Jeshua always acts as he feels.

OTHNIEL (*to* AHOLIBAH.) You spoke quite differently about him last summer, if I do not err?

AHOLIBAH. We sometimes change and know not why. Hagar. In my life, nothing changes. One day is like the other, full of pain.

HANNAH (*enters barefooted; she perceives* JESHUA, *and stands as if in a dream; the languid voluptuousness of Southern climes takes for a moment possession of her soul.*)

TABEA. Queer I could never understand Jeshua.

OTHER GIRLS. Nor I!—Nor I!

AHOLIBAH. What is there strange about it? Is he not the son of Mother Maria? Sons take after their mother. (*Aside.*) God forgive me for saying this. How I have loved that man! Milk exuded from my nipples from very joy, when I thought of him. And he rejected me!

EVA. Jeshua deserves everyone's love.

RECHA. There they come! (*Music is heard, slaves appear waving perfumed kerchiefs and strewing flowers, carmine, and gold dust on the road. Coins are thrown among the crowd, who shout Hosanna!*)

JESHUA. So everybody is saluted, whether friend or foe, as long as curiosity is satisfied. (*Enter* CAMILLUS *and attendants, some on horseback.* ZENOBIA, *dressed in striped black and golden yellow, is borne on a palanquin.* PRINCE PARSONDES *rides in a chariot. The village girls hail them with palm leaves.*)

PARSONDES. What a vile place!

ZENOBIA, We shall linger here over night.

PARSONDES. In your embrace the humblest spot; on earth converts into a place of bliss.

MURMURING OF THE CROWD. Isn't she just splendid!—She looks like the queen of abomination!—What sumptuous, saturated brilliancy!—What merciless glare and glitter!—Not half as dazzling as I thought!—Observe the luring glances of her emerald eye!—I wonder if the vermilion of her lips is real I—How grey those many-colored tunics look!—Will I be able to hallow her afterimage by my art?

ZENOBIA. How they stare at me! I am used to the shouting of multitudes. Soulless creatures, insipid fools, they envy me, and do not know that I am the unhappiest creature of them all. In my mighty passion I absorb all other ones. I stand smiling in the arena of the world, and shed my heart-blood unseen, in the carmine and gold dust of my poetry. (*Suddenly perceives* JESHUA, *and stares at him.* HANNAH *anxiously watches the queen.*)

CAMILLUS. What ails you, my queen?

ZENOBIA. Find out the name of yonder swain.

CAMILLUS (*aside.* May the gods of your forefathers preserve you from her luring smiles, young Jew.

ZENOBIA. I have never met the man of whom I desired children until now. Embracing him I could fall into eternal slumber. And mine he will be. An ocean of light surrounds me. Oh, could I but throw myself into its clear and steady flames, that it might purify and burn up ail that is foul within me!

AHOLIBAH. She has cast an eye upon the coyish dreamer. Ha! wait now and see, if he can resist that virulent demon of passion.

HANNAH. I knew it, I knew it! (ZENOBIA *and procession exit; the crowd follows them. A few remain, speaking about the event, then slowly disperse in different directions. Only* HANNAH *and* JESHUA *remain on the stage. It grows dark during the following scene.*)

HANNAH (*slowly approaches* JESHUA, *and whispers with sisterly affection.*) Beware! Beware!

Long pause.

JESHUA. Who are you?

HANNAH. A part of you. All else I love in you. Take what I am, it is yours!

JESHUA. Who are you? Hannah. I know no more, I simply feel that I belong to you, and to nobody else on earth. (*They gaze at each other for a long while, then embraced.*)

JESHUA. The first long, slumbering kiss confirms all that god and the heavens decreed.

HANNAH (*quivering with bliss.*) Hold me fast!

Pause.

JESHUA. Also upon us lingers the silent sadness known to all who listen to the woeful song of life and death. We soar above the dust and bitterness of human cares. When our lips meet, they touch—

HANNAH. Infinitude.

JESHUA, Infinitude. Our Love is as healthy and strong as the noon of summer days. Ages may sink into the past, yet our friendship would not change, not even with death, for we would continue—

HANNAH, Beyond.

JESHUA. Beyond. The waves of our mind meet on the vibrating ocean of air, and wandering to and fro, from soul to soul, call forth responsive thoughts.

BOTH (*as in a trance, hardly audible,* HANNAH *speaking more softly than* JESHUA, *like music accompanying a song.*) Our Love fills the world with the thunder of unearthly joy! We penetrate into all the kindred parts of the universe. Like eagles, we cleave the ambient realms of dark and darker blue, and break the dreariness of Northern darkness as inconstant lights. We sweep over vast, variegated plains, and sink with the roaring waters into the depth of the wild, unresting sea!

How glorious is our Love! We float with the jubilating songs of nightingales on the silver beams of night. We rest on the lips of lovers; we bloom with the flowers that fade unseen, and smile through the mist of tears at morn. We rest on Nature's bosom, and dream her naked dream of grace; we feel the burning passion of all mankind, and the body becomes as sacred as the soul!

How old and new is our Love! We are buried by hurricanes that crush the homes of peaceful men; we drown in seas of blood shed for a future state of joy. And, with enthusiasm's blazing flames our Love soars to the suns of heaven, and falls into the sunless gulfs of hell. We leap into the boundlessness of space, and taste in the rapture of one moment, the eternity of time!

We laugh at the violence of fate; we laugh at wealth, wisdom, beauty, power. We sink into each other's arms. Dark immensity of night surround us! We are in Love! (*In their kisses, body and soul are trembling in a rapturous embrace!*)

The heavens open! The widening infinite! Spirits of heaven and hell, they cast their sickles upon earth, and stars are falling from the clouds, and earthquakes split the realms, and still we cry for Love, more Love!

And from the unfathomed depth of this restless world rise thousands of gigantic visions. We tremble in the laments of life; we feel the holy agony, the godlike sufferings of the past; and our bodies crumble into dust, while our souls mount: to those wonderful, brooding stars, which flame through the sky in endless variation.

(Hermit enters)

Oh, everchanging orbs of God, you are the symbol of Love! Myriads of falling stars, that whirl around each other, you are like the maddening yearning of humanity itself the nameless longing of life and Love to throw itself into another life and Love, until you dash together in the fury of a glorious, overwhelming light! (*Meteors shoot across heaven.*)

HERMIT. Oh, world of fire-balls, destined to be embodied in one star, in you mankind can read, night for night, the secret of the universe, how glowing suns transform into cold and glittering stars of ice, till they collide to become once more the ardent suns of time and space. And like creation's cycling course the stars form circles, rolling forth in endless chains to nothingness. The fires of the universe prophecy their destiny in your immortal Love, (*extends his arms to* HANNAH *and* JESHUA,) when at last, in the far-distant future, all the ambitious suns of heaven tumble into one mighty, burning giant star, who will shed a light of redemption over the final union of hostile elements, sleeping mysteriously and motionless in the dark immensity of time. Then Love, the one colossal soul of the departed worlds, will dreamingly begin a new existence for decillions of ages to come. (*The old hermit exits, the lovers remain as petrified, in an embrace expressing the triumph of purity in Love. The stars are sparkling like diamonds on the turquoise vault. After a long pause, the curtain drops.*)

ACT II.
SCENE I.

SCENE.—*An interior of Mother Maria's cottage. The deep violet light of dawn streams through the windows. Jeshua's brothers and sisters sleep picturesquely grouped on mats, divans, and cushions, around a hearth of clay.*

JESHUA (*dreaming a morning dream.*) Oh, Hannah, star of my life, you shall not go! Can it be true that even you will fade from the heaven of my hopes? Your lips are twitching with secret wishes, yet your eyes are staring in bitter hate. Let us then part! No love proves true within these whirling spheres. Farewell, grey walls of my mother's home! Farewell to the sandhills and vineyards where I have roamed in hours of careless innocence! Farewell to all the interests of youth! Farewell, beloved one; farewell to all the sacred hours, the hopeful dreams of our love!

And hail to thee, thou dismal land, where the restive joys of our past will grow to unknown fates!—It is so dark around me now. No love proves true within these whirling spheres. Yet you I must remember in all eternity.

Day and night, roll on, roll on, and sweep I away my paradise of dreams! All better thoughts flee from my memory! Swift-gliding years in restless works are all that I behold.

Oh, nature, fill me with the violent energy of life! I wish to conquer and command. Now see me kneeling at the feet of those who wear the diadems of fame. I flatter them. I rise, and all their sins I own. Swift-gliding years in restless works are all that I behold, and thus: all former virtues turn but fugitive lights in the; haunting shadows of my self. Now I am king! Woe to you all! Like sultry winds, the breath of death lolls on the plain.

Humanity make no demands on me I You: speak of innocence, how it suffers in this fleeting dream; but what is that to me? Let them perish in this world of moan. Begone, with words you cannot threaten me! Away, detested race, I hate you. Do not curse me; accurse yourselves, for you have petrified my soul.

Oh, that I knew a being on whose breast I could forget that immortality is the fate of every living object on the earth! Oh, that I knew a place where I could rest when, in dark and dreary hours, the horror of loneliness steals on my weary heart! Yet all my life is vain. My soul knows love no more, and all my sufferings are eternal, creep into the infinite.

Oh, nature, you majestic queen of all, come with your storms, and let them desolate the lands! Open your deepest depth of hell, my mother earth, and take me back into thy burning lap! Fall upon me, ye proud and dazzling walls of heaven; bury the remnants of my life; oh, still under the ruins my reeling brain would feel the tortures of that thought from which is no escape!

Prophet star, thy light is fading in the purple rain of sin. Hope is dying, hope is dying, loud and louder grows the din. Blood, blood, blood through all the ages, from beginning to the end! Blood, blood, blood in every dwelling—glint of steel in clinching hand! Tears, tears, tears in every valley where the seeds of life are sown. Tears, tears, tears on every summit where a fruitful tree has grown!

Enough laments, enough of woe! Here I lie prostrate and forlorn before thy mighty throne, god of my better days; dead while living, waiting for a deathless death I pray! Hark! Hear I right? A voice is calling. "Human sins will be forgiven through your faith in Hannah's faith."

Oh, dreams of my youth, you golden memories of the past, help me to find my soul again! Oh, love, let sound thy melodies! Oh, morning sun of love, of first and only love, shine into my aching soul, that it may learn to hope again!

Dawn, aurora, a new life! The infinite sufferings of years are melting into tears of joy. Leave me, black night! Dark shadows, fly! Oh, slumbering world, awake! I pray to the star of immortality—to pure, unselfish love.

Curtain.

ACT II.
SCENE II.

SCENE.—*Among the sandhills. A road leads across the stage. At the right, a view on the sublime solitude of the desert.*

HERMIT. Oh, sunshine, sunshine, how you dazzle, and spread your light upon the vast and silent I plain. Here is rest from the turmoil of the t world. Everywhere silence: deep, sad silence; nothing torments me; it is as if I knew everything, and was set free from all earthly bonds. And yet as I feel at my heart, and listen to its peaceful hymns, pictures of the past are rising. Once more I stand in the golden light of youth. I longingly open my arms, as I was wont to do in the days when I was young, and I clasp the empty air. The desert lies before me. The hoped for happiness was but a dream of youth. Self-improvement has taught me to accept success and failure as they come. Hope is justified through nothing on this earth, for existence is illusion, and human efforts but a grand mistake. Even the greatest success is a failure. The sage alone never fails, because he never attempts to act. So I patiently wait, until I go to those regions, where neither weal nor woe can influence us, where ideas melt into the oblivion of Nirvana: a realm of perfect peace, without even a suggestion of the absence of ideas.

JESHUA (*enters in deep meditation.*) Will I succeed?

HERMIT. My son!

JESHUA. Will I teach mankind to lead a happier life than they do now?

HERMIT. How can sorrow be extinguished by a mortal?

JESHUA. By hope in all adversity.

HERMIT. Will it give them hours of absolute serenity, undarkened by the gloom of care?

JESHUA. Yes, if all human beings considered themselves the members of one family; if we assisted each other to overcome every evil that befalls us.

HERMIT. You speak of something, that can never be ours in all lights and shades of eternity.

JESHUA. Some glorious inspiration may form mysterious clouds around me— the shadows of the greatest light.

HERMIT. Vain endeavors! The eternal light may shine, but the darkness will

231

not comprehend it. Tell them to live without demands, and happiness will be theirs unawares. If we abandon appetites and restrain our passions, we escape all troubles and anxiety. We bring joy and pain upon ourselves. The highest phase of life is to be self-contained, immutable.

JESHUA. Who but a sage can do it? Inferiors cannot depend upon their strength alone. The reward of virtue by a higher power will give them self-enjoyment, rectitude, and peace.

HERMIT. Nature alone could do it. No promise can be more exalted than the voice which speaks in wind and water. Let nature sound its echoes in the human soul, and it will rise above nations, lands, and seas; above the world, above the stars, to search in the vast wastes of ether for its original home.

JESHUA. You are like the lily on the placid waters, sublime in mystery. Wait for the day of revelation.

HERMIT. The unknown will never be known, the unconscious will never be conscious.

JESHUA. You cannot rob me of my faith. If men and women had *no secrets* from each other, and felt that the intention is as good or bad as the deed itself, they would not hesitate to pity and pardon, to trust and assist each other. Then love would find its final utterance in all embracing sympathy. The rest I leave to the wisdom of my people.

HERMIT. On whose help do you depend in this gigantic task?

JESHUA. I trust in myself alone.

HERMIT. A man Who trusts in himself is isolated.

JESHUA. A man with new and bold ideas expects no help from others.

HERMIT. Bold youth, what is your will against that power that formed substance, life, and space from the chaos of time?

JESHUA. I know one man is nothing, fate everything, but some men become their own fate.

HERMIT. Kingdoms have fallen to ruins, the gods of old stand lonesome at their shrines, whole civilizations have been swept away in the furious run of time, the sand of the desert may swallow up all in Palestine—the loving arms that embraced me in childhood have withered long ago. Why should the laws of your new faith prove irresistible? Human life is a continual up-and-down, never-ending, never-changing, until everything has passed away.

JESHUA. If everything is transitory, if nothing can resist the gnawing tooth of time, if everything! that our eyes behold must gradually decay, let us at least wander towards the future, hand in hand, like lovers, like brothers and sisters, like the children of one god!

HERMIT. Progress will Welcome every gleam and glimmer of true light. (*Bugles sound; both listen. The Roman soldiers pass by.*)

SEMAJA. Farewell, Jeshua! Manhood is made to wander, and so am I. God alone knows whither. My love to Recha, and a farewell to all!

YOUNG MEN (*exit, shouting and singing.*)

JESHUA (*standing on a rock. Now and then the bugles sound, gradually dying away.*) God be with you! May everyone reach satisfaction at the end. I do not envy you. True, it is great, banner in hand, to lead an army of strong, armed warriors to victory. To march, crowned with the laurel wreath of fame, under triumphal arches to the Capitol! To sit on golden thrones, and have proud foreign queens kneel at one's feet. Alas! my road will also lead over battle fields, with mangled, festering corpses, pass through odious seas of stenchening blood; but it will lead to truth.

HERMIT. And what is truth?

JESHUA (*crosses his arms on his breast, and looks up to heaven.*)

HERMIT (*softly shakes his head, and exits.*)

Pause.

JESHUA (*prays.*) Oh, god of truth, I have listened so often to the captious and minatious words of my brethren; for years I have meditated if thou art truly existent, and always with the same result—reason denies thee, feeling affirms thee still. Oh, god of truth, thou art inexplicable! Who dares to manifest thee? Thou art to men and women what they should be to themselves. And yet the highest thought to which my urgent, auguring mind can rise, art thou: my property, nobody else's. Faith in thee is only in its totality alike, giving to every creature a different ideal of thy existence.—I am no Jew.—I belong to no creed.—I belong to everyone.—I endeavor to be god man.—Better voice within myself, thou art my god! Brethren, my god is within me. I am myself my god! (*Railing asleep, he murmurs.*) Dark spots and sparks of fire—streaks of red—a deluge of unknown colors—a luminous orb is drowning fast—familiar scenes rise reddish-brown—an unseen smile is floating by; the sin of love in a serpent eye.

Desert weaving.

ZENOBIA (*enters, dressed like the Assyrian Istar, with bow and quiver slung over her shoulder. She makes a sign to her female attendants to depart, then looks at* JESHUA *for a long while before she speaks.*) Why do my knees tremble as I loosen my girdle? Zenobia's pride has humbled the most audacious self-esteem, and shall not fail this time!

JESHUA (*raves in his dream.*) On sunny shades I creation's music—refluent waves of after-bliss I a cross is rising within the white and bluish mist —black, gigantic; it tills the universe—save one red flower climbing up the shaft, all else grows dark—and dead—also the flower breaks, and—(ZENOBIA *kisses* JESHUA's *mouth.*) falls upon my mouth like soft, human lips. (*He awakes.*) What fragrant dream of beauty blurs my sight? Ha! whom do I behold?

ZENOBIA. Zenobia, queen of the East! Cling to me, and leave on my lips the voluptuous breath of life, a deluge of fire, boundless desires for never-ending bliss. The yearning for an ideal existence as a curse on our head, and the wonderful flower of passion in the suffocating heat of our hearts, we wander lonesome on the shore of cold reality, extending our arms towards a home of joy, which will never be ours.

JESHUA. We two have nothing in common.

ZENOBIA. Nothing but ambition. Are not our kisses like lamentations from the depths of the earth? Are not our sighs like the hungry cry of two majestic beasts of prey, searching for glowing flesh and blood in the desert of sensation?

JESHUA. Woman, I do not understand your passion nor your sadness, for sad you are. I long for deep affection which is lasting, like the love of a mother to her child; the love of twin brothers and sisters; of the artist for his art, destined by higher decrees to mingle and be one.

ZENOBIA. Oh, listen to the flow of my tears over the nothingness of life, in the elegies off those nights when my body can find no rest it the limitation of its sphere; when my better self! is praying for an eternal sleep, in the arms of deathless joy. Then there is within me a chaos in which good and evil spirits crowd together in indescribable confusion. My body, as if possessed by madness, devoured by passions gloomy and imperishable, is in a desperate war with my better self, which strives for the serene perfection of a god.

JESHUA. If nothing can satisfy you, what do you want of me?

ZENOBIA. Give me peace in pleasure, and the riches of Judea shall be yours! I will make you the ruler of vast domains; nations shall kneel at your feet, and hail you king! Your name shall be carried over land and sea; it shall even reach distant Lundinium. The kings of all the world, shall pay homage to you!

JESHUA. Worldly enjoyments are valueless to me.

ZENOBIA. Then I renounce them. (*Scatters gold.*) I tear the jewels from my limbs! (*Throws off her jewels.*) Take me as I am, I am yours!

JESHUA. Woman, what is your aim in this? If you think of tempting me, your efforts shall prove vain.

ZENOBIA. Oh, come to the festivals of my native land; to flower beds in enchanted groves, near shimmering lakes! There, before the sacred shrines of our shadowy gods, wrapt in clouds of incense, men and women dance to the tinkling of cymbals and the wailing of flutes. Bare shoulders and naked breasts glow in the tepid atmosphere, flowing garments are floating in an ocean of light, and myrrh and orange blossoms sink fading to the ground. How the torchlight dwells upon the half-veiled limbs! Louder and louder the music sounds, swifter and swifter the footsteps glide over the glittering sand! Look at those bacchantes! Their dark eyes—what wild desires they express—their trembling nostrils and moist, quivering lips! In emulous ardor every movement tempts with boundless bliss! Thought and feeling are forgotten, only the body lives!

JESHUA. Cease to speak! I will listen no further.

ZENOBIA. Oh, for the days of soft rubescence, ere my free, fresh inflorescence was unmarred by violation's glow! The nightingales sang softly on sycamore and cypress tree, mild southern winds caressed the blushing rose in all her maiden bashfulness. The odors of the dew-lit chalice stole softly into the silent air of night, and in her burning chastity of passion the flower yielded all her sweet virginity. The leaves fell fading to the ground, and only stem and spine looked up to the blackest sky.

JESHUA. Life is to all a mournful dream.

ZENOBIA. Should I have thrown away the withered wreath which has ornamented my hair, hung my rumpled garment on the thorny hedge and donned a servant's garb?

JESHUA. I pity you.

ZENOBIA. No, I continue to drink the bacchanalian joys of life! I kindle the evanescent sparks of the hearth to a mighty flame, enrapture and drink enraptures, receive and give, think and feel with the ambitious energy of youth, though spring has left my features and the noonday sun has passed the summit. Follow me to fragrant bowers! The wrinkled garments fall from my limbs, while the languid, half-closed eyes look around in search. You, the lover, sink down at my side.

JESHUA. Temptress, leave me! I can never be yours!

ZENOBIA. Press closer and closer to me! Listen to nature's voice. It is the expression of our overflowing lives. The forests sound, the waters roar, and in the trembling air the fire flies build their heaven of sparkling light, like fickle stars that crowd the firmament of night.

JESHUA. Let me go! Inordinate love can gain no power over me.

ZENOBIA. Behold me as I am! (*Rends her garment.*) This godlike form is yours!

JESHUA (*yields for one moment, then suddenly frees himself.*) I still resist!

ZENOBIA.—What woman's son are you?—I see my efforts to conquer you are in vain; but in my I body boils a sea of blood. Now I give vent to all inhuman feelings that find shelter in my belly's flame! (*Seizes her dagger!*) I'll limb and laniate the body of my wayward suitor; lacerate his selfish heart, and amidst writhing mutilations and smoking sloughs of blood, I shall stand triumphant! (*Stands for one moment transfigured as the incarnation of lust, then throws herself upon* JESHUA, *who disarms and forces her to the ground. A groan comes from* ZENOBIA'S *lips, she murmurs*) Forgive! (*and clings to the burning sand in voluptuous despair. The sun bums intensely!*)

JESHUA. Oh, woman, your incessant, fearful struggle of the body with the soul, of light with darkness, j reality with the ideal, is like the universal song of life and death. You are immortal, even with your faults, which fetter you to the shadow of shadows, and your virtues, which lift you to the light of lights.

Curtain.

ACT II,
SCENE III.

SCENE AS IN ACT I.—JESHUA'S *brothers and sisters, eating dried dates and drinking camel's milk, sit in the garden.* JESHUA *mends his Sabbath breeches.*

MAGDALEN. Brother, what is love?

JESHUA. A flower growing in the human soul. Its buds break forth and open to a life of sunshine. At first a zephyr gently kisses the trembling leaves; suddenly a storm starts up, and the chill, dark earth consumes its fading charms. For the flower of love has no abode on earth; her yearning is for an eternally faraway home, from whence she has come, to which she must return. And if she reveals herself in her serenest beauty, she stands on the grave of two human beings, who have drunk from her chalice the benediction of another world.

MAGDALEN. This is very sad; and does love never dwell upon earth in any other form?

JESHUA. Never.

MOTHER MARIA (*sings inside the cottage.*) Unhappy lovers, young widows and widowers, parents sit ting at the empty cradle, beggars, all diseased and deformed beings, poets and artists without success,

Toil along, toil along!

(*Calls*). Come in, my children. Leave Jeshua alone!

MAGDALEN. Never tell me such a story again, for it makes me weep. I feel as if the angels had to weep in heaven to see such sorrow upon earth. (*Opens her eyes wide, with an expression of innocence, as if her glance should penetrate all the world. Children exit.*)

JESHUA. Who can understand the soul of children? —They should be taught by the young.—We will never get farther than this child—. What will my future Magdalen be?—Last night I beheld a world sublime beneath the sky; how can I speak such bitter words of sorrow now? (HANNAH *enters.*) Strange feelings have come over me. I hardly know myself. (*Breaks a lily and plucks out the stamens.*)

Pause.

BOTH (*as before.*) The chaos of our childlike dreams have merged into unsatisfied desires. Our love is poisoned by heart-corroding thoughts, and the mysteries of creation have become the temptation in our Eden-like dream. (*Their voices falter, tears fall from their eyes, profound sobs convulse their throats,* JESHUA *kneels at* HANNAH's *feet, lowers his head in bitter supplication, and weeps. She looks at him with an expression of indescribable sadness, her whole body trembles, then the sunshine breaks through the clouds, an angelic smile glides over her face, and the drapery unveils itself from the divine beauty of her body. Music.—*HANNAH *hastily arranges her drapery, which formed a background to her denudation!*)

JESHUA. Your nakedness was a prayer! (*To* ELLOSAR, *who enters!*) Soon you will hear from me. The mission of my life begins this very hour. (MOTHER MARIA *enters the garden, and converses with* HANNAH.)

ELLOSAR. People, nowadays, believe only in signs and wonders.

JESHUA. Then I will stoop to do them.

ELLOSAR. Oh, that I could always stay with you!

JESHUA. You could forget yourself, but not your art.

ELLOSAR. Oh, my beloved art!

JESHUA. Fair for a day.

ELLOSAR. Fair for ages to come! Art eternizes whatever is beautiful; each idea by purity composed has right to breathe the vital air. Inspirations of color, sound, or thought will yet survive when the pyramids have fallen to ruins, and the temple of Jerusalem no longer lifts its golden dome against the azure of the timeless sky.

JESHUA. May be, but to what end?

ELLOSAR. To beautify—to beautify!

JESHUA. Proceed, my prophet, and with the crown of martyrdom enter the kingdom of heaven!

ELLOSAR. I wonder who is the greater dreamer of us two? (*Sits down near the well.*)

MAGDALEN (*enters.*) Brother, take a walk with me! (JESHUA *takes her hand.*)

MOTHER MARIA. Bring me home some flowers.

MAGDALEN. I am not to break any flowers.

MOTHER MARIA. Why, my darling?

MAGDALEN. I think that flowers have a soul like human beings.

MOTHER MARIA. Angel, a flower yourself! (JESHUA *and* MAGDALEN *exit.*)

HANNAH. I love him more than god and all existences! Oh, Mother, do you know those moments when a soul in ecstacy of bliss rises to the eye in shape of tears, moments when our faltering lips would murmur words of wonder, what mighty incomprehensible thoughts the human mind can hide, which give us a glimpse into infinity which give us the right to hope?

MOTHER MARIA. I do, my child, only too well.

HANNAH. Thus I have felt since his first kiss which still glows upon my lips. If there is a Paradise on earth, it is this, it is this!

TUBAL CAIN (*passes by.*)

MOTHER MARIA. Your words return to me all that I have lost. Cod of my forefathers, send thy blessing upon these two until they find repose in thy omnipotence. (*Exits.*)

ELLOSAR (*watching* HANNAH, *aside.*) Oh, Jeshua, let thyself sink deep into the inward smile of loving souls.

HANNAH. If I could make him happy!

AHOLIBAH (*followed by* ZENOBIA, *disguised.*) Hasten, he may soon return.

ZENOBIA. Leave me! (*Hands gold to* AHOLIBAH, *who joins* ELLOSAR.) I have arranged my plans. (*Laughs wildly.*) How That homely mendicant in patched clothes can make him dream of love! (*To* HANNAH.) Where are your thoughts?

HANNAH (*absent minded.*) With him, alas!

ZENOBIA. You recognise me?

HANNAH (*nods.*) What do you want of him?

ZENOBIA. Fear not that I come to do him injury.

HANNAH (*murmurs.*) He is invulnerable.

ZENOBIA. I also love him.

HANNAH. Who can help loving him?—How I pity you.

ZENOBIA (*aside.*) Audacious one!—You know the ambition of his life?

HANNAH. I feel what it might he. He will succeed.

ZENOBIA (*aside.*) Oh, for her faith! And yet one obstacle exists.

HANNAH, Name it.

ZENOBIA. It would make you more unfortunate than human lips can devise.

HANNAH. I do not understand. No service which I could render him would bring unhappiness to me. Name it, I implore you.

ZENOBIA. He loves his ambition most of all. Your faithfulness would hinder him in its fulfillment.

Pause.

HANNAH. That my dream should come to such an end! Life without him will be a void, for I loved him, not love.

ZENOBIA. He loves love.

HANNAH. I obey.

ZENOBIA. Your self-denial will bear fruit, though you may never witness it

HANNAH. I will gladly bear all in his name, unworthy as I am. And now away, far away, over burning deserts! Zenobia. Remain with me in your distress. You shall be my bosom friend, (*aside*) my slave! Hannah. Lead me forth!

ZENOBIA. We both will mourn for him. (*Aside.*) Now I may hope for victory.

Hannah. Farewell, lord of my soul, farewell! (*Exits with* ZENOBIA.)

AHOLIBAH. Oh, Ellosar, you despise me because I like to be caressed and kissed by those I love? Does not the bee also prefer to suck the thyme because it gives the sweetest honey? Am I so different to other girls? Show me one who does not go astray before her marriage. (OTHNIEL *and* REUBEN, EVA *and* TABEA *enter.*)

ELLOSAR. No embroidered garments, however flaunting they may be, can hide the leprous sores of vice. And many a female, though virgin-knotted still, may be a greater harlot than she who is the odious friend of every man.

AHOLIBAH. You are cruel and unjust. How can a woman remain pure. Has nature fashioned her to live an abstemious life? Women have, perhaps, more right to expect chastity of men, than you of us.

ELLOSAR. I bear you no ill. Yet some night when your hands are toying with your breasts, or glide listlessly between your thighs, make an effort, stop your willful play, and ponder on maternity.

OTHNIEL. Who knows how you will speak thirty years hence? Perhaps like bald-pated Habakuk around the corner, who did not succeed in reforming the world, and now is doing trade in bread and cheese. He grumbles, "Fine arts are very nice; but to make money in this damned country one has to sell something that turns into dung."

ELLOSAR. A person who listens to a dirty story without disgust, should be spit at.

OTHNIEL (*laughs.*) You better change humanity into a spitting dish, moral philosopher!

ELLOSAR. What is the use of art for Othniels? My consolation is that every human being is of some use. So also my efforts will not be in vain. Should I die unknown they will be like the blossoms which the trees shake off in spring; if I succeed, like those who defy the threatening siege of rain and storm, and finally bear fruit.

TUBAL CAIN (*enters.* Mother Maria, *standing at the door, leaves on perceiving him.*) She does not wish to see me. Well, Mother Maria, I will get there after all. If it could only be done without wooing. Why not simply say, I am male, you are female—let us marry; let us have offspring. The animals have more sense than we.

HAGAR *and other girls come home singing from the fields.*

TABEA. A weird song!

EVA (*dressed in dark blue, with red girdle and red blossoms in her hair.*) Like the curious question. What comes after death?

ELLOSAR. Look at these flowers, just gathered from the field. How beautiful they are! What fragrant smell! Now, look at these that fade away. O'er what regions do their odors roam? Your answer tells what human minds of immortality may know.

OTHNIEL. What a wonderful imagination!

REUBEN (*shaking his head.*) Onanism!

OTHNIEL. A peculiar association of ideas!

REUBEN. Why, human beings are after all nothing but degenerated animals, degenerated by mental self-abuse.

OTHNIEL. I believe you would make an owl of your mother, if it would serve your argument.

REUBEN. Why not, as long as I am in the right?

TABEA. I fear nobody exactly knows what is right or wrong.

REUBEN. Right is where conviction is.

ELLOSAR. Then everyone is right, and all controversy ends.

OTHNIEL. No generation is ripe for the revelation of two geniuses.

ELLOSAR. Tabea hinted at the truth. One human being never learns to understand another; even parents and children, brothers and sisters, husbands and wives walk side by side, like perfect strangers, through this life.

TUBAL CAIN. And well for them that it is so. How could a man succeed otherwise?

OTHNIEL. I am sure you have grown fat by the ignorance of others.

REUBEN, Nature gave him cupidity, and he made use of it.

TABEA. Could not success spring from a purer source?

ELLOSAR. It often does, but the waters grow turbid: as they onward flow. I

TUBAL CAIN. Every word you speak is dirt; he, he. A man succeeds only by patience, cunning, and hard labor. In the beginning be a sycophant, adnescent to everyone you need. Sell your conscience, turn a hypocrite, pry for the weakness of superiors, seize every opportunity by which to rise, and by persistent knavery—clandestine, of course—success is sure to come. Then kick aside superfluous friends, and profit by your slyness. Be a blood-sucker, incendiary, virgin violator, the most infamous wretch that ever breathed, all the same they'll come and lick your feet. Believe old Tubal Cain; he may be wrong in many things, but he is right in this. Now for a flask of wine with Habakuk! (*Exits;* OTHNIEL, REUBEN, *and* TABEA *follow.*)

HAGAR. I understand nothing of their talk. I work the whole day in the fields, and when I come home I take care of my younger sisters and brothers. I have not even time to pray. I am happy only when I am asleep. A terrible guilt must rest upon us that we can be so unhappy, (*Slowly exits.*)

ELLOSAR (*watching* EVA.) For ages could I look at her latent, luscious limbs. Each of her motions reveals the sumptuous sensuousness of all terrestrial scenes. The fiery flame of twilight gold on her white marble limbs, the distant blue, the pink and green suggestions, mysterious tints, sighs of virginity, sweet music to the eye! Her arms, her heaving breast, the chaste line of her tender, swelling hips, the night of ebon hair. And then her lap, night within light, dark star of future's hope, the unattainable of vital strength—creative beauty, sempiternal, forming the uniting link between man and the infinite! An angel lost between heaven and earth, the light of god upon her head and her feet wrapt in the shadow of fleeting days! (*Joins* EVA *at the well.*) Will you share this drink with me?

EVA (*looks dreamfully at him, then drinks.*) Oh, if it were the draught of oblivion! (*A heavenly smile plays around* ELLOSAR's *lips; he presses a kiss on her sad, dark eyes, her pale cheeks begin to glow, a warm, melodious mystery quivers through every atom of her soul.*)

Long pause.

EVA. My love died without the crowning glory of a woman's fate. A life-long ache in a nightless life has sealed the surrender of my yesterdays.

Pause.

ELLOSAR. Eva, confide in me! The secret, long sorrowing of your soul is sacred to me. Oh, do not blush! You have loved, but in vain. You are childless against your will. Be not ashamed! I am as healthy in body and mind as you. One fierce embrace suffices. The *idea* alone shall reign when we are linked together. Take this kiss unto the welfare of the child which now we shall create. *(He kisses her forehead, leading her away.)* Come, lie with me, muse of my body! Uncover your nakedness! Let flesh be flesh, let soul be soul! Perfume of maternity, rise into the air! We create our children, not in tepid chambers with lurking sensations in the regions of shame, nor on debauchment's bed of flowers of soft, sirenic power, but undraped in the open air, on the life-kindling bosom of mother earth. The Philistines will cry; "The land has fallen to abomination!" The prophets of mankind will murmur: "The dawn of another race!" *(Exits with* EVA.)

JESHUA *(enters, carrying* MAGDALEN *in his arms; he carries her into the cottage; re-enters, and stands at the garden gate.)* An unredeemable dreariness of thought has come over me. I have a strange presentiment that something terrible will happen before the close of this day. Where is Hannah? I see her nowhere. Hannah! Hannah! No answer! Where can she be?

AHOLIBAH *(timidly, having remained in the background durmg the preceding scenes.)* I know where Hannah is.

JESHUA. Speak!

AHOLIBAH. She has left the village, with the foreign queen.

Jeshua *(utters a cry of despair, and falls backwards; his mother and a few passing friends gather around him. It grows dark, as before a coming storm. He rises suddenly.)* Follow me!

Curtain.

ACT III.

SCENE—*Camp in the desert, Before a tent, to the right,* Zenobia, *crowned and in gold and crimson drapery, rests on a couch, like a personification of the world's agony. An orgy, magnificent and unrestrained, occupies the remainder of the stage. A feast of colors, as suggested in the pictures of Hans Makart, pervades the scene. In the background, a group of palm trees, behind it a view on the desert.*

ZENOBIA. Oh, voluptuous breath of life, burst from the intestines of the earth, and overwhelm me in thy furious majesty! Simoons, come from the desert, devour me in your burning heat! I can no longer breathe in this dark solitude. Pent-up rivers, descend in torrents, embrace me with your foaming waves, and carry me back to the watery chaos! Oh, glowing fires above my head, fall from heaven and burn these mighty limbs to ashes!

There is a fire in my breast! Bring me some palm-wine! Some wine, I say! *(Tears the goblet with a threatening gesture from the slave, empties it in one gulp, and hurls it to the ground; to the slave.)* Ha! you are strong and nobly built.—Take him away! My Lybian lions roar for food. Strike the cymbals, eat and drink, glorify my divinity!

Life glares at me like the empty black bottomless eye-sockets of my punished slaves. The god of this land separated light from darkness, why not in me? When will the sun break through the storm-cloud of my sorrow? A ghost of barrenness is doomed forever to haunt the labyrinth beneath these fervid breasts. I have given orders that the poems of Sappho should be demolished, and my golden verses distributed instead. I have sent hundreds of sculptors to Mount Sinai to change that mountain into one mighty, colossal bust of me. I shall have temples erected all over this floating sphere, and everyone shall mock at the Ephesians' arrogance. All this, however, leaves the same frost and fire within me. Oh, had I the power to chain the tempests, and move the mountains at my command! Oh, had I thousand bodies that I could lie with thousand kings at one mad moment of inebriation! Oh, were the ocean a goblet of blood, that I could gulp it down in one draught! Would that satisfy me?—No!

Where are my stewards, Camillus, Koa, and the rest? Gold, gold, more gold, I cry! (*Scatters gold.*) I want a hundredfold Croesean wealth to build a road to heaven, that I may visit unknown worlds.

What are these fireballs that dance before my eyes? These grinning faces—myriads of faces! Now they unite into one Cyclopean head, with the same abominable grin around its haggard lips. Hand me a flaming sword! I'll chop it off from the misshapen shoulders of the universe, that I may be alone with myself and the eternity of my despair. This world is too narrow for more than one.—I am queen of earth, lady of heaven, mother of all existences! Kneel and tremble! (*Her vassals kneel.*) Kill me, gods, or I'll kill you! (*Stares motionless at heaven.*) There is a blot upon my brain, and I see life in different colors to the rest. What power has a god? Can they forget the past? No, even the deathless gods are deprived of making that which is past, undone. (*Aside, showing her teeth.*) All this is but a vulgar comedy, and I play the fool myself. (*To the stewards.*) Distribute some precious stones among my guests—sapphires, as hard as they. (*To* CAMILLUS.) Let your hand rest upon my forehead, Camillus. All seem satisfied, save I.

CAMILLUS. My queen, a passion like yours will never be understood.

ZENOBIA. What shall I do?

CAMILLUS. How can a mortal counsel god?

ZENOBIA. There must be something which could radiate the empty void around the earth, within my soul.

CAMILLUS. To squander love, and ask for no return.

ZENOBIA. To squander love, and ask for no return would be the birthday of another life. Yet 1 cannot stand at the portals of glory and bestow such benevolence. My world-wide passion yells for sempiternal sin.

Oh, Tammuz, why didst thou betray me? At thy breast of fire I would never have felt the power of darkness which now pervades my life. Love is the light which illumines all, and once extinguished nothing remains but perdition. Oh, Tammuz, return with thy purple flood of light; let me sink into thy languid stream of gold; let me dissolve in thy glorious heat—lost, lost forever!

CAMILLUS. Alas! who has not experienced the pangs of love?

ZENOBIA. You also, Camillus?

CAMILLUS. Yes, my queen. I also roamed through the garden of Aphrodite, dreaming that its roads were strewn with roses, sonnets, and laurel crowns. The brilliant skies have lost their brightness. We left those beautiful shores of golden sand, and the waves which caressed the sea shells on the strand have lost their crest of silver foam. We have departed from that island, with its verdant hills. The melancholy dreams of future bliss no longer visit us in the sylvan groves of hope, and the roads, where we wandered arm in arm, are desolate, overgrown with weeds, like lonesome walks in the historical gardens of the past. Only the marble temple of our love still stands in all its majesty, amidst the changing scenes of autumn, but the fire of its altar is long extinguished, and the garlands of luminous flowers which entwined the columns have long withered, and only the sweet sadness of our childish faith still lingers in that realm of peace. At times, dreamlike melodies carry me back to the classic shores of Greece, where the human body in all its naked purity, sculptures lines of poetry into the marble blocks of Paros. Oh, could I wander again along the villas near the sea, and there under the dark foliage of the cypress trees, while yellow leaves sweep over marble steps, dream the dreams of a happy past.

PARSONDES. Zenobia, so deep in thought?

ZENOBIA. And you shouting for pleasure as loud as ever?

PARSONDES. That alone is joy in living! To dress in the finest shades of green and blue; to carry a sharp sword; to bridle a fire-striking mare; to be wasteful to excess in drink and food! To force some cold, bright beauty to the ground, to carnalize a stubborn, struggling sacrifice, while strained eyeballs and meandering tongue still indicate desires indomitable! Let me unkiss the wanton sorrow between your lips incarnadine!

ZENOBIA. Camillus, something to while away the time.

CAMILLUS. My queen? A fight of female gladiators— the rites of violation—a sanguinarian tragedy—the dythirambs of northern bards—Atma, the dancing woman.

ZENOBIA. Let her appear!

ATMA, (*of lush and lithsome shape, draped in silvery gauze, veiling her as water veils a bather, enters. Her loose, dark hair is interwoven with golden threads. Her saint-like visage, with its deep, sad eyes, bears Pre-Raphculitic reminiscences. She stretches her limbs in full enjoyment of life, and endeavors to express by the most rhythmical motions, accompanied by soft music, all phases of love. Beginning with the purely physical, her dance becomes more and more dignified and spiritualized until at last it represents the ecstasy of perfect purity in love. Her limbs reveal the highest poetic beauty capable of being expressed by the human body, and Dancing reaches in this new, ideal way of revealing abstract beauty, the glory of her sister arts.*)

CAMILLUS. What suggestions for an artist! What s inspiration for a poet's soul! What ethereal flights toward the infinite!

ZENOBIA (*to* ATMA.) Take this tiara!

PARSONDES. How, my love's oblation!

ZENOBIA (*to* ATMA.) Be free! You gave me for one moment oblivion of myself.

CAMILLUS. That woman has driven all repose from my breast. The Lydian dreams of her marble limbs make me tremble. The Greek statues are awakened to musical life. A new art has risen from the past.

PARSONDES. And all this you see in that lean woman over there?

CAMILLUS. I do. Form-language seems to be incomprehensible to you; there are but few who understand it.

PARSONDES (*shrugs his shoulders?*) Zenobia, the night is cool and it grows late. The waters deluged the red nelumbus long ago. Oblivion from the hungry, idle monotony of day beckons from yonder tent, and where the giant tiger skin is spread, let your lyre sound the song of love's great rage; let me, like night upon the darkening world, descend upon your trembling, glowing frame.

ZENOBIA. It would not tremble nor glow for you. Hours of unknown joys soar from my darksome bed, and luxuries unseen, unfelt, obliviate my tremulent past. The sea of lust recedes, and the sound of the softest kiss sojourns in sylvan scenes, where the nightingale is sweetly singing, where brisk morning breezes sway, and where the bee is humming from flower to flower.

PARSONDES. Fluid sighs and weaving pain—golden cataracts bursting through love's domain—all creation sinks low as the waters glow, as we absorb the scaturient flow—deep, darkling desires—fire in fire—daedalian coition—antemundane nihilation—(*seizes her with violence.*)

ZENOBIA. Begone! Take away your wanton face; all vices of humanity cry from your earth-drawn limbs! One step nearer, and this dagger will be plunged into your venomous breast!

PARSONDES (*staggering, hisses forth.*) Your immane pride shall have its fall,
poor, wasted, aging godling! I cease to be your paramour. In amorous
fever search in vain for other kings of ideal adulation—while I in wild
delight, roam night for night through variegated fields of fornication!
Women serving but as drains for men are indistinguishable to me. (*To
partakers of the bacchanal.*) Fair hoiden, come! (*gropes at her lactescent
bosom.*) or your flesh in venerous heat will burst through its pregnant
vesture to-night. And you, dumb statue of maidenhood demure, I swear
your cold carnation will yet be inflamed, that like Zuleikha's glossy
skin, it will be irradiant of all carnal sin. Come all, undrape, nudate,
and in amorous confusion form Prince Parsondes' cushion, cover, and
couch! (*The courtezans shrink brfore him in sexual disgust or hope, as they
accompany him.*)

ZENOBIA (*to the rest.*) Leave me!

CAMILLUS. Good night, fair queen. May your heart be at rest, may the gods
grant you extended years of glory! (*Exit.*)

ZENOBIA. The present is born in agony and sinks with agony into the past.
Night and day pass each other in dreadful silence, and stare into my de-
spairing face. What pleasures have been floating down on my rapid stream
of life? Its rushing torrents brought me nothing but desire, brutal acts, and
then disgust. And now, having met the man who could change my whole
existence, in repugnant pity he turns from me, despises me for her, this
beggar-child. (*Seizes her lyre, and sings softly.*)

When gardens lie dreaming in moonlight, the nocturnal flower begins
her reign, unfastening her mantle of glimmering white, perfuming the air
with a sinful strain.

The night moths are lured to the dangerous fire, each sips from the
nectar of her desire, while her soul is yearning for unknown treasures that
can never be hers in her life of pleasures.

(*It grows silent in the camp. The cries of hyenas now and then interrupt
the stillness.*)

Oh, night, send a mild and balmy influence o'er my frame! The sins
I have committed turn to righteousness in the restless sable clouds of thy
mysterious power. Lull my thoughts into quiescence; lowery darkness loom
before my lurid inward eye, and give me sleep—sleep—death!

Death? Death is my bitterest foe! Dreadful vision of decay, do not
grind thy yellow, jagged teeth at me; drag thee aside, or my fist will break
thy monstrous gaping jaw of black, unfath omable mystery! There it comes
crawling towards me, and rolls its eyes in furious rage. Its pointed, wind-

ing tongue jerks for my breasts. Its boiling, putrid breath stagnates the air. Diseased claws dig deep and deeper into my angry flesh. Help, help! I will depopulate the world, and feed you with its carcasses. Gnaw away my outward beauty; let me rot, but let me live! Strike me blind, deaf, dumb, immovable, and I will thank thee still, if you but let me live! I beg thee, I command thee, let me live! Who is there? (*Runs up to* HANNAH, *who enters.*) Ah I it is you—through whom I suffer. By what magic did you win his love? Confess, or I will kill you.

HANNAH. I loved him, and he—loved me.

ZENOBIA. What else?

HANNAH. I know not.

ZENOBIA. You lie! (*Strikes her.*)

HANNAH. I forgive you.

ZENOBIA. Speak!

HANNAH. Strike me again.

ZENOBIA. You refuse? Then you must die.

HANNAH. May it be so.

ZENOBIA (*claps her hands.* CAMILLUS *enters.*) Strike off her head, and hurl it into some hyena's jaw.

CAMILLUS. I cannot.

ZENOBIA. Do it, or suffer death yourself.

CAMILLUS. I cannot.

ZENOBIA. I'll do it myself!—I cannot. (*Sits down. An attendant enters in haste, and whispers to* CAMILLUS.)

CAMILLUS. My queen, the young Jew stands at the entrance of the camp, and asks admittance.

ZENOBIA (*takes a deep breath.*) Is he alone?

CAMILLUS. No, a tall Jewish woman stands at his side, and a few friends accompany him.

ZENOBIA. If you value your life, let them not enter! (Camillus *exit.*) What will the coming hour reveal to me?

HANNAH, He calls me. I hear it, and I must welcome him.

ZENOBIA (*aside.*) Now I must venture all; now or never. His she shall not be at any cost! How now, Camillus?

CAMILLUS (*enters.*) He has entered.

ZENOBIA. Have I no body guard Are my servants all asleep? They shall suffer for it, and so shall you, ungrateful hound!

CAMILLUS. The guards are as blameless as I. Nobody can use violence if the earnest, piercing glance of that young Jew is fastened upon one's face.

ZENOBIA (*looks at a ring on her finger, which contains poison, seizes a goblet, puts the poison into the drink.*) Hannah, your lover has come, and you shall follow him. Come, drink with me to his happy return!

HANNAH (*drinks.*) Jehovah be praised for his-wonderful guidance that led Jeshua back to my arms!

CAMILLUS. My queen, they come. (JESHUA *enters, followed by* MOTHER MARIA, ELLOSAR, AHOLIBAH, *and a few villagers.*)

JESHUA. Queen, return my love to me.

ZENOBIA. Take her, there she stands.

HANNAH (*bursts forth with a cry of joy. Enraptured she throws her arms wide open, makes a few steps towards* Jeshua, *then staggers and faints away.*)

JESHUA. Hannah, what has befallen you? Speak, look up, your love has come, and waits for you. Hannah, awake! Open your eyes, and speak to me! No answer. Your hands are of eburnean hue, your limbs are stiff and lifeless. Could it be? (*To* CAMILLUS.) Speak, if you know! Is she dead?

CAMILLUS (*firmly.*) She is poisoned.

JESHUA (*stands for a moment, as if petrified, then makes a sign to his mother and friends to be calm.*) Peace! Be still! She speaks.

HANNAH. Let me fall into slumber. It is better so. I had nothing to do in this world but to make you happy, and for that you are not in need of me. I do not wish to darken the splendor of the sun. Do not mourn for me, yet think of me often when I am no more. Farewell, beloved, farewell! Is it the last farewell? (*She looks for a long while up to heaven, then turns her eyes on* JESHUA, *and dies.*)

MOTHER MARIA. Woman, restore her life, or I will strangle thee with these, a mother's hands. Do you hear me?

ZENOBIA (*absentminded.*) I see but him. Who are you?

MOTHER MARIA. His mother, who will avenge her death, if such a crime can be avenged.

JESHUA. Mother, use no violence; you have no right to do so.

MOTHER MARIA. How! No retribution?

JESHUA. No, Mother, no. (*To the others.*) Respect the dead!

MOTHER MARIA. Maranatha! Maranatha!—Oh, that that demon could feel no pity for this tender flower!

JESHUA. Yes, Hannah, thou art like a broken flower. Thus far thou couldst blossom in this garden of transitoriness, now bloom on over the grave! The beautiful has no abode on earth. (AHOLIBAH, *in mute despair, draws close her robe over her breasts.*)

ELLOSAR (*aside.*) Oh, Jeshua, the fire of your soul is so prolific that every spark will kindle conflagrations in countless lives of countless generations!

ZENOBIA (*lost in wonder, steps to* JESHUA, *kneels at his feet, her head bent low. He takes her head between his hands, and looks with sublime sadness into her eyes. An idea of immortality begins to dawn upon* ZENOBIA'S *mind. She speaks in a trembling voice.*) Master, judge your slave!

JESHUA. I have no right to judge. We all are sinners, and need salvation. Let the god of truth forgive us all! (*In an undertone.*) All for giving love is the redemption of my faith. (*For the first time a halo is seen around* JESHUA'S *head, caused by a concentration of light on his back. All kneel or bow their heads in reverence.*)

Curtain.

SUGGESTIONS
FOR A PERFORMANCE OF
"CHRIST."

In case the author could not be present to supervise the first production of his drama "Christ," the following demands are made by him, the fulfilment of which he deems not only desirable, but essential for a satisfactory performance:

1. A well-ventilated theatre, with comfortable seats, each commanding a perfect view of the whole stage.

2. An intelligent audience, not indulging in the naughty caprice of coming too late, of leaving their seats regularly during the intermission, of wearing colossal hats, of chatting and laughing during the performance, and of applauding at the most inappropriate occasions.

3. An invisible orchestra of first-class musicians, (the dramatic music to be descriptive in the style of Massenet).

4. A proscenium enclosed by a large, broad, golden frame, so that every situation on the stage is made to appear like the representation of a painting, and that from curtain to curtain the action proceeds like a series of pictures, each worthy of a painter of repute.

5. A stage manager who, in his directions and arrangements, will borrow freely from all arts, and prove bold enough to gain a laurel wreath in introducing successfully the nude into the dramatic art. (If he should grow a little nervous at the"undrape"of Hannah and Zenobia, and the orgy in the camp, he is kindly asked to remember that tact and bold artistic inspiration will overcome all obstacles).

6. Actors and actresses who are not exclusively mercenary in their views, and believe that the dramatic art has other ends besides that of amusing. (The author would like to see a Duse or Clara Morris as Aholibah, a Possart or Got as Tubal Cain).

7. Supernumeraries, superior to those of the Saxon Meiningen Company, i.e. who are more natural and artistic, by displaying a greater variety of movement and expression, without becoming conspicuous.

8. Light and atmospheric effects as perfect as contemporary science, skill, and taste can produce, (for instance an adaptation of those used at the Urania lectures).

9. Panorama-like scenery, with effects of impressionism always in harmony with costumes and accessories.

10. Costumes revealing a close study of the innumerable pictures that relate to the old and new testaments.

11. Picturesque and natural looking, if necesssary, solid properties.

Conversations with Walt Whitman

Sadakichi Hartmann

URING MY PHILADELPHIA STUDENT DAYS I discovered in the parlor of my relatives—plebeian, philistine grand uncle and aunt of mine; peace be with their souls!—a volume of poetry, I believe, the only one in the house and not remarkable at that, which lay there lonesome as if in state. It had been presented to them by their daughter, who had made a good match by marrying lumber, and in the eyes of the parents was equipped with all those excellent qualities which a modem American lady should possess. The book was cherished accordingly; now and then the mother's hand glided caressingly over the gold embossed covers, but it was never read. It was an edition of Stoddard's poems. I perused them, recognized their worth, and laid them aside for ever. I did not know that indirectly through them, I should make the acquaintance of the most American intellectual individuality these States have hitherto produced. It came about in the following way.

At that period of life, like Ulrich von Hutten, I was more anxious about my spiritual than bodily welfare, and really abused my body to a shameful degree. I had given up all regular work in order to study. How I subsisted then as at many subsequent periods, I really cannot tell. I enjoyed the humorous weekly allowance of three dollars, that went largely towards the purchase of second-hand books, for which purpose I rummaged for hours through all the different stores, and of course Ninth Street was also my favorite hunting ground.

On one of these expeditions I entered a little store which hitherto had escaped my invasions. It looked as if it had never been swept, the dust lay a quarter of an inch thick on the shelves. The proprietor, dusty like his books, with a rich layer of dandruff on his back and shoulders, his coat and shirt front spotted with tokens of his meals, was sitting on a box, a cigar clenched in his mouth, and reading very intensely. He was a man of middle age, with quite a fierce interesting physiognomy, and as I soon found out, different to the ordinary booksellers—also his stock was more select—being the author of several excellent poems.

I soon became a regular frequenter of this place, where amongst others I made the acquaintance of an old, well to do Quaker—dressed in old fashioned drab suit, clerical neckwear, and broad brim, exactly as the Friends had walked about Independence Hall a hundred years before—who played an important part in my drama of life, as he launched me into a more intellectual society than hitherto had been my deplorable fate to associate with.

And all this happened simply because I accidentally mentioned the author of the volume of poetry lying in state in my relatives' parlor. The dusty bookseller was highly astonished, that I, only a late edition to the conglomeration called Americans, knew Stoddard's poems. A conversation about American literature ensued, he became interested in me, and introduced me to his acquaintances.

We had regular little meetings in this shop, and discussed one literary subject after the other, and during one of these, the dusty bookseller advised me to call on Walt Whitman. "He is living right across the river, in Camden, he likes to see all sorts of people. "The Quaker argued that it had always been his intention to go over, but somehow he never got to it, and as he was an old man, I should do it instead. A young Jewish lawyer present remarked with triumphant glee that he has crossed the ferry with Whitman sitting at his side.

So I decided to go.

MY FIRST VISIT.

IT WAS IN NOVEMBER, 1884, THAT I paid my first visit to Walt Whitman.

After crossing the Delaware—in my excitement to get there I took the wrong ferry, which lands the passengers a few blocks higher up the river than the other—I asked a policeman if he knew where Whitman resided. "Of course, I know—" he directed me: "—and then you see a little two story frame house, grey, that's the place."

Arrived in Mickle Street, one of the most quiet and humble in provincial Camden, I easily found number 328 and rang the bell.

It was a disagreeable day, snow was lying on the ground, and though it was thawing, the wind felt cold as it sped through the streets and rattled at the shutters.

An old man with a long grey beard, flowing over his open shirt front—the first thing I actually saw of Whitman was his naked breast—half opened the door and looked out.

SADAKICHI: "I would like to see Walt Whitman."

WHITMAN: "That's my name. And you are a Japanese boy, are you not?"

(Except very small boys the only person I met in those years who recognized my nationality at the first glance).

SADAKICHI: "My father is a German, but my mother was a Japanese and I was born in Japan."

WHITMAN: "H'm—Come in."

And he led me into the small and humble two windowed little parlor, with its chilly atmosphere, as no fire was lit, and everything in great disorder. The first color impression of the interior, was a frugal grey. He sat down at the right window, where he was generally to be seen, with his face turned towards the street. Visitors seated themselves at the opposite side. Between the host and guest stood a table, actually covered with books, magazines, newspaper clippings, letters, manuscripts. A demijohn, which looked very suspicious to me until I was better informed, occupied a conspicuous place on the table, and during the summer a glass with flowers, brought by some lady-friend, was always within his reach. The rest of the room looked very much like the table; a varitable sea of newspapers, books, magazines, circulars, rejected manuscripts, etc., covered the floor in a topsy-turvy fashion, and only here and there odd pieces of furniture, a trunk, a large heap of his own publications loomed up like rocks. On the mantlepiece stood an old clock, surrounded by photographs of celebrities and friends, on my first visit also a few apples and onions were lying there. On one side of the mantlepiece hung the portrait of his father, on the other side that of his mother: two strong, highly interesting physiognomies. As I studied them one day, he remarked: "I never forget that my ancestors were Dutch."

There was nothing overwhelming to me in Whitman's face, but I liked it at once for its healthy manliness. It seemed to me a spiritually deepened image of contemporary Americans: an ideal laborer, as the Americans are really a nation of laborers. Above all else I was attracted by the free flow of his grey hair and beard, and his rosy complexion, Boucher like, only healthier and firmer in tone. Of his features the large distance between his heavy eyebrows and his bluish grey eyes, (calm and cold in their expression) denoting frankness, boldness, haughtiness, according to my physiognomical observations, particularly interested me. His forehead was broad and massive, not furrowed by Kantean meditation, but rather vaulted by spontaneous *prophecies* (in the sense in which Whitman applies this word to Carlyle, viz: II 169).[1] His broad nose with dilated nostrils showed with what joy of living he had inhaled life.

---

1 Volume and page quotations from the 1891-3 edition, David McKay, publisher. 33 South Ninth Street, Philadelphia, Pa., recommended by Whitman as the most complete and satisfactory.

He was dressed as usual in a grey suit, and negligé shirt with a broad turn-over collar. I was too much impressed by the passive power of his personality, and occupied in studying his appearance and the *milieu* in which he lived to be able to remember much of this first conversation.

At that time I was stage-struck, and of course mentioned my intention to devote myself to the histrionic art; I contemplated a special study of Shakespeare's fools (though I was rather too tall for them, they should be played by Marshall Wilders).

WHITMAN: (shaking his head): "I fear that won't go. There are so many traits, characteristics, Americanisms, inborn with us, which you would never get at. One can do a great deal of propping. After all one can't grow roses on a peach tree."

I spoke of Japan, of the beautiful bay of Nagasaki though I did not know much about it from personal recollection.

WHITMAN: "Yes, it must be beautiful."

On leaving he gave me a proof sheet copy of "After all Not to Create Only," saying paternally: "Read it over six or eight times and you may understand it."

"Come again, come again!" he shouted after me.

VISITS DURING 1886, MARCH—OCTOBER.

ONE OF MY FIRST VISITS, AFTER I had returned to Philadelphia from my first European trip, was to the "good gray poet." I told him about my studies, my stay in Hamburg, Berlin and principally Munich, where I had enjoyed a delightful series of conversation with Paul Heyse, the foremost living author of Germany; also that I had written an article "Ein Besuch bei Walt Whitman" for the "*Münchner Nueste Nachrichten*" in which I had made some comparison of his works with the old Greek literature, a comparison I was rather ashamed of.

I felt relieved, however, when he remarked: "The Greek nation was the most remarkable one after all."

Speaking of Germany, he observed with paternal good-will, "The old countries have also their destiny—there is no such thing as decay."

I purchased from him two copies of the 1882 McKay edition of his literary work.

"One is for you?"he asked, "I let you have it for half price."

"Do you sell many?"I inquired.

"Very few, very few," and he shook his head, "I believe not more than two hundred a year,"he added with slight mockery.

Whitman was always very fond of speaking of his literary achievements, and remarked on various occasions:

"There is a certain idea in my works—to glorify industry, nature, and pure instinct."

After commenting on Browning. "If anything has a destiny, the English language has a destiny. In my books, in my prose as well as my poetry are many knots to untie."

"*Leaves of Grass* are the reflections of American life and ideas which reflect again."

Leaves of Grass! How adequate a title! Truly his poems are chaotic in appearance like clusters of wild grass. As we loll amongst them, looking from blade to blade, they seem to us so prosaic, and yet so rhythmical in their hieroglyphic simplicity and munificent utility. And considering them from some distance we observe with what master hand these spears are grouped together, as if Gothic Dürer had outlined them, as if we were gazing into the forest-like halls of nature's cathedral.

As my hesitancy at calling too often had been allayed once for all by his cheerful "Come again, come again!" only a short time elapsed before I was again wending my way to Camden. I read to him a little treatise on beauty, my first original literary effort in English that I had flogged out of my brain with considerable exertion during an afternoon in Fairmount Park.

I read a sentence that sounded very much like Millet's: "All is proper to be expressed, provided one's aim is only high enough," and which he quotes as a motto (II, 302).

"Where did you get that from?" he started up, most eagerly.

I explained, and continued to read; when I had finished I asked: "Well, what is your opinion about it?"

There was a pause, as if he wanted to indicate that my writing did not call forth any opinion in him, then he said leisurely: "They are truisms—I am no worshipper of beauty. I do not believe in abstract beauty."

At that time I did not exactly know what he meant by abstract beauty, so I merely nodded and uttered a long drawn 'Ye-es' with a knowing air.

As I was leaving, he pointed towards a bunch of red carnations that were standing in a glass before him.

"Take a pink!"

I took one, pressed it among my "Leaves of Grass," and have kept it ever since.

Many of his visitors have complained that Whitman was unbearably selfish in his social intercourse. Of course they gave in, that they could walk straight into his parlor, shake hands with him, and sit down whenever they liked, but right there all privileges ceased, as it was simply impossible to make him speak, and after a few vain endeavors, shy at first and then more or less indignant, they had to give it up as a hopeless task. True enough. Whitman had a peculiar habit of being absent-minded in company, especially that of strangers—which Dr. Max Nordau considers one of the strongest proofs of Whitman's moral insanity—and to the despair of uninitiated visitors he answered all their questions with his favorite ejaculation: oy! oy? or oy!? This peculiarity excited the ire of many visitors, and with right, as some had come all the way from England and were full of expectancy about the harvest they were to reap of wise oracular utterances—but why should a man always feel like talking, at any time of the day, with any person who might have taken it into his head to call, often out of sheer curiosity or egotistical purpose! I personally found him sociable enough. At times I also found it extremely difficult to induce him to take an actual active part in a conversation, and do something else hut listen and ejaculate, but I generally found a successful remedy in simply talking on, jumping from one subject to the other, until finally he became interested in one thing or another, and when he had once begun, it was comparatively easy to proceed. On several exceptional occasions we talked for two or three hours without interruption, which clearly revealed to me, however, that he had no remarkable conversational power. He was no Johnson, no ready wit, or speculative monologist, had nothing whatever of the fluent delivery of learned men, or of the French *causeur littéraire*. He was always awkward in his utterances, often clipping verbs and conjunctions, making abrupt halts, leaving sentences unfinished—in short applying somewhat the style of his shorter poems—which really made it laborious to get anything of literary value from his conversation.

AN IMPORTANT VISIT.

I have read your books right through," I exclaimed beamingly as I entered.

"Oy! oy?—Did you make anything out of it?"

I then told him the various impressions his writings had made upon me, and finally asked: "Do you believe that mankind can be improved by books?"

WHITMAN: "I can hardly say that I had the idea to better mankind. I grew up like a tree—the poems are the fruit. Good literature ought to be the Roman cement; the older it grows—the better it serves its purpose."

An old peddler passed by. Whitman waved his hand, his famous *Salut au Monde*, as he did to nearly every passer-by.

The ragged old man stopped before the window and displayed his ware.

Whitman greeted him with a cordial "How do you do, sir?" and leaning a little out the window pointed at a set of collar buttons: "How much are they?"

PEDDLER: (holding them up to him) "Five cents."

WHITMAN: "No, thanks, I don't need any to-day."

Then followed an awkward pause.

I produced the copy of "After all Not to Create Only" with which he had presented me, handsomely bound.

"Why how nice it looks!" he exclaimed, scrutinizing it from all sides.

"Won't you inscribe something in it?" I asked.

"Thanks," he answered, and holding the book on his knee, his habitual way of writing, he penned down the words, 'Given to C. S. H., by Walt Whitman' in his immense, uncouth, heavy-stroked handwriting, which offers marvelous opportunities to chirographists.

After this performance another pause, and a few vain attempts on my side to get him interested in some topic.

I mentioned at haphazard that my old Quaker friend had been one of his very first admirers, having studied the 1856 edition.

"Why I must go to see him," he exclaimed enthusiastically. "Yes, that's what I am going to do!" He never did, but we talked for a while quite seriously about how it could be accomplished without exerting him.

"I want you to do me a favor—" and Whitman suddenly rose, dragging himself slowly step by step, with the help of a stick in a sideward direction through the room and upstairs. I looked after him for an explanation, but as none came, glanced over some books on the table, and was attracted by an old voluminous edition of Walter Scott's poems with numerous margin notes in red ink. He returned with a clipping of a German newspaper, handed it to me, and asked me to translate it. It was an ordinary newspaper concoction on "Leaves of Grass," comparing his style with that of the psalmists.

WHITMAN smiled: "I don't know why some men compare my book with the Bible."

Another pause ensued.

For at least half an hour I spoke of a dozen different subjects or more, without getting anything else but an occasional oy! oy? as answer, nevertheless, one could presume from the way Whitman poised his head, that he was listening quite attentively most of the time.

At last I broke this silence by mentioning that I had read Bryant's "Thanatopsis." "There is something large about it," I remarked.

WHITMAN: "He is our greatest poet. He had a smack of Americanism, American individuality, smack of outdoor life, the wash of the sea, the mountains, forests, and animals. But he is too melancholy for a great representative of American poetry."

SADAKICHI: "It seems that the New England States have produced nine tenths of all our American literati (a word I had learnt from Whitman, which he used with preference instead of authors, poets etc). I cannot understand the worship of Emerson. Many of his ideas one can find in the Alexandrian philosophers."

WHITMAN: "Emerson's deficiency is that he doubts everything. He is a deep thinker, though he had hardly any influence on me; but people say so; maybe, without my knowledge. He had much of the Persians and Oriental people. He is only the offspring of other suns tumbling through the universe."

For a moment I thought of Whitman and Emerson, arguing under the old elms of Boston Common about certain passages in the "Children of Adam" and Whitman, after listening for two hours to the well nigh indisputable logic of Emerson, being "more settled than ever to adhere to his own theory." (American genre painters should tackle that subject!)

WHITMAN: "Did you read Holmes?"

SADAKICHI: Very little. He serves his humor in a dainty fashion; yet I cannot digest it, it is too dry for me."

WHITMAN: "He is very witty, very smart, not first rank and not second rank; man of fine culture, who knows how to move in society; he takes the same place in modem society as the court singers and troubadours in the Middle

Ages, who had a taste for castles, ladies' festivals, etc., who knew exactly how to move among kings and princes; but something was failing, that very thing which would have made him a poet."

His opinion about Mark Twain was similar.

SADAKICHI: "It seems to me, as if all these men produced nothing new. They are like imitators, for instance, was Washington Irving anything but a clever English essayist?"

WHITMAN: "Some people think they are poets if they have a feeling for jewels, paste gems, feathers, birds, flowers, perfume, etc. In a barbaric country among uncivilized people they would deserve some praise, but not in our time, when everybody can imagine these things."

SADAKICHI: "Like Gilder and Stoddard?"

WHITMAN: "Who?"

SADAKICHI: "Stoddard, for instance?"

WHITMAN: "Stoddard is fair, but many are like him."

SADAKICHI: "Whittier seems to reflect more of the *milieu* of his creed and country?"

WHITMAN: "Whittier was a strong poet, the favorite of Horace Greeley—as good and powerful in his old days as in his young. Much earnestness and fierceness bends all his Quaker peace."

SADAKICHI: "And the critical element, is it entirely lacking? Whipple? (I shrugged my shoulders) Lowell, of course."

WHITMAN: (nodded) "Cute, elegant, well dressed, somewhat of a Yankee—student—college."

SADAKICHI: "I think Stedman is after all the best we have."

WHITMAN: "Oy? (pause—smiling) Stedman is, after all, nothing but a sophisticated dancing master. If Hercules or Apollo himself would make their appearance he would look at them only from the standpoint of a dancing master. Now I have to be excused. I feel tired."

So I shook hands with him, and left satisfied with that afternoon's conversation at any rate.

During this as well as the following visits, I made it my object to practice Boswellean tactics, I generally prepared my questions beforehand. Sitting opposite him, I never let any words of importance escape from his lips without repeating them several times rapidly to myself, and as soon as I was on the ferry I jotted them down on scraps of paper, word by word.

These estimates of contemporary American authors aroused quite a storm of indignation when I published them in the New York Herald in 1889, which was the more strange as Whitman made similar statements in his writings, for instance on Longfellow (II, 481). Mr. Th. B. Hamed, of Camden, even went as far as to write to me, after I had published them once more in the Boston *Weekly Review* in '93:

"I have been shown in the Review your article containing alleged sayings of Walt Whitman respecting certain authors. It is not fair to reprint this after Whitman's death. This article caused considerable trouble when it was first published. Walt repudiated the whole article and told me that you manufactured it. You make him call Stedman a 'sophisticated dancing master' and this caused no end of mischief. Walt has the greatest possible regard for Stedman and there was a strong attachment between these two men. Walt assured Stedman at that time that you had coined the expression out of your own unaided imagination."

To this I can only reply, that Walt Whitman has said every word that I attribute to him, and that I feel obliged to leave various utterances of interest, for instance on Howells, etc., unpublished because I am not quite certain whether the wording, as I have it, is absolutely correct. What object had I in coining these critical remarks! And as far as Whitman's repudiation is concerned, I simply do not believe in it. The Whitman, I knew, never repudiated. I saw Whitman quite often after the publication of the *Herald* article, and he never mentioned a word to me about it. And could Whitman and Stedman not frankly express opinions about each other, and yet entertain a strong attachment? From the conventional point of view Stedman's comments on Walt (which are quoted later on; to me the most reasonable criticism ever made on certain traits of Whitman's open and yet so complex character) were just as straightforward. Besides what did Whitman mean by calling Stedman 'a sophisticated dancing master' but that all critics—and Stedman is our best critic of the old school—are sophisticated dancing masters in comparison to creative minds, eternity-souls (like Walt Whitman). There is, however, still another point on which the Philistines may attack me most cruelly. What right have I or any person to repeat what so and so remarked about so and so in private conversation! Was I a malicious scandal-loving tale-bearer, a literary spy in service of sensational journalism! Indeed I was not. All I received for the publication of these notes was twelve dollars, and that only three years after the conversations had happened. My code of morals simply differs on the point of discretion with that of these people. I believe implicitly that no person should say anything about another, which they would not be willing to repeat or have repeated face to face with the person discussed. To practice this principle—I am convinced that men of the Whitman type share this view—comes absolutely natural to me, and I have acted accordingly (always ingenuously, of course) since childhood, despite the endless inconveniences that have ensued out of it for me.

A LUNCHEON WITH WHITMAN.

W̶E HAD BEEN TALKING ABOUT POLITICS.

WHITMAN: "It does not matter much who's in Washington. Certainly they must have one—and I think Cleveland tries to do his best."

SADAKICHI: "Then you consider all party contests unnecessary from an ideal point of view?"

WHITMAN: "Americans are allowed to be different. The theory of our government is to give to every man the freedom of his activity—to work, study, electrify."

'Yes in theory,' I thought, 'but not in practise' and wondered at his apparent indifference to present conditions. I soon learnt that Whitman looked at all things from the most cosmic point of view possible.

Then our conversation drifted to Bismarck.

SADAKICHI: "Bismarck refounded the German nation, and Wagner gave to it a national art."

WHITMAN: "Yes, Bismarck's work of life is to make Germany strong. Stanton was very much like him. I excuse a great deal of tyranny, even cruelty in the government of a nation. Stanton was a steady supplement to Lincoln."

Whenever he spoke of Lincoln his voice seemed to assume a tone of reverence. His estimate of the martyr president was almost idolatrous. He considered himself nothing in comparison, and several times in my presence murmured, as if to remind himself: "Lincoln is our greatest man. I sometimes ask myself what would have become of us if he hadn't been president during those terrible years, 1862-5."

Nothing was more natural than Whitman's love for Lincoln. Lincoln as a man of deed was as true a representative of our American conglomeration and the "Democratic Vista" of its future, as the literary prophet himself; and as a character-study Lincoln was even more suggestive of grandeur, for as Whitman has written "four sorts of genius, four mighty and primal hands, will be needed to the complete limning of this man's future portrait—the eyes and brains and finger touch of Plutarch and Eschylus and Michael Angelo, assisted by Rabelais."

Who knows if in centuries to come, when so much has clarified that now confuses our view, Lincoln and Whitman will not stand distinct in the mists of the past like Pericles and Phidias.

How sincere and persistent Whitman was in his Lincoln cult everybody knows who has heard him read his Memorial lecture, or 'Captain my captain' with which he generally concluded. His very life blood throbbed in every word, as he slowly proceeded, sentence after sentence, with that noble simplicity which only strong personalities can apply successfully, as their individuality alone is sufficient to satisfy the curiosity of intelligent audiences. I, for my part, shall never forget how he read the simple words, 'the hospitals, oh, the hospitals.' The 'Paradox on the Comedian' could never produce such an effect.

SADAKICHI: "What is your estimate of Washington?"

WHITMAN (in an almost humorous tone): "George Washington had the power of organization, the ability to identify the power of the States. He was an Englishman, an English Franklin—wealthy—well educated—with high morals."

Then Billie, a railroad newsboy, who boarded with Whitman's housekeeper, Mrs. Davis, came bouncing in, kissed Whitman repeatedly and asked whether luncheon was ready.

WHITMAN (rising) "Mrs. Davis is out, but we'll manage to get something. Come on, Mr. Sadakichi."

We sojourned into the kitchen. Billie was sent out to get a can of lobster, and there was quite a dispute between the two as to what kind they wanted, one being a few cents more expensive.

Then Whitman set the table, and I assisted him.

WHITMAN (limping to the range and frying several eggs): "The American nation is not much at present, but will be some day the most glorious one on earth. At first the cooking must be done, the table set, before one can sit down to a square meal. We are now tuning the instruments, afterwards comes the music."

Then he brought out some California claret, and when Billie returned with the lobster, we sat down—several hens running in and out the half open door through which one could catch a glance of the red and green of a sunlit yard—and had a very jolly repast.

Whitman was in the best of humor and ate heartily.

WHITMAN: "Have you been West?"

SADAKICHI: "No—but I have a brother in Denver, who has written to me about his adventures out there."

WHITMAN (enthusiastically): "In Denver I would like to live!" and he began to relate his Denver impressions, of the smelting works, etc., several sentences with an astonishing similarity to those in his Specimen Days (II, 146).

Whitman always succeeded in putting the most vital essence of things into his rhapsodical writings, and his conversation on the same topics, even after years, could be nothing else but repetitions of what he had already expressed in the jagged structures of his poetry or prose.

The restless commercial activity of the Americans, our strongest social trait, is not favorable to the cultivation of an independent spiritual life. Even in the acquirements of educational mediums the same haste is applied, as if Stanford universities and metropolitan art schools could produce culture.

The reticent inward growth in artistic domains was therefore rendered extremely difficult, and, though Whitman was a creative genius of the first magnitude, he lacked the constructive ability of great European minds.

We had nearly finished when Whitman remarked: "In New York, Boston, the East, they eat their bread and beef and digest it for the Western world, but in the valley of the Mississippi there is quite another life." After we had returned into the front room, Billie came and fondled around him, asking if we could not have a drink of whiskey, he would go upstairs and get it.

WHITMAN: "Not today! Not today!" (and took a drink of the demijohn on the table).

SADAKICHI: "What is that?"

WHITMAN: "Spring water."

When the boy saw that his begging was useless he kissed Whitman several times, and left.

ANOTHER LITERARY AFTERNOON.

SADAKICHI: "Sidney Lanier, weak as he is, seems to me after all our most modern poet."

WHITMAN: "Oy! oy?"

SADAKICHI: "At any ray, though only a flute player, he is more powerful than Dempster Sherman, Bliss Carman, or Paul Hayne."

WHITMAN: "Who! Paul Hayne? I don't know much about him; quite a poet, I presume, genteel, etc., nothing dazzling."

SADAKICHI: "Strange how America could ever produce such a genius like Poe."

WHITMAN (indifferently): "Poe had a tendency for the gloomy side of life."

SADAKICHI: "I presume, you have also no special liking for Hawthorne?"

WHITMAN: "About Hawthorne I have nothing particular to say. The multitude likes him. I have read his novels. In my opinion, they do not amount to much. His works are languid, melancholy, morbid. He likes to dwell on crimes, on the sufferings of the human heart, which he analyzes by far too much. Our literature will come! The newspapers indicate it, miserable as they are, miserable and grand too as they are."

SADAKICHI: "Do you not think that the present literary shortcomings are due to the spirit of our time?"

WHITMAN: "Our time? We must settle a little more, but there seems to be a demand for this hurly-burly time."

MRS. DAVIS (at the door): "The luncheon is ready."

WHITMAN: "Come, Mr. Sadakichi have a bite."

Once more we sat down at the kitchen table and displayed our strong, healthy appetites. I, at last, had found my peer in eating.

WHITMAN (eating): "Just as we always prefer a dish that our mother cooked—it tastes better than anything else we get in after life—I like those books best, I read when I was young. Everybody who reads novels not for mere pleasure will admire Walter Scott. He had a Shakespearean variety of subject. He did not analyze and anatomize his subjects."

SADAKICHI: "Which of his novels do you like best?"

WHITMAN: "The Heart of Midlothian. I read it over and over again."

I wanted to know his opinion on Victor Hugo, and spoke of the marvelous description of the battle of Waterloo, but Whitman had no word of admiration. "I do not like him much."

SADAKICHI: "What do you think about Byron?"

WHITMAN: "Byron became bitter through the ups and downs of his career, his life—specially the downs. A desperate fierceness is predominant in his works. But I like something more free—Homer, Shakespeare, Walter Scott, Emerson."

In the parlor we resumed our review of literati. A few of his remarks were:

"Taine's Literature is one of the productions of our age."

"Rousseau I have never read, of Voltaire now and then a quotation."

"Chinese literature, I think, is empirical."

Probably, to protect himself against draughts, he had wrapped a shawl of an Oriental pattern around his shoulders, and with his white beard streaming over this reddish orange cloth, he looked very much like one of those biblical characters, Rubens and his pupils have painted.

SADAKICHI (rising to leave): "May I kiss you?"

WHITMAN: "Oh, you are very kind."

I touched his forehead with my lips. "Thanks, thanks!" ejaculated Whitman. With a blush of false shame I offered him this tender tribute of youthful ardor, ambition, enthusiasm with which my soul was overflowing; I felt that I had to show to this man some emotional sign of the love, I bore his works or those of any remarkable individuality.

One afternoon I took an acquaintance with me to photograph his house, the right window with Whitman looking out waving his *Salut au Monde,* and the interior of the parlor.

Sorry to report, the negative of the first was broken, and the other two did not come out well, as the shy young man, who felt rather uncomfortable in the presence of the great man, was not far enough advanced in amateur photography. The first negative, of course, can be replaced at any time, but in regard to the others it is a great pity, for, as far as I know, no such photographs have ever been taken, and even Whitman's own descriptions cannot give us an exact idea of the peculiar atmosphere of his last years' retreat.

Now, everything is changed.

A visit to the humble frame building in Mickle Street hardly repays the trouble at present. The almost historically noted room looks like any other ordinary parlor, as everything of interest has been removed, and some new furniture added instead. Some of Walt Whitman's admirers have privately agreed to buy the house and hand it down to posterity in its present state, making a sort of Whitman museum of it. How stupid these rooms will look, with well swept floors, solemnly adorned with busts and neatly hung with photographs!

Why not try and be original—original in the manner that Walt Whitman would have liked—and give a perfect fac-simile of the room as it was during the lifetime of the poet—the floor strewn with newspapers, magazines, and books; on the table a demijohn with spring water; on the mantelpiece photographs; on the walls pictures of his parents; in one comer a large heap of his own books? It would be the work of an artistic person, who was familiar with Walt Whitman's way of living, to rearrange the room; but it could be done and would be unique.

On one of my visits I was accompanied by Miss E. Whitman at once shook hands with the young lady, and asked for her name.

After some commonplaces had been exchanged. Whitman got up and said: "I am going out for a drive in a moment. There's the team. Stay here with Mrs. Davis, she will entertain you. Do as if you were at home. (To Miss E.) You must come again. Good bye, good bye!"

Then we talked commonplaces for a while with Mrs. Davis. I, who was subject to a frightful temper at the time, asked the housekeeper if Whitman were always so calm, of that friendly but stoic nature, if nothing could disturb him.

MRS. DAVIS: "He is always that way. I am now with him for several years."

SADAKICHI: "But does he not even scold?"

MRS. DAVIS: "Oh, no."

I myself had later on a proof of the truth of this statement. One day he wished to show me an original letter by Stanton. He looked over the various unruly heaps of papers and books, at first in vain, but at last found it in some book in a 'rather dilapidated condition, as if somebody had willfully torn it. He simply gazed at it for a long while, and then exclaimed in a grieved voice: "Why, I would give ten dollars if this was not done!"

IMPERTINENT QUESTIONS.

THE NEXT TIME AN AUTOGRAPH COLLECTOR was on the scene, coaxing Whitman to give him some photographs and sign them.

AUTOGRAPH FIEND: "They will be valuable some day."

WHITMAN (looking up): "What are you doing now?"

SADAKICHI: "I read your 'Pieces in Early Youth,' what do you think of them?"

WHITMAN: "Pretty bad—pretty bad."

SADAKICHI: "I looked everywhere for your 'Frank Evans,' your novel on metropolitan city life, but no body seems to know anything about it."

WHITMAN: "Oy!?"

AUTOGRAPH FIEND: "Is this gentleman also a writer?"

WHITMAN: "No, Mr. Sadakichi is interested a little in everything."

AUTOGRAPH FIEND (patronizingly): "I believe Mr. Whitman will some day be considered a great author." I ignored him, and Whitman silently handed him the signed photographs, then the fiend made his exit.

I pointed at some of Whitman's favorite books and asked:

"What will become of all these things, when you die? Surely they are of great value."

I don't know whether he was annoyed at this question, but he responded rather growlingly, "I never think of that."

Did he dislike to talk about death like Johnson, Carlyle and many others?

Then I launched upon a still more impertinent topic, on his relation to women.

WHITMAN (evading the question): "One cannot say much about women. The best ones study Greek or criticise Browning—they are no women."

SADAKICHI (rather brusquely): "Have you ever been in love?"

WHITMAN (rather annoyed by my cross examining): "Sensuality I have done with. I have thrown it out, but it is natural, even a necessity."

I do not believe that Whitman was ever absorbed in a love of the Petrarch or Dante type, he stood most likely between the ideal free lover and the ideal varietist.

To entertain him I had brought with me the photographs of a number of celebrities I had met in Germany. Showing him a photograph of the German actor, Ernst Possart as Napoleon, he ardently exclaimed: "Very fine—very fine! "Of the others Paul Heyse's beautiful Christ-like face interested him most. He looked at it steadily for at least two minutes, and then with an outpouring of his very soul he uttered a long drawn, "Beautiful—beautiful!" The sound still rings in my ears.

How rugged and true, he appeared in comparison with the European poet who is more polished and beautiful.

I remarked that Paul Heyse had written to me about him, and had compared "his staff rhymes to the sounds of an Æolian harp, and traditional poetry to the music of a well tuned piano," and had also stated that he preferred "flowers and fruit to leaves of grass."

WHITMAN: "Strange!"

WHITMAN (pointing at a bundle of manuscript): "Will you take it to the Express for me? Mr. Keimedy, a gentleman who lives near Boston, has written about me."

SADAKICHI: "Of course.—How is it, satisfactory?"

WHITMAN: "Passable. To write the life of a human being takes many a book, and after all the story is not told."

SADAKICHI: "Shall I pay for it?"

WHITMAN (hesitating a moment): "No—let him pay."

LAST VISIT IN 1886.

SADAKICHI: "I attended the seance of a medium a few nights ago."

WHITMAN: "Oy!"

SADAKICHI: "She told me a few truisms about myself besides a great deal of nonsensical stuff. I believe these mediums are merely clever women who have a motley knowledge of society and life, of physiognomy, and pathognomy, and above all else the gift of the gab, though in rare cases they may be capable of clairvoyance."

WHITMAN (absent-minded): "There are so many other miracles in this world just like them, that can't be explained."

This opening brought us to religion.

WHITMAN: "There is no worse devil than man."

SADAKICHI: "But what do you think of churches, where heaven and hell theories are continually expounded?"

WHITMAN: "If the common consent of people think churches a necessity, they ought to be."Then, referring to an East Indian native who was trying to introduce Brahmanism into America, he said in a slow, fault finding tone: "I don't think he is right."

SADAKICHI: "Do you consider the Christian religion superior to others?"

WHITMAN: "No, religions."

SADAKICHI: "I as an artistic nature, always felt drawn towards the Catholic religion. Of course only on account of its picturesqueness and mysticism."

WHITMAN: "Men should do as they please. Nobody has the right to interfere with another man's business, religion, or habits. That's what I have told to Ingersoll."

Referring to church music. Whitman branched off on music in general. He spoke of a German street band that now and then played in the neighborhood, "very well." He was only superficially acquainted with Wagner and the new school.

WHITMAN: "Verdi I think is one of the best musicians; he is a storm with the intention of being a real storm. Mendelssohn is my favorite. I always like to hear him. Music is the only art where we get something."

Painting and sculpture was never mentioned in our conversations; of course Whitman admired Millet, but the fact that he, who was so anxious

269

to leave to posterity a correct description of his personality, never induced a first-class painter or sculptor to portray him, shows that he was not intimate with contemporary art. His figure as well as face were a wonderful subject for the chisel or brush of a great artist. The opportunity is lost, and photographs are all we have.

SADAKICHI: "I am sailing next week."

WHITMAN: "Sailing to Europe, eh? Well, if you meet young men in Germany—artists—poets—tell them that the liberty and equality of which Freiligrath and other classics sung, have been quacked over enough. Here in America we do the thing they talk of."

SADAKICHI: "Well, I think I must go. Good bye."

WHITMAN: "Good bye, never forget to study the old, grand poets—but do not imitate them. We want something which pays reverence to our time."

During my absence Miss E. visited Whitman, brought him some flowers and a greeting from me. Thereupon he decided to call her Emma. They spoke about me.

MISS E.: "He is studying life in Paris."

WHITMAN: "Studying life, eh! Let him take care, studying human life is like looking at the stars. If you look too close, there is a dazzle."

I never corresponded with Whitman; the only communication I received from him is a postal card acknowledging the receipt of some money for several of his books I had bought. It said, covering the entire card:

"Yours rec'd—With many thanks—Walt Whitman."

1887.

The conversations during the summer of 1886 were really the most interesting I had with Whitman. Already in July, 1887, there was a decided difference in his deportment; old age and bad health were telling on him, he became more taciturn than ever, and it was principally I who had to make up the large bulk of the conversation.

In the meantime I had become a very close student of his work, produced a number of prose poems in imitation of him, among them a 'To Walt Whitman.' My youthful enthusiasm extended so far as to cause me to starve in order to purchase his works and present them to leading European critics, so that they might write about him; at one period I even thought of becoming his voluntary nurse.

I had pitched my Bohemian tent in Boston, with the intention of re-introducing Whitman into New England. Whitman being rather badly off financially, a collection was made to enable him to keep a horse and buggy. It looked to, me very much like charity, and I hoped to remedy it, by founding a Whitman Society which all Whitman admirers would join in order to give him a permanent pension and do away once for all with donations and charitable gifts. Other aims of the Society were to further the propagation of his works in cheap or gratuitous editions, to make the Whitman society a sort of literary club, with the establishment of a library of the master pieces of foreign literature in the original language and a complete Whitman bibliography as main interest.

All this was undoubtedly praiseworthy but as I could invest only $100 in the scheme, (largely spent for circulars sent all over the globe) and only two Philadelphia gentlemen. Mr. David McKay, Whitman's publisher, and Mr. C. L. Moore, an amateur poet, had the enthusiasm to pay the initial fee of twelve dollars, the project was never carried out. True enough in my youthful fervor I acted rather undemocratically by electing the officers of the Society myself, which were as follows:

President: D. R. M. Bucke.

Vice-President: W. S. Kennedy.

Director: Your humble servant.

Committee: C. E. Dallin, a sculptor; Sylvester Baxter, of the *Boston Herald*, F. A. Nichols, literary editor of the *Boston Globe*, Max Elliot (Mrs. A. M. B. Ellis) correspondent of the *Boston Herald*, J. C. Chamberlain, of the *Boston Transcript*.

Honorary Members:

Mme. Th. Bentzon, Paris.

Rudolf Schmidt, Copenhagen.

Enrico Nencione, Firenze.

The only meeting we ever had in the Boston Globe Building, was opened with the witty remark that' also the Secession was had begun in such an humble way, and a censure to me that I had elected the officers, like a despot, without even asking their leave. It was proposed by Mr. Sylvester Baxter that all interested in the project should dine together and talk the matter over. Nobody seconded the motion.

Although the enterprise was a failure, I learnt a good deal by it, as I met personally or corresponded with nearly all Whitman admirers here and abroad.

Among others I tried to induce Oliver Wendell Holmes and John Greenleaf Whittier to join us. The first I saw smirking, sitting near a framed Mona Lisa, in a little back room with a view on the Charles River, and the latter in a long linen ulster in his Danvers home. Holmes said, nervously twitching his lips in various directions, that he would be willing to give his name if Whittier was, and Whittier assured me that he also was willing only that Mr. Holmes would have to say the first word.

How much cowardice there is practiced even by stars of second or third magnitude in evading a simple truthful answer that would settle such a matter at once!

Diplomatic Holmes would not express himself regarding Whitman but continually smirked.

Old Whittier said candidly: "I bear Whitman no ill will. He does what he thinks right. I, however, can not fully appreciate him. Perhaps it is my fault. I have been brought up too differently. They say to the pure everything is pure, yet it grieves me to see the noblest trailing in the dust, and the very lowest put on high."

1887.

I never mentioned the Society to Whitman himself, whom I saw again twice during a visit to Philadelphia, July 1887.

"Ah, Mr. Sadakichi, are you back again? "He greeted me as cordially as ever.

I told him about Mme. Th. Bentzon's article in the *Revue des Deux Mondes* of 1872, which had introduced him into France, as a powerful individuality, though she was partial in preferring his war poems to all others; also that he was known and appreciated among the younger generation of poets, several of them imitating his diction without rhyme and rhythm. Gabriel Sarrazin had not written his article as yet. I also showed him several articles about himself that had appeared in the German press and periodicals, none however as comprehensive as Freiligrath's short notice in the *Augsburger Allgemeine Zeitung* comparing him with Wagner, which is the more marvelous as it was written as early as 1868, when nearly all failed to grasp the meaning of Whitman's literary innovations.

Also from Italy progress could be reported, Enrico Nencione had written a book on American literature giving Whitman and Poe the foremost rank, had commented upon him repeatedly in the *Nuovo Antologia*, and called him in a letter to me "the great humanitarian poet of the new world." Carducci had expressed his admiration, and the Verists of course, found much of interest in him.

That his Democratic Vistas in the Danish translation by Rudolph Schmidt had quite a circulation, and that Schmidt in his correspondence with me had expressed himself on the lines in *Salut au Monde* beginning with "I see the places of the sagas"(I 116) as being the best perhaps ever written on Scandinavia. On ending my report Whitman jovially burst out: "Why you are my expounder of Leaves of Grass in Europe!" But the next moment he leaned back in his huge yellow polished arm chair, and let his chin drop on his chest as if a thought absorbed all his attention.

Did he feel that the contents of his books by being uncorked and rebottled into other languages and 'Weltanschauungen' evaporated their most intense and individual efflorescence, the aroma of his rugged, sunburnt American youth (Whitman had really accomplished his mission before he was 40) before foreigners could enjoy them!

SADAKICHI: "Schmidt intends to write a great novel, a consume of Danish society."

WHITMAN: "He undertakes a great deal."

SADAKICHI: "By the by, Schmidt complained to me in a letter that he had written repeatedly to you about the great sorrow of his life, his wife suffering from some mental disease, but that he had never received a word of sympathy from your great humane soul, as he expressed himself."

WHITMAN: "Pshaw!"

SADAKICHI: "You probably think why should I feel more sympathy for him than others. The world is full of misery. But will you not write to him? "

WHITMAN: "Most likely."

Whitman had not the glance of Indian sadness which in every pain mirrors its own fate, nor the trembling smile which we love in the images of the Greek. He was one of these stoic natures which we find in new countries, who knew how many human sacrifices have to be made, before even the uncultivated soil will yield the bare necessities of subsistence. In his time he had also suffered for others, for few men have looked so deep into human life, and scarcely anything could happen in this wide world of ours which did not awake "recallé's" in him, but his sympathy had become passive, and had dissolved in that peaceful state of the soul that the Germans call 'Lebensruhe,' which Goethe possessed in such an eminent degree.

The next time we talked of Boston.

SADAKICHI: "Your books are still in the locked shelves."

WHITMAN: "In the locked shelves, are they, isn't it funny!" (smiling good-humoredly).

SADAKICHI (taking up Carpenter's "Democracy"): "They say his work resembles yours."

Whitman (dryly): "Do they say that?"

Talking of his Boston friends and admirers, mentioning one name or another, he asked quite anxiously: "Quite a clever man, isn't he?" or "I hear, quite a man?"

It was a rather unfriendly day, and as he sat there in his grey suit against the dark grey of the dreary street seen through the dusty window panes—he who had been for so many years not only not understood, but even not misunderstood, and who now in his old age still sat there in world-distracted poverty, secluded from the loud gaieties and soothing comforts of human life—the question: "Do you never long for the company of noble, intellectual, genuine women?" was involuntarily uttered by me.

WHITMAN (after a long pause): "Yes, I think old men like me should have a lady to take care of them; just as Montaigne had his Marie."

This was the only time that I saw this stoic bent by a despondent melancholy mood. And then it was but a quickly passing cloud, as he remarked a few minutes later in a cheerful tone: "After all my staunchest friends have been O'Connor, Burroughs, and Rossetti in England."

I could only nod approval. These men were really worthy of his friendship. O'Connor I have never met, but his fervent, eloquent vindication won my sympathy at once. W. M. Rossetti's acquaintance I made during a stay in London. And John Burroughs I paid a visit to during a pedestrian trip along the Hudson, which I must relate as he represented to me just what I imagine a friend of Whitman's should be.

A VISIT TO JOHN BURROUGHS.

WHEN I ARRIVED AT HIS LITTLE ESTATE near West Park, over-looking the Hudson, he was picking berries.

"Greetings from Walt Whitman," I called out as I approached him.

He, without looking up, continued picking berries, I joined him in the work.

BURROUGHS (throwing a side glance at me): "How is Whitman?" and a conversation on this topic ensued.

He showed me over the grounds, while we talked chiefly about literature; the particulars of the conversation are entirely obliterated from my memory, I only recall that we passed a critical review on a motley crowd of authors and dwelt for quite a while on Victor Hugo. I liked his clear judgment and sturdy simplicity of deportment.

Then we entered the house—simple but tasteful interiors—when he introduced me to his taciturn wife and little boy; and we had a luncheon with wine.

After luncheon Burroughs excused himself as he had to go to Poughkeepsie for a few hours. "But you stay right here, act as if you felt perfectly at home; if you wish to read go into my study, perhaps, you prefer a plunge."

For a while I glanced over Burroughs' works in his study, an ideal little place, a one room cottage, covered with bark on the outside, filled with books, and every convenience for writing; and with a vista on the Hudson through the windows. Later during the afternoon his little son asked me to play with him: we rambled over the ground, climbed into the cherry trees, and had 'a rattling good time all around.'

After Burroughs' return, supper was served, by his ever taciturn wife, and soon after I seized my knapsack and staff, ready to pursue my wandering to the Catskills.

He accompanied me to the gate, and cordially shook hands with me: "I am sorry that I can't accommodate you over night, but we have no servant girl at present. Drop in if you come this way again—and best wishes to Walt."

And as I strolled along the dusty highway, while the mists of evening wove their veils over the distance, I wondered at the hospitality of this man to a perfect stranger, for he had not even asked me for my name.

1888.

Next time I saw Whitman was in May 1888, a few days before my departure for England.

SADAKICHI: "Have you done anything with your "November Boughs?""

WHITMAN: "Here they are!" (pointing down at a bundle of ragged manuscripts, tied together, which he used as a footrest).

SADAKICHI: "Would you present me with a piece of original manuscript?"

WHITMAN (without answering, got up, untied a bundle of manuscript and handed me "Roaming in Thought"(I 216) written on the back of a creditor's letter): "This will do."

SADAKICHI: "What do you think about St. Gaudens' Lincoln?"

WHITMAN: "——I really don't know what I think about it."

Whitman like most of our American writers was not well posted on foreign literature, in particular on foreign contemporary literature. Nietzsche, Ibsen, the Verists, the Symbolists, etc. etc. he had not heard of or they had made no impression on him.

SADAKICHI: "You read Tolstoi?"

WHITMAN: "Not much. In translation—I don't think he has written anything more powerful than his *King Lear of the Steppes*. It has some of the quality of *King Lear*, not merely a resemblance to the plot. I read *War and Peace*. I couldn't make much out of it. The translation seems to be very superficial, poor.—A good book should be like Roman cement, the older it grows, the better it sticks."

SADAKICHI: "Could you give me an introduction to Tennyson?"

WHITMAN: "Rather not. Some time ago I sent several ladies to him, and they had a royal time out of it."

SADAKICHI: "Would you not do the same for me?"

WHITMAN: "Rather not. He is getting old and is bothered too much. Go and see young Gilchrist."

Then we talked about Mrs. Gilchrist, the author of a "Woman's Estimate of Whitman."

SADAKICHI: "She was one of your very best friends, was she not?"

WHITMAN: "Yes, she was very much to me," and his voice trembled, the only time that I felt something like tears in his voice.

WHITMAN (as I departed): "Tell my English friends that I feel well—and many thanks to them—that I live very economically, but you don't know what support I get from my friends; besides I write for the magazines and get well paid. The state of my affairs is at present very bright. Why should I trouble myself, I have only a few years to live."

A MEETING WITH E. C. STEDMAN.

I DID NOT SEE WHITMAN AGAIN BEFORE September, 1889. My feelings towards him had somewhat changed, as I was developing into a writer myself; I feared that Whitman might have too strong an influence upon me, and I had freely given away the various scraps, proof sheets, pictures of him, etc., he had given me, and even disposed of his books, in order not to read them anymore.

I do not remember anything Whitman said at this particular visit as I did not take any notes. I recall, however, that I related to him my meeting with E. C. Stedman:

When I called one evening at Mr. Stedman's he had visitors, but he asked me to stay and made me wait over two hours. At last he appeared and addressed me: "I do not know anything about you except that you look like a gentleman."

I introduced myself as the young fanatic of the Walt Whitman Society notoriety.

STEDMAN: "I hope you are not one of those Whitmaniacs?"

I denied the insinuation.

STEDMAN (with fervor): "I have no patience with them at all. I mean those men who say Whitman's books are their Bible, who must always carry a copy of Leaves of Grass about their person, and put it under their pillows when they go to sleep. They are absolutely disgusting to me and I have told them so."

SADAKICHI: "Yes, you are right I have never in my life met a more narrow-minded set of philistines than these Whitman worshippers. How they crouch on their knees before him and whine silly admirations in praise of him, whom they do not comprehend in the least, for there is really not a spark of Whitman's grandeur in any of them. A true Whitmanite would try to be like Whitman in character and action; independent, not looking up to him as to a God."

STEDMAN: "It is a good deal the fault of Whitman himself. He always liked to see himself worshipped, and he is not grateful at all after one does it."

SADAKICHI: "You knew Whitman well?"

STEDMAN: "Oh my, yes, we have often been together, talked and drank beer together. In those days he paraded on Broadway, with a red shirt on, open in front to show the 'scented herbage of his breast' and compared himself with Christ and Osiris. That is absurd!"

SADAKICHI: "Do you think he affected it?"

STEDMAN: "I do. Now it is quite different; sitting there in his grey suit in Camden, quite gentlemanlike. I was always one of his admirers; of course, I object to his 'smell of the armpits,' and that sort of a thing, but I always defended him. Mrs. Ellen McKay Hutchinson, my co-operator, in compiling "The Library of American Literature"would give him no place at all. But no, I said, that cannot be, in a hundred years people will think a good deal more about him than now. He will grow."

Yes, Mr. Stedman and Co., with all due respect, Whitman will grow. We poor critics can not fell this mighty tree, whose foliage is destined to overshadow these states and, perhaps, the entire world.

Poe was a genius that could have lived in any country. All the other authors did not express America as an entity, but only parts of it, like Hawthorne, Whittier, Thoreau, Bret Hart, Cable, Wilkins, etc. Walt Whitman, however, dragged the ever evolutionizing civilization of these States as far as his own development went, which is typical for the ideal American spirit of to-day, free from foreign idolatry. It is as if the murmuring of a multitude of people were moving through his Leaves of Grass. And should the Americans ever become a patriotic democratic race, how much national enthusiasm and pride will jubilate in return around his memory.

1890.

June 1890 brought me once more to Philadelphia.

He had already permanently retired to the rooms on the second floor.

He spoke but little. Asking him for his health he answered. "Oh, I am well taken care of, I eat plenty of berries and milk."

After a long pause, he suddenly asked me. "Did you ever meet Ingersoll? You should meet him. He is really a fine fellow."

The rest of this call's conversation consisted almost entirely of questions on my part, and extremely brief answers in the affirmative or negative.

I mentioned the German translation of *Leaves of Grass* "Grasshalme," by Karl Knortz and T. W. Roueston, published in Zurich, 1889.

WHITMAN: "Is it—good?"

SADAKICHI: "Yes the selections make a good impression."

WHITMAN: "That's all what non-Americans can expect."

FINALE.

IN MARCH 1891 I TOOK MY WIFE TO see him. He was very ill. Contrary to the easy access I generally had, Mrs. Davis had to go up stairs first and ask him, if he could see me. "Yes, for a moment."

So we went up stairs. All his former buoyancy seem to have left him, he was really a very old man.

"This is my wife, Mr. Whitman."

"Oy! oy!" he exclaimed, "be seated madam."

I asked about his health, if he was still writing a line now and then.

WHITMAN: "Yes, I keep it up to the last, but it is now good bye to my fancy."

I entertained him with the report of the progress his works were making, spoke again of Nencione.

He was very eager to get his address.

We were hardly seated for five minutes when a meal was brought in on a tray: coffee, meat, bread and butter, fruit and pie.

SADAKICHI: "Well, we had better go. I hope you will soon feel better."

WHITMAN: "It is clouded now, possibly, it'll pass by."

These were the last words Walt Whitman spoke to me.

When the report of his death reached me, I was in New York. I felt very much like running over to Camden and speaking a few words at the funeral, but as my means were very limited at the time, and as my presence was really unnecessary where so many had to pay their tribute of condolence, I went into Central Park instead, and held a silent communion with the soul atoms of the good gray poet, of which a few seemed to have wafted to me on the mild March winds.

This memorandum has come to an end. Intentionally I abstained from all analytical criticism of his works, and pycho-physiological investigation into his character.

My old Quaker friend once humorously remarked that some day I might be able to publish something like Erckmann—Chatrians "Gespraeche with Goethe." Of course this pamphlet has no such pretentious aim. I merely wished to relate my personal relation with Walt Whitman, truthfully and without embellishment, and by so doing, to give as faithful a picture as can be given of the living Walt Whitman, slowly ebbing in the sands of seventy, when at last the storm of derision had ceased, and his fame was flaming up all over the world.

Whitman's estimate of me, I presume was less favorable than one might imagine from my intimacy with him. I was a mere lad of nineteen when, we had the most striking conversations, and thought I was a much more brilliant and less phlegmatic conversationalist than now, our relation was after all very much like that of a disciple to his master. Besides my independent, despotic nature, which never flatters, must have annoyed him at times, for instance when I remarked that the writings of his old age would not add a particle to the glory of the work of his manhood, or that other poets would rise and treat him as he has treated the past.

He had arrived at that point of life when even eternity souls become steady. There is a boundary line, in particular for prophets and innovators, beyond which they search no longer for new realms, but stop to rotate around themselves. In short it is that period in a great man's life, when he has acquired his indisputable and greatest, more or less universal reputation; for when such a mighty spirit stops to proceed, his few apostles can also stop on the laborious march and take a rest, and the stragglers will approach in a medley crowd and no longer consider themselves stragglers. Criticism, abuse, calumniation which persecute each growing greatness, grow silent; all come to shake hands with him and laud him to the skies. And the great man gazes around and is astonished that he has got so far, and he feels religious, and mild, and forgiving towards all—except those who disturb the peace, those who want to proceed. For he who has been a leader, wants to remain a leader.

Nevertheless, what the old Quaker, shortly before his death, remarked about his intercourse with me, I could repeat in regard to Walt Whitman. "When I summon up all the incidents of our acquaintance, it was perfectly satisfactory in every way." I would only add 'the most satisfactory one I ever had, without exception.'

It was calm, invigorating, softly flowing on like a summer day in the open fields or on the ocean.

MRS. SPRING FRAGRANCE

SUI SIN FAR (EDITH MAUD EATON)

Mrs Spring Fragrance

I

WHEN MRS. SPRING FRAGRANCE FIRST ARRIVED IN SEATTLE, she was unacquainted with even one word of the American language. Five years later her husband, speaking of her, said: "There are no more American words for her learning." And everyone who knew Mrs. Spring Fragrance agreed with Mr. Spring Fragrance. Mr. Spring Fragrance, whose business name was Sing Yook, was a young curio merchant. Though conservatively Chinese in many respects, he was at the same time what is called by the Westerners, "Americanized." Mrs. Spring Fragrance was even more "Americanized."

Next door to the Spring Fragrances lived the Chin Yuens. Mrs. Chin Yuen was much older than Mrs. Spring Fragrance; but she had a daughter of eighteen with whom Mrs. Spring Fragrance was on terms of great friendship. The daughter was a pretty girl whose Chinese name was Mai Gwi Far (a rose) and whose American name was Laura. Nearly everybody called her Laura, even her parents and Chinese friends. Laura had a sweetheart, a youth named Kai Tzu. Kai Tzu, who was American-born, and as ruddy and stalwart as any young Westerner, was noted amongst baseball players as one of the finest pitchers on the Coast. He could also sing, "Drink to me only with thine eyes," to Laura's piano accompaniment.

Now the only person who knew that Kai Tzu loved Laura and that Laura loved Kai Tzu, was Mrs. Spring Fragrance. The reason for this was that, although the Chin Yuen parents lived in a house furnished in American style, and wore American clothes, yet they religiously observed many Chinese customs, and their ideals of life were the ideals of their Chinese forefathers. Therefore, they had betrothed their daughter, Laura, at the age of fifteen, to

281

the eldest son of the Chinese Government school-teacher in San Francisco. The time for the consummation of the betrothal was approaching.

Laura was with Mrs. Spring Fragrance and Mrs. Spring Fragrance was trying to cheer her.

"I had such a pretty walk today," said she. "I crossed the banks above the beach and came back by the long road. In the green grass the daffodils were blowing, in the cottage gardens the currant bushes were flowering, and in the air was the perfume of the wallflower. I wished, Laura, that you were with me."

Laura burst into tears. "That is the walk," she sobbed, "Kai Tzu and I so love; but never, ah, never, can we take it together again." "Now, Little Sister," comforted Mrs. Spring Fragrance "you really must not grieve like that. Is there not a beautiful American poem written by a noble American named Tennyson, which says:

> "'Tis better to have loved and lost,
> Than never to have loved at all?"

Mrs. Spring Fragrance was unaware that Mr. Spring Fragrance, having returned from the city, tired with the day's business, had thrown himself down on the bamboo settee on the veranda, and that although his eyes were engaged in scanning the pages of the *Chinese World*, his ears could not help receiving the words which were borne to him through the open window.

> "'Tis better to have loved and lost,
> Than never to have loved at all,"

repeated Mr. Spring Fragrance. Not wishing to hear more of the secret talk of women, he arose and sauntered around the veranda to the other side of the house. Two pigeons circled around his head. He felt in his pocket for a lichi which he usually carried for their pecking. His fingers touched a little box. It contained a jadestone pendant, which Mrs. Spring Fragrance had particularly admired the last time she was down town. It was the fifth anniversary of Mr. and Mrs. Spring Fragrance's wedding day.

Mr. Spring Fragrance pressed the little box down into the depths of his pocket.

A young man came out of the back door of the house at Mr. Spring Fragrance's left. The Chin Yuen house was at his right.

"Good evening," said the young man. "Good evening," returned Mr. Spring Fragrance. He stepped down from his porch and went and leaned over the railing which separated this yard from the yard in which stood the young man.

"Will you please tell me," said Mr Spring Fragrance, "the meaning of two lines of an American verse which I have heard?"

"Certainly," returned the young man with a genial smile. He was a star student at the University of Washington, and had not the slightest doubt that he could explain the meaning of all things in the universe.

"Well," said Mr. Spring Fragrance, "it is this:

> "'Tis better to have loved and lost,
> Than never to have loved at all."

"Ah!" responded the young man with an air of profound wisdom. "That, Mr. Spring Fragrance, means that it is a good thing to love anyway—even if we can't get what we love, or, as the poet tells us, lose what we love. Of course, one needs experience to feel the truth of this teaching."

The young man smiled pensively and reminiscently. More than a dozen young maidens "loved and lost" were passing before his mind's eye.

"The truth of the teaching!" echoed Mr. Spring, Fragrance, a little testily. "There is no truth in it whatever. It is disobedient to reason. Is it not better to have what you do not love than to love what you do not have?"

"That depends," answered the young man, "upon temperament."

"I thank you. Good evening," said Mr. Spring Fragrance. He turned away to muse upon the unwisdom of the American way of looking at things.

Meanwhile, inside the house, Laura was refusing to be comforted.

"Ah, no! no!" cried she. "If I had not gone to school with Kai Tzu, nor talked nor walked with him, nor played the accompaniments to his songs, then I might consider with complacency, or at least without horror, my approaching marriage with the son of Man You. But as it is—oh, as it is—!"

The girl rocked herself to and fro in heartfelt grief.

Mrs. Spring Fragrance knelt down beside her, and clasping her arms around her neck, cried in sympathy:

"Little Sister, oh, Little Sister! Dry your tears—do not despair. A moon has yet to pass before the marriage can take place. Who knows what the stars may have to say to one another during its passing? A little bird has whispered to me—"

For a long time Mrs. Spring Fragrance talked. For a long time Laura listened. When the girl arose to go, there was a bright light in her eyes.

II

MRS. SPRING FRAGRANCE, IN SAN FRANCISCO on a visit to her cousin, the wife of the herb doctor of Clay Street, was having a good time. She was invited everywhere that the wife of an honorable Chinese merchant could go. There was much to see and hear, including more than a dozen babies who had been born in the families of her friends since she last visited the city of the Golden Gate. Mrs. Spring Fragrance loved babies. She had had two herself, but both had been transplanted into the spirit land before the completion of even one moon. There were also many dinners and theatre-parties given in her honor. It was at one of the theatre-parties that Mrs. Spring Fragrance met Ah Oi, a young girl who had the reputation of being the prettiest Chinese girl in San Francisco, and the naughtiest. In spite of gossip, however, Mrs. Spring Fragrance took a great fancy to Ah Oi and invited her to a tête-à-tête picnic on the following day. This invitation Ah Oi joyfully accepted. She was a sort of bird girl and never felt so happy as when out in the park or woods.

On the day after the picnic Mrs. Spring Fragrance wrote to Laura Chin Yuen thus:

MY PRECIOUS LAURA,—May the bamboo ever wave. Next week I accompany Ah Oi to the beauteous town of San José. There will we be met by the son of the Illustrious Teacher, and in a little Mission, presided over by a benevolent American priest, the little Ah Oi and the son of the Illustrious Teacher will be joined together in love and harmony—two pieces of music made to complete one another.

The Son of the Illustrious Teacher, having been through an American Hall of Learning, is well able to provide for his orphan bride and fears not the displeasure of his parents, now that he is assured that your grief at his loss will not be inconsolable. He wishes me to waft to you and to Kai Tzu—and the little Ah Oi joins with him—ten thousand rainbow wishes for your happiness.

My respects to your honorable parents, and to yourself, the heart of your loving friend,

JADE SPRING FRAGRANCE

To Mr. Spring Fragrance, Mrs. Spring Fragrance also indited a letter:

GREAT AND HONORED MAN,—Greeting from your plum blossom,[1] who is desirous of hiding herself from the sun of your presence for a week of seven days more. My honorable cousin is preparing for the Fifth Moon Festival, and wishes me to compound for the occasion some American "fudge," for which delectable sweet, made by my clumsy hands, you have sometimes shown a slight prejudice. I am enjoying a most agreeable visit, and American friends, as also our own, strive benevolently for the accomplishment of my pleasure. Mrs. Samuel Smith, an American lady, known to my cousin, asked for my accompaniment to a magniloquent lecture the other evening. The subject was "America, the Protector of China!" It was most exhilarating, and the effect of so much expression of benevolence; leads me to beg of you to forget to remember that the barber charges you one dollar for a shave while he humbly submits to the American man a bill of fifteen cents. And murmur no more because your honored elder brother, on a visit to this country, is detained under the roof-tree of this great Government instead of under your own humble roof. Console him with the reflection that he is protected under the wing of the Eagle, the Emblem of Liberty. What is the loss of ten hundred years or ten thousand times ten dollars compared with the happiness of knowing oneself so securely sheltered? All of this I have learned from Mrs. Samuel Smith, who is as brilliant and great of mind as one of your own superior sex.

For me it is sufficient to know that the Golden Gate Park is most enchanting, and the seals on the rock at the Cliff House extremely entertaining and amiable. There is much feasting and merrymaking under the lanterns in honor of your Stupid Thorn.

I have purchased for your smoking a pipe with an amber mouth. It is said to be very sweet to the lips and to emit a cloud of smoke fit for the gods to inhale.

Awaiting, by the wonderful wire of the telegram message, your gracious permission to remain for the celebration of the Fifth Moon Festival and the making of American "fudge," I continue for ten thousand times ten thousand years,

Your ever loving and obedient woman,

JADE

P.S. Forget not to care for the cat, the birds, and the flowers. Do not eat too quickly nor fan too vigorously now that the weather is warming.

Mrs. Spring Fragrance smiled as she folded this last epistle. Even if he were old-fashioned, there was never a husband so good and kind as hers. Only on

---

1 The plum blossom is the Chinese flower of virtue. It has been adopted by the Japanese, just in the same way as they have adopted the Chinese national flower, the chrysanthemum.

one occasion since their marriage had he slighted her wishes. That was when, on the last anniversary of their wedding, she had signified a desire for a certain jadestone pendant, and he had failed to satisfy that desire.

But Mrs Spring Fragrance, being of a happy nature, and disposed to look upon the bright side of things, did not allow her mind to dwell upon the jadestone pendant. Instead, she gazed complacently down upon her bejeweled fingers and folded in with her letter to Mr. Spring Fragrance a bright little sheaf of condensed love.

III

Mr. Spring Fragrance sat on his doorstep. He had been reading two letters, one from Mrs. Spring Fragrance, and the other from an elderly bachelor cousin in San Francisco. The one from the elderly bachelor cousin was a business letter, but contained the following postscript:

Tsen Hing, the son of the Government schoolmaster, seems to be much in the company of your young wife. He is a good-looking youth, and pardon me, my deaf cousin; but if women are allowed to stray at will from under their husbands' mulberry roofs, what is to prevent them from becoming butterflies?

"Sing Foon is old and cynical," said Mr. Spring Fragrance to himself. "Why should I pay any attention to him? This is America, where a man may speak to a woman, and a woman listen, without any thought of evil."

He destroyed his cousin's letter and re-read his wife's. Then he became very thoughtful. Was the making of American fudge sufficient reason for a wife to wish to remain a week longer in a city where her husband was not?

The young man who lived in the next house came out to water the lawn.

"Good evening," said he. "Any news from Mrs. Spring Fragrance?"

"She is having a very good time," returned Mr. Spring Fragrance.

"Glad to hear it. I think you told me she was to return the end of this week."

"I have changed my mind about her," said Mr. Spring Fragrance. "I am bidding her remain a week longer, as I wish to give a smoking party during her absence. I hope I may have the pleasure of your company."

"I shall be delighted," returned the young; fellow. "But, Mr. Spring Fragrance, don't invite any other white fellows. If you do not I shall be able to get in a scoop. You know, I'm a sort of honorary reporter for the *Gleaner*."

"Very well," absently answered Mr. Spring Fragrance.

"Of course, your friend the Consul will be present. I shall call it 'A high-class Chinese stag party!'"

In spite of his melancholy mood, Mr. Spring Fragrance smiled.

"Everything is 'high-class' in America," he observed.

"Sure!" cheerfully assented the young man.

"Haven't you ever heard that all Americans are princes and princesses, and just as soon as a foreigner puts his foot upon our shores, he also becomes of the nobility—I mean, the royal family."

"What about my brother in the Detention Pen?" dryly inquired Mr. Spring Fragrance.

"Now, you've got me," said the young man, rubbing his head. "Well, that is a shame—'a beastly shame', as the Englishman says. But understand, old fellow, we that are real Americans are up against that—even more than you. It is against our principles."

"I offer the real Americans my consolations that they should be compelled to do that which is against their principles."

"Oh, well, it will all come right some day. We're not a bad sort, you know. Think of the indemnity money returned to the Dragon by Uncle Sam."

Mr. Spring Fragrance puffed his pipe in silence for some moments. More than politics was troubling his mind.

At last he spoke. "Love," said he, slowly and distinctly, "comes before the Wedding in this country, does it not?"

"Yes, certainly."

Young Carman knew Mr. Spring Fragrance well enough to receive with calmness his most astounding queries.

"Presuming," continued Mr. Spring Fragrance—"presuming that some friend of your father's, living—presuming—in England—has a daughter that he arranges with your father to be your wife. Presuming that you have never seen that daughter, but that you marry her, knowing her not. Presuming that she marries you, knowing you not.—After she marries you and knows you, will that woman love you?"

"Emphatically, no," answered the young man.

"That is the way it would be in America—that the woman who marries the man like that—would not love him?"

"Yes, that is the way it would be in America. Love, in this country, must be free, or it is not love at all."

"In China, it is different!" mused Mr. Spring Fragrance.

"Oh, yes, I have no doubt that in China it is different."

"But the love is in the heart all the same," went on Mr. Spring Fragrance.

"Yes, all the same. Everybody falls in love some time or another. Some"—pensively—"many times."

Mr. Spring Fragrance arose.

"I must go down town," said he.

As he walked down the street he recalled the remark of a business acquaintance who had met his wife and had had some conversation with her: "She is just like an American woman."

He had felt somewhat flattered when this remark had been made. He looked upon it as a compliment to his wife's cleverness; but it rankled in his mind as he entered the telegraph office. If his wife was becoming as an American woman, would it not be possible for her to love as an American woman—a man to whom she was not married? There also floated in his memory the verse which his wife had quoted to the daughter of Chin Yuen. When the telegraph clerk handed him a blank, he wrote this message:

"Remain as you wish, but remember that 'Tis better to have loved and lost, than never to have loved at all.'"

When Mrs. Spring, Fragrance received this message, her laughter tinkled like falling water. How droll! How delightful! Here was her husband quoting American poetry in a telegram. Perhaps he had been reading her American poetry books since she had left him! She hoped so. They would lead him to understand her sympathy for her dear Laura and Kai Tzu. She need no longer keep from him their secret. How joyful! It had been such a hardship to refrain from confiding in him before. But discreetness had been most necessary, seeing that Mr. Spring Fragrance entertained as old-fashioned, notions concerning marriage as did the Chin Yuen parents. Strange that that should be so, since he had fallen in love with her picture before *ever* he had seen her, just as she had fallen in love with his! And when the marriage veil was lifted and each beheld the other for the first time in the flesh, there had been, no disillusion—no lessening of the respect and affection, which those who had brought about the marriage had inspired in each young heart.

Mrs. Spring fragrance began to wish she could fall asleep and wake to find the week flown, and she in her own little home pouring tea for Mr. Spring Fragrance.

IV

Mr. Spring Fragrance was walking to business with Mr. Chin Yuen. As they walked they talked.

"Yes," said Mr. Chin Yuen, "the old order is passing away, and the new order is taking its place, even with us who are Chinese. I have finally consented to give my daughter in marriage to young Kai Tzu."

Mr. Spring Fragrance expressed surprise. He had understood that the marriage between his neighbor's daughter and the San Francisco school-teacher's son was all arranged.

"So 'twas," answered Mr. Chin Yuen; "but it seems the young renegade, without consultation or advice, has placed his affections upon some untrustworthy female, and is so under her influence that he refuses to fulfill his parents' promise to me for him."

"So!" said Mr. Spring Fragrance: The shadow on his brow deepened.

"But," said Mr. Chin Yuen, with affable resignation, "it is all ordained by Heaven. Our daughter, as the wife of Kai Tzu, for whom she has long had a loving feeling, will not now be compelled to dwell with a mother-in-law and where her own mother is not. For that, we are thankful, as she is our only one and the conditions of life in this Western country are not as in China. Moreover, Kai Tzu, though not so much of a scholar as the teacher's son, has a keen eye for business and that, in America, is certainly much more desirable than scholarship. What do you think?"

"Eh! What!" exclaimed Mr. Spring Fragrance, The latter part of his companion's remarks had been lost upon him.

That day the shadow which had been following Mr. Spring Fragrance ever since he had heard his wife quote, "'Tis better to have loved," etc., became so heavy and deep that he quite lost himself within it.

At home in the evening he fed the cat the bird, and the flowers. Then, seating himself in a carved black chair—a present from his wife on his last birthday—he took out his pipe and smoked. The cat jumped into his lap. He stroked it softly and tenderly. It had been much fondled by Mrs. Spring Fragrance, and Mr. Spring Fragrance was under the impression that it missed her. "Poor thing!" said he. "I suppose you want her back!" When he arose to go to bed he placed the animal carefully on the floor, and thus apostrophized it:

"O Wise and Silent One, your mistress returns to you, but her heart she leaves behind her, with the Tommies in San Francisco."

The Wise and Silent One made no reply. He was not a jealous cat.

Mr. Spring Fragrance slept not that night; the next morning he ate not. Three days and three nights without sleep and food went by.

There was a springlike freshness in the air on the day that Mrs. Spring Fragrance came home. The skies overhead were as blue as Puget Sound stretching its gleaming length toward the mighty Pacific, and all the beautiful green world seemed to be throbbing with springing life.

Mrs. Spring Fragrance was never so radiant.

"Oh," she cried light-heartedly, "is it not lovely to see the sun shining so clear, and everything so bright to welcome me?"

Mr. Spring Fragrance made no response. It was the morning after the fourth sleepless night.

Mrs. Spring Fragrance noticed his silence, also his grave face.

"Everything—everyone is glad to see me but you," she declared, half, seriously, half jestingly.

Mr. Spring Fragrance set down her valise. They had just entered the house.

"If my wife is glad to see me," he quietly replied, "I also am glad to see her!"

Summoning their servant boy, he bade him look after Mrs. Spring Fragrance's comfort.

"I must be at the store in half an hour," said he, looking at his watch. "There is some very important business requiring attention."

"What is the business?" inquired Mrs. Spring Fragrance, her lip quivering with disappointment.

"I cannot just explain to you," answered her husband.

Mrs. Spring Fragrance looked up into his face with honest and earnest eyes. There was something in his manner, in the tone of her husband's voice, which touched her.

"Yen," said she, "you do not look well. You are not well. What is it?"

Something arose in Mr. Spring Fragrance's throat which prevented him; from replying.

"O darling one! sweetest one!" cried a girl's joyous voice. Laura Chin Yuen ran into the room and threw her arms around Mrs. Spring Fragrance's neck.

"I spied you from the window," said Laura, "and I couldn't rest until I told you. We are to be married next week, Kai Tzu and I. And all through you, all through you—the sweetest jade jewel in the world!"

Mr. Spring Fragrance passed out of the room.

"So the son of the Government teacher and little Happy Love are already married," Laura went on, relieving Mrs. Spring Fragrance of her cloak, her hat, and her folding fan.

Mr. Spring Fragrance paused upon the doorstep.

"Sit down, Little Sister, and I will tell you all about it," said Mrs. Spring Fragrance, forgetting her husband for a moment.

When Laura Chin Yuen had danced away, Mr. Spring Fragrance came in and hung up his hat.

"You got back very soon," said Mrs. Spring Fragrance, covertly wiping away the tears which had begun to fall as soon as she thought herself alone.

"I did not go," answered Mr. Spring Fragrance. "I have been listening to you, and Laura."

"But if the business is very important, do not you think you should attend to it?" anxiously queried Mrs. Spring Fragrance.

"It is not important to me now," returned Mr. Spring Fragrance. "I would prefer to hear again about Ah Oi and Man You and Laura and Kai Tzu."

"How lovely of you to say that!" exclaimed Mrs. Spring Fragrance, who was easily made happy. And she Taegan to chat away to her husband in the friendliest and wifeliest fashion possible. When she had finished she asked him if he were not glad to hear that those who loved as did the young lovers whose secrets she had been keeping, were to be united; and he replied that indeed he was; that he would like every man to be happy with a wife as he himself had ever been and ever would be.

"You did not always talk like that," said Mrs. Spring Fragrance slyly. "You must have been reading my American poetry books!"

"American poetry!" ejaculated Mr. Spring Fragrance almost fiercely, "American poetry is detestable, *abhorrable!*"

"Why! why!" exclaimed Mrs. Spring Fragrance, more and more surprised.

But the only explanation which Mr. Spring Fragrance vouchsafed was a jadestone pendant.

THE INFERIOR WOMAN

I

MRS. SPRING FRAGRANCE WALKED THROUGH THE leafy alleys of the park, admiring the flowers and listening to the birds singing. It was a beautiful afternoon with the warmth from the sun cooled by a refreshing breeze. As she walked along she meditated upon a book which she had some notion of writing. Many American women wrote books. Why should not a, Chinese? She would write a book about Americans for her Chinese women friends. The American people were So interesting and mysterious. Something of pride and pleasure crept into Mrs. Spring Fragrance's heart as she pictured Fei and Sie and Mai Gwi Far listening to Lae-Choo reading her illuminating paragraphs.

As she turned down a by-path she saw Will Carman, her American neighbor's son, coming towards her, and by his side a young girl who seemed to belong to the sweet air and brightness of, all "the things around her. They were talking very earnestly and the eyes of the young man were on the girl's face.

"Ah!" murmured Mrs. Spring Fragrance, after one swift glance. "It is love."

She retreated behind a syringa bush, which completely screened her from view.

Up the winding path Went the young couple.

"It is love," repeated Mrs. Spring Fragrance, "and it is the 'Inferior Woman.'"

She had heard about the Inferior Woman from the mother of Will Carman.

After tea that evening Mrs. Spring Fragrance stood musing at her front window. The sun hovered over the Olympic mountains like a great, golden red-bird with dark purple wings, its long tail of light trailing underneath in the waters of Puget Sound.

"How very beautiful!" exclaimed Mrs. Spring Fragrance; then she sighed.

"Why do you sigh?" asked Mr. Spring Fragrance.

"My heart is sad," answered his wife.

"Is the cat sick?" inquired Mr. Spring Fragrance.

Mrs. Spring Fragrance shook her head. "It is not our Wise One who troubles me today," she replied. "It is our neighbors. The sorrow of the

Carman household is that the mother desires for her son the Superior Woman, and his heart enshrines but the Inferior. I have seen them together today, and I know."

"What do you know?"

"That the Inferior Woman is the mate for young Carman."

Mr. Spring Fragrance elevated his brows, Only the day before, his wife's arguments had all been in favor of the Superior Woman. He uttered some words expressive of surprise, to which Mrs. Spring Fragrance retorted:

"Yesterday, O Great Man, I was a caterpillar!"

Just then young Carman came strolling up the path. Mr. Spring Fragrance opened the door to him. "Come in, neighbor," said he. "I have received some new books from Shanghai."

"Good," replied young Carman, who was interested in Chinese literature. While he and Mr. Spring Fragrance discussed the "Odes of Chow" and the "Sorrows of Han," Mrs. Spring Fragrance, sitting in a low easy-chair of rose-colored silk, covertly studied her visitor's countenance. Why was his expression so much more grave than gay? It had not been so a year ago—before he had known the Inferior Woman. Mrs. Spring Fragrance noted other changes, also, both in speech and manner. "He is no longer a boy," mused she. "He is a man, and it is the work of the Inferior Woman."

"And when, Mr. Carman," she inquired, "will you bring home a daughter to your mother?"

"And when, Mrs. Spring Fragrance, do you think I should?" returned the young man.

Mrs. Spring Fragrance spread wide her fan and gazed thoughtfully' over its silver edge.

"The summer moons will soon be over," said she. "You should not wait until the grass is yellow."

> "The woodmen blows responsive ring,
>   As on the trees they fail,
> And when the birds their sweet notes sing.
>   They to each other call.
> From the dark valley comes a bird,
>   And seeks the lofty tree,
> *Ying* goes its voice, and thus it cries:
>   'Companion, come to me.'
> The bird, although a creature small
>   Upon its mate depends,

And shall we men, who rank o'er all,
    Not seek to have our friends?"

quoted Mr. Spring Fragrance.

Mrs. Spring Fragrance tapped his shoulder approvingly with her fan.

"I perceive," said young Carman, "that you are both allied against my peace."

"It is for your mother," replied Mrs. Spring Fragrance soothingly. "She will be happy when she knows that your affections are fixed by marriage."

There was a slight gleam of amusement in the young man's eyes as he answered: "But if my mother has no wish for a daughter—at least, no wish for the daughter I would want to give her?"

"When I first came to America," returned Mrs. Spring Fragrance, "my husband desired me to wear the American dress. I protested and declared that never would I so appear. But one day he brought home a gown fit for a fairy, and ever since then I have worn and adored the American dress."

"Mrs. Spring Fragrance," declared young Carman, "your argument is incontrovertible."

II

A YOUNG MAN WITH A DETERMINED SET to his shoulders stood outside the door of a little cottage perched upon a bluff overlooking the Sound. The chill sea air was sweet with the scent of roses, and he drew in a deep breath of inspiration before he knocked.

"Are you not surprised to see me?" he inquired of the young person who opened the door.

"Not at all," replied the young person demurely.

He gave her a quick almost fierce look. At their last parting he had declared that he would not come again unless she requested him, and that she assuredly had not done.

"I wish I could make you feel," said he.

She laughed—a pretty infectious laugh which exorcised all his gloom. He looked down upon her as they stood together under the cluster of electric lights in her cozy little sitting-room. Such a slender, girlish figure! Such a soft cheek, red mouth, and firm little chin! Often in his dreams of her he had A taken her into his arms and coaxed her into a I good humor. But, alas! dreams are not realities, and the calm friendliness of this young person made any demonstration of tenderness well-nigh impossible. But for the shy regard of her eyes, you might have thought that he was no more to her than a friendly acquaintance.

"I hear," said she, taking up some needlework, "that your Welland case comes on tomorrow."

"Yes," answered the young lawyer, "and I have all my witnesses ready."

"So, I hear, has Mr. Greaves," she retorted. "You are going to have a hard fight."

"What of that, when in the end I'll win."

He looked over at her with a bright gleam in his eyes.

"I wouldn't be too sure," she warned demurely. "You may lose on a technicality?"

He drew his chair a little nearer to her side and turned over the pages of a book lying on her work-table. On the fly-leaf was inscribed in a man's writing: "To the dear little woman whose friendship is worth a fortune."

Another book beside it bore the inscription: "With the love of all the firm, including the boys," and a volume of poems above it was dedicated to the young person "with the high regards and stanch affection" of some other masculine person.

Will Carman pushed aside these evidences of his sweetheart's popularity with his own kind and leaned across the table.

"Alice," said he, "once upon a time you admitted, that you loved me."

A blush suffused the young person's countenance.

"Did I?" she queried.

"You did, indeed."

"Well?"

"Well! If you love me and I love you—"

"Oh, please!" protested the girl, covering her ears with her hands.

"I *will* please," asserted the young man.

"I have come here tonight, Alice, to ask you to marry me—and at once."

"Deary me!" exclaimed the young person; but she let her needlework fall into her lap as her lover, approaching nearer, laid his arm around her shoulders and, bending his face close to hers, pleaded his most important case.

If for a moment the small mouth quivered, the firm little chin lost its firmness, and the proud little head yielded to the pressure of a lover's arm, it was only for a moment so brief and fleeting that Will Carman had hardly become aware of it before it had passed.

"No," said the young person sorrowfully but decidedly. She had arisen and was standing on the other side of the table facing him. "I cannot marry you while your mother regards me as beneath you."

"When she knows you she will acknowledge you are above me. But I am not asking you to come to my mother, I am asking you to come to me, dear. If you will put your hand in mine and trust to me through all the coming years, no man or woman born can come between us."

But the young person shook her head.

"No," she repeated. "I will not be your wife unless your mother welcomes me with pride and with pleasure."

The night air was still sweet with the perfume of roses as Will Carman passed out of the little cottage door; but he drew in no deep breath of inspiration. His impetuous Irish heart was too heavy with disappointment. It might have been a little lighter, however, had he known that the eyes of the young person who gazed after him were misty with a love and yearning beyond expression.

III

WILL CARMEN HAS FAILED TO SNARE HIS BIRD," said Mr. Spring Fragrance to Mrs. Spring Fragrance. Their neighbor's son had just passed their veranda without turning to bestow upon them his usual cheerful greeting.

"It is too bad," sighed Mrs. Spring Fragrance sympathetically. She clasped her hands together and exclaimed:

"Ah, these Americans! These mysterious, inscrutable, incomprehensible Americans! Had I the divine right, of learning I would put them into an immortal book!"

"The divine right of learning," echoed Mr. Spring Fragrance, "Humph!"

Mrs. Spring Fragrance looked up into her husband's face in wonderment. "Is not the authority of the scholar, the student, almost divine?" she queried.

"So 'tis said," responded he. "So it seems."

The evening before, Mr. Spring Fragrance, together with several Seattle and San Francisco merchants, had given a dinner to a number of young students who had just arrived from China. The morning papers had devoted several columns to laudation of the students, prophecies as to their future, and the great influence which they would exercise over the destiny of their nation; but no comment whatever was made on the givers of the feast, and Mr. Spring Fragrance was therefore feeling somewhat unappreciated. Were not he and his brother merchants worthy of a little attention? If the students had come to learn things in America, they, the merchants, had accomplished things. There were those amongst them who had been instrumental in bringing several of the students to America. One of the boys was Mr. Spring Fragrance's own young brother, for whose maintenance and education he had himself sent the wherewithal every year for many years. Mr. Spring Fragrance, though well read in the Chinese classics, was not himself a scholar. As a boy he had come to the shores of America, worked his way up, and by dint of painstaking study after working hours acquired the Western language and Western business ideas. He had made money, saved money, and sent money home. The years had flown, his business had grown. Through his efforts trade between his native town and the port city in which he lived had greatly increased. A school in Canton was being built in part with funds furnished by him, and a railway syndicate, for the purpose of constructing a line of railway from the big city of Canton to his own native town, was under process of formation, with the name of Spring Fragrance at its head.

No wonder then that Mr. Spring Fragrance muttered "Humph!" when Mrs. Spring Fragrance dilated upon the "divine right of learning," and that he should feel irritated and humiliated, when, after explaining to her his grievances, she should quote in the words of Confutze: "Be not concerned that men do not know you; be only concerned that you do not know them." And he had expected wifely sympathy.

He was about to leave the room in a somewhat chilled state of mind when she surprised him again by pattering across to him and following up a low curtsy with these words:

"I bow to you as the grass bends to the wind. Allow me to detain you for just one moment."

Mr. Spring Fragrance eyed her for a moment with suspicion.

"As I have told you, O Great Man," continued Mrs. Spring Fragrance, "I desire, to write an immortal book, and now that I have learned from you that it is not necessary to acquire the 'divine right of learning' in order to accomplish things, I will begin the work without delay. My first subject will be 'The Inferior Woman of America.' Please advise me how I shall best inform myself concerning her."

Mr. Spring Fragrance, perceiving that his wife was now serious, and being easily mollified, sat himself down and rubbed his head. After thinking for a few moments he replied:

"It is the way in America, when a person is to be illustrated, for the illustrator to interview the person's friends. Perhaps, my dear, you had better confer with the Superior Woman."

"Surely," cried Mrs. Spring Fragrance, "no sage was ever so wise as my Great Man."

"But I lack the 'divine right of learning,'" dryly deplored Mr. Spring Fragrance.

"I am happy to hear it," answered Mrs. Spring Fragrance. "If you were a scholar you would have no time to read American poetry and American newspapers."

Mr. Spring Fragrance laughed heartily.

"You are no Chinese woman," he teased. "You are an American."

"Please bring me my parasol and my folding fan," said Mrs. Spring Fragrance. "I am going out for a walk."

And Mr. Spring Fragrance obeyed her.

IV

T HIS IS FROM MARY CARMAN, WHO IS IN PORTLAND," said the mother of the Superior Woman, looking up from the reading of a letter, as her daughter came in from the garden.

"Indeed," carelessly responded Miss Evebrook.

"Yes, it's chiefly about Will."

"Oh, is it? Well, read it then, dear. I'm interested in Will Carman, because of Alice Winthrop."

"I had hoped, Ethel, at one time that you would have been interested in him for his own sake. However, this is what she writes:

"I came here chiefly to rid myself of a melancholy mood which has taken possession of me lately, and also because I cannot bear to see my boy so changed towards me, owing to his infatuation for Alice Winthrop. It is incomprehensible to me how a son of mine can find any pleasure whatever in the society of such a girl. I have? traced her history, and find that she is not only uneducated in the ordinary sense, but her environment, from childhood up, has been the sordid and demoralizing one of extreme poverty and ignorance. This girl, Alice, entered a law office at the age of fourteen, supposedly to do the work of an office; boy. Now, after seven years in business, through the friendship and influence of men far above her socially, she holds the position of private secretary to "this most influential man in Washington—a position which by rights belongs only to a well-educated young woman of good family. Many such applied. I myself sought to have Jane Walker appointed. Is it not disheartening to out woman's cause to be compelled to realize that girls such as this one can win men over to be their friends and lovers, when there are so many splendid young women who have been carefully trained to be companions and comrades of educated men?"

"Pardon me, mother," interrupted Miss Evebrook, "but I have heard enough. Mrs. Carman is your friend and a well-meaning woman sometimes; but a woman suffragist, in the true sense, she certainly is not. Mark my words: If any young man had accomplished for himself what Alice Winthrop has, accomplished, Mrs. Carman could not have said enough in his praise. It is women such as Alice Winthrop who, in spite of every drawback, have raised themselves to the level of those who have had every advantage, who are the pride and glory of America. There are thousands of them, all over this land: women who have been of service to others all their years and who have graduated from the university of life with honor. Women Such as I, who are called the Superior Women of America, are after all nothing but schoolgirls in comparison.

Mrs. Evebrook eyed her daughter mutinously. "I don't see why you should feel like that," said she. "Alice is a dear bright child, and it is prejudice engendered by Mary Carman's disappointment about you and Will which is the real cause of poor Mary's bitterness towards her; but to my mind, Alice does not compare with my daughter. She would be frightened to death if she had to make a speech."

"You foolish mother!" rallied Miss Evebrook. "To stand upon a platform at woman suffrage meetings' and exploit myself is certainly a great recompense to you and father for all the sacrifices you have made in my behalf. But since it pleases you, I do it with pleasure even on the nights when my beau should 'come a courting.'"

"There is many a one who would like to come, Ethel. You're the handsomest girl in this Western town—and you know it."

"Stop that, mother. You know very well I have set my mind upon having ten years' freedom; ten years in which to love, live, suffer, see the world, and learn about men (not schoolboys) before I choose one."

"Alice Winthrop is the same age as you are, and looks like a child beside you."

"Physically, maybe; but her heart and mind are better developed. She has been out in the world all her life,, I only a few months."

"Your lecture last week on 'The Opposite Sex' was splendid."

"Of course. I have studied, one hundred books on the subject and attended fifty lectures. All that was necessary was to repeat in an original manner what was not by any means original."

Miss Evebrook went over to a desk and took a paper therefrom.

"This," said she, "is what Alice has written me in reply to my note suggesting that she attend next 'week the suffrage meeting, and give some of the experiences of her business career. The object I had in view when I requested the relation of her experiences was to use them as illustrations of the suppression; and oppression of women by f men. Strange to say, Alice and I have never conversed on this particular subject. If we had I would not have made this request of her, nor written her as I did. Listen:

"I should dearly love to please you, but I am afraid that my experiences, if related, would not help the cause. It may be, as you say, that men prevent' women from rising to their level; but if there are, such men, I have not met them. Ever since, when a little girl, I walked into a law office' and asked for work, and the senior member kindly looked me over through his spectacles and inquired if I thought I could learn to index-books, and the junior member glanced under my hat and said: "This is a pretty little girl and we must be pretty to her," I have loved and respected the men amongst whom I have worked and wherever I have worked. I may have been exceptionally fortunate, but I know this: the men for whom I have worked and amongst whom I have spent my life, whether they have been business or professional men, students or great lawyers and politicians, all alike have upheld me, inspired me, advised me, taught me, given me a broad outlook upon life for a woman; interested me in themselves and' in their work. As to corrupting my mind and my morals, as you say so many men do, when they have young and innocent girls to deal with: As a woman. I look back over my years spent amongst business and professional men, and see myself, as I was at first, an impressionable, ignorant little girl, born a Bohemian, easy to lead and easy to win, but borne aloft and morally supported by the goodness of my brother men, the men amongst whom I worked. That is why, dear Ethel, you will have to forgive me, because I cannot carry out your design, and help your work, as otherwise I would like to do."

"That, mother," declared Miss Evebrook, "answers all Mrs. Carman's insinuations, and should make her ashamed of herself. Can anyone know the sentiments which little Alice entertains toward men, and wonder at her winning out as she has?"

Mrs. Evebrook was about to make reply, when her glance happening to stray out of the window, she noticed a pink parasol.

"Mrs. Spring Fragrance!" she ejaculated, while her daughter went to the door and invited in the owner of the pink parasol, who was seated in a veranda rocker calmly writing in a note-book.

"I'm so sorry that we did not hear your ring, Mrs. Spring Fragrance," said she.

"There is no necessity for you to sorrow," replied the little Chinese woman. "I did not expect you to hear a ring which rang not. I failed to pull the bell."

"You forgot, I suppose," suggested Ethel Evebrook.

"Is it wise to tell secrets?" ingenuously inquired Mrs. Spring Fragrance.

"Yes, to your friends. Oh, Mrs. Spring Fragrance, you are *so* refreshing."

"I have pleasure, then, in confiding to you. I have an ambition to accomplish an immortal book about the Americans, and the conversation I heard through the window was" so interesting to me that I thought I would take some of it down for my book before I intruded myself. With your kind permission I will translate for your correction."

"I shall be delighted—honored," said Miss Evebrook, her cheeks glowing and her laugh rippling, "if you will promise me that you will also translate for our friend, Mrs. Carman."

"Ah, yes, poor Mrs. Carman! My heart is so sad for her," murmured the little Chinese woman.

V

WHEN THE MOTHER OF WILL CARMAN returned from Portland, the first person upon whom she called was Mrs. Spring Fragrance. Having lived in China while her late husband was in the customs service there, Mrs. Carman's prejudices did not extend to the Chinese, and ever since the Spring Fragrances had become the occupants of the villa beside the Carmans, there had been social good feeling between the American and Chinese families. Indeed, Mrs. Carman was wont to declare that amongst all her acquaintances there was not one more congenial and interesting than little Mrs. Spring Fragrance. So after she had sipped a cup of delicious tea, tasted some piquant candied limes, and told Mrs. Spring Fragrance all about her visit to the Oregon city and the Chinese people she had met there she reverted to a personal trouble confided to Mrs. Spring Fragrance some months before and dwelt upon it for more than half an hour. Then she checked herself and gazed at Mrs. Spring Fragrance in surprise. Hitherto she had found the little Chinese woman sympathetic and consoling, of Chinese ideas of filial duty chimed in with her own. But today Mrs. Spring Fragrance seemed strangely uninterested and unresponsive.

"Perhaps," gently suggested the American woman, who was nothing if not sensitive, "you have some trouble yourself. If so, my dear, tell me all about it."

"Oh, no!" answered Mrs. Spring Fragrance brightly. "I have no troubles to tell; but all the while I am thinking about the book I am writing."

"A book!"

"Yes, a book about Americans, an immortal book."

"My dear Mrs. Spring Fragrance!" exclaimed her visitor in amazement.

"The American woman writes books about the Chinese. Why not a Chinese woman write books about the Americans?"

"I see what you mean. Why, yes, of course. What an original idea!"

"Yes, I think that is what it is. My book I shall take from the words of others."

"What do you mean, my dear?"

"I listen to what is said, I apprehend, I write it:, down. Let me illustrate by the 'Inferior Woman' subject. The Inferior Woman is most interesting to me because you have told me that your son is in much love with her. My husband advised me to learn about the Inferior Woman from the Superior Woman. I go to see the Superior Woman. I sit on the veranda of the Superior Woman's house. I listen to her converse with her mother about the Inferior Woman. With the speed of flames I write down all I hear. When I enter the house the Superior Woman advises me that what I write is correct. May I read to you?"

"I shall be pleased to hear what you have written; but I do not think you were wise in your choice of subject," returned Mrs. Carman somewhat primly.

"I am sorry I am not wise. Perhaps I had better not read?" said Mrs. Spring Fragrance with humility.

"Yes, yes, do, please."

There was eagerness in Mrs. Carman's voice. What could Ethel Evebrook have to say about that girl!

When Mrs. Spring Fragrance had finished reading, she looked up into the face of; her American friend—a face in which there was nothing now but tenderness.

"Mrs. Mary Carman," said she; "you are so good as to admire my husband because he is what the Americans call 'a man who has made himself.' Why then do you not admire the Inferior Woman who is a woman who has made herself?"

"I think I do," said Mrs. Carman slowly.

VI

I
T WAS AN EVENING THAT INVITED TO REVERIE. The far stretches of the sea were gray with mist, and the city itself, lying around the sweep of the Bay, seemed dusky and distant. From her cottage window Alice Winthrop looked silently at the open world around her. It seemed a long time since she had heard Will Carman's whistle. She wondered if he were still angry with her. She was sorry that he had left her in anger, and yet not sorry. If she had not made him believe that she was proud and selfish, the parting would have been much harder; and perhaps had he known the truth and realized that it was for his sake, and not for her own, that she was sending him away from her, he might have refused to leave her at all. His was such an imperious nature. And then they would have married—right away. Alice caught her breath a little,

and then she sighed. But they would not have been happy. No, that could not have been possible if his mother did not like her. When a gulf of prejudice lies between the wife and mother of a man, that man's life is not what it should be. And even supposing she and Will could have lost themselves in each other, and been able to imagine themselves perfectly satisfied with life together, would it have been right? The question of right and wrong was a very real one to Alice Winthrop. She put herself in the place of the mother of her lover—a lonely elderly woman, a widow with an only son, upon whom she had expended all her love and care ever since, in her early youth, she had been bereaved of his father. What anguish of heart would be hers if that son deserted her for one whom she, his mother, deemed unworthy! Prejudices are prejudices. They are like diseases.

The poor, pale, elderly Woman, who cherished bitter and resentful feelings towards the girl whom her son loved, was more an object of pity than condemnation to the girl herself.

She lifted her eyes to the undulating line of hills beyond the water. From behind them came a silver light. "Yes," said she aloud to herself—and, though she knew it not, there was an infinite pathos in such philosophy from one so young—"if life cannot be bright and beautiful for me, at least it can be peaceful and contended."

The light behind the hills died away; darkness crept over the sea. Alice withdrew from the window, and went and knelt before the open fire in her sitting-room. Her cottage companion, the young woman who rented the place with her, had not yet returned from town.

Alice did not turn on the light. She was seeing pictures in the fire, and in every picture was the same face and form—the face and form of a fine, handsome young man with love and hope in his eyes. No, not always love and hope. In the last picture of all there was an expression which she wished she could forget. And yet she would remember—ever—always—and with it, these words; "Is it nothing to you nothing to tell a man that you love him, and then to bid him go?" Yes, but when she had told him she loved him she had not dreamed that her love for him and his for her would estrange him from one who, before ever she had come to this world, had pillowed his head on her breast.

Suddenly this girl, so practical, so humorous, so clever in every-day life, covered her face with her hands and sobbed like a child. Two roads of life had lain before her and she had chosen the hardest.

The warning hell of an automobile passing the cross-roads checked her tears. That reminded, her that Nellie Blake would soon be home. She turned on the light and went to the bedroom and bathed her eyes. Nellie must have forgotten her key. There she was knocking.

The chill sea air was sweet with the scent of roses as Mary Carman stood upon the threshold of the little cottage, and beheld in the illumination from within the young girl whom she had called "the Inferior Woman."

"I have come, Miss Winthrop," said she, "to beg of you to return home with me. Will, reckless boy, met with a slight accident while out shooting, so could not come for you himself. He has told me that he loves you, and if you love him, I want to arrange for the prettiest wedding of the season. Come, dear!"

"I am so glad," said Mrs. Spring Fragrance, "that Will Carman's bird is in his nest and his felicity is assured."

"What about the Superior Woman?" asked Mr. Spring Fragrance.

"Ah, the Superior Woman! Radiantly beautiful, and gifted with the divine right of learning! I love well the Inferior Woman; but, O Great Man, when we have a daughter, may Heaven ordain the she walk in the groove of the Superior Woman."

The Americanizing of Pau Tsu

I

WHEN WAN HOM HING CAME TO SEATTLE to start a branch of the merchant business which his firm carried on so successfully in the different ports of China, he brought with him his nephew, Wan Lin Fo, then eighteen years of age. Wan Lin Fo was a well-educated Chinese youth, with bright eyes and keen ears. In a few years' time he knew as much about the business as did any of the senior partners. Moreover, he learned to speak and write the American language with such fluency that he was never at a loss for an answer, when the white man, as was sometimes the case, sought to pose him. "All work and no play," however, is as much against the principles of a Chinese youth as it is against those of a young American, and now and again Lin Fo Would while away an evening at the Chinese Literary Club, above the Chinese restaurant, discussing with some chosen companions the works and merits of Chinese sages—and some other things. New Year's Day, or rather, Week, would also see him, business forgotten, arrayed in national costume of finest silk, and color "the blue of the sky after rain," visiting with his friends, both Chinese and American, and scattering silver an old coin amongst the youngsters of the families visited.

It was on the occasion of one of these New Year's visits that Wan Lin Fo first made known to the family of his firm's silent American partner, Thomas Raymond, that he was betrothed. It came about in this wise: One of the young ladies of the house, who was fair and frank of face and friendly and cheery in manner, observing as she handed him a cup of tea that Lin Fo's eyes wore a rather wistful expression, questioned him as to the wherefore:

"Miss Adah," replied Lin Fo, "may I tell you something?"

"Certainly, Mr. Wan," replied the girl.

"You know how I enjoy hearing your tales."

"But this is no tale. Miss Adah, you have inspired in me a love—"

Adah Raymond started. Wan Lin Fo spake slowly.

"For the little girl in China to whom I am betrothed."

"Oh, Mr. Wan! That is good news. But what have I to do with it?"

"This, Miss Adah! Every time I come to this house, I see you, so good and so beautiful, dispensing tea and happiness to all around, and I think, could I have in my home and ever by my side one who is also both good and beautiful, what a felicitous life mine would be!"

"You must not flatter me, Mr. Wan!" "All that I say is founded on my heart. But I will speak not of you. I will speak of Pau Tsu."

"Pau Tsu?"

"Yes. That is the name of my future wife. It means a pearl."

"How pretty! Tell me all about her!"

"I was betrothed to Pau Tsu before leaving China, My parents adopted her to be my wife. As I remember, she had shining eyes and the good-luck color was on her cheek. Her mouth was like a red vine leaf, and her eyebrows most exquisitely arched. As slender as a willow was her form, and when she spoke, her voice lilted from note to note in the sweetest melody."

Adah Raymond softly clapped her hands.

"Ah! You were even then in love with her."

"No," replied Lin Fo thoughtfully. "I was too young to be in love—sixteen years of age. Pau Tsu was thirteen. But, as I have confessed, you have caused me to remember and love her."

Adah Raymond was not a self-conscious girl, but for the life of her she could think of no reply to Lin Wo's speech.

"I am twenty-two years old now," he continued. "Pau Tsu is eighteen. To-morrow I will write to my parents and persuade them to send her to me at the time of the spring festival. My elder brother was married last year, and his wife is now under my parents' roof, so that Pau Tsu, who has been the daughter of the house for so many years, can now be spared to me."

"What a sweet little thing she must be," commented Adah Raymond.

"You will say that when you see her," proudly responded Lin Fo. "My parents say she is always happy. There is not a bird or flower or dewdrop in which she does not find some glad meaning."

"I shall be so glad to know her. Can she speak English?"

Lin Fo's face fell.

"No," he replied, "but,"—brightening—"when she comes I will have her learn to speak like you and be like you."

II

Pau Tsu came with the spring, and Wan Lin Fo was one of the happiest and proudest of bridegrooms. The tiny bride was really very pretty—even to American eyes. In her peach and plum colored robes, her little arms and hands sparkling with jewels, and her shiny black head decorated with wonderful combs and pins, she appeared a bit of Eastern coloring amidst the Western lights and shades.

Lin Fo had not been forgotten, and her eyes, and under their downcast lids discovered him at once, as he stood awaiting her amongst a group of young Chinese merchants on the deck of the vessel.

The apartments he had prepared for her were furnished in American style, and her birdlike little figure in Oriental dress seemed rather out of place at first. It was not long, however, before she brought forth from the great box, which she had brought overseas, screens and fans, vases, panels, Chinese matting, artificial flowers and birds, and a number of exquisite carvings and pieces of antique porcelain. With these she transformed the American flat into an Oriental bower, even setting up in her sleeping-room a little chapel, enshrined in which was an image of the Goddess of Mercy, two ancestral tablets, and other emblems of her faith in the Gods of her fathers.

The Misses Raymond called upon her soon after arrival, and she smiled and looked pleased. She shyly presented each girl with a Chinese cup and saucer, also a couple of antique vases, covered with whimsical pictures, which Lin Fo tried, his best to explain.

The girls were delighted with the gifts, and having fallen, as they expressed themselves, in love with the little bride, invited her through her husband to attend a launch party, which they intended giving the following Wednesday on Lake Washington.

Lin Fo accepted the invitation in behalf of himself and wife. He was quite at home with the Americans and, being a young man, enjoyed their rather effusive appreciation of him s as an educated Chinaman. Moreover, he was of the opinion that the society of the American young ladies would benefit Pau Tsu in helping her to acquire the ways and language of the land in which he hoped to make a fortune.

Wan Lin Fo was a true son of the Middle Kingdom and secretly pitied all those who were born far away from its influences; but there was much about the Americans that he admired. He also entertained sentiments of respect for a motto which hung in his room which bore the legend: "When in Rome, do as the Romans do."

"What is best for men is also best for: women in this country," he told Pau Tsu when she wept over his suggestion that she should take some lessons in English from a white woman.

"It may be best for a man who goes out in the street," she sobbed, "to learn the new language, but of what importance is it to a woman who lives only within in the house and her husband's heart?"

It was seldom, however, that she protested against the wishes of Lin Fo. As her mother-in-law had said, she was a docile, happy little creature. Moreover, she loved her husband.

But as the days and weeks went by the girl bride whose life hitherto had been spent in the quiet retirement of a Chinese home in the performance of filial duties, in embroidery work and lute playing, in sipping tea and chatting with gentle girl companions, felt very much bewildered by the novelty and stir of the new world into which she had been suddenly thrown. She could not understand, for all Lin Fo's explanations, why it was required of her to learn the strangers' language and adopt their ways. Her husband's tongue was the same as her own. So also her little maid's. It puzzled her to be always seeing this, and hearing that—sights and sounds which as yet had no meaning for her. Why also was it necessary to receive visitors nearly every evening?—visitors who could neither understand nor make themselves understood by her, for all their curious smiles and stares, which she bore like a second visitor Vashti—or rather, Esther. And why, oh! why should she be constrained to eat her food with clumsy, murderous looking American implements instead of with her own elegant and easily manipulated ivory chopsticks?

Adah Raymond, who at Lin Fo's request was a frequent visitor to the house, could not fail to observe that Pau Tsu's small face grew daily smaller and thinner, and that the smile with which she invariably greeted her, though sweet, was tinged with melancholy. Her woman's instinct told her that something was wrong, but what it was the light within her failed to discover. She would reach over to Pau Tsu and take within her own firm, white hand the small, trembling fingers, pressing them lovingly and sympathetically; and the little Chinese woman would look up into the beautiful face bent above hers and think to herself: "No wonder he wishes me to be like her!"

If Lin Fo happened to come in before Adah Raymond left he would engage the visitor in bright and animated conversation. They had so much of common interest to discuss, as is always the way with young people who have lived any length of time in a growing city of the West. But to Pau Tsu, pouring tea and dispensing sweetmeats, it was all Greek, or rather, all American.

"Look, my pearl, what I have brought you," said Lin Fo one afternoon as he entered his wife's apartments, followed by a messenger-boy, who deposited in the middle of the room a large cardboard box.

With murmurs of wonder Pau Tsu drew near, and the messenger-boy having withdrawn Lin Fo cut the string, and drew forth a beautiful lace evening dress and dark blue walking costume, both made in American style.

For a moment there was silence in the room. Lin Fo looked at his wife in surprise. Her face was pale and her little body was trembling, while her hands were drawn up into her sleeves.

"Why, Pau Tsu!" he exclaimed, "I thought to make you glad."

At these word the girl bent over the dress of filmy lace, and gathering the flounce in her hand smoothed it over her knee; then lifting a smiling face to her husband, replied: "Oh, you are too good, too kind to your unworthy Pau Tsu. My speech is slow, because I am overcome with happiness."

Then with exclamations of delight and admiration she lifted the dresses out of the box and laid them carefully over the couch.

"I wish you to dress lite an American woman when we go out or receive," said her husband. "It is the proper thing in America to do as the Americans do. You will notice, light of my eyes, that it is only on New Year and our national holidays that I wear the costume of our country and attach a queue. The wife should follow the husband in all things."

A ripple of laughter escaped Pau Tsu's lips.

"When I wear that dress," said she, touching the walking costume, "I will look like your friend, Miss Raymond."

She struck her hands together gleefully, but when her husband had gone to his business she bowed upon the floor and wept pitifully.

III

URING THE RAINY Reason Pau Tsu was attacked with a very bad cough. A daughter of Southern China, the chill, moist climate of the Puget Sound winter was very hard on her delicate lungs. Lin Fo worried much over the state of her health, and meeting Adah Raymond on the street one afternoon told her of his anxiety. The kind-hearted girl immediately returned with him to the house. Pau Tsu was lying on her couch, feverish and breathing hard. The American girl felt her hands and head.

"She must have a doctor," said she, mentioning the name of her family's physician.

Pau Tsu shuddered. She understood a little English by this time.

"No! No! Not a man, *not* a man!" she cried.

Adah Raymond looked up at Lin Fo.

"I understand," said she. "There are several women doctors in this town. Let us send for one."

But Lin Fo's face was set.

"No!" he declared. "We are in America. Pau Tsu shall be attended to by your physician."

Adah Raymond was about to protest against this dictum when the sick wife, who had also heard it, touched her hand and whispered: "I not mind now. Man all right."

So the other girl closed her lips, feeling that if the wife would not dispute her husband's will it was not her place to do so; but her heart ached with compassion as she bared Pau Tsu's chest for the stethoscope.

"It was like preparing a lamb for slaughter," she told her sister afterwards. "Pau Tsu was motionless, her eyes closed and her lips sealed, while the doctor remained; but after he had left and we two were alone she shuddered and moaned' like one bereft of reason. I honestly believe that the examination was worse than death to that little Chinese woman. The modesty of generations of maternal ancestors was crucified as I rolled down the neck of her silk tunic."

It was a week after the doctor's visit, and Pau Tsu, whose cough had yielded to treatment, though she was still far from well, was playing on her lute, and whisperingly singing this little song, said to have been written on a fan which was presented to an ancient Chinese emperor by one of his wives:

> "Of fresh new silk,
> All snowy white,
> And round as a harvest moon,
> A pledge of purity and love,
> A small but welcome boon.
>
> While summer lasts,
> When borne in hand,
> Or folded on thy breast,
> 'Twill gently soothe thy burning brow,
> And charm thee to thy rest.
>
> But, oh, when Autumn winds blow chill,
> And days are bleak and cold,
> No longer sought, no longer loved,
> 'Twill lie in dust and mould.
>
> This silken fan then deign accept,
> Sad emblem of my lot,
> Caressed and cherished for an hour,
> Then speedily forgot."

"Why so melancholy, my pearl?" asked Lin Fo, entering from the street.

"When a bird is about to die, its notes are sad," returned Pau Tsu.

"But thou art not for death—thou art for life," declared Lin Fo, drawing her towards him and gazing into a face which day by day seemed to grow finer and more transparent.

IV

A CHINESE MESSENGER-BOY RAN UP THE STREET, entered the store of Wan Hom Hing & Co. and asked for the junior partner. When Lin Fo came forward he handed him a dainty, flowered missive, neatly folded and addressed. The receiver opened it and read:

DEAR AND HONORED HUSBAND,—Your unworthy Pau Tsu lacks the courage to face the ordeal before her. She has, therefore, left you and prays you to obtain a divorce, as is the custom in America, so that you may be happy with the Beautiful One, who is so much your Pau Tsu's superior. This, she acknowledges, for she sees with your eyes, in which, like a star, the Beautiful One shineth. Else, why should you have your Pau Tsu follow in her footsteps? She has tried to obey your will and to be as an American woman; but now she is very weary, and the terror of that is before her has overcome.

Your stupid thorn,

PAU TSU

Mechanically Lin Fo folded the letter and thrust it within his breast pocket. A customer inquired of him the price of a lacquered tray. "I wish you good morning," he replied, reaching for his hat. The customer and clerks gaped after him as he left the store.

Out in the street, as fate would have it, he met Adah Raymond. He would have turned aside had she not spoken to him.

"Whatever is the matter with you, Mr. Wan?" she inquired. "You don't look yourself at all."

"The density of my difficulties you cannot understand," he replied, striding past her.

But Adah Raymond was persistent. She had worried lately over Pau Tsu.

"Something is wrong with your wife," she declared.

Lin Fo wheeled around.

"Do you know where she is?" he asked with quick suspicion.

"Why, no!" exclaimed the girl in surprise.

"Well, she has left me."

Adah Raymond stood incredulous for a moment, then with indignant eyes she turned upon the deserted husband.

"You deserve it!" she cried, "I have seen it for some time: your cruel, arbitrary treatment of the dearest, sweetest little soul in the world."

"I beg your pardon, Miss Adah," returned Lin Fo, "but I do not understand. Pau Tsu is heart of my heart. How then could I be cruel to her?"

"Oh, you Stupid!" exclaimed the girl. "You're a Chinaman, but you're almost as stupid as an American. Your cruelty consisted in forcing Pau Tsu to be—what nature never intended her to be—an American woman; to adapt and adopt in a few months' time all our ways and customs. I saw it long ago, but as Pau Tsu was too sweet and meek to see any faults in her man I had not the heart to open her eyes—or yours. Is it not true that she has left you for this reason?"

"Yes," murmured Lin Fo. He was completely crushed; "And some other things."

"What other things?"

"She—is—afraid—of—the—doctor."

"She is!"—fiercely—"Shame upon you!"

Lin Fo began to walk on, but the girl kept by his side and continued:

"You wanted your wife to be an American woman while you remained a Chinaman. For all your clever adaptation of our American ways you are a thorough Chinaman. Do you think an American would dare treat his wife as you have treated yours?"

Wan Lin Fo made no response. He was wondering how he could ever have wished his gentle Pau Tsu to be like this angry woman. Now his Pau Tsu was gone. His anguish for the moment made him oblivious to the presence of his companion and the words she was saying. His silence softened the American girl. After all, men, even Chinamen, were nothing but big, clumsy boys, and she didn't believe in kicking a man after he was down.

"But, cheer up, you're sure to find her," said she, suddenly changing her tone. "Probably her maid has friends in Chinatown who have taken them in."

"If I find her," said Lin Fo fervently, "I will not care if she never speaks an American word, and I will take her for a trip to China, so that our son may be born in the country that Heaven loves."

"You cannot make too much amends for all she has suffered. As to Americanizing Pau Tsu—that will come in time. I am quite sure that were I transferred to your country and commanded to turn myself into a Chinese woman in the space of two or three months I would prove a sorry disappointment to whomever built their hopes upon me."

Many hours elapsed before any trace could be found of the missing one. All the known friends and acquaintances of little Pau Tsu were called upon and questioned; but if they had knowledge of the young wife's hiding place they refused to divulge it. Though Lin Fo's face was grave with an unexpressed fear, their sympathies were certainly not with him.

The seekers were about giving up the search in despair when a little boy, dangling in his hands a string of blue beads, arrested the attention of the young husband. He knew the necklace to be a gift from Pau Tsu to the maid, A-Toy, He had bought it himself. Stopping and questioning the little fellow he learned to his great joy that his wife and her maid were at the boy's home, under the care of his grandmother, who was a woman learned in herb lore.

Adah Raymond smiled in sympathy with her companion's evident great relief.

"Everything will now be all right," said she, following Lin Fo as he proceeded to the house pointed out by the lad. Arrived there, she suggested that the husband enter first and alone. She would wait a few moments.

"Miss Adah," said Lin Fo, "ten thousand times I beg your pardon, but perhaps you will come to see my wife some other time—not today?"

He hesitated, embarrassed, and humiliated.

In one silent moment Adah Raymond grasped the meaning of all the morning's trouble—of all Pau Tsu's sadness.

"Lord, what fools we mortals be!" she soliloquized as she walked home alone. "I ought to have known. What else could Pau Tsu have thought?— coming from a land where women have no men friends save their husbands. How she must have suffered under her smiles! Poor, brave little soul!"

In The Land of the Free

I

SEE, LITTLE ONE—THE HILLS IN the morning sun. There is thy home for years to come. It is very beautiful and thou wilt be very happy there."

The Little One looked up into his mother's face in perfect faith. He was engaged in the pleasant occupation of sucking a sweetmeat; but that did not prevent him from gurgling responsively.

"Yes, my olive bud; there is where thy father is making a fortune for thee. Thy father! Oh, wilt thou not be glad to behold his dear face. "'Twas for thee I left him."

The Little One ducked his chin sympathetically against his mother's knee. She lifted him on to her lap. He was two years old, a round, dimple-cheeked boy with bright brown eyes and a sturdy little frame.

"Ah! Ah! Ah! Ooh! Ooh! Ooh!" puffed he, mocking a tugboat steaming by.

San Francisco's waterfront was lined with ships and steamers, while other craft, large and small, including a couple of white transports from the Philippines, lay at anchor here and there off shore. It was some time before the *Eastern Queen* could get docked, and even after that was accomplished, a lone Chinaman who had been waiting on the wharf for an hour was detained that much longer by men with the initials U. S. C. on their caps, before he could board the steamer and welcome his wife and child.

"This is thy son," announced the happy Lae Choo.

Hom Hing lifted the child, felt of his little body and limbs, gazed into his face with proud and joyous eyes; then turned inquiringly to a customs officer at his elbow.

"That's a fine boy you have there," said the man. "Where was he born?"

"In China," answered Hom Hing, swinging the Little One on his right shoulder, preparatory to leading his wife off the steamer.

"Ever been to America before?"

"No, not he," answered the father with a happy laugh.

The customs officer beckoned to another.

"This little fellow," said he, "is visiting America for the first time."

The other customs officer stroked his chin reflectively.

"Good day," said Hom Hing.

"Wait!" commanded one of the officers.

"You cannot go just yet."

"What more now?" asked Hom Hing.

"I'm afraid," said the first customs officer, "that we cannot allow the boy to go ashore. There is nothing in the papers that you have shown us—your wife's papers and your own—having any bearing upon the child."

"There was no child when the papers were made out," returned Hom Hing. He spoke calmly; but there was apprehension in his eyes and in his tightening grip on his son.

"What is it? What is it?" quavered Lae Choo, who understood a little English.

The second customs officer regarded her pityingly.

"I don't like this part of the business," he muttered.

The first officer turned to Horn Ming and in an official tone of voice, said:

"Seeing that the boy has no certificate entitling him to admission to this country you will have to leave him with us."

"Leave my boy!" exclaimed Hom Hing.

"Yes; he will be well taken care of, and just as soon as we can hear from Washington he will be handed over to you."

"But," protested Hom Hing, "he is my son."

"We have no proof," answered the man with a shrug of his shoulders; "and even if so we cannot let him pass without orders from the Government."

"He is my son," reiterated Hom Hing, slowly and solemnly. "I am a Chinese merchant and have been in business in San Francisco for many years. When my wife told to me one morning that she dreamed of a green tree with spreading branches and one beautiful red flower growing thereon, I answered her that I wished my son to be born in our country, and for her to prepare to go to China. My wife complied with my wish. After my son was born my mother fell sick and my wife nursed and cared for her; then my father, too, fell sick, and my wife also nursed and cared for him. For twenty moons my wife care for and nurse the old people, and when they die they bless her and my son, and I send for her to return to me. I had no fear of trouble. I was a Chinese merchant and my son was my son."

"Very good, Hom Hing," replied the first officer. "Nevertheless, we take your son."

"No, you not take him; he my son too."

It was Lae Choo. Snatching the child from his father's arms she held and covered him with her own.

The officers conferred together for a few moments; then one drew Hom Hing aside and spoke in his ear.

Resignedly Hom Hing bowed his head, then approached his wife. "'Tis the law," said he speaking in Chinese, "and 'twill be but for a little while—until tomorrow's gun arises."

"You, too," reproached Lae Choo in a; voice eloquent with pain. But accustomed to obedience she yielded the boy to her husband who in turn delivered him to the first officer. The Little One protested lustily against the transfer; but his mother covered her face with her sleeve and his father silently led her away. Thus was the law of the land complied with.

II

D AY WAS BREAKING. LAE CHOO, WHO had been awake all night, dressed herself, then awoke her husband.

"'Tis the morn," she cried. "Go, bring our son."

The man rubbed his eyes and arose upon his elbow so that he could see out of the window. A pale star was visible in the sky. The petals of a lily in a bowl on the windowsill were unfurled.

"'Tis not yet time," said he, laying his head down again.

"Not yet time. Ah, all the time that I lived before yesterday is not so much as the time that has been since my little one was taken from me."

The mother threw herself down beside the bed and covered her face.

Hom Hing turned on the light, and touching his wife's bowed head with a sympathetic hand inquired if she had slept.

"Slept!" she echoed, weepingly. "Ah, how could I close my eyes with my arms empty of the little body that has filled them every night for more than twenty moons! You do not know—man—what it is to miss the feel of the little fingers and the little toes and the soft round limbs of your little one. Even in the darkness his darling eyes used to shine up to mine, and often have I fallen into slumber with his pretty babble at my ear. And now, I see him not; I touch him not; I hear him not. My baby, my little fat one!"

"Now! Now! Now!" consoled Hom Hing, patting his wife's shoulder reassuringly; "there is no need to grieve so; he will soon gladden you again. There cannot be any law that would keep a child from its mother!"

Lae Choo dried her tears.

"You are right, my husband," she meekly murmured. She arose and stepped about the apartment, setting things to rights. The box of presents she had brought for her California friends had been opened the evening before; and silks, embroideries, carved ivories, ornamental lacquer-ware, brasses, camphor wood boxes, fans, and chinaware were scattered around in confused heaps. In the midst of unpacking the thought of her child in the hands of strangers had overpowered her, and she had left everything to crawl into bed and weep.

Having arranged her gifts in order she stepped out on to the deep balcony.

The star had faded from view and there were bright streaks in the western sky. Lae Choo looked down the street and around. Beneath the flat occupied by her and her husband were quarters for a number of bachelor Chinamen, and she could hear them from where she stood, taking their early morning breakfast. Below their dining-room was her husband's grocery store. Across the way was a large restaurant. Last night it had been resplendent with gay colored lanterns and the sound of music. The rejoicings over "the completion of the moon," by Quong Sum's firstborn, had been long and loud, and had caused her to tie a handkerchief over her ears. She, a bereaved mother, had it not in her heart to rejoice with other parents. This morning the place was more in accord with her mood. It was still and quiet. The revellers had dispersed or were asleep.

A roly-poly woman in black sateen, with long pendant earrings in her ears, looked up from the street below and waved her a smiling greeting. It was her old neighbor, Kuie Hoe, the wife of the gold embosser, Mark Sing. With her was a little boy in yellow jacket and lavender pantaloons. Lae Choo remembered him as a baby. She used to like to play with him in those days when she had no child of her own. What a long time ago that seemed! She caught her breath in a sigh, and laughed instead.

"Why are you so merry?" called her husband from within.

"Because my Little One is coming home," answered Lae Choo. "I am a happy mother—a happy mother."

She pattered into the room with a smile on her face.

The noon hour had arrived. The rice was steaming in the bowls and a fragrant dish of chicken and bamboo shoots was awaiting Hom Hing. Not for one moment had Lae Choo paused to rest during the morning hours; her activity had been ceaseless. Every now and again, however, she had raised her eyes to the gilded clock on the curiously carved mantelpiece. Once, she had exclaimed:

"Why so long, oh I why so long?" Then apostrophizing herself: "Lae Choo, be happy. The Little One is coming! The Little One is coming!" Several times she burst into tears: and several times she laughed aloud.

Hom Hing entered the room; his arms hung down by his side.

"The Little One!" shrieked Lae Choo.

"They bid me call tomorrow."

With a moan the mother sank to the floor.

The noon hour passed. The dinner remained on the table.

III

THE WINTER RAINS WERE OVER: the spring had come to California, flushing the hills with green and causing an ever-changing pageant of flowers to pass over them. But there was no spring in Lae Choo's heart, for the Little One remained away from her arms. He was being kept in a mission. White women were caring for him, and though for one full moon he had pined for his mother and refused to be comforted he was now apparently happy and contented. Five moons or five months had gone by since the day he had passed with Lae Choo through the Golden Gate; but the great Government at Washington still delayed sending the answer which would return him to his parents.

Hom Hing was disconsolately rolling up and down the balls in his abacus box when a keen-faced young man stepped into his store.

"What news?" asked the Chinese merchant.

"This!" The young man brought forth a typewritten letter. Hom Hing read the words:

"Re Chinese child, alleged to be the son of Hom Hing, Chinese merchant, doing business at 425 Clay street, San Francisco.

"Same will have attention as soon as possible."

Hom Hing returned the letter, and without a word continued his manipulation of the counting machine.

"Have you anything to say?" asked the young man.

"Nothing, they have sent the same letter fifteen times before. Have you not yourself showed it to me?"

"True!" The young man eyed the Chinese merchant furtively. He had a proposition to make and he was pondering whether or not the time was opportune.

"How is your wife?" he inquired solicitously—and diplomatically.

Hom Hing shook his head mournfully.

She seems less every day," he replied. "Her food she takes only when I bid her and her tears fall continually. She finds no pleasure in dress or flowers and cares not to see her friends. Her eyes stare all night. I think before another moon she will pass into the land of spirits."

"No!" exclaimed the young man, genuinely startled.

"If the boy not come home I lose my wife sure," continued Hom Hing with bitter sadness.

"It's not right," cried the young man indignantly. Then he made his proposition.

The Chinese father's eyes brightened exceedingly.

"Will I like you to go to Washington, and make them give you the paper to restore my son?" cried he. "How can you ask when you know my heart's desire?"

"Then, said the young fellow, "I will start next week. I am anxious to see this thing through if only for the sake of your wife's peace of mind."

"I will call her. To hear what you think to do will make her glad," said Hom Hing.

He called a message to Lae Choo upstairs through a tube in the wall.

In a few moments she appeared, listless, wan, and hollow-eyed; but when her husband told her the young lawyer's suggestion she became as one electrified; her form straightened, her, eyes glistened; the color flushed to her cheeks.

"Oh," she cried, turning to James Clancy, "You are a hundred man good!"

The young man felt somewhat embarrassed; his eyes shifted a little under the intense gaze of the Chinese mother.

"Well, we must get your boy for you," he responded. "Of course"—turning to Hom Hing—"it will cost a little money. You can't get fellows to hurry the Government for you without gold in your pocket."

Hom Hing stared blankly for a moment. Then: "How much do you want, Mr. Clancy?" he asked quietly.

"Well, I will need at least five hundred to start with."

Hom Hing cleared his throat.

"I think I told to you the time I last paid you for writing letters for me and seeing the Custom boss here that nearly all I had was gone!"

"Oh, well then we won't talk about it, old fellow. It won't harm the boy to stay where he is, and your wife may get over it all right."

"What that you say?" quavered Lae Choo.

James Clancy looked out of the window.

"He says," explained Hom Hing in English, "that to get our boy we have to have much money."

"Money! Oh, yes."

Lae Choo nodded her head.

"I have not got the money to give him."

For a moment Lae Choo gazed wonderingly from one face to the other; then, comprehension dawning upon her, with swift anger, pointing to the lawyer, she cried: "You not one hundred man good; you just common white man."

"Yes, ma'am," returned James Clancy, bowing and smiling ironically.

Hom Hing pushed his wife behind him and addressed the lawyer again: "I might try," said he, "to raise something; but five hundred—it is not possible."

"What about four?"

I tell you I have next to nothing left and my friends are not rich."

"Very well!"

The lawyer moved leisurely toward the door, pausing on its threshold to light a cigarette.

"Stop, white man; white man, stop!"

Lae Choo, panting and terrified, had started forward and now stood beside him, clutching his sleeve excitedly.

"You say you can go to get paper to bring my Little One to me if Hom Hing give you five hundred dollars?"

The lawyer nodded carelessly; his eyes were intent upon the cigarette which would not take the fire from the match.

"Then you go, get paper. If Hom Hing not can give you five hundred dollars—I give you perhaps what more that much."

She slipped a heavy gold bracelet from her wrist and held it out to the man. Mechanically he took it.

"I go get more!"

She scurried away, disappearing behind the door through which she had come.

"Oh, look here, I can't accept this," said James Clancy, walking back to Hom Hing and laying down the bracelet before him.

"It's all right," said Hom Hing, seriously, "pure China gold. My wife's parent give it to her when we married."

"But I can't take it anyway," protested the young man.

"It is all same as money. And you want money to go to Washington," replied Hom Hing in a matter of fact manner.

"See, my jade earrings—my gold buttons—my hairpins—my comb of pearl and my rings—one, two, three, four, five rings; very good—very good—all same much money. I give them all to you. You take and bring me paper for my Little One."

Lae Choo piled up her jewels before the lawyer.

Hom Hing laid a restraining hand upon her shoulder. "Not all, my wife," he said in Chinese. He selected a ring—his gift to Lae Choo when she dreamed of the tree with the red flower. The rest of the jewels he pushed toward the white man.

"Take them and sell them," said he. "They will pay your fare to Washington and bring you back with the paper."

For one moment James Clancy hesitated. He was not a sentimental man; but something within him arose against accepting such payment for his services.

"They are good, good," pleadingly asserted Lae Choo, seeing, his hesitation.

Whereupon he seized the jewels; thrust them into his coat pocket, and walked rapidly away from the store.

IV

LAE CHOO FOLLOWED AFTER THE MISSIONARY woman through the mission nursery school. Her heart was beating so high with happiness that she could scarcely breathe. The paper had come at last—the precious paper which gave Hom Hing and his wife the right to the possession of their own child. It was ten months now since he had been taken from them—ten months since the sun had ceased to shine for Lae Choo.

The room was filled with children—most of them were tots, but none so wee as her own. The mission woman talked as she walked. She told Lae Choo that little Kim, as he had been named by the school, was the pet of the place, and that his little tricks and ways amused and delighted everyone. He had been rather difficult to manage at first and had cried much for his mother; "but children so soon forget, and after a month he seemed quite at home and played around as bright and happy as a bird."

"Yes," responded Lae Choo. "Oh, yes, yes!"

But she did not hear what was said to her. She was walking in a maze of anticipatory joy.

"Wait here, please," said the mission woman, placing Lae Choo in a chair. "The very youngest ones are having their breakfast."

She withdrew for a moment—it seemed like an hour to the mother—then she reappeared leading by the hand a little boy dressed in blue cotton overalls and white-soled shoes. The little boy's face was round and dimpled and his eyes were very bright.

"Little One, ah, my Little One!" cried Lae Choo.

She fell on her knees and stretched her hungry arms toward her son.

But the Little One shrunk from her and tried to hide himself in the folds of the white woman's skirt.

"Go 'way, go 'way!" he bade his mother.

Lin John

IT WAS NEW YEAR'S EVE. LIN JOHN mused over the brightly burning fire. Through ii the beams of the roof the stars shone, far away in the deep night sky they shone down upon him, and he felt their beauty, though he had no words for it. The long braid which was wound around his head lazily uncoiled and fell down his back; his smooth young face was placid and content. Lin John was at peace with the world. Within one of his blouse sleeves lay a small bag of gold, the accumulated earnings of three years, and that gold was to release "his only sister from a humiliating and secret bondage. A sense of duty done led him to dream of the To-Come. What a fortunate fellow he was to have been able to obtain profitable work, and within three years to have saved four hundred dollars! In the next three years, he might be able to establish a little business and send his sister to their parents in China to live like an honest woman. The sharp edges of his life were forgotten in the drowsy warmth and the world faded into dreamland.

The latch was softly lifted; with stealthy step a woman approached the boy and knelt beside him. By the flickering gleam of the dying fire she found that for which she searched, and hiding it in her breast swiftly and noiselessly withdrew.

Lin John arose. His spirits were light—and so were his sleeves. He reached for his bowl of rice, then set it down, and suddenly his chopsticks clattered on the floor. With hands thrust into his blouse he felt for what was not there. Thus, with bewildered eyes for a few moments. Then he uttered a low cry and his face became old and gray.

A large apartment, richly carpeted; furniture of dark and valuable wood artistically carved ceiling decorated with beautiful Chinese ornaments and gold incense burners; walls hung from top to bottom with long bamboo panels covered with silk, on which, were printed Chinese characters; tropical plants, on stands; heavy curtains draped over windows. This, in the heart of Chinatown. And in the midst of these surroundings a girl dressed in a robe of dark blue silk worn over a full skirt richly embroidered. The sleeves fell over hands glittering with rings, and shoes, of light silk were on her feet. Her hair was ornamented with flowers made of jewels; she wore three or four pairs of bracelets; her jewel earrings were over an inch long.

The girl was fair to see in that her face was smooth and oval, eyes long and dark, mouth small and round, hair of jetty hue, and figure petite and graceful.

Hanging over a chair by her side was a sealskin sacque, such as is worn by fashionable American women. The girl eyed it admiringly and every few moments stroked the soft fur with caressing fingers.

"Pau Sang," she called.

A curtain was pushed aside and a heavy, broad-faced Chinese woman in blouse and trousers of black sateen stood revealed.

"Look," said the beauty. "I have a cloak like the American ladies. Is it not fine?"

Pau Sang nodded. "I wonder at Moy Loy," said she. "He is not in favor with the Gambling Cash Tiger and is losing money."

"Moy Loy gave it not to me. I bought it myself."

"But from whom did you obtain the money?"

"If I let out a secret, will you lock it up?"

Pau Sang smiled grimly, and her companion, sidling closer to her, said: "I took the money from my brother—it was my money; for years he had been working to make it for me, and last week he told me that he had saved four hundred dollars to pay to Moy Loy, so that I might be free. Now, what do I want to be free for? To be poor? To have no one to buy me good dinners and pretty things—to be gay no more? Lin John meant well, but he knows little. As to me, I wanted a sealskin sacque like the fine American ladies. So two moons gone by I stole away to the country and found him asleep. I did not awaken him—and for the first day of the New Year I had this cloak. See?"

"Heaven frowns on me," said Lin John sadly, speaking to Moy Loy. "I made the money with which to redeem my sister and I have lost it. I grieve, and I would have you say to her that for her sake, I will engage myself laboriously and conform to virtue till three more New Years have grown old, and that though I merit blame for my carelessness yet I am faithful unto her."

And with his spade over his shoulder he shuffled away from a house, from an upper window of which a woman looked down and under her breath called "Fool!"

TALES OF CHINESE CHILDREN

The Inferior Man

KU YUM, THE LITTLE DAUGHTER OF WEN HING, the schoolmaster, trotted into the school behind her father and crawled under his desk. From that safe retreat, her bright eyes looked out in friendly fashion upon the boys. Ku Yum was three years old and was the only little girl who had ever been in the schoolroom. Naturally, the boys were very much interested in her, and many were the covert glances bestowed upon the chubby little figure in red under the schoolmaster's desk. Now and then a little lad, after an unusually penetrating glance, would throw his sleeve over or lift his slate up to his face, and his form would quiver strangely. Well for the little lad that the schoolmaster wore glasses which somewhat clouded his vision.

The wife of Wen Hing was not very well, which was the reason why the teacher had been bringing the little Ku Yum to school with him for the last three weeks. Wen Hing, being a kind husband, thought to help his wife, who had two babies besides Ku Yum to look after.

But for all his troubled mind, the schoolmaster's sense of duty to his scholars was as keen as ever; also his sense of smell.

Suddenly he turned front the blackboard upon which he had been chalking.

"He who thinks only of good things to eat is an inferior man," and pushing back his spectacles, declared in a voice which caused his pupils to shake in their shoes:

"Some degenerate son of an honorable parent is eating unfragrant sugar."

"Unfragrant sugar! honorable sir!" exclaimed Han Wenti.

"Unfragrant sugar!" echoed little Yen Wing.

"Unfragrant sugar!"

"Unfragrant sugar!"

The murmur passed around the room.

"Silence!" commanded the teacher.

There was silence.

"Go Ek Ju," said the teacher, "why is thy miserable head bowed?"

"Because, wise and just one, I am composing," answered Go Ek Ju.

"Read thy composition."

"A wild boar and a sucking pig were eating acorns from the bed of a sunken stream," shrilly declaimed Go Ek Ju.

"Enough! It can easily be perceived what thy mind is on. Canst thou look at me behind my back and declare that thou art not eating unfragrant sugar?"

"To thy illuminating back, honorable sir, I declare that I am not eating unfragrant sugar."

The teacher's brow became yet sterner.

"You, Mark Sing! Art thou the unfragrant sugar eater?"

"I know not the taste of that confection, most learned sir."

The teacher sniffed.

"Someone," he reasserted, "is eating unfragrant sugar. Whoever the miserable culprit is, let him speak now, and four strokes from the rattan is all that he shall receive."

He paused. The clock ticked sixty times; but there was no response to his appeal. He lifted his rattan.

"As no guilty one," said he, "is honorable enough to acknowledge that he is dishonorably eating unfragrant sugar, I shall punish all for the offense, knowing that thereby the offender will receive justice "Go Ek Ju, come forward, and receive eight strokes from the rattan."

Go Ek Ju went forward and received the eight strokes. As he stood trembling with pain before the schoolmaster's desk, he felt a small hand grasp his§ foot. His lip tightened. Then he returned to his seat, sore, but undaunted, and unconfessed. In like manner also his schoolmates received the rattan.

When the fifteen aching but unrepentant scholars were copying industriously, "He who thinks only of good things to eat is an inferior man," and the schoolmaster, exhausted, had flung himself back on his seat, a little figure in red emerged from under the schoolmaster's desk and attempted to clamber on to his lap. The schoolmaster held her back.

"What! What!" he exclaimed. "What! what!" He rubbed his head in puzzled fashion. Then he lifted up the little red figure, turning its face around to the schoolboys. Such a chubby, happy little face as it was. Dimpled cheeks and pearly teeth showing in a gleeful smile. And the hands of the little, red figure grasped two sticky balls of red and white peppermint candy—unfragrant sugar.

"Behold!" said the teacher; with a twinkle in his spectacles, "the inferior man!"

Whereupon the boys forgot that they were aching. You see, they loved the little Ku Yum and believed that they had saved her from eight strokes of the rattan.

The Little Fat One

LEE CHU AND LEE YEN SAT ON a stone beneath the shade of a fig tree. The way to school seemed a very long way and the morning was warm, the road dusty.

"The master's new pair of goggles can see right through our heads," observed Lee Chu.

"And his new cane made Horn Wo's fingers blister yesterday," said Lee Yen. They looked sideways at one another and sighed.

"The beach must be very cool today," said Lee Chu after a few moments.

"Ah, yes! It is not? far from here." Thus Lee Yen.

"And there are many; pebbles."

"Of all colors."

"Of all colors."

The two little boys turned and looked at each other.

"Our honorable parents need never know," mused one.

"No!" murmured the other. "School is so far from home. And there are five new scholars to keep the schoolmaster busy."

Yes, the beach was cool and pleasant, and the pebbles were many, and the finest in color and shape that Lee Chu and Lee Yen had ever seen. The tide washed up fresh ones every second—green, red, yellow, black, and brown; also white and transparent beauties. The boys exclaimed with delight as they gathered them. The last one spied was always the brightest sparkler.

"Here's one like fire and all the colors in the sun," cried Lee Chu.

"And this one—it is such a bright green, there never was another one like it!" declared Lee Yen.

"Ah! most beautiful!"

"Oh! most wonderful!"

And so on until they had each made an iridescent little pile. Then they sat down to rest and eat their lunch—some rice cakes which their mother had placed within their sleeves.

As they sat munching these, they became reflective. The charm of the sea and sky was on them though they knew it not.

"I think," said Lee Chu, "that these are the most beautiful pebbles that the sea has ever given to us."

"I think so too," assented Lee Yen.

"I think," again said Lee Chu, "that I will give mine to the Little Fat One."

"The Little Fat One shall also have mine," said Lee Yen. He ran his fingers through his pebbles and sighed with rapture over their glittering. Lee Chu also sighed as his eyes dwelt on the shining heap that was his.

The Little Fat One ran to greet them on his little fat legs when they returned home at sundown, and they poured their treasures into his little tunic.

"Why, where do these come from?" cried Lee Amoy, the mother, when she tried to lift the Little Fat One on to her lap and found him too heavy to raise.

Lee Chu and Lee Yen looked away.

"You bad boys!" exclaimed the mother angrily. "You have been on the beach instead of at school. When your father comes in I shall tell him to cane you."

"No, no, not bad!" contradicted the Little Fat One, scrambling after the stones which were slipping from his tunic. His mother picked up some of them, observing silently that they were particularly fine,

"They are the most beautiful pebbles that ever were seen," said Lee Chu sorrowfully. He felt sure that his mother would cast them away.

"The sea will never give up as fine again," declared Lee Yen despairingly.

"Then why did you not each keep what you found?" asked the mother.

"Because—" said Lee Chu, then looked at the Little Fat One.

"Because—" echoed Lee Yen, and also looked at the Little Fat One.

The mother's eyes softened.

"Well," said she, "for this one time we will forget the cane."

"Good! Good!" cried the Little Fat One.

A Chinese Boy-Girl

I

THE WARMTH WAS DEEP AND ALL-PERVADING. The dust lay on the leaves of the palms and the other tropical plants that tried to flourish in the Plaza. The persons of mixed nationalities lounging on the benches within and without the square appeared to be even more listless and unambitious than usual. The Italians who ran the peanut and fruit stands at the corners were doing no business to speak of. The Chinese merchants' stores in front of the Plaza looked as quiet and respectable and drowsy as such stores always do. Even the bowling alleys, billiard halls, and saloons seemed under the influence of the heat, and only a subdued clinking of glasses and roll of balls could be heard from behind the half-open doors. It was almost as hot as an August day in New York City, and that is unusually sultry for Southern California.

A little Chinese girl, with bright eyes and round cheeks, attired in blue cotton garments, and wearing her long, shining hair in a braid interwoven with silks of many colors, paused beside a woman tourist who was making a sketch of the old Spanish church. The tourist and the little Chinese girl were the only, persons visible who did not seem to be affected by the heat. They might have been friends; but the lady, fearing for her sketch, bade the child run off. Whereupon the little thing shuffled across the Plaza, and in less than five minutes was at the door of the Los Angeles Chinatown school for children.

"Come in, little girl, and tell me what they call you," said the young American teacher, who was new to the place.

"Ku Yum be my name," was the unhesitating reply; and, said Ku Yum 'walked into the room, seated herself complacently on an empty bench in the first row, and informed the teacher that she, lived on Apablaza street, that her parents were well, but her mother was dead, and her father, whose name was Ten Suie, had a wicked and tormenting spirit in his foot.

The teacher gave her a slate and pencil, and resumed the interrupted lesson by indicating with her rule ten lichis (called "Chinese nuts" by people in America) and counting them aloud.

"One, two, three, four, five, six, seven, eight, nine, ten," the baby class, repeated.

After having satisfied herself by dividing the lichis unequally among the babies, that they might understand the difference between a singular and a plural number, Miss Mason began a catechism on the features of the face. Nose, eyes, lips, and cheeky! were property named, but the class was mute when it came? to the forehead.

"What is this?" Miss Mason repeated posing her finger on the fore part of her head.

"Me say, me say," piped a shrill voice, and the new pupil stepped to the front, and touching the forehead of the nearest child with the tips of her fingers, christened it "one," named the next in like fashion "two," a third "three," then solemnly pronounced the fourth a "four head."

Thus Ku Yum made her debut in school, and thus began the trials and tribulations of her teacher.

Ku Yum was bright and learned easily, but she seemed to be possessed with the very spirit of mischief; to obey orders was to her an impossibility, and though she entered the school a voluntary pupil, one day at least out of every week found her a truant.

"Where is Ku Yum?" Miss Mason would ask on some particularly alluring morning, and a little girl with the air of one testifying to having seen a murder committed, would reply: "She is running around with the boys." Then the rest of the class would settle themselves back in their seats like a jury that has found a prisoner guilty of some heinous offense, and, judging by the expression on their faces, were repeating a silent prayer somewhat in the strain of "O Lord; I thank thee that I am not as Ku Yum is!" For the other pupils were demure little maidens who, after once being gathered into the fold, were very willing to remain.

But if ever the teacher broke her heart over anyone it was over Ku Yum. When she first came, she took an almost unchildlike interest in the rules and regulations, even at times asking to have them repeated to her; but her study of such rules seemed only for the purpose of finding a means to break them, and that means she never failed to discover and put into effect.

After a disappearance of a day or so she would reappear, bearing a gorgeous bunch of flowers. These she would deposit on Miss Mason's desk with a little bow; and though one would have thought that the sweetness of the gift and the apparent sweetness of the giver needed but a gracious acknowledgment, something like the following conversation would ensue:

"Teacher, I plucked these flowers for you from the Garden of Heaven." (They were stolen from some park).

"Oh, Ku Yum, whatever shall I do with you?"

"Maybe you better see my father."

"You are a naughty girl. You shall be punished. Take those flowers away."

"Teacher, the eyebrow over your little eye is very pretty."

But the child was most exasperating when visitors were present. As she was one of the brightest scholars, Miss Mason naturally expected her to reflect' credit on the school at the examinations. On one occasion she requested her to say some verses which the little Chinese girl could repeat as well as any young American, and with more expression than most. Great was the teacher's chagrin when Ku Yum hung her head and said only: "Me 'shamed, me 'shamed!"

"Poor little thing," murmured the bishop's wife. "She is too shy to recite in public."

But Miss Mason, knowing that of all children Ku Yum was the least troubled with shyness, was exceedingly annoyed.

Ku Yum had been with Miss Mason about a year when she became convinced that some steps would have to be taken to discipline the child, for after school hours she simply ran wild on the streets of Chinatown, with boys for companions.. She felt that she had a duty to perform towards the motherless little girl; and as the father, when apprised of the fact that his daughter was growing up in ignorance of all home duties, and, worse than that, shared the sports of boy children on the street, only shrugged his shoulders and drawled: "Too ball! Too bad!" she determined to act.

She interested in Ku Turn's case the president of the Society for the Prevention of Cruelty to Children, the matron of the Rescue Home, and the most influential ministers, and the result, after a month's work, was that an order went forth from the Superior Court of the State decreeing that Ku Yum, the child of Ten Suie, should be removed from the custody of her father, and, under the auspices of the Society for the Prevention of Cruelty to Children, be put into a home for Chinese girls in San Francisco?

Her object being accomplished, strange to say, Miss Mason did not experience that peaceful consent which usually follows a benevolent, action. Instead, the question as to whether, after all, it was right, under the circumstances, to deprive a father of the society of his child, and a child of the love and care of a parent, disturbed her mind, morning, noon, and night. What had previously seemed her distinct duty no longer appeared so, and she began to wish with all her heart that she had not interfered in the matter.

II

Ku Yum had not been seen for weeks, and those who were deputed to brings her into the sheltering home were unable to find her. It was suspected that the little thing purposely kept out of the way—no difficult matter, all Chinatown being in sympathy with her and arrayed against Miss Mason. Where formerly the teacher had met with smiles and pleased greetings, she now beheld averted faces and downcast eyes, and her school had within a week dwindled from twenty-four scholars to four. Verily, though acting with the best of intentions, she had shown a lack of diplomacy.

It was about nine o'clock in the evening. She had been visiting little Lae Choo, who was lying low with typhoid fever. As she wended her way home through Chinatown, she did not feel at all easy in mind; indeed, as she passed one of the most unsavory corners and observed some men frown and mutter among themselves as they recognised her, she lost her dignity in a little run. As she stopped to take breath, she felt her skirt pulled from behind and heard a familiar little voice say:

"Teacher, be you afraid?"

"Oh, Ku Yum," she exclaimed, "is that you?" Then she added reprovingly: "Do you think it is right for a little Chinese girl to be out alone at this time of the night?"

"I be not alone," replied the little creature, and in the gloom Miss Mason could distinguish behind her two boyish figures.

She shook her head.

"Ku Yum, will you promise me that you will try to be a good little girl?" she asked.

Ku Yum answered solemnly:

"Ku Yum *never* be a good girl."

Her heart hardened. After all, it was best that the child should be placed where she would be compelled to behave herself.

"Come, see my father," said Ku Yum pleadingly.

Her voice was soft, and her expression was so subdued that the teacher could hardly believe that the moment before she had defiantly stated that she would never be a good girl. She paused irresolutely. Should she make one more appeal to the parent to make her a promise which would be a good excuse for restraining the order of the Court? Ah, if he only would, and she only could prevent the carrying out of that order!

They found Ten Suie among his curiosities, smoking a very long pipe with a very small ivory bowl. He calmly surveyed the teacher through a pair of gold-rimmed goggles, and under such scrutiny it was hard indeed for her to broach the subject that was on her mind. However, after admiring the little carved animals, jars, vases, bronzes, dishes, pendants, charms, and snuff-boxes displayed in his handsome showcase, she took courage.

"Mr. Ten Suie," she began, "I have come to speak to you about Ku Yum."

Ten Suie laid down his pipe and leaned over the counter. Under his calm exterior some strong; excitement was working, for his eyes glittered exceedingly.

"Perhaps you speak too much about Ku Yum already," he said; "Ku Yum be my child. I bring him up as I please. Now, teacher, I tell you something. One, two, three, four, five, seven, eight, nine years go by, I f have five boy. One, two, three, four, five, six, seven years go. I have four boy. One, two, three, four, five, six years go by, I have one boy. Every year for three year evil spirit come, look at my boy, and take him. Well, one, two, three, four, five, six years go by, I see but one boy, he four year old. I say to me: Ten Suie, evil spirit be jealous. I believed he want my one boy. I dress him like one girl. Evil Spirit think him one girl, and go away; no want girl."

Ten Suie ceased speaking, and settled back into his seat.

For some moments Miss Mason stood uncomprehending. Then the full meaning of Ten Suie's; words dawned upon her, and she turned to Ku Yum, and taking the child's little hand in hers, said:

"Goodbye, Ku Yum. Your father, by passing you off as a girl, thought to keep ail evil spirit away from you; but just by that means he brought another, and one which nearly took you from him too."

"Goodbye, teacher," said Ku Yum, smiling wistfully. "I never be good girl, but perhaps I be good boy."

Pat and Pan

I

THEY LAY THERE, IN THE ENTRANCE to the joss house, sound asleep in each other's arms. Her tiny face was hidden upon his bosom and his white, upturned chin rested upon her black, rosetted head.

It was that white chin which caused the passing Mission woman to pause and look again at the little pair. Yes, it was a white boy and a little Chinese girl; he, about five, she, not more than three years old.

"Whose is that boy?" asked the Mission woman of the peripatetic vendor of Chinese fruits and sweetmeats.

"That boy! Oh, him is boy of Lum Yook that make the China gold ring and bracelet."

"But he is white."

"Yes, him white; but all same, China boy. His mother, she not have any white friend, and the wife of Lum Yook give her lice and tea, so when she go to the land of spirit, she give her boy to the wife of Lum Yook. Lady, you want buy lichi?"

While Anna Harrison was extracting a dime from her purse the black, rosetted head slowly turned and a tiny fist began rubbing itself into; a tiny face.

"Well, chickabiddy, have you had a nice nap?" "Tjo ho! tjo ho!"

The black eyes gazed solemnly and disdainfully at the stranger.

"She tell you to be good," chuckled the old man.

"Oh, you quaint little thing!"

The quaint little thing hearing herself thus apostrophized, turned herself around upon the bosom of the still sleeping boy and, reaching her arms up to his neck, buried her face again under his chin. This, of course, awakened him. He sat up and stared bewilderedly at the Mission woman.

"What is the boy's name?" she asked, noting his gray eyes and rosy skin.

His reply, though audible, was wholly unintelligible to the American woman.

"He talk only Chinese talk," said the old man,

Anna Harrison was amazed. A white, hoy in America talking only Chinese talk! She placed her bag of lichis beside him and was amused to see the little girl instantly lean over her companion and possess herself of it. The boy made no attempt to take it from her, and the little thing opened the bag and cautiously peeped in. What she saw evoked a chirrup of delight. Quickly she brought forth one of the browny-red fruit nuts, crushed and pulled off its soft shell But to the surprise of the Mission woman, instead of putting it into her own mouth, she thrust the sweetish, dried pulp into that of her companion. She repeated this operation several times, then cocking her little head on one side, asked:

"Ho 'm ho? Is it good or bad?"

"Ho! ho!" answered the boy, removing several pits from his mouth and shaking his head to signify that he had had enough. Whereupon the little girl tasted herself of the fruit.

"Pat! Pan! Pat! Pan!" called a woman's voice, and a sleek-headed, kindly-faced matron in dark blue pantalettes and tunic, wearing double hooped gold earrings, appeared around the corner. Hearing her voice, the boy jumped up with a merry laugh and ran out into the street. The little girl more seriously and slowly followed him.

"Him mother!" informed the lichi man.

II

WHEN ANNA HARRISON, SOME MONTHS LATER, opened her school for white and Chinese children in Chinatown, she determined that Pat, the adopted son of Lum Yook, the Chinese jeweler, should learn to speak his mother tongue. For a white boy to grow up as a Chinese was unthinkable. The second time she saw him, it was some kind of a Chinese holiday, and he was in great glee over a row of red Chinese candles and punk which he was burning on the curb of the street, in company with a number of Chinese urchins. Pat's candle was giving a brighter and bigger flame than any of the others, and he was jumping up and down with his legs doubled under him from the knees like an India-rubber ball, while Pan, from the doorstep of her father's store, applauded him in vociferous, infantile Chinese.

Miss Harrison laid her hand upon the boy's shoulder and spoke to him. It had not been very difficult for her to pick up a few Chinese phrases. Would he not like to come to her school and see some pretty pictures? Pat shook his ruddy curls and looked at Pan. Would Pan come too? Yes, Pan would. Pan's memory was good, and so were lichis and shredded cocoanut candy.

Of course Pan was too young to go to school—a mere baby; but if Pat could not be got without Pan, why then Pan must come too. Lum Yook and his wife, upon being interviewed, were quite willing to have Pat learn English. The foster-father could speak a little of the language himself; but as he used it only when in business or when speaking to Americans, Pat had not benefited thereby. However, he was more eager than otherwise to have Pat learn "the speech of his ancestors," and promised that he would encourage the little ones to practise "American" together when at home.

So Pat and Pan went to the Mission school, and for the first time in their lives suffered themselves to be divided, for Pat had to sit with the boys and tiny Pan had a little red chair near Miss Harrison, beside which were placed a number of baby toys. Pan was not supposed to learn, only to play.

But Pan did learn. In a year's time, although her talk was more broken and babyish, she had a better English vocabulary than had Pat. Moreover, she could sing hymns and recite verses in a high, shrill voice; whereas Pat, though he tried hard enough, poor little fellow, was unable to memorize even a sentence. Naturally, Pat did not like school as well as did Pan, and it was only Miss Harrison's persistent ambition for him that kept him there.

One day, when Pan was five and Pat was seven, the little girl, for the first time, came to school alone.

"Where is Pat?" asked the teacher.

"Pat, he is sick today," replied Pan.

"Sick!" echoed Miss Harrison. "Well, that is too bad. Poor Pat! What is the matter with him?"

"A big dog bite him."

That afternoon, the teacher, on her way to see the bitten Pat, beheld him up an alley busily engaged in keeping five tops spinning at one time, while several American boys stood around, loudly admiring the Chinese feat.

The next morning Pat received five strokes from a cane which Miss Harrison kept within her desk and used only on special occasions. These strokes made Pat's right hand tingle smartly; but he received them with smiling grace.

Miss Harrison then turned to five year old Pan, who had watched the caning with tearful interest.

"Pan!" said the teacher, "you have been just as haughty as Pat, and you must be punished too."

"I not stay away from school!" protested Pan.

"No,"—severely—"you did not stay away from school; but you told me a dog had bitten Pat, and that was not true. Little girls must not say what is not true. Teacher does not like to slap Pan's hands, but she must do it, so that Pan will remember that she must not say what is not true. Come here!"

Pan, hiding her face in her sleeve, sobbingly arose.

The teacher leaned forward and pulling down the uplifted arm, took the small hand in her own and slapped it. She was about to do this a second time when Pat bounded from his seat, pushed Pan aside, and shaking his little list in the teacher's face, dared her in a voice hoarse with passion:

"You hurt my Pan again! You hurt my Pan again!"

They were not always lovers—those two. It was aggravating to Pat, when the teacher finding he did not know his verse, would turn to Pan and say:

"Well, Pan, let us hear you."

And Pan, who was the youngest child in school and unusually small for her years, would pharisaically clasp her tiny fingers and repeat word for word the verse desired to be heard.

"I hate you, Pan!" muttered Pat on one such occasion.

Happily Pan did not hear him. She was serenely singing:

"Yesu love me, t'is I know,
For the Bible tell me so."

But though a little seraph in the matter of singing hymns and repeating verses, Pan, for a small Chinese girl, was very mischievous. Indeed, she was the originator of most of the mischief which Pat carried out with such spirit. Nevertheless, when Pat got into trouble, Pan, though sympathetic, always had a lecture for him, "Too bad, too bad! Why not you be good like me?" admonished she one day when he was suffering "consequences."

Pat looked down upon her with wrathful eyes.

"Why," he asked, "is bad people always so good?"

III

THE CHILD OF THE WHITE WOMAN, who had been given a babe into the arms of the wife of Lum Yook, was regarded as their own by the Chinese jeweler and his wife, and they bestowed upon him equal love and care with the little daughter who came two years after him. If Mrs. Lum Yook showed any favoritism whatever, it was to Pat. He was the first she had cradled to her bosom; the first to gladden her heart with baby smiles and wiles; the first to call her Ah Ma; the first to love her. On his eighth birthday, she said to her husband: "The son of the white woman is the son of the white woman, and there are many tongues wagging because he live under our roof. My heart is as heavy as the blackest heavens."

"Peace, my woman," answered the easygoing man. "Why should we trouble before trouble comes?"

When trouble did come it was met calmly and bravely. To the comfortably off American and wife who were to have the boy and "raise him as an American boy should be raised," they yielded him without protest. But deep in their hearts was the sense of injustice and outraged love. If it had not been for their pity for the unfortunate white girl, their care and affection for her helpless offspring, there would have been no white boy for others to "raise."

And Pat and Pan? "I will not leave my Pan! I will not leave my Pan!" shouted Pat.

"But you must!" sadly urged Lum Yook.

"You are a white boy and Pan is Chinese."

"I am Chinese too! I am Chinese too!" cried Pat.

"He Chinese! He Chinese!" pleaded Pan. Her little nose was swollen with crying; her little eyes red-rimmed.

But Pat was driven away.

Pat, his schoolbooks under his arm, was walking down the hill, whistling cheerily. His roving glance down a side street was suddenly arrested.

"Gee!" he exclaimed. "If that isn't Pan! Pan, oh, Pan!" he shouted.

Pan turned. There was a shrill cry of delight, and Pan was clinging to Pat, crying:

335

"Nice Pat! Good Pat!"

Then she pushed him away from her and scanned him from head to foot.

"Nice coat! Nice boot! How many dollars?" she queried.

Pat laughed good-humoredly. "I don't know," he answered. "Mother bought them."

"Mother!" echoed Pan. She puckered her brows for a moment.

"You are grown big, Pat," was her next remark.

"And you have grown little, Pan," retorted Pat. It was a year since they had seen one another and Pan was much smaller than any of his girl schoolfellows.

"Do you like, to go to the big school?" asked Pan, noticing the books.

"I don't like it very much. But, say, Pan, I learn lots of things that you don't know anything about."

Pan eyed him wistfully. Finally she said: "O Pat! A-Toy, she die."

"A-Toy! Who is A-Toy?"

"The meow, Pat; the big gray meow! Pat, you have forgot to remember."

Pat looked across A-Toy's head and far away.

"Chinatown is very nice now," assured Pan. "Hum Lock has two trays of brass beetles in his store and Ah Ma has many flowers!"

"I would like to see the brass beetles," said Pat.

"And father's new glass case?"

"Yes."

"And Ah Ma's flowers?"

"Yes."

"Then come, Pat."

"I can't, Pan!"

"Oh!"

Again Pat was walking home from school this time in company with some boys. Suddenly a glad little voice sounded in his ear. It was Pan's.

"Ah, Pat!" cried she joyfully. "I find you! I find you!"

"Hear the China kid!" laughed one of the boys.

Then Pat turned upon Pan. "Get away from me," he shouted. "Get away from me!"

And Pan did get away from him—just as fast as her little legs could carry her. But when she reached the foot of the hill, she looked up and shook her little head sorrowfully. "Poor Pat!" said she. "He Chinese no more; he Chinese no more!"

Leaves from the Mental Portfolio

of an Eurasian

Sui Sin Far (Edith Maud Eaton)

WHEN I LOOK BACK OVER THE years I see myself, a little child of scarcely four years of age, walking in front of my nurse, in a green English lane, and listening to her tell another of her kind that my mother is Chinese. "Oh, Lord!" exclaims the informed. She turns me around and scans me curiously from head to foot. Then the two women whisper together. Tho the word "Chinese" conveys very little meaning to my mind, I feel that they are talking about my father and mother and my heart swells with indignation. When we reach home I rush to my mother and try to tell her what I have heard. I am a young child. I fail to make myself intelligible. My mother does not understand, and when the nurse declares to her, "Little Miss Sui is a story-teller," my mother slaps me.

Many a long year has past over my head since that day—the day on which I first learned that I was something different and apart from other children, but tho my mother has forgotten it, I have not.

I see myself again, a few years older. I am playing with another child in a garden. A girl passes by outside the gate. "Mamie," she cries to my companion. "I wouldn't speak to Sui if I were you. Her mamma is Chinese."

"I don't care," answers the little one beside me. And then to me, "Even if your mamma is Chinese, I like you better than I like Annie."

"But I don't like you," I answer, turning my back on her. It is my first conscious lie.

I am at a children's party, given by the wife of an Indian officer whose children were schoolfellows of mine. I am only six years of age, but have attended a private school for over a year, and have already learned that China is a heathen country, being civilized by England. However, for the time being, I am a merry romping child. There are quite a number of people present. One, a white haired old man, has his attention called to me by the hostess. He adjusts his eyeglasses and surveys me critically. "Ah, indeed!" he exclaims, "Who would have thought it at first glance. Yet now I see the difference between her and other children. What a peculiar coloring! Her mother's eyes and hair and her father's features, I presume. Very interesting little creature!"

I had been called from my play for the purpose of inspection. I do not return to it. For the rest of the evening, I hide myself behind a hall door and refuse to show myself until it is time to go home.

My parents have come to America. We are in Hudson City, N.Y., and we are very poor. I am out with my brother, who is ten months older than myself. We pass a Chinese store, the door of which is open. "Look!" says Charlie, "Those men in there are Chinese!" Eagerly I gaze into the long low room. With the exception of my mother, who is English bred with English ways and manner of dress, I have never seen a Chinese person. The two men within the store are uncouth specimens of their race, drest in working blouses and pantaloons with queues hanging down their backs. I recoil with a sense of shock.

"Oh, Charlie," I cry, "Are we like that?"

"Well, we're Chinese, and they're Chinese too, so we must be!" returns my seven-year-old brother.

"Of course you are," puts in a boy who has followed us down the street, and has followed us down the street, and who lives near us and has seen my mother: "Chinky, Chinky, Chinamen, yellow-face, pig-tail, rat-eater." A number of other boys and several little girls join in with him.

"Better than you," shouts my brother, facing the crowd. He is younger and smaller than any there, and I am even more insignificant than he; but my spirit revives.

"I'd rather be Chinese than anything else in the world," I scream.

They pull my hair, they tear my clothes, they scratch my face, and all but lame my brother; but the white blood in our veins fights valiantly for the Chinese half of us. When it is all over, exhausted and bedraggled, we crawl home, and report to our mother that we have "won the battle."

"Are you sure?" asks my mother doubtfully.

"Of course. They ran from us. They were frightened," returns my brother.

My mother smiles with satisfaction.

"Do you hear? She asks my father.

"Umm," he observes, raising his eyes from his paper for an instant. My childish instinct, however, tells me that he is more interested than he appears to be.

It is tea time, but I cannot eat. Unobserved I crawl away. I do not sleep that night. I am too excited and I ache all over. Our opponents had been so very much stronger and bigger than we. Toward morning, however, I fall into a doze from which I awaken myself, shouting:

"Sound the battle cry;
See the foe is nigh."

My mother believes in sending us to Sunday school. She has been brought up in a Presbyterian college.

The scene of my life shifts to Eastern Canada. The sleigh which has carried us from the station stops in front of a little French Canadian hotel. Immediately we are surrounded by a number of villagers, who stare curiously at my mother as my father assists her to alight from the sleigh. Their curiosity, however, is tempered with kindness, as they watch, one after another, the little blackheads of my brothers and sisters and myself emerge out of the buffalo robe, which is part of the sleigh's outfit. There are six of us, four girls and two boys, being only seven years of age. My father and mother are still in their twenties. "*Les pauvres enfants*," the inhabitants murmur, as they help to carry us into the hotel. Then in lower tones: "*Chinoise, Chinoise.*"

For some time after our arrival, whenever we children are sent for a walk, our footsteps are dogged by a number of young French and English Canadians, who amuse themselves with speculations as to whether, we being Chinese, are susceptible to pinches and hair pulling, while older persons pause and gaze upon us, very much in the same way that I have seen people gaze upon strange animals in a menagerie. Now and then we are stopt and plied with questions as to what we eat and drink, how we go to sleep, if my mother understands what my father says to her, if we sit on chairs or squat on floors, etc., etc., etc.

There are many pitched battles, of course, and we seldom leave the house without being armed for conflict. My mother takes a great interest in our battles, and usually cheers us on, tho I doubt whether she understands the depth of the troubled waters thru which her little children wade. As to my father, peace is his motto, and he deems it wisest to be blind and deaf to many things.

School days are short, but memorable. I am in the same class with my brother, my sister next to me in the class below. The little girl whose desk my sister shares shrinks close against the wall as my sister takes her place. In a little while she raises her hand.

"Please, teacher!"

"Yes, Annie."

"May I change my seat?"

"No, you may not!"

The little girl sobs. "Why should we have to sit beside a———"

Happily my sister does not seem to hear, and before long the two little girls become great friends. I have many such experiences.

My brother is remarkably bright; my sister next to me has a wonderful head for figures, and when only eight years of age helps my father with his night work accounts. My parents compare her with me. She is of sturdier build than I, and, as my father says, "Always has her wits about her." He thinks her more like my mother, who is very bright and interested in every little detail of practical life. My father tells me that I will never make half the woman that my mother is or that my sister will be. I am not as strong as my sisters, which makes me feel somewhat ashamed, for I am the eldest little girl, and more is expected of me. I have no organic disease, but the strength of my feelings seems to take from me the strength of my body. I am prostrated at times with attacks of nervous sickness. The doctor says that my heart is unusually large; but in the light of the present I know that the cross of the Eurasian bore too heavily upon my childish shoulders. I usually hide my weakness from the family until I cannot stand. I do not understand myself, and I have an idea that the others will despise me for not being as strong as they. Therefore, I like to wander away alone, either by the river or in the bush. The green fields and flowing water have a charm for me. At the age of seven, as it is today, a bird on the wing is my emblem of happiness.

I have come from a race on my mother's side which is said to be the most stolid and insensible to feeling of all races, yet I look back over the years and see myself so keenly alive to every shade of sorrow and suffering that is almost a pain to live.

If there is any trouble in the house in the way of a difference between my father and mother, or if any child is punished, how I suffer! And when harmony is restored, heaven seems to be around me. I can be sad, but I can also be glad. My mother's screams of agony when a baby is born almost drives me wild, and long after her pangs have subsided I feel them in my own body. Sometimes it is a week before I can get to sleep after such an experience.

A debt owing by my father fills me with shame. I feel like a criminal when I pass the creditor's door. I am only ten years old. And all the while the question of nationality perplexes my little brain. Why are we what we are? I and my brothers and sisters. Why did God make us to be hooted and stared at? Papa is English, mamma is Chinese. Why couldn't we have been either one thing or the other? Why is my mother's race despised? I look into the faces of my father and mother. Is she not every bit as dear and good as he? Why? Why? She sings us the songs she learned at her English school. She tells us tales of China. Tho a child when she left her native land she remembers it well, and I am never tired of listening to the story of how she was stolen from her home. She tells us over and over again of her meeting with my father in Shanghai and the romance of their marriage. Why? Why?

I do not confide in my father and mother. They would not understand. How could they? He is English, she is Chinese. I am different to both of them—a stranger, tho their own child. "What are we? I ask my brother. "It doesn't matter, sissy," he responds. But it does. I love poetry, particularly heroic pieces. I also love fairy tales. Stories of everyday life do not appeal to me. I dream dreams of being great and noble; my sisters and brothers also. I glory in the idea of dying at the stake and a great genie arising from the flames and declaring to those who have scorned us: "Behold, how great and glorious and noble are the Chinese people!"

My sisters are apprenticed to a dressmaker; my brother is entered in an office. I tramp around and sell my father's pictures, also some lace which I make myself. My nationality, if I had only known it at that time, helps to make sales. The ladies who are my customers call me "The Little Chinese Lace Girl." But it is a dangerous life for a very young girl. I come near to "mysteriously disappearing" many a time. The greatest temptation was in the thought of getting far away from where I was known, to where no mocking cries of "Chinese!" "Chinese!" could reach.

Whenever I have the opportunity I steal away to the library and read every book I can find on China and the Chinese. I learn that China is the oldest civilized nation on the face of the earth and a few other things. At eighteen years of age what troubles me is not that I am what I am, but that others are ignorant of my superiority. I am small, but my feelings are big—and great is my vanity.

My sisters attend dancing classes, for which they pay their own fees. In spite of covert smiles and sneers, they are glad to meet and mingle with other young folk. They are not sensitive in the sense that I am. And yet they understand. One of them tells me that she overheard a young man say to another that he would rather marry a pig than a girl with Chinese blood in her veins.

In course of time I too learn shorthand and take a position in an office. Like my sister, I teach myself, but, unlike my sister, I have neither the perseverance nor the ability to perfect myself. Besides, to a temperament like mine, it is torture to spend the hours in transcribing other people's thoughts. Therefore, altho I can always earn a moderately good salary, I do not distinguish myself in the business world as does she.

When I have been working for some years I open an office of my own. The local papers patronize me and give me a number of assignments, including most of the local Chinese reporting. I meet many Chinese persons, and when they get into trouble am often called upon to fight their battles in the papers. This I enjoy. My heart leaps for joy when I read one day an article signed by a New York Chinese in which he declares "The Chinese in America owe an everlasting debt of gratitude to Sui Sin Far for the bold stand she has taken in their defense."

The Chinaman who wrote the article seeks me out and calls upon me. He is a clever and witty man, a graduate of one of the American colleges and as well a Chinese scholar. I learn that he has an American wife and several children. I am very much interested in these children, and when I meet them my heart throbs in sympathetic tune with the tales they relate of their experiences as Eurasians. "Why did papa and mamma born us?" asks one. Why?

I also meet other Chinese men who compare favorably with the white men of my acquaintance in mind and heart qualities. Some of them are quite handsome. They have not as finely cut noses and as well developed chins as the white men, but they have smoother skins and their expression is more serene; their hands are better shaped and their voices softer.

Some little Chinese women whom I interview are very anxious to know whether I would marry a Chinaman. I do not answer No. They clap their hands delightedly, and assure me that Chinese are much the finest and best of all men. They are, however, a little doubtful as to whether one could be persuaded to care for me, full-blooded Chinese people having a prejudice against the half white.

Fundamentally, I muse, all people are the same. My mother's race is as prejudiced as my father's. Only when the whole world becomes as one family will human beings be able to see clearly and hear distinctly. I believe that some day a great part of the world will be Eurasian. I cheer myself with the thought that I am a pioneer. A pioneer should glory in suffering.

"You were walking with a Chinaman yesterday," accuses an acquaintance.

"Yes, what of it?"

"You ought not to. It isn't right."

"Not right to walk with one of my own mother's people? Oh, indeed!"

I cannot reconcile his notion of righteousness with my own.

I am living in a little town away off on the north shore of a big lake. Next to me at the dinner table is the man for whom I work as a stenographer. There are also a couple of business men, a young girl and her mother.

Someone makes a remark about the cars full of Chinamen that past that morning. A transcontinental railway runs thru the town.

My employer shakes his rugged head. "Somehow or other," says he, "I cannot reconcile myself to the thought that the Chinese are humans like ourselves. They may have immortal souls, but their faces seem to be utterly devoid of expression that I cannot help but doubt."

"Souls," echoes the town clerk. "Their bodies are enough for me. A Chinaman is, in my eyes, more repulsive than a nigger."

"They always give me such a creepy feeling," puts in the young girl with a laugh.

"I wouldn't have one in my house," declares my landlady.

"Now, the Japanese are different altogether. There is something bright and likeable about those men," continues Mr. K.

A miserable, cowardly-feeling keeps me silent. I am in a Middle West town. If I declare what I am, every person in the place will hear about it the next day. The population is in the main made up of working folks with strong prejudices against my mother's countrymen. The prospect before me is not an enviable one—if I speak. I have no longer an ambition to die at the stake for the sake of demonstrating my greatness and nobleness of the Chinese people.

Mr. K. turns to me with a kindly smile.

"What makes Miss Far so quiet?" he asks.

"I don't suppose she finds the 'washee washee men' particularly interesting subjects of conversation," volunteers the young manager of the local bank.

With great effort I raise my eyes from my plate. "Mr. K.," I say, addressing my employer, "the Chinese people may have no souls, no expression on their faces, be altogether beyond the pale of civilization, but whatever they are, I want you to understand that I am—I am a Chinese."

There is silence in the room for a few minutes. Then Mr. K. pushes back his plate and standing up beside me, says:

"I should not have spoken as I did. I know nothing whatever about the Chinese. It was pure prejudice. Forgive me!"

I admire Mr. K's moral courage in apologizing to me; he is a conscientious Christian man, but I do not remain much longer in the little town.

I am under a tropic sky, meeting frequently and conversing with persons who are almost as high up in the world as birth, education and money can set them. The environment is peculiar, for I am also surrounded by a race of people, the

reputed descendants of Ham, the son of Noah, whose offspring, it was prophe-
sied, should be the servants of the sons of Shem and Japheth. As I am a descen-
dant, according to the Bible, of both Shem and Japheth, I have perfect right to
set my heel upon the Ham people; but tho I see others around me following
out the Bible suggestion, it is not in my nature to be arrogant to any but those
who seek to impress me with their superiority, which the poor black maid who
has been assigned to me by the hotel certainly does not. My employer's wife
takes me to task for this. "It is unnecessary," she says, "to thank a black person
for a service."

The novelty of life in the West Indian island is not without its charm. The
surroundings, people, manner of living, are so entirely different from what I
have been accustomed to up North that I feel as if I were "born again." Mixing
with people of fashion, and yet not of them, I am not of sufficient importance
to create comment or curiosity. I am busy nearly all day and often well into the
night. It is not monotonous work, but it is certainly strenuous. The planters and
business men of the island take me as a matter of course and treat me with kind-
ly courtesy. Occasionally an Englishman will warn me against the "brown boys"
of the island, little dreaming that I too am of the "brown people" of the earth.

When it begins to be whispered about the place that I am not all white,
some of the "sporty people seek my acquaintance. I am small and look much
younger than my years. When, however, they discover that I am a very serious
and sober-minded spinster indeed, they retire quite gracefully, leaving me a few
amusing reflections.

One evening a card is brought to my room. It bears the name of some naval
officer. I go down to my visitor, thinking he is probably someone who, having
been told that I am a reporter for the local paper, has brought me an item of
news. I find him lounging in an easy chair on the veranda of the hotel—a big,
blond, handsome fellow, several years younger than I.

"You are Lieutenant ———?" I inquire.

He bows and laughs a little. The laugh doesn't suit him somehow—and it
doesn't suit me, either.

"If you have anything to tell me, please tell it quickly, because I'm very busy."
"Oh, you don't really mean that," he answers, with another silly and offensive
laugh. "There's always plenty of time for good times. That's what I am here for.
I saw you at the races the other day and twice at King's House. My ship will be
here for ——— weeks."

"Do you wish that noted?" I ask.

"Oh, no! Why—I came just because I had an idea that you might like
to know me. I would like to know you. You look such a nice little body. Say,

wouldn't you like to go out for a sail this lovely night? I will tell you all about the sweet little Chinese girls I met when we were at Hong Kong. They're not so shy!"

I leave Eastern Canada for the Far West, so reduced by another attack of rheumatic fever that I only weigh eighty-four pounds. I travel on an advertising contract. It is presumed by the railway company that in some way or other I will give them full value for their transportation across the continent. I have been ordered beyond the Rockies by the doctor, who declares that I will never regain my strength in the East. Nevertheless, I am but two days in San Francisco when I start out in search of work. It is the first time that I have sought work as a stranger in a strange town. Both of the other positions away from home were secured for me by home influence. I am quite surprised to find that there is no demand for my services in San Francisco and that no one is particularly interested in me. The best I can do is to accept an offer from a railway agency to typewrite their correspondence for $5 a month. I stipulate, however, that I shall have the privilege of taking in outside work and that my hours shall be light. I am hopeful that the sale of a story or a newspaper article may add to my income, and I console myself with the reflection that, considering that I still limp and bear traces of sickness, I am fortunate to secure any work at all.

The proprietor of one of the San Francisco papers, to whom I have a letter of introduction, suggests that I obtain some subscriptions from the people of Chinatown, that district of the city having never been canvassed. This suggestion I carry out with enthusiasm, tho I find that the Chinese merchants and people generally are inclined to regard me with suspicion. They have been imposed upon so many times by unscrupulous white people. Another drawback—save for a few phrases, I am unacquainted with my mother's tongue. How, then, can I expect these people to accept me as their own countrywoman? The Americanized Chinamen actually laugh in my face when I tell them that I am of their race. However, they are not all "doubting Thomases." Some little women discover that I have Chinese hair, color of eyes and complexion, also that I love rice and tea. This settles the matter for them—and for their husbands.

My Chinese instincts develop. I am no longer the little girl who shrunk against my brother at the first sight of a Chinaman. Many and many a time, when alone in a strange place, has the appearance of even an humble laundryman given me a sense of protection and made me feel quite at home. This fact of itself proves to me that prejudice can be eradicated by association.

I meet a half Chinese, half white girl. Her face is plastered with a thick white coat of paint and her eyelids and eyebrows are blackened so that the shape of her eyes and the whole expression of her face is changed. She was born in the East, and at the age of eighteen came West in answer to an advertisement. Living for many years among the working class, she had heard little but abuse of the Chinese. It is not difficult, in a land like California, for a half Chinese, half white girl to pass as one of Spanish or Mexican origin. This the poor child does, tho she lives in nervous dread of being "discovered." She becomes engaged to a young man, but fears to tell him what she is, and only does so when compelled by a fearless American girl friend. This girl, who knows her origin, realizes that the truth sooner or later must be told, and better soon than late, advises the Eurasian to confide in the young man, assuring her that he loves her well enough not to allow her nationality to stand, a bar sinister, between them. But the Eurasian prefers to keep her secret, and only reveals it to the man who is to be her husband when driven to bay by the American girl, who declares that if the half-breed will not tell the truth she will. When the young man hears that the girl he is engaged to has Chinese blood in her veins, he exclaims: "Oh, what will my folks say?" But that is all. Love is stronger than prejudice with him, and neither he nor she deems it necessary to inform his "folks."

The Americans, having for many years manifested a much higher regard for the Japanese than for the Chinese, several half Chinese young men and women, thinking to advance themselves, both in a social and business sense, pass as Japanese. They continue to be known as Eurasians; but a Japanese Eurasian does not appear in the same light as a Chinese Eurasian. The unfortunate Chinese Eurasians! Are not those who compel them to thus cringe more to be blamed than they?

People, however, are not all alike. I meet white men, and women, too, who are proud to mate with those who have Chinese blood in their veins, and think it a great honor to be distinguished by the friendship of such. There are also Eurasians and Eurasians. I know of one who allowed herself to become engaged to a white man after refusing him nine times. She had discouraged him in every way possible, had warned him that she was half Chinese; that her people were poor, that every week or month she sent home a certain amount of her earnings, and that the man she married would have to do as much, if not more; also, most uncompromising truth of all, that she did not love him and never would. But the resolute and undaunted lover swore that it was a matter of indifference to him whether she was a Chinese or a Hottentot, that it would be his pleasure and privilege to allow her relations double what it was in her power to bestow, and as to not loving him—that did not matter at all. He loved her. So, because the young woman had a married mother and married sisters, who were always picking at her and gossiping over her independent manner of living, she finally consented to marry him, recording the agreement in her diary thus:

"I have promised to become the wife of s——— ——— on ——— ———, 189-, because the world is so cruel and sneering to a single woman—and for no other reason."

Everything went smoothly until one day. The young man was driving a pair of beautiful horses and she was seated by his side, trying very hard to imagine herself in love with him, when a Chinese vegetable gardener's cart came rumbling along. The Chinaman was a jolly-looking individual in blue cotton blouse and pantaloons, his rakish looking hat being kept in place by a long queue which was pulled upward from his neck and wound around it. The young woman was suddenly posset with the spirit of mischief. "Look!" she cried, indicating the Chinaman, "there's my brother. Why don't you salute him?"

The man's face fell a little. He sank into a pensive mood. The wicked one by his side read him like an open book.

"When we are married," said she, "I intend to give a Chinese party every month."

No answer.

"As there are very few aristocratic Chinese in this city, I shall fill up with the laundrymen and vegetable farmers. I don't believe in being exclusive in democratic America, do you?"

He hadn't a grain of humor in his composition, but a sickly smile contorted his features as he replied:

"You shall do just as you please, my darling. But—but—consider a moment. Wouldn't it be just a little pleasanter for us if, after we are married, we allowed it to be presumed that you were—er—Japanese? So many of my friends have inquired of me if that is not your nationality. They would be so charmed to meet a little Japanese lady."

"Hadn't you better oblige them by finding one?"

"Why—er—what do you mean?"

"Nothing much in particular. Only—I am getting a little tired of this," taking off his ring.

"You don't mean what you say! Oh, put it back, dearest! You know I would not hurt your feelings for the world!"

"You haven't. I'm more than pleased. But I do mean what I say."

That evening the "ungrateful" Chinese Eurasian diaried, among other things, following:

"Joy, oh, joy! I'm free once more. Never again shall I be untrue to my own heart. Never again will I allow anyone to 'hound' or 'sneer' me into matrimony."

I secure transportation to many California points. I meet some literary people, chief among whom is the editor of the magazine who took my first Chinese stories. He and his wife give me a warm welcome to their ranch. They are broadminded people, whose interest in me is sincere and intelligent, not affected and vulgar. I also meet some funny people who advise me to "trade" upon my nationality. They tell me that if I wish to succeed in literature in America I should dress in Chinese costume, carry a fan in my hand, wear a pair of scarlet beaded slippers, live in New York, and come of high birth. Instead of making myself familiar with the Chinese-Americans around me, I should discourse on my spirit acquaintance with Chinese ancestors and quote in between the "Good mornings" and "How d'ye dos" of editors,

> "Confucius, Confucius, how great is Confucius,
> Before Confucius, there never was Confucius.
> After Confucius, there never came Confucius,"
> etc., etc., etc.,

or something like that, both illuminating and obscuring, don't you know. They forget, or perhaps they are not aware that the old Chinese sage taught "The way of sincerity is the way of heaven."

My experiences as an Eurasian never cease; but people are not now as prejudiced as they have been. In the West, too, my friends are more advanced in all lines of thought than those whom I know in Eastern Canada—more genuine, more sincere, with less of the form of religion, but more of its spirit.

So I roam backward and forward across the continent. When I am East, my heart is West. When I am West, my heart is East. Before long I hope to be in China. As my life began in my father's country it may end in my mother's.

After all I have no nationality and am not anxious to claim any. Individuality is more than nationality. "You are you and I am I," says Confucius. I give my right hand to the Occidentals and my left to the Orientals, hoping that between them they will not utterly destroy the insignificant "connecting link." And that's all.

SEATTLE, WASH.

MISS NUMÈ OF JAPAN

ONOTO WATANNA (WINNIFRED EATON)

Chapter I. Parental Ambitions.

WHEN ORITO, SON OF TAKASHIMA SACHI, was but ten years of age, and Numè, daughter of Watanabe Omi, a tiny girl of three, their fathers talked quite seriously of betrothing them to each other, for they had been great friends for many years, and it was the dearest wish of their lives to see their children united in marriage. They were very wealthy men, and the father of Orito was ambitious that his son should have an unusually good education, so that when Orito was seventeen years of age, he had left the public school of Tokyo and was attending the Imperial University. About this time, and when Orito was at home on a vacation, there came to the little town where they lived, and which was only a very short distance from Tokyo, certain foreigners from the West, who rented land from Sachi and became neighbors to him and to Omi.

Sachi had always taken a great deal of interest in these foreigners, many of whom he had met quite often while on business in Tokyo, and he was very much pleased with his new tenants, who, in spite of their barbarous manners and dress, seemed good-natured and friendly. Often in the evening he and Omi would walk through the valley to their neighbors' house, and listen to them very attentively while they told them of their home in America, which they said was the greatest country in the world. After a time the strange men went away, though neither Sachi nor Omi forgot them, and very often they talked of them and of their foreign home. One day Sachi said very seriously to his friend:

"Omi, these strangers told us much of their strange land, and talked of the fine schools there, where all manner of learning is taught. What say you that I do send my unworthy son, Orito, to this America, so that he may see much of the world, and also become a great scholar, and later return to crave thy noble daughter in marriage?"

Omi was fairly delighted with this proposal, and the two friends talked and planned, and then sent for the lad.

Orito was a youth of extreme beauty. He was tall and slender; his face was pale and oval, with features as fine and delicate as a girl's. His was not merely a beautiful face; there was something else in it, a certain impassive look that rendered it almost startling in its wonderful inscrutableness. It was not expressionless, but unreadable—the face of one with the noble blood of the Kazoku and Samourai—pale, refined, and emotionless.

He bowed low and courteously when he entered, and said a few words of gentle greeting to Omi, in a clear, mellow voice that was very pleasing. Sachi's eyes sparkled with pride as he looked on his son. Unlike Orito, he was a very impulsive man, and without preparing the boy, he hastened to tell him at once of their plans for his future. While his father was speaking Orito's face did not alter from its calm, grave attention, although he was unusually moved. He only said, "What of Numè, my father?"

Sachi and Omi beamed on him.

"When you return from this America I will give you Numè as a bride," said Omi.

"And when will that be?" asked Orito, in a low voice.

"In eight years, my son, and you shall have all manner of learning there, which cannot be acquired here in Tokyo or in Kyushu, and the manner of learning will be different from that taught anywhere in Japan. You will have a foreign education, as well as what you have learned here at home. It shall be thorough, and therefore it will take some years. You must prepare at once, my son; I desire it."

Orito bowed gracefully and thanked his father, declaring it was the chief desire of his life to obey the will of his parent in all things.

Now Numè was a very peculiar child. Unlike most Japanese maidens, she was impetuous and wayward. Her mother had died when she was born, and she had never had anyone to guide or direct her, so that she had grown up in a careless, happy fashion, worshiped by her father's servants, but depending entirely upon Orito for all her small joys. Orito was her only companion and friend, and she believed blindly in him. She told him all her little troubles, and he in turn tried to teach her many things, for, although their fathers intended to betroth them to each other as soon as they were old enough, still Numè was only a little girl of ten, whilst Orito was a tall man-youth of nearly eighteen years. They loved each other very dearly; Orito loved Numè because she was one day to be his little wife, and because she was very bright and pretty; whilst Numè loved big Orito with a pride that was pathetic in its confidence.

That afternoon Numè waited long for Orito to come, but the boy had gone out across the valley, and was wandering aimlessly among the hills, trying to make up his mind to go to Numè and tell her that in less than a week he must leave her, and his beautiful home, for eight long years. The next day a great storm broke over the little town, and Numè was unable to go to the school, and because Orito had not come she became very restless and wandered fretfully about the house. So she complained bitterly to her father that Orito had not come. Then Omi, forgetting all else save the great future in store for his prospective son-in-law, told her of their plans. And Numè listened to him, not as Orito had done, with quiet, calm face, for hers was stormy and rebellious, and she sprang to her father's side and caught his hands sharply in her little ones, crying out passionately:

"No! no! my father, do not send Orito away."

Omi was shocked at this display of unmaidenly conduct, and arose in a dignified fashion, ordering his daughter to leave him, and Numè crept out, too stunned to say more. About an hour after that Orito came in, and discovered her rolled into a very forlorn little heap, with her head on a cushion, and weeping her eyes out.

"You should not weep, Numè," he said. "You should rather smile, for see, I will come back a great scholar, and will tell you of all I have seen—the people I have met—the strange men and women." But at that Numè pushed him from her, and declared she wanted not to hear of those barbarians, and flashed her eyes wrathfully at him, whereat Orito assured her that none of them would be half as beautiful or sweet as his little Numè—his plum blossom; for the word Numè means plum blossom in Japanese. Finally Numè promised to be very brave, and the day Orito left she only wept when no one could see her.

And so Orito sailed for America, and entered a great college called "Harvard." And little Numè remained in Japan, and because there was no Orito now to tell her thoughts to, she grew very subdued and quiet, so that few would have recognized in her the merry, wayward little girl who had followed Orito around like his very shadow. But Numè never forgot Orito for one little moment, and when everyone else in the house was sound asleep, she would lie awake thinking of him.

Chapter II. Cleo.

N O USE LOOKING OVER THERE, MY DEAR. Takie has no heart to break—never knew a Jap that had, for that matter—cold sort of creatures, most of them."

The speaker leaned nonchalantly against the guard rail, and looked half-amusedly at the girl beside him. She raised her head saucily as her companion addressed her, and the willful little toss to her chin was so pretty and wicked that the man laughed outright.

"No need for *you* to answer in words," he said. "That wicked, willful look of yours bodes ill for the Jap's—er—heart."

"I would like to know him," said the girl, slowly and quite soberly. "Really, he is very good-looking."

"Oh! yes—I suppose so—for a Japanese," her companion interrupted.

The girl looked at him in undisguised disgust for a moment.

"How ignorant you are, Tom!" she said, impatiently; "as if it makes the slightest difference *what* nationality he belongs to. Mighty lot *you* know about the Japanese."

Tom wilted before this assault, and the girl took advantage to say: "Now, Tom, I want to know Mr.—a—a—Takashima. *What* a name! Go, like the dear good boy you are, and bring him over here."

Tom straightened his shoulders.

"I utterly, completely, and altogether *refuse* to introduce you, young lady, to any other man on board this steamer. Why, at the rate you're going there won't be a heart-whole man on board by the time we reach Japan."

"But you said Mr. Ta—Takashima—or 'Takie,' as you call him, had no heart."

"True, but you might create one in him. I have a great deal of confidence in you, you know."

"Oh! Tom, *don't* be ridiculous now. Horrid thing! I believe you just want to be coaxed."

Tom's good-natured, fair face expanded in a broad smile for a moment. Then he tried to clear it.

"*Always* disliked to be coaxed," he choked.

352

"Hem!" The girl looked over into the waters a moment, thinking. Then she rose up and looked Tom in the face.

"Tom, if you don't I'll go over and speak to him without an introduction."

"Better try it," said Tom, aggravatingly. "Why, you'd shock him so much he wouldn't get over it for a year. You don't know these Japs as I do, my dear— dozens of them at our college—awfully strict on subject of etiquette, manners, and all that folderol."

"Yes, but I'd tell him it was an American custom."

"Can't fool Takashima, my dear. Been in America eight years now—knows a thing or two, I guess."

Takashima, the young Japanese, looked over at them, with the unreadable, quiet gaze peculiar to the better class Japanese. His eyes loitered on the girl's beautiful face, and he moved a step nearer to them, as a gentleman in passing stood in front, and for a moment hid them from him.

"He is looking at us now," said the girl, innocently.

Tom stared at her round-eyed for a moment.

"How on earth do you know that? Your head is turned right from him."

Again the saucy little toss of the chin was all the girl's answer.

"He's right near us now. Tom, please, please—now's your chance," she added, after a minute.

The Japanese had come quite close to them. He was still looking at the girl's face, as though thoroughly fascinated with its beauty. A sudden wind came up from the sea and caught the red cape she wore, blowing it wildly about her. It shook the rich gold of her hair in wondrous soft shiny waves about her face, as she tried vainly to hold the little cap on her head. It was a sudden wild wind, such as one often encounters at sea, lasting only for a moment, but in that moment almost lifting one from the deck. The girl, who had been clinging breathlessly to the railing, turned toward Takashima, her cheeks aflame with excitement, and as the violent gust subsided, they smiled in each other's faces.

Tom relented.

"Hallo! Takie—you there?" he said, cordially. "Thought you'd be laid up. You're a pretty good sailor, I see." Then he turned to the girl and said very solemnly and as if they had never even discussed the subject of an introduction, "Cleo, this is my old college friend, Mr. Takashima—Takie, my cousin, Miss Ballard."

"Will you tell me why," said the young Japanese, very seriously, "you did not want that I should know your cousin?"

"Don't mind Tom," the girl answered, with embarrassment, as that gentleman threw away his cigar deliberately; and she saw by his face that he intended saying something that would mislead Takashima, for he had often told her of the direct, serious and strange questions the Japanese would ask, and how he was in the habit of leading him off the track, just for the fun of the thing, and because Takashima took everything so seriously.

"Why—a—" said Tom, "the truth of the matter is—my cousin is a—a flirt!"

"Tom!" said the girl, with flaming cheeks.

"A flirt!" repeated the Japanese, half-musingly. "Ah! I do not like a flirt— that is not a nice word," he added, gently.

"Tom is just teasing me," she said; and added, "But how did you know Tom did not want you to know me?"

"I heard you tell him that you want to know me, and I puzzle much myself why he did not want."

"I was sorry for you in advance, Takie," said Tom, wickedly, and then seeing by the girl's face that she was getting seriously offended, he added: "Well, the truth is—er—Cleo—is—a so—young, don't you know. One can't introduce their female relatives to many of their male friends. You understand. That's how you put it to me once."

"Yes!" said Takashima, "I remember that I tell you of that. Then I am most flattered to know your relative."

As Tom moved off and left them together, feeling afraid to trust himself for fear he would make things worse, he heard the gentle voice of the Japanese saying very softly to the girl:

"I am most glad that you do not flirt. I do not like that word. Is it American?"

Tom chuckled to himself, and shook his fist, in mock threat, at Cleo.

Chapter III. Who Can Analyze a Coquette?

CLEO BALLARD WAS A COQUETTE; SUCH AN alluring, bright, sweet, dangerous coquette. She could not have counted her adorers, because they would have included everyone who knew her. Such a gay, happy girl as she was; always looking about her for happiness, and finding it only in the admiration and adoration of her victims; for they *were* victims, after all, because, though they were generally willing to adore in the beginning, she nevertheless crushed their hopes in the end; for that is the nature of coquettes. Hers was a strange, paradoxical nature. She would put herself out, perhaps go miles out of her way, for the sake of a new adorer, one whose heart she knew she would storm, and then perhaps break. She would do this gayly, thoughtlessly, as unscrupulously and impetuously as she tore the little silk gloves from her hands because they came not off easily. And yet, in spite of this, it broke her heart (and, after all, she had a heart) to see the meanest, the most insignificant of creatures in pain or trouble. With a laugh she pulled the heart-strings till they ached with pain and pleasure commingled; but when the poor heart burst with the tension, then she would run shivering away, and hide herself, because so long as she did not see the pain she did not feel it. Who can analyze a coquette?

Then, too, she was very beautiful, as all coquettes are. She had sun-kissed, golden-brown hair,—dark brown at night and in the shadow, bright gold in the daytime and in the light. Her eyes were dark blue, sombre, gentle eyes at times, wicked, mischievous, mocking eyes at others. Of the rest of her face, you do not need to know, for when one is young and has wonderful eyes, shiny, wavy hair and even features, be sure that one is very beautiful.

Cleo Ballard *was* beautiful, with the charming, versatile, changeable, wholly fascinating beauty of an American girl—an American beauty.

And now she had a new admirer, perhaps a new—lover. He was so different from the rest. It had been an easy matter for her to play with and turn off her many American adorers, because most of them went into the game of hearts with their eyes open, and knew from the first that the girl was but playing with them. But how was she to treat one who believed every word she said, whether uttered gayly or otherwise, and who, in his gentle, undisguised way, did not attempt, even from the beginning, to hide from her the fact that he admired her so intensely?

Ever since the day Tom Ballard had introduced Takashima to her, he had been with her almost constantly. Among all the men, young and old, who paid her court on the steamer, she openly favored the Japanese. Most Japanese have their full share of conceit. Takashima was not lacking in this. It was pleasant for him to be singled out each day as the one the beautiful American girl preferred to have by her. It pleased him that she did not laugh or joke so much when with him, but often became even as serious as he, and he even enjoyed hearing her snub some of her admirers for his sake.

"Cleo," Tom Ballard said to her one day, as the Japanese left her side for a moment, "have mercy on Takashima; spare him, as thou wouldst be spared."

She flushed a trifle at the bantering words, and looked out across the sea.

"Why, Tom! he understands. Didn't you say he had lived eight years in America?"

Tom sighed. "Woman! woman! incorrigible, unanswerable creature!"

After a time Cleo said, almost pleadingly, as if she were trying to defend herself against some accusation:

"Really, Tom, he *is* so nice. I can't help myself. You haven't the slightest idea how it feels to have anyone—anyone like that—on the verge of being in love with you."

Takashima returned to them, and took his seat by the girl's side.

"To-night," he told her, "they are going to dance on deck. The band will play a concert for us."

Cleo smiled whimsically at his broken English, for, in spite of his long residence in America, he still tripped in his speech.

"Do you dance?" she asked, curiously.

"No! I like better to watch with you."

"But I dance," she put in, hastily.

Takashima's face fell. He looked at her so dejectedly that she laughed. "Life is so serious to you, is it not, Mr. Takashima? Every little thing is of moment."

He gravely agreed with her, looking almost surprised that she should consider this strange.

"We are always taught," he said, gently, "that it is the little things of life which produce the big; that without the little we may not have the big. So, therefore, we Japanese measure even the smallest of things just as we do the large things."

Cleo repeated this speech later to Tom, and an Englishman who had been paying her a good deal of attention. They both laughed, but she felt somewhat ashamed of herself for repeating it.

"I suppose, then, you will not dance," said the Englishman. Cleo did not specially like him. She intended fully to dance, that night, but a contrary spirit made her reply, "No; I guess I will not."

She glanced over to where the young Japanese sat, a little apart from the others. His cap was pulled over his eyes, but the girl felt he had been watching her. She recrossed the deck and sat down beside him.

"Will you be glad," she asked him, "when we reach Japan?"

A shadow flitted for a moment across his face before he replied.

"Yes, Miss Ballard, most glad. My country is very beautiful, and I wish very much to see my home and my relations again."

"You do not look like most Japanese I have met," she said, slowly, studying his face with interest. "Your eyes are larger and your features more regular."

"That is very polite that you say," he said.

The girl laughed. "No! I didn't say it for politeness," she protested, "but because it is true. You are really very fine looking, as Tom would say;" she halted shyly for a moment, and then added, "for—for a Japanese."

Takashima smiled. "Some of the Japanese do not have very small eyes. Very few of the Kazoku class have them. That it is more pretty to have them large we do not say in Japan."

"Then," said the girl, mischievously, "you are not handsome in Japan."

This time Takashima laughed outright.

"I will try and be modest," he said. "Therefore, I will let *you* be the judge when we arrive there. If you think I am, as you say, handsome, then shall I surely be."

MARION
THE STORY OF AN ARTIST'S MODEL

ONOTO WATANNA (WINNIFRED EATON)

I

IN DAT FAMILEE DERE ARE ELEVEN CHEELDREN, and more—they come! See dat leetle one? She is très jolie! Oui, très jolie, n'est-ce pas? De father he come from Eengland about ten year ago. He was joost young man, mebbe twenty-seven or twenty-eight year ol', and he have one leetle foreign wife and six leetle cheeldren. They were all so cold. They were not use to dis climate of Canada. My wife and I, we keep de leetle 'otel at Hochelaga, and my wife she take all dose leetle ones and she warm dem before the beeg hall stove, and she make for dem the good French pea-soup."

Mama had sent me to the corner grocer to buy some things. Monsieur Thebeau, the grocer, was talking, and to a stranger. I felt ashamed and humiliated to hear our family thus discussed. Why should we always be pointed out in this way and made to feel conspicuous and freaky? It was horrid that the size of our family and my mother's nationality should be told to everyone by that corner grocer. I glared haughtily at Monsieur Thebeau, but he went garrulously on, regardless of my discomfiture.

"De eldest—a boy, monsieur—he was joost nine year old, and my wife she call him, 'Le petit père.' His mother she send him out to walk wiz all hees leetle sisters, and she say to him: 'Charles, you are one beeg boy, almost one man, and you must take care you leetle sisters; so, when de wind she blow too hard, you will walk you on de side of dat wind, and put yourself between it and your sisters.' 'Yes, mama,' il dit. And we, my wife and I, we look out de window, and me? I am laugh, and my wife, she cry—she have lost her only bebby, monsieur—to see dat leetle boy walk him in front of his leetle sisters, open hees coat, comme ça, monsieur, and spread it wiz hees hands, to make one shield to keep de wind from his sisters."

The man to whom Monsieur Thebeau had been speaking, had turned around, and was regarding me curiously. I felt abashed and angry under his compelling glance. Then he smiled, and nodding his head, he said:

"You are right. She *is* pretty—quite remarkably pretty!"

I forgot everything else. With my little light head and heart awhirl, I picked up my packages and ran out of the store. It was the first time I had been called pretty, and I was just twelve years old. I felt exhilarated and utterly charmed.

When I reached home, I deposited the groceries on a table in the kitchen and ran up to my room. Standing on a chair, I was able to see my face in the oval mirror that topped a very high and scratched old chiffonier. I gazed long and eagerly at the face I had often heard Monsieur Thebeau say was "très jolie," which French words I now learned must mean: "Pretty—quite remarkably pretty!" as had said that Englishman in the store.

Was I really pretty then? Surely the face reflected there was too fat and too red. My! my cheeks were as red as apples. I pushed back the offending fat with my two hands, and I opened my eyes wide and blinked them at myself in the glass. Oh! if only my hair were gold! I twisted and turned about, and then I made grimaces at my own face.

Suddenly I was thrilled with a great idea—one that for the moment routed my previous ambition to some day be an artist, as was my father. I would be an actress! If I were pretty, and both that Frenchman and Englishman had said so, why should I not be famous?

I slipped into mama's room, found a long skirt, and put it on me; also a feather which I stuck in my hair. Then, fearing detection, I ran out on tiptoe to the barn. There, marching up and down, I recited poems. I was pausing, to bow elaborately to the admiring audience, which, in my imagination, was cheering me with wild applause, when I heard mama's voice calling to me shrilly:

"Marion! Marion! Where in the world is that girl?"

"Coming, mama."

I divested myself hastily of skirt and feather, and left the barn on a run for the house. Here mama thrust our latest baby upon me, with instructions to keep him quiet while she got dinner. I took that baby in my arms, but I was still in that charmed world of dreams, and in my hand I clasped a French novel, which I had filched from my brother Charles' room. Charles at this time was twenty years of age, and engaged to be married to a girl we did not like.

I tried to read, but that baby would not keep still a minute. He wriggled about in my lap and reached a grimy hand after my book. Irritated and impatient, I shook him, jumped him up and down, and then, as he still persisted,

I pinched him upon the leg. He simply yelled. Mama's voice screamed at me above the baby's:

"If you can't take better care of that baby, and keep him quiet, you shall not be allowed to paint with your father this afternoon, but shall sit right here and sew," a punishment that made me put down the book, and amuse the baby by letting him pull my hair, which seemed to make him supremely happy, to judge from his chuckles and shouts of delight.

After dinner, which we had at noon, I received the cherished permission, and ran along to papa's room. Dear papa, whose gentle, sensitive hands are now at rest! I can see him sitting at his easel, with his blue eyes fixed absently upon the canvas before him. Papa, with the heart and soul of a great artist, "painting, painting," as he would say, with a grim smile, "pot-boilers to feed my hungry children."

I pulled out my paints and table, and began to work. From time to time I spoke to papa.

"Say, papa, what do I use for these pink roses?"

"Try rose madder, white and emerald green—a little naples yellow," answered papa patiently.

"Papa, what shall I use for the leaves?"

"Oh, try making your greens with blues and yellows."

From time to time I bothered him. By and by, I tired of the work, and getting up with a clatter, I went over and watched him. He was painting cool green waves dashing over jagged rocks, from a little sketch he had taken down at Lachine last summer.

"Tell me, papa," I said after a moment, "if I keep on learning, do you think I will ever be able to earn my living as an artist?"

"Who? What—you? Oh!" Absently papa blew the smoke about his head, gazed at me, but did not seem to see me. He seemed to be talking rather to himself, not bitterly, but just sadly:

"Better be a dressmaker or a plumber or a butcher or a policeman. There is no money in art!"

II

NEXT TO OUR GARDEN, SEPARATED ONLY by a wooden fence, through which we children used to peep, was the opulent and well-kept garden of Monsieur Prefontaine, who was a very important man, once Mayor of Hochelaga, the French quarter of Montreal, in which we lived. Madame

Prefontaine, moreover, was an object of unfailing interest and absorbing wonder to us children. She was an enormously fat woman, and had once taken a trip to New York City, to look for a wayward sister. There she had been offered a job as a fat woman for a big circus. Madame Prefontaine used to say to the neighbors, who always listened to her with great respect:

"Mon dieu! That New York—it is one beeg hell! Never do I feel so hot as in dat terrible city! I feel de grease it run all out of me! Mebbe, eef I stay at dat New York, I may be one beeg meelionaire—oui! But, non! Me? I prefer my lee-tle home, so cool and quiet in Hochelaga than be meelionaire in dat New York, dat is like purgatory."

We had an old straggly garden. Everything about it looked "seedy" and uncared for and wild, for we could not afford a gardener. My sisters and I found small consolation in papa's stout assertion that it looked picturesque, with its gnarled old apple trees and shrubs in their natural wild state. I was sensitive about that garden. It was awfully poor-looking in comparison with our neighbors' nicely kept places. It was just like our family, I sometimes treacherously thought—unkempt and wild and "heathenish." A neighbor once called us that. I stuck out my tongue at her when she said it. Being just next to the fine garden of Monsieur Prefontaine, it appeared the more ragged and beggarly, that garden of ours.

Mama would send us children to pick the maggots off the currant bushes and the bugs off the potato plants and, to encourage us, she would give us one cent for every pint of bugs or maggots we showed her. I hated the bugs and maggots, but it was fascinating to dig up the potatoes. To see the vegetables actually under the earth seemed almost like a miracle, and I would pretend the gnomes and fairies put them there, and hid inside the potatoes. I once told this to my little brothers and sisters, and Nora, who was just a little tot, wouldn't eat a potato again for weeks, for fear she might bite on a fairy. Most of all, I loved to pick strawberries, and it was a matter of real grief and humiliation to me that our own strawberries were so dried-up looking and small, as compared with the big, luscious berries I knew were in the garden of Monsieur Prefontaine.

On that day, I had been picking strawberries for some time, and the sun was hot and my basket only half full. I kept thinking of the berries in the garden adjoining, and the more I thought of them, the more I wished I had some of them.

It was very quiet in our garden. Not a sound was anywhere, except the breezes, making all kinds of mysterious whispers among the leaves. For some time, my eye had become fixed, fascinated, upon a loose board, with a hole in it near the ground. I looked and looked at that hole, and I thought to myself: "It is just about big enough for me to crawl through." Hardly had that thought occurred to me, when down on hands and knees I dropped, and into the garden of the great Monsieur Prefontaine I crawled.

The strawberry beds were right by the fence. Greedily I fell upon them. Oh, the exquisite joy of eating forbidden fruit! The fearful thrills that even as I ate ran up and down my spine, as I glanced about me on all sides. There was even a wicked feeling of fierce joy in acknowledging to myself that I was a thief.

"Thou shalt not steal!" I repeated the commandment that I had broken even while my mouth was full, and then, all of a sudden, I heard a voice, one that had inspired me always with feelings of respect and awe and fear.

"How you get in here?"

Monsieur Prefontaine was towering sternly above me. He was a big man, bearded, and with a face of preternatural importance and sternness.

I got up. My legs were shaky, and the world was whirling about me. I thought of the jail, where thieves were taken, and a great terror seized me. Monsieur Prefontaine had been the Mayor of Hochelaga. He could have me put in prison for all the rest of my life. We would all be disgraced.

"Well? Well? How you get in here?" demanded Monsieur Prefontaine.

"M'sieu, I—I-*crawled in*!" I stammered, indicating the hole in the fence.

"Bien! *Crawl out*, madame!"

"Madame" to me, who was but twelve years old!

"*Crawl out!*" commanded Monsieur, pointing to the hole, and feeling like a worm, ignominiously, under the awful eye of that ex-mayor of Hochelaga, on hands and knees and stomach, I crawled out.

Once on our side, I felt not the shame of being a thief so much as the degradation of *crawling out* with that man looking.

Feeling like a desperate criminal, I swaggered up to the house, swinging my half-filled basket of strawberries. As I came up the path, Ellen, a sister just two years older than I, put her head out of an upper window and called down to me:

"Marion, there's a beggar boy coming in at the gate. Give him some of that stale bread mama left on the kitchen table to make a pudding with."

The boy was about thirteen, and he was a very dirty boy, with hardly any clothes on him. As I looked at him, I was thrilled with a most beautiful inspiration. I could regenerate myself by doing an act of lovely charity.

"Wait a minute, boy."

Disregarding the stale bread, I cut a big slice of fresh, sweet-smelling bread that Sung Sung, our one very old Chinese servant, had made that day. Heaping it thick with brown sugar, I handed it to the boy.

"There, beggar boy," I said generously, "you can eat it all."

He took it with both hands, greedily, and now as I looked at him another, a fiendish, impulse seized me. Big boys had often hit me, and although I had always fought back as valiantly and savagely as my puny fists would let me, I had always been worsted, and had been made to realize the weakness of my sex and age. Now as I looked at that beggar boy, I realized that here was my chance to hit a big boy. He was smiling at me gratefully across that slice of sugared bread, and I leaned over and suddenly pinched him hard on each of his cheeks. His eyes bulged with amazement, and I still remember his expression of surprise and pained fear. I made a horrible grimace at him and then ran out of the room.

III

THERE WAS A LONG, BLEAK PERIOD, when we knew acutely the meaning of what papa wearily termed "Hard Times." Even in "Good Times" there are few people who buy paintings, and no one wants them in Hard Times.

Then descended upon Montreal a veritable plague. A terrible epidemic of smallpox broke out in the city. The French and not the English Canadians were the ones chiefly afflicted, and my father set this down to the fact that the French Canadians resisted vaccination. In fact, there were anti-vaccination riots all over the French quarter, where we lived.

And now my father, in this desperate crisis, proved the truth of the old adage that "Blood will tell." Ours was the only house on our block, or for that matter the surrounding blocks, where the hideous, yellow sign, "PICOTTE" (smallpox), was not conspicuously nailed upon the front door, and this despite the fact that we were a large family of children. Papa hung sheets all over the house, completely saturated with disinfectants. Every one of us children was vaccinated, and we were not allowed to leave the premises. Papa himself went upon all the messages, even doing the marketing.

He was not "absent-minded" in those days, nor in the grueling days of dire poverty that followed the plague. Child as I was, I vividly recall the terrors of that period, going to bed hungry, my mother crying in the night and my father walking up and down, up and down. Sometimes it seemed to me as if papa walked up and down all night long.

My brother Charles, who had been for some time our main support, had married (the girl we did not like) and although he had fervently promised to continue to contribute to the family's support, his wife took precious care that the contribution should be of the smallest, and she kept my brother, as much as she could, from coming to see us.

A day came when, with my mother and it seemed all of my brothers and sisters, I stood on a wharf waving to papa on a great ship. There he stood, by the railing, looking so young and good. Papa was going to England to try to induce grandpa—that grandfather we had never seen—to help us. We clung about mama's skirts, poor little mama, who was half distraught and we all kept waving to papa, with our hats and hands and handkerchiefs and calling out:

"Good-bye, papa! Come back! Come back soon!" until the boat was only a dim, shadowy outline.

The dreadful thought came to me that perhaps we would never see papa again! Suppose his people, who were rich and grand, should induce our father never to return to us!

I had kept back my tears. Mama had told us that none of us must let papa see us cry, as it might "unman" him, and she herself had heroically set the example of restraining her grief until after his departure. Now, however, the strain was loosened. I fancied I read in my brothers' and sisters' faces—we were all imaginative and sensitive and excitable—my own fears. Simultaneously we all began to cry.

Never will I forget that return home, all of us children crying and sobbing, and mama now weeping as unconcealedly as any of us, and the French people stopping us on the way to console or commiserate with us; but although they repeated over and over:

"Pauvre petites enfants! Pauvre petite mère!" I saw their significant glances, and I knew that in their minds was the same treacherous thought of my father.

But papa did return! He could have stayed in England, and, as my sister Ada extravagantly put it, "lived in the lap of luxury," but he came back to his noisy, ragged little "heathens," and the "painting, painting of pot-boilers to feed my hungry children."

IV

MONSIEUR DE ST. VIDAL IS RINGING the doorbell," called Ellen, "why don't you open the door, Marion? I believe he has a birthday present for you in his hand."

It was my sixteenth birthday, and Monsieur de St. Vidal was my first beau! He was a relative of our neighbors, the Prefontaines, and I liked him pretty well. I think I chiefly liked to be taken about in his stylish little dogcart. I felt sure all the other girls envied me.

"You go, Ellen, while I change my dress."

I was anxious to appear at my best before St. Vidal. It was very exciting, this having a beau. I would have enjoyed it much more, however, but for the interfering inquisitiveness of my sisters, Ada and Ellen, who never failed to ask me each time I had been out with him, whether he had "proposed" yet or not.

Ellen was running up the stairs, and now she burst into our room excitedly, with a package in her hand.

"Look, Marion! Here's your present. He wouldn't stop—just left it, and he said, with such a Frenchy bow—whew! I don't like the French!—'Pour Mamselle Marion, avec mes compliments!'" and Ellen mimicked St. Vidal's best French manner and voice.

I opened the package. Oh, such a lovely box of paints—a perfect treasure!

"Just exactly what I wanted!" I cried excitedly, looking at the little tubes, all shiny and clean, and the new brushes and palette.

Ada was sitting reading by the window, and now she looked up and said:

"Oh, did that French *wine merchant* give that to Marion?"

She cast a disparaging glance at the box, and then, addressing Ellen, she continued:

"Marion is disgustingly old for sixteen, but, of course, if he gives her *presents*" (he had never given me anything but candy before) "he will propose to her, I suppose. Mama married at sixteen, and I suppose *some* people—" Ada gave me another look that was anything but approving—"*are* in a hurry to get married. *I* shall never marry till I am twenty-five!" Ada was twenty.

This time, Ellen, who was eighteen, got the condemning look. Ellen was engaged to be married to an American editor, who wrote to her every day in the week and sometimes telegraphed. They were awfully in love with each other. Ellen said now:

"Oh, he'll propose all right. Wallace came around a whole lot, you know, before he actually popped."

"Well, maybe so," said Ada, "but I think we ought to know that French wine merchant's intentions pretty soon. I'll ask him if you like," she volunteered.

"No, no, don't you dare!" I protested.

"Well," said Ada, "if he doesn't propose to you soon, you ought to stop going out with him. It's bad form."

I *wished* my sisters wouldn't interfere in my affairs. They nagged me everlastingly about St. Vidal, and it made me conscious when I was with him. They acted like self-appointed monitors. The minute I would get in, they would begin:

"Well, did he propose?" and I would feel ashamed to be obliged to admit, each time, that he had not. Ada had even made some suggestions of how I might "bring him to the point." She said men had to be led along like sheep. Ellen, however, had warmly vetoed those suggestions, declaring stoutly that Wallace, her sweetheart, had needed no prodding. In fact, he had most eloquently and urgently pleaded his own suit, without Ellen "putting out a finger" to help him, so she said.

That evening St. Vidal called and took me to the rink, and I enjoyed myself hugely. He was a graceful skater, and so was I, and I felt sure that everyone's eye was upon us. I was very proud of my "beau," and I secretly wished that he was blond. I did prefer the English type. However, conscious of what was expected of me by my sisters, I smiled my sweetest on St. Vidal, and by the time we started for home, I realized, with a thrill of anticipation, that he was in an especially tender mood. He helped me along the street carefully and gallantly.

It was a clear, frosty night, and the snow was piled up as high as our heads on each side of the sidewalks. Suddenly St. Vidal stopped, and drawing my hand through his arm, he began, with his walking stick, to write upon the snow:

"Madame Marion de St. Vida—"

Before he got to the "l," I was seized with panic. I jerked my hand from his arm, took to my heels and ran all the way home.

Now it had come—that proposal, and I did not want it. It filled me with embarrassment and fright. When I got home, I burst into Ada's room, and gasped:

"It's done! He did propose! B-but I said—I said—" I hadn't said anything at all.

"Well?" demanded Ada.

"Why, I'm not going to, that's all," I said.

Ada returned to the plaiting of her hair. Then she said sceptically:

"Hm, that's very queer. Are you *sure* he proposed, because *I* heard he was all the time engaged to a girl in Côte des Neiges."

"Oh, Ada," I cried, "do you suppose he's a bigamist? I think I'm fortunate to have escaped from his snare!"

The next day Madame Prefontaine told mama that St. Vidal had said he couldn't imagine what in the world I had run away suddenly from him like that for, and he said:

"Maybe she had a stomach ache."

V

ELLEN, DON'T YOU WISH SOMETHING WOULD HAPPEN?"
Ellen and I were walking up and down the street near the English church.

"Life is so very dull and monotonous," I went on. "My! I would be glad if something real bad happened—some sort of tragedy. Even that is better than this deadness."

Ellen looked at me, and seemed to hesitate.

"Yes, it's awful to be so poor as we are," she answered, "but what I would like is not so much money as fame, and, of course, love. That usually goes with fame."

Ellen's fiancé was going to be famous some day. He was in New York, and had written a wonderful play. As soon as it was accepted, he and Ellen were to be married.

"Well, I tell you what I'd like above everything else on earth," said I sweepingly. "I would love to be a great actress, and break everybody's heart. It must be perfectly thrilling to be notorious, and we certainly are miserable girls!"

We were chewing away with great relish the contents of a bag of candy.

"Anyhow," said Ellen, "you seem to be enjoying that candy," and we both giggled.

Two men were coming out of the side door of the church. Attracted by our laughter, they came over directly to us. One of them we knew well. He was Jimmy McAlpin, the son of a fine old Scotch, very rich, lady, who had always taken an especial interest in our family. Jimmy, though he took up the collection in church, had been, so I heard the neighbors whisper to mama, once very dissipated. He had known us since we were little girls, and always teased us a lot. He would come up behind me on the street and pull my long plait of hair, saying:

"Oh, pull the string, gentlemen and ladies, and the figure moves!"

Now he came smilingly up to us, followed by his friend, a big, stout man, with a military carriage and gray mustache. I recognized him, too, though we did not know him. He was a very rich and important citizen of our Montreal. Of him also I had heard bad things. People said he was "fast." That was a word they always whispered in Montreal, and shook their heads over, but whenever

I heard it, its very mystery and badness somehow thrilled me. Ada said there was a depraved and low streak in me, and I guiltily admitted to myself that she was right.

"What are you girls laughing about?" asked Jimmy, a question that merely brought forth a fresh accession of giggles.

Colonel Stevens was staring at me, and he had thrust into his right eye a shining monocle. I thought him very grand and distinguished-looking, much superior to St. Vidal. Anyway we were tired of the French, having them on all sides of us, and, as I have said, I admired the blond type of men. Colonel Stevens was not exactly blond, for his hair was gray (he was bald on top, though his hat covered that), but he was typically British, and somehow the Englishmen always appeared to me much superior to our little French Canucks, as we called them.

Said the Colonel, pulling at his mustache:

"A laughing young girl in a pink cotton frock is the sweetest thing on earth."

I had on a pink cotton frock, and I was laughing. I thought of what I had heard Madame Prefontaine say to mama—in a whisper:

"He is one dangerous man—dat Colonel Steven, and any woman seen wiz him will lose her reputation."

"Will I lose mine?" I asked myself. I must say my heart beat, fascinated with the idea.

Looking at me he added: "May I send you some roses just the color of your cheeks?"

Something now was really happening, and I was excited and delighted.

"Can't we take the ladies—" I nudged Ellen—"some place for a little refreshment," said the Colonel.

"No," said Ellen, "mama expects us home."

"Too bad," murmured the Colonel, very much disappointed, "but how about some other night? To-morrow, shall we say?" Looking at me, he added: "May I send you some roses, just the color of your cheeks?"

I nodded from behind Ellen's back.

"Come on," said Ellen brusquely, "we'd better be getting home. You know you've got the dishes to do, Marion."

She drew me along. I couldn't resist looking back, and there was that fascinating Colonel, standing stock-still in the street, still pulling at his mustache, and staring after me. He smiled all over, when I turned, and blew me an odd little kiss, like a kind of salute, only from his lips.

That night, when Ellen and I were getting ready for bed, I said:

"Isn't the Colonel thrillingly handsome though?"

"Ugh! I should say not," said Ellen. "Besides he's a married man, and a flirt."

"Well, I guess he doesn't love his old wife," said I.

"If she is old," said Ellen, "so is he—maybe older. Disgusting."

All next day I waited for that box of roses, and late in the afternoon, sure enough, it came, and with it a note:

"DEAR MISS MARION:

Will you and your charming sister take a little drive with me and a friend this evening? If so, meet us at eight o'clock, corner of St. James and St. Denis streets. My friend has seen your sister in Judge Laflamme's office" (Ellen worked there) "and he is very anxious to know her. As for me, I am thinking only of when I shall see my lovely rose again. I am counting the hours!

Devotedly,

FRED STEVENS."

The letter was written on the stationery of the fashionable St. James Club. Now I was positive that Colonel Stevens had fallen in love with me. I thought of his suffering because he could not marry me. In many of the French novels I had read men ran away from their wives, and, I thought: "Maybe the Colonel will want me to elope with him, and if I won't, perhaps, he will kill himself," and I began to feel very sorry to think of such a fine-looking soldierly man as Colonel Stevens killing himself just because of me.

When I showed Ellen the letter, after she got home from work, to my surprise and delight, she said:

"All right, let's go. A little ride will refresh us, and I've had a hard week of it, but better not let mama know where we're going. We'll slip out after supper, when she's getting the babies to sleep."

Reaching the corner of St. James and St. Denis Streets that evening, we saw a beautiful closed carriage, with a coat of arms on the door, and a coachman in livery jumped down and opened the door for us. We stepped in. With the Colonel was a middle-aged man, with a dry, yellowish face and a very black—it looked dyed—mustache.

"Mr. Mercier," said the Colonel, introducing us.

"Oh," exclaimed Ellen, "are you the Premier?"

"Non, non, non," laughed Mr. Mercier, and turning about in the seat, he began to look at Ellen and to smile at her, until the ends of his waxed mustache seemed to jump up and scratch his nose. Colonel Stevens had put his arm just at the back of me, and as it slipped down from the carriage seat to my waist, I sat forward on the edge of the seat. I didn't want to hurt his feelings by telling him to take his arm down, and still I didn't want him to put it around me. Suddenly Ellen said:

"Marion, let's get out of this carriage. That beast there put his arm around me, and he pinched me, too." She indicated Mercier.

She was standing up in the carriage, clutching at the strap, and she began to tap upon the window, to attract the attention of the coachman. Mr. Mercier was cursing softly in French.

"Petite folle!" he said, "I am not meaning to hurt you—joost a little loving. Dat is all."

"You ugly old man," said Ellen, "do you think I want *you* to love me? Let me get out!"

"Oh, now, Miss Ellen," said the Colonel, "that is too rude. Mr. Mercier is a gentleman. See how sweet and loving your little sister is."

"No, no," I cried, "I am not sweet and loving. He had no business to touch my sister."

Mr. Mercier turned to the Colonel.

"For these children did you ask me to waste my time?" and putting his head out of the carriage, he simply roared:

"Rue Saint Denis! Sacré!"

They set us down at the corner of our street. When we got in a friend of papa's was singing to mama and Ada in the parlor:

"In the gloaming, oh, my darling,
When the lights are dim and low."

He was one of many Englishmen, younger sons of aristocrats, who, not much good in England, were often sent to Canada. They liked to hang around papa, whose family most of them knew. This young man was a thin, harmless sort of fellow, soft-spoken and rather silly, Ellen and I thought; but he could play and sing in a pretty, sentimental way and mama and Ada would listen by the hour to him. He liked Ada, but Ada pretended she had only an indifferent interest in him. His father was the Earl of Albemarle, and Ellen and I used to make Ada furious by calling her "Countess," and bowing mockingly before her.

Walking on tiptoe, Ellen and I slipped by the parlor door, and up to our own room. That night, after we were in bed, I said to Ellen:

"You know, I think Colonel Stevens is in love with me. Maybe he will want me to elope with him. Would you if you were me?"

"Don't be silly. Go to sleep," was Ellen's cross response. She regretted very much taking that ride, and she said she only did it because she got so tired at the office all day, and thought a little ride would be nice. She had no idea, she said, that those "two old fools" would act like that.

I was not going to let Ellen go to sleep so easily, however.

"Listen to this," I said, poking her to keep her awake. "This is Ella Wheeler Wilcox, Ellen, and they call her the Poet of Passion." Ellen groaned, but she had to listen:

> "Just for one kiss that thy lips had given
> Just for one hour of bliss with thee,
> I would gladly barter my hopes of heaven,
> And forfeit the joys of eternity;
> For I know in the way that sins are reckoned
> That this is a sin of the deepest dye,
> But I also know if an angel beckoned,
> Looking down from his home on high,
> And you adown by the gates Infernal
> Should lift to me your loving smile,
> I would turn my back on the things Eternal,
> Just to lie on your breast awhile."

"Ugh!" said Ellen, "I would scorn to lie on Colonel Stevens' old fat breast."

VI

WALLACE, ELLEN'S SWEETHEART, HAD NOT SOLD his play, but he expected to any day. He was, however, impatient to be married—they had now been engaged over a year—and he wrote Ellen that he could not wait, anyway more than two or three months longer. Meanwhile Ellen secured a better position.

The new position was at a much greater distance from our house, and as she had to be at the office early, she decided to take a room farther down town. Papa at first did not want her to leave home, but Ellen pointed out that Hochelaga was too far away from her office, and then she added, to my delight, that she'd take me along with her. I could make her trousseau and cook for us both, and it wouldn't cost any more for two than for one.

Mama thought we were old enough to take care of ourselves. "For," said she, "when I was Ellen's age I was married and had two children. Besides," she added, "we are crowded for room, in the house, and it will only be for a month or two."

So Ellen secured a little room down town. I thought the house was very grand, for there was thick carpet on all the floors and plush furniture in the parlor.

We were unpacking our trunk, soon after we arrived, when there was a knock at our door, and in came Mrs. Cohen, our landlady and a big fat man. Mrs. Cohen pointed at us with a pudgy finger:

"There they are!" she explained. "Ain't they smart? Look at that one," pointing to Ellen, "she is smart like a lawyer, and the sister," pointing to me, "she is come to work and sew like she was the wife, see."

She turned about then and yelled at the top of her voice:

"Sarah! Sarah! Where is that lazy Sarah? Come! Directly!"

A young, thin girl with a clear skin and enormous black eyes came slowly up the stairs and into the room.

"See, Sarah," cried Mrs. Cohen, "there is two girls that is more smart than you. That one, she is just the same age as you, and she makes good money, yes. She makes twelve dollar a week. *You* cannot do that. Oh, no!"

Sarah looked at us sullenly, and to our greeting: "How do you do?" she returned: "How's yourself?" Then turning savagely on her father and stepmother, she snarled:

"And if I can't make money, whose fault is it? I have to work more hard than a servant even, with all those children of yours!"

"Sarah, Sarah! be more careful of your speech!" cried her mother. "Did not the God above give to you those six little brothers? You should thank Him for His kindness."

She started down the stairs, followed by her husband. Sarah, however, stayed in the room, and now she smiled at us in a friendly way.

"Say, Miss— What's your names?"

"Ellen and Marion."

"Well, say, my stepmother is the limit. Gosh! I wish we were not Jews. Nobody likes us."

"You ought not to say that," said Ellen, severely, "the Jews were God's chosen people, remember."

"Gosh!" said Sarah, "I wish He didn't choose me."

That evening, Sarah thrust her face in at our door, and called in a loud whisper:

"Say, girls, do youse want to see two old fools? Come on then."

She led us, all tiptoeing, into a room next to one occupied by a little English old maid named Miss Dick, who gave music lessons for twenty-five cents a lesson, and who always spoke in a sort of hissing whisper, so that a little spit came from her lips. Mrs. Cohen called it the "watering can."

"Kneel down there," said Sarah, pointing to a crack in the wall. I peeped through, and this is what I saw: Seated in the armchair was a funny little old man—I think he was German—with a dried, wrinkled face. Perched on the arm of the chair was Miss Dick. They were billing and cooing like turtle doves, and she was saying:

"Am I your little Dicky-birdie?" and he was looking proud and pleased.

Ellen and I burst into fits of laughter, but Sarah pulled us away, and we covered our mouths and stifled back the laughter. When we got to our room, Sarah told us that the old man, Schneider, had come to her father and mother and asked them to find him a wife. Her mother agreed to do so for the payment of ten dollars. She had spoken to Miss Dick, and the latter had also agreed to pay ten dollars.

About a week after we had been there, Miss Dick and Mr. Schneider were married. They had packed up all Miss Dick's things and were going down the stairs with bags in their hands, when Mrs. Cohen ran out into the hall.

"Now please, like a lady and gentleman, pay me the ten dollars each as we made the bargain, for I make you acquainted to get married."

"Ten dollars!" screamed Miss Dick.

"Yes, you make the bargain with me."

"I made no such bargain," cried the bride shrilly. "We met and loved at first sight." Turning to Schneider, who was twirling his thumbs, she said: "Protect me, dearie."

He said:

"I say nutting. I say nutting."

"*Will* you pay that debt?" demanded Mrs. Cohen and then, as Miss Dick did not answer, she pointed dramatically to my sister Ellen, who was standing with me laughing at the head of the stairs. "You see that lady. She is just the same as a lawyer, and she say you should pay. Pay for your man like a lady, that smart lady up there say you should."

"Oh, oh! you old Shylock!" screamed Miss Dick hissingly. Mrs. Cohen was obliged to wipe her face and, backing away, she cried:

"Don't you Shylock me with your watering can."

Ellen and I were doubled up with laughter, and Mrs. Cohen seized hold of a broom, and literally swept bride and groom from the house, shouting at them all sorts of epithets and curses.

VII

WE HAD BEEN AT COHEN'S LESS THAN a month, when Wallace wrote he could wait no longer.

He had not sold his play, but he had a very good position now as associate editor of a big magazine, and he said he was making ample money to support a wife. So he was coming for his little Ellen at once. We were terribly excited, particularly as Wallace followed up the letter with a telegram to expect him next day, and sure enough the next day he arrived.

He did not want any "fussy" wedding. Only papa and I were to be present. Wallace did not even want us, but Ellen insisted. She looked sweet in her little dress (I had made it), and although I knew Wallace was good and a genius and adored my sister, I felt broken-hearted at the thought of losing her, and it was all I could do to keep from crying at the ceremony.

As the train pulled out, I felt so utterly desolate that I stretched out my arms to it and cried out aloud:

"Ellen, Ellen, please don't go. Take me, too."

I never realized till then how much I loved my sister. Dear little Ellen, with her love of all that was best in life, her sense of humor, her large, generous heart, and her absolute purity. If only she had stayed by my side I am sure her influence would have kept me from all the mistakes and troubles that followed in my life, if only by her disgust and contempt of all that was dishonorable and unclean. But Wallace had taken our Ellen, and I had lost my best friend, my sister and my chum.

That night I cried myself to sleep. I thought of all the days Ellen and I played together. Even as little girls mama had given us our special house tasks together. We would peel potatoes and shell peas or sew together, and as we worked we would tell each other stories, which we invented as we went along. Our stories were long and continuous, and full of the most extravagant and unheard of adventures and impossible riches, heavenly beauty and bravery that was wildly reckless.

There was one story Ellen continued for weeks. She called it: "The Princess who used Diamonds as Pebbles and made bonfires out of one-hundred-dollar bills." I made up one called: "The Queen who Tamed Lions and Tigers with a Smile," and more of that kind.

Mama would send Ellen and me upon messages sometimes quite a distance from our house, for we had English friends living at the other side of the town. The French quarter was cheaper to live in and that was why we lived in Hochelaga. Ellen and I used to walk sometimes three miles each way to Mrs. McAlpin's house on Sherbrooke Street. To vary the long walk we would hop along in turn, holding one another's legs by the foot, or we would walk backward, counting the cracks in the sidewalks that we stepped over. One day a young man stood still in the street to watch us curiously. Ellen was holding one of my feet and I was hopping along on the other. He came up to us and said:

"Say, sissy, did you hurt your foot?"

"No," I returned, "we're just playing Lame Duck."

It was strange now, as I lay awake, crying over the going of my sister, that all the queer little funny incidents of our childhood together came thronging to my mind. I vividly remembered a day when mama was sick and the doctor said she could have chicken broth. Well, there was no one home to kill the chicken, for that was the time papa went to England. Ellen and I volunteered to kill one, for Sung Sung, our old servant, believed it would be unlucky to kill one with the master away—one of his everlasting superstitions. Ellen and I caught the chicken. Then I held it down on the block of wood, while Ellen was to chop the head off. Ellen raised the hatchet, but when it descended she lowered it very gently, and began to cut the head off slowly. Terrified, I let go. Ellen was trembling, and the chicken ran from us with its head bleeding and half off.

"Qu'est-ce que c'est? Qu'est-ce que c'est? De little girl, she is afraid. See me, I am not scared of nutting."

It was the French grocer boy. He took that unfortunate chicken, and placing its bleeding head between the door and jamb, he slammed the door quickly, and the head was broken. I never did like that boy, now I hated him. Ellen looked very serious and white. When we were plucking the feathers off later, she said:

"Marion, do you know we are as guilty as Emile and if it were a human being, we could be held as accomplices."

"No, no, Ellen," I insisted. "I did not kill it. I am not guilty. I wouldn't be a murderer like Emile for anything in the world."

"You're just as bad," said Ellen severely, "perhaps worse, because to-night you'll probably eat part of your victim."

I shuddered at the thought, and I did not eat any chicken that night.

When I was packing my things, preparatory to leaving Mrs. Cohen's next morning, for I was to return home, now that Ellen was married, Mrs. Cohen came in with a large piece of cake in her hand. She was very sorry for me because I had lost my sister.

"There," she said, "that will make you feel better. Taste it. It is good." I could not eat their cake, because she used goose grease instead of butter, but I didn't want to hurt her feelings and I pretended to take a bite. When she was not looking I stuffed it into the wastepaper basket.

"Now never mind about your sister no more," she said kindly. "The sun will shine in your window some day."

I was still sniffing and crying, and I said:

"It looks as if it were going to rain to-day."

"Vell then," she said, "it vill not be dry."

VIII

I WAS AT AN AGE—NEARLY EIGHTEEN NOW—when girls want and need chums and confidantes. I was bubbling over with impulses that needed an outlet, and only foolish young things like myself were capable of understanding me. With Ellen gone, I sought and found girl friends I believed to be congenial.

My sister Ada, because of her superiority in age and character to me, would not condescend to chum with me. Nevertheless, she heartily disapproved of my choice in friends, and constantly reiterated that my tastes were low. Life was a serious matter to Ada, who had enormous ambitions, and had already been promised a position on our chief newspaper, to which she had contributed poems and stories. To Ada, I was a frivolous, silly young thing, who needed constantly to be squelched, and she undertook to do the squelching, unsparingly, herself.

"Since we are obliged," said Ada, "to live in a neighborhood with people who are not our equals, I think it a good plan to keep to ourselves. That's the only way to be exclusive. Now, that Gertie Martin" (Gertie was my latest friend) "is a noisy American girl. She talks through her nose, and is always criticizing the Canadians and comparing them with the Yankees. As for that Lu Fraser" (another of my friends) "she can't even speak the Queen's English properly, and her uncle keeps a saloon."

Though I stoutly defended my friends, Ada's nagging had an unconscious effect upon me, and for a time I saw very little of the girls.

Then one evening, Gertie met me on the street, and told me that, through her influence, Mr. Davis (also an American) had decided to ask me to take a part in "Ten Nights in a Bar Room," which was to be given at a "Pop" by the Montreal Amateur Theatrical Club, of which he was the head. I was so excited and happy about this that I seized hold of Gertie and danced with her on the sidewalk, much to the disgust of my brother Charles, who was passing with his new wife.

Mr. Davis taught elocution and dramatic art, and he was a man of tremendous importance in my eyes. He was always getting up concerts and entertainments, and no amateur affair in Montreal seemed right without his efficient aid. The series of "Pops" he was now giving were patronized by all the best people of the city and he had an imposing list of patrons and patronesses. Moreover the plays were to be produced in a real theatre, not merely a hall, and so they had somewhat the character of professional performances.

To my supreme joy, I was given the part of the drunkard's wife, and there were two glorious weeks in which we rehearsed and Mr. Davis trained us. He said one day that I was the "best actress" of them all, and he added that although he charged twenty-five dollars a month to his regular pupils he would teach me for ten, and if I couldn't afford that, for five, and if there was no five to be had, then for nothing. I declared fervently that I would repay him some day, and he laughed, and said: "I'll remind you when that 'some day' comes."

Well, the night arrived, and I was simply delirious with joy. I learned how to "make up," and I actually experienced stage fright when I first went on, but I soon forgot myself.

When I was crawling on the floor across the stage, trying to get something to my drunken husband, a voice from the audience called out:

"Oh, Mar-ri-on! Oh, Ma-ri-on! You're on the bum! You're on the bum!"

It was my little brother Randle, who, with several small boys had got free seats away up in front, by telling the ticket man that his sister was playing the star part. I vowed mentally to box his ears good and hard when I got home.

When the show was over, Mr. Davis came to the dressing room, and said, right before all the girls:

"Marion, come to my studio next week, and we'll start those lessons, and when we put on the next 'Pop,' which I believe will be 'Uncle Tom's Cabin,' we will find a good part for you."

"Oh, Mr. Davis," I cried, "are you going to make an actress of me?"

"We'll see! We'll see!" he said, smiling. "It will depend on yourself, and if you are willing to study."

"I'll sit up all night long and study," I assured him.

"The worst thing you could do," he answered. "We want to save these peaches," and he pinched my cheek.

Mr. Davis did lots of things that in other men would have been offensive. He always treated the girls as if they were children. People in Montreal thought him "sissified," but I am glad there are some men more like the gentler sex.

So I began to take lessons in elocution, and dramatic art. Oh! but I was a happy girl in those days. It is true, Mr. Davis was very strict, and he would make me go over lines again and again before he was satisfied, but when I got them finally right and to suit him, he would rub his hands, blow his nose and say:

"Fine! Fine! There's the real stuff in you."

And what with Nora crying with sympathy and excitement.

He once said that I was the only pupil he had who had an atom of promise in her. He declared Montreal peculiarly lacking in talent of that sort, though he said he had searched all over the place for even a "spark of fire." I, at least, loved the work, was deadly in earnest and, finally, so he said, I was pretty, and that was something.

We studied "Camille," "The Marble Heart" and "Romeo and Juliet." All of my spare time at home, I spent memorizing and rehearsing. I would get a younger sister, Nora, who was absorbedly interested, to act as a dummy. I would make her be Armand or Armand's father.

"Now, Nora," I would say, "when I come to the word 'Her,' you must say: 'Camille! Camille'!"

Then I would begin, addressing Nora as Armand:

"You are not speaking to a cherished daughter of society, but a woman of the world, friendless and fearless. Loved by those whose vanity she gratifies, despised by those who ought to pity her—her—*Her*—"

I would look at Nora and repeat: "Her—!" and Nora would wake up from her trance of admiration of me and say:

"Camel! Camel!"

"No, no!" I would yell, "*That* is—" (pointing to the right—Mr. Davis called that "Dramatic action") "*your* way! *This* way—" (pointing to the left) "is mine!"

Then throwing myself on the dining-room sofa, I would sob and moan and cough (Camille had consumption, you may recall), and what with Nora crying with sympathy and excitement, and the baby generally waking up, there would be an awful noise in our house.

I remember papa coming half-way down the stairs one day and calling out:

"What in the devil is the matter with that Marion? Has she taken leave of her senses?"

Mama answered from the kitchen:

"No, papa, she's learning elocution and dramatic art from Mr. Davis; but I'm sure she's not suited to be an actress, for she lisps and her nose is too short. But do make her stop, or the neighbors will think we are quarreling."

"Stop this minute!" ordered papa, "and don't let me hear any more such nonsense."

I betook myself to the barn.

IX

THE SNOW WAS CRISP AND THE AIR as cold as ice. We were playing the last performance of "Uncle Tom's Cabin." We had been playing it for two weeks, and I had been given two different parts, Marie Claire, in which, to my joy, I wore a gold wig and a lace tea-gown—which I made from an old pair of lace curtains and a lavender silk dress mama had had when they were rich and she dressed for dinner—and Cassy. I did love that part where Cassy says:

"Simon Legree, you are afraid of me, and you have reason to be, for I have got the devil in me!"

I used to hiss those words at him and glare until the audience clapped me for that. Ada saw me play Cassy one night, and she went home and told mama that I had "sworn like a common woman before all the people on the stage" and that I ought not to be allowed to disgrace the family. But little I cared for Ada in those days. *I* was learning to be an actress!

On this last night, in fact, I experienced all the sensations of a successful star. Someone had passed up to me, over the footlights if you please, a real bouquet of flowers, and with these clasped to my breast, I had retired smiling and bowing from the stage.

To add to my bliss, Patty Chase, the girl who played Topsy, came running in to say that a gentleman friend of hers was "crazy" to meet me. He was the one who had sent me the flowers. He wanted to know if I wouldn't take supper with him and a friend and Patty that night.

My! I felt like a regular professional actress. To think an unknown man had admired me from the front, and was actually seeking my acquaintance! I hesitated, however, because Patty was not the sort of girl I was accustomed to go out with. I liked Patty pretty well myself, but my brother Charles had one day come to the house especially to tell papa some things about her—he had seen me walking with Patty on the street—and papa had forbidden me to go out with her again. As I hesitated, she said:

"It isn't as if they are strangers, you know. One of them, Harry Bond, is my own fellow. You know who his folks are, and but for them we'd have been married long ago. Well, Harry's friend, the one who wants to meet you, is a swell, too, and he hasn't been out from England long. Harry says his folks are big nobs over there, and he is studying law here. His folks send him a remittance and I guess it's a pretty big one, for he's living at the Windsor, and I guess he can treat us fine. So come along. You'll not get such a chance again."

"Patty," I said, "I'm afraid I dare not. Mama hates me to be out late, and, see, it's eleven already."

"Why, the night's just beginning," cried Patty.

There was a rap at the door, and Patty exclaimed:

"Here they are now!"

All the girls in the room were watching me—enviously, I thought—and one of them made a catty remark about Patty, who had gone out in the hall, and was whispering to the men. I decided not to go, but when I came out of the room there they were all waiting for me and Patty exclaimed:

"Here she is," and, dragging me along by the hand, she introduced me to the men.

I found myself looking up into the face of a tall young man of about twenty-three. He had light curly hair and blue eyes. His features were fine and clear-cut, and, to my girlish eyes, he appeared extraordinarily handsome and distinguished, far more so even than Colonel Stevens, who had, up till then, been my ideal of manly perfection. Everything he wore had an elegance about it from his evening suit and the rich fur-lined overcoat to his opera hat and gold-topped cane. I felt flattered and overwhelmingly impressed to think that such a fine personage should have singled me out for especial attention. What is more, he was looking at me with frank and undisguised admiration. Instead of letting go my hand, which he had taken when Patty introduced us, he held it while he asked me if he couldn't have the pleasure of taking me out to supper. As I hesitated, blushing and awfully thrilled by the hand pressing mine, Patty said:

"She's scared. Her mother won't let her stay out late at night. She's never been out to supper before."

Then she and Harry Bond burst out laughing, as if that were a good joke on me, but Mr. Bertie (his name was the Honorable Reginald Bertie—pronounced Bartie) did not laugh. On the contrary, he looked very sympathetic, and pressed my hand the closer. I thought to myself:

"My! I must have looked lovely as Marie St. Claire. Wait till he sees me as Camille."

"I'm not afraid," I contradicted Patty, "but mama will be worried. She sits up for me."

This was not strictly true, but it sounded better than to say that Ada was the one who always sat up for anyone in the house who went out at night. She even used to sit up for my brother Charles before he was married, and I could just imagine the cross-questioning she would put me through when I got in late. Irritated as I used to be in those days at what I called Ada's interference in my affairs, I know now that she always had my best good at heart. Poor little delicate Ada! with her passionate devotion and loyalty to the family and her fierce, antagonistic attitude to all outside intrusion. She was morbidly sensitive.

Mr. Bertie quieted my fears by dispatching a messenger boy to our house with a note saying that I had gone with a party of friends to see the Ice Palace.

Even with Ada in the back of my mind, I was now, as Patty would say, "out for a good time," and when Mr. Bertie carefully tucked the fur robes of the sleigh about me, I felt warm, excited and recklessly happy.

We drove over to the Square, where the Ice Palace was erected. The Windsor Hotel was filled with American guests who were on the balconies watching the torchlight procession marching around the mountain. My brother Charles was one of the snow-shoers, and the men were all dressed in white and striped blanket overcoats with pointed capuchons (cowls) on their backs or heads, and moccasins on their feet.

It was a beautiful sight, that procession, and looked like a snake of light, winding about old Mount Royal, and when the fireworks burst all about the monumental Ice Palace, inside of which people were dancing and singing, really it seemed to me like a scene in fairyland. I felt a sense of pride in our Montreal, and looking up at Mr. Bertie, to note the effect of so much beauty upon him, I found him watching me instead.

The English, when they first come out to Canada, always assume an air of patronage toward the "Colonials," as they call us, just as if, while interested, they are also highly amused by our crudeness. Now Mr. Bertie said:

"We've seen enough of this Ice Palace's hard, cold beauty. Suppose we go somewhere and get something warm inside us. Gad, I'm dry."

Harry told the driver to take us to a place whose name I could not catch, and presently we drew up before a brilliantly lighted restaurant. Harry Bond jumped out, and Patty after him. I was about to follow when I felt a detaining hand upon my arm, and Bertie called out to Bond:

"I've changed my mind, Bond. I'll be hanged if I care to take Miss Ascough into that place."

Bond was angry, and demanded to know why Bertie had told him to order supper for four. He said he had called the place up from the theatre. I thought that queer. How could they have known I would go, since I had not decided till the last minute?

"Never mind," said Bertie. "I'll fix it up with you later. Go on in without us. It's all right."

Harry and Patty laughed, and, arm-in-arm, they went into the restaurant. All the time Bertie had kept a hand on my arm. I was too surprised and disappointed to utter a word, and after he had again tucked the rug about me, he said gently:

"I wouldn't take a sweet little girl like you into such a place, and that Patty isn't a fit person for you to associate with."

I said:

"You must think I'm awfully good."

I was disappointed and hungry.

"Yes, I do think so," he said gravely.

"Well, I'm not," I declared. "Besides, I'm going to be an actress, and actresses can do lots of things other people get shocked about. Mr. Davis says they are privileged to be unconventional."

"You, an actress!" he exclaimed. He said the word as if it were something disgraceful, like Ada might have said it.

"Yes," I returned. "I'll die if I can't be one."

"Whatever put such an idea in your head. You're just a refined, innocent, sweet, adorable little girl, far too sweet and pure and lovely to live such a dirty life."

He was leaning over me in the sleigh, and holding my hand under the fur robe. I thought to myself: "Neither St. Vidal nor Colonel Stevens would make love as thrillingly as he can, and he's certainly the handsomest person I've ever seen."

I felt his arm going about my waist, and his young face come close to mine. I knew he was going to kiss me, and I had never been kissed before. I became agitated and frightened. I twisted around and pulled away from him so that despite his efforts to reach my lips his mouth grazed, instead, my ear. Much as I really liked it, I said with as much hauteur as I could command:

"Sir, you have no right to do that. How dare you?"

He drew back, and replied coldly:

"I beg your pardon, I'm sure. I did not mean to offend you."

He hadn't offended me at all, and I was debating how on earth I was to let him know he hadn't, and at the same time keep him at the "proper distance" as Ada would say, when we stopped in front of our house. He helped me out, and lifting his hat loftily, was bidding me good-bye when I said shyly:

"M-Mr. Bertie, you—you d-didn't offend me."

Instantly he moved up to me and eagerly seized my hand. His face looked radiant, and I did think him the most beautiful man I had ever seen. With a boyish chuckle, he said:

"I'm coming to see you to-morrow night. May I?"

I nodded, and then I said:

"You mustn't mind our house. We're awfully poor people." I wanted to prepare him. He laughed boyishly at that and said:

"Good heavens, that's nothing. So are most of my folks—poor as church mice. As far as that goes, I'm jolly poor myself. Haven't a red cent except what the governor sends out to me. I'm going to see *you* anyway, and not your house."

He looked back at the driver whose head was all muffled up under his fur collar. Then he said:

"Will you give me that kiss now?"

I returned faintly:

"I c-can't. I think Ada's watching from the window."

He looked up quickly.

"Who's Ada?"

"My sister. She watches me like a hawk."

"Don't blame her," he said softly, and then all of a sudden he asked:

"Do you believe in love at first sight?"

"Yes," I answered. "Do you?"

"Well, I didn't—till to-night, but, by George, I do—now!"

X

I AM NOT LIKELY TO FORGET THAT FIRST call of Reginald Bertie upon me. I had thought about nothing else, and, in fact, had been preparing all day.

I fixed over my best dress and curled my hair. I cleaned all of the lower floor of our house, and dusted the parlor and polished up the few bits of furniture, and tried to cover up the worn chairs and horsehair sofa.

Every one of the children had promised to "be good," and I had bribed them all to keep out of sight.

Nevertheless, when the front doorbell rang that evening, to my horror, I heard the wild, noisy scampering of my two little brothers down the stairs, racing to see which should be the first to open the door; and trotting out from the dining-room right into the hall came Kathleen, aged three, and Violet, four and a half. They had been eating bread and molasses and had smeared it all over their faces and clothes, and they stood staring solemnly at Mr. Bertie as though they had never seen a man before. On the landing above, looking over the banister, and whispering and giggling, were Daisy, Lottie and Nellie.

Oh, how ashamed I felt that he should see all those dirty, noisy children. He stood there by the door, staring about him, with a look of amazement and amusement on his face; and, as he paused, the baby crawled in on hands and knees. She had a meat bone in her hand, and she squatted right down at his feet, and while staring up at him, wide-eyed, she went right on loudly sucking on that awful bone.

My face was burning, and I felt that I never could live down our family. Suddenly he burst out laughing. It was a boyish, infectious laugh, which was quickly caught up and mocked and echoed by those fiendish little brothers of mine.

"Are there any more?" he demanded gaily. "My word! They are like little steps and stairs."

I said:

"How do you do, Mr. Bertie?"

He gave me a quizzical glance, and said in a low voice:

"What's the matter with calling me 'Reggie?'"

Nora had run down the stairs and now, to my intense relief, I could hear her coaxing the children to come away, and she would tell them a story. Nora was a wonderful story-teller, and the children would listen to her by the hour. So would all the neighbors' children. I had told her that if she kept the children out of sight I would give her a piece of ribbon on which she had set her heart. So she was keeping her word, and presently I had the satisfaction of watching her go off with the baby on one arm, Kathleen and Violet holding to her other hand and skirt, and the boys in the rear.

Mr. Bertie, or "Reggie," as he said I was to call him, followed me into the "parlor." It was a room we seldom used in winter on account of the cold, but I had coaxed dear papa to help me clean out the fireplace—the only way it was heated—our Canadian houses did not have furnaces in those days—and the boys had brought me in some wood from the shed. So, at least, we had a cheerful fire crackling away in the grate, and although our furniture was old, it did not look so bad. Besides he didn't seem to notice anything except me, for as soon as we got inside he seized my hands and said:

"Give you my word, I've been thinking about you ever since last night."

Then he pulled me up toward him, and said:

"I'm going to get that kiss to-night."

Just then in came mama and Ada, and feeling awfully embarrassed and confused, I had to introduce him. Mama only stayed a moment, but Ada settled down with her crochet work by the lamp. She never worked in the parlor on other nights, but she sat there all of that evening, with her eye on Mr. Bertie and occasionally saying something brief and sarcastic. Mama said, as she was going out:

"I'll send papa right down to see Mr. Bertie. He looks so much like papa's brother who died in India. Besides, papa always likes to meet anyone from home."

Papa came in later, and he and Mr. Bertie found much to talk about. They had lived in the same places in England, and even found they knew some mutual friends and relatives. Papa's sisters were all famous sportswomen and hunters. One was the amateur tennis champion, and, of course, Mr. Bertie had heard of her.

Then papa inquired what he was doing in Montreal, and Bertie said he was studying law, and hoped to pass his finals in about eight months.

Then, he added that as soon as he could get together a fair practice, he expected to marry and settle down in Montreal. When he said that, he looked directly at me, and I blushed foolishly, and Ada coughed significantly and sceptically.

I really didn't get a chance to talk to him all evening, and even when he was going I could hardly say good-bye to him for mama came back with Daisy and Nellie, the two girls next to me, and what with Ada and papa there besides and everybody wishing him good-bye and mama inviting him to call again, I found myself almost in the background. He smiled, however, at me over mama's head, and he said, while shaking hands with her:

"I'll be delighted. May I come—er—to-morrow night?"

I saw Ada glance at mama, and I knew what was in their minds. Were they to be forced to go through this all again? The dressing up, the suppressing of the children, the using of the unused parlor, the burning of our fuel in the fireplace, etc. Papa, however, said warmly:

"By all means. I've some pretty good sketches of Macclesfield I'd like to show you."

"That will be charming," said my caller and, with a smile and bow that included us all, he was gone.

I did not get that kiss after all, and I may as well confess I was disappointed.

ME

A BOOK OF REMEMBRANCE

ONOTO WATANNA (WINNIFRED EATON)

I

IT WAS A COLD, BLIZZARDY DAY IN THE MONTH of March when I left Quebec, and
my weeping, shivering relatives made an anxious, melancholy group about my
departing train. I myself cried a bit, with my face pressed against the window;
but I was seventeen, my heart was light, and I had not been happy at home.

My father was an artist, and we were very poor. My mother had been a
tight-rope dancer in her early youth. She was an excitable, temperamental crea-
ture from whose life all romance had been squeezed by the torturing experience
of bearing sixteen children. Moreover, she was a native of a far-distant land, and
I do not think she ever got over the feeling of being a stranger in Canada.

Time was when my father, a young and ardent adventurer (an English-Irish-
man) had wandered far and wide over the face of the earth. The son of rich
parents, he had sojourned in China and Japan and India in the days when few
white men ventured into the Orient. But that was long ago.

This story is frankly of myself, and I mention these few facts merely in the
possibility of their proving of some psychological interest later; also they may ex
plain why it was possible for a parent to allow a young girl of seventeen to leave
her home with exactly ten dollars in her purse (I do not think my father knew
just how much money I did have) to start upon a voyage to the West Indies!

In any event, the fact remains that I had overruled my father's weak and
absentminded objections and my mother's exclamatory ones, and I had accepted
a position in Jamaica, West Indies, to work for a little local newspaper called
The Lantern.

It all came about through my having written at the age of sixteen a crude,
but exciting, story which a kindly friend, the editor of a Quebec weekly paper,
actually accepted and published.

386

I had always secretly believed there were the strains of genius somewhere hidden in me; I had always lived in a little dream world of my own, wherein, beautiful and courted, I moved among the elect of the earth. Now I had given vivid proof of some unusual power! I walked on air. The world was rose-colored; nay, it was golden.

With my story in my hand, I went to the office of a family friend. I had expected to be smiled upon and approved, but also lectured and advised. My friend, however, regarded me speculatively.

"I wonder," said he, "whether you couldn't take the place of a girl out in Jamaica who is anxious to return to Canada, but is under contract to remain there for three years."

The West Indies! I had heard of the land somewhere, probably in my school geography. I think it was associated in my mind in some way with the fairy-stories I read. Nevertheless, with the alacrity and assurance of youth I cried out that of course I would go.

"It's a long way off," said my friend, dubiously, "and you are very young."

I assured him earnestly that I should grow, and as for the distance, I airily dismissed that objection as something too trivial to consider. Was I not the daughter of a man who had been back and forth to China no fewer than eighteen times, and that during the perilous period of the Tai-ping Rebellion? Had not my father made journeys from the Orient in the old-fashioned sailing-vessels, being at sea a hundred-odd days at a time? What could not his daughter do?

Whatever impression I made upon this agent of the West Indian newspaper must have been fairly good, for he said he would write immediately to Mr. Campbell, the owner of *The Lantern*, who, by the way, was also a Canadian, and recommend me.

I am not much of a hand at keeping secrets, but I did not tell my parents. I had been studying short hand for some time, and now I plunged into that harder than ever, for the position was one in which I could utilize stenography.

It was less than two weeks later when our friend came to the house to report that the West Indian editor had cabled for me to be sent at once.

I was the fifth girl in our family to leave home. I suppose my father and mother had become sadly accustomed to the departing of the older children to try their fortunes in more promising cities than Quebec; but I was the first to leave home for a land as distant as the West Indies, though two of my sisters had gone to the United States. Still, there remained a hungry, crushing brood of little ones younger than I. With what fierce joy did I not now look forward to getting away at last from that same noisy, tormenting brood, for whom it had been my particular and detested task to care! So my father and mother put no obstacle in the way of my going. I remember passionately threatening to "run away" if they did.

My clothes were thick and woolen. I wore a red knitted toque, with a tassel that wagged against my cheek. My coat was rough and hopelessly Canadian. My dress a shapeless bag belted in at the waist. I was not beautiful to look at, but I had a bright, eager face, black and shining eyes, and black and shining hair. My cheeks were as red as a Canadian apple. I was a little thing, and, like my mother, foreign-looking. I think I had the most acute, inquiring, and eager mind of any girl of my age in the world.

A man on the train who had promised my father to see me as far as my boat did so. When we arrived in New York he took me there in a carriage the first carriage in which I had ever ridden in my life!

I had a letter to the captain, in whose special charge I was to be, that my Jamaica employer had written. So I climbed on board the *Atlas*. It was about six in the morning, and there were not many people about just a few sailors washing the decks. I saw, however, a round-faced man in a white cap, who smiled at me broadly. I decided that he was the captain. So I went up to him and presented my letter, addressing him as "Captain Hollowell." He held his sides and laughed at me, and another man this one was young and blond and very good-looking; at least so he seemed to the eyes of seventeen came over to inquire the cause of the merriment. Greatly to my mortification, I learned from the new arrival that the man I had spoken to was not the captain, but the cook. He himself was Mr. Marsden, the purser, and he was prepared to take care of me until Captain Hollowell arrived.

The boat would not sail for two hours, so I told Mr. Marsden that I guessed I'd take a walk in New York. He advised me strenuously not to, saying that I might "get lost." I scorned his suggestion. What, *I* get lost? I laughed at the idea. So I went for my "walk in New York."

I kept to one street, the one at the end of which my boat lay. It was an ugly, dirty, noisy street, noisy even at that early hour, for horrible-looking trucks rattled over the cobblestoned road, and there were scores of people hurrying in every direction. Of the streets of New York I had heard strange, wonderful, and beautiful tales; but as I trotted along, I confess I was deeply disappointed and astonished. I think I was on Canal Street, or another of the streets of lower New York.

I was not going to leave the United States, however, without dropping a bit of my ten dollars behind me. So I found a store, in which I bought some post cards, a lace collar, and some ribbon pink. When I returned to the boat I possessed, instead of ten dollars, just seven. However, this seemed a considerable sum to me, and I assured myself that on the boat itself, of course, one could not spend money.

I was standing by the rail watching the crowds on the wharf below. Everyone on board was saying good-by to someone else, and people were waving and calling to one another. Everybody seemed happy and excited and gay. I felt suddenly very little and forlorn. I alone had no one to bid me good-by, to wave to me, and to bring me flowers. I deeply pitied myself, and I suppose my eyes were full of tears when I turned away from the rail as the boat pulled out.

The blond young purser was watching me, and now he came up cheerfully and began to talk, pointing out things to me in the harbor as the boat moved along. He had such nice blue eyes and shining white teeth, and his smile was quite the most winning that I had ever seen. Moreover, he wore a most attractive uniform. I forgot my temporary woes. He brought me his "own special" deck chair, at least he said it was his, and soon I was comfortably ensconced in it, my feet wrapped about with a warm rug produced from somewhere also his. I felt a sense of being under his personal charge. A good part of the morning he managed to remain near me, and when he did go off among the other passengers, he took the trouble to explain to me that it was to attend to his duties.

I decided that he must have fallen in love with me. The thought delightfully warmed me. True, nobody had ever been in love with me before. I was the Ugly Duckling of an otherwise astonishingly good-looking family. Still, I was sure I recognized the true signs of love (had I not in dreams and fancies already been the heroine in a hundred princely romances?), and I forthwith began to wonder what life as the wife of a sailor might be like.

At dinner-time, however, he delivered me, with one of his charming smiles, to a portly and important personage who proved to be the real captain. My place at table was to be at his right side. He was a red-faced, jovial, mighty-voiced Scotchman. He called me a "poor little lassie" as soon as he looked at me. He explained that my West Indian employer (also a Scotch-Canadian) was his particular friend, and that he had promised to take personal care of me upon the voyage. He hoped Marsden, in his place, had looked after me properly, as he had been especially as signed by him to do. I, with a stifling lump of hurt vanity and pride in my throat, admitted that he had.

Then he was not in love with me, after all!

I felt cruelly unhappy as I stole out on deck after dinner. I disdained to look for that special deck chair my sailor had said I could have all for my own, and instead I sat down in the first one at hand.

Ugh! how miserable I felt! I suppose, said I to myself, that it was I who was the one to fall in love, fool that I was! But I had no idea one felt so wretched even when in love. Besides, with all my warm Canadian clothes, I felt chilly and shivery.

A hateful, sharp-nosed little man came poking around me. He looked at me with his eyes snapping, and coughed and rumbled in his throat as if getting ready to say something disagreeable to me. I turned my back toward him, pulled the rug about my feet, closed my eyes, and pretended to go to sleep. Then he said:

"Say, excuse me, but you've got my chair and rug."

I sat up. I was about to retort that "first come, first served" should be the rule, when out on deck came my friend Marsden. In a twinkling he appeared to take in the situation, for he strode quickly over to me, and, much to my indignation, took me by the arm and helped me to rise, saying that my chair was "over here."

I was about to reply in as haughty and rebuking a tone as I could command when I was suddenly seized with a most frightful surge of nausea. With my good-looking blond sailor still holding me by the arm, and murmuring something that sounded both laughing and soothing, I fled over to the side of the boat.

II

FOR FOUR DAYS I NEVER LEFT MY STATE-ROOM. "A sea-voyage is an inch of hell," says an old proverb of my mother s land, and to this proverb I most heartily assented.

An American girl occupied the "bunk" over mine, and shared with me the diminutive state-room. She was even sicker than I, and being sisters in great misery, a sweet sympathy grew up between us, so that under her direction I chewed and sucked on the sourest of lemons, and undermine she swallowed lumps of ice, a suggestion made by my father.

On the second day I had recovered somewhat, and so was able to wait upon and assist her a bit. Also. I found in her a patient and silent listener (Heaven knows she could not be otherwise, penned up as she was in that narrow bunk), and I told her all about the glorious plans and schemes I had made for my famous future; also I brought forth from my bag numerous poems and stories, and these I poured into her deaf ears in a voluble stream as she lay shaking and moaning in her bunk.

It had been growing steadily warmer so warm, in deed, that I felt about the room to ascertain whether there were some heating-pipes running through it.

On the fourth day my new friend sat up in her bunk and passionately went "on strike." She said:

"Say, I wish you'd quit reading me all that stuff. I know it's lovely, but I've got a headache, and honestly I can't for the life of me take an interest in your poems and stories."

Deeply hurt, I folded my manuscripts. She leaned out of her berth and caught at my arm.

"Don't be angry," she said. "I didn't mean to hurt you."

I retorted with dignity that I was not in the slightest degree hurt. Also I quoted a proverb about casting one's pearls before swine, which sent her into such a peal of laughter that I think it effectually cured her of her lingering remnants of seasickness. She jumped out of her bunk, squeezed me about the waist, and said:

"You re the funniest girl I've ever met a whole vaudeville act." She added, however, that she liked me, and as she had her arm about me, I came down from my high horse, and averred that her affection was reciprocated. She then told me her name and learned mine. She was bookkeeper in a large department store. Her health had been bad, and she had been saving for a long time for this trip to the West Indies.

We decided that we were now well enough to go on deck. As I dressed, I saw her watching me with a rather wondering and curious expression. My navy-blue serge dress was new, and although it was a shapeless article, the color at least was becoming, and with the collar purchased in New York, I felt that I looked very well. I asked her what she thought of my dress. She said evasively:

"Did you make it yourself?"

I said:

"No; mama did."

"Oh," said she.

I didn't just like the sound of that "Oh," so I asked her aggressively if she didn't think my dress was nice. She answered:

"I think you've got the prettiest hair of any girl I ever knew."

My hair did look attractive, and I was otherwise quite satisfied with my appearance. What is more, I was too polite to let her know what I thought of her appearance. Although it was March, she, poor thing, had put on a flimsy little muslin dress. Of course it was suffocatingly hot in our close little state-room, but, still, that seemed an absurd dress to wear on a boat. I offered to lend her a knitted woolen scarf that mama had made me to throw over her shoulders, but she shook her head, and we went up on deck.

To my unutterable surprise, I found a metamorphosis had taken place on deck during my four days absence. Everyone appeared to be dressed in thin white clothes; even the officers were all in white duck. Moreover, the very atmosphere had changed. It was as warm and sultry as midsummer, and people were sipping iced drinks and fanning themselves!

Slowly it dawned upon me that we were sailing toward a tropical land. In a hazy sort of way I had known that the West Indies was a warm country, but I had not given the matter much thought. My father, who had been all over the world, had left my outfit ting to mama and me (we had so little with which to buy the few extra things mama, who was more of a child than I, got me!), and I had come away with clothes fit for a land which often registered as low as twenty-four degrees below zero!

My clothes scorched me; so did my burning shame. I felt that everyone's eyes were bent upon me.

Both Captain Hollowell and Mr. Marsden greeted me cordially, expressing delight at seeing me again, but although the captain said (in a big, booming voice that everyone on deck could hear) that I looked like a nice, blooming peony, I sensitively fancied I detected a laugh beneath his words.

Tragedies should be measured according to their effects. Trifles prick us in youth as sharply as the things that ought to count. I sensitively suffered in my pride as much from the humiliation of wearing my heavy woolen clothes as I physically did from the burden of their weight and heat. I was sure that I presented a ridiculous and hideous spectacle. I felt that everyone was laughing at me. It was insufferable; it was torture.

As soon as I could get away from that joking captain, who would keep patting me on the head, and that purser, who was always smiling and showing his white teeth, I ran down to my room, which I had hoped to see as little of as possible for the rest of the voyage.

I sat down on the only chair and began to cry. The ugly little room, with its one miserable window, seemed a wretched, intolerable prison. I could hear the soughing of the waves outside, and a wide streak of blue sky was visible through my port-hole window. The moving of the boat and the thud of the machinery brought home to me strongly the fact that I was being carried resistlessly farther and farther away from the only home I had ever known, and which, alas! I had yearned to leave.

It was unbearably hot, and I took off my woolen dress. I felt that I would never go on deck again; yet how was I going to endure it down here in this little hole? I was thinking miserably about that when my room-mate came back.

"Well, here you are!" he exclaimed. "I've been looking for you everywhere! Now what's the matter?"

"N-nothing," I said; but despite myself the sob would come.

"You poor kid!" she said. "I know what's the matter with you. I don't know what your folks were thinking of when they sent you off to the West Indies in Canadian clothes. Are they all as simple as you there? But now don't you worry. Here, I've got six pretty nice-looking shirt-waists, besides my dresses, and you're welcome to any of them you want. You're just about my size. I'm thirty-four."

"Thirty-four!" I exclaimed, astonished even in the midst of my grief. "Why, I thought you were only about twenty."

"Bust! Bust!" she cried, laughing, and got her waists out and told me to try them on. I gave her a kiss, a big one, I was so delighted; but I insisted that I could not borrow her waists. I would, however, buy some of them if she would sell them.

She said that was all right, and she sold me three of them at a dollar-fifty each. They fitted me finely. I never felt happier in my life than when I put on one of those American-made shirt-waists. They were made sailor-fashion, with wide turnover collars and elbow sleeves; with a red silk tie in front, and with my blue cloth skirt, I really did look astonishingly nice, and, anyway, cool and neat. The fact that I now possessed only two dollars and fifty cents in the world gave me not the slightest worry, and when I ran out of my room, humming, and up the stairs and bang into the arms of Captain Hollowell, he did not say this time that I looked like a peony, but that, "By George!" I looked like a nice Canadian rose.

III

D O YOU KNOW," SAID MY ROOM-MATE on the night before we reached Jamaica, "that that four-fifty you paid me for those waists just about covers my tips."

"Tips?" I repeated innocently. "What are tips?"

She gave me a long, amazed look, her mouth wide-open.

"Good heavens!" at last she said, "where have you lived all of your life?"

"In Quebec," I said honestly.

"And you never heard of tips people giving tips to waiters and servants?"

I grew uncomfortably red under her amused and amazed glance. In the seven days of that voyage my own extraordinary ignorance had been daily brought home to me. I now said lamely:

"Well, we had only one servant that I can ever re member, a woman named Sung-Sung whom papa brought from China; but she was more like one of our family, a sort of slave. We never gave her tips, or whatever you call it."

Did I not know, pursued my American friend, that people gave extra mon- ey that is, "tips" to waiters at restaurants and hotels when they got through eating a meal?

I told her crossly and truthfully that I had never been in a hotel or restau- rant in all my life. She threw up her hands, and pronounced me a vast object of pity. She then fully enlightened me as to the exact meaning of the word "tips," and left me to calculate painfully upon a bit of paper the division of two dollars and fifty cents among five people; to wit, stewardesses, cabin boys, waiters, etc.

I didn't tell her that that was the last of my money that two-fifty. However, I did not expend any thought upon the subject of what was to become of me when I arrived in Jamaica sans a single cent.

We brought our bags and belongings out on deck before the boat docked next day. Everyone was crowded against the rails, watching the approaching land.

A crowd seemed to be swarming on the wharves, awaiting our boat. As we came nearer, I was amazed to find that this crowd was made up almost entirely of negroes. We have few negroes in Canada, and I had seen only one in all my life. I remember an older sister had shown him to me in church he was pure black and told me he was the "Bogy man," and that he'd probably come around to see me that night. I was six. I never took my eyes once from his face during the service, and I have never forgotten that face.

It was, therefore, with a genuine thrill of excitement and fear that I looked down upon that vast sea of upturned black and brown faces. Never will I forget that first impression of Jamaica. Everywhere I looked were negroes men and women and children, some half naked, some with bright handkerchiefs knot- ted about their heads, some gaudily attired, some dressed in immaculate white duck, just like the people on the boat.

People were saying good-by, and many had already gone down the gang- plank. Several women asked me for my address, and said they did not want to lose me. I told them I did not know just where I was going. I expected Mr. Campbell to meet me.

As Mr. Campbell had not come on board, however, and as Captain Hol- lowell and Mr. Marsden seemed to have forgotten my existence in the great rush of arrival, I, too, at last descended the gang-plank. I found myself one of that miscellaneous throng of colored and white people.

A number of white men and women were hurrying about meeting and welcoming expected passengers, who were soon disposed of in various vehicles.

Soon not one of the boat's passengers remained, even my room-mate being one of a party that climbed aboard a bus marked, "The Crystal Springs Hotel."

I was alone on that Jamaica wharf, and no one had come to claim me!

It was getting toward evening, and the sky in the west was as red as blood. I sat down on my bag and waited. Most of the people left on the dock were laborers who were engaged in unloading the ship's cargo. Women with heavy loads on their heads, their hands on their shaking hips, and chattering in a high singsong dialect (I didn't recognize it for English at first!), passed me. Some of them looked at me curiously, and one, a terrifying, pock-marked crone, said something to me that I could not understand.

I saw the sun slipping down in the sky, but it was still as bright and clear as mid-day. Sitting alone on that Jamaica wharf, I scarcely saw the shadows deepening as I looked out across the Caribbean Sea, which shone like a jewel under the fading light. I forgot my surroundings and my anxiety at the failure of my employer to meet me; I felt no fear, just a vague sort of enchantment and interest in this new land I had discovered.

But I started up screaming when I felt a hand on my shoulder, and looking up in the steadily deepening twilight, I saw a smiling face approach my own, and the face was black!

I fled toward the boat, crying out wildly:

"Captain Hollowell! O Captain Hollowell!"

I left my little bag behind me. Fear lent wings to my feet, and I kept crying out to Captain Hollowell as I ran up that gang-plank, mercifully still down. At the end of it was my dear blond purser, and right into his arms unhesitatingly I ran. He kept saying: "Well! well! well!" and he took me to Captain Hollowell, who swore dreadfully when he learned that Mr. Campbell had not met me. Then my purser went to the dock wharf to get my bag, and to "skin the hide off that damned black baboon "who had frightened me.

I ate dinner with Captain Hollowell and the officers of the *Atlas* that night, the last remaining passenger on the boat. After dinner, accompanied by the captain and the purser, I was taken by carriage to the office of *The Lantern*.

I don't know what Captain Hollowell said to Mr. Campbell before I was finally called in, for I had been left in the outer office. Their voices were loud and angry, and I thought they were quarreling. I devoutly hoped it was not over me. I was tired and sleepy. In fact, when Captain Hollowell motioned to me to come in, I remember rubbing my eyes, and he put his arm about me and told me not to cry.

In a dingy office, with papers and books scattered about in the most be-wildering disorder, at a long desk-table, likewise piled with books and journals and papers, sat an old man who looked exactly like the pictures of Ibsen. He was sitting all crumpled up, as it were, in a big arm-chair; but as I came forward he sat up straight. He stared at me so long, and with such an expression of amazement, that I became uneasy and embarrassed. I remember holding on tight to Captain Hollowell's sleeve on one side and Mr. Marsden's on the other. And then at last a single sentence came from the lips of my employer. It came explosively, despairingly:

"My God!" said the owner of *The Lantern*.

It seems that our Quebec friend had been assigned to obtain for *The Lantern* a mature and experienced journalist. Mr. Campbell had expected a woman of the then approved, if feared, type of bluestocking, and behold a baby had been dropped into his lap!

The captain and Marsden had departed. I sat alone with that old man who looked like Ibsen, and who stared at me as if I were some freak of nature. He had his elbows upon his desk, and his chin propped up in the cup of his hands. He began to ask me questions, after he had literally stared me down and out of countenance, and I sat there before him, twisting my handkerchief in my hand.

"How old are you?"

"Seventeen. I mean I'm going on eighteen." Eighteen was, in fact, eleven months off.

"Have you ever worked before?"

"I've written things." After a silent moment, during which he glared at me more angrily than ever, he demanded:

"What have you written?"

"Poetry," I said, and stopped because he said again in that lost voice, "My God!"

"What else?"

"I had a story published in *The Star* I said. "I've got it here, if you'd like to see it."

He made a motion of emphatic dissent.

"What else have you done?"

"I taught myself shorthand," I said, "and I can take dictation as fast as you can talk."

He looked frankly skeptical and in no wise impressed.

"How can you do that if you've had no experience as a stenographer?"

"I got a shorthand book," I said eagerly. "It's not at all hard to teach yourself after you learn the rudiments. My sister showed me that. She's secretary to the Premier of Canada. As soon as I had learned shorthand, I acquired practice and speed by going to church and prayer-meetings and taking down sermons."

After a moment he said grudgingly:

"Not a bad idea." And then added, "What do you think you are going to do here?"

"Write for your paper," I said as conciliatingly as I could.

"What?" he inquired curiously.

"Why anything poetry

He waved his hand in such a dismissing manner that I got up, though it was my poetry, not I, he wished to be rid of just then. I went nearer to him.

"I know you don't want me," I said, "and I don't want to stay. I'm sorry I came. I wouldn't if I had known that this was a hot, beastly old country where nearly everybody is black. If you'll just get me back to the boat, I know Captain Hollowell will let me go back with him, even if I have n t the money for my fare."

"What about the money I paid for you to come here?" he snarled. "Think I'm going to lose that?"

I did not answer him. I felt enervated, homesick, miserable, and tired. He got up presently, limped over to another table, he was lame, poured a glass of water, brought it to me with a big fan, and said gruffly, "Sit!"

The act, I don't know why, touched me. In a dim way I began to appreciate his position. He was a lame old man running a fiery, two-sheet little newspaper in this tropical land far from his native Canada. There was no staff, and, indeed, none of the ordinary appurtenances of a newspaper office. He employed only one able assistant, and as he could not get such a person in Jamaica and could not afford to pay a man s salary, being very loyal to Canada, he had been accustomed to send there for bright and expert young women reporters to do virtually all the work of running his newspaper. Newspaper women are not plentiful in Canada. The fare to Jamaica is, or was then, about $55. Mr. Campbell must have turned all these things over in his mind as he looked at this latest product of his native land, a green, green girl of seven teen, whose promise that she would "look older next day," when her "hair was done up," carried little re assurance as to her intelligence or ability.

He did a lot of "cussing" of our common friend in Canada. Finally he said that he would take me over to the Myrtle Bank Hotel, where accommodations had been arranged for me, and we could talk the matter over in the morning.

While he was getting his stick and hat, the latter a green-lined helmet, I couldn't resist looking at some of his books. He caught me doing this, and asked me gruffly if I had ever read anything. I said:

"Yes, Dickens, George Eliot, and Sir Walter Scott; and I've read Huxley and Darwin, and lots of books on astronomy to my father, who is very fond of that subject." As he made no comment, nor seemed at all impressed by my erudition, I added proudly: "My father's an Oxford man, and a descendant of the family of Sir Isaac Newton."

There was some legend to this effect in our family. In fact, the greatness of my father s people had been a sort of fairy-story with us all, and we knew that it was his marriage with mama that had cut him off from his kindred. My Jamaica employer, however, showed no interest in my distinguished ancestry. He took me roughly by the arm, and half leaning upon, half leading me, hobbled with me out into the dark street.

It was about nine o'clock. As we approached the hotel, which was only a short distance from the office of *The Lantern*, it pleased me as a happy omen that somewhere within those fragrant, moonlit gardens a band began to play most beautifully.

Mr. Campbell took me to the room of the girl whose place I was to take, and who was also from Quebec. She had already gone to bed, but she rose to let me in. Mr. Campbell merely knocked hard on the door and said:

"Here's Miss Ascough. You should have met her," and angrily shoved me in, so it seemed to me.

Miss Foster, her hair screwed up in curl-papers, after looking at me only a moment, said in a tired, complaining voice, like that of a sick person, that I had better get to bed right away; and then she got into bed, and turned her face to the wall. I tried to draw her out a bit while undressing, but to all my questions she returned monosyllabic answers. I put out the light, and crept into bed beside her. The last thing she said to me, and very irritably, was:

"Keep to your own side of the bed."

I slept fairly well, considering the oppressiveness of the heat, but I awoke once when something buzzed against my face.

"What's that?" I cried, sitting up in bed.

She murmured crossly:

"Oh, for heaven s sake lie down! I haven't slept a wink for a century. You'll have to get used to Jamaica bugs and scorpions. They ought to have screens in the windows!"

After that I slept with the sheet over my head.

IV

I WAS AWAKENED AT SIX THE following morning. A strange, singsong voice called into the room:

"Marnin, missee! Heah's your coffee."

I found Miss Foster up and dressed. She was sit ting at a table drinking coffee. She put up the shade and let the light in. Then she came over to the bed, where the maid had set the tray. I was looking at what I supposed to be my breakfast. It consisted of a cup of black coffee and a single piece of dry toast.

"You'd better drink your coffee," said Miss Foster, wearily. "It will sustain you for a while."

I got a good look at her, standing by my bed. The yellowness of her skin startled me, and I wondered whether it could be possible that she, too, was "colored." Then I remembered that she was from my home. Moreover, her eyes were a pale blue, and her hair a light, nondescript brown. She had a peevish expression, even now while she made an effort at friendliness. She sat down on the side of my bed, and while I drank my coffee and nibbled my piece of toast she told me a few things about the country.

Jamaica, she said, was the beastliest country on the face of the earth. Though for a few months its climate was tolerable, the rest of the year it was almost unbearable. What with the crushing heat and the dirty, drizzling rain that followed, and fell without ceasing for months at a time, all ambition, all strength, all hope were slowly knocked out of one. There were a score of fevers, each one as bad as the others. She was suffering from one now. That was why she was going home. She was young, so she said, but she felt like an old woman. She pitied me, she declared, for what was before me, and said Campbell had no right to bring healthy young girls from Canada without first telling them what they were coming up against.

I put in here that perhaps I should fare better. I said:

"I'm almost abnormally healthy and strong, you know, even if I look thin. I'm the wiry kind."

She sniffed at that, and then said, with a shrug:

"Oh, well, maybe you will escape. I'm sure I wish you better luck than mine. But one thing's certain: you'll lose that Canadian complexion of yours all right."

My duties, she said, would be explained to me by Mr. Campbell himself, though she was going to stay over a day or two to help break me in. My salary would be ten dollars a week and free board and lodging at the Myrtle Bank Hotel. I told her of the slighting reception I had received at the hands of Mr. Campbell, and she said:

"Oh, well, he's a crank. You couldn't please him, no matter what you did." Then she added: "I don't see, anyhow, why he objected to you. Brains aren't so much needed in a position like this as legs and a constitution of iron."

As the day advanced, the heat encroached. Miss Foster sat fanning herself languidly by the window, looking out with a far-away expression. I told her about my clothes, and how mortified I was to find them so different from those of the others on the boat. She said:

"You can have all my clothes, if you want. They won't do for Canada."

That suggested a brilliant solution of my problem of how I was to secure immediately suitable clothes for Jamaica. I suggested that as she was going to Canada, she could have mine, and I would take hers. The proposition seemed to give her a sort of grim amusement. She looked over my clothes. She took the woolen underwear and heavy, hand-knitted stockings (that Sung-Sung had made for an older brother, and which had descended to me after two sisters had had them!), two woolen skirts, my heavy overcoat, and several other pieces.

She gave me a number of white muslin dresses, they seemed lovely to me, an evening gown with a real low neck, cotton underwear, hose, etc.

I put my hair up for the first time that morning. As I curled it a bit, this was not difficult to do. I simply rolled it up at the back and held the chignon in place with four bone hair-pins that she gave me. I put on one of her white muslin dresses but it was so long for me that we had to make a wide tuck in it. Then I wore a wide Leghorn hat, the only trimming of which was a piece of cream-colored mull twisted like a scarf about the crown.

I asked Miss Foster if I looked all right, and was suitably dressed, and she said grudgingly:

"Yes, you'll do. You re quite pretty. You'd better look out."

Asked to explain, she merely shrugged her shoulders and said:

"There's only a handful of white women here, you know. We don't count the tourists. You'll have all you can do to hold the men here at arm's length." "This last prospect by no means bothered me. I had the most decided and instinctive liking for the opposite sex.

The hotel was beautiful, built somewhat in the Spanish style, with a great inner court, and an arcade that ran under the building. Long verandas ran out

like piers on each side of the court, which was part of the wonderful garden that
extended to the shores of the Caribbean.

The first thing I saw as we came out from our room upon one of the long-
pier verandas was an enormous bird. It was sitting on the branch of a fantastic
and incredibly tall tree that was all trunk, and then burst into great fan-like
foliage at the top. Subsequently I learned that this was a cocoanut tree.

The proprietor of the hotel, who was dark, smiling, and deferential, came
up to be introduced to me, and I said, meaning to pay a compliment to his
country:

"You have fine-looking birds here."

He looked at me sharply and then snickered, as if he thought I were joking
about something.

"That's a scavenger," he said. "There are hundreds, thousands of them here
in Jamaica. Glad you like them."

I thought it an ugly name for a bird, but I said:

"It's a very interesting bird, I think."

Miss Foster pulled me along and said sharply that the birds were vultures.
They called them scavengers in Jamaica because they really acted as such. Every
bit of dirt and filth and refuse, she declared with dis gust, was thrown into the
streets, and devoured shortly by the scavengers. If a horse or animal died or was
killed, it was put into the street. Within a few minutes it had completely dis-
appeared, the scavengers having descended like flies upon its body. She darkly
hinted, moreover, that many a human corpse had met a similar fate. I acquired
a shuddering horror for that "interesting bird" then and there, I can tell you,
and I thought of the unscreened windows, and asked Miss Foster if they ever
had been known to touch living things. She shrugged her shoulders, which was
not reassuring.

Miss Foster took me into the hotel s great dining-room, which was like a
pleasant open conservatory, with great palms and plants everywhere. There we
had breakfast, for it seems coffee and toast were just an appetizer. I never be-
came used to Jamaica cooking. It was mushy, hot, and sweet.

After breakfast we reported at *The Lantern*, where Mr. Campbell, looking
even fiercer in the day, impatiently awaited us. He wished Miss Foster to take
me directly out to Government House and teach me my duties there, as the
Legislative Council was then in session. He mumbled off a lot of instructions
to. Miss Foster, ignoring me completely. His apparent contempt for me, and
his evident belief that there was no good to be expected from me, whetted
my desire to prove to him that I was not such a fool as I looked, or, rather, as
he seemed to think I looked. I listened intently to everything he said to Miss

Foster, but even so I received only a confused medley of "Bills attorney-general Representative So and So Hon. Mr. So and So," etc.

I carried away with me, however, one vivid instruction, and that was that it was absolutely necessary for *The Lantern* to have the good-will of the Hon. Mr. Burbank, whom we must support in everything. It seemed, according to Mr. Campbell, that there was some newspaper libel law that was being pressed in the House that, if passed, would bring the Jamaica press down to a pusillanimous condition.

Mr. Burbank was to fight this bill for the newspapers. He was, in fact, our representative and champion. *The Lantern*, in return, was prepared to support him in other measures that he was fathering. Miss Foster and I were to remember to treat him with more than common attention. I did not know, of course, that this meant in our newspaper references to him, and I made a fervent vow personally to win the favor of said Burbank.

We got into a splendid little equipage, upholstered in tan cloth and with a large tan umbrella top, which was lined with green.

We drove for several miles through a country remarkable for its beautiful scenery. It was a land of color. It was like a land of perpetual spring a spring that was ever green. I saw not a single shade that was dull. Even the trunks of the gigantic trees seemed to have a warm tone. The flowers were startlingly bright yellow, scarlet, and purple.

We passed many country people along the road. They moved with a sort of languid, swinging amble, as if they dragged, not lifted, their flat feet. Women carried on their heads enormous bundles and sometimes trays. How they balanced them so firmly was always a mystery to me, especially as most of them either had their hands on their hips, or, more extraordinary, carried or led children, and even ran at times. Asses, loaded on each side with produce, ambled along as draggingly as the natives.

Miss Foster made only three or four remarks during the entire journey. These are her remarks. They are curious taken altogether:

"This carriage belongs to Mr. Burbank. He sup plies all the vehicles, by the way, for the press."

"Those are the botanical gardens. Jamaica has Mr. Burbank to thank for their present excellent condition. Remember that."

"We are going by the Burbank plantation now. He has a place in Kingston, too, and a summer home in the mountains."

"If we beat that newspaper libel law, you'll have a chance to write all the funny things and rhymes you want about the mean sneaks who are trying to push it through."

Even during the long drive through the green country I had been insensibly affected by the ever-growing heat. In the long chamber of Government House, where the session was to be held, there seemed not a breath of air stirring. It was insufferably hot, though the place was virtually empty when we arrived. I had a shuddering notion of what it would be like when full.

Miss Foster was hustling about, getting "papers" and "literature" of various kinds, and as the legislators arrived, she chatted with some of them. She had left me to my own devices, and I did not know what to do with myself. I was much embarrassed, as everyone who passed into the place took a look at me. We were the only two girls in the House.

There was a long table in the middle of the room, at which the members of Parliament and the elected members had their seats, and there was a smaller table at one side for the press. I had remained by the door, awaiting Miss Foster s instructions. The room was rapidly beginning to fill. A file of black soldiers spread themselves about the room, standing very fine and erect against the walls. At the council table, on one side, were the Parliament members, Englishmen, every one of whom wore the conventional monocle. On the other side were the elected members, who were, without an exception, colored men. I was musing over this when a very large, stout, and handsome personage (he was a personage!) entered ponderously, followed by several younger men. Everyone in the room rose, and until he took his seat (in a big chair on a little elevated platform at the end of the room) they remained standing. This was his Excellency Sir Henry Drake, the Governor-General of Jamaica. The House was now in session.

By this time I experienced a natural anxiety to know what was to become of me. Surely I was not supposed to stand there by the door. Glancing across at the press table, I presently saw Miss Foster among the reporters. She was half standing, and beckoning to me to join her. Confused and embarrassed, I passed along at the back of one end of the council table, and was proceeding in the direction of the press table, when suddenly the room reverberated with loud cries from the soldiers of, "Order! order! order!"

I hesitated only a moment, ignorant of the fact that that call was directed against me, and, as I paused, I looked directly into the purpling face of the Governor of Jamaica. He had put on his monocle. His face was long and preternaturally solemn, but there was a queer, twisted smile about his mouth, and I swear that he winked at me through that monocle, which fell into his hand. I proceeded to my seat, red as a beet.

"Great guns!" whispered Miss Foster, dragging me down beside her, "you walked in front of the governor! You should have gone behind his chair. What will Mr. Campbell say when he knows you were called to order the first day! A fine reflection on *The Lantern*!" She added the last sentence almost bitterly.

What went on at that session I never in the world could have told. It was all like an incomprehensible dream. Black men, the elected members, rose, and long and eloquently talked in regard to some bill. White men (government) rose and languidly responded, sometimes with a sort of drawling good humor, sometimes satirically. I began to feel the effect of the oppressive atmosphere in a way I had not yet experienced. An unconquerable impulse to lay my head down upon the table and go to sleep seized upon me, and I could scarcely keep my eyes open. At last my head did fall back against the chair; my eyes closed. I did not exactly faint, but I succumbed slightly to the heat. I heard a voice whispering at my ear, for the proceedings went on, as if it were a common thing for a woman to faint in Government House.

"Drink this!" said the voice, and I opened my eyes and looked up into a fair, boyish face that was bending over mine. I drank that cool Jamaica kola, and recovered myself sufficiently to sit up again. Said my new friend:

"It'll be cooler soon. You'll get used to the climate, and if I were you, I wouldn't try to do any work to-day."

I said:

"I've got to learn. Miss Foster sails to-morrow, and after that"

"I'll show you after that," he said, and smiled reassuringly.

At one there was an adjournment for luncheon. I then became the center of interest, and was introduced by Miss Foster to the members of the press. Jamaica boasted three papers beside ours, and there were representatives at the Parliament s sessions from other West Indian islands. I was also introduced to several of the members, both black and white.

I went to luncheon with Miss Foster and two members of Parliament (white) and three reporters, one of them the young man who had given me the kola, and whose name was Verley Marchmont. He was an Englishman, the younger son in a poor, but titled, family. We had luncheon at a little inn hard by, and while there I made three engagements for the week. With one of the men I was to go to a polo match (Jamaica had a native regiment whose officers were English), with another I was to attend a ball in a lighthouse, and young Marchmont, who was only about eighteen, was to call upon me that evening.

At the end of the afternoon session, which was not quite so wearing, as it had grown cooler, I was introduced by Miss Foster to the governor s secretary, Lord George Fitzpatrick, who had been smiling at me from behind the governor s back most of the day. By him I was introduced to the governor, who seemed to regard me as a more or less funny curiosity, if I am to judge from his humorous expression. Lord George also introduced me to other government members, and he asked me if I liked candies. I said I did. He asked me if I played golf or rode horseback. I said I didn't, but I could learn, and he said he was a great teacher.

By this time I thought I had met everyone connected with the House, when suddenly I heard someone I think it was one of the reporters call out:

"Oh, all right, Mr. Burbank. I'll see to it."

Miss Foster was drawing me along toward the door. It was time to go. Our carriage was waiting for us. As we were going out, I asked her whether I had yet met Mr. Burbank, and she said she supposed so.

"I don't remember meeting him," I persisted, "and I want very specially to meet Mr. Burbank."

On the steps below us a man somewhat dudishly attired in immaculate white duck, and wearing a green-lined helmet, turned around and looked up at us. His face was almost pure black. His nose was large and somewhat hooked. I have subsequently learned that he was partly Hebrew. He had an enormous mouth, and teeth thickly set with gold. He wore gold-rimmed glasses with a chain, and these and his fine clothes gave a touch of distinction to his appearance. At least it made him stand out from the average colored man. As I spoke, I saw him look at me with a curious expression; then smiling, he held out his big hand.

"I am the Hon. Mr. Burbank," he said.

I was startled to find that this man I had been planning to cultivate was black. I do not know why, but as I looked down into that ingratiating face, I was filled with a sudden panic of almost instinctive fear, and although he held out his hand to me, I did not take it. For that I was severely lectured by Miss Foster all the way back. She reminded me that I could not afford to snub so powerful a Jamaican as Burbank, and that if I had the slightest feeling of race prejudice, I had better either kill it at once or clear out of Jamaica. She said that socially there was absolutely no difference between the white and colored people in Jamaica.

As a matter of fact, I had literally never even heard the expression "race prejudice" before, and I was as far from feeling it as any person in the world. It must be remembered that in Canada we do not encounter the problem of race. One color there is as good as another. Certainly people of Indian extraction are well thought of and esteemed, and my own mother was a foreigner. What should I, a girl who had never before been outside Quebec, and whose experience had been within the narrow confines of home and a small circle, know of race prejudice?

Vaguely I had a feeling that all men were equal as men. I do not believe it was in me to turn from a man merely because of his race, so long as he himself was not personally repugnant to me. I myself was dark and foreign-looking, but the blond type I adored. In all my most fanciful imaginings and dreams I had always been golden-haired and blue-eyed.

V

I GOT ON BETTER WITH MR. CAMPBELL after Miss Foster went. He told me it was necessary for us to keep on the right side of Mr. Burbank, who was one of the greatest magnates and philanthropists of Jamaica, but he took occasion to contradict some of Miss Foster s statements. It was not true, he said, that there was no social distinction between black and white in Jamaica. That was the general opinion of tourists in Jamaica, who saw only the surface of things, but as a matter of fact, though the richest people and planters were of colored blood; though they were invited to all the governor s parties and the various official functions; though they were in vast evidence at polo and cricket matches; though many of them were talented and cultivated, nevertheless, there was a fine line drawn between them and the native white people who counted for anything. This he wished me to bear in mind, so that while I should always act in such a way as never in the slightest to hurt or offend the feelings of the colored element, whose good-will was essential to *The Lantern*, I must retain my dignity and stoop to no familiarity which would bring me and *The Lantern* into disrepute with the white element, whose good-will was equally essential.

I think in less than a week my employer began grudgingly to approve of me; in about two weeks we were friends. His eyes no longer glared at me through his thick glasses. Once when I timidly proffered one of my "poems," those same fierce eyes actually beamed upon me. What is more, he published the poem!

Of course it was chiefly my work that won me favor with Mr. Campbell. I came back every day from Government House with accurate and intelligent reports of the debates. I wonder what Mr. Campbell would have said to me had he known that nearly all my first reports were written for me by young Verley Marchmont of *The Daily Call*, *The Lantern's* deadliest rival! For the life of me, I never could grasp the details of the debates clearly enough to report them coherently, and so young Marchmont obligingly "helped" me. However, these debates were only a part of my work, though at this time they constituted the chief of my duties.

For a young person in a hot country I was kept extremely busy. Even after my day's work was over I had to bustle about the hotel and dig up society notes and stories, or I had to attend meetings, functions, and parties of various kinds.

One morning after I had been on *The Lantern* about a week, Mr. Campbell handed me a list of my duties as an employee of *The Lantern*. Perhaps you would like to know exactly what they were:

1. To attend and report the debates of the Legislative Council when in session.
2. To report City Council proceedings.
3. To report court cases of interest to the public.
4. To keep posted on all matters of interest to Great Britain and Jamaica.
5. To make calls upon and interview at intervals His Excellency the Governor-General, the Colonial Secretary, the Commander of the Forces, the Attorney-General, and other Government officials.
6. To interview elected members when matters of interest demand it.
7. To interview prominent Americans or those who are conspicuous on account of great wealth.
8. To report political speeches.
9. To report races, cricket matches, polo, etc.
10. To represent *The Lantern* at social functions.
11. To visit stores, factories, etc., and to write a weekly advertising column.
12. To prepare semi-weekly a bright and entertaining woman's column, into which must be skillfully woven the names of Jamaica s society women.
13. To review books and answer correspondence.
14. To correct proof in the absence of the proof reader.
15. To edit the entire paper when sickness or absence of the editor prevents him from attending.

Mr. Campbell watched my face keenly as I read that list, and finally, when I made no comment, he prompted me with a gruff, "Well?" To which I replied, with a smile:

"I think what you want, Mr. Campbell, is a mental and physical acrobat."

"Do I understand from that," he thundered, "that you cannot perform these necessary duties?"

"On the contrary," I returned coolly, "I think that I can perform them all, one at a time; but you have left out one important item."

"Well, what?"

"Poetry," I said.

My answer tickled him immensely, and he burst into loud laughter.

"Got any about you?" he demanded. "I believe you have it secreted all over you."

I said:

"I've none of my own this morning, but here's a fine little verse I wish you'd top our editorial page with," and I handed him the following:

> For the cause that lacks assistance;
> For the wrong that needs resistance;
> For the future in the distance,
> And the good that we can do!

With such a motto, we felt called upon to be pugnacious and virtuous, and all of that session of Parliament our little sheet kept up a peppery fight for the rights of the people.

Mr. Campbell said that I looked strong and impudent enough to do anything, and when I retorted that I was not the least bit impudent, but, on the contrary, a dreamer, he said crossly:

"If that's the case, you'll be incompetent."

But I was a dreamer, and I was not incompetent.

It was all very well, however, to joke with Mr. Campbell about these duties. They were pretty hard just the same, and I was kept rushing from morning till night. There was always a pile of work waiting me upon my return from Government House, and I could see that Mr. Campbell intended gradually to shift the major part of the work entirely upon me.

The unaccustomed climate, the intense heat, and the work, which I really loved all contributed to make me very tired by evening, when my duties were by no means ended.

Miss Foster's warning that I should have to keep the men at arm's-length occasionally recurred to me, but I dare say she exaggerated the matter. It is true that considerable attention was directed at me when I first came to Jamaica, and I received no end of flowers and candies and other little gifts; but my work was so exacting and ceaseless that it occupied all of my time. I could do little more than pause a moment or two to exchange a word or joke with this or that man who sought flirtations with me. I was always in a hurry. Rushing along through the hotel lobby or parlors or verandas, I scarcely had time to get more than a confused impression of various faces.

There was a ball nearly every night, and I always had to attend, for a little while, anyway; but I did not exactly mingle with the guests. I never danced, though lots of men asked me. I would get my list of guests and the description of the women's dresses, etc., write my column, and dispatch it by boy to *The Lantern*, and I would go to bed while the music was still throbbing through the hotel. Often the guests were dancing till dawn.

Now I come to Dr. Manning. He was the one man in the hotel who persistently sought me and endeavored to make love to me. He was an American, one of a yachting party cruising in the Caribbean. I was not attracted to him at all, and as far as I could, I avoided him; but I could not come out upon the verandas or appear anywhere about the hotel without his seeming to arise from somewhere, and come with his flattering smiles and jokes. His hair was gray, and he had a pointed, grizzled beard. He was tall, and carried himself like a German officer.

He was always begging me to go to places with him, for walks, drives, or boat-trips, etc., and finally I did accept an invitation to walk with him in the botanical gardens, which adjoined, and were almost part of our own grounds.

That evening was a lovely one, with a great moon overhead, and the sea like a vast glittering sheet of quicksilver. The Marine Band was playing. People were dancing in the ball-room and on the verandas and out in a large pagoda in the gardens. Down along the sanded paths we passed numerous couples strolling, the bare shoulders of the women gleaming like ivory under the moonlight. The farther we strolled from the hotel, the darker grew the paths. Across the white backs of many of the women a black sleeve was passed. Insensibly I felt that in the darkness my companion was trying to see my face, and note the effect upon me of these "spooners." But he was not the first man I had walked with in the Jamaica moonlight. Verley Marchmont and I had spent a few brief hours from our labors in the gardens of the hotel.

Dr. Manning kept pressing nearer to me. Officiously and continuously, he would take my arm, and finally he put his about my waist. I tried to pull it away, but he held me firmly. Then I said:

"There are lots of people all around us, you know. If you don't take your arm down, I shall scream for help."

He took his arm down.

After a space, during which we walked along in silence, I not exactly angry, but irritated, he began to reproach me, accusing me of disliking him. He said he noticed that I was friendly with everyone else, but that when he approached me my face always stiffened. He asked if I disliked him, and I replied that I did not, but that other men did not look at or speak to me as he did. He laughed unbelievingly at that, and exclaimed:

"Come, now, are you trying to make me believe that the young men who come to see you do not make love to you?" I said thoughtfully:

"Well, only one or two come to see me, and no none of them has yet. I suppose it's because I'm always so busy; and then I'm not pretty and rich like the other girls here."

"You are pretty," he declared, "and far more interesting than any other girl in the hotel. I think you exceedingly captivating."

For that compliment I was truly grateful, and I thanked him for saying it. Then he said:

"Let me kiss you just once, won't you?" Again he put his arm about me, and this time I had to struggle considerably to release myself. When he let me go, he said almost testily:

"Don't make such a fuss. I'm not going to force you," and then after a moment, "By the way, why do you object to being kissed?" just as if it were unusual for a girl to object to that.

"I'll tell you why," I said tremulously, for it is impossible for a young girl to be unmoved when a man tries to kiss her, "because I want to be in love with the first man who kisses me."

"And you cannot care for me?"

I shook my head.

"Why?"

"Because you are an old man," I blurted out

He stopped in the path, and I could feel him bristling with amazement and anger. Somewhat of a fop in dress, he had always carried himself in the gay manner of a man much younger than he probably was. His voice was very nasty:

"What?"

I repeated what I had said:

"You are an old man."

"What on earth makes you think that?" he demanded.

"Because your hair is gray," I stammered, "and because you look at least forty."

At that he broke into a loud chuckle.

"And you think forty old?"

I nodded. For a long moment he was silent, and then suddenly he took my arm, and we moved briskly down the path. We came to one of the piers, and he assisted me up the little stone steps. In silence we went out to the end of the pier. There was a little rustic enclosure at the end, covered with ivy from some sort of tree that seemed to grow out of the water. We sat down for a while and looked out across the sea. Everything was very dark and still. Presently he said:

"What would you do if I were to take you into my arms by force now?"

"I would scream," I said childishly.

"That wouldn't do you much good, for I could easily overpower you. You see, there is not a soul anywhere near us here."

I experienced a moment s fear, and stood up, when he said in a kind and humorous way:

"Sit down, child; I'm not going to touch you. I merely said that to see what you would do. As a matter of fact, I want to be your friend, your very particular friend, and I am not going to jeopardize my chances by doing something that would make you hate me. Do sit down."

Then as I obeyed, he asked me to tell him all about myself. It was not that I either trusted or liked him, but I was very lonely, and something in the quiet beauty of our surroundings affected me, I suppose. So long as he did not make love to me, I found him rather attractive. So I told him what there was to tell of my simple history up to this time, and of my ambitions.

He said a girl like me deserved a better fate than to be shut up in this country; that in a few weeks the hot season would set in, and then I would probably find life unbearable, and surely have some fever. He advised me very earnestly, therefore, not to remain here, but suggested that I go to America. There, he said, I would soon succeed, and probably become both famous and rich. His description of America quickened my fancy, and I told him I should love to go there, but, unfortunately, even if I could get away from this position, and managed to pay my fare to America, I did not know what I would do after arriving there virtually penniless.

When I said that, he turned and took both my hands impulsively and in a nice fatherly way in his, and said:

"Why, look here, little girl, what's the matter with your coming to work for me? I have a huge practice, and will need a secretary upon my return. Now, what do you say?"

I said:

"I say, Thank you, and I'll remember."

At the hotel he bade me good night rather perfunctorily for a man who had recently tried to kiss a girl, but I lay awake some time thinking about what he had said to me.

I suppose every girl tosses over in her mind the thought of that first kiss that shall come to her. In imagination, at least, I had already been kissed many many times, but the ones who had kissed me were not men or boys. They were strange and bewildering heroes, princes, kings, knights, and great nobles. Now, here was a real man who had wanted to kiss me. I experienced no aversion to him at the thought; only a cool sort of wonder and a flattering sense of pride.

VI

I T WAS A CRUEL COINCIDENCE THAT THE DREADFUL thing that befell me next day should have followed at a time when my young mind was thus dreamily engrossed.

The day had been a hard one, and I know not why, but I could not concentrate my mind upon the proceedings. I felt inexpressibly stupid, and the voices of the legislators droned meaninglessly in my ears. As I could not follow the debates intelligently, I decided that I would stay a while after the council had adjourned, borrow one of the reporter's notes, and patch up my own from them.

So, with a glass of kola at my elbow, and Verley Marchmont's notes before me, I sat at work in the empty chamber after everyone, I supposed, had gone, though I heard the attendants and janitors of the place at work in the gallery above. Young Marchmont waited for me outside.

A quiet had settled down over the place, and for a time I scribbled away upon my pad. I do not know how long I had worked not more than ten or fifteen minutes when I felt someone come up behind me, and a voice that I recognized from having heard it often in the House during the session said:

"May I speak to you a moment, Miss Ascough?"

I looked up, surprised, but not alarmed. Mr. Burbank was standing by my chair. There was something in his expression that made me move my chair back a little, and I began gathering up my papers rapidly. I said politely, however:

"Certainly, Mr. Burbank. What can *The Lantern* do for you?"

I sat facing the table, but I had moved around so that my shoulder was turned toward him. In the little silence that followed I felt his breath against my ear as he leaned on the table and propped his chin upon his hand, so that his face came fairly close to mine. Before he spoke I had shrunk farther back in my chair.

He said, with a laugh that was an odd mixture of embarrassment and assurance:

"I want nothing of *The Lantern*, but I do want something of you. I want to ask you to marry me. God! how I love you!"

If someone had struck me hard and suddenly upon the head, I could not have experienced a greater shock than the words of that negro gave me. All through the dreaming days of my young girlhood one lovely moment had stood

412

out like a golden beam in my imagination my first proposal. Perhaps all girls do not think of this; but *I* did, I who lived upon my fancies. How many gods and heroes had I not created who had whispered to me that magical question? And now out of that shining, beautiful throng of imaginary suitors, what was this that had come? A great black man, the "bogy man" of my childhood days!

Had I been older, perhaps I might have managed that situation in some way. I might even have spoken gently to him; he believed he was honoring me. But youth revolts like some whipped thing before stings like this, and I was so hurt, so terribly wounded, that I remember I gasped out a single sob of rage. Covering my face with my hands, I stood up. Then something happened that for a moment robbed me of all my physical and mental powers.

Suddenly I felt myself seized in a pair of powerful arms. A face came against my own, and lips were pressed hard upon mine.

I screamed like one gone mad. I fought for my freedom from his arms like a possessed person. Then blindly, with blood and fire before my eyes and burning in my heart, I fled from that terrible chamber. I think I banged both my head and hands against the door, for later I found that my forehead and hands were swollen and bruised. Out into the street I rushed.

I heard Verley Marchmont call to me. I saw him like a blur rise up in my path, but behind him I fancied was that other that great animal who had kissed me.

On and on I ran, my first impulse being to escape from something dreadful that was pursuing me. I remember I had both my hands over my mouth. I felt that it was unclean, and that rivers and rivers could not wash away that stain that was on me.

I think it was Marchmont's jerking hold upon my arm that brought me to a sense of partial awakening.

"Miss Ascough, what is the matter? What is the matter?" he was saying.

I looked up at him, and I started to speak, to tell him what had happened to me, and then suddenly I knew it was something I could tell no one. It loomed up in my child's imagination as something filthy.

"I can't tell you," I said.

"Did something frighten you? What is it, dear?"

I remember, in all my pain and excitement, that he called me "dear," that fair-haired young Englishman; and like a child unexpectedly comforted, it brought the sobs stranglingly to my throat.

"Come and get into the carriage, then," he said. "You are ill. Your hands and face are burning. I'm afraid you have fever. You'd better get home as quickly as possible."

The driver of our carriage, who had followed, drew up beside us; but even as I turned to step into the carriage, suddenly I remembered what Miss Foster had said that first day:

This carriage is owned by Mr. Burbank. He supplies all the carriages for the press."

"I can't ride in that!" I cried.

"You've got to," said Marchmont. "It's the last one left except Mr. Burbank's own."

"I'm going to walk home," I said.

I was slowly recovering a certain degree of self-possession. Nevertheless, my temples were throbbing; my head ached splittingly. I was not crying, but gasping sobs kept seizing me, such as attack children after a tempestuous storm of tears.

"You can't possibly walk home," declared Marchmont."It is at least four and a half miles, if not more."

"I am going to walk just the same," I said. "I would rather die than ride in that carriage."

He said something to the driver. The latter started up his horses, and drove slowly down the road. Then Marchmont took my arm, and we started.

That interminable walk in the fearful Jamaica heat and sun recurs sometimes to me still, like a hectic breath of hateful remembrance. The penetrating sun beat its hot breath down upon our backs. The sand beneath our feet seemed like living coals, and even when we got into the cooler paths of the wooded country, the closeness and oppressive heaviness of the atmosphere stifled and crushed me.

At intervals the driver of that Burbank carriage would draw up beside us on the road, and Marchmont would entreat me to get in; but always I refused, and a strength came to me with each refusal.

Once he said:

"If you would let me, I could carry you."

I looked up at his anxious young face. His clothes were thicker than mine, and he had a number of books under his arm. He must have been suffering from the heat even as I was, but he was ready to sacrifice himself for what he must have thought was a sick whim on my part. He was nothing but a boy, very little older than I; but he was of that plugging English type which sticks at a task until it is accomplished. The thought of his carrying me made me laugh hysterically, and he, thinking I was feeling better, again urged me to get into the carriage, but in vain.

We met many country people on the road, and he bought from one a huge native umbrella. This he hoisted over my head; I think it did relieve us somewhat. But the whole of me, even to my fingers, now seemed to be tingling and aching. There was a buzzing and ringing in my head. I was thirsty. We stopped at a wayside spring, and an old woman lent me her tin cup for a drink. Marchmont gave her a coin, and she said in a high, whining voice:

"Give me another tuppence, Marster, and I'll tell missee a secret." He gave her the coin, and then she said:

"Missee got the fever. She better standoff n dat ground."

"For God's sake!" he said to me, "let me put you in the carriage!"

"You would not want to, if you knew," I said, and my voice sounded in my own ears as if it came from some distance.

On and on we tramped. Never were there five such miles as those.

Many a time since I have walked far greater distances. I have covered five and six miles of links, carrying my own golf-clubs. I've climbed up and down hills and valleys, five, ten, and more miles, and arrived at my destination merely healthily tired and hungry.

But five miles under a West Indian sun, in a land where even the worms and insects seemed to wither and dry in the sand!

It was about four-forty when we left Government House; it was seven when we reached the hotel. I was staggering as we at last passed under the great arcade of the Myrtle Bank. Though my eyes were endowed with sight, I saw nothing but a blurred con fusion of shadows and shapes.

Mr. Marchmont and another man I think the manager of the hotel took me to my room, and someone I suppose the maid put me to bed. I dropped into a heavy sleep, or, rather, stupor, almost immediately.

The following day a maid told me that everyone in the hotel was talking about me and the sick condition in which I had returned to the hotel, walking! Everyone believed I was down with some bad fever and had lost my mind, and there was talk of quarantining me somewhere until my case was properly diagnosed. I sent a boy for Mr. Campbell.

He came over at once. Grumbling and muttering something under his breath, he stumped into my room, and when he saw I was not sick in bed, as report had made me, he seemed to become angry rather than pleased. He cleared his throat, ran his hand through his hair till it stood up straight on his head, and glared at me savagely.

"What's the matter with you?" he demanded. "Why did you not report at the office last evening? Are you sick or is this some prank? What's this I've been hearing about you and that young cub of The Call?"

"I don't know what you've been hearing," I said, "but I want to tell you that I'm not going to stay here any longer. I'm going home."

"What do you mean by that?" he shouted at me.

"You asked me what happened to me?" I said excitedly. "I'll tell you."

And I did. When I was through, and sat sobbingly picking and twisting my handkerchief in my hands, he said explosively:

"Why in the name of common sense did you remain behind in that place?"

"I told you I wanted to go over my notes. I had not been able to report intelligently the proceedings, as I felt ill."

"Don't you know better than to stay alone in any building where there are likely to be black men?"

No, I did not know better than that.

And now began a heated quarrel and duel between us. I wanted to leave Jamaica at once, and this old Scotchman desired to keep me there. I had become a valuable asset to *The Lantern*. But I was determined to go. After Mr. Campbell left I sought out Dr. Manning. He had offered to help me if I went to America. To America, then, I would go.

Dr. Manning watched my face narrowly as I talked to him. I told him of the experience I had had, and he said:

"Now, you see, I warned you that this was no place for a girl like you."

"I know it isn't," I said eagerly, "and so I'm going to leave. I want to take the first boat that sails from Jamaica. One leaves for Boston next Friday, and I can get passage on that. I want to know whether you meant what you said the other night about giving me a position after I get there."

"I certainly did," he replied. "I live in Richmond, and when you get to Boston, telegraph me, and I will arrange for you to come right on. I myself am leaving to-night. Have you enough money?" I said I had, though I had only my fare and a little over.

"Well," he said, "if you need more when you reach Boston, telegraph me, and I'll see that you get it at once."

"This relieves me of much anxiety," I said. "And I'm sure I don't know how to thank you."

He stood up, took my hand, and said:

"Perhaps you won't thank me when you see what a hard-worked little secretary you are to be."

Then he smiled again in a very fatherly way, patted my hand, and wished me good-by.

I now felt extremely happy and excited. Assured of a position in America, I felt stronger and more re solved. I put on my hat and went over to *The Lantern* office. After another quarrel with Mr. Campbell, I emerged triumphant. He released me from my contract.

That evening Verley Marchmont called upon me, and of course I had to tell him I was leaving Jamaica, a piece of information that greatly disheartened him. We were on one of the large verandas of the hotel. The great Caribbean Sea was below us, and above, in that marvelous, tropical sky, a sublime moon looked down upon us.

"Nora," said Verley, "I think I know what happened to you yesterday in Government House, and if I were sure that I was right, I'd go straight out and half kill that black hound."

I said nothing, but I felt the tears running down my face, so sweet was it to feel that this fine young Englishman cared. He came over and knelt down beside my chair, like a boy, and he took one of my hands in his. All the time he talked to me he never let go my hand.

"Did that nigger insult you?" he asked.

I said:

"He asked me to marry him."

Verley snorted.

"Anything else?"

A lump came up stranglingly in my throat.

"He kissed me!" The words came with difficulty.

"Damn him!" cried young Verley Marchmont, clenching his hands.

There was a long silence between us after that. He had been kneeling all this time by my chair, and at last he said:

"I don't blame you for leaving this accursed hole, and I wish I were going with you. I wish I were not so desperately poor. Hang it all!" he added, with a poor little laugh. "I don't get much more than you do."

"I don't care anything about money," I said. "I like people for themselves."

"Do you like me, Nora?" He had never called me Nora till this night.

I nodded, and he kissed my hand.

"Well, someday then I'll go to America, too, and I'll find you, wherever you may be."

I said chokingly, for although I was not in love with this boy, still I liked him tremendously, and I was sentimental:

"I don't believe we'll ever meet again. We're just little ships passing in the night.

Marchmont was the only person to see me off. He called for me at the hotel, arranged all the details of the moving of my baggage, and then got a hack and took me to the boat. He had a large basket with him, which I noticed he carried very carefully. When we went to my state-room, he set it down on a chair, and said with his bright, boyish laugh:

"Here's a companion for you. Every time you hear him, I want you to think of me."

I heard him almost immediately; a high, questioning bark came out that package of mystery. I was delighted. A dear little dog fox terrier, the whitest, prettiest dog I had ever seen. Never before in my life had I had a pet of any kind; never have I had once since. I lifted up this darling soft little dog he was nothing but a puppy and as I caressed him, he joyfully licked my face and hands. Marchmont said he was a fine little thoroughbred of a certain West Indian breed. His name, he said, was to be "Verley," after my poor big "dog" that I was leaving behind.

"Are you pleased with him?" he asked.

"I'm crazy about him," I replied.

"Don't you think I deserve some reward, then?" he demanded softly.

I said:

"What do you want?"

"This," he said, and, stooping, kissed me.

I like to think always that that was my first real kiss.

VII

THE TRIP HOME WAS UNEVENTFUL, AND, on account of Verley, spent for the most part in my state room. The minute I left the room he would start to whine and bark so piercingly and piteously that of course I got into trouble, and was obliged either to take him with me or stay with him.

I used to eat my meals with Verley cuddled in my lap, thrusting up his funny, inquiring little nose, and eating the morsels I surreptitiously gave him from my plate, much to the disgust of some of the passengers and the amusement of others.

Once they tried to take Verley from me, some of the ship's people, but I went to the captain, a friend of Captain Hollowell, about whom I talked, and I pleaded so fervently and made such promises that when I reached the tearful stage he relented, and let me keep my little dog.

I had an address of a Boston lodging-house, given me by a woman guest of the Myrtle Bank. A cab took me to this place, and I was fortunate in securing a little hall room for three dollars a week. There was a dining-room in the basement of a house next door where for three dollars and fifty cents I could get meal-tickets enough for a week. My landlady made no objection to Verley, but she warned me that if the other lodgers objected, or if Verley made any noise,

I'd have to get rid of him. She gave me a large wooden box with straw in it. This was to be his bed. I didn't dare tell her that Verley slept with me. He used to press up as closely to my back as it was possible to get, and with his fore paws and his nose resting against my neck, he slept finely. So did I. I kept him as clean as fresh snow. I had tar soap, and I scrubbed him every day in warm water, and I also combed his little white coat. If I found one flea on him, I killed it.

The first day I went into the dining-room next door with little Verley at my heels, everyone turned round and looked at him, he was such a pretty, tiny little fellow, and so friendly and clean. The men whistled and snapped their fingers at him. He ran about from table to table, making friends with everyone, and being fed by everyone.

I was given a seat at a table where there was just one other girl. Now here occurred one of the co incidences in my life that seem almost stranger than fiction. The girl at the table was reading a newspaper when I sat down, and I did not like to look at her at once; but presently I became aware that she had lowered her paper, and then I glanced up. An exclamation escaped us simultaneously, and we jumped to our feet.

"Nora!" she screamed.

"Marion!" I cried.

She was one of my older sisters!

As soon as we recognized each other, we burst out hysterically laughing and crying. Excited words of explanation came tumbling from our lips.

"What are you doing here?"

"What are you?"

"Why aren't you in Jamaica?"

"Why aren't you in Quebec?"

I soon explained to Marion how I came to be in Boston, and then, crying and eating at the same time, she told me of her adventures. They were less exciting, but more romantic, than mine. She had left Quebec on account of an unhappy love-affair. She had quarreled with the young man to whom she was engaged, and "to teach him a lesson, and because, anyway, I hate him," she had run away. She had been in Boston only one day longer than I. She said she had been looking for work for two days, but only one kind had been offered her thus far. I asked her what that was. Her eyes filled with tears, and she said bitterly, that of an artist's model.

Marion could paint well, and papa had taught her considerably. It was her ambition, of course, to be an artist. In Quebec she had actually had pupils, and made a fair living teaching children to draw and paint on china. But here in Boston she stood little chance of getting work like that. Nevertheless, she had gone the rounds of the studios, hoping to find something to do as assistant and pupil. Nearly every artist she had approached, however, had offered to engage her as a model.

Marion was an unusually pretty girl of about twenty-two, with an almost perfect figure, large, luminous eyes, which, though fringed with black lashes, were a golden-yellow in color; hair, black, long, and glossy; small and charmingly shaped hands and feet; and a perfectly radiant complexion. In fact, she had all the qualities desirable in a model. I did not wonder that the artists of Boston wanted to paint her. I urged her to do the work, but poor Marion felt as if her best dreams were about to be shattered. She, who had cherished the hope of being an artist, shrank from the thought of being merely a model. However, she had scarcely any money. She said she would not mind posing in costume; but only one of the artists had asked her to do that, a man who wanted to use her in "Oriental studies."

In her peregrinations among the studios she had come across other girls who were making a profession of posing, and one of them had taken her to a large art school, so that she could see exactly what the work was. This girl, Marion said, simply stripped herself "stark naked," and then went on before a large room full of men and women. Marion was horrified and ashamed, but her friend, a French girl, had laughed and said:

"Que voulez-vous? It ees nutting."

She told Marion that she had felt just as she did at first; that all models experienced shame and embarrassment the first time. The plunge was a hard thing; and to brace the girl up for the ordeal, the model was accustomed to take a drink of whisky before going on. After that it was easy. Marion was advised to do this.

"Just tek wan good dreenk," said the French girl; "then you get liddle stupid. After zat it doan matter."

Marion remarked hysterically that whisky might not make her stupid. She might be disposed to be hilarious, and in that event what would the scandalized class do?

However, Marion was hopeful, and she expected to get the costume work with the artist mentioned before.

As for me, just as I advised Marion to take this easy work that was offered her, so she most strenuously advised me not to waste my time looking for work in Boston, but to go on to Richmond, where a real position awaited me.

It is curious how natural it is for poor girls to slip along the path of least resistance. We wanted to help each other, and yet each advised the other to do something that upon more mature thought might have been inadvisable; for both courses held pitfalls of which neither of us was aware. However, we seized what was nearest to our hand.

Marion got the work to pose in Oriental studies next day, and I, who had telegraphed Dr. Manning, received by telegraph order money for my fare. I at once set out for Richmond, and I did not see my sister again for nearly five years. I left her crying at the station.

JAPANESE AMERICAN AUTHORS

A Japanese Robinson Crusoe

Jenichiro Oyabe

PREFACE

"The kingdom of Nippon," says St. Xavier, "is the delight of my soul" And to one whose ideas have been trained in accordance with the habits of European civilization, Japan is indeed the land of surprises; not, however, the country, but its people. But how can a foreigner know about them?" Of course, by reading their biographies, that is, by means of written language," must be the answer. But, in the first place, must the foreigner learn our language, or shall we study his? The first is more difficult than the last, as the Japanese is a language limited to that island empire exclusively, while the English or French is almost universal. So, then, in this book let my imperfect English triumph over my own mother tongue.

My object in composing this work is partly to secure the attention and interest of the young people. For I see some dangers arising from the effect of the wonderful progress of this country in the development of machinery, and from the tremendous power of money. These two are most convenient substances, and have saved a great deal of time and of human labor. But, on the other hand, they corrupt the hearts of many of the younger generation; leading them to seek after pleasure, luxury, and a life without labor. The "Japanese Crusoe" will tell them that there is nothing which can be bought without a price; even for the Gospel one must pay faith and devotion.

Another reason for this publication is, that in the social and religious gatherings to which I have been invited during my stay in America, I have always been asked by my friends, how I happened to leave Japan, what strange experiences I had during my roving, and how I was converted? When I was a student in the United States, I disliked to tell others in public about my early adventures. But now I have no objection whatever to relate the story of my wandering life; if there be any benefit in it for others. Moreover, it would be disloyal in me to bury myself in the Far East, keeping my unique experience to myself and the lesson of it hidden. So I propose to write out my story for the use of aspiring young people in the future. If anyone who reads this narrative shall find any lesson of warning or of inspiration in my checkered life, and so take it as a compass for his life voyage, I shall be truly rewarded.

I entitle this book "A Japanese Robinson Crusoe," because my wandering life much resembles that of the fictitious Robinson Crusoe. The difference between the old and the new Crusoe consists in this, that the former drifted away unintentionally to a desolate island, while the latter wandered purposely from island to island, looking for a "land of saints," and finally reached the shores of America, leading there, during nine years, a struggling life in pursuit of a higher education.

I take this opportunity to extend most sincere thanks to these kind friends for their generous assistance during my wanderings: President J. E. Rankin, D.D., LL.D., of Howard University; Rev. S. M. Newman, D.D., of Washington, D.C.; the late Gen. S. C. Armstrong, LL.D., of Virginia; Prof. L. O. Brastow and Prof. G. E. Day, of Yale University, New Haven, Conn.; Rev. Secretary O. P. Emerson, Hon. W. F. Frear, Rev. E. G. Beckwith, D.D., Hon. A. F. Judd, LL.D., of Honolulu; and many others.

JENICHIRO OYABE.

NEW HAVEN, CONNECTICUT,
JANUARY, 1898.

CHAPTER I
ORIGIN— CHILDHOOD

EARLY ONE SUMMER EVENING, WHEN THE AIR was pure, the earth moist, and graceful old pine trees, waving in the breeze, were playing their peculiar music together with the surge's roar which broke on the cragged beach, "Shipwreck! shipwreck! fire! fire!" was suddenly shouted by the simple-hearted fishermen who were mending their nets on a peaceful shore.

While these men were preparing a life-saving boat, several strange black vessels rushed, amid circling clouds of smoke, into the bay. Soon the "stars and stripes" were flung to the gentle wind, and the sailors boldly cast anchor into waters where no foreign vessels ever lay before.

These were the squadron of well-equipped ships under the orders of the American expedition to Japan in 1853; and they were commanded by a gallant United States naval officer, Matthew Calbraith Perry, the young brother of the hero of Lake Erie.

In those days most people in Japan believed that Nippon, the land of the Rising Sun, was the only divinely blessed country in the world. But the formidable appearance of the powerful foreign steamers greatly surprised the self-conceited sons of the Mikado. With the chief of the feudal lords, called Siogun, the United States made a treaty, and afterward, though slowly, other countries followed her example. These treaties, however, did not receive the sanction of the Emperor, but were negotiated by the Siogun's independent action. Thereupon the imperialists were stirred with intense wrath against the Siogun. A civil war followed, bringing ruin and desolation. After the memorable battle of Fushimi, the Siogun made peace with the Emperor, and formally resigned his office. About the same time, the Emperor died at the old Capital. The young Crown Prince was thereupon declared sole sovereign, and the whole empire was placed under his direct rule. The old imperial palace which had been the residence of many Mikados was removed to Tokyo, formerly Yedo. The old record of dates, which had been kept for many centuries, was at once changed for the European calendar. An excellent system of civil and commercial law was adopted from European countries. Post-offices, a national bank, and a school system were established. Newspapers were printed and circulated for the first time; the coast was made bright with lighthouses; the first railroads were opened, telegraphs connected the important cities, and many other features of Western civilization, including the latest army and naval improvements, were copied.

In those busy days of New Japan, amid its earliest scenes of splendor, I was born in Akita," in the province of Dewa, on the twenty-third day of December, third year of Kieoli, according to the old Japanese calendar. My great grandfather was of noble descent. He was the prince of Mogami in the province of Uzen. My grandfather was a soldier and a noted teacher of fencing, though afterward he was adopted by a worthy merchant in Akita. My father was more cultured, and had a profound knowledge of law and politics. In his early boyhood he was sent to a Buddhist high priest in order to obtain philosophical knowledge.

One day he was called to his home on account of his father's sudden illness. When he arrived at home, he found his father lying in bed, and dangerously ill. The father grasped the hand of his son, and said: "I was born of a noble family, but in my boyhood I was treated very unkindly by my parents. So, one day, leaving a letter for my father, I departed from my father's palace without his permission. My desire was to go to Satsuma to find the best teacher in philosophy. On the way to that province my money was stolen by a highwayman. I became a helpless wanderer, and was rescued by a noble-looking traveller. The gentleman advised me to come with him to his house. I thought he was a Samurai class man; so I followed. But after I arrived at his house, I found that he was a wealthy business man. Soon I was adopted as his son, and was obliged to marry his daughter."

While speaking this, the tears ran down his face and he was almost overcome by emotion. Still he continued: "But, in the first place, I was mistaken in thinking my father cruel and lacking in affection; for was there ever a parent who did not love his own children? My father, the prince, chastised me because he wished me to be a wiser and better son in the future. My present repentance, however, is too late. But take this as an example for yourself. Correct your best beloved child for his own benefit. For no man can understand the truest meaning of a gratification unless he pays the proper price. It should be the outcome of toil in his early years. Above all, let not your son, as an offspring of my noble family, ever disgrace it."

After giving many such instructions, the poor fugitive prince's soul was at rest and the body returned to the dust. I realized afterward that his last word was the very cause of my long wandering life.

My father devoted himself to studying the laws and politics which had been newly introduced to our country from the West. His name became known to the regent of Iwasaki, and he was invited to the palace as a civil adviser. Shortly before the civil war broke out my father advised the regent to obey the orders of the Mikado. But his suggestion was not accepted. My father retired from his office and devoted himself again to study.

His silent, cottage life was like a hermit's, and even my mother had no idea what his desire for the future was. She often asked my father to undertake some practical work, instead of digging at the pages of books. But he did not pay any attention to her requests, nor change his mind. His habitual reticence enervated my mother and caused the sickness which led to her death at the early age of twenty-four. I was then only five years old. Immediately after her death I was taken to my grandmother's house, because it was too much for my patriotic father to take care of his young boy himself.

At about this time political troubles occurred between the governments of Japan and Corea. A warlike spirit filled the empire. My father could no longer stay at his humble cottage. "Why do I sit here and study in quiet?" he said. "This is the time to give my life for my country!" He started for Tokyo, the capital, leaving his aged mother and myself at home.

Soon my good grandmother sent me to a common school where my father's intimate friend was the principal. The schoolmaster was very kind, and was, indeed, a father to me. He paid special attention to me in all branches of knowledge. But again there came a painful trial upon me. It was the death of my grandmother. "Though I depart from you, yet my soul will live with you until you become a man," was her last word to the unfortunate boy, myself. I was then taken and cherished by my aunt.

Although I was born in a heathen family, yet it was my chief impulse to become an anti-idolater, and it came from the death of my grandmother. In the beginning of her last sickness the doctors said that she could not live more than a week. As soon as I heard this I determined to pray to the gods for her life, and even to sacrifice my own, as in Japan there is connected with prayer for the life of a relative the religious ceremony of offering the suppliant's life for that of the sick person. It was a cold winter's day when I got up at one or two o'clock in the morning to worship in a dozen of the Shinto temples, and came back home before the people were up. Sometimes I bowed down and worshipped gods while the priests poured many bucketsful of cold water upon my body according to the Shinto custom.

All my prayers were in vain, as the idols gave no answer to them. Finally, my sick grandmother's breath was gone. My patience was dead. I said to the idols: "You have eyes, but cannot see; you have ears, but cannot hear; of what good are you?" From that time on, I did not worship Shinto or Buddhist idols.

One day we, the schoolboys, went to the yard of a large Buddhist temple. When I saw the stone and bronze idols in the yard, I told my playmates that the idols were not gods, and those who worship them would have severe punishment from heaven. I bade the boys break them in pieces, perhaps in the same manner as is suggested in the book of Psalms: "Thou shalt break them with a rod of iron; thou shalt dash them in pieces like a potter's vessel." Without waiting for anyone, I went up to a large stone idol and pushed it backward with my full strength. It was thrown to the ground and broken into pieces by its heavy weight. This so pleased the other boys that they all followed my example and tried the same way with each of those idols.

Just as we were leaving the yard, we saw two priests coming toward us, so we all ran homeward, but, unfortunately, two of the youngest were caught by them. The next day, an old, dignified priest came to my house and told my aunt that I was the leader at that notorious sport of breaking the idol gods in the temple yard. The priest asked her to pay the full expense for the damage.

My aunt was very angry with me. She sent me to the house of her country relative, who was a Buddhist priest, for punishment. While I was there I had a good opportunity for studying the Buddhist philosophy under the guidance of the priest.

The village was situated at the foot of a high mountain. Once a rumor went through the village that there was a living god in that mountain. The hunters and mountaineers told me often that they saw the living god clothed with grass and leaves. I did not believe the story, for my conclusion was that gods were spirits and have no shape like man.

One day, through curiosity, I went up to the mountain without speaking of it to my priest. I missed the road, and so climbed up the mountain through forests, resting in the caves at night and seeking after the living god in the day. And, of course, I found out that it was nonsense.

During my absence, however, the priest and his people were looking for me all through the village, without success. They thought that while I was swimming in the river, I had met death by drowning. So the priest employed a dozen small boats, and men with fishing-nets to search the water for my supposed dead body. In the midst of this great confusion and trouble I came home weary and disappointed. When I saw the terrified priest, he exclaimed: "Where have you been all these days? and what will you do next, I wonder? I think I must punish you this time; back to your aunt's house."

He then sent me to my aunt's with a servant. When I returned home my aunt's patience was already exhausted. But she welcomed me heartily, and the very next day she sent me to a government school, where I enjoyed the study of Western art and science, and after being there four years, I was graduated.

CHAPTER IV
ON TO AMERICA

THE HOAR-FROST LAY GLITTERING OVER THE tender grass. The forest leaves had changed their deep green color to yellow and red, and the first winter-winds were wearily sighing."

"Oh, how wondrous rare the autumn scenes are! But yesterday the summertide was here, and now it is dead. So comes and goes our life. At the longest, how short it is! But though so short and so full of meaning, yet here, on this desolate isle, for no crime I have done, I find myself a lonely exile. I have no relative to comfort me, neither do I see any prospect before me but to be pitied by the poor Ainos," I soliloquized. Then I began to pray in a loud voice as though addressing someone near my side: "Father in heaven, have mercy on me! Come now and take full possession of my soul. And if thou wilt, let me soon leave for the land of light and happiness."

"Why will you forsake us now, and go away for the land of light and happiness, you cruel man?" was the sudden, anxious word of the chiefs daughter, who had come close to my window and heard the last words of my prayer, and now gazed straight into my eyes.

For a maiden of no more experiences, it was natural, perhaps, that she should have such a suspicious idea. But it was a very painful extremity for me. Since my arrival at the island, it had been my custom to love all people; and it is the law of nature that if we love others, they will return the love. Among such people, however, things are often misunderstood, such for example as pure affection for a worldly love; nobleness for pride; servileness for humility, and for stinginess economy, etc.

"May be so, but you must not mind me at all. I have a great duty to undertake for the good of the whole community. I must leave here for America sooner or later." I spoke kindly, yet my heart was beating fast, and I felt exceedingly sad and gloomy. But my intense love of the truth overcame all this difficulty.

"Oh, you wicked, wicked person!" she cried. Surely she must have thought of me as a cold-minded youth, for she was not intelligent enough to understand that my plans, as well as my experience and education, obliged me to act as one indifferent, although my heart was tender and full of sympathy.

"You wicked young man! I will tell my father all the cruel things that you have spoken to me.

Soon the color flew into her face, and she gathered the brown cloak closer about her eyes, and ran into her father's house.

The faithful and noble-looking chief and three of his younger brothers walked quietly toward my abode. When I said to them "Good afternoon, attenas [elders]," they cordially raised their hands and stroked their beards, as was the custom of the Ainos in their hearty salutations.

"My young prince," said the chief, "did I not look upon you with favor? and have you any disagreement with me? I pray you, abide with us."

"Thank you a thousand times. I want you to listen now to my speech and hear the reason for my departure," I said to him with fervent devotion. "Just now we have no true religion. The dark curtain of immorality and cruelty covers all classes of society. Charity is unknown even among worthy people. Thus those of the poor class are forever poor. The majority of them have no social standing and are treated but little better than brutes. For example, see the condition of your own people. In this glorious age you live as your ancestors lived a thousand years ago. Let me ask why? Because none of our able and worthy men ever paid any attention to you, or gave any sympathy. Indeed, this proscription, this galling yoke of bondage, must and shall be broken, if my heavenly Father will permit me to undertake the work. The causes of all these things are undoubtedly to be found in Buddhism. See the condition of the people of India where it had its origin. So with Siam, Anam, China and Corea, the most prominent Buddhist countries, many centuries ago. They are now just dying before the superior power of modern civilization. Let, then, their wreck be our warning. I must save my country from such desolation. And for that cause I must leave this country for the land of saints to learn first, under the guidance of my kind Providence, how to deliver you."

The amiable old chief and his staff were so much excited by my long speech that the tears rolled down their cheeks, and they said that I was not a man, but an angel sent by the Spirit.

"Go, my prince, and bring us the precious things from the land of saints," was the chief's encouraging word to me.

After a few days I bundled together all the things which had been prepared for my long, snowy journey, such as a suit of winter clothes, a snow cap, a bag which was just large enough to put my body into, and one pair of boots—the materials of all which were made of bearskin; plenty of dried meat and smoked fish, dried, cooked rice, beans and some raisins, etc. The chief brought a young native to carry my heavy provisions, and told me that he could accompany me until I reached the very end of the island, where I would depart for America.

A large number of Ainos came to me with presents of skin-cloth, shoes, and some dried fish and food, and bade me an affectionate farewell. I did not take any gifts, for I had as much of my own provisions as we could carry.

The chill of autumn was in the air, and the white flakes of snow covered the tops of the mountains. Now, as the wise men followed the star, I started with my young native servant from the old island home toward the United States of America.

I turned my feet toward the northeast, directed by my pocket compass. After about three days of hard travelling, we came to a deep valley in Kitami. While we were passing through the wild, lonesome forest, we saw a dozen human skeletons and corpses lying here and there. I thought it was a very strange thing to find them in such a remote mountainous region. In my curiosity I determined to examine the cause of it. But my poor Aino servant, buoyant and adventurous as he was, was greatly frightened and began to cry like a child. I encouraged him, and we climbed up the wooded mountain. Midway up, the day became dark. Still pressing on far up, we saw a small light, which at last we reached. There we found an old house and a man sitting near the fireplace. We quietly walked near to the window to see what that man was doing.

"Hush! hush! my master, the man is preparing some poison from Kuma grass. Oh, what a devilish look he has!" my man whispered to me.

I knew that the hunters often made some kind of poison to put on the tip of their arrows and spears to kill wild animals, yet, at the same time, I had some doubt whether the place was not, perhaps, a resort of mountain thieves and murderers. So I tried to escape without meeting with the man. Just then we were discovered by two wolf-like dogs. They barked after us very loudly, so that the man took notice of it and came out to the entrance of the house.

"Is there any stranger at this time of the night?" the man cried, and when he found us outside, he continued in a deep, thoughtful voice: "Come in, friends. This is a mountain inn, and, if you like, we can give you some warm dishes, too."

We had no place in which to hide ourselves, so I gave a solemn command to my servant that when we went inside the house he must not eat or touch anything; also that we must be very careful to guard ourselves from any danger.

The host seemed to me between forty and fifty years old, and he had a repulsive appearance. When we entered the house, he cleared all things away into a closet; then he served us tea and some sweetmeats. We did not touch either of them, as we had previously promised.

After I had narrated several wonderful stories of my journey, I remarked to the man that we had seen many human skeletons in the valley. When he heard this, he broke into a laugh, yet I noticed in his face that he looked surprised.

"Nothing strange about it, my young fellow. Some years ago this place was occupied by two men, and they kept it as a lodging house. I heard afterward that they were thieves who robbed the travellers and murdered them, then cast their bodies into the valley. That was what you saw, I suppose."

He then began to light his old pipe with the most spiteful expression of face that I ever saw. "Oh, was that all about it?" I replied to him, but in my heart I doubted whether that man was not doing the very same thing.

After we went to our chamber, my man told me, in a very low voice, that the host was surely a thief and murderer, as he had heard about him before. He then advised me to escape before the old man should come to kill us. I, of course, agreed with him, and we noiselessly gathered our things. After we were ready to start, I threw from the window some dried fish and meat to the watch-dogs. While they came and were eating the food, we jumped out from the window and ran directly toward the east without being disturbed by the dogs or the man. Soon we found a good road, and after two days of difficult journeying, we reached Nemuro, one of the seaports on the northeastern coast of Yezo Island.

Someone, perhaps, will laugh at me because I took such a strange way to reach America, since there are so many fine steamers on the Pacific nowadays. But my nature was such that I desired to do what others did not try. Because of such a peculiar nature, I have met with many hardships and much misery in my life; but, on the other hand, I have acquired a great deal of experience. A man cannot learn how to swim without getting wet. There is no other way to get wisdom except by toil and study. Though a young artist may have a serviceable machine to copy and enlarge the photograph for his canvas, still let him use freely his own hand to draw a portrait from life. So must it be with the young business man and the scholar. Though he be brought up in a worthy family, yet he needs the bitter tonic of the world. He will become strong, and get a wisdom out of his own experience that the universities cannot give.

CHAPTER XI
VOYAGE TO AMERICA

COURAGE AND PERSEVERANCE CARRY ALL BEFORE THEM. I had overcome many difficulties, and had now arrived at the city of Tien-Tsin. After I had rested two or three days, my friend told me of an American merchant ship that was anchored in the port. He told the captain all about me, and asked him to take me to the United States at the cheapest rate possible.

The captain was a kind-hearted man. He told my friend that he would take me to America at the cost of my rations. I paid the money and remained in the ship, and two days afterward she sailed away from the port. I was told by the captain that the ship was going to Japan first, and from there would start for America.

Our voyage was very peaceful until we came near the coast of Kiushu in Japan. One evening we met a terrible storm. The water rose high, and the ship rolled like a ball. When she went up to the top of the giant wave it looked like ascending to the summit of the high mountains, and when she went down into the trough of the sea, I felt as though she were falling into the deep caverns. A grievous thought came to my mind, and I resolved that if I could not go to America this time I would either die or go directly home to my earthly father, and be like one of his servants, as I was not worthy to be called his son, and would never run myself into such miseries as these anymore.

All this while the storm increased more and more, and I heard very sudden-ly the fire-bell and the shouting of men, "Fire! fire!" Soon all the sailors came out, and while every effort was being made to extinguish the fire which had broken out in the lamp-room, the captain ordered the men to prepare the life-boats. He now turned the ship's bow toward the nearest land.

After a few hours the ship came along the coast of Tani Island. The fire was soon past all control and so we jumped overboard. Most of us who knew how to swim, got the life-boat which had been lowered; but two men who were not skilled in swimming were drowned.

While we were on the way to the shore, we met two life-boats each rowed by four natives. They did us great service, and when we got to the shore, a crowd of people were watching for us, and we were very hospitably treated by the natives.

We stayed on that island about two days; then we were sent by an official junk to Kagoshima, and from there a steamer conveyed us to Kobe, one of the five open ports in Japan. In that city, our men were all discharged.

After a few days, the chief officer, who was a native of Massachusetts, and I, went to a Nova Scotia ship which was in port and ready to sail for New York within a day or two. He had told the captain about our wreck, and asked him to take us to America on his vessel. The captain, a good-hearted old man, at once employed my friend as his shipmate, and he promised him that he would take me to America free of charge.

When I heard this news, my heart was filled with joy. I thanked the captain and returned to the shore to prepare for my departure. At the city of Kobe, I visited several noted places and old historical spots for my last sight of the loved native land, and on the way home, I bought many English books, among them an English and Japanese dictionary and a Bible.

That night, thinking many things about the future, I could not sleep at all until morning.

To go had been my one desire, but a poor stranger with an unknown tongue, how could I live, and support myself in that vast mysterious world? Such questions came to my mind. But casting myself on the providence of my heavenly Father, I left my friend's house and started on my search for truth.

When I came to the end of the wharf, for the first time I expressed my unspeakable feeling of sorrow and loneliness. "This toil and misery are not for my own sake," I said, "but all for the good of my countrymen, yet none give me any sympathy whatever. Not only so, but while most young men who are going abroad for study or business, are surrounded by a great many friends and kinsmen who bid them good-by, no one congratulates me.

> The bell is ringing,
> It bids me hurry away;
> But love is abiding.

No one, but thou, O God:
Thou only knowest my heart
Of sweet and tender love.

I left the shore in a small boat, and was cordially received on board the schooner by the captain. The next morning the ship spread her sails and moved out for the great ocean. This was on the 15th day of June, in the year 1888, according to the European calendar. The ship's name was "Thomas Perry." By that name I recalled my country's royal friend. Commodore Perry and his merit.

This is all for thee.
Fairest Queen of the East!
Perry, thy honored friend
Carries thy son away.
To give thee peace;
Farewell! God will bless thee.

As I kept no diary during my voyage, I must necessarily trust entirely to my memory, giving here such facts as were indelibly impressed on my mind while on board the schooner on which I spent over half of a year.

June 15th. The day was clear and warm. As the green mountains of my native country faded from my vision and disappeared, very sad thoughts filled my heart. I took an empty bottle, put some letters into it and tied its mouth with a cork, then threw it into the water, expecting that it would reach my beloved people.

June 16th. The weather was quite stormy. The captain was very anxious about my seasickness. He gave me some medicine, and told me that if I would take some deck work, I would have no more seasickness. So I did, and I enjoyed it very much. I was also interested to listen to the wonderful stories told by the sailors who represented almost all nationalities.

June 17th. The wind blew hard and the sea was still wild. I got cold, and my sickness was so bad that I could not come to the dinner-table. I had a terrible homesickness, too.

June 18th. I felt much better. I began to study English as my daily task until I should get to the shore. I had a very fine time with my study, for there was nothing to interrupt me whatever.

June 18th. The day was very hot. The ship's fresh provisions were all out, such things as meat, vegetables and eggs. I asked the captain in what month we would get to New York. He said that we would reach there perhaps at the end of the year. The answer surprised me a great deal, for there was nothing to eat save some salt beef and potatoes. The ship-cook encouraged me saying that we might catch plenty of fish by and by.

June 20th. From this day to the first of July, there was nothing worthy of mention excepting the sight of the blue waters and sky.

July 1st. We entered the China Sea. The weather was cloudy. A strong gale of wind blew the whole day, and the sea was very rough. The waves often rose higher than our main mast. The ship was in a dangerous condition.

July 2nd. The wind was still blowing hard. The captain thought that it was best to cut the masts, in order to save the ship, or at least the lives of the men. The sailors came on deck each with an axe, waiting simply the captain's last order to cut down the wings of the ship. But God did not forsake us. The wind gradually abated, and thus we all escaped from the danger of being lost.

Here, my exact records of the diary are exhausted. I think it was in the last part of August that we came to the great Indian Ocean.

Early one morning, while we were yet asleep, "All hands!" was suddenly called out by the watch officer. Soon the men took in all sail from the yards, and while they were doing so, a monstrous waterspout which had a rapid, whirling motion rose up just a few yards beyond our vessel. Had it struck us, our ship would surely have been broken in pieces. But we escaped from it as if by a miracle.

When I first came on board, the captain kindly advised me to do some deck work because I had seasickness. But now the sailors rudely urged me to do part of their menial work as my everyday duty. One of them especially insulted me every time I met him. I endured it for over a month. My patience, however, was gone at last, and my youthful heart was burning like fire. I forgot all my plans for the future. I took the pistol which belonged to the captain and had been kept in his cabin. I determined to shoot the man, and then throw myself into the sea.

Madness comes like lightning in the night. When a man's heart is in the dark, he cannot see even himself. But it is just for a moment, and after all, he will return to himself and exercise judgment of right and wrong.

When I seized the captain's pistol and went near to the man to kill him and then commit suicide, my conscience awakened instantly. "Nay! nay!" I said, "to demolish a temple is easier than to build it. This flesh and blood does not belong to no one but to God. I cannot steal it nor kill it. I must make myself useful to him and to my fellow countrymen!" My mind turned again to the right course, and thus calmed my passions, and I meekly submitted to the indignity.

I remember that, during the month of September, a fresh-water tank was empty, so the ship-carpenter opened the other one. That, too, he found was empty. The water had leaked out from a hole underneath the old iron tank. It gave us a surprise and much grief. After we discovered it, every rainy day kept us quite busy, some carrying the rain-water to fill the empty tanks, and others taking the opportunity for washing and bathing.

We now came near the coast of the Cape of Good Hope. The tide was very strong around here. The ship did not move ahead, but kept in almost the same position for over three weeks. It was not our ship alone, for we saw three or four sailing vessels in a similar condition along these waters.

One evening when I stood on the bow, watching the African coast and its beautiful sunset, I saw a shoal of man-eating sharks, perhaps eight or nine feet long, swimming round our vessel. When I saw them, my pragmatic nature moved me to fish for them just for fun.

I got a sharp harpoon and a long cord from the carpenter's room. I went to the extreme end of the bow and sat upon a wire rope which is called a martingale. I tied the cord to the end of my harpoon and the other end of it to the ship's figurehead. When things were all ready, I cast my harpoon at a shark. Just at that moment both of my feet slipped down from the wire rope and I tumbled overboard. In my fall, I did not relax my hold of the cord, and, as soon as I realized my position, I knew that my life depended on my ability to hold to the cord, so inch by inch I climbed up into the ship.

When I was safely on deck and on the way to my cabin, my friend, the second mate, asked me: "What is the matter with you, Charley? Your face is pale and white." I wished to tell him the story, but no voice came from my mouth.

When I got into my cabin, I lay down on the floor, offered an earnest prayer to my unseen Father, and thanked him for my wonderful deliverance. In my prayer I made a solemn vow that I would give myself hereafter to God and devote my whole life for the salvation of mankind, and more especially for the poor and needy.

We came now to the coast of the West Indies. We saw many seaweeds floating on the water, and I was told by an officer that Columbus was assured of the land when he came as far as to these waters and found the seaweed floating on the surface.

As we came farther north, the climate suddenly changed. The day became very cold. So I tried to make a fire in the stove which was placed in our cabin.

The captain was sitting in an easy chair with a chart in his hand, watching me carefully, and after I had made a nice fire, he said: "You can make a fire at very short notice. I suppose you have a good brain. Do tell me now, Charley, what will you do when you get to New York? Wouldn't you like to go with me to Nova Scotia?"

I told him that I was going to the United States for study.

He assured me that if I stayed in that country, without money or friends, I would starve to death.

"I think you might better come with me to my home; then you will be safe, and my wife will teach you the books which you wish to study," said the good old commander.

I thanked him and said that it had long been my desire to come to America, so I would rather go ashore and die. "I believe that I shall not become a helpless wanderer and starve to death while the noble spires of the house of God, that I have so often read about, stand in the land."

While I was saying this, a voice by the watch office suddenly came from the upper deck, "A pilot-boat coming, sir!" So the captain left the cabin.

Now, though my faith and patience had been painfully tried on the long voyage, yet gladness came again, on the joyful Christmas Day, in the year 1888, when the good ship, "Thomas Perry," carried us safely to our destined port and dropped anchor at the foot of the great statue of "Liberty" in New York. I was newly born to the American home like a Christmas gift from the Orient!

CHAPTER XII
DARKEST AMERICA

THE OLD ROBINSON CRUSOE WAS CAST UPON an uninhabited island of the sea, but nature had abundantly provided him with food; the climate was always warm, so that a man would not suffer though he had no house or clothing.

But I, the poor stranger, was now landed in a thickly inhabited and most civilized and thriving city. My heart was not at ease, for my situation was more dangerous than in a bare island where one could freely get fruits and game. I had far more difficulties than Robinson had, for though there were all sorts of things in the market, and homes and restaurants were plentiful, yet nobody would welcome me unless I had my pockets full of the almighty dollar, which seemed the only deity which many of these people worshiped. Without it I was not allowed to take either fruit or flower, both of which were offered to Robinson Crusoe by nature.

Still, like the other Robinson Crusoe, I walked about on the shore, lifting up my hands; and my whole being, as I may say, wrapped up in contemplation of my deliverance, making a thousand gestures and motions, which I cannot describe.

New York is a stupendous city, the largest in the United States; a city of commercial magnificence. The streets are everywhere lively; the people are busy, and life is tuned to the key of hurry, bustle and excitement. The whole city is served with electric and cable-cars.

The down-town of New York is that part of the city usually given up to business, and, in general, may be said to consist of the district south of Union Square. It is the busiest part of the busiest town in the world. Some of the buildings are so high that they look like attempts of Jack, of beanstalk fame, to build a step-ladder to heaven. When I came to a broad street with my American friend, the shipmate, he pointed out to me a large queer-looking chair which was ornamented with shining brass and silver nails, and was placed on the side of the open street, and told me to sit on it.

"You ought to sit down on that big, funny-looking chair, and not I," I told him, as a joke.

"Oh, no, my shoes are too clean just now, Charley, you had better do it; I will pay for you," says my friend.

"I beg your pardon. I came to this country not for a show. You think, because I am a stranger, that while I am sitting in that chair you will exhibit me to the people, and then perhaps you will collect some pennies from the spectators," I said, and refused to do it.

My friend laughed at me and then he seated himself in the big chair. Two boys came, blacking-brush in hand, and a cigarette in each little mouth, and began to shine my old mate's shoes. I understood it then; so I sat in the other chair, when two other boys came, with similar implements, and worked upon my boots also.

"The little children are smoking in Christendom, and spending their most valuable school years in nothing but shining boots. Is it a part of their practical Christian education to imitate the Master in washing one another's feet?" I thought to myself.

As we left there, my friend said: "You'd better be careful, for pickpockets are plentiful all round on these streets, you know."

As soon as I was told so I thrust my hand into my pocket to see if my money was safe; alas! a little purse that contained three gold coins was gone somewhere, and I could not find it.

"Did I not tell you so, Charley?" says my friend.

"Yes, but your advice has done me no good, as you gave it after the purse was stolen. A wonderful Christendom!" I said, as my excited mind and eyes first caught a faint view of the facts of the case.

While we were walking on Broadway I met with a very odd-looking white man. He wore a long yellow overcoat and had on an old silk hat; his face was painted with white and red color. He carried two boards, which were covered with white linen and had some inscription on each. He hung one board on his chest and the other at his back, and he walked very slowly on the street. I thought, perhaps, the man was a criminal who was condemned to death, and now the poor victim was driven away on the public thoroughfares, as I had often heard that such things were practised upon the Christians in my old country, some two or three hundred years ago.

My friend explained to me, however, that he was a "sandwich-man," an advertiser.

"The man who uses the image of God for such a foolish purpose, and also disturbs the public order, is far worse than he who keeps a negro slave around his house, "I whispered within, in surprise.

Everything in America was strange and new to me, and my eyes were quite busy looking everywhere. At one corner of the entrance of a house, I saw a very queer-looking figure of a red-colored man, with a feather helmet on, and a battle-ax in his hand.

"Oh, a heathen god of war! Do these Christian people worship such an idol, too?" I inquired, and I was told that it was a sign of a cigar store.

"Charley, would not you like to stand up there with a silk hat on?" he said, and laughed at me, though I did not understand exactly what that meant.

Now the sun was down, and the evening wind was very cold. My friend took me into one of the liquor saloons which were so abundant in that city.

The bar was in the cellar. In there I saw more than twenty men and women drinking, dancing, laughing, talking, and quarreling. The appearance was that of an insane asylum. When I saw the condition of these men and women I grieved for their future. What a miserable old age they will spend! For, though they look so young and gay now, yet they will go on, one year after another, until their hair becomes gray, and, at last, unable to work, even for their own living, they must starve to death. Knives and pistols are not the only weapons that can kill a person; but the fire-water destroys our fellow men by the thousands. "O God, curse and sweep away all these savage, no, civilized cannibals, these liquors, from the face of the earth!" I cried, and my heart was excited with wonder, perhaps in the same manner as when the true Crusoe found the skulls, hands, feet and other bones of human bodies in the place where the savages did their inhuman feastings.

Now the moon was shining beautifully, together with the gas and electric lights, and the street was almost as light as day. Along the Bowery we met with several strangely-dressed women. When I saw them I thought an old barbarism was still practised by these American females, for they had holes in their ears and in them they hung bangles and rings; their necks and shoulders were covered with furs; their heads tricked out with feathers and dead birds. Some of them looked upon us and saluted us with a sweet little voice. The language I, a stranger, could not understand. I thought, however, that it was a very sympathetic and polite manner of the women of Christendom to give such a welcome word to a stranger on the street! Alas! I did not understand their meaning, nor how they led souls down to death.

We soon arrived at a down-town hotel to have our dinner. I notice the people never eat their meat cooked in small pieces as we do at our home. It is carried into the room in large chunks, often half raw, and then they cut and slash and tear it apart. They eat with knives and prongs, and they use an immense quantity of strong liquor. After the dinner, when we went into the parlor, I saw more than a dozen respectable-looking gentlemen. They were smoking cigars enough to fill the whole parlor with the acrid vapor. One of them was sitting on an easy chair, and he put his feet up on a side-table, and looked at the illustrations of a magazine which was printed on red paper. I thought if I wished to be like an American gentleman, I must smoke a cigar anyway, so I went to a tobacco store and bought a few cigars. On the way to my place I met with a big, fat man who wore a blue uniform with a silver badge on his chest.

"Aee, Jimmie, give me one and a match; if ye say No, oill club yez," and he begged my cigar.

Was he an officer or a rascal? I did not know. I afterwards found he was one of the New York policemen.

When I came home again I sat near the window in the hotel parlor, and while I was putting my feet up on the table and smoking a cigar, my friend came in and looked at me with wonder:

"Charley, what does that mean?"

"Do I not look like an American gentleman?" I said, with an air of superior wisdom.

"Of course not, you young goose," he said scornfully.

About ten o'clock we retired. My bedroom was near an old gentleman's apartment. Shortly before he retired, he said to himself: "Foolish city people! while we sleep, what need of light?"

In a minute or two I smelled gas. Soon I heard somebody knock at the man's door. I, too, got up and went there, and we found the gentleman had blown out the gaslight; the gas was leaking out, and the old man was lying in bed, unconscious of danger. I wondered at him and said: "Even an uneducated heathen knows how to treat the gaslight. What a shame for an American, who calls himself a civilized man, not to understand it."

One day when I went to Brooklyn, crossing the East River by the ferry-boat, I saw quarreling between a woman and a ferryman. The cause was that the woman had put her boy into a big basket and covered it with some clothes and then carried it on her head and paid only one fare. After she came into the boat, she let the boy out of the basket.

My feeling at that time was as follows: "I heard America was the richest country in the world, but here a poor woman carries her young boy on her head to save only three cents fare!"

After a few weeks I went into a barber shop to have my hair trimmed: "Aee, John, git out from here. Oi don't cut a Chinaman's hair!" I was scorned by the old barber. I told him that I was not such a man, but a Japanese. "Ou, ye Javanese, a country of lots coffee! All right; sit dan, my goot fellar." The barber charged me twenty-five cents; so I gave him a dollar, and he paid me the balance of money, which was seventy-five cents.

After I came out, I went into a bookstore to buy a map of New York City. I paid for it a half silver dollar which the barber had just given to me; but the clerk said that fifty-cent piece was a counterfeit, so I brought it back to the barber shop and told him so. "No! oh, no, sar! Oi don't give you any such bad money. Oi are doin' 'onest bizinez like de Bible," was the barber's false assertion; and the half-dollar piece became forever useless. This was American civilization!

I thought America was the land of Christian civilization and general education, but I soon lost my confidence in her, for the language was imperfect, the man was knavish and with a strong race prejudice, much stronger than in China, a pagan kingdom, so called by the Christian missionaries.

The people in America have no sense of dignity, and they serve woman as their deity. Yet the women are to be pitied, too. On festive occasions they are compelled to appear almost naked before every man who likes to look at them, and then they are dragged around a room to the accompaniment of noisy music.

One evening when I went to the theater, accompanied by my friend, I found more horror and luxury of this people. When I was in my old country I saw some pretty pictures on a cigarette box of a half-naked white woman with a fan, lifting her foot and hand. I, who knew only the modest, graceful Oriental women, could hardly believe such a female figure was ever copied from life. But in that house I saw the reality; and also it was a very strange sight to see the men and women who look at such things dressed in their best, and gazing with mouths wide open. What impression would these men and women get from such fascinating play of frail beauties clad in tights and profligate actors? Yet these people of Christendom had a peculiar proclivity to it, as, in the city of New York alone, there were over fourteen hundred such houses, besides many hundred music-halls, all in full operation.

Next to that was the savage wrestling, two stout-necked men fighting each other in a ring until one was bruised to helplessness, the spectators, both men and women, staking money upon it, as in horse-races or cock-fights. It was indeed more inhuman than the Spanish bull-fights; and it was, of course, one of the unchristian features of Christendom!

I had spent over a month in the city, and now I was longing after my native food, rice and fish. Some of my companions told me that if I went to Chinatown I could eat all such food as much as I wanted. It is situated in the neighborhood of Five Points. The best day to see the place is Sunday, when the laundry business is closed and the almond-eyed fellow takes things easy after the manner of his American customer, and comes to that place to disport himself in gambling, drinking, and smoking his favorite pipe. When I went inside the restaurant I found everything was in Chinese fashion. The little images of pagan gods were on the shelf with flowers and burning incense. I noticed also quite a number of young American females, together with the pig-tailed men, sitting round a table, eating the Chinese macaroni and enjoying the heathen cups. What and who were these eccentric damsels? Alas! the women of the demi-monde the same with those of the opium dens. If the visitor has any curiosity to penetrate into the interior of the cellar, he will see three or more rooms divided into cabins by thin partitions, and in each cabin three or more wooden couches arranged. The smoker lies down on one of these couches. He inhales a few breaths of the smoke of the burning opium, and then is wrapped in a dream-laden atmosphere of lethargy. This evil was not practised simply by the Chinamen, but there were several such houses exclusively for the use of white people. They were established in the neighborhood of Five Points, and farther up town. These places were known as "joints" by the white opium smokers.

Though this is a democracy, yet the people are crazy after titles. At the small hotel down town, one young man was invariably addressed as "General," and another who lives on his father's money, as I was told, was called "King." Though these were only nicknames, yet the tendency thus shown is seen to prevail in higher circles. Even the educated newspaper editors are addicted to this titleism. In the daily papers such items will be seen as: "The Hon. E." and "ex-Secretary of State F." said this; "His Excellency the Governor of B," and "General H." did that; "Madame S." and "Lady W." organized so and so; "Doctor P." and "Professor G." have returned from Europe; "Colonel L," and "Captain M." killed so many Indians in such battle, etc. College presidents are given the degree of Doctor of Laws, and Doctor of Divinity is conferred upon clergymen. "In no country in Europe," says a French writer, "do you hear so many titles, or see so many insignia worn."

When I was in my old country, I used to call America "The Home of Christians," and the image of it, as pictured upon my mind, was that of a real Paradise. I suffered and toiled, on land and sea, for many years simply to come to that high ideal home to be educated. Here I was. After my brief inspection of all such customs as I have mentioned above, I made the following note in my memorandum: "Is this the civilization of which we were taught in our home? I was deceived indeed! Apparently a prosperous country, but really going to decay. She has conquered the British and the Southern slaveholder, but now luxury and intemperance are restricting her liberty. With what shame-facedness should the missionaries teach our people about the superiority of Christian civilization over pagan countries, and call us miserable sinners and poor heathen!" My trust in a highly regarded Christendom was for the time almost driven away from my mind.

I had had many experiences, however, in strange countries long before I had reached the American shore, and I knew pretty well about human nature and society. As I spent day after day in the city, I came to understand gradually that I was looking among too low a class of people in the American republic. "If such customs were universal, how could this be the home of Washington, Franklin, Webster, Lincoln, Patrick Henry, John Brown, and Ulysses Grant?" I said to myself.

"The eye, which sees all things, cannot see itself." If I looked at such low-class people in my old country, what horrible things should I find? With a beam in my own eye, I was trying to pull out the mote out of another man's eye! That is not altogether wise. Truly, I was observing an inferior part of society which had been recently brought over from the old European countries.

In the early history of America a multitude of black-skinned Hamites had been imported to America, while a multitude of white-skinned poor descendants of Japheth had come of their own accord. The difference in them was this, that the former were sent to work for a master, while the latter came in freedom to work for mammon; and to some extent both were slaves just the same.

The walls of the vast republic were surrounded largely by these people. "Look not upon one's outward appearance," was a very applicable word for the Yankee society. And at last I will advocate her right with one word:—Judge not the honeycomb by its look, for the honey cannot be found on the outside.

CHAPTER XIII
LIGHT OF AMERICA

AMERICANS ARE NOT AN ISOLATED, INDEPENDENT race like the Chinese, but embrace peoples of all nationalities that have been naturalized or were born in the United States. Once I heard a speech from a curly-haired black man at the anniversary of Washington's birthday. "Gentlemen! we are born 'Merican citizen, de children ov George Washington!" The name, American citizenry was a matter of pride even to that black man. I knew a young Jew in New York, whose father had lived in that city about fifteen or sixteen years, who was forbidden to eat pork or anything that was cooked with lard, and who had no knowledge of English. Still, he did a large business in the city, and called himself an American citizen. Once I was told that "the newspaper of the largest circulation, and of the most unsavory reputation, in New York City, is owned by a Jew; and not long ago Boston itself had an Irish Catholic as its mayor." Even in a small Puritan city like New Haven there were Jewish, French, German, and English churches, with preaching in the mother-tongue of each nationality. It is not, therefore, very easy for a stranger to judge the great American republic from its exterior.

But the danger to which superficial travelers in the United States are exposed is that they "see her by candlelight," and never look into the inner heart of the nation. Their note-books are filled with references to the corruptions of American society and the degradation of the Christian religion.

Years ago America was visited by Charles Dickens, who subsequently wrote an indiscreet book about the country, with glaringly ridiculous statements. Taine, the French author, also has written a book about America after a short stay there, and the result was almost equally unfortunate. So with our Japanese observers. Some years ago, for example, a company of our young students whose acquaintance with the Caucasian race in Japan had been mostly with missionaries, came to America for study. Until the very landing at "Frisco," these men thought that the people in America were all saintly men, whose hearts were filled with noble Christian purposes; who sang hymns from morning till evening; and that the whole nation praised the Lord with harps and horjis, with hosannas, hallelujahs, and amens. But soon they saw degraded and vicious society, as I have portrayed it in the other chapter. The young men were shockingly disappointed and began to feel that there must be much truth in the statement of the antichristians in their home: "Christianity has already begun to lose its power in the West." They all reported to their influential newspapers and magazines about what they heard and saw in America. Gradually, the native theologians and the preachers of the gospel began to think that they were too restricted by the old theology which was far behind the time. The cry "Japan for Japanese," became strong; they tried to establish a pure Japanized Christian church in their own kingdom. Next to that was a partial reformation of our girls' education. The old literature, poetry, and the suitable housekeeping training were abolished; and instead of it, philosophy, German and French languages and sciences took the old place. Ungraceful, impudent, and affected "American" girlhood was introduced. Free marriages and woman's rights were proclaimed from her sweet little mouth, out of which it seemed impossible that such language should come. She was walking arrogantly like a man, with a foreign bonnet with the back side in front. She was proud of her education, and she loved to attend political and scientific lectures which had little or no connection with her line of work; and with all that she neglected, her own business, which is to win the heart by her natural sweetness and attraction.

This state of things was brought about mostly by the misleading of one-sided advocates. But he who knows thoroughly the true American society would never forget its charming, modest, generous, patriotic, and friendly people; and really one cannot avoid a homesickness for that land of stars, though he comes back to his own native country.

But to return to my story. My friend, the old shipmate, went to sea again; but sometime before he departed he placed me in one of the best academies in the city, and I was taught there daily.

Although there were so many fine places to visit in the city, yet loneliness in the heart is unavoidable to any sojourner in a strange country. "Alone!" Ah, what more sorrowful word is there in the language, than that single one, "Alone"? Alone I was living among a different race of people, with a limited knowledge of their language. In the school, no one could teach me with the tongue which I learned from my mother's lips; but, word after word, I must struggle with my dictionary. In the boarding-house, I could not enjoy any of my native food; and the old mistress was scornful if I neglected to pay a week's room-rent and board in advance.

"By lying down and eating, even a mountain may be consumed," is a saying common among my countrymen. My pocket was growing empty, and I was anxious about my future. How could I feed and clothe myself when all my money was gone? I knew that if I told my poor condition to the hostess, she would be glad to employ me as her house servant; but I was too proud, and would not ask anything as a favor, so the old lady did not think of me as a poor young man. No one knew of all I suffered save myself and my Father in heaven.

"Skin for skin, yea, all that a man hath will he give for his life. But put forth thine hand now, and touch his bone and his flesh," was the suggestion of Satan to Job's Master.

My next trial was suffering with a dangerous illness. One day, when I walked home from school, I got a severe cold. The sickness was the first I ever experienced in my life. I spent all my money for medicine and for a doctor. When I was lying helplessly in bed, my schoolmate came and asked me why I did not use some medicine. I told him that I had spent all my money, and now I could not ask the doctor anymore. He then accompanied me to a dispensary at Centre Street, where I was examined kindly by a doctor, and medicine was given without charge. One morning, when I went there as usual, the doctor told me if I wanted to be cured quicker, I had better go to the hospital.

"But, doctor, I have no friend to pay my expenses," I said to him.

"Never mind that; we are good friends to Japan," he said.

And that encouraged this helpless patient, myself. He gave me a letter addressed to a head officer in the hospital. After I went there my schoolmate removed all my things from the boarding-house into his residence, and he visited my sick-bed as often as he could. The following note was translated from my Japanese pen, which was written in my memorandum shortly before I left the hospital:

"Bellevue Hospital is situated on the banks of East River, a beautiful eight-storied stone building. It has a large fine garden with a view of the river. The rooms are nicely decorated and heated with steam. When I came here, four weeks ago, a doctor examined me first; then I was put into a nice room. Soon two nurses came and taking off all my garments, gave me a warm bath, then put on me new white clothes. The meals and medicine were brought by an attendant. Every morning two nurses came and wiped my face and hands, and combed my hair, etc. I, the motherless refugee, now became a happy child in a Christian family. Last Sunday a company of children came and sung for us a beautiful hymn, 'Behold a stranger at the door!' My eyes were filled with tears, and they ran down and wet all my pillow. A wealthy Christian lady has been visiting our room quite often, and she gave me flowers, cakes, fruits, books, and all necessary things. She also told me to come straight to her residence when I got well, and she would send me to school. I write these lines in this memorandum in honor of the doctors, the kind-hearted lady, nurses, and, last of all, the Bellevue Hospital."

Time passes like the running water. It was on a glorious day in spring, I was made whole, and my life was again saved from the fate of death. I thanked the Lord and Saviour. My faith, which was small as a grain of mustard seed, now sprang over into a large portion of my heart, and my interest in God's work grew so strong that I forgot everything else, even the kind word of the lady who had told me to come to her home. With all that I left the hospital like a bird which is flying away from a cage.

When I met with my old friend, he told me that he had provided for me already a nice place to work and study. The next day he accompanied me to a government hospital in the city, and I was very gladly employed there. The officers and men were very kind; a nice clean room was offered me, a library and reading-room were furnished freely with new books and periodicals, and I could keep up with my studies, too.

Now, I had no trouble with my own living, and I had time enough to observe the very heart of Christendom.

When I was in my old home, I thought my country was the center of all beauties, both in scenery and custom. Her soil is fertile, climate mild, seas deep and mountains high, such as could be found nowhere else but in Japan; and the land itself was the very abode of gentlemen and gods. But when I saw the banks of the Hudson River, moonlight nights on High Bridge and Washington Heights, the interior of New Jersey, and Long Island, I was surprised. The picturesque mountains, solitary lakes, passionate streams, pine-clad hills, velvet lawns, and green pastures were simply grand. Along the coast of Staten Island and Sandy Hook, the water and sky are as clear and blue as a maiden's eyes. Many fine mansions appear in the woods, and the white smoke curls out from each chimney like a beauty's forelock. A small house away from the crowd is more highly esteemed than a large house in the crowd. A white yacht perhaps is sailing swiftly with her shadow on the water, which is tranquil as a mirror. The full spring moon is bright, calm, splendid. On the whole, the scenery is more like a picture than a reality.

Besides these attractive natural views, there were many valuable art galleries and fine museums in the city. There were also over six hundred houses of God whose doors were thrown open on every Sabbath. The melodious notes of the organ were heard along the aisles of the church, and the bells were ringing out sweet notes of music. All the stores, even the saloons, were closed on that day. The crowded markets now became as quiet as a graveyard, and everybody seemed busy for churchgoing. These houses of God were mostly built of fine stones, broad on the ground, with massive columns and high spires. The interior of the buildings was beautifully decorated. The floors and aisles were carpeted, the pews all cushioned, and hymn-books, Bibles, and fans provided and laid in these pews. The preaching was practical and timely, and the singing was very charming. It is a place of worship, enjoyment, and public education.

On the other hand, charity works in that city are very active and successful, and are instituted to relieve the suffering of a vast number of persons of every condition, religion, or want. There are almshouses for the needy, societies for the friendless, houses of shelter for the fallen, reformatories for the erring, homes for boys and girls, all of them watched over and superintended by men and matrons who understand their work thoroughly. Free libraries, reading-rooms, night schools are opened for everybody without distinction of race. Free dispensaries and hospitals are plenty on every hand; and the merciful hand of Christ touches all the sick people; not his direct hand, but, by his wonderful name, the people throw money voluntarily into such work to save the millions of poor sick men and women, as in the days of their Saviour along the sea of Galilee.

Important auxiliaries in the moral sphere of things in the city are the Young Men's Christian Association and the Midday Fulton Prayer Meeting. The former is on Twenty-third Street, and is a large, handsome erection, five stories high, with numerous apartments, including halls, lecture-rooms, offices, etc. Many young men have received good by coming to these rooms; and it is calculated that over seven hundred persons enter the rooms of the Association every day, and that upwards of one hundred thousand come to the reading room every year. The Midday Fulton Prayer Meeting is held in a large hall in Fulton Street. Working men, merchants, and earnest people in general come here for an hour at midday; they return to their business and occupations carrying with them increased strength and joy.

"Oh, what a delightful land, thou Christendom!" was now for the first time impressed upon my mind. Soon my pride in the old native country was gone, and an idea caught my mind that she was yet a whitewashed grave. And little by little, my heart was converted to Americanism. Yet let me widely wake up and look at these two strange people with an impartial eye.

Although the color of skin is different, yet we are the same human beings who live nowhere else but on this one small planet beneath the marvelous sky, and with a short earthly life less than a century long. Then, whole is a king, or a peasant? It seems to me a man in this world is more like an ant which is creeping on a sugar bowl. The difference in mind and thought of each race chiefly depends upon the religion which they believe. We, the Orientals, were led by Buddha and Confucius. They taught our people a strict obedience to a master, father, and a woman to her husband. Although a man has a heart full of gratitude, or of love for another, yet he will not express it in words readily, but will wait for a chance to show it by his action. "Please guess at and discern my heart," was common to use in our conversation. A person is bound to do everything under a sense of obligation more than for the exact reward of money. On the contrary, the Americans are a people of genuine sentiment. They are ready to express their feelings of joy or sorrow in language without any form of crookedness or in indirect ways. Hugging and kissing his relatives before the eyes of a stranger was not contrary to custom. In his heart there were nothing but truthfulness, sympathy, and love. Such a beautiful custom must be the result of the religion of Jesus, whose heart was filled with truthfulness, sympathy, and love!

> "Blest are the men whose feelings move,
> And melt with sympathy and love:
> From Christ the Lord shall they obtain
> like sympathy and love again."

CHAPTER XIV
IN AMERICAN SCHOOLS

MY ACADEMY WAS STRICTLY CHRISTIAN; the principal was a well-known Christian worker in the city. In my studies I was interested in my Bible above all other books. My service in the government hospital was very prosperous, too. The head doctor was a man who took thorough interest in me and gave me his confidence and love. I had no trouble whatever with my living, as I was receiving a stated salary from the government, besides the nice board, a room, and everything else.

But, once in a while, when I thought of my poor Aino people, how they were living in their rude cabins in the severe cold weather of the northern province of Japan, my heart was sore with sympathy. At last I determined that I should not stay content with such an easy life any longer; for I came to the United States, not to settle down permanently in joy and comfort, but to get a true, Christian education. Moreover, I had so many times faced death since I resolved to get to America that I realized the life which I possessed was not mine but belonged to God. Consequently "I do not live to eat, I eat to live;" and I live not for display nor for vain honor, neither for earthly riches. If I can do some good, and commend the word and character of Christ to the poor young men and helpless heathen young women, sometime before my name is registered in an obituary, I shall be truly satisfied, and shall want nothing more.

But above all, I must first learn how to teach and save my fellow men. Over a prima donna, princes, emperors, and thousands of listeners often rejoice, but we must remember that their rejoicing is at the price of her pain. Jesus died to give us life; so with all his apostles and saints. The noble churches and all Christian institutions are the price of the martyr's blood. And I must prepare to shed mine in the future, too. I prayed my heavenly Father to guide me into a noble Christian institution where I could learn the right methods for my future plan.

I learned about a large industrial school in Virginia. It was exactly such an institution as I had looked for, and desired to establish for my people. I wrote a letter in my broken English and forwarded it to the principal of that school. After a few days I received his answer, a handwritten letter which was filled with the spirit of love for his fellow men, and a fatherly affection toward this new-found stranger. Part of his letter read as follows:

"I am interested in you and wish to help you as much as I can. Now I wish to see you. Please meet me at the Everett House, Union Square, New York City, next Monday morning. I will talk with you, and you can come with me to this school."

The word, "I will never leave thee nor forsake thee," became real to me. My unseen Father had now committed this unrepentant sinner to the hand of his faithful servant. And, except by God's guidance, who could say such accurate and trustful words to a stranger? This real man, the servant of God, and the Christlike volunteer, was the late General Samuel Chapman Armstrong.

I found now a benefactor, and a light on the way of my path. But, ah! what shall I do with my kindhearted superintendent, the head doctor? If I say that I am going to Virginia, what disappointment will I give him? "Well! I will rather speak nothing to him, but simply ask him for my discharge from the hospital," I thought. Such was the self-restraint of the Oriental mind, and such was the Eastern custom!

When I asked the doctor about my discharge, "Oh, no! no! no! what the d——l now have you in your mind? Certainly, you must stay with us," cried the dignified old officer.

But I told him my determination, and asked him again and again.

He, at last, sadly said to me: "This is a free country. I've no right to keep you if you have made up your mind to go!" He summoned his high officers into his office, wrote my certificate and read it before the council, then handed it to me with a parting word. The letter read as follows:

U. S. N. H., New York, Sept. 4, 1889. I have the greatest pleasure in certifying to the invariably estimable, commendable and perfect behavior of J. O., during the time he has been in my employ at this Hospital, and I have no hesitancy in recommending him as worthy of implicit trust and as industrious and zealous in the discharge of whatever duty he may undertake.

A. L. G.

MEDICAL DIRECTOR U. S. N.,

IN CHARGE OF HOSPITAL.

The distinguished senior officer of the United States Government crowned me with such words, although I had done him very poor service. With much feeling of gratitude for his kindness, I left the hospital. Then I went to my old academy to bid farewell to the friends. The principal gave me a worthy letter of recommendation, and told me that he would be glad to help me at any time.

The days slipped by, and then came the "Monday morning" which was the promised day to see my unknown benefactor.

When I went into the Everett House on Union Square, I found many persons in the parlor. I sat down and waited for the gentleman. Though I had never met him before, yet I knew that his title was the "General." So the appearance of that soldier, as pictured in my mind, was of a dignified man in full dress uniform with gold medals and ornaments. I did not pay attention to any gentlemen, because there was no such person in the parlor. After about half an hour a middle-aged, slender looking gentleman in citizen's dress laid aside his morning paper, and looked at me closely, and then addressed me: "Is this not my young man whom I love and am looking for?"

His face was rather pale, his mouth was small and tight, his eyes were narrow and long; he had no moustache but had a thin beard on both of his cheeks, and his hair was almost white. I could hardly believe that such a meek man was a gallant soldier who had smashed the southern army into pieces.

Half in doubt, I answered, "Is this the General?"

Now he came close to me and shook my hand. "Yes, yes! very happy to meet you, my son. Your thought in the letter which you sent to me was very fine, too. I will look after you, and pay all your school expenses for you so far as I can. Come now with me to my home."

Was this man a soldier or a saint? Neither name was too good for him. The world bestowed on him the title of a "genuine philanthropist."

We left the city by the train, and soon arrived at his home in Virginia. By his kindness I was placed in the agricultural department for practice, and also I attended the normal school.

I chose agriculture for my trade, because it is the source of the country's wealth and because it was my purpose to teach it to my pupils who would prepare for the ministry and look for a foreign field, and also because I could take my physical exercise without losing time and money for it. By the kindness of the General I was specially permitted to take one or two months' practice in each section throughout the agricultural department: such as in the nursery and in the barn, out in the field for general farm-work, taking care of horses, feeding hundreds of pigs and chickens, milking cows, making butter, out in the pasture, and in the butchery, etc.

One morning, while I was working in the cornfield along the roadside, I met with two Japanese high officials who came to inspect the institution. One of them asked me in English: "Will this road lead us to the school?"

I thought he was a very proud and affected person, because he spoke to his countryman in English, as, generally, we never do.

Soon nine o'clock came. I changed my clothes in haste, and went to the recitation room, as usual. There I met with the Japanese visitors, shook hands with them, and began to talk in my mother-tongue. The officials were surprised at me, and they said that when they met me at the road side, they thought I was a black farmer boy. So the reader may easily judge how I looked in those days.

Once in a while the General inspected our department, and when he found me in the field he always encouraged me. "If all your countrymen do like yourself, Japan will soon become a first-class nation!" It was a golden word to me. Truly, if such a method were taken with all young men, we could sweep out the ugly words pauper, cockney, prodigal, etc., from our dictionary.

The "industrial school" was well named. The General and all his officers were industrious and zealous in their work, and it was characteristic of the school. There were over fifty young lady teachers, besides the numerous male instructors, and they were all fresh from New England colleges. I had thought that ladies are generally weak, feeble, and tender, but here all the misses were active, earnest, studious, and sensible, like men. "Woman can rule as well as men" was manifested to me without any doubt. One of the school dames went to Japan and did splendid work among our women and for the empress. She came back to her old school in triumph, and wrote an admirable book on our girls and women. She was indeed a heroine, and certainly she is a product of Christian America. Comparing this lady with our Eastern females, whom I used to call graceful, tender, and gentle, I find a vast difference, and the modest Oriental womanhood cannot bring forth any equal.

All my associations here were Christian, and even the dogs and cats in the school grounds seemed to have some idea of religion. I could no longer keep my old heathenism; and at last my heart was modeled into Christian shape. By the help of the General and other friends, I was baptized in the name of the Trinity by our chaplain. I cast off my old garment, and now I was clothed with the new raiment of light.

Once when I was feeding the cows, the director of our department came and pointed out to me a fine Jersey cow, and told me not to give her any food or water for a whole day and night. I thought that he was doing so because he disliked that cow, or else he was fooling me, for it must be hard for any animal to live without food or water for a day and night. I pitied her and I could not sleep all that night. About ten o'clock in the night I went into the barn and gave the poor cow plenty of bran, barley, and hay. I returned to my room with much satisfaction.

The next morning when I came to the barn I found a veterinary doctor, the director, and two or three other persons surrounding a dying cow.

When I saw the director, he asked me:

"Did you not feed her yesterday after I told you not to do so?"

I did not know what answer I should give him.

Suppose I say No, I will break the divine law; but if I say Yes, what punishment will I get, though I did it in sympathy toward the animal? Still I could not keep silent, so I told him the truth.

"I thought so! I asked you not to feed her because we were expecting that she would have a calf. Now you have killed both the mother and the calf. Two hundred dollars in property has gone!" he said to me.

On the following day the cow was dead; the director had reported it to the General. I was summoned to his office. My feet stumbled, and my face became pale.

When I went into his office the General stood up and closed the door; then he put his hand upon my shoulder and very tenderly said: "I do not regret losing a cow. I am glad you have had such a tangible example of the danger of disobedience by killing an animal. Plenty of people in this world are wanting food, but be careful with your sympathy. If you think that charity is only giving them food and money, and if you neglect to give them the bread of life, which is the Word of God, you will spoil them." Then he smiled on me gently, and that smiling face to me was worth more than a thousand dollars.

By the generous treatment of the General and all his officers I learned everything very quickly. I was privately instructed also in Greek and Latin by a kind lady teacher. I observed all I wanted, and now I was looking for a higher school. The only trouble was the expense. I knew, however, that if I should ask the General he would be glad to help me and send me to any college or university; but according to my Oriental mind, which was imbued with the doctrines of ancient magians, I did not ask him, neither did I consult with him about the matter.

Soon the General went on his annual tour round the United States, and he did not come home for some time. I felt quite lonesome, though I had many good friends all around me. I was now trying to go to a higher school to prepare for my life work. But who would help me? No one; but my unseen Benefactor was still looking after me with the loving word, "I will instruct thee and teach thee in the way which thou shalt go."

As the result of my earnest prayer I found many Christian colleges in Iowa, Oberlin, New Haven, Boston, New York, and in Washington City. But I could not ask about choosing these schools openly of any of my school friends; at least, I feared to injure the feelings of my loved teachers; and such was the peculiar Oriental mind, too.

When a person is desiring or thinking something in his mind, and cannot express it to others but keeps it all to himself, it gives him anxiety, pain, and disquiet. I was perplexed, indeed, and was tired from my inexpressible suffering. I lay on a sofa, and read Smiles' "Self Help," and there I found how Grant and his two brothers went to search after a fortune, and judge the place by lot; that is, they took the cane, and stood it before them and they went in the direction in which it fell, and became rich and famous. My heart was wakened again. I took a paper and cut it in many pieces; I wrote the name of one school on each paper, and cast the lot. The first one which I found was the name of Howard University, in the city of Washington. But I wanted to go to New Haven for my study. So I cast the lot again with most hearty prayer to my unseen Father; and again I found the same name, Howard University. Thus, now, I decided to go to the university at the capital.

Although I had no superstitious ideas, yet I believe divine direction comes to those who seek it. I do not believe in the existence of any visible angels, but this conscious, yet indescribable sense of divine guidance I called an angel, a messenger of God to me. So I believe here that my way was appointed by my heavenly Father.

Though I had no friend in the capital, yet by faith I made up my mind to go to the university as a wealthy young scholar who could help himself. But I was poor, and yet rich spiritually. To my eyes, the gold and silver were worth nothing more than a piece of rock or stone. Can a man carry all his earthly treasures into heaven? Nay! "Nothing in our hands we bring," and in the same manner we must go! But how many young men are ruined inwardly and spiritually by their intense desire to get riches! Remember that the corruption of each nation has sprung from their worship of mammon instead of the true God in heaven. See the last days of Babylonia, Egypt, and the great Roman Empire. So must it be with each individual.

After I made my decision to go to the university in the capital, there came another thought that if I lived in Washington until I was through with my course of study, I should be benefited by finding many new things both in public museums and in good society, besides the knowledge of books; and it must be a liberal education for a heathen convert like myself to be in such a city.

Now I addressed a letter to the President of the University, whose name is so well known everywhere as the author of the famous hymn, "God be with you till we meet again," and other fine lyrics. I told him what I wanted and asked him, "How can I learn Christian civilization among these wild Indians?"

It is most astonishing to see how the mind and heart of the true sons of God are drawn to each other, as in the cases of David to Jonathan, and Paul to Timothy. Although I never met with the president, nor was recommended to him by any friend, yet, only by one communication, he looked through my heart at once, and knew this poor refugee from bottom to top. He answered my letter with the following words:

"We have concluded that you can enter one of our departments. I need not remind you of your duty to your kind teachers there. You must secure their assent and approval. You seem to understand that very well. It is not certain that we can do as well by you as they. But, if you come here, we will try and do the best we can. You can ask for me. I live on the university grounds. Till I see you, good-bye.

YOURS VERY TRULY," ETC.

CHAPTER XV
AT THE CAPITAL—UNIVERSITY LIFE

FOR MANY DAYS I HAD WRESTLED IN PRAYER for the higher education, and now I had the answer. I could not let go this opportunity, for I had my long-cherished plan still in view; and, also, I heard that my father in Japan was getting old and waiting for my return. Moreover, the spring term of the university had just begun, and my promise to the kind-hearted president must not be broken. For these reasons I could no longer wait for the arrival of the General. I left a letter to him, and finished all my business with the secretary and with a sad heart left the old Virginian home and many good friends.

I took a river boat and steamed up the Potomac, and soon arrived at the capital of the nation. The first thing that I wondered at was the Washington obelisk or national monument, which is the loftiest construction of masonry in the world. In the city the streets are broad and paved with stone or concrete, and everything is nice and clean as in a parlor. The trees are planted along the sidewalks, and the whole city was decorated with a beautiful green. The dwellings and public buildings were fine and large. The characteristic of the people was a special refinement, and it seemed to me that they were not so hurried in the street as the New Yorkers or Bostonians.

To the eyes of a Washingtonian, my appearance must have been quite strange, for my old black hat had faded into brown, my half-broken shoes had not been brushed for many days. I was miserably clad in an old worn-out suit, with a big satchel in my hand, together with an old umbrella and a cane.

In such a condition I entered the university gate. When I appeared at the secretary's office, "Johnny, what do you want now?" asked the secretary.

"I want to see the head man of this university," I answered." What! whom do you mean? the President?"

"Yes, I suppose he is expecting me here."

"Oh, you are the one whom the Doctor is so highly speaking of? You had better sit down here, sir; I will send a boy to the President?" he said very courteously.

My heart was not at ease, for in a minute or two I must have audience with a man who had the high titles of D.D. and LL.D., and who could undoubtedly look through a person's heart by one glance of his keen eye; and whether I would be accepted or refused was wholly to depend on that interview. But, behold, when the door of the secretary's office was opened, there came in a gentleman somewhere near sixty years of age, with a brisk business air, but clothed with meekness and humility. He introduced himself to this half-read scholar, and with kind welcome words he clasped my hand unusually tight.

"Why!" I said to myself, "what country does this man belong to?" And in my heart I answered, "A Christian country." I asked at once for daily Bible study, and was told I should have all the Bible I wanted.

Although it was my first interview with the gentleman, yet I soon felt as though I had known him for years, and this feeling must have been the same with the president, for I noticed it in all his ways of talking. He soon accompanied me to his residence, and introduced me to his family. It was about midday, and after I had dined with his family, the kind Doctor invited me to his private study. He handed me a family Bible and bade me read the twenty-second chapter in the book of Proverbs. After I read it, he knelt and offered a prayer to God,—the tenderest prayer that I ever heard from the voice of man.

"I know men, and I tell you that Jesus Christ was not a man," was the saying of Napoleon Bonaparte. So I might say, "I know men, and that this president was not simply a man but a Christian." Indeed, outside of true Christendom, where can we find such a godly race? All persons have the same sensibilities; that is, if a white man can test sugar as sweet, a black man also will test it the same; and so through all the range of his faculties. Then, we must know that everyone can tell something about good and bad. If Christianity is a bad religion, how is it, since its Founder taught only three years, that his disciples, who were the meanest fishermen, carried it along the shores of Galilee, and finally it has spread all over Europe and America, and is spreading over Asia and Africa, and all the islands of the sea? Ah, stupid idolaters! how long will they stay in their blindness and keep away from Him who is the true Light which came from the bosom of our Father in heaven and lighteth every man that cometh into the world?

A few years ago, at the Chicago World's Fair, a company of Japanese Buddhist priests came and preached to the American public. In the city of Washington the priests had a distinguished audience, and among them was the wife of the president, and some other leading society ladies. After these priests went back to their home land, they said that the Americans were eagerly seeking after the mercy and blessing of Buddha; and they were already tired of the corrupt religion of Jesus. I must laugh at these obstinate priests, for they could not make a distinction between science and religion. A few Americans listened to them as lecturers on an ancient philosophy or science, and that was all. The priests had not sense enough even to understand about the generosity of the people of Christendom, who had treated them with such brotherly love and courtesy, not at all as the first Christian missionaries to their country were treated, who were cruelly persecuted and put to death.

Now, my American patron, the president, knew my heart better than my own parents; and the close friendship between the Doctor and myself was increased day by day. He called me "Isaiah," and I was often his page and companion whenever he was invited to various noted public meetings, and by his introduction, I met with several illustrious men of the day.

One of the great missionary meetings, the Moody meeting, is certainly worthy to be recorded here. That wonderful man had labored in the capital about thirty days. The meeting was held in the largest hall in the city. Every time the service was opened by the great choir of sixteen hundred voices, massed on a rising, semicircular platform. Mr. Sankey's solo singing was most marvelous. All noise instantly ceased when he took the seat to sing. On the platform, beside Mr. Moody, were nearly all the leading pastors of the city, prominent professional men, members of Congress, the president's wife and her lady friends. Over six thousand people made up the regular evening audience during the thirty days' assembly. Every morning, afternoon, and evening, Mr. Moody preached with mighty power. I cannot fully describe this eminent Christian soldier. I might say one word, however, that he was "a man sent from God," and that would be sufficient for him and for all. On the last evening of the mission over four thousand Christians rose to testify that they had been revived; and I was one of them. Soon I was kindly recommended by President Rankin to a well-known pastor in the city, and I became a member of his blessed church which has one thousand fellow members. It was the church of which he himself had been fifteen years pastor.

The president was always very busy, and had no resting-day in the week, not even on Sunday, as he preached on that day in the college chapel. But whenever he had a vacant hour we both took a walk and visited the public places in the city, such as the White House, the Capitol, libraries, the National Museum, the Smithsonian Institution, the art gallery, the Zoological Park, and various public gardens. The most worthy to mention here was the capitol. Here are some of my notes about it: "It occupies a lofty seat on the western edge of the plateau of Capitol Hill. The surrounding park comprises about fifty-two acres. The building is 751 feet by 324 feet, including porticos. The whole structure is of the Corinthian order. The original building was of Potomac Creek freestone, but an enormous marble terrace and grand stairway erected on the north, west, and south gives the structure an imposing appearance. The interior of the capitol is divided into the House of Representatives, the Senate Chamber, Supreme Court, Library, Rotunda and Statuary Hall, etc. Entering the capitol by the east front, a visitor is at once struck with the fine appearance of the door. It is all of bronze, and cost $30,000." I feel sorry that I can describe only the outward building, and cannot attempt to show the backbone of the capitol, that is, the members of the house. But it is enough for a person if he knows that the chaplains of the Congress are both blind men—blind, but they see all spiritual things with a most clear eye, and we should judge no man by his bodily eyes!

The most disappointing thing to a visitor's expectation is the White House, the official residence of the President, comparing it with the homes of the emperors and kings in the old world. There are no military officials at its gates. A stranger may enter without obstruction or questions. The mansion is a plain two-storied building. But such is the plainness and simplicity of the American republic and the home of liberty! Once I saw the inauguration of a new president. It was a cold, sleety day in March, yet the newcomer rode in his carriage from the capitol to the White House with bared head, taking off his silk hat almost all the way, as the crowds of people cheered him unceasingly. Comparing this to the coronation of the present Czar of Russia, which was conducted with enormous extravagance, there was a vast difference. The characteristics of the days of the "Mayflower" and the old Pilgrim Fathers are still carried out, and it is the spirit of America; but if she loses it, her condition will be like the salt which has lost its savor.

The Doctor and I were not only visiting and walking together, but for our physical exercise we both went to the market every day in the early morning before breakfast, to buy a day's provisions and other things. One day we bought a lawn-mower. I carried it all the way up to our house. The Doctor told me to draw it instead of carrying it, but I did not obey him.

"I suppose you have forgotten all your lessons in science. The machine has two wheels, and you must let them work instead of using your hands," was his advice.

"No, no! this is my principle, not to depend on others, so far as my strength will allow. But, of course, for my greater work, such as saving men, I must wholly depend upon good-hearted benefactors," I said to him, and it was more like a boy preaching philosophy to Plato. But such discussions were always brought up while we were walking on the streets of Washington.

At home, I was the Doctor's pet, but in the recitation-room he was a very strict master, and often he was pretty hard on me as well as on all his pupils, in catechetics and examinations. Sometimes I appealed to my affectionate mistress, and the Doctor was always playfully taken to task by the madam for his treatment of his boy.

In the president's classes I studied moral philosophy, Christian evidences, and other high branches of science. I had eight other classes to attend every day, as my studies were extended into two different departments. I liked all the professors. The professor of literature and oratory was the jolliest man I ever met. Once I was chosen to speak at the oratorical contest before the large public audience, the judges being some of the leading men in the capital. The place was the college chapel. Everything was in grand style. The hall was decorated with colors, the band played, and there were six speakers in all. After the young scholars presented their emphatic discourses, the chief judge, who was one of the editors of the Washington "Star," announced the opinion of his fellow judges. I did not get a prize, but he conferred upon me this title instead: "Born English orator." And then, the pride of my loving Doctor and the mistress was very excessive! All my other public speeches, such as those delivered at the anniversary of Washington's Birthday, presenting the president's portrait, which was drawn by myself, to the First Congregational Church, and in various missionary meetings in the city, were highly spoken of by the Washington papers. Everybody was kind to me. With most humble and thankful heart, I must return all my honor to my teachers. My instructor in drawing and painting was a goodhearted, refined lady, whose father had been a brigadier-general in the war.

I drew several portraits of distinguished personages, and earned more than a hundred dollars during one school year. The "Standard." a weekly paper, published the following notice: "Among the attractions in the University Chapel is a new portrait of Professor Bascom, by Mr. J. Oyabe of Japan. This young artist has done other very fine work, having made three crayons of ex-Senator Pomeroy, two of Madame Sono, and one of Doctor Rankin. Professor Bascom's portrait, too, is a very faithful and excellent one."

The professor of history and "dead languages" was a very devoted, strict, hard master. If his pupil missed one word in a sentence or the exact date of a certain event in the pages of history, he would not pass his examination. Largely on that account, when we reached the end of the senior term, there remained only five young men, though while we were in the junior year there were more than a dozen classmates.

Although my kind president was looking after my interests and all my needs, yet it was my nature to hate to ask anything of my friends, or to depend at all upon the care of others. So it was my usual custom to go out every summer vacation to work and earn some money for my own expenses.

One summer vacation day, in the city of New York, a friend of mine, who was a member of a respectable club, said to me: "Do prepare for us a lecture on Japan. It would be interesting to us, indeed!" I followed his advice, and did prepare a lecture entitled "An Evening Trip to Japan." He secured many places for me, at which I lectured, with good enough success to encourage me, though I think my English was better written than spoken.

A PROPOSAL TO AMERICAN POETS

YONE NOGUCHI

Hokku (seventeen-syllable poem) is like a tiny star, mind you, carrying the whole sky at its back. It is like a slightly-open door, where you may steal into the realm of poesy. It is simply a guiding lamp. Its value depends on how much it suggests. The Hokku poet's chief aim is to impress the reader with the high atmosphere in which he is living. I always compare an English poem with a mansion with windows widely open, even the pictures of its drawing-room being visible from outside. I dare say it does not tempt me much to see the within.

> "A cloud of flowers!
> Is the bell from Uyeno
> Or Asakusa?"
> (Basho.)

Yes, cloud of flowers, of course, in Mukojima, the odorous profusion shutting out every prospect! Listen to the bell sounding from the distance! Does it come from the temple of Uyeno or Asakusa? Doesn't the poem suggest a Spring picture of the river Sumida?

> "On a Withered branch,
> Lo! the crows are sitting there,
> Oh, this Autumn eve!"
> (Basho.)

What a suggestion for the solitariness of a Japanese Autumn evening!
The crows—what a monotonous "Kah! Kah, Kah!"—are the image of melancholy for Japanese.

Basho was a master of Hokku, a great suggester. He made long excursions to the remotest spots frequently, leaving behind him traces which remain to this day in the shapes of stones with his inscription. His monuments are said to number more than one thousand.

Pray, you try Japanese Hokku, my American poets!
You say far too much, I should say.
Here are some of my own attempts in the seventeen-syllable verse:

"My girl's lengthy hair
Swung o'er me from Heaven's gate:
Lo, Evening's shadow!"

"Lo, light and shadow
Journey to the home of night:
Thou and I—to Love!"

"Where the flowers sleep,
Thank God! I shall sleep, to-night.
Oh, come, butterfly!"

"Fallen leaves! Nay, spirits?
Shall I go downward with thee
'Long a stream of Fate?"

Selected Poems of Yone Noguchi, Selected By Himself

Yone Noguchi

In Memory

of

Basho,

a Hokku Poet

of the

Seventeenth Century

FOREWORD

I often wonder at the difference between the words of English Poets and the daily speech of common people; and I think that it is not necessary to go to Milton or Dryden for the proof. The poetical words used by Tennyson, Browning, Francis Thompson, and even Yeats, are certainly different from those spoken in the London streets or an English village shadowed by a church spire or darkened by dense foliage. But, on the other hand, how similar are the words of Japanese poets and those of the common people! Is it that the Japanese poets, whether they be Uta poets or Hokku writers, are condescending to the common people? Or is it that the common people of Japan are entering into the realm of poesy? Or is it that our Japanese phraseology belongs to either of them, or does not belong to either of them, through its virtue of being neutral in nature?

Suppose a pensive young lady is standing by a veranda opened to the garden with blooming cherry trees, and her eyes are following the snow-white petals of cherry blossoms hastening to the ground. And suppose she murmurs with a sigh, "Why do the flowers fall in such a flurry?" Now compare such an exclamation with the following Uta poem by Ki no Tomonori:

"'Tis the spring day
With lovely far-away light . . .
Why must the flowers fall
With hearts unquiet?"

It is plain to see how the words of Japanese poets and common people join hands. This particular point is most worthy of notice in the discussion of the differences and similarities between the East and West in literature.

It is said in the West that the poets are a race apart. The fact that our Japanese poets are not a race apart should be the very focus for a discussion of Japanese poets. While in the West the poets claim special regard and, indeed, immortality for themselves, we in Japan treat the poet as a natural phenomenon, as natural as a flower or bird.

I admit that we Japanese as poets are lacking in creative power, and do not aim, like many Western poets, at becoming rebuilders of life. We are taught not to deal with poetry as a mere art, but to look upon it as the most necessary principle along which our real life shall be developed. When we kneel before poetry, it is our desire to create a clarified pure realm where we can, through the inspiration of rhythm, arrange our own minds. And then we recognise its existence of the compromising ground of passion, where we as members of society find our safety. What great uncompromising creators of passion were Shelley, Byron, Browning and Swinburne! They were so earnest in their desire for the recreation of life, and not afraid were they, when their desire reached its climax, even to risk reaching a condition of confused intricacy. They were indeed great and wonderful heroes. We cannot help thinking, on the other hand, what cowards the majority of Japanese poets have been.

I respect that attitude of Western poets in wiping to rebuild or recreate their own lives; and also I can well understand why they ascribe importance to their intellectual power. A great literary danger lies in this, of course, because there is nothing more sad and terrible for poets than to enslave themselves to intellect.

But we have also our own literary danger. I mean that we often mistake a simple and cold morality for an art. I should like to know what is a more dangerous thing for poets than this sad morality. There are only a few Japanese poets who have failed from their abuse of moods and passions; but we know so many cases wherein their poetical failure was quite complete under the stifling breath of conventional morality. This damage would not necessarily be below that inflicted by intellect; it might be greater. We notice that the Western poets often attempt to discover a poetical theory even in the waving plaits of Apollo's robe and analyse intellectually a little cloud flying in the sky. Admitting that their poetical theory and intellectual power are doubtless great, I have no hesitation in declaring that it is they who harden, shrink, and wither their own art. It is true to say that they owe much to the matter of form for the great development of their epics and dramas. Also it is true that the undeveloped form of Japanese poetry has given a mighty freedom for our poets to fly into an invisible spiritual domain. We can say again that if these poets both of the West and the East often stray into the field of non-poetry, it is the result of their too close attachment to forms.

Of course we want more passion and intellect in our Japanese poets, and also properly tempered patience and effort. And at the same time we should hope that the Western poets would forget their passion and intellect to advantage and enter into the real poetical life born out of awakening from madness. I have no quarrel with a critic when he applies the word "mad" to his Western poets; but we Japanese would be pleased to see and admire the rare moment when madness grows strangely calm and returns to its normal condition, and there we will find our own real poetry. Not the moving dynamic aspect of all the phenomena, but their settled still aspect inspired the Japanese poets—at least the Japanese poets of olden days—to real poetry. But I know that the times are changing when we must, I think, cultivate the really living dynamic life. And I am afraid, with many others, that such a new literary step may bring us into an unhappy compromise with Western literature. Of course there are poets and writers both of the East and West who know only how to compromise. But, on the other hand, we have a natural-born Easterner, for instance, Wordsworth, in the West, and there may be a natural-bom Westerner in the East, who will bring the East and West together into true understanding, not through faint-hearted compromise but by the real strength of independence which alone knows the meaning of harmony.

Today we must readjust the meanings of all things or give a new interpretation to all the old meanings; and we must solve the problem of life and the world from our real obedience to laws and knowledge that will make the inevitable turn to a living song, and learn the true meaning of time from the evanescence of psychical life; then our human lives will become true and living.

We must realise the ephemeral aspect of moments when time moves, and also the still aspect of infinity when it settles down; seek the meaning of moments out of the bosom of infinity, and again that of infinity from the changing heart of moments—that is the secret of real poetry. The moments suggest the still aspect of infinity are accidental, therefore; again the infinity that is nothing but another revelation of moments is absolute, therefore quiet and full of strength and truth. The real poetry should be accidental and also absolute. See the river and trees, see the smiling garden flowers, see the breaks clouds of the sky. See also the lonely moon walking a precipitate pathless way through the clouds. The natural phenomena are, under any circumstances, revealing both meanings of the accidentalism which is born from the absolute. When our great poets of Japan write only of a shiver of a tree or a flower, of a single isolated aspect of nature, that means that they are singing of infinity from its accidental revelation.

The poetical attitude of Wordsworth was anarchical when, singing of the small celandine, daisy, and daffodils, he gave even a little natural phenomenon a great sense of dignity by making it a center of the universe, and broke the stupid sense of proportion by looking on things without discrimination; he was pantheistic, like nearly all Japanese poets and painters, because he was never troubled by any intellectual differentiation, and his clear and guileless eyes went into the simplicity that joined the universe and himself into one. His poetical sensibility was very true and plain, and he gained a real sense of the depth of space, the amplitude of time, and the circle of the universal law, and made his life's exigency a new turn of rhythm. I am glad to think of Wordsworth as the first Easterner of English literature.

I do not know what one critic means when he calls Robert Bridges the father of the new poetry, unless he means that Bridges has regained the artless bent of the poetical mind which was lost under the physical vulgarisation of the Mid-Victorian age, and that he has opened his honest eyes upon nature and life. He, like our Japanese Uta or Hokku poets, gazes on life's essential aspects. If the Japanese poets teach the Western poets anything, it is how to return to the most important feature of poetry after clearing away all the debris of literature; their expression is ample, therefore myterious in many respects; as it is mysterious, it is vivid and fresh, here is nothing more wonderful than the phrase "Seeing poetry exactly;" nobody who has never lived in poetry fully, aims to see its exact existence. And you cannot be taught to to live in it by reason of argument; you must have a sense of adoration that comes only from poetical concentration.

The time is coming when, as with international politics where the under-standing of the East with the West is already an unmistakable fact, the poetries of these two different worlds will approach of one another and exchange their cordial greetings. If I am not mistaken, the writers of free verse of the West will be ambassadors to us.

MY ACKNOWLEDGMENTS ARE DUE TO THE EDITOR OF THE OUTLOOK, NEW YORK, FOR PERMISSION TO REPRINT THIS ESSAY WHICH HAS APPEARED IN HIS PAGES.

FROM "SEEN AND UNSEEN" (1887)

What About My Songs

The known-unknown-bottomed gossamer waves of the field are coloured by the
  travelling shadows of the lonely, orphaned meadow lark:
At shadeless noon, sunful-eyed,—the crazy, one-inch butterfly (dethroned an-
  gel?) roams about, her embodied shadow on the secret-chattering hay-tops,
  in the sabre-light.
The Universe, too, has somewhere its shadow;—but what about my songs?
An' there be no shadow, no echoing to the end,—my broken-throated flute will
  never again be made whole!

Where Is the Poet

The inky-garmented, truth-dead Cloud—woven by dumb ghost alone in the
  darkness of phantasmal mountain-mouth—kidnapped the maiden Moon,
  silence-faced, love-mannered, mirroring her golden breast in silvery rivu-
  lets:
The Wind, her lover, grey-haired in one moment, crazes around the Universe,
  hunting her dewy love-letters, strewn secretly upon the oat-carpets of the
  open field.
O, drama! never performed, never gossiped, never rhymed! Behold to the blind
  beast, ever tearless, iron-hearted, the Heaven has no mouth to interpret
  these tidings!
Ah, where is the man who lives out of himself?—the poet inspired often to
  chronicle these things?

The Desert of 'No More'

Until Nothing muffles over the Universe of No More, my soul lives with the god, darkness and silence.

Ah, great Nothing?

Ah, the all-powerful Desert of No More!—where myriads of beings sleep in their eternal death; where the god dies, my soul dies, darkness dies, silence dies; where nothing lives, but the Nothing that lives to the End.

Listen to the cough of Nature!

After the cough, the Universe is silent again, my soul kissing the ever nameless idol faces of the Universe, as in a holy heathen temple.

Seas of Loneliness

Underneath the void-coloured shade of the trees, my 'self' passed as a drowsy cloud into Somewhere.

I see my soul floating upon the face of the deep, nay the faceless face of the deepless deep—

Ah, the Seas of Loneliness!

The mute-waving silence-waters, ever shoreless, bottomless heavenless, colourless, have no shadow of my passing soul.

Alas, I, without wisdom, without foolishness, without goodness, without badness,—am like God, a negative god at least!

Is that a quail? One voice out of the back-hill jumped into the ocean of loneliness.

Alas, what sound resounds; what colour returns; the bottom. the heaven, too, reappears!

There is no place of muteness! Yea, my paradise is lost in this moment!

I want not pleasure, sadness, love, hatred, success, unsuccess, beauty, ugliness—only the mighty Nothing in No More.

The Garden of Truth

Untimely frosts wreathe over the garden—the staid bottom were air the sea.

Alas! from her honeyed rim, frosts steal down like love-messengers from the Lady Moon.

A light-walled corridor in Truth's palace; a humanity-guarded chapel of God, where brave divinities kneel, small as mice, against the shoreless heavens,— the midnight garden, where my naked soul roams alone, under the guidance of Silence.

The God-beloved man welcomes, respects as an honoured guest, his own soul and body, in his solitude.

Lo! the roses under the night dress themselves in silence, and expect no mortal applaud,—content with that of their voiceless God.

Like a Paper Lantern

"Oh, my friend, them wilt not come back to me this night!"

I am lonely in this lonely cabin, alas, in the friendless Universe, and the snail at my door hides stealishly his horns.

"Oh, for my sake, put forth thy honourable horns!"

To the Eastward, to the Westward? Alas, where is Truthfulness?—Goodness?—Light?

The world enveils me; my body itself this night enveils my soul.

Alas, my soul is like a paper lantern, its pastes wetted off under the rainy night, in the rainy world.

FROM "THE VOICE OF THE VALLEY" (1898)

I Hail Myself as I Do Homer

The heart of God, the unpretending heaven, concealing the midnight stars in glassing the day of earth.

Showers his brooding love upon the green-crowned goddess, May Earth, in heart-lulling mirth.

O Poet, begin thy flight by singing of the hidden soul in vaporous harmony;

Startle the lazy noon drowsing in the full-flowing tide of the sunbeams nailing thy chants in Eternity!

The melody breathing peace in the name of Spring, calms tear to smile, envy to rest.

Ah thou, world of this day, sigh not of the poets who have deserted thee—aye, I hail myself as I do Homer!

Behold, a baby flower hymns the creation of the universe in the breeze, charming my soul as the lover-moon!

O Yone,—a ripple of the vanity-water, a rain drop from the vanity-cloud,—lay thy body under the sun-enamelled shade of the trees.

As a heathen idol in an untrodden path awakening in spirit sent by the unseen genius of the sphere!

The earth, a single-roomed hermitage for mortals, shows not, unto me a door to Death on the joy-carpeted floor—

Aye, I call the once dead light of day from the dark-breasted slumber of night!—

I repose in the harmonious difference of the divine Sister and Brother,—Voice and Silence in Time.

O Yone, return to Nature in the woodland,—thy home, where Wisdom and Laughter entwine their arms!

Ah Cities, scorning the order of the world, ye plunder rest from night, paint day with snowy vice,—

Alas, the smoke-dragon obscures the light of God; the sky measuring steeple speaks of discontent unto the Heaven!

O Yone, wander not city-ward—there thou art sentenced to veil thy tears with smiles!

Behold, the cloud hides the sins of the cities—regiments of redwood-giants guard the holy gates of the woodland against the shames!

Chant of Nature, O Yone,—sing thy destiny—hymn of darkness for the ivory-browed dawn—

Behold, the deathless Deity blesses thee in silence from the thousand temples of the stars above!

The Night Reverie in the Forest

"Buy my tears that I sucked from the breast of Truth—tears, sister spirits of Heaven's smile!" sobs the Wind.

Thou pale Wind, tear-vendor of the hideous night, no one welcomes thee with thy unsold tears!

Thou Gipsy-Wind, my fellow-wanderer who fears light, cease thy plaintive strain of the sweet home ever lost!

"O Poet, sole midnight comforter, share my tears in thy heart ever tenanted by Autumn!"

Kiss me, Wind, to whom the gates of Spring never swing open, let us sleep under the weeping candle-star!

O Repose, whose bosom harbours the heavenly dream-ships, welcome me, an exiled soul!

Thou Forest, where Peace and Liberty divide their wealth with even a homeless convict.

Let me sleep in thy arm-boughs, safer far than a king's iron castle guarded by mortal power!

Lull thy guest to reverie, master-spirit of the forest, with thy solemn love tales of ancient gods!

Here Ease and Grandeur lodge in the forest's heart, where Time ever reveals his changeless youth.

Five miles I travelled—the black-robed bird-monk had ended his last prayer, a good-night hymn;

Ten miles,—I lost the home window-light that bids Sorrow and Tears depart like masterless dogs;

Twenty miles,—the eloping mother-moon had abandoned her child, my lonely soul.

Thou Darkness, bewailing thy desertion by Light, I deplore my like fate, echoing thy saddest strain!—

Friend Night, my tears overflow from the love-fountain unto the sorrow-made dells!

I, an idle singer, fleeing from the world's shame, make a pilgrimage to an unknown land—O Heaven—or Hell?

Thou Silence, who never responds to mortal's voice, where is the secret door of Paradise?—Speak once unto me!

O Star, thou radiant spirit of the blessed Beatrice who once guided a mortal unto Heaven, brighten now my darksome path!

I, a lone pilgrim, knock at the gate of Heaven—nay, the silent castle of Repose—O Repose!

Rhyme on, Lady-Rivulet from thy mountain Memnon, thy tunable song awakening mortals' vanity-dreams!

Ah, Nakedness! Nakedness—to whom Shame and Pride arc buried in the peaceful tomb of Faith!

Ah, Loneliness! Loneliness—to whom a boatman of God is the sole saviour on the vast Sea of Eternity!

I repose under the forest's arm-bough—if I awaken not forever, pray, brother mortal.

Make my grave under the greenest grass and carve this line: *"Here sleeps a nameless Poet."*

Song of Day in Yosemite Valley

O thunderous opening of the unseen gate of solemn Heaven's Eternal Court!

Behold, clouds, tenants of the sky, sweep down from the Heavens unto a secret palace under the Earth!—

Aye, mighty Yosemite!—a glorious troop of the unsuffering souls of gods

Marches on with battle-sound against the unknown castle of Hell!—

Aye, a divine message of Heaven unto Earth—the darksome house of mortals—to awake!

Hark—the heart-broken cry of a great Soul!—

Nay, the tempestuous song of Heaven's organ throbbing wild peace through the sky and land!

The Shout of Hell wedded to the Silence of Heaven completes the Valley concert, forms the true symphony—

The Female-light kissing the breast of the Male-shadow chants the sacred Union!

I, a muse from the Orient, where is revealed the light of dawn,

Harken to the welcome strains of genii from the heart of the great Sierras—

I repose under the forest-boughs that invoke the Deity's hymn from the
Nothing-air.

Here, brother mortal, lies the path like Beauty's arm, guiding thee into the
Heaven afar!—

Alone I stray by the mountain walls that support the enamelled mirror-sky,

Enfolding my free-born soul in the vice-purifying odours of the forest from an
unknown corner of Paradise.

Art thirsty?—here roils the snow-robed water for thy fulfillment;

Does dullness veil thee?—here a stone chamber invites thee into the world of
dreams through an unseen door.

O return, brother mortal, from Samsara unto the great Valley!

Yea, the mighty Temple of the World, everlasting with the heaven and earth,
welcomes thee!

Behold! Yosemite, sermoning Truth and Liberty, battles in spirit with the Pacific
Ocean afar!

O unfading wonder, eternal glory! I pray a redemption from the majesty that
chains me—

(Lo, Hell offers a great edifice unto Heaven!) O, I bid my envy and praise rest
against thee;

I am content in the sounding Silence, in the powerless Time that holds the
Valley in the age of gold;

I proffer my stainful body and leprous soul with blackest shame unto thee;

I am united with the Universe, and the Universe with me.

O hail, brother mortal! the true joy is revealed unto thee—

Be thou a wave ebbing and flowing with the air of Heaven!

Behold! The genii of the forest chant Peace unto the Lord from an unknown
shrine in the Valley temple.

O mighty chapel of God! Thou knowest not an iron chariot stained with hostile
blood;—

Aye, idle spears and foolish shields dare not ruin thee, proclaiming War in
Eternity!

Song of Night in Yosemite Valley

Hark! The prophecy-inciting windquake of the unfathomable concave of darkest Hell!

O, the God-scorning demon's shout against the truth-locked gate of mighty Heaven!

Heaven and Hell joining their palace and dungeon, remould the sinful universe to an ethereal paradise—

O, the sphere is shaken by the Master-Mechanic working from the surface of the world to its center!

Alas, the sun has fled in saddest woe!—O mortal, breathe thy silent prayer unto mighty Yosemite for mirth!

Behold, the light of day leaves the white mansion to the care of dolorous night!—

The genii of the Valley fly from the roar of a thousand lions to the sacred peace above—

Lo, an unknown jeweller decks the black, velvety heaven with treasure-stars—

Yea, the Mother-Goddess, mantling the earth with the night, forbids Yosemite disturb her baby-angel's dream in the heaven!

Hark! the night disconcord of the eternal falling of waters sounding discontent throughout the earth—

O, a chariot is rushing down to an unknown hollow in wild triumph!

Behold, a dragon reveals divinity in the ghostly-odorous sky of night—

Nay, the mighty sword of the Judgment Day blazes down the Heaven to the gate of Hell!

FROM "FROM THE EASTERN SEA" (1903)

Apparition

'Twas morn;
I felt the whiteness of her brow
Over my face; I raised my eyes and saw
The breezes passing on dewy feet.

'Twas noon;
Her slightly trembling lips of passion
I saw, I felt, but where she smiled
Were only yellow flakes of sunlight.

'Twas eve;
The velvet shadows of her hair enforded me;
I eagerly stretched my hand to grasp her.
But touched the darkness of eve.

'Twas night;
I heard her eloquent violet eyes
Whispering love, but from the heaven
Gazed down the stars in gathering tears.

O Cho San

Dream was in the soul of the garden brook,
Spring in its song: O Cho San
Leaned her down to face her image
In the brook; both smiled in greeting.
In sudden thought she looked behind;
The sadness of a midnight star

Abode in her unmoving eyes;
The mists of silence filled the gate of her lips.
The moments slipped by: the sunlight fell
Over her face, as a golden message;
The kiss of beauty graced her hair;
The soft odour of womanhood beautifully rose;
The butterflies surrounding her forgot to part;
She was in indolence. Slowly she
Began a dreamy smile, silently facing
Toward a calm sea of fancy: her smile
Was that of an April-night cherry-blossom
To the wind. Softly she looked round and whispered:
"At the return of my lord I will thus smile.
My sweet lover, when Anata shall return!"
And smiling bravely with a sweet intent, she said
"Look what a beautiful smiling O Cho San!"
Then much she blushed, and started up, and, with a sigh,
Began a languid, graceful walk along the path;
Her walk was that of an afternoon breeze
With the fragrance of cherry-blossoms.
The petals of the flower, like butterflies.
Abruptly fell, some on her shoulders
And her hair; the brook gossiped of Spring.
She walked amid the solemn loveliness of eve:
And solitude and dreams were with her soul;
Her poems rose around her like odours
Unto the moon. She was beautiful as one
Who smiling, enters in the gate of Sorrow:
The earth upturned her melancholy face
Toward the heavens; the evening bell
Tolled as the last song of a sea.
Beloved! Beloved! she cried;
Her streaming eyes beheld a silent star.

Address to a Soyokaze[1]

O Soyokaze,
From the golden bower of the morning sun,
In gracefully loose gown,
Your eyes strewing the wealth of aerial beauty
That is half shadow, half odour,
Up with me, Soyokaze!
I've left behind the mortal love,
And all the books dear next to woman.
Up, up, and seek with me
A thousand stars
Lost beyond the skies!
Sail afar with me,
O Soyokaze, on light-gleaming step;
Sail into the garden strange yet my own!
I'll build there my home in the moonbeams,
I'll gather the poems from the flowers.
And from the hearts of birds.
Sail, sail, my Soyokaze!
When I am tired,
We'll rest, my head on your shoulder,
And I'll listen to your tales
That you heard under the roses
Passing through the woodland.
When the tree throws its shadow on the ground
(The shadow is its written song),
And I see not its real meaning,
You will instantly rise,
And play the harp of the leaves.
And make me fully understand.
O beloved Soyazake,
My dear comrade,
Be with my soul eternally
Since I am sundered from the world,
And am alone!

1 'Soyokaze' is 'zephyr' in Japanese.

Under the Moon

The autumn night had a sad impressive beauty.
I turned to my face as a flower,
In indolence: the sweet mystery of indolence
Whispered me an alien legend. I, with lips apart,
With the large mindless eyes, stood
As one fresh from a fairy dream:
The ecstasy of the dream was not yet dry
On my face. The strangest stillness,
As exquisite as if all the winds
Were dead, surrounded me; I idly thought,
What a poem, and what love were hidden behind
The moon, and how great to be beyond mortal breath,
Far from the human domain. My moon fancy,
Aimless as a breeze of summer eve,
Drowsy as a rose of Spring morning, has passed:
My fancy was a fragrance as from an unknown isle
Where Beauty smiled her favourite smile.
How glad I was, being wounded by
The beautiful rush of yellow rays!
The sad sobbing charm of the moon
Was that of the face of an ancient fairy.
The moon gracefully kept her perfect silence
Until a greater muse shall restore the world
From demon's sword and unworthy death.
I was in the lullaby of the moon,
As a tree snugly wrapped in the mist:
I lost all my earthly thoughts.
The moon was voiceless as a nun
With eyes shining in beauteous grief:
The mystic silence of the moon
Gradually revived in me the Immortality,
The sorrow that gently stirred
Was melancholy-sweet: sorrow is higher
Far than joy, the sweetest sorrow is supreme
And all the passions. I had

No sorrow of mortal heart: my sorrow
Was one given before the human sorrows
Were given me. Mortal speech died
From me: my speech was one spoken before
God bestowed on me human speech.
There is nothing like the moon-night
When I, parted from the voice of the city.
Drink deep of Infinity with peace
From another, a stranger sphere. There is nothing
Like the moon-night when the rich noble stars
And maiden roses interchange their long looks of love.
There is nothing like the moon-night
When I raise my face from the land of loss
Unto the golden air, and calmly learn
How perfect it is to grow still as a star.
There is nothing like the moon-night
When I walk upon the freshest dews,
And amid the warmest breezes,
With all the thought of God
And all the bliss of man, as Adam
Not yet driven from Eden, and to whom
Eve was not yet born. What a bird
Dreams in the moonlight is my dream:
What a rose sings is my song.

O Hana San

It was many and many a year ago.
In a garden of the cherry-blossom
Of a far-off isle you may know
By the fairy name of Nippon,
That a maiden who was dressing her hair
Against the mirror of a shining spring,
Casting over me her sudden heavenly glance,
Entreated me to break a beautiful branch
Of the cherry-tree: I cannot forget
I was a boy on the way home
From my school; I threw aside

All my books and slate, and I climbed
Up the tree, and looked down
Over her little anxious butterfly face;
Oh, how the wind blew fanning me
With a love that was more than earthly love,
In a garden of the cherry-blossom
Of a far-off isle you may know
By the fairy name of Nippon!
I broke a branch, slowly dropped it
To her up-raised hands that God shaped
With best art and pain; she smiled
Toward me an angel smile; she,
Speaking no word, ran away as a breeze,
Leaving behind the silver evening moon,
And hid from me in the shadow of a pine-tree
In a garden of the cherry-blossom
Of a far-off isle you may know
By the fairy name of Nippon.
I stole toward her on tiptoe.
As a silent moonbeam to a sleeping flower,
And frightened her with a shout of 'Mitsuketa wa,'[1]
And I ran away from her, smiling and blushing,
In a garden of the cherry-blossom
Of a far-off isle you may know
By the fairy name of Nippon.
And I hid me beneath the gate of a temple.
That was a pathway to the heavens;
She stepped softly as the night.
Found me and looked upon me with a smile like a star.
Tapped my head with the branch,
Speaking fondly, 'My sweetest one!'
I had no answer but a glad laugh
That was taught by the happy wind
In a garden of the cherry-blossom
Of a far-off isle you may know
By the fairy name of Nippon,
And that maiden who was known
By the pretty name of O Hana San,

---

1   "'I found thee out'" in English.

Ran away gracefully as a Spring cloud
Into the heavens, blushing and smiling,
Then I followed O Hana's steps.
Into the heavens, in the realm of Love.

The Myoto[1]

The woman whispered in the voice that roses have lost:
'My love!'
The man said, 'Yes, dear!'
In the voice that seas cannot utter.

The woman whispered in the voice of velvet-footed moonbeams:
'My love!'
The man said, 'Yes, dear!'
In the voice that mountains keep in bosom.

The woman whispered in the voice of eve calling the stars to appear:
'My love!'
The man said, 'Yes, dear!'
In the voice of dawn for Spring and Life.

The woman whispered in the voice of a young summer rivulet:
'My love!'
The man said, 'Yes, dear!'
In the voice of forests into the sky.

The Goddess: God

The goddess spins the wool of the rivulet to its length
O silver song of the female spinner!
O golden silence of the male spinner!
God spinning with the wheel of Time,
White of day and darkness of the night to eternity.

---

1 'Myoto' is Japanese for 'couple' in English.

By the Sea

The moon came sadly out of a hill;
I from the city silently stole:
Many an hour had passed since I shook
The sorrow-thoughts to the winds.
The moon's beautiful cold steps were my steps.
In silvery peace, apart from paths of men:
The dewy mysterious beams, as love-whispers,
Stole in my hair which zephyr stirred
As cloud; I was as in the mazy sweet,
I knew not why. I smiled unto the moon;
The moon understood me: the silence was profound.
On the sea-face unearthly dreams
And greenly melancholic autumn voicelessly stepped:
The moon threw a large soft smile over the sea.
The sea was verily proud to sing:
The sea's passions wooing the shore.
Taught me the secret how to win woman;
But the love of woman was left far behind.
I slowly thought how beautiful to sink
Into the moon-sea and to rise
With worshipping face unto the moon:
A sea-bird suddenly sprung from the wave,
Scattering sea-pearls with lavish wing,
I sat me down on the shore.
With tragic eyes upon the stars,
With my ears unto the sea:
The silence of the stars was as great
As the voice of the sea; it is so
Since the First day, that the stars
Keep the silence and the sea the voice.
I walked with the moon, by the sea,
Till the dawn: what I thought was that
The moon thought, I knew not what.

Homekotoba[1]

I

I hear, O lovely lady, in thy voice,
The music of a hidden flower valley,
Anear yet distant; from thy face
The beauty of Spring flashes:
I linger around thee, faithful and ecstatic.
The murmur of a rose,
Or of a white star that peeps
Out of another world of poetry,
Is the murmur of thy gracious eyes:
Thine eyes are veiled by the misty breezes.
Thy lips of infinity are beautifully wet
With human kisses and with the breath of life;
On thy cheeks bloom the flowers of moonbeams;
Thy bosom holds the mystery of the sky;
The laughter of the air is thy laughter.
The freshness of a sea at morn
Is like unto thy fragrant thought of woman;
A wood with leaves glistening with dewdrops
And a singing bird are symbols of thy fancy;
A flower of morning prayer is thy upturned look
Into the sunlight that, like organ melody,
Rolls up the vault of heaven from the east;
On thy hair flutters the gossip of heaven.
A vision of heavenly leauty in a haze
Is thy lithe form reclining upon the grasses;
A lily appearing from the gossamer
Is thy face looking out from the bewilderment?
Thy soul is a divine complexity
In which I lose my way as in a dream.
Thy smile was born in light of summer blessedness;
The dark-browed wind in Spring rain is thy melancholy;

---

1 'Homekotoba' means 'praising words.'

Thy breath is the whisper along a violet road;
Thy shadow on my breast is thy heart's history.

II

I read, O lovely lady, in thy face
All the religions of beauty
(They are nothing else but Love);
Thy silence musical and commanding
Is that of a harp set in the windless air.
Whenever I see thee my new page of life begins,
With the moon of another light,
With the fresh stir of a new field of wealth;
If I was not born for anything else,
I was born with one aim to adore thee:
One aim is enough for any life.
Thy head is thrust up into the breath of gods,
Yet thy feet on the dandelion ground;
Each pool of the sky woos thy beauty,
Every shadow of earth-tree gossips of thee;
The fancy road of thy song I pursue,
I loiter in the blessed vale of thy heart.
O how proud I feel to see thy face
Hasting to meet my face, as a flower
Hurries to the silken shower of sunshine!
I dare to say that thou art fed
With my praising words lavished over thee;
I dream in the odour of thy womanhood.
Since thou belongst me, my life begins
To be very important; I have to walk
Safely oil the clear road of emerald light,
Safely along the flower-rimmed path of poesy.
With my hand upon thy bosom,
I will feed all the mystery of thy love;
With thy hand upon my brow,
I ask thee what a confidence thou feelst in me;
Casting two shadows on the stream of Life,
We will whistle of the sweet world to the moon.

III

Thy divinely large eyes, O lovely lady,
Gaze beyond our world into a hid kingdom
Of coral-hued beauty and sapphire thought;
The fragrance from thy lips which are a rose
Speaks more than thy golden speech:
The gossamers tarry around thy rose-lips.
Thou seemst unto me a vaporous beauty
Which I saw upon the Spring seas,
Laying me down on the silvery sand of the shore,
With my soul in the song of the seas;
I fear that thou mayest vanish any moment:
What a fear and joy I feel
In my sacred marriage with thee!
The moon marred by clouds is beautiful:
Joy mingled with fear has a deeper thrill.
How often before my lips opened,
Wishing thy impressive kisses;
How often before my hands stretched,
Wishing to feel thy deep bosom:
I ever dreamed of thee amid the breezes,
Under the shadows of flowers and stars:
If my present union with thee be a dream,
The dream has to be eternal.
Everything has a silent hour at whiles:
'Tis sweet to bathe in the silence by thy side;
'Tis sweeter to raise the head from the sea-silence,
And to stare on thy high-born face,
Like a sea-ear gatherer on the sea-waves
With eyes turned toward the abandoned shore.
Then in the stillness of eve (yet stirring
Enough to make one sweetly sad), I
Bind my body with thine own, and send
My soul along the road of the Divine Unseen.

IV

The soul of flower, O lovely lady,
Is the soul of poem; the soul of poem
Is thy soul: thou art like a faithful-eyed caravan
Across the waste, bringing heavenly jewels.
The winds come from east and west.
But thy wind of heart only comes from
The singing woodland of Love.
The air around thy bosom grows roseate
By the fire within; from the ground
Under thy feet has blossomed a daffodil:
Thy presence is the presence of Sun.
My old memory and new dream jauntily come
Riding on thy eye-flash of pearl:
Thou art the soul of all the dawns.
In thy soul I see a brook
Whose song of silvery happiness I love most,
Since I tired of iron-buskined song;
Thy soul with a far-away voice
Like that of an eve of a thousand stars.
Calls me to a task of high yearning;
I see my face in the mirror of thy heart;
And triumphantly smile, thinking that
I am thy husband and slave.
Under the tree-shade I lay me down,
And smell thy balsam breath stealing
Around me like a sweet ancient tale;
Upturning my face I draw
Thy lovely shape in the purple sky:
Since I love thee, my life grows plain,
My dream being only to be faithful to thee,
My toil being only to entertain thee.
The life of simplicity is the life of beauty:
With the beauty and with thee I remain forever.

Upon the Heights

And victor of life and silence,
I stood upon the Heights; triumphant.
With upturned eyes, I stood,
And smiled unto the sun, and sang
A beautifully sad farewell unto the dying day,
And my thoughts and the eve gathered
Their serpentine mysteries around me,
My thoughts like alien breezes.
The eve like a fragrant legend.
My feeling was that I stood as one
Serenely poised for flight, as a muse
Of golden melody and lofty grace.
Yea, I stood as one scorning the swords
And wanton menace of the cities.
The sun had heavily sunk into the seas beyond,
And left me a tempting sweet and twilight.
The eve with trailing shadows westward
Swept on, and the lengthened shadows of trees
Disappeared: how silently the songs of silence
Steal into my soul! And still I stood
Among the crickets, in the beauteous profundity
Sung by stars; and I saw me
Softly melted into the eve. The moon
Slowly rose: my shadow on the ground
Dreamily began a dreamy roam,
And I upward smiled silent welcome.

The Poet

Out of the deep and the dark,
A sparkling mystery, a shape.
Something perfect,
Comes like the stir of the day:
One whose breath is an odour.

Whose eyes show the road to stars,
The breeze in his face.
The glory of Heaven on his back.
He steps like a vision hung in air,
Diffusing the passion of Eternity;
His abode is the sunlight of morn,
The music of eve his speech;
In his sight.
One shall turn from the dust of the grave,
And move upward to the woodland.

The Face in the Mirror

'Why do you cry so, dear little girl?
Come, dry your tears,' I said,
'Like a dew-bathed butterfly in the sun rays,
And then tell me of yourself.'
The girl said;
'My kind Danna San, 'twas this morn
When the breath of Spring blew along the mountain path.
That I went up alone to gather wild-flowers,
And there naughty neighbour's children shouted at me;
Look at that dirty motherless girl!"
Then I retorted that I had my mother in the mirror,
And I ran home and I saw the mirror,—
Alas! my mother's face was crying,
Because I cried.
Then I felt still more sad.
And cried still more,
And now still I cry.'
I said to the girl:
"Sweet child, the face in the mirror
Is not your mother's, but your own.'
The girl flinging a quick opposing look,
Impatiently said:
'So many many years older than I you are,
So much more wiser than I you are,
But, my great lord, you know nothing of my mirror.

The face in the mirror is mother's,
So mother said:
My dear mother never told a lie.
The mirror was left me
When she died, and she said:
"Whenever you want to see me,
You'll find me in the mirror,
I a thousand times have looked in it,
And hidden there my truest face."
Since then, every eve at dusk.
When the church bell sounds to me like mother's call,
I hurry to my mirror,
And I see my mother looking at me.'
Then I said:
'Listen, dear little maiden,
I will adorn your hair with the flowers,
I will give you money for a new Spring dress.
And you shall smile, that's a good girl!
Aren't you happy?
Now look at your mirror, gentle child.'
The girl looked in the mirror, and joyfully exclaimed:
'Mother is happy,
Because I am happy.
I'll not cry any more,
You'll cry no more, my dear mother.'
Then we lay down in the sunlight,
With her pretty head on my knee.
I told many a tale of fairy queens far and near.
My voice was music to her ears,
Her head languidly drooped.
Her innocent sleeping face in the mirror by her side:
I saw the breezes playing with the tassels of her hair.

How Near to Fairyland

The spring warmth steals into me, drying up all the tears of my soul,
And gives me a flight into the vastness,—into a floorless, unroofed reverie-hall.

Lo, such greenness, such velvety greenness, such a heaven without heaven above!
Lo, again, such grayness, such velvety grayless, such an earth without earth below!
My soul sails through the waveless mirror-seas.

Oh, how near to Fairyland!
Blow, blow, gust of wind!
Sweep away my soul-boat against that very shore!

Lines

I love the saintly chant of the winds touching their odorous fingers to the harp
    of the angel Spring;
I love the undiscording sound of thousands of birds, whose concord of song
    echoes on the rivulet afar;
I muse on the solemn mountain which waits in sound content for the time
    when the Lord calls forth;
I roam with the wings of high-raised fantasy in the pure universe;
Oh, I chant of the garden of Adam and Eve!

Spring

Spring,
Winged Spring,
A laughing butterfly,
Flashes away,
Rosy-cheeked Spring,
Angel of a moment.
The little shadow of my lover perfumed,
Maiden Spring,
Now fades,
The shadow,
The golden shadow,
With all the charm.
Spring,
Naughty sweet Spring,
A proud coquette,
Born to laugh but not to live.
Spring,
Flying Spring,
A beautiful runaway,
Leaves me in tears.
But my soul follows after.
Till I catch her.
Next March.
Spring,
Spring!

FROM "THE SUMMER CLOUDS" (1906)

Prose Poems

"The Summer clouds rise in shape of fantastic peaks."

I

Wave, wave, black hair of my Beauty, wave, and wave, and show me where the love deepens, and the forest silence thickens; show me where Peace is buried with heavy wings, and where hours never grow gray!

Wave, wave, black hair of my Beauty, wave, and wave, and show me where the shadows are gold, and the airs are honey, show me the heart—joy of Life and world; wave and wave, black hair of my Beauty!

II

Touch me with thy soft hands, O Yuki San! They are soft as moonbeams on the singing sands, O Yuki San!

They are soft as kisses of the eve, thy soft hands; they are soft as rivulets over the Spring lands, O Yuki San!

Oh, touch me again with thy soft hands, O Yuki San! I feel the passion and Truth of forgotten ages in their touches, O Yuki San! I feel the songs and incense in their touches, O Yuki San!

Here by the sea I sit from dawn till the dusk, O Yuki San! I dream of thy soft hands, soft as soft foams on the laughing shore, O Yuki San! The sun is gone and the soft moon is rising, but never thy soft hands again, O Yuki San!

III

The rain stopped suddenly, when the moon made her way in the sky. O Moon! thou art not the ball of fire and poetry, but thou art the mirror of my Lady Beauty who inerts her own Beauty and Truth, day and night!

Here upon the garden of roses (roses are my Lady Beauty's favourite flowers) I stand. My soul rises from the odours and earth, and comes close to the moon. O Moon! my Lady Beauty's mirror, make my soul and Love nobler by Beauty and Truth which my Lady Beauty imparts. I think only of my Lady Beauty whose work of life was to turn my soul and Love to gold. Oh, where is she, this very moment?

IV

Out of the gray forest (forest? It is the forest. But I doubt whether it was not a shadow) I hear the gray voice of a bird. Oh, lonely bird, art thou still sad? Art thou still keeping comradeship with Death and Darkness? So am I—a poet quietly leaning on the wall of sadness, I burn incense and pray once in a while. How afraid I am to stir up the air of silence! Spring is coming so slow. My soul is kissing the Heart of Voicelessness.

I hear the gray voice of the bird sinking and sinking far down like a dead leaf. Where does it go? It is like my soul which started somewhere without purpose, and is sailing without end. Oh, where does my soul aim to go?

And again I hear another gray voice of another bird out of the gray forest.

Dear lonely Voice, tell me where thou want'st to go! Art thou going into the silver temple of the immortal moonlight? Art thou going into the dusky bosom of the Mother-Rest? Pray, take my soul with thee, O comrade!

V

The happy little songs go to-day under the arms of a wind: my heart will go with them, wherever they go. As the little voices of the leaves they go, laughing and singing. Now they are suddenly still, when the white dews fail under the stars. Is it not the time for them to hurry to their beds in the House of Peace by the mountain flowers? My heart will be happy and go with them wherever they go.

VI

I hear you call, Pine-tree, I hear you upon the hill; by the silent pond where the lotus flowers bloom, I hear you call, Pine-tree!

What is it you call, Pine-tree, when the nuns fall, when the winds blow, and when the stars appear, what is it you call, Pine-tree?

I hear you call. Pine-tree, but I am blind, and do not know how to reach you, Pine-tree. Who will take me to you, Pine-tree?

VII

Out of the cradle of great Silence, from under the grave (do you feel Silence's touch?) the poet, the singer of Seen and Unseen, still sings his voiceless song—the song of the land of shadow and agelessness, the song of the land of peace and memory, the song of the land of Silence and mist! I hear, O poet, thy new melody of voicelessness, thy sweet song of eternal Spring eve, thy song like that of the moon over the land of sleep, thy song of Heaven and love! O poet, thy song fills my heart with sweet unrest and with dreams like passing clouds! O poet, thy song comes from under the grave—out of the cradle of Silence, like the flowing tide!

VIII

The Spring field, calm, odorous, like the breast of Heaven, waving in red and green, like a flowing sea in tune of breeze. A thousand birds, like ships, singing of Spring hope, searching after a joyous life. (O bird-ships on the newest sea!)

"What news, speak, dear ships from another land?"

"Only a love-message, my lord!"

IX

I and Nature are one in sweet weariness: my soul slowly fades into Sleep. Is this earth? Or Heaven? The summer odour sweetens Nature to dream: the trees and birds murmur with a breeze.

"I am blind, deaf, and also dumb; I am a traveller toward God, alas! without a guide," I say.

Oh, deathlessness! Oh, happiness! I and Summer spirits play upon a vast sea of fancy.

FROM "PILGRIMAGE" (1909)

"The New Art"

She is an art (let me call her so)
Hung as a web in the air of perfume,
Soft yet vivid, she sways in music:
(But what sadness in her saturation of life!)
Her music lives in the intensity of a moment, and then dies;
To her suggestion is life.
She left behind the quest of beauty and dream;
Is her own self not the song of dream and beauty itself?
(I know she is tired of ideal and problem and talk.)
She is the moth-light playing on reality's dusk.
Soon to die as a savage prey of the moment;
She is a creation of surprise (let me say so),
Dancing gold on the wire of impulse.
What an elf of light and shadow!
What a flash of tragedy and beauty!

By the Engakuji Temple: Moon Night

Through the breath of perfume,
(O music of musics!)
Down creeps the moon
To fill my cup of song
With memory's wine.

Across the song of night and moon,
(O perfume of perfumes!)
My soul, as a wind
Whose heart's too full to sing,
Only roams astray . . ,

Down the tide of the sweet night
(O the ecstasy's gentle rise!)
The birds, flowers and trees
Are glad at once to fall
Into Oblivion's ruin white.

To a Nightingale

Creator of the only one song!
Triumph, rapture and art thou tellest
But with thy self-same word, what mystery!
I have a few more songs and dreams than thou,
(Alas, my words not serving at my command!)
I tremble, hesitate before I sing:
What carelessness in thy rush with song,
Splendour is thine to sing into air, be forgotten!
Thou singest out, thou pushest thy song's way,
Without regard to the others waiting their turns,
(Pity the other birds and poets!)
What a sweet bit of thy barbarism!
I know not technically what thy song means:
I take thee not only for a bird but the poet
Thou art a revolter against prosody:
What a discoverer of the newest language!
A man's life and art are disturbed by thy song,
(What exhaustion in thy voice,
What a feast and sensation of thy life!)
When thou changest him to become thy kin,—
A thing of simplicity and force;
Thy song stops, thou fliest away.
Oh, can thy work be done so swift?
Didst thou see thy song's future in him?
Thou art suggestion; what a fragment of art!

I Am like a Leaf

The silence is broken: into the nature
    My soul sails out,
Carrying the song of life on his brow,
    To meet the flowers and birds.

When my heart returns in the solitude,
    She is very sad,
Looking back on the dead passions
    Lying on Love's ruin.

I am like a leaf
    Hanging over hope and despair,
Which trembles and joins
    The world's imagination and ghost.

To the Sunflower

Thou burstest from mood:
How sad we have to cling to experience!
Marvel of thy every atom burning of life,
How fully thou livest!
Didst thou ever think to turn to cold and shadow?
Passionate liver of sunlight,
Symbol of youth and pride;
Thou art a lyric of thy soaring colour;
Thy voicelessness of song is action.
What absorption of thy life's meaning,
Wonder of thy consciousness,—
Mighty sense of thy existence!

Shadow

My song is sung, but a moment . . . . .
The song of voice is merely the body, (the body dies,)
And the real part of the song, its soul, remains after it is sung:
Yea, it remains in the vibration of thy waves of heart-sea
Echoing still my song, (O shadow my song threw!)
In thy heart's thrill I see my far truer and whiter soul,
And through my soul thou soarest out of thy dust and griefs.
. . . . Spring passed,
(Spring in roses and birds is merely the body,)
And I see the greater Spring (O soul-shadow she left!)
In the Summer forest, luminous in green and dream:
Oh to be that Spring over the word's Summer valley,
O shadow I may cast in the after-age, O my shadow of soul!

The Fantastic Snow-Flakes

Bah! What fantastic snow-flakes, eh,
Dancing merrily, ha! ha! ha!
Lo, their tiny feet reusing so!

Death is sweet, to be sure.
Laughing they go to death,
What delicious teeth, ha! ha! ha!

Suppose we die together, eh,
With the snow dying upon a pond?
What a fantastic end, ha! ha! ha!

What a fantastic end to die
In the dying music of ancient love!
Behold the snow and music die!

What a coward, ha! ha! ha!
Are you afraid to die, eh?
Still you love a little caprice of world?

What fantastic snow-flakes, ha! ha! ha!
To leave no sorrow and to die!
Such a coward, you my beloved!

Ghost of Abyss

My dreams rise when the rain falls: the sudden songs
Flow about my ears as the clouds in June;
And the footsteps, lighter than the heart of wind,
Beat, now high, then low, before my dream-flaming eyes.

"Who am I?" said I. "Ghost of abyss," a Voice replied,
"Piling an empty stone of song on darkness of night,
Dancing wild as a fire, only to vanish away."

Autumn Song

The gold vision of a bird-wind sways on the silver foam of song,
The oldest song rises again on the Autumn heart of dream.

The ghost castle of glory is built by the sad magic of Time,
With the last laughter of sorrow, and with the red tempest of leaves.

My little soul born out of the dews of singing dawn,
Bids farewell to the large seas of Life and speech.

Fantasia

Bits of straw and clay and woman's hair,—
So shall be builded my house:
Oh to lose the world and gain a song!
Let the clouds flit through the window at the left;
The dancer shapeless in pain and pride,
From the right dance in as a tide:
A spirit of pagan days, sick in joy,
That rose at the sound of their stamping feet,
I'll sing a song that makes the seas the hills.
(Morality begins, I am afraid, where I stop my song.)
Rags to roll me in, pieces of dream,
So with my heart of nocturnal fear;
I have chose of the sky red in memory and art.
Let the stars fall in the garden rose:
The leaves and my souls in a thousand guises
Hurry to the ground to build a grave.

The Temple Bell

Trembling in its thousand ages,
Dark as its faith,
It wails, hunting me,
(It's a long time since I lost my faith,)
Up through the silence with a scorn,
Heavy but not unkind,
Out of the dusk of the temple and night
Into my heart of dusk,
Hushed after my song of cities played,
Weary and grey in thought.
My heart replies to the wail of the bell.
Slow-bosomed in sadness and faith,
With my memory rising from dusts,
Namu amida butsu! Namu amida butsu!

To the Cicada

What a sudden pun of ancient soul,—
A tear that is a voice, a voice that is a tear!
What unforgotten tragedy thou tellest in thy break of heart
Min, min, min, min, minminminminmin . . . . !

Grey singer of the forest with heart of fire.
Dost thou cry for the world, or for my love and life?
Is thy monotony of voice the tragedy of my song?
Min, min, min, min, minminminminmin . . . . !

The soul that reads the sorrow of life knows thy heart:
Cry till the world and life gain the triumph of death!
Let us earn Death through the tragedy of Faith!
O singer of sad Faith and only one song,—
Cry out thy old dream of life and tears!
Min, min, min, min, minminminminmin . . . . !

The Lady of Utamaro's Art

Too common to say she is the beauty of line,
However, the line old, spiritualised into odour,
(The odour soared into an everlasting ghost from life and death,)
As a gossamer, the handiwork of dream,
'Tis left free as it flaps:
The lady of Utamaro's Art is the beauty of zephyr flow.
I say again, the line with the breath of love,
Enwrapping my heart to be a happy prey:
Sensuous? To some so she may appear,
But her sensuousness divinised into the word of love.
To-day I am with her in silence of twilight eve,
And am afraid she may vanish into the mist.

The Buddha Priest in Meditation

He is a style of monotony,
His religion is aloofness,
Is there any simplicity more beautiful?
What a grand leisure in his walk
On the road of mystery:
Is there any picture more real,
More permanent than he?
He surrenders against faith:
He walks on mystery's road,—that is enough.
He never quests why.
He feels a touch beyond word,
He reads the silence's sigh,
And prays before his own soul and destiny:
He is a pseudonym of the universal consciousness,
A person lonesome from concentration.
He is possessed of Nature's instinct,
And burns white as a flame;
His morality and accident of life
No longer exist,
But only the silence and soul of prayer.

In the Inland Sea

Here the waters of wine with far-off desires,
Here the April breezes with purple flashes familiar and yet forgotten.
Oh, here the twilight of the Inland Sea!
Here I hear a song without a word,
(Is it the song of my flying soul?)
That's the song of my dream I dreamed a thousand years ago.
Oh, my dream of the fairy world, oh, the beauty of the Inland Sea!
I sail and sail to-day in this fairy sea,
(O my heart, hear the sailors' song of life!)
I sail leaving the welcoming isles far behind,

(Hear the isles bidding adieu, O my heart!)
I sail toward the chanting sky.
O birds with white souls, steer my soul with white love,
Here the sea of my dream, Oh, the beauty of the Inland Sea!

Kyoto

Mist-born Kyoto, the city of scent and prayer,
Like a dream half-fading, she lingers on:
The oldest song of a forgotten pagoda bell
Is the Kamo River's twilight song.

The girls, half whisper and half love,
As old as a straying moonbeam,
Flutter on the streets gods built.
Lightly carrying Spring and passion.

"Stop a while with me," I said.
They turned their powdered necks. How delicious!
"No, thank you, some other time," they replied.
Oh, such a smile like the breath of a rose!

My Little Bird

My little bird,
My bird born in my Mother's tears,
She flies,
Stretching her wings so,
And from under her wings she drops my Mother's message;
"Come home, Beloved!"

Running out from my Mother's bosom,
My little river.
She suddenly stopped her song,
And looking up to the sun.
She in her ripples flashed my Mother's message:
"Beloved, come home!"

My roses,
My little roses grow in my Mother's breath,
They are sad to-day,
Casting their faces down;
On their petals I read my Mother's message:
"Come home. Beloved!"

Her Weapons Are a Smile and a Little Fan

Her weapons are a smile and a little fan.
Sayonara, sayonara . . .
Her bent neck like that of a stork
Seeking a jewel of heart in the ground!
Her wisdom is folded sweet in her bosom.
Sayonara, sayonara . . .
Her flapping robe like a cloud
That follows a lyric of butterfly!
Her song is on her tips of naked feet.
Sayonara, sayonara . . .
Beat of her wooden clogs
Playing the unseen strings of love!

My Heart

Oh Lord, is it the reflection of my heart of fire?
Is it, my Lord, the sunset flashes of the Western sky?
Oh Lord, is it the echo of my heart of unrest?
Is it, my Lord, the cry of a sea breaking on the sand?
Oh Lord, is it the voice of my sorrowful heart?
Is it, my Lord, the wail of a wind seeking the road in the dark?
Oh Lord, is it the dripping tears of my heart?
Is it, my Lord, the rain carrying tragedy from the Heavens?

The Lotus Worshippers

From dale and hill the worshippers steal
In whitest robes: yea, with whitest souls.
They sit around the holy pond, the lotus home.
Their finger-tips folded like the hushing lotus-buds
Thrust through the water and twilight, nun-like.
And they pray (the silent prayer that is higher than the prayer of speech).
The stars and night suddenly cease their song.
The air and birds begin to stir.
(O Resurrection, Resurrection of World and Life!)
Lo, Sun ascending! The lotus buds flash with hearts parted.
With one chant "Namu, Amida!"
The stars disappear, nay, they fall in their hearts.
The worshippers turn their silent steps toward their homes,
Learning that the stars will fall in their truthful souls.
And the road of sunlight is the road of prayer.
And for Paradise.
Their faces shining under the sun's blessing gold.
They chant the divine name along the woodland.

Lines

The sun I worship,
Not for the light, but for the shadows of the trees he draws:
O shadows welcome like an angel's bower,
Where I build Summer-day dreams!
Not for her love, but for the love's memory,
The woman I adore;
Love may die, but not the memory eternally green—
The well where I drink Spring ecstasy.
To a bird's song I listen.
Not for the voice, but for the silence following after the song;
O Silence fresh from the bosom of voice!—
Melody from the Death-Land whither my face does ever turn!

The Eastern Sea

I say my farewell to the Western cities;
I will return to the Eastern Sea,—
To my isle kissed first ever by the sun,—
I will now go to my sweetest home,
And lay there my griefs on a mountain's breast,
And give all my songs to the birds, and sleep long,
A wind may stir the forest, I may awake,
I will whistle my joy of life up to a cloud:
The life of the cloud will be my life there.
How tall my lover now will be!
She was two inches shorter than I long ago.
When mid the wistarias the moon-lantern is lit,
She and I will steal to measure our heights
By their drooping flowers—drooping calm like peace.
Should she win, I will pay her my kisses seven:
I will take her seven kisses if I win:
So all the same the kisses shall be mine.
Then we will walk by the idols—the saint's and the poet's,
And assure them that Life is but Love;
With Love and chrysanthemum I will remain forever.

To a Sparrow

Sudden ghost
That danced out again from the shadow and rest,
Hunter of the memory and colour of thy last life,
Dost thou find the same humanity, the same dream?
Consecrator of every moment,
Holder of the genius for living,
Thy one moment might be our ten years:
Does it tempt, console and frighten thee?
Ghost of nerve,
If thy voice be curse,
It is with all thy soul
If it be repentance,

It is with all thy body.
Oh, would that I could relish the same sensation as thou!

Right and Left

The mountain green at my right:
The sunlight yellow at my left:
The laughing winds pass between.

The river white at my left:
The flowers red at my right:
The laughing girls go between.

The clouds sail away at my right:
The birds flap down at my left:
The laughing moon appears between.

I turned left to the dale of poem;
I turned right to the forest of Love:
But I hurry Home by the road between.

In Japan Beyond

Do you not hear the sighing of a willow in Japan,
(In Japan beyond, in Japan beyond)
In the voice of a wind searching for the sun lost,
For the old faces with memory in eyes?

Do you not hear the sighing of a bamboo in Japan,
(In Japan beyond, in Japan beyond)
In the voice of a sea urging with the night,
For the old dreams of a twilight tale?

Do you not hear the sighing of a pine in Japan,
(In Japan beyond, in Japan beyond)
In the voice of a river in quest of the Unknown,
For the old ages with gold in heart?

Do you not hear the sighing of a reed in Japan,
(In Japan beyond, in Japan beyond)
In the voice of a bird who long ago flew away,
For the old peace with velvet-sandalled feet?

Cradle Songs

I

Sleep, my love, your way of dream
By the fireflies shall be lighted,
That I gather from the heart of night
Your father is off, good night,
To buy the honey from the stars:
The city of stars is away a hundred miles.
But by the dawn he will return,
Riding on the horse of the dews.
For you, with a drum as big as the sun.

II

The flowers are nodding
Above your head;
The flowers arc made with sorrows seven.
And laughters three which are the best.

The sorrows seven your mother keeps,
(Mother's way is that of pain,)
But the laughters three make you fair and gay,
I rock you, fairy boat on the tide of love.

Sleep, my own, till the bell of dusk
Bring the stars laden with a dream;
With that dream you shall awake
Between the laughters and song.

FROM "JAPANESE HOKKUS" (1920)

JAPANESE HOKKUS

I

What is life? A voice,
A thought, a light on the dark,
Lo, crow in the sky.

II

Sudden pain of earth
I hear in the fallen leaf.
"Life's autumn," I cry.

III

The silence-leaves from Life,
Older than dream or pain,—
Are they my passing ghost?

IV

Is it not the cry of a rose to be saved?
Oh, how could I
When I, in fact, am the rose!

V

But the march to Life . . .
Break song to sing the new song!
Clouds leap, flowers bloom,

VI

Fallen leaves! Nay, spirits?
Shall I go downward with thee
By a stream of Fate?

VII

Speak not again, Voice!
The silence washes off sins:
Come not again, Light!

VIII

It is too late to hear a nightingale?
Tut, tut, tut, . . . some bird sings,—
That's quite enough, my friend,

IX

I shall cry to thee across the years?
Wilt thou turn thy face to respond
To my own tears with thy smile?

X

Where the flowers sleep,
Thank God! I shall sleep, to-night.
Oh, come, butterfly!

XI

My Love's lengthened hair
Swings o'er me from Heaven's gate:
Lo, Evening's shadow!

XII

Is there anything new under the sun?
Certainly there is.
See how a bird flies, how flowers smile!

Tanka: Poems in Exile

Jun Fujita

For permission to reprint certain of these poems, I am grateful to the editors of *Poetry: A Magazine of Verse, The Wave, Caprice,* and other periodicals. Especially I take this opportunity to express my long felt gratitude to *Miss Harriet Monroe,* editor of *Poetry.*

I also wish to thank *Miss Florence Mae Carr* for her valuable advice and assistance in preparing this, volume. *J.F.*

To *Mrs. Edward H. Taylor*

Winter

Under the scowling sky
The frozen sand plain stretches.
Curled and crisp, two leaves
Scud away.

Falling slowing, whirling swiftly—
The horizon lost in the snow.
On a gaunt skeleton
A crow with wings drooping
Peers.

Among the brittled grasses,
Frosting in the moon glare,
Tombstones are
Whiter tonight.

The glamorous night is fading
Over the rolling hills, hoary bare.
On the paled sky; the moon
Has forgotten to vanish.

From the clear depth, inlaid with stars,
An echo of the glittering snow.
A fleeting song and bell, over the icy horizon,
Have left a vibrant void.

The death-like expanse of snow,
The low leaden sky—
From the drift, now and then,
Thin fangs dart.

The rocking horse,
A half built block house—
Stillness echoes.
Lost laughter.

Spring

Milky night;
Through slender trees in drowse
A petal—
Falling.

The air is still
And grasses are wet;
Thread-like rain
Screens the dunes.

On the pond rain-drops are bubbling;
From the hem of heaven
Dyed in black
The frog echoes.

The sloping sand plain
Fades into pale night air;
A black tree skeleton
Casts no shadow.

Above the settling mist,
Above the phantom isles upon the settling mist,
In the opalized moonlight,
The whinny of a horse careers by.

Down the slope, white with flowers,
Toward the hills, hazy blue,
A butterfly
Floats away.

While you pant deliriously, I awake
To the bold moon,
The somber hills,
And myself.

Summer

Against the gulls that play in the gale
The black waves dart
White fangs
In vain.

Midnight;
Over the lifeless sand plain,
The moon and I
Are alone.

The night is bare and pale
Over the charred down trees.
Daring the empty space and drifting mist
A gaunt skeleton stands.

Over the undulating expanse, grey glare,
A last glint of day is fading;
On the shore the same tired waves
Splash.

There is no time here.
From giant trunks hoary moss
Hangs through the air of shadowy green.
And cool dew drips.

By the sunflowers
A cat sniffs the grass—
Her tail curls in the air.

A strange muteness—
The grey door of your boat-house alone
Listens to ripples,
Tonight.

Autumn

The brook has gone.
Over the leaves that lie so still
A bird,
Startled.

A sudden caw, lost in the air,
Leaves the hillside to the autumn sun;
Save, a leaf or two curling
Not a sound is here.

On a country road
An old woman walks;
The autumn sun casts her shadow
Long and thin.

Against the cold sky
Where the day fades swiftly
A scarecrow stands
With its torn sleeve swaying.

The November sky without a star
Droops low over the midnight street;
On the pale pavement, cautiously
A leaf moves.

Across the frozen marsh
The last bird has flown;
Save a few reeds
Nothing moves.

On a pale sand-hill
A bare tree stands;
The death-wind has snatched
The last few leaves.

Graves are frozen.
A few leaves
Stood, whirled,
And have gone.

I know it is not she,
Yet, I listen
To distant laughter,
Fleeting away.

Others

Gypsy Taylor

"G-y-p, oh, G-y-y-p!"
In mute blackness where my call vanishes
Your voiceless laughter
Flickers.

To Elizabeth

Against the door dead leaves are falling;
On your window the cobwebs are black.
Today, I linger alone.

The foot-step?
A passer-by.

Miriam

A sigh among the trees;
A sudden shower of large rain-drops—
I hear no voice, today.

On the wet grass
Paper, crumpled, flaps.

Ecstasy

The night is still,
So, you,
Panting secretly, relaxed on the grass,
With languorous eyes half closed.
You smile
As the cool breeze flows—
Flows over your dishevelled hair.

Summer Moon

The rain, crazed like horses
In the flare of lightning, has gone.

Against the clear washed sky
Rain-drops on the twigs
Reflect the moon.

A Moon

Why so weird, Moon?
Grey-haired, wind-combed,
Hastening through the torn clouds
With pale stare fixed beyond the horizon,
What are you searching for?
Dried and crazed, the sands are rising
Against a broken face in laughter.

A Picture

The roads are frozen; no moving thing is there.
Upon the red opening across the black sky
A headless, giant form,
Hanging by its arms stretched,
Glides on.
Dead and pale, the roads are far.

Diminuendo

Into the evening haze
Out of giant stacks, the smoke
Winds and fades.

Din and whistles have dwindled away
And stillness chants an empty echo.

Michigan Boulevard

A row of black tombs—tall and jagged,
The buildings stand in the drizzly night.
With vacant stare the boulevard lamps in rain
Amuse the green gleams they cast.
Beyond the lamps, among the tomb,
Drip, and drip,
The hollow sound rises.

Chicago River

Slowly, by the slimy wooden wharves,
Through the stillness of rain
The Chicago River glides into night.
From the silhouette of a black iron bridge,
The watchman's light is dripping—
Dripping like melting tallow.
Out of darkness
Comes a woman,
Hellos to me; her wet face glares;
Casually she turns and goes
Into the darkness.

Through the stillness of rain
The Chicago River glides on.

My Sister

Across the meadow
The breeze is fragrant;
In a tree a bird
Disturbs the petals
Over these tombstones, still and content.

A melodious afternoon years ago;
My sister
With pig-tail flying
Chased a dragon-fly
And laughed over nothing.

The deaf vision stands today—
When I pledged
Tidings and gifts
Her strained lips quivered in vain—
Before me, the tombstone, still and content.

The chirp of a bird among the trees—
It too has died away.

TIMELINE

1848	James W. Marshall discovers gold along the American River in California.
1849	Gold Rush brings waves of Chinese immigrants to California.
1855	Yung Wing graduates from Yale, first Asian American to graduate from an American university.
1861	Start of Civil War.
1863	Abraham Lincoln issues the Emancipation Proclamation.
1865	Assassination of Abraham Lincoln. Robert E. Lee surrenders in Virginia, ending the Civil War. Eaton family emigrates from England to Hudson, NY.
1869	The First Transcontinental Railroad is completed.
1872	Yung Wing organizes the Chinese Educational Mission and sends 120 students to study in New England. Eaton family moves to Montreal, QC.
1875	Page Act bars immigration of Chinese women due to suspicions of prostitution.
1879	Thomas Edison invents the electric lightbulb.
1882	President Chester A. Arther signs the Chinese Exclusion Act.
1884	Sadakichi Hartmann's first visit to Walt Whitman.
1885	Rock Springs massacre kills 28 Chinese coal miners.
1887	Yan Phou Lee publishes *When I Was a Boy in China* and gives his speech "Graduating Address of Yan Phou Lee at Yale College."
1888	Scott Act prohibits Chinese who left the US for reentry.
1892	Death of Walt Whitman. The Geary Act replaces the expired Chinese Exculsion Act and adds additonal restrictions to Chinese immigration. Chinese American immigrants must now prove certificates of residency or face deportation.
1893	Sadakichi Hartmann publishes *Christ: A Dramatic Poem in Three Acts.*
1895	Sadakichi Hartmann publishes *Conversations with Walt Whitman.*
1896	Edith Maud Eaton adopts her pen name Sui Sin Far in Jamaica.
1898	Spanish-American War. United States acquire Cuba and the Philippines from the Treaty of Paris.
1898	Jenichiro Oyabe publishes *A Japanese Robinson Crusoe.*
1899	Onoto Watanna publishes *Miss Numè of Japan.*

1903   Lee Chew publishes "The Biography of a Chinaman."

1904   Publication of *As a Chinaman Saw Us: Passages from his Letters to a Friend at Home.*

        Yone Noguchi publishes "A Proposal to American Poets."

1907   Gentleman's Agreement suspends Japanese immigration. Expatriation Act rules relinquishment of American identity if a woman marries a foreign man.

1909   Sui Sin Far publishes "Leaves from the Mental Portfolio of an Eurasian."

        Yung Wing publishes *My Life in China and America.*

1912   Sui Sin Far publishes *Mrs. Spring Fragrance.*

1913   Alien Land Law in California prohibits aliens from purchasing land, targeting Japanese immigrants.

1915   Onoto Watanna publishes *Me: A Book of Remembrance.*

        Tingfang Wu publishes *America Through the Spectacles of an Oriental Diplomat.*

1916   Onoto Watanna publishes *Marion: The Story of an Artist's Model.*

1917   US enters World War I. Immigration Act bars immigration from the Asia-Pacific and imposes literacy tests on immigrants.

1920   19th Amendment grants women's suffrage.

1922   Cable Act reverses the 1907 Expatriation Act. Supreme Court rules in *Takao Ozawa v. United States* that Japanese are ineligible for naturalization.

1922   Yone Noguchi publishes *Selected Poems of Yone Noguchi, Selected by Himself.*

1923   Jun Fujita publishes *Poems in Exile.*

1924   Immigration Act continues to bar immigration from the Asia-Pacific.

1941   Japan attacks Pearl Harbor.

1943   Chinese Exclusion Act is repealed.

1944   Executive Order 9066 incarcerates Japanese Americans in internment camps. Hartmann is one of a few Japanese Americans to avoid the mass incarceration.

1945   Dropping of the atomic bomb in Hiroshima and Nagasaki. End of World War II.

Suggested Reading

Adams, Bella. *Asian American Literature*. Edinburgh University Press, 2008.

As a Chinaman Saw Us: Passages from His Letters to a Friend at Home. D. Appleton and Co., 1904.

Bieler, Stacey. *Patriots or Traitors: A History of American Educated Chinese Students*. Routledge, 2003.

Boggs, Lucinda P. *Chinese Womanhood*. Jennings and Graham, 1913. Print.

Chang, Sharon. *Raising Mixed Race: Multiracial Asian Children in a Post-Racial World*. Routledge, 2015.

Cheung, King-Kok. *Articulate Silences: Hisaye Yamamoto, Maxine Hong Kingston, Joy Kogawa*. Cornell University Press, 1993.

Chin, Frank, et al., editors. *Aiiieeeee! An Anthology of Asian-American Writers*. Howard University Press, 1974.

Chin, Frank, et al., editors. *The Big Aiiieeeee!*. Plume, 1991.

Condit, Ira M. *The Chinaman as We See Him and Fifty Years of Work for Him*. Fleming H. Revell Co., 1900.

Davis, Rocio G. *Relative Histories: Mediating History in Asian American Family Memoirs*. University of Hawaii Press, 2010.

Duncan, Patti. *Tell This Silence: Asian American Women Writers and the Politics of Speech*. University of Iowa Press, 2004.

Far, Sui Sin. *Mrs. Spring Fragrance: A Collection of Chinese-American Short Stories*. Dover Publications, 2013.

Porter, Katherine. Franking, Holly, editor. *Mae Franking's My Chinese Marriage: An Annotated Edition*. University of Texas Press, 1991.

Ghymn, Esther M. *The Shapes and Styles of Asian American Prose Fiction*. Peter Land,1992.

Hartmann, Sadakichi. Lawton, Harry, and George Knox, editors. *Budda, Confucius, Christ: Three Prophetic Plays*. Herder and Herder, 1971.

Hartmann, Sadakichi. Cheung, Floyd, editor. *Memento: Collected Poems, 1886-1944*. Little Island Press, 2016.

Hartmann, Sadakichi. "Permanent Peace: Is it a Dream?" Bruno Chap Books, 1915.

Hartmann, Sadakichi. *Schopenhauer in the Air*. New York, 1899.

Koshy, Susan. *Sexual Naturalization: Asian Americans and Miscegenation*. Stanford University Press, 2005.

Kuo, Helena. *I've Come a Long Way*. D. Appleton-Century Co., 1942.

Lee, Erika. *The Making of Asian America*. Simon and Schuster, 2015.

Lee, Yan Phou. *When I was a Boy in China*. D. Lothrop Co., 1887.

Lim, Shirley G., et. al., editors. *The Forbidden Stitch: An Asian American Women's Anthology*. CALYX Books, 1989.

Ling, Amy. *Between Worlds: Women Writers of Chinese Ancestry*. Pergamon Press, 1990.

Ling, Huping. *Chinese Chicago: Race, Transnational Migration, and Community Since 1870*. Stanford University Press, 2012.

Madsen, Deborah L. *Asian American writers*. Thomas Gale, 2005.

McCunn, Ruthanne. *Chinese American Portraits: Personal Histories 1828-1988*. Chronicle Books, 1988.

Noguchi, Yone. *The American Diary of a Japanese Girl*. Frederick A. Stokes Company, 1902.

Noguchi, Yone. *The Story of Yone Noguchi Told by Himself*. George W. Jacobs & Co., 1915.

Osia, N. H. *Hansu's Journey: A Korean Story*. Philip Jaisohn & Co., 1921.

Oyabe, Jenichiro. *A Japanese Robinson Crusoe*. The Pilgrim Press, 1898.

Parikh, Crystal, editor. *The Cambridge Companion to Asian American Literature*. Cambridge University Press, 2015.

Peters, James S. *Sadakichi Hartmann: Alien Son*. Sunstone Press, 2017.

Prchal, Tim, and Tony Trigilio, editors. *Visions and Divisions: American Immigration Literature, 1870-1930*. Rutgers, The State University, 2008.

Rau, Santha R. *Home to India*. Harper & Brothers, 1945.

Sollors, Werner. *Neither Black nor White yet Both: Thematic Explorations of Interracial Literature*. Oxford University Press USA-OSO, 1997.

Sueyoshi, Amy H.. *Queer Compulsions: Race, Nation, and Sexuality in the Affairs of Yone Noguchi*. University of Hawaii Press, 2012.

Takaki, Ronald. *Strangers from a Different Shore: A History of Asian Americans, Updated and Revised Edition*. Little, Brown and Co., 1998.

Tamagawa, Kathleen. *Holy Prayers in a Horse's Ear*. Butgers University Press, 2008.

Uno, Roberta, editor. *Unbroken Thread: An Anthology of Plays by Asian American Women*. The University of Massachusetts Press, 1993.

Villa, José G. Cowen, John E., editor. *Doveglion: Collected Poems*. Penguin Books, 2008.

Watanna, Onoto. Moser, Linda T., and Elizabeth Rooney, editors. *"A Half Caste" and Other Writings*. University of Illinois Press, 2003.

Watanna, Onoto. *A Japanese Nightingale*. Harper & Brothers, 1901.

Watanna, Onoto. *Marion: The Story of an Artist's Model*. W. J. Watt & Company, 1916.

Watanna, Onoto. *Me: A Book of Remembrance*. The Century Co., 1915.

Watanna, Onoto. *Miss Numè of Japan*. Rand, McNally & Co., 1899.

Watanna, Onoto. *Sunny-San*. George H. Doran Company, 1922.

Wing, Yung. *My Life in China and America*. Earnshaw Books, 2007.

Wong, Sau-Ling Cynthia, et al. *Reading Asian American Literature: From Necessity to Extravagance*. Princeton University Press, 1993.

Wong, Shawn, editor. *Asian American Literature: A Brief Introduction and Anthology*. Pearson, 1996.

Wu, Frank. *Yellow: Race in America Beyond Black and White*. Basic Books, 2003.

Wu, Tingfang. *America Through the Spectacles of an Oriental Diplomat*. Frederick A. Stokes Co., 1914.

Xu, Wenying. *Historical Dictionary of Asian American Literature and Theater*. Lanham: Scarecrow Press, 2012.

"'Yellow Slavery,'" Narratives of Rescue, and Sui Sin Far/Edith Maud Eaton's 'Lin John.'" *Journal of Asian American Studies,* Vol. 12, 2009.

Yin, Xiao-huang. *Chinese American Literature since the 1850s*. University of Illinois Press, 2006.

Yung, Judy. *Unbound Voices: A Documentary History of Chinese Women in San Francisco*. University of California, 1999.

Yutang, Lin. *My Country and My People*. Hesperides Press, 2008.

Zia, Helen. *Asian American Dreams: The Emergence of an American People*. Farrar, Straus and Giroux, 2001.